Mathematica
Graphics Tom Wickham-Jones

TECHNIQUES

&

APPLICATIONS

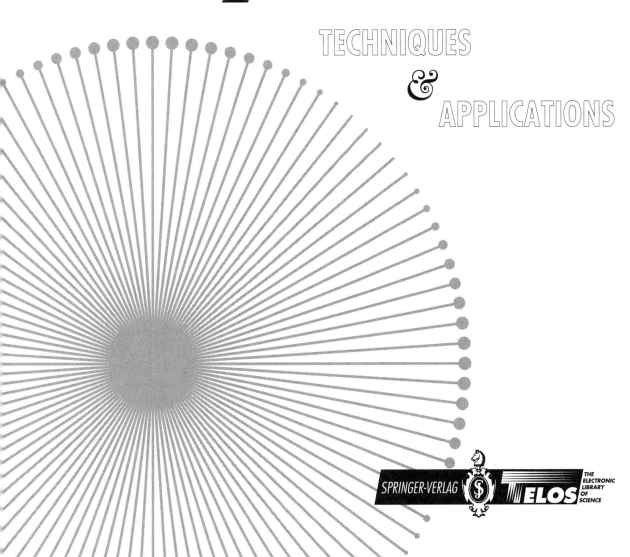

SPRINGER-VERLAG $ TELOS THE ELECTRONIC LIBRARY OF SCIENCE

Tom Wickham-Jones
Wolfram Research, Inc.
100 Trade Center Drive
Champaign, IL 61820-7237 USA

Publisher: Allan M. Wylde
Publishing Assistant: Kate McNally Young
Product Manager: Carol Wilson
Produced and Prepared by: Jan Benes, Black Hole Publishing Service
Text and Cover Designer: John Bonadies
Production Artist: Joe Kaiping
Copy Editor: John T. Selawsky/Jan Progen
Editorial Consultant: Paul Wellin

Library of Congress Cataloging–in–Publication Data

Wickham-Jones, Tom, 1958-
    Computer graphics with Mathematica / by Tom Wickham-Jones.
        p.   cm.
    Includes bibliographical references and index.
    ISBN 0-387-94047-2
    1. Computer graphics.   2. Mathematica (Computer file)   I. Title.
T385.W543   1994
006.6'.7—dc20   94–12680
                                                                                  CIP

THE
ELECTRONIC
LIBRARY
OF
SCIENCE

TELOS, The Electronic Library of Science, is an imprint of Springer-Verlag New York, with publishing facilities in Santa Clara, California. Its publishing domain encompasses the natural and physical sciences, computer science, mathematics, and engineering. All TELOS publications have a computational orientation to them, as TELOS' primary publishing strategy is to wed the traditional print medium with the emerging new electronic media in order to provide the reader with a truly interactive multimedia information environment. To achieve this, every TELOS publication delivered on paper has an associated electronic component. This can take the form of book/diskette combinations, book/CD-ROM packages, books delivered via networks, electronic journals, newsletters, plus a multitude of other exciting possibilities. Since TELOS is not committed to any one technology, any delivery medium can be considered.

The range of TELOS publications extends from research level reference works through textbook materials for the higher education audience, practical handbooks for working professionals, as well as more broadly accessible science, computer science, and high technology trade publications. Many TELOS publications are interdisciplinary in nature, and most are targeted for the individual buyer, which dictates TELOS publications be priced accordingly.

Of the numerous definitions of the Greek work "telos," the one most representative of our publishing philosophy is to "to turn," or "turning point." We perceive the establishment of the TELOS publishing program to be a significant step towards attaining a new plateau of high quality information packaging and dissemination in the interactive learning environment of the future. TELOS welcomes you to join us in the exploration and development of this frontier as a reader and user, and author, editor, consultant, strategic partner, or in whatever other capacity might be appropriate.

TELOS, The Electronic Library of Science
Springer-Verlag Publishers
3600 Pruneridge Avenue, Suite 200
Santa Clara, CA 95051

TELOS Diskettes

Unless otherwise designated, computer diskettes packaged with TELOS publications are 3.5" high-density DOS-formatted diskettes. They may be read by any IBM-compatible computer running DOS or Windows. They may also be read by computers running NEXTSTEP, by most UNIX machines, and by Macintosh computers using a file exchange utility.

In those cases where the diskettes require the availability of specific software programs in order to run them, or to take full advantage of their capabilities, then the specific requirements regarding these software packages will be indicated.

TELOS CD-ROM Discs

It is also clearly indicated to buyers of TELOS publications containing CD-ROM discs, or in cases where the publication is a standalone CD-ROM product, the exact platform, or platforms, on which the disc is designed to run. For example, Macintosh only; MPC only; Macintosh and Windows (cross-platform), etc.

TELOSpub.com (Online)

New product information, product updates, TELOS news and FTPing instructions can be accessed by sending a one-line message: **send info** to: **info@TELOSpub.com**. The TELOS anonymous FTP site contains catalog product descriptions, testimonials and reviews regarding TELOS publications, data-files contained on the diskettes accompanying the various TELOS titles, order forms and price lists.

To Liz, Daniel and James

Preface

Mathematica introduced two important innovations to computer graphics. The first was the close integration of high-quality graphics in a computational system. Before *Mathematica*, graphics systems tended to be separated from computational systems. This meant that after results had been generated in the latter they needed to be exported to the former. *Mathematica* demonstrated that graphics were an indispensable component. Integration was more than a matter of convenience; it expanded the type of work that could be attempted.

The other innovation, more far-reaching, is the way that *Mathematica* treats graphics objects in symbolic or object form using a high-level programming language. This allows graphical elements to be developed that build upon lower-level primitives and can themselves be combined into yet more complex elements. In addition to these programming capabilities *Mathematica* provides a huge set of functions that range from file input and output, through numerical functions, to symbolic mathematics. With all these tools *Mathematica* works well for a wide range of graphical applications, from creating specific plots to constructing very general diagrams and figures.

The Purpose of this Book

A powerful computer application must provide useful functionality and clearly describe how that functionality works. *Mathematica* provides powerful graphics capabilities and this book shows how they can be put to practical uses. It does this by providing a detailed reference to all of the graphics in *Mathematica* as well as presenting a large number of examples of real-world applications. One of my personal aims has been to collect the large body of results and functions that I have developed over my years working on *Mathematica*. Much of the material in this book, especially in Part III, is a collation of these results, presented as useful and documented functions. These are some of the important aims of this book:

- Introduce graphics in *Mathematica* to beginners

- Provide a detailed reference and description of graphics in *Mathematica*

- Describe visualization problems and their solution by *Mathematica*

- Collect useful results implemented in *Mathematica*

- Share ideas for implementing new features in *Mathematica*

- Show how to customize pictures with *Mathematica*

- Demonstrate real-world applications of graphics in *Mathematica*

The Sources for this Book

I joined the research and development staff at Wolfram Research in 1990 and have worked primarily on the *Mathematica* kernel as the main developer for graphics. I have also been engaged in areas such as the low-level kernel functions and data structures. Consequently, I have a large amount of firsthand knowledge on exactly how the graphics functions work and the types of problem to which *Mathematica* is especially well suited.

I'd like to demonstrate how *Mathematica* is used to solve real problems. It is not sufficient to know how to use the graphics functions, it is also necessary to recognize what to use them for. One important influence for the type of problem to tackle with *Mathematica* has been the time I spent engaged in scientific research into molecular physics. At that time, I had many different graphics problems. For example, I needed to make data plots of experimental results, construct diagrams of molecular properties, and plot computational results. Invariably, these were solved by writing Fortran programs, sometimes many lines of code for simple tasks. I look back now at these tasks and see how they could be carried out with *Mathematica* much more efficiently.

When I came to work at Wolfram Research, I started to add the experiences of *Mathematica* users to my own. One important source for these is the Technical Support department at Wolfram Research. Each week, I respond to many of the graphics questions that technical support engineers receive from users: "How do I make a plot such as this?", or "How do I get this to work like so?" Many of these questions I have turned into improvements in the system and many have become examples in *Mathematica Graphics*.

Another important source for material is from conferences and events at which I give talks and tutorials on graphics. Many of the people attending these events come to me with questions and ideas for making *Mathematica* do some special type of thing. Many of the more complicated examples in this book were conceived at a conference.

The Features of this Book

Mathematica Graphics is divided into four parts:

Part I describes the fundamental ways to use *Mathematica* to generate pictures by using the built-in functionality. It will be of interest both to elementary users and to those who are more advanced. Regardless of experience, this is a good place to start.

Part II takes a detailed look at the structure of graphics in conjunction with programming features. There are many examples given throughout, and a last chapter concentrates on solving a variety of problems, giving a detailed description to each. Also provided is important information about the way that graphical objects are put together to form pictures. This part lays the foundations for the techniques of graphics programming and demonstrates some of the unique features of *Mathematica*.

Part III studies the application of *Mathematica* to solve real-world problems. These include the visualization of numerical data, the design of effective data plots, and applications in geometry. The material here will be attractive to readers who want to solve particular problems as opposed to learning more about *Mathematica*.

Part IV is a reference to all the different types of graphics objects in *Mathematica*. This is provided as a detailed reference with examples for each of these objects.

The diskette included in the back of the book contains a large number of packages described and used in the text. These extend the graphics functionality of *Mathematica*. Some of these packages make use of *MathLink* binaries. The source code that build these is included, as are actual binaries compiled for Microsoft Windows and Macintosh systems. Also included are data sets that are used in some of the examples in the book. The diskette is written in a DOS format, which can be read by most computers. The material is stored in separate DOS, Macintosh, and Unix and NeXT archives, so that file transfer problems will be prevented. The appendix includes an extensive description of how to install and test the diskette.

Another noteworthy feature of the book is the chapter on color; Chapter 11 is printed entirely in four color. This combines the text description with the pictures, making it more convenient for the reader.

Which Version of *Mathematica*

This book has been prepared with the version of *Mathematica* that will follow Version 2.2. The vast majority of the examples will work in Version 2.2, and with older versions. When an example is known not to work in one of these versions, the text points this out.

Acknowledgements

There are many people who have contributed to this project. I would like to thank all of them for their ideas, enthusiasm, and encouragement.

My publisher, Allan Wylde, from the very beginning has been a powerful force driving to complete the project and at the same time maintain the highest standards of quality. He has also been extremely responsive, something which I really appreciated during some of the more stressful moments. Paul Wellin has been an essential help, being available to hear my ideas, make comments on particular parts of the manuscript as it developed, and provide general encouragement. Stephen Wolfram, as ever, has encouraged me to think of the book as a whole and of its place in the *Mathematica* pantheon. It is easy to be sidetracked by details in a book; while these are important, the project as a cohesive whole must also be nurtured. The reviewers of the manuscript have provided invaluable comments and ideas: Paul Abbott, John Novak, Mark Yoder, Troels Petersen, and Steve Christensen. Joe Kaiping implemented TEX macros and many design features for the book; he also cut the PostScript pages. In addition he worked with me on lots of little software tools that made the production of the book go smoothly. These tools were also fun to put together. John Bonadies designed the cover, the part and chapter openers, and gave expert advice on a variety of other design issues. Jan Benes worked on the production of the book. Proofreading and other invaluable work was carried out by Jan Progen. A special recognition must be given to all the technical support engineers here at Wolfram Research for passing so many interesting questions to me. There are many people at Wolfram Research who have given me invaluable input and help on the book. These include: Jerry Keiper, Dave Withoff, Joe Grohens, Shawn Sheridan, George Beck, Jean Buck, Andre Kuzniarek, Glenn Scholebo, Oleg Perelet, Tom Sherlock, Thomas Chin, Jane Rich, Dara Pond, and Laurie Scoggins. Finally I would like to recognize all the great people at Wolfram Research who make it a stimulating, entertaining, and friendly place to work.

In Conclusion

It has taken me more than two years to write this book, and I trust you will find it useful. I am always interested in hearing of noteworthy pictures that people have made. Please feel free to communicate these to me, along with any ideas or comments you have about matters related to graphics and *Mathematica*.

Tom Wickham-Jones (graphics@wri.com)
August 1994
Wolfram Research

Contents

PART I
The Built-in Functions

Chapter 1
Introduction to Mathematica

In order to make use of this book readers should be familiar with certain concepts. They should be capable of launching *Mathematica*, entering input, and receiving output. They should also have some understanding of the different types of expression that *Mathematica* can work with.

For those who are very new to *Mathematica*, the documentation with which it comes will describe how it can be launched and how simple evaluations can be carried out. There will be documentation that describes the specifics of interacting with *Mathematica* on their particular computer. Also included is a book, *Mathematica: A System for Doing Mathematics by Computer*, Second Edition, by Stephen Wolfram, the standard reference to the system. The student version of *Mathematica* now ships with an adapted edition of this book. In the *Mathematica* book is a section called "The Tour of *Mathematica*" (in some versions this is also available in an electronic form). This tour is probably a good place to start to get some idea of the different functionality available in *Mathematica*. Working through these examples is a useful excercise for the novice *Mathematica* user.

The rest of this chapter is a very brief description of some key concepts that will be used throughout *Mathematica Graphics*. It is provided here as a refresher for readers who so desire. People should be able to comprehend these simple examples before proceeding.

1.1 Basic Input and Output

For these examples the text that follows each input prompt `In[x]:=` can be entered, it can be evaluated, and then the result will be displayed after the output prompt `Out[x]:=`. *Mathematica* works by getting an input and displaying the result.

Enter an input to *Mathematica*, such as a simple sum, and the result is returned.

```
In[1]:= 12 + 25
Out[1]= 37
```

Here there is an implicit multiplication operator, a space, for this integer arithmetic.

```
In[2]:= 25 + 12 43
Out[2]= 541
```

Mathematica will work with floating-point numbers as well as integers.

```
In[3]:= 4.5 / 45.9
Out[3]= 0.0980392
```

Sqrt is one example of the many built-in mathematical functions.

```
In[4]:= Sqrt[56.9]
Out[4]= 7.54321
```

% refers to the result of the previous evaluation. Here the previous result is squared.

```
In[5]:= %^2
Out[5]= 56.9
```

%*num* utilizes the result `Out[num]`, here `Out[2]`. This cannot evaluate to an integer without loss of precision and returns in this partially evaluated form.

```
In[6]:= Sqrt[%2]
Out[6]= Sqrt[541]
```

The command N converts expressions to real numbers. The exact square root is now evaluated.

```
In[7]:= N[%]
Out[7]= 23.2594
```

Note that *Mathematica* has built-in complex arithmetic. Here a complex number is returned.

```
In[8]:= ArcSin[%]
Out[8]= 1.5708 - 3.83939 I
```

Mixed arithmetic with all the different types of numbers can be carried out.

```
In[9]:= % + 9.5
Out[9]= 11.0708 - 3.83939 I
```

Mathematical functions work with complex numbers in the expected way. There is no changing of arithmetic modes.

```
In[10]:= Exp[%]
Out[10]= -49244.7 + 41293.6 I
```

?fun will display a message of descriptive text about a function.

```
In[11]:= ?ArcSin
ArcSin[z] gives the arc sine of the complex number z.
```

1.2 *Mathematica* Expressions

One can enter sequences of numbers and apply mathematical operations to them, in a similar way to using an electronic calculator. Of course *Mathematica* can do much more. This can be seen by considering the different types of expression that *Mathematica* understands.

Number	1, 1/2, 1.5, 1.5 + 5.6 I
Symbol	a, b, foo
String	"This is a string"
Normal Expression	f[x, y]

Different types of *Mathematica* expressions.

Symbols

Symbol expressions are extremely useful since they can hold values. The value of a symbol can be any other *Mathematica* expression. Symbols are an atomic type of expression, *i.e.*, they have no sub-parts.

This creates the symbol x and gives it a value of 52.

```
In[12]:= x = 52
Out[12]= 52
```

The symbol x evaluates to return its value.

```
In[13]:= x
Out[13]= 52
```

y has no value so it evaluates to itself.

```
In[14]:= y^5
          5
Out[14]= y
```

Assign a value to y.	*In[15]:=* **y = 53**
	Out[15]= 53
y now has a value and we get a different result.	*In[16]:=* **y∧5**
	Out[16]= 418195493

Strings

String expressions hold raw textual data. They are also atomic expressions.

A string expression is made by placing text inside double quotes, " ". In this example these are dropped when the result prints. A string expression evaluates to itself.	*In[17]:=* **"This is a string"**
	Out[17]= This is a string
StringQ tests to see if its argument is a string expression.	*In[18]:=* **StringQ[%]**
	Out[18]= True
Since the string evaluates to itself the result comes back unchanged.	*In[19]:=* **"54 + 31"**
	Out[19]= 54 + 31
ToExpression will take a string expression and interpret it as *Mathematica* input.	*In[20]:=* **ToExpression[%]**
	Out[20]= 85

Normal Expressions

Normal expressions provide a way to collect atomic expressions into groups. Each part of the group is itself a *Mathematica* expression.

This is an example of a List, here containing numbers. It is saved as the value of the symbol list1.	*In[21]:=* **list1 = {1,2,3,4}**
	Out[21]= {1, 2, 3, 4}
This general expression has parts. First returns the first element.	*In[22]:=* **First[list1]**
	Out[22]= 1
The Head of an expression identifies it.	*In[23]:=* **Head[list1]**
	Out[23]= List
This returns the second element.	*In[24]:=* **Part[list1, 2]**
	Out[24]= 2
[[*num*]] is a shorthand notation for Part.	*In[25]:=* **list1[[3]]**
	Out[25]= 3
Length as its name implies returns the number of elements in an expression.	*In[26]:=* **Length[list1]**
	Out[26]= 4

Here we call the function `Table` to generate a list. Often this is faster and more convenient than entering each element explicitly.

```
In[27]:= list2 = Table[i, {i, 10}]

Out[27]= {1, 2, 3, 4, 5, 6, 7, 8, 9, 10}
```

Just as normal expressions have heads so do atomic expressions.

```
In[28]:= {Head[a], Head[5], Head[6.3], Head["foo bar"]}

Out[28]= {Symbol, Integer, Real, String}
```

Expressions are the only objects in *Mathematica*.

Number expressions represent numbers.

String expressions hold raw text.

Symbol expressions can be assigned values.

Normal expressions are composed of a head and zero or more elements.

The head and elements of an expression are themselves expressions.

Summary on *Mathematica* expressions.

1.3 Different Interfaces to *Mathematica*

Mathematica is split into two parts. The kernel is the computational engine of the system, it carries out computations that are sent to it. It receives *Mathematica* expressions and evaluates them. The front end is concerned with interface issues, such as how input is entered and how the results are displayed. The kernel provides essentially the same set of functions for all the different computer systems on which *Mathematica* runs. The front end is not identical on all these different systems, rather it depends on the type of computer being used.

On many computers *Mathematica* provides a sophisticated front end that supports interactive documents mixing computations, text, and graphics. Such a document is called a notebook. One difference, relevant to this book, between a notebook and a non-notebook front end is how graphics work. Typically when graphics are produced on a notebook front end they appear in the document immediately below the input. On a non-notebook front end a separate window will appear with the graphic.

The notebook front end provides many useful facilities for working with *Mathematica* graphics. Many of these are also available with the non-notebook front end though not in such a convenient form. Chapters 6 and 26 describe these features and discuss the difference between the notebook and non-notebook front ends in more detail.

1.4 Learning More about *Mathematica*

Material about *Mathematica* is available in books as well as in electronic forms (sometimes these two are combined). The many books about *Mathematica* range from elementary guides for getting started to those covering topics such as *Mathematica* programming, numerical analysis, or calculus, to references on specific topics such as graph theory or financial modeling. In addition there are two journals, *The Mathematica Journal* and *Mathematica in Education*. Many of the books and both of the journals possess electronic supplements.

The electronic forms of *Mathematica* material include *MathSource* the repository of *Mathematica* material that is maintained by Wolfram Research, Inc. This can be accessed by email from `mathsource@wri.com` or through anonymous FTP, Gopher, or World Wide Web at `mathsource.wri.com` [IP\# 140.177.10.5]. *Mathematica* is a frequent topic of discussion on many Internet news groups; the group `sci.math.symbolic` is one favorite. A moderated forum accessible through `mathgroup@yoda.physics.unc.edu` is devoted to *Mathematica* questions and information. For people who have questions or observations this is often a suitable place where these can be asked or aired.

Chapter 2
A Tour of Plotting

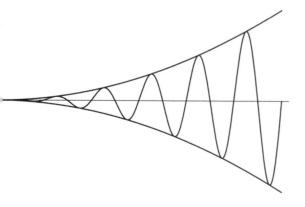

This chapter introduces the basic types of *Mathematica* plots. There are commands that can make a variety of different pictures from functions and from numeric data. In all of *Mathematica* there are many ways plots can be made. This chapter introduces the simplest and most basic.

2.1 Function Plotting

Mathematica can produce two-dimensional plots, contour plots, and three-dimensional surface plots of functions.

`Plot`	two-dimensional graphic
`ParametricPlot`	two-dimensional graphic
`Plot3D`	three-dimensional surface
`ParametricPlot3D`	three-dimensional surface
`ContourPlot`	contour plot
`DensityPlot`	density plot

Mathematica commands that graph functions.

Plot is one of the simplest plotting commands. It generates a two-dimensional plot, the *y* value derived by evaluating a function over a range of *x* values.

In[1]:= `Plot[Sin[x], {x,0,2Pi}]`

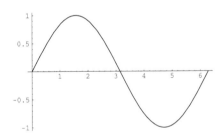

ParametricPlot makes a two-dimensional plot. The *x* and *y* values are determined by a pair of functions of a single variable.

In[2]:= `ParametricPlot[{3.5 Sin[t], 2.5 Cos[t]}, {t,0,2Pi}]`

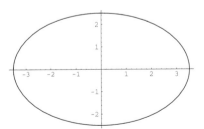

Plot3D is the three-dimensional equivalent of Plot. Here the height of the surface is determined by evaluating the function for different values of x and y.

In[3]:= **Plot3D[Sin[x y], {x,0,2Pi}, {y,0,Pi}]**

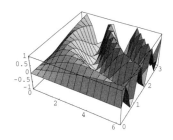

The syntax for ContourPlot is very similar to Plot3D. One of the strengths of *Mathematica* is the common syntax of related functions.

In[4]:= **ContourPlot[x^2 - y^2, {x,-2,2}, {y,-2,2}]**

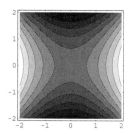

DensityPlot shows a bitmap representation of a function.

In[5]:= **DensityPlot[Sin[x y], {x,-1,1}, {y,-1,1}]**

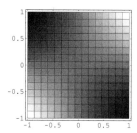

This is the three-dimensional equivalent of ParametricPlot. With a two-dimensional parametrization a surface is generated.

```
In[6]:= ParametricPlot3D[
            {2 Sin[z] Sin[t], 2 Sin[z] Cos[t],z},
            {z,-Pi,Pi}, {t,0,2Pi}]
```

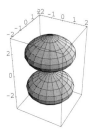

With a one-dimensional parametrization ParametricPlot3D generates a space curve.

```
In[7]:= ParametricPlot3D[{Sin[t], Cos[t],t}, {t,0,4Pi}]
```

▶ *What Do These Images Show?*

These pictures can be categorized according to the type of image generated and the type of input required. Part IV of *Mathematica Graphics* describes in detail the type of result produced by all these commands and how they are rendered.

Plot and ParametricPlot

Both functions plot lines in two dimensions that represent a function. ParametricPlot is a generalization of Plot: Plot[*fun*[*x*], {*x*, *x1*, *x2*}] is equivalent to ParametricPlot[{*x*,*fun*[*x*]}, {*x*,*x1*,*x2*}]. Plot is more compact and is preferable when applicable.

Plot3D and ParametricPlot3D

Both functions produce three-dimensional surfaces with differences somewhat analogous to those between Plot and ParametricPlot. Plot3D has a more compact input notation, executes faster, and produces a smaller result. ParametricPlot3D can plot more general surfaces. Another difference is that ParametricPlot3D can also plot a space curve whereas Plot3D can only plot a surface.

ContourPlot and DensityPlot

A contour plot of a function, $f[x, y]$, shows contours or level sets representing particular values of the function. It displays the loci of x and y that represent values of z from the equation $f[x, y] = z$. The space between the lines is normally shaded to help to distinguish them. A contour plot tends to show the long-range behavior of a function. It can show how the values of the function in one region of the $x\,y$ plane compare with values in another. Also a contour plot is suitable for looking at functions that do not vary rapidly.

A density plot is related to the contour plot. It is similar to a shaded contour plot with a large number of shaded regions. The density plot tends to show the short-range behavior of a function and is suitable for looking at functions that vary rapidly, for example with singularities. The contour plot and density plot are complementary to one another.

▶ *What Functions Can Be Plotted?*

All functions plotted by these commands must return real numbers over the plotting range. If this is not the case an error will result. The plot will show those parts for which the function returns real numbers.

When x is negative `Sqrt[Sin[x]]` is imaginary. `Plot` must receive a real number and thus an error message is generated.

`In[8]:= Plot[Sqrt[Sin[x]], {x,0,5Pi}]`

`Plot::plnr: CompiledFunction[x, Sqrt[Sin[x]], -CompiledCode-][x]`
`            is not a machine-size real number at x = 3.27249.`

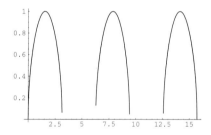

For this function, real values are ensured by wrapping it in `Re`.

`In[9]:= Plot[Re[Sqrt[Sin[x]]], {x,0,5Pi}]`

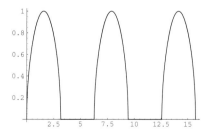

The same constraint exists for all function plotting commands. The function *must* return a real number.

```
In[10]:= Plot3D[ArcSin[x y],{x,-2,2}, {y,-2,2}]
```

```
Plot3D::gval:
    Function value 1.5708 - 2.06344 I at grid point xi = 1, yi =
    1 is not a real number.
```

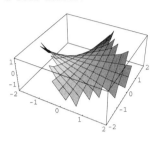

Of course, complex valued functions can easily be plotted using other tools available in *Mathematica*. For example, the absolute value of a function can be plotted (using Abs) with shading according to the argument or some other characteristic (using Arg or Im). There are a number of other techniques that can be used.

2.2 Data Plotting

When a plot is to be made of some data or numbers then different commands must be used. It is slightly more complicated to demonstrate data rather than function plotting since the data must be generated in some way. These could come from an external source, maybe a spreadsheet program, or from some external measurement. Alternatively, the data may have come from inside *Mathematica*. The examples in this section generate data from within *Mathematica*, a simple way to construct data. Chapter 4 page 54 shows how data can be read into *Mathematica*. In general the topic of plotting data is quite involved and Part III of *Mathematica Graphics* devotes several chapters to it.

The main method that *Mathematica* provides to hold a group of objects such as a data set is a List. Therefore the data plotting commands are called list plotting commands. For the function plotting commands there are equivalent list plotting commands.

Function Plotting	Data Plotting
Plot [*fun*, *xrng*]	ListPlot [*data*]
Plot3D [*fun*, *xrng*, *yrng*]	ListPlot3D [*data*]
ContourPlot [*fun*, *xrng*, *yrng*]	ListContourPlot [*data*]
DensityPlot [*fun*, *xrng*, *yrng*]	ListDensityPlot [*data*]

Function and data plotting commands in *Mathematica*.

To show data plotting a data set must be generated. One way to do this is a Table command.

In[11]:= **data1 = Table[i∧2, {i,20}]**

Out[11]= {1, 4, 9, 16, 25, 36, 49, 64, 81, 100, 121, 144, 169, 196, 225, 256, 289, 324, 361, 400}

This plots **data1**. The ith point has, by default, coordinates {i,Part[data1,i]}.

In[12]:= **ListPlot[data1]**

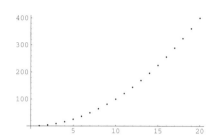

In order to join the points with a line the option PlotJoined is set to True. Options are described in the next chapter.

In[13]:= **ListPlot[data1, PlotJoined -> True]**

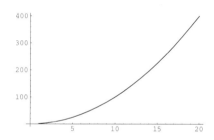

To set the *x* coordinate explicitly it can be explicitly placed in the list. ListPlot will accept a list of pairs of numbers, each pair giving a coordinate {x, y}.

A list of pairs of numbers is generated. The output is suppressed with the semicolon.

In[14]:= **data2 = Table[{i, Sqrt[i]}, {i,0,.5,.025}];**

The ith point has *x* and *y* coordinates Part[data2,i,1] and Part[data2,i,2].

In[15]:= **ListPlot[data2]**

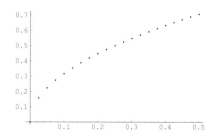

The list plotting functions ListPlot3D, ListContourPlot, and ListDensityPlot all have a command syntax that is closely related. Here an example using ListPlot3D is given; it could have used either of the other commands by using ListContourPlot or ListDensityPlot in place of ListPlot3D. The data that are passed to these commands must form an array or grid of z values and not a set of $\{x, y, z\}$ values. Part III discusses how plots can be made from data in more general forms.

The data to be plotted. It is a grid of the z values.

In[16]:= **data3 = Table[x - y, {y, -1, 1}, {x, -1, 1}]**

Out[16]= {{0, 1, 2}, {-1, 0, 1}, {-2, -1, 0}}

A surface is plotted over the data.

In[17]:= **ListPlot3D[data3]**

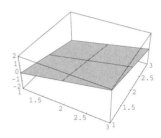

▶ *A Common Problem with Axes*

In the picture above the axes are not labeled with the expected values. The Table command had x and y going from -1 to 1, but the axes did not show this. The input given to ListPlot3D did not describe the x and y values at all, the input just gave z values describing the height of the various parts of the surface.

This problem is solved by specifying the range of coordinates in x and in y with the MeshRange option. The next chapter will give a fuller discussion of options but since this is a common problem it is discussed here.

ListPlot3D[*data*, MeshRange -> {{x_{min}, x_{max}}, {y_{min}, y_{max}}}]

ListContourPlot[*data*, MeshRange -> {{x_{min}, x_{max}}, {y_{min}, y_{max}}}]

ListDensityPlot[*data*, MeshRange -> {{x_{min}, x_{max}}, {y_{min}, y_{max}}}]

Using the MeshRange option.

Passing the proper ranges of *x* and *y* to the option MeshRange will give the axes the correct values.

In[18]:= **ListPlot3D[data3, MeshRange -> {{-1,1}, {-1,1}}]**

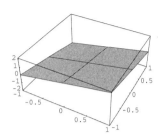

▸ *Suitable Data*

The data that can be plotted with the list plotting commands are restricted as expected from the restrictions for the function plotting commands. The data must be capable of being turned into real numbers.

Mathematica keeps this data in its exact form.

In[19]:= **data = Table[Sqrt[i], {i,10}]**

Out[19]= {1, Sqrt[2], Sqrt[3], 2, Sqrt[5], Sqrt[6], Sqrt[7],

2 Sqrt[2], 3, Sqrt[10]}

ListPlot will attempt to convert its data into real numbers. Here this conversion succeeds.

In[20]:= **ListPlot[data]**

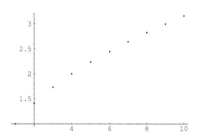

Here one of the items does not convert to a number. In this case a gap is left in the plot.

In[21]:= **ListPlot[{1,4,a,16,25,36}]**

Graphics::gptn:

Coordinate a in {3, a} is not a floating-point number.

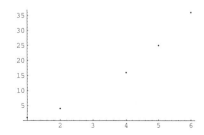

2.3 *Mathematica* Graphics Objects

For every input that is sent to *Mathematica* a result is returned. For these graphics commands it may appear that the result is the picture. This is incorrect. The result of these commands is a *Mathematica* expression; it could not be anything else. The result is printed after the output prompt. In most parts of *Mathematica Graphics* the result is not printed after the picture. In these examples it is shown to demonstrate that *Mathematica* really returns a result.

The result of this command follows the output prompt Out. The result is printed in a special way that does not expose its structure. The PlotPoints option, described later in the chapter, is decreased to reduce the size of this structure for when it is printed.

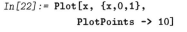

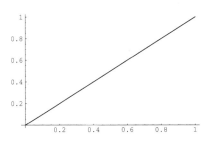

```
Out[22]= -Graphics-
```

The actual contents of the result can be exposed by printing it in InputForm [1]. It has a Head of Graphics and contains primitives that describe the picture to be drawn.

```
In[23]:= InputForm[%]

Out[23]//InputForm=
  Graphics[{{Line[{{1.111111111111111*10^-7,
        1.111111111111111*10^-7},
       {0.1068671554305544, 0.1068671554305544},
       {0.2214117887013872, 0.2214117887013872},
       {0.3295903217847181, 0.3295903217847181},
       {0.4356468214722153, 0.4356468214722153},
       {0.545136843319434, 0.545136843319434},
       {0.6525048317708188, 0.6525048317708188},
       {0.7633063423819251, 0.7633063423819251},
       {0.8719858195971976, 0.8719858195971976},
       {0.9785432634166363, 0.9785432634166363},
       {0.9999998888888889, 0.9999998888888889}}]}},
  {PlotRange -> Automatic, AspectRatio -> GoldenRatio^(-1),
   DisplayFunction :> $DisplayFunction,
   ColorOutput -> Automatic, Axes -> Automatic,
   AxesOrigin -> Automatic, PlotLabel -> None,
   AxesLabel -> None, Ticks -> Automatic, GridLines -> None,
   Prolog -> {}, Epilog -> {}, AxesStyle -> Automatic,
   Background -> Automatic, DefaultColor -> Automatic,
   DefaultFont :> $DefaultFont, RotateLabel -> True,
   Frame -> False, FrameStyle -> Automatic,
   FrameTicks -> Automatic, FrameLabel -> None,
   PlotRegion -> Automatic}]
```

---

[1]The default style of output is OutputForm. InputForm prints in a style that can be used as input to *Mathematica*.

This graphics object can be redisplayed with the command Show.

In[24]:= **Show[%]**

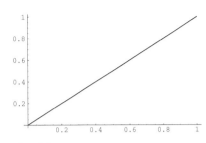

Out[24]= -Graphics-

Just as the command Plot produces a Graphics object all the graphics commands produce different graphics objects. Each of these graphics objects contains the information that can be displayed to produce the desired picture. Since the result is a *Mathematica* expression it can be used and manipulated like any other expression. This will prove to be extremely useful. One simple thing that can be done is to assign this result to be the value of a symbol.

For a graphics object like the one above, a Graphics object, the contents are a collection of graphical primitives such as a Line primitive. Part II of *Mathematica Graphics* introduces the primitives in more detail and Part IV has a detailed description of what all these graphics objects can contain.

Plot	ListPlot	Graphics
ContourPlot	ListContourPlot	ContourGraphics
DensityPlot	ListDensityPlot	DensityGraphics
Plot3D	ListPlot3D	SurfaceGraphics
ParametricPlot3D		Graphics3D

Graphics commands and the objects they produce.

▸ *Show*

The command Show was shown above redisplaying the image. It is a key *Mathematica* command for working with graphics with several uses: it can be used to redisplay a picture, it can change an option setting for an existing picture, and it can combine several pictures.

Show[*image*]   display *image*

Show[*image*, *option* -> *value*]   redisplay *image* with *option* set to *value*

Show[*image₁*, *image₂*, ...]   combine *image₁*, *image₂*, ...

Uses of Show.

Reseting Options

The previous section showed how it was necessary to set the MeshRange option of ListPlot3D. This can be done as follows with Show. The next chapter describes options in much more detail.

The grid of *z* values.

```
In[25]:= data3 = Table[x - y, {y, -1, 1}, {x, -1, 1}]

Out[25]= {{0, 1, 2}, {-1, 0, 1}, {-2, -1, 0}}
```

The axes are not labeled with the *x* and *y* values used in the Table command.

```
In[26]:= ListPlot3D[data3]
```

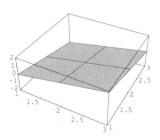

To reset the MeshRange option the new setting can be combined with a call to Show.

```
In[27]:= Show[%, MeshRange -> {{-1,1}, {-1,1}}]
```

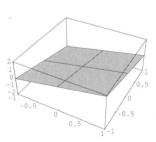

Combining Pictures

A first picture generated by Plot.

In[28]:= **Plot[Sin[x], {x,0,2Pi}]**

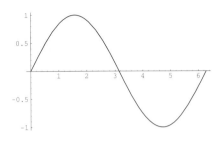

Another picture shows some data plotted by ListPlot.

In[29]:= **ListPlot[**
　　　　Table[{i, Sin[i] + Random[Real, {-0.1, 0.2}]},
　　　　　{i,0,2Pi,0.1}]]

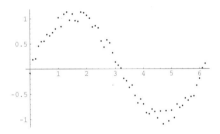

Calling Show with two graphics objects will cause them to be displayed together in one picture.

In[30]:= **Show[%, %%]**

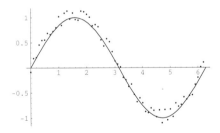

　　　In this example we combine the results of Plot and the result of ListPlot. Both results are Graphics objects and it is not surprising that the result of the combination is a Graphics object. In fact all the different types of *Mathematica* graphics can be combined.

2.4 GraphicsArray

A final type of picture to be demonstrated in this chapter is `GraphicsArray`. This is a collection of other plots.

Here a single plot is made.

In[31]:= **p1 = Plot[Sin[x], {x,0,2Pi}]**

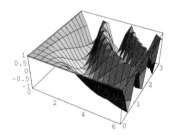

Another plot is constructed.

In[32]:= **p2 = Plot3D[Cos[x y], {x,0,2Pi}, {y,0,Pi}]**

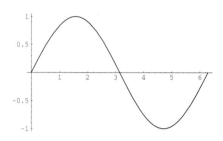

A collection of pictures is made by placing an array inside `GraphicsArray`. The result is displayed with a call to `Show`.

In[33]:= **Show[GraphicsArray[{{p1,p2}, {p2,p1}}]]**

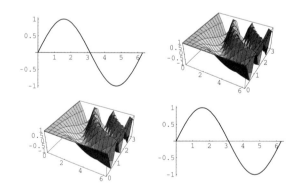

The Frame option of GraphicsArray
draws a frame around all the images.
This makes it a convenient way to draw a
border around a single picture.

In[34]:= **Show[GraphicsArray[{p1}], Frame -> True]**

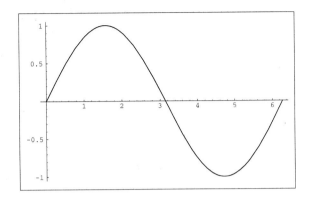

2.5 Advanced Function Plotting

This last section looks at some more features and details of the Plot command. These will go beyond the
basic uses that have been examined so far. They will look at some useful features and explain certain details
that sometimes cause problems.

▶ *Multiple Plots*

The previous section demonstrated how Show could combine graphical images into one picture. It is
possible to do this directly from the Plot command.

Here three functions are plotted.

In[35]:= **Plot[{x^2, -x^2, x^2 Sin[x]}, {x, 0, 12Pi}]**

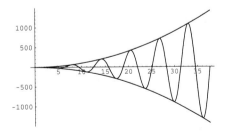

ParametricPlot can also plot multiple functions.

```
In[36]:= ParametricPlot[{
            LegendreP[2, Cos[t]] {Cos[t]/3, Sin[t]/3},
            LegendreP[4, Cos[t]] {Sin[t]/3, Cos[t]/3}
          }, {t,0,2Pi}]
```

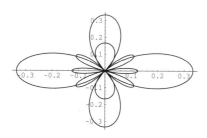

The plots that are combined can be distinguished using the PlotStyle option. This and the other options are discussed in the next chapter.

▶ *The Evaluation of Plot*

Evaluation and Hold

Mathematica works by evaluating expressions. An input expression is passed into an evaluation process. The result of evaluation forms the output expression. *Mathematica Graphics* will not present a detailed description of the *Mathematica* evaluator since that is described in Chapter 2.5 of the *Mathematica* book. Here only a brief description relevant to a discussion of plotting will be given.

The input evaluates to 2.

```
In[37]:= 1+1
Out[37]= 2
```

The argument of the expression with head f evaluates to 2. This is standard evaluation.

```
In[38]:= f[1+1]
Out[38]= f[2]
```

The attribute HoldAll specifies non-standard evaluation of the arguments of Hold.

```
In[39]:= Attributes[Hold]
Out[39]= {HoldAll}
```

The argument of the expression with head Hold does not evaluate to 2. This is non-standard evaluation.

```
In[40]:= Hold[1+1]
Out[40]= Hold[1 + 1]
```

The standard evaluation sequence is that the arguments of expression are evaluated. However, when an expression has a head with the HoldAll attribute the arguments will be evaluated in a non-standard way.

Plot and HoldAll

The HoldAll attribute means that the arguments to Plot are not evaluated before it is called.

```
In[41]:= Attributes[Plot]
Out[41]= {HoldAll, Protected}
```

The non-standard evaluation of Plot allows the plot variable to be local to the Plot command. This is useful if the variable already has a value.

The symbol x is given a value.

```
In[42]:= x = 1
Out[42]= 1
```

Since Plot is HoldAll the x does not evaluate to 1, *i.e.,* it does not try to do Plot[Sin[1], {1,0,5}].

```
In[43]:= Plot[Sin[x], {x,0,5}]
```

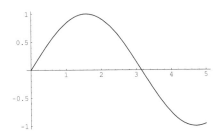

If Plot were not HoldAll the x would evaluate and this would be the input received by the Plot command. An error would result.

```
In[44]:= Plot[Sin[1], {1,0,5}]
Plot::itraw: Raw object 1 cannot be used as an iterator.
Out[44]= Plot[Sin[1], {1, 0, 5}]
```

Since Plot has the HoldAll attribute a problem can arise when an inner expression must evaluate before plotting is done. An example follows.

This fails because Plot is HoldAll. The Table function does not evaluate to a real number and errors are generated.

```
In[45]:= Plot[Table[t^n, {n,4}], {t,0,5}]

Plot::plnr: CompiledFunction[t, <<1>>, -CompiledCode-][t]
    is not a machine-size real number at t = 0.200376.
```

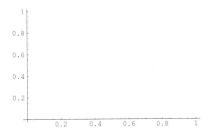

Evaluate overrides the HoldAll
attribute and causes the Table to
evaluate before plotting is started.

In[46]:= `Plot[Evaluate[Table[t^n, {n,5}]], {t,0,5}]`

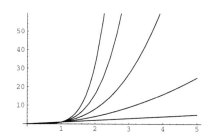

▸ *Adaptive Sampling*

Plot and ParametricPlot work by sampling a function at certain points. These points are then placed inside Line primitives to form lines. These primitives can be exposed by printing them in InputForm as was shown previously. Plot and ParametricPlot use an adaptive sampling technique that samples more points in regions where the function changes rapidly. This allows a better looking plot to be generated.

As the function becomes more oscillatory
more points are chosen.

In[47]:= `Plot[Sin[x^3], {x,0,Pi}]`

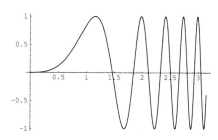

If the step size was fixed, as in this data
generated from Table, the sampling will
be either not frequent enough for the
oscillating parts or redundant for the
smooth parts.

In[48]:= `ListPlot[Table[{x, Sin[x^3]}, {x,0,Pi,0.05}],
          PlotJoined -> True]`

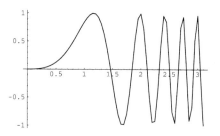

As the function oscillates more rapidly the adaptive sampling algorithm may not make enough samples.

In[49]:= `Plot[Sin[x], {x,0,60Pi}]`

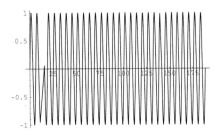

One simple way to sample more points is to increase the setting of the `PlotPoints` option.

In[50]:= `Plot[Sin[x], {x,0,60Pi}, PlotPoints -> 50]`

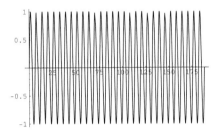

It should be noted that only `Plot` and `ParametricPlot` implement adaptive plotting. When other graphics commands such as `Plot3D` are being used it may be necessary to increase the number of points at which the function is evaluated. This is done with the `PlotPoints` option and is discussed in the next chapter. The adaptive algorithm is documented in Part IV.

2.6 Summary

This chapter has shown the simplest and most basic ways to generate *Mathematica* graphics. It has shown two and three-dimensional plots as well as contour and density plots all made from functions and data sets. When functions are used they must return real numbers and when data are plotted they must consist of real numbers. All the graphics commands return *Mathematica* expressions that describe a particular type of graphics object. For example, `Plot` returns a `Graphics` object. Finally, *Mathematica* graphics objects can be redisplayed with the command `Show`.

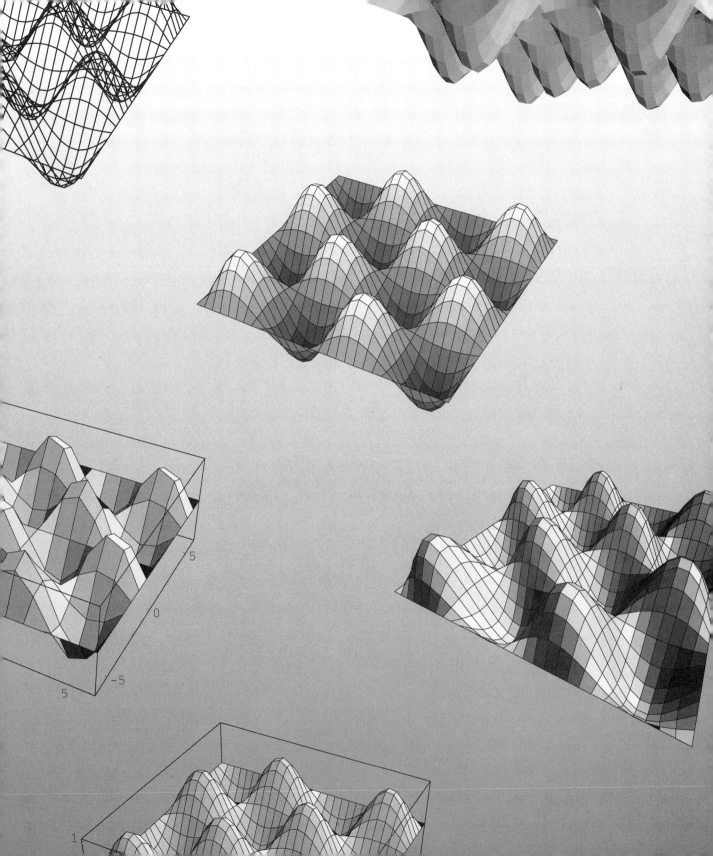

5

0

-5

5

Chapter 3
Graphics Options

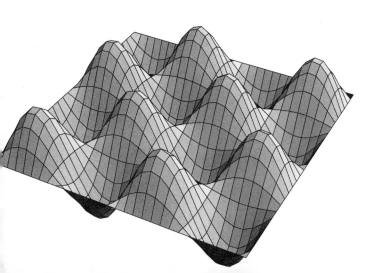

This chapter shows how the appearance of pictures made in *Mathematica* can be altered. It will show how to contruct two and three-dimensional graphical images and then add embellishments suitable for use in a paper or report. The chapter does not provide a detailed description of every option of every graphics function, as this is done in Part IV. It does demonstrate some of the more important options and discusses reasons why it may be necessary to make use of them.

3.1 Using *Mathematica* Options

When *Mathematica* makes a picture, or executes any command, there are often a number of choices as to how that command is carried out. These choices can be controlled with the use of options. The description of options given here applies throughout *Mathematica*.

command [*arg1* , ... *opt* -> *val*]	execute *command* with option *opt* set to *val*
Options [*command*]	return the options of *command*
Options [*command* , *opt*]	return just the option *opt*
SetOptions [*command* , *option* -> *value*]	set the default of *opt* to *val*
SetOptions [*command* , *opt*$_1$ -> *val*$_1$, *opt*$_2$ ->*val*$_2$, ...]	
	set the default for several options
FullOptions [*obj* , *opt*]	return the setting of option *opt* in object *obj*

Mathematica utilities for working with options.

An option can be set when a graphics command is issued.

In[1]:= **Plot[Sin[x], {x,0,2Pi}, Frame -> True]**

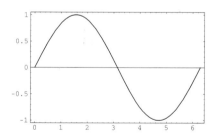

These are all the options of `Plot` and their default values.

```
In[2]:= Options[Plot]

Out[2]= {AspectRatio ->  ----1----- , Axes -> Automatic,
                          GoldenRatio

   AxesLabel -> None, AxesOrigin -> Automatic,

   AxesStyle -> Automatic, Background -> Automatic,

   ColorOutput -> Automatic, Compiled -> True,

   DefaultColor -> Automatic, Epilog -> {}, Frame -> False,

   FrameLabel -> None, FrameStyle -> Automatic,

   FrameTicks -> Automatic, GridLines -> None, MaxBend -> 10.,

   PlotDivision -> 30., PlotLabel -> None, PlotPoints -> 25,

   PlotRange -> Automatic, PlotRegion -> Automatic,

   PlotStyle -> Automatic, Prolog -> {}, RotateLabel -> True,

   Ticks -> Automatic, DefaultFont :> $DefaultFont,

   DisplayFunction :> $DisplayFunction}
```

The default setting for the `AspectRatio` option of `Plot`.

```
In[3]:= Options[Plot, AspectRatio]

Out[3]= {AspectRatio ->  ----1-----}
                         GoldenRatio
```

The default setting of the `AspectRatio` option is changed to be `Automatic`.

```
In[4]:= SetOptions[Plot, AspectRatio -> Automatic];
```

Now the default setting is different.

```
In[5]:= Options[Plot, AspectRatio]
Out[5]= {AspectRatio -> Automatic}
```

Now the same plot command as `In[1]` is given. However the result now has a different shape.

```
In[6]:= Plot[Sin[x], {x,0,2Pi}, Frame -> True]
```

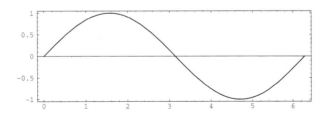

The default setting of `AspectRatio` is restored.

```
In[7]:= SetOptions[Plot, AspectRatio -> 1/GoldenRatio];
```

In general `SetOptions` should be used when some option is to be changed for every graphic generated in a *Mathematica* session. When some special option setting is only required for a few graphs it is usually better to set the option just in those cases.

▸ *Show*

When a picture has been made it is sometimes necessary to experiment with a range of option values. This can be done with the command Show as was demonstrated in the previous chapter. Once the settings that give the desired results have been found they can be made to be the default.

A picture is generated with Plot and saved as the value of a symbol pic1.

*In[8]:= * **pic1 = Plot[x^5 - 4 x^3 + 2 x, {x,-2,2}]**

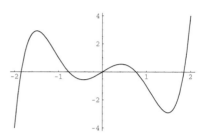

Show will use this value pic1 to re-create the picture.

*In[9]:= * **Show[pic1]**

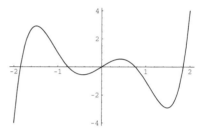

Now pic1 is displayed again with the value of the option Frame set to True. This causes frame axes, axes around the frame of the picture, to be drawn.

*In[10]:= * **Show[pic1, Frame -> True]**

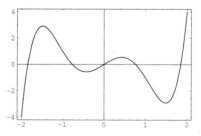

Thus the names of options and their default settings are shown by Options. These defaults can be changed with SetOptions. Options can be set when a command is originally executed and can be altered by Show. Now some ways to use options will be demonstrated.

▶ *FullOptions*

For certain commands *Mathematica* returns special objects, which can be used later. Graphics objects are an important class of these though other examples include InterpolatingFunction and CompiledFunction objects. As was explained in Chapter 2 page 20 graphics objects are created by the graphics commands. This is very useful since they can be manipulated and redisplayed after they have been created. Changing an option with Show, as was just demonstrated, is one example; more sophisticated uses involving programming techniques are explored throughout Part II.

A graphics object may well contain options that were inserted as it was created. Sometimes it is useful to find out what the actual values of these options were. One way to do this would be to look in the object itself. This would require details of the structure of graphics objects as described in Part IV. A more convenient way to find out is to use FullOptions.

A simple plot.   *In[11]:=* **p1 = Plot[x, {x,0,1}]**

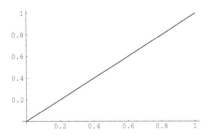

This is the setting of the AspectRatio   *In[12]:=* **FullOptions[p1, AspectRatio]**
option.
                                   Out[12]= 0.618034

For important options, such as AspectRatio and PlotRange in two-dimensional graphics, FullOptions returns the actual numerical equivalent even if a setting such as Automatic had been used.

Now the AspectRatio option is changed   *In[13]:=* **p2 = Plot[x, {x,0,1}, AspectRatio -> Automatic]**
to Automatic.

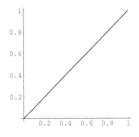

Even though the setting of   *In[14]:=* **FullOptions[p2, AspectRatio]**
AspectRatio is Automatic,
FullOptions returns a numerical   *Out[14]=* 1.
value.

3.2 Two-Dimensional Graphics Options

Mathematica provides many methods to annotate its images. In this section several examples of annotating and other features will presented. Each consists of a sequence of different commands adding elements to a picture to construct a final result.

▷ *Example 1: Frame Axes*

First some data to be plotted are made. The large output is suppressed with the trailing semicolon, ";".

In[15]:= **Table[{i, Sin[i^2] + Random[ ]/10}, {i, 0, 4, .1}];**

When ListPlot is executed, the default behavior of *Mathematica* is to draw axes.

In[16]:= **plot1 = ListPlot[%]**

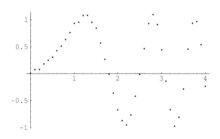

The default setting of the Axes option of ListPlot. This is why the axes were drawn in the previous picture.

In[17]:= **Options[ListPlot, Axes]**

Out[17]= {Axes -> Automatic}

The plot is now drawn with no axes. This is a naked picture that may be useful for an overlay.

In[18]:= **Show[plot1, Axes -> False]**

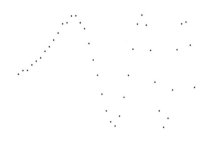

Here frame axes, a different type of axes, are drawn. These surround the image and consequently never obscure any of the graphical elements.

In[19]:= **Show[%, Frame -> True]**

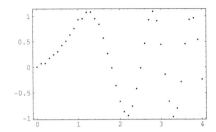

Labels can be added to the frame axes with the FrameLabel option.

In[20]:= **Show[%, FrameLabel -> {"Impetus", "Response"}]**

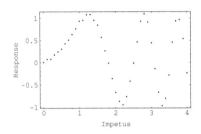

The PlotLabel option places a label at the top of the picture.

In[21]:= **Show[%, PlotLabel -> "Data Collected 11-11-92"]**

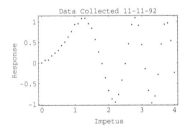

Now the font in which the text in the picture is displayed is altered.

In[22]:= **Show[%, DefaultFont -> {"Helvetica", 6}]**

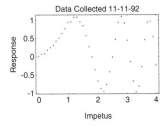

As a final effect FontForm gives the
PlotLabel a different font.

```
In[23]:= Show[%, PlotLabel ->
              FontForm["Data Collected 11-11-92",
                  {"Times-Roman", 8}]]
```

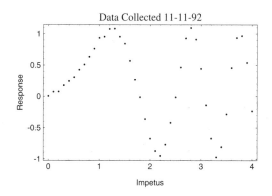

Here the plot was made and then experiments with different option settings were carried out. Finally a plot style considered to be optimal for displaying the information was produced. In Chapter 14 the principles that determine such a style are discussed. Often the desired style conforms to a norm for the data being presented. In this case, experimentation with options can find desirable style settings and then SetOptions can set that style for subsequent plots.

▶ *Example 2: A Range Plot*

Table is usually an efficient method to
generate a collection of numbers in
Mathematica.

```
In[24]:= data = Table[{i, i + 2 Random[ ]}, {i,5, 25}];
```

ListPlot shows the data. However the
axes obscure one of the points.

```
In[25]:= ListPlot[%]
```

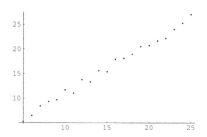

Frame axes would have worked. Instead AxesOrigin, the point where the axes cross, is changed. Since the setting is outside of the the range of coordinates the axes do not cross.

In[26]:= **Show[%, AxesOrigin -> {0,0}]**

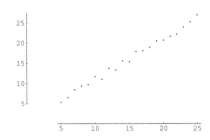

AspectRatio sets the shape of the picture. Automatic instructs *Mathematica* to use the same scale in *x* and *y*.

In[27]:= **Show[%, AspectRatio -> Automatic]**

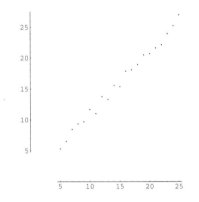

This final image shows pairs of numbers in an economical fashion that concentrates on the data. Chapter 14 discusses similar ways to generate effective plots. A plot like this can be described as a range plot. In such a picture the axes show both the actual values of the points and the range of values in the *x* and *y* directions.

▷ *The PlotRange Option*

This sequence of examples demonstrates how the range of points that *Mathematica* chooses to show in a picture can be altered to focus attention on some region.

A function is investigated by Plot. Some of the detail in the picture is not very clear.

In[28]:= **plot2 = Plot[Exp[-x^2] Cos[x], {x,-3,3}]**

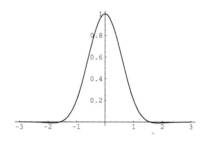

More detail is shown by using a PlotRange of -0.01 to 0.05 in the y direction.

In[29]:= **Show[%, PlotRange -> {-0.01, 0.05}]**

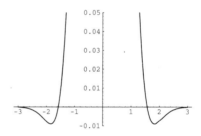

The default setting of PlotRange is Automatic. This instructs *Mathematica* to choose a representative sample of points.

In[30]:= **Options[Plot, PlotRange]**

Out[30]= {PlotRange -> Automatic}

plot2 was drawn with the default setting of Automatic. The actual range of coordinates used can be displayed with FullOptions as was shown in this chapter page 35.

In[31]:= **FullOptions[plot2, PlotRange]**

Out[31]= {{-3.15, 3.15}, {-0.0342304, 1.02522}}

▶ *Text Labels*

Mathematica possesses a variety of tools with which to format the text that is placed on plots with options such as PlotLabel, AxesLabel, and FrameLabel.

The setting of PlotLabel can be a string. This will be rendered in the default font.

```
In[32]:= Plot[Exp[-x^2] Cos[x], {x,-3,3},
             PlotLabel -> "This is a label"]
```

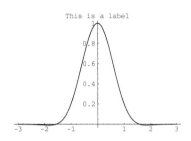

PlotLabel can take an expression other than a string. In this case the expression is formatted.

```
In[33]:= Plot[Exp[-x^2] Cos[x], {x,-3,3},
             PlotLabel -> Exp[-x^2] Cos[x]]
```

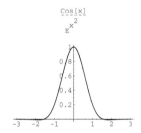

A formatted expression can be placed inside a string by means of StringForm. The control sequence `1` gives the position for the first argument of StringForm after the string.

```
In[34]:= Plot[Exp[-x^2] Cos[x], {x,-3,3},
             PlotLabel ->
               StringForm["This is a plot of `1`",
                 Exp[-x^2] Cos[x]]]
```

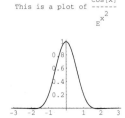

More sophisticated labels that are more compact, use nonfixed-width fonts, and mix roman, greek, and other characters can be made by using a typeset formatting type. These include `StandardForm`, which generates *Mathematica* style formatting, and `TraditionalForm`, which approximates traditional mathematical notation. Some examples of this capability are now shown. These did not work in Version 2.2 (or earlier) *Mathematica*.

The typeset format `StandardForm` produces a typeset layout for *Mathematica* syntax. The syntax `\[Alpha]` represents a greek alpha.

```
In[35]:= Plot[Sin[x]^2, {x, 0,2Pi},
            AxesLabel -> {StandardForm[\[Alpha]],
                StandardForm[Sin[\[Alpha]]^2]}]
```

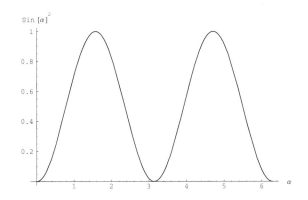

`TraditionalForm` produces a typeset layout for traditional mathematics notation.

```
In[36]:= Plot[Sin[x]^2, {x, 0,2Pi},
            AxesLabel -> {TraditionalForm[\[Alpha]],
                TraditionalForm[Sin[\[Alpha]]^2]}]
```

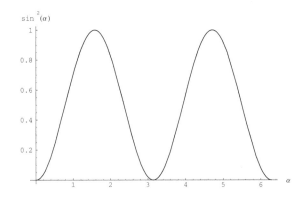

The label is built up separately. This label uses `StringForm`.

```
In[37]:= lab1 =
            StringForm["This is a plot of `1`",
                Exp[-x^2] Cos[x]];
```

Placing the label expression inside `TraditionalForm` typesets it. In addition, the font for the graphic is changed.

```
In[38]:= Plot[Exp[-x^2] Cos[x], {x,-3,3},
            PlotLabel ->
              TraditionalForm[lab1],
            DefaultFont -> {"Helvetica", 8}]
```

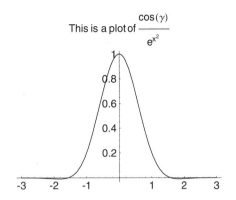

Another label is built up. This one contains an integral to be formatted. To prevent it from evaluating it is wrapped in `HoldForm`. `\[Gamma]` represents a greek gamma.

```
In[39]:= lab2 =
          HoldForm[Integrate[Exp[-\[Gamma]/3] Cos[\[Gamma]],
                    {\[Gamma],0,x}]];
```

The integral is evaluated numerically with `NIntegrate`. Again the font for the graphic is altered.

```
In[40]:= Plot[NIntegrate[Exp[-t/3]Cos[t],{t,0,x}] ,{x,0,15},
            PlotLabel ->
              TraditionalForm[lab2],
            AxesLabel -> {TraditionalForm[\[Gamma]], None},
            DefaultFont -> {"Helvetica", 8}]
```

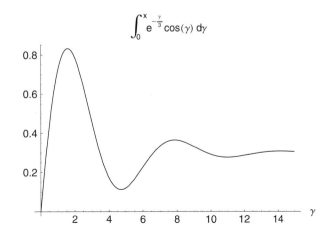

One simple way to put a border around the picture is to draw it in a GraphicsArray with the Frame option set to True.

In[41]:= **Show[GraphicsArray[{%}], Frame -> True]**

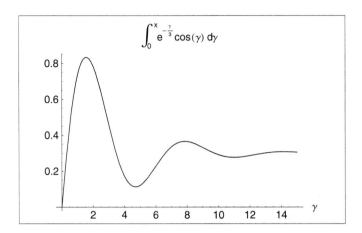

▸ *The DisplayFunction*

DisplayFunction is an option of all the graphics commands. Its setting governs the way in which graphics objects are displayed. One of its common uses is to suppress the output of a picture while still producing a *Mathematica* expression. Some of the syntax used in this discussion has not been introduced before now and is discussed in later sections of *Mathematica Graphics*. This should not divert attention from the use of the DisplayFunction to suppress graphical output.

The DisplayFunction option has a default value governed by the global variable $DisplayFunction. The :> syntax is described in Chapter 7 page 108; it means that the value is taken when the rule is used rather than when the rule is entered into *Mathematica*.

In[42]:= **Options[Graphics, DisplayFunction]**

Out[42]= {DisplayFunction :> $DisplayFunction}

The actual value of $DisplayFunction is not the same in all versions of *Mathematica*. However, this value is typical, it invokes the function Display. The syntax involving the # and the & describes a pure function; these are described in Chapter 7 page 110.

In[43]:= **$DisplayFunction**

Out[43]= Display[$Display, #1] &

A common reason for resetting the DisplayFunction is to set it to Identity. When this is done no picture will be generated but the same graphics object will be returned.

In[44]:= **Plot[Sin[x], {x,0,2Pi},**
          DisplayFunction -> Identity]

Out[44]= -Graphics-

If Show is called on the graphics object no picture is displayed. The DisplayFunction is still Identity.

```
In[45]:= Show[%]
Out[45]= -Graphics-
```

When the DisplayFunction is set to $DisplayFunction a picture is produced.

```
In[46]:= Show[%, DisplayFunction -> $DisplayFunction]
```

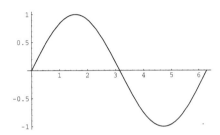

The DisplayFunction determines the function that is called by Show. By default it is set to generate pictures. This is done by using the function Display, the function that *Mathematica* uses to turn a graphics object into PostScript. On occasion, if for example a group of pictures is being made, it is necessary to suppress any intermediate pictures that are produced. This can be done by setting the DisplayFunction to Identity.

A much more advanced use of the DisplayFunction is to set it to use some program other than *Mathematica* to render graphics. If this application could render the primitives of *Mathematica* graphics then connecting it to $DisplayFunction would ensure that the graphics commands of *Mathematica* would all work. They would just use this different rendering method. *MathLink* provides a powerful method for this to be implemented[2]. It is one of the strengths of *Mathematica* graphics that the preparation of graphical objects is so clearly separated from their display. Chapter 26 discusses this and the implementation of $DisplayFunction in more detail.

3.3 Graphics Commands

The previous chapter demonstrated how graphics commands render a picture and return a *Mathematica* expression describing the picture. For example, Plot returns an expression with head of Graphics. The Plot expression evaluates to a Graphics expression and this is displayed. Just as Plot has a set of options so does Graphics. In fact all of the options of Graphics are also options of Plot. The Plot command passes them to the Graphics object. However, some options of Plot control the way that Plot itself works and alter the Graphics object that it creates. These options are obviously not passed to the Graphics object. Since they are not options of Graphics they cannot be altered with Show.

These are the options of Plot that are different from the options of Graphics.

```
In[47]:= Complement[
              Options[Plot], Options[Graphics]]
Out[47]= {Axes -> Automatic, Compiled -> True, MaxBend -> 10.,
          PlotDivision -> 30., PlotPoints -> 25, PlotStyle -> Automatic}
```

---

[2]*MathLink* is a method for *Mathematica* to communicate with external processes. Chapter 13 page 285 has an example of the use of *MathLink*.

The option PlotStyle changes the style in which lines are drawn. Here the lines are dashed.

```
In[48]:= Plot[BesselJ[0, x], {x,0,10},
             PlotStyle -> {Dashing[{0.02}]}]
```

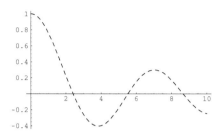

The PlotStyle option cannot be reset with Show.

```
In[49]:= Show[%, PlotStyle -> {Dashing[{0.01}]}]
Graphics::optx: Unknown option PlotStyle in -Graphics-.
Out[49]= -Graphics-
```

PlotStyle is not an option of Graphics.

```
In[50]:= Options[Graphics, PlotStyle]
Options::optnf: PlotStyle is not a known option for Graphics.
Out[50]= {}
```

Options that are specific to Plot cannot be altered by a call to Show. The same applies to ListPlot; certain options are not passed to the resulting Graphics object and these cannot be altered with Show.

```
In[51]:= Table[{i, Sin[i]}, {i,0,2Pi, .1}];
```

The PlotJoined option of ListPlot joins the points together.

```
In[52]:= ListPlot[%, PlotJoined -> True]
```

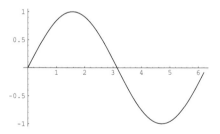

PlotJoined cannot be reset by Show.

```
In[53]:= Show[%, PlotJoined -> False]
Graphics::optx: Unknown option PlotJoined in -Graphics-.
Out[53]= -Graphics-
```

3.4 Three-Dimensional Graphics Options

Three-dimensional *Mathematica* graphics have similar embellishments to two-dimensional graphics. In addition, there are special options specific to three dimensions.

Only the *z* axis is drawn; the *x* and *y* axes are omitted.

```
In[54]:= Plot3D[Sin[x y], {x,0,2Pi}, {y,0,Pi},
              Axes -> {False, False, True}]
```

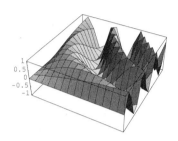

Now no axes at all are drawn, though there is still a box around the image. The box helps to enhance the three-dimensional appearance.

```
In[55]:= Show[%, Axes -> False]
```

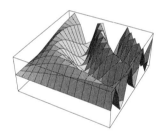

Now only the surface is drawn.

```
In[56]:= Show[%, Boxed -> False]
```

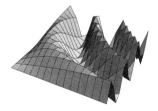

The viewpoint that is used to view the surface is changed so that the surface is presented more obliquely.

In[57]:= **Show[%, ViewPoint -> {1.3, -2.4, .3}]**

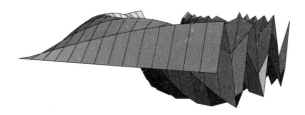

Many versions of the *Mathematica* front end provide a three-dimensional ViewPoint selector that allows the ViewPoint of a three-dimensional object to be altered dynamically. This allows one to experiment and find the most informative view of a surface. The viewpoint selector is described in Chapter 6 page 94.

The command Plot produces a Graphics object. The three-dimensional plotting command Plot3D produces a SurfaceGraphics object. All the options of SurfaceGraphics can be set in Plot3D. However there are some options of Plot3D that are not passed on. One example is the PlotPoints option, which sets the number of points used to construct the surface.

These are the options of Plot3D that are different from the options of SurfaceGraphics.

In[58]:= **Complement[**
            Options[Plot3D], Options[SurfaceGraphics]]

Out[58]= {Axes -> True, Compiled -> True, PlotPoints -> 15}

The default PlotPoints is used to determine the selection of points for the surface.

In[59]:= **Plot3D[Sin[x] Sin[y],**
            {x,-2Pi, 2Pi}, {y,-2Pi, 2Pi}]

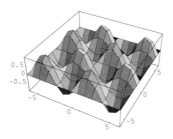

Here PlotPoints is increased so that the surface is sampled more frequently.

In[60]:= **Plot3D[Sin[x] Sin[y],**
            {x,-2Pi, 2Pi}, {y,-2Pi, 2Pi},PlotPoints -> 30]

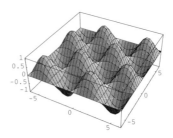

3.5 Contour Plots

All graphics objects have options to control the way they appear. The contour drawing commands have options that are similar to other graphics functions. In addition they have options special to contour plots. These control features such as whether or not the contour is shaded and the selection and appearance of contour lines.

The default option settings are used.   *In[61]:=* **ContourPlot[x y, {x,-2,2},{y,-2,2}]**

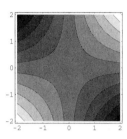

Now the contour plot is not shaded.   *In[62]:=* **Show[%, ContourShading -> False]**

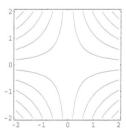

The Contours option sets the number and values of the contour lines.   *In[63]:=* **Show[%, Contours -> 4]**

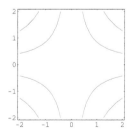

The style of the contour lines is set by the ContourStyle option.

In[64]:= **Show[%, ContourStyle -> Dashing[{0.01}]]**

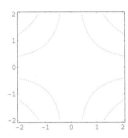

The options of the contour plotting commands are considered in more detail in Chapter 23.

3.6 Density Plots

Density plots have options that are similar to those of other graphics objects. They also have options unique to density plots that control features such as whether or not the mesh is drawn. An example here plots a map of Gaussian integers (complex numbers that have integral real and imaginary parts) in the complex plane. If they are Gaussian prime they are drawn in black otherwise they are drawn in white.

This tests integers in part of the complex plane. The array contains 0 if they are Gaussian prime and 1 otherwise.

In[65]:= **data =**
    Table[If[x^2 + y^2 < 625 &&
        PrimeQ[x + I y, GaussianIntegers -> True],
        0, 1], {x,-25,25},{y,-25,25}];

Here the mesh is turned off; it would interfere with the picture. The MeshRange option is set to make the labels come out properly.

In[66]:= **ListDensityPlot[data,**
    MeshRange -> {{-25, 25}, {-25,25}},
    Mesh -> False]

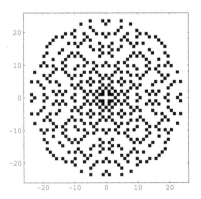

Here the FrameTicks are turned off making a starker plot.

In[67]:= **Show[%, FrameTicks -> None]**

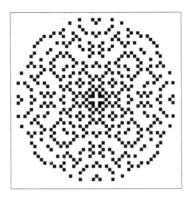

3.7 Summary

This chapter has examined the options available for graphics commands. It first looked at the tools that *Mathematica* provides to work with options. It is to be noted that these tools are available not only for graphics options but for *all* commands in *Mathematica* with options. This was followed by a variety of examples of the use of graphics options. These showed how changing options can improve the annotation and appearance of particular images.

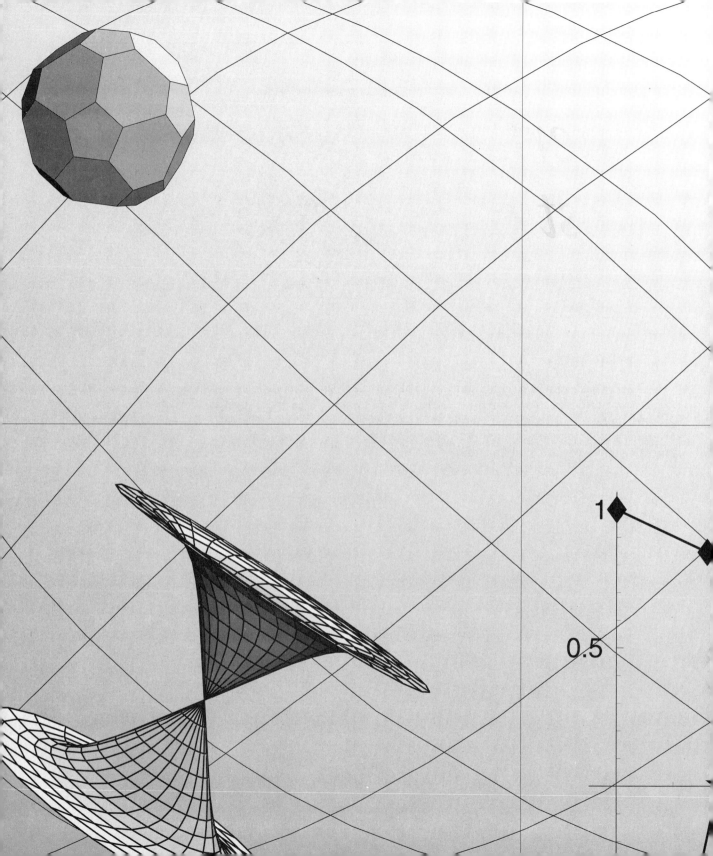

Chapter 4
Interfacing with the Rest of Mathematica

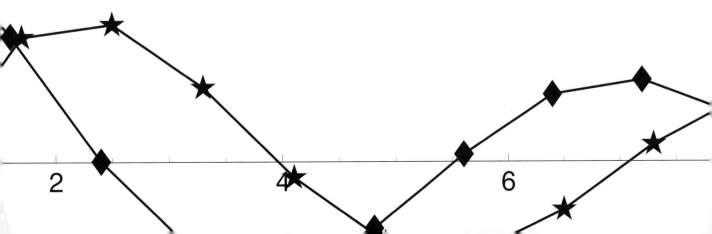

This chapter looks at some of the facilities available in the rest of *Mathematica*. There are many tools that provide important functionality for generating pictures with *Mathematica*. The file reading functions are essential for importing data as are the numerical functions for processing that data. In addition to these built-in functions a large and important collection of additional functions is available in *Mathematica* packages.

4.1 Importing and Manipulating Data

Mathematica provides a number of powerful tools to import (and export) data. If the file contains ASCII text its contents can easily be imported. One way to confirm that a file contains text is to inspect it with the !! mechanism that *Mathematica* provides, another is to examine it with a text editor. The first input here is shown to create the data file.

These commands will build the file that will be read in. The actual commands are not explained in the text.

```
In[1]:= (Do[WriteString["file1.dat", i, " ", i^3, "\n"],
              {i,1,10,2}]; Close["file1.dat"])
Out[1]= file1.dat
```

Display the contents of this file.

```
In[2]:= !!file1.dat

1 1
3 27
5 125
7 343
9 729
```

ReadList will read the contents of the file into a list. They are interpreted as numbers.

```
In[2]:= ReadList["file1.dat", Number]
Out[2]= {1, 1, 3, 27, 5, 125, 7, 343, 9, 729}
```

In this command every number in the file is read into one list. However, each line of the file consists of two numbers. In order to maintain this organization, which might be useful for plotting or data analysis, the ReadList command can be amended.

Now pairs of numbers are formed into sub-lists.

```
In[3]:= ReadList["file1.dat", {Number, Number}]
Out[3]= {{1, 1}, {3, 27}, {5, 125}, {7, 343}, {9, 729}}
```

ReadList reads the contents of a file into a list. It can interpret the contents as numbers as shown above. It can also interpret the contents as other types of data. The first input here is shown to create the data file.

These commands will build the file that will be read in. The actual commands are not explained in this text[3].

```
In[4]:= (Do[WriteString["file2.dat", "a" <> ToString[i],
              "   ", Random[ ], "\n"], {i,1,5}];
              Close["file2.dat"])
Out[4]= file2.dat
```

---

[3]File input and output are described in detail in Chapter 2.10 of the *Mathematica* book.

This file contains expressions that cannot be made into numbers.

```
In[5]:= !!file2.dat
a1    0.0560708
a2    0.6303
a3    0.359894
a4    0.871377
a5    0.858645
```

If an attempt is made to use the Number type, an error results. a1 cannot be interpreted as a number.

```
In[5]:= ReadList["file2.dat", Number]
Read::readn: Syntax error reading a real number from file2.dat.
Out[5]= {$Failed}
```

These first elements can be read in with the type Word.

```
In[6]:= d1 = ReadList["file2.dat", {Word, Number}]
Out[6]= {{a1, 0.0560708}, {a2, 0.6303}, {a3, 0.359894},
   {a4, 0.871377}, {a5, 0.858645}}
```

Looking at the result with InputForm these first elements are seen to be string expressions.

```
In[7]:= InputForm[d1]
Out[7]//InputForm=
  {{"a1", 0.0560708}, {"a2", 0.6303}, {"a3", 0.359894},
   {"a4", 0.871377}, {"a5", 0.8586449999999999}}
```

If this collection of data is to be plotted a problem will arise. This is because it contains both numbers and strings and the latter cannot be plotted. The problem could be solved by going back to the file and editing it. There is however a much neater solution: to use *Mathematica* to extract the numbers.

The Map command travels down a normal expression and applies a function to every element. Here the last element of every sub-list is extracted.

```
In[8]:= Map[Last, d1]
Out[8]= {0.0560708, 0.6303, 0.359894, 0.871377, 0.858645}
```

This result can be plotted by ListPlot.

```
In[9]:= ListPlot[%, PlotJoined -> True]
```

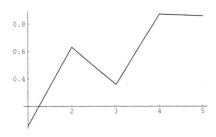

An alternative method to extract the numbers is to take the last element of the Transpose.

```
In[10]:= Last[Transpose[d1]]
Out[10]= {0.0560708, 0.6303, 0.359894, 0.871377, 0.858645}
```

The list and expression manipulation commands of *Mathematica* are extremely useful for working with data that have been read in from a file. There will be many examples of this in *Mathematica Graphics*. Using *Mathematica* to do this type of manipulation is efficient and straightforward.

▹ *Reading Different Parts of a File*

The simplest way to use `ReadList` is to read all the data in the file at once. However, different parts of a file can be read with different input commands. This is useful if for example the beginning of the file contains a header that describes its contents. This is done by opening the file with `OpenRead` and keeping the stream object that this generates. Streams are described in the *Mathematica* book Chapter 2.10. As above, the first command here will generate the file that will be used in the example.

These commands will build the file that will be read in. The actual commands are not explained in the text.

```
In[11]:= (OpenWrite["file3.dat"];
    WriteString["file3.dat", "X-range", " ", -2," ", 2,
    "\n"];
    WriteString["file3.dat", "Y-range", " ", -2," ", 2,
    "\n"];
    Do[Do[WriteString["file3.dat",  x+y, " "], {x, -2,2}];
        WriteString["file3.dat", "\n"], {y,-2,2}];
    Close["file3.dat"])
Out[11]= file3.dat
```

Different parts of this file contain different data.

```
In[12]:= !!file3.dat
X-range  -2   2
Y-range  -2   2
-4  -3  -2  -1   0
-3  -2  -1   0   1
-2  -1   0   1   2
-1   0   1   2   3
 0   1   2   3   4
```

`OpenRead` opens the file for input returning an `InputStream` object. This can be used for subsequent input operations.

```
In[12]:= stream = OpenRead["file3.dat"]
Out[12]= InputStream[file3.dat, 11]
```

The third argument to `ReadList` specifies that two objects are to be read. Each has the format {Word, Number, Number}.

```
In[13]:= ReadList[stream, {Word, Number, Number}, 2]
Out[13]= {{X-range, -2, 2}, {Y-range, -2, 2}}
```

The range will be used with the `MeshRange` option to set the axes properly.

```
In[14]:= range = Map[Rest, %]
Out[14]= {{-2, 2}, {-2, 2}}
```

Now the rest of the file is read. Setting `RecordLists` to be True puts everything from one record, here one line, into a sub-list.

```
In[15]:= d2 = ReadList[stream, Number, RecordLists -> True]
Out[15]= {{-4, -3, -2, -1, 0}, {-3, -2, -1, 0, 1},
    {-2, -1, 0, 1, 2}, {-1, 0, 1, 2, 3}, {0, 1, 2, 3, 4}}
```

It is a good thing to close the stream after it has been used.

```
In[16]:= Close[stream]
Out[16]= file3.dat
```

Now the data can be used in a contour plot.

In[17]:= **ListContourPlot[d2, MeshRange -> range]**

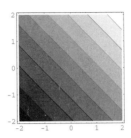

Alternatively a surface can be plotted over the data.

In[18]:= **ListPlot3D[d2, MeshRange -> range]**

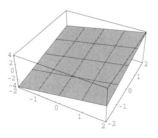

In this example these commands are given one after another to build up the data that will be plotted. Chapter 7 discusses *Mathematica* programming and will show how these steps can be combined to form a simple program. The problem of generating surfaces and other plots from data is covered in detail in Chapter 18.

ReadList[*file*, *type*]	a general function to import data
ReadList[*file*, Number]	import numbers
ReadList[*file*, {Number, Number}]	import pairs of numbers
ReadList[*file*, Word]	import text into a string
ReadList[*file*, *type*, RecordLists -> True]	
	place the contents of each line into a sub-list
OpenRead[*file*]	open a file and read an InputStream object
ReadList[*stream*, *type*]	accept a stream object instead of a file

Reading data with ReadList.

4.2 Saving and Restoring a Graphics Object

The command ReadList is useful for reading a complicated file that contains different sorts of information. It is also useful for reading a file that was not prepared by *Mathematica*. A related task is to save and restore *Mathematica* expressions and there is an easy way to do this. The functionality is useful for graphics since a complex collection of graphics may be generated. Saving them in a file will allow them to be read back in and displayed later. For objects that take a long time to generate this will be worthwhile.

A graphics object can be generated.   `In[19]:= p = Plot[x^2 Sin[x], {x,-2Pi,2Pi}]`

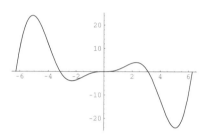

This saves the value of p into the file `file4.dat`. >> is shorthand notation for Put.   `In[20]:= p >> file4.dat`

This reads the file `file4.dat`. As the file is read the contents are evaluated. The result of the last evaluation is saved as the value of p1. << is shorthand notation for Get.

`In[21]:= p1 = << file4.dat`

`Out[21]= -Graphics-`

A call to Show will display the graphics that were saved in the file.   `In[22]:= Show[p1]`

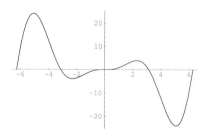

When a graphics object is generated it can be written to a file with the command Put. The contents of such a file can be read back in with the command Get. Put and Get have shorthand notations of >> and << respectively. This makes it very simple to save and restore any result generated by *Mathematica*. The result can be graphics objects, as in this example, but it could be any other expression.

Chapter 26 describes how to export *Mathematica* pictures into other formats such as PostScript files. It is important to remember that if a graphics object is to be worked on by *Mathematica* the *Mathematica* graphics expression should be saved or it will have to be regenerated. This is because it is not possible to convert a PostScript file or some other format back to a *Mathematica* expression. This section has shown how easy these are to save and restore.

4.3 Numerical Functions

There are strong similarities between graphical and numerical functionality. This is because something that is plotted must ultimately consist of numbers. In *Mathematica* this means that the graphical functions are related to the N functions. For example, Plot can be compared with the NIntegrate function.

If the integrand was some symbolic function such as f[x], NIntegrate could not work.

In[23]:= **NIntegrate[Sin[x]∧2, {x,0,Pi}]**

Out[23]= 1.5708

The syntax is very similar to that of NIntegrate.

In[24]:= **Plot[Sin[x]∧2, {x,0,Pi}]**

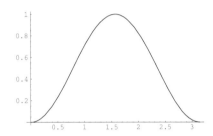

▶ *Fit*

Some examples of using the numeric and graphical functions together will now be presented. The first example will examine the function Fit. This is used in a basic form of data analysis that fits data with some function such as a polynomial or a series of trigonometric functions. Once this is done it is often useful to make a picture to allow a visual inspection of the goodness of fit. There is often a need for a mixture of symbolic computation, numeric computation, and graphics. *Mathematica* meets this requirement.

Here some data is generated. If it came from some source outside *Mathematica* it could be imported with ReadList.

In[25]:= **data =**
        Table[{i, Sin[i] - .5 Random[ ]}, {i, 0, 2, .05}];

A picture of the data is made with
ListPlot. The result is saved by the
symbol dataplot.

In[26]:= **dataplot = ListPlot[data]**

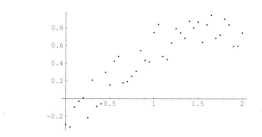

A least-squares fit is made using the
basis functions {1, x, x^2}. The
resulting best-fit function is returned.

In[27]:= **fun = Fit[data, {1, x, x^2}, x]**

Out[27]= $-0.316838 + 1.23247 x - 0.350231 x^2$

The best-fit function is plotted.

In[28]:= **fitplot = Plot[fun, {x,0,2}]**

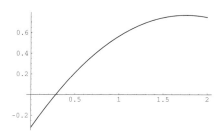

Show combines the two plots into one
picture.

In[29]:= **Show[dataplot, fitplot]**

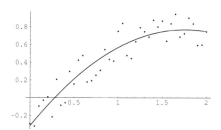

Some labels are added to the picture.

```
In[30]:= Show[%,
            AxesLabel -> { "Time/s", "Height/cm"}]
```

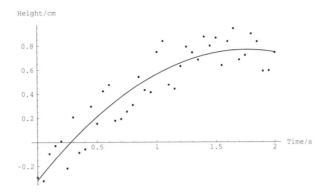

▶ *Solving Differential Equations*

The NDSolve function provides another important numeric capability to *Mathematica*. It uses numerical techniques to solve sets of ordinary differential equations. Having solved a differential equation it is useful and straightforward to graph the result.

A damped oscillator problem is solved. The result is a set of replacement rules typical of the solving functions of *Mathematica*.

```
In[31]:= NDSolve[{ x''[t] + .3 x'[t] + x[t] == 0 ,
                  x[0] == 2,
                  x'[0] == 0}, x[t], {t,0,20}]
Out[31]= {{x[t] -> InterpolatingFunction[{0., 20.}, <>][t]}}
```

The solution can be plotted immediately. The /. syntax substitutes the InterpolatingFunction result for x[t]. Evaluate is necessary since Plot is HoldAll[4].

```
In[32]:= Plot[Evaluate[x[t] /. %], {t,0,20}]
```

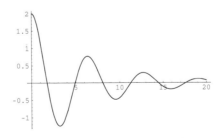

---

[4]The HoldAll attribute of Plot is discussed in Chapter 2 page 26. Replacement rules are discussed in Chapter 7 page 107.

NDSolve can also solve coupled
equations.

```
In[33]:= sol =
            NDSolve[
                {
                x''[t] + x[t] == 0,
                y''[t] + 2 y[t] == 0,
                x[0] == 2, x'[0] == 0,
                y[0] == 2, y'[0] == 0}, {x[t], y[t]}, {t,0,40}]
Out[33]= {{x[t] -> InterpolatingFunction[{0., 40.}, <>][t],
            y[t] -> InterpolatingFunction[{0., 40.}, <>][t]}}
```

Both solutions can be plotted
simultaneously.

```
In[34]:= Plot[Evaluate[{x[t], y[t]} /. sol], {t, 0, 20}]
```

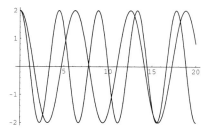

Instead of plotting both solutions as a
function of the independent variable the
x value can be plotted against the *y* value
to form a phase plot.

```
In[35]:= ParametricPlot[
            Evaluate[{x[t], y[t]} /. First[sol]], {t,0,40}]
```

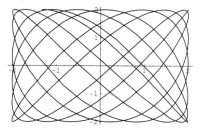

▶ *FindRoot*

A last example of the combination of graphical and numerical functions will involve `FindRoot`. This finds the numerical solution to an equation. `FindRoot` requires an initial guess for the root. One way to find this is by inspecting the graph of the function. For example, plotting `Sin[x] + Sin[x^1.1]` can reveal the approximate location of the roots.

The function has a number of roots, one of them is proximate to 6.

In[36]:= `Plot[Sin[x] + Sin[x^1.1], {x, 0, 4Pi}]`

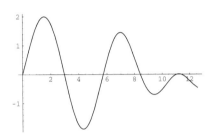

FindRoot will find the root that is proximate to 6.

In[37]:= `FindRoot[Sin[x] + Sin[x^1.1], {x, 6}]`

Out[37]= `{x -> 5.73582}`

The combination of graphical and numerical functions can be made more useful if one writes procedures to combine them automatically. The way that this can be done, so that the extensibility of *Mathematica* can be taken advantage of, is discussed in Part II of *Mathematica Graphics*.

4.4 *Mathematica* **Graphics Packages**

▶ *Mathematica Is Extensible*

Different *Mathematica* functions fit together naturally. The commands that read data from a file fit with graphics functions to plot that data. The commands that make a fit of some data combine with the commands that plot the fit. Since there are often groups of tasks that work together it is natural to combine these together to form new functions making it easier to repeat the process. When this is done *Mathematica* has been extended.

Part II of *Mathematica Graphics* describes *Mathematica* programming. It shows how functions can be joined to form programs. The emphasis is on extending graphics functionality but the methods apply generally. Before starting to write a program for some functionality it is worth checking that it does not already exist. It may be built into the kernel or it may exist in what are called the *Mathematica* standard packages. These are a large collection of *Mathematica* programs (packages is the term used to describe them) that are distributed with *Mathematica*. They are well documented in the *Guide to Standard Packages* but are often overlooked by users. Some versions of the *Mathematica* notebook front end support a facility called a Function Browser. This allows the packages to be browsed and studied.

This section will look at some of the *Mathematica* standard packages that have an application in the area of graphics. It will show how to use the packages and some of the functionality they provide. It will not give a detailed description of every package since that is done in the *Guide to Standard Packages*. However, the rest of this book will make continuous use of these packages since they provide a large amount of useful functionality.

Arrow	arrow primitive
ComplexMap	graphical description of complex functions
ContourPlot3D	implicit function plotting in three dimensions
FilledPlot	shading beneath a plot
Graphics	a variety of basic two-dimensional functions
Graphics3D	a variety of basic three-dimensional functions
ImplicitPlot2D	implicit function plotting in two dimensions
Legend	placing a legend on a plot
MultipleListPlot	general data plots
ParametricPlot3D	more three-dimensional plots
PlotField	two-dimensional vector field plots
PlotField3D	three-dimensional vector field plots
Polyhedra	polyhedra
Shapes	three-dimensional shapes
Spline	splines
SurfaceOfRevolution	surface of revolution

Some of the graphics packages available with *Mathematica*.

▷ *MultipleListPlot: Using a Package*

ListPlot will plot a single data set. When there are several data sets to be plotted it is still possible to use ListPlot for each and to combine them. However, this can be done directly with the command MultipleListPlot which is defined in the package Graphics`MultipleListPlot`. When a package is to be used it must first be loaded. The best way to do this is with Needs since this protects against multiple loading.

MultipleListPlot in versions of *Mathematica* including Version 2.2 (or earlier) did not possess all the functionality that is described here. For example, the legend and the plotting of error bars will not work, neither will the functions for changing plotting symbols. For these versions it is possible to update the package Graphics`MultipleListPlot`.

Using the backquotes, `, makes sure that this command will work on *all Mathematica* platforms. A machine-specific filename could be used but this is not portable from one type of machine to another.

```
In[38]:= Needs["Graphics`MultipleListPlot`"]
```

The usage message provides initial information about a function.

```
In[39]:= ?MultipleListPlot
```

MultipleListPlot[data,(opts)] plots the data, using symbols
    determined by the options. MultipleListPlot[data1,
    data2,...] plots multiple sets of data. Data are either a
    list of numbers (whose x coordinates are implicitly the
    positions in the list), or as pairs of {x, y} coordinates.
    Each data point can be accompanied by an error, indicated by
    an ErrorBar object indicating the error as positive and
    negative offsets (see ErrorBar for more information).

A first data set can be constructed.

```
In[40]:= data1 = Table[{x, BesselJ[0, x]}, {x,0,10,0.8}];
```

A second data set can be constructed.

```
In[41]:= data2 = Table[{x, BesselY[0, x]}, {x,0.1,10,0.8}];
```

MultipleListPlot will plot both data sets.

```
In[42]:= MultipleListPlot[data1, data2]
```

PlotJoined set to True will join the points.

```
In[43]:= MultipleListPlot[data1, data2, PlotJoined -> True]
```

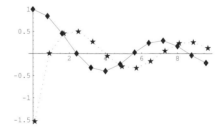

The names of the options of
MultipleListPlot that are different
from those of Graphics. These allow
the style of the lines and the points to
be altered as well as adding a legend
and plotting error bars.

```
In[44]:= Map[First,
            Complement[Options[MultipleListPlot],
                       Options[Graphics]]]
Out[44]= {Axes, ErrorBarFunction, LegendBackground,
    LegendBorder, LegendBorderSpace, LegendLabel,
    LegendLabelSpace, LegendOrientation, LegendPosition,
    LegendShadow, LegendSize, LegendSpacing, LegendTextDirection,
    LegendTextOffset, LegendTextSpace, PlotJoined, PlotLegend,
    PlotStyle, SymbolLabel, SymbolShape, SymbolStyle}
```

The PlotStyle sets the style for the lines.
They are now drawn with the same style:
thicker and dashed.

```
In[45]:= MultipleListPlot[data1, data2,
            PlotJoined -> True,
            PlotStyle ->
                {{Thickness[0.004], Dashing[{0.02}]}}]
```

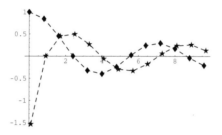

Changing the Plotting Symbols

The symbol that is placed at each data point is controlled by the option SymbolShape. The function
PlotSymbol is provided to return different symbols that can be used.

This uses boxes for the plotting symbols.

```
In[46]:= MultipleListPlot[data1,
            SymbolShape -> PlotSymbol[Box]]
```

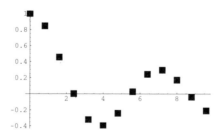

PlotSymbol returns a value that can be used by SymbolShape. The second argument sets the size of the symbol.

```
In[47]:= sym1 = PlotSymbol[Box, 2]

Out[47]= Polygon[{Offset[{-2, 2}, #1], Offset[{2, 2}, #1],
        Offset[{2, -2}, #1], Offset[{-2, -2}, #1],
        Offset[{-2, 2}, #1]}] &
```

PlotSymbol can take the option Filled that determines whether or not the symbol appears in outline.

```
In[48]:= sym2 = PlotSymbol[Triangle, Filled -> False]

Out[48]= Line[{Offset[{0, 2.5}, #1],
        Offset[{-2.165, -1.25}, #1], Offset[{2.165, -1.25}, #1],
        Offset[{0, 2.5}, #1]}] &
```

The two different symbol styles are used.

```
In[49]:= MultipleListPlot[data1, data2,
            SymbolShape -> {sym1, sym2},
            PlotJoined -> True]
```

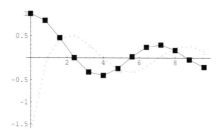

Labeling with a Legend

The option PlotLegend draws a legend beside the plot that associates text with a representation of the plot styles. This is extremely helpful in understanding the different data sets.

The PlotLegend option adds a legend to the image.

```
In[50]:= MultipleListPlot[data1, data2,
            PlotJoined -> True,
            PlotLegend -> {"Data 4-27", "Data 4-24"}]
```

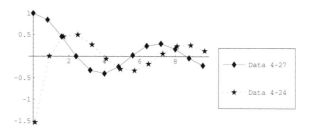

A shadow can be added with
LegendShadow; the default setting of
{0,0} omits the shadow. The position of
the legend is set by the option
LegendPosition.

```
In[51]:= MultipleListPlot[data1, data2,
            PlotJoined -> True,
            PlotLegend -> {"Data 4-27", "Data 4-24"},
            LegendShadow -> {0.02,-0.02},
            LegendPosition -> {-2,-0.5}]
```

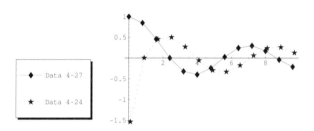

Plotting Error Bars

MultipleListPlot can plot error bars with the data. The error is included in the data set as $\{pt, err\}$ where *pt* is the $\{x,y\}$ coordinate and *err* error in the form ErrorBar$[\{y_{min}, y_{max}\}]$ for the y error or ErrorBar$[\{x_{min}, x_{max}\}, \{y_{min}, y_{max}\}]$ for the x and y errors.

This is a simulated set of data with
error information.

```
In[52]:= data3 =
            Table[err = 0.2+Random[ ];
                {{i, Sin[i]+err}, ErrorBar[{-err,err}]},
                {i,0,4Pi,1}];
```

Each datum includes the error in the y
direction.

```
In[53]:= First[data3]
Out[53]= {{0, 1.03643}, ErrorBar[{-1.03643, 1.03643}]}
```

The error bars are plotted with the data.

```
In[54]:= MultipleListPlot[data3]
```

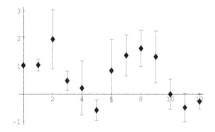

Other data can be plotted as well and all the options of `MultipleListPlot` work in the normal way.

`In[55]:= MultipleListPlot[data2, data3,`
              `PlotJoined -> {True,False}]`

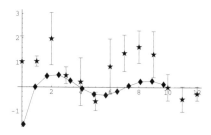

Since the result of `MultipleListPlot` is a `Graphics` object, all the options of `Graphics` can be changed with `Show`.

`In[56]:= Show[%, Frame -> True]`

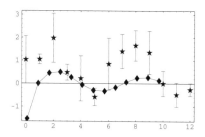

Plotting a List of Data Sets

`MultipleListPlot` requires that each data set is given as a separate argument. In the earlier examples each data set was assigned to a symbol that was then placed as an argument. If the data sets are all collected together in a list then it is possible to use `Apply` to plot them.

`data` consists of a collection of two data sets.

`In[57]:= data = {data1, data2};`

Using `Apply` means that the individual data sets do not need to be separated.

`In[58]:= Apply[MultipleListPlot, data]`

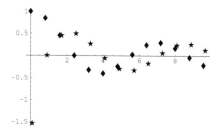

In order to set an option of
MultipleListPlot it is necessary to use
a pure function. These are described in
Chapter 7.

```
In[59]:= Apply[
            MultipleListPlot[##, PlotJoined -> True]&,
            data]
```

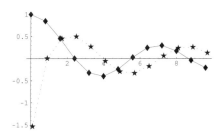

Apply and pure functions are described in more detail in Chapter 7, which discusses *Mathematica* programming.

Summary of MultipleListPlot

Since MultipleListPlot is such an important graphics function this is a summary of its functionality. As described earlier some of the functionality was not present in Version 2.2 *Mathematica*. Some of this functionality, such as including a legend and error bars, and changing the plotting symbols will not work as described. In this case it is possible to update the package Graphics`MultipleListPlot`.

MultipleListPlot[*data₁*, *data₂*, ... , *opts*]

$\qquad\qquad\qquad$ plot *data₁, data₂, ...*

{{x_1, y_1}, {x_2, y_2}, ... } $\qquad$ data with no errors

{{x_1, y_1}, ErrorBar[{y_{min},y_{max}}]} $\qquad$ datum with *y* coordinate error

{{x_1, y_1}, ErrorBar[{x_{min},x_{max}},{y_{min},y_{max}}]}

$\qquad\qquad\qquad$ datum with *x* and *y* coordinate error

Data formats for MultipleListPlot.

PlotJoined -> True $\qquad\qquad$ join the points

PlotJoined -> {True, False, ... } $\qquad$ join the points for certain data sets

PlotStyle -> *style* $\qquad\qquad$ the style for all lines

PlotStyle -> {*style₁*, *style₂*, ... } $\qquad$ the styles for different data sets

---

Style options for MultipleListPlot.

SymbolShape -> *sym*	use plot symbol *sym*
PlotSymbol[*shape*]	plot symbol of certain shape
PlotSymbol[*shape*, *size*]	plot symbol of certain shape and size
PlotSymbol[*shape*, Filled -> *bool*]	whether the symbol is filled
Star	a shape for PlotSymbol
Triangle	a shape for PlotSymbol
Box	a shape for PlotSymbol
Diamond	a shape for PlotSymbol

Symbol options for MultipleListPlot.

PlotLegend -> {*text₁*, *text₂*}	text for the legend
LegendPosition -> {*x*, *y*}	position for the legend
LegendShadow -> {*x*, *y*}	position for the legend shadow

Legend options for MultipleListPlot.

▷ *The Pie Chart*

There are many different types of pictures that can be made with the graphics packages. These include bar charts, pie charts, log plots, and so on. The types of pictures that can be made and their strengths and weaknesses are reviewed in Chapter 14. Here some simple examples will be demonstrated. The package Graphics`Graphics` contains definitions for these different types of plots. Here is an example of making a pie chart.

Here is some data to plot with a pie chart.

```
In[60]:= data =
          {{30, "English"}, { 30, "French"}, {30, "German"}}
Out[60]= {{30, English}, {30, French}, {30, German}}
```

The Graphics`Graphics` package is loaded.

```
In[61]:= Needs["Graphics`Graphics`"]
```

The usage message provides basic information.

```
In[62]:= ?PieChart
PieChart[{y1, y2, ...}] generates a pie chart of the values yi.
    The values yi need to be positive. Several options
    (PieLabels, PieStyle, PieLineStyle, PieExploded) are
    available to modify the style of the pie.
```

A simple pie chart is made.

In[63]:= **PieChart[data]**

The function has a number of options.

In[64]:= **Options[PieChart]**

Out[64]= {PieLabels -> Automatic, PieStyle -> Automatic,
PieLineStyle -> Automatic, PieExploded -> None}

In this way the slices can be moved out.

In[65]:= **PieChart[data, PieExploded -> {1,2,3}]**

▷ *Log Plots*

The package Graphics`Graphics` contains many types of two-dimensional plots. This includes support for several different logarithmically scaled plots.

Needs can be executed more than once. It will not load the package if this has already taken place.

In[66]:= **Needs["Graphics`Graphics`"]**

The logarithmically scaled plotting functions can be listed. There are commands to plot both functions and data.

In[67]:= **??*Log*Plot**

```
LinearLogListPlot  LogLinearPlot      LogLogPlot
LinearLogPlot      LogListPlot        LogPlot
LogLinearListPlot  LogLogListPlot
```

LogListPlot plots data with the *y* coordinate logarithmically scaled.

In[68]:= **?LogListPlot**

LogListPlot[{y1, y2, ...}] or LogListPlot[{{x1, y1}, {x2, y2},
    ...}] generates a plot of Log[yi] against the xi.

A data set is generated with Table. Random is used with different arguments to change the range of numbers generated.

```
In[69]:= data =
            Table[{x, Exp[-x 3] Random[Real,{.5, 1.5}]},
              {x,0.1,4,.05}];
```

The data can be plotted with ListPlot.

```
In[70]:= ListPlot[data]
```

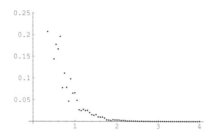

LogListPlot will give a better picture of the data.

```
In[71]:= LogListPlot[data]
```

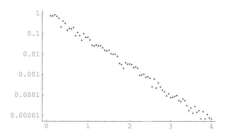

If the PlotRange is changed this is applied to the data after it has been logarithmically scaled. This may not be the desired effect.

```
In[72]:= Show[%, PlotRange -> {0.01, 1}]
```

The simplest way to change the range of numbers that are plotted is to return to the original command.

In[73]:= `LogListPlot[data, PlotRange -> {0.01, 1}]`

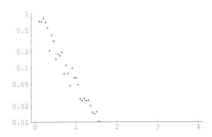

▹ *Another Way to Load Packages*

Mathematica provides a mechanism to load the standard packages automatically. This is done with the master packages. Each collection of packages has a master package that can be loaded like any other package.

The master package will set up the other graphics packages to load automatically.

In[74]:= `Needs["Graphics`Master`"]`

Now when a symbol from a graphics package is referred to that package will load automatically. This will be demonstrated using the package `Graphics`Polyhedra`. This contains code to plot the Platonic solids and to stellate and truncate them.

`Graphics`Polyhedra` is automatically loaded, then the plot of the icosahedron is made.

In[75]:= `Show[Polyhedron[Icosahedron]]`

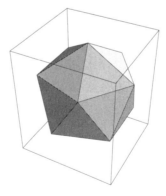

The icosahedron is truncated.   *In[76]:=* **Show[Truncate[Polyhedron[Icosahedron]]]**

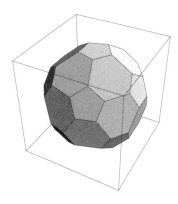

▶ *Surface Of Revolution*

A final demonstration of the graphics packages will show the package `Graphics`SurfaceOfRevolution`` that plots a surface of revolution. This combines the symbolic and graphical capabilities of *Mathematica*.

The package is loaded. If the master package was loaded previously, as demonstrated earlier, this is unnecessary.

In[77]:= **Needs["Graphics`SurfaceOfRevolution`"]**

A simple two-dimensional curve.   *In[78]:=* **Plot[2 x^2 - x^3, {x, 0,2}]**

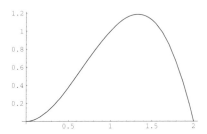

The curve can be rotated around the *z* axis.

In[79]:= **SurfaceOfRevolution[2 x^2 - x^3, {x, 0,2}]**

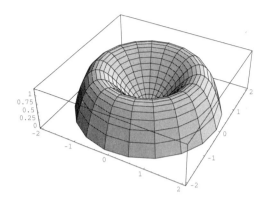

The curve can be defined parametrically.

In[80]:= **SurfaceOfRevolution[{Sin[t], t}, {t, -Pi,Pi}]**

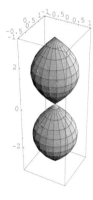

The axis of revolution can be set with the option RevolutionAxis.

In[81]:= **SurfaceOfRevolution[{Sin[t], t}, {t, -Pi,Pi},**
   RevolutionAxis -> {1,1,1}]

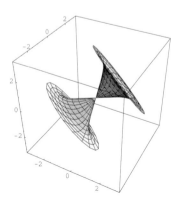

4.5 Summary

This chapter has shown how to use *Mathematica* graphics with the rest of the system. *Mathematica* is not just a graphics system any more than it is just a symbolic algebra system or just a numerical calculator. *Mathematica* is an environment that contains functionality in *all* of these areas. The examples shown in the chapter involved importing a data set with the function `ReadList` and then manipulating it to be suitable for plotting. Other examples depicted how to save and restore graphics objects in a file, and looked at plotting the results of a fit and the solution of a differential equation.

The last section of the chapter introduced the *Mathematica* standard packages. These collections of *Mathematica* code provide useful functionality in many areas. The packages are distributed with the system and are documented in the *Guide to Standard Packages*. The text did not provide a detailed description of every function with graphics functionality; these are numerous and they are already well documented. The chapter merely showed how to use the packages and some simple examples. One of the most important graphics packages is the `Graphics‘MultipleListPlot‘` package that provides general functions for plotting data. This and the other *Mathematica* standard packages will be used frequently throughout the rest of *Mathematica Graphics*.

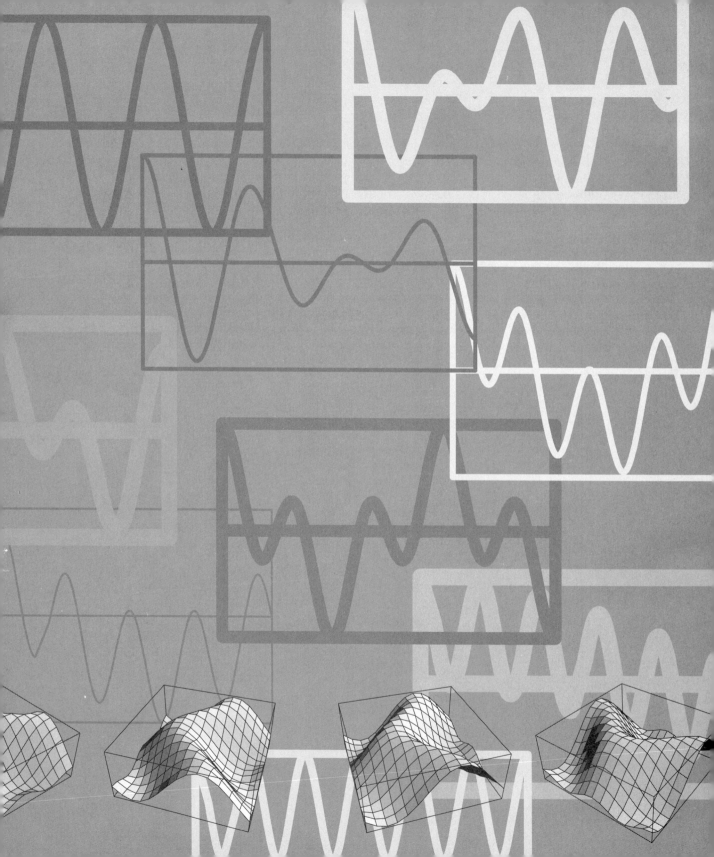

Chapter 5
Animating Graphics

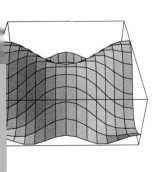
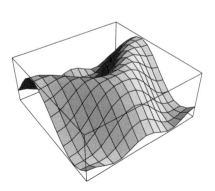
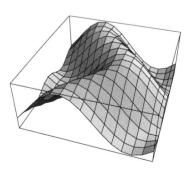
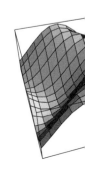

There are several ways to use *Mathematica* to produce animations. These depend upon whether a notebook or a non-notebook interface[5] is used to connect to the *Mathematica* kernel. In order that the animations work in the same way irrespective of the particular interface it is highly recommended that the animation package be used. This chapter concentrates on the kernel commands that are relevant to animations. The next chapter, page 91, discusses some front end issues concerned with animations.

5.1 Animation Methods

There are different ways that animations can be carried out. *Mathematica* produces a sequence of different pictures that are then displayed in rapid succession. This is a very simple but effective method. There are other ways to produce animations; a more complex method involves storing the differences between frames rather than each frame in its entirety, thereby saving memory. Another way to generate an animation is through a system of interactive graphics. Here the actual objects being displayed are moved under control of some application. *MathLink* provides a powerful method for using the *Mathematica* kernel to implement such animations.

In a book it is hard to document animation since only static pictures can be demonstrated. It is possible to print the different frames on different pages. The animation is then made by flipping through the pages. Wolfram Research has produced a number of *Mathematica* animations using this method. The solution of last resort is to show an array of different frames of the animation. There is a package that does this in a convenient fashion called `FlipBookAnimation`. The name suggests that this generates a flip book but in fact it just produces a static array. It should only be used when no other method is available.

5.2 The Animation Package

The animation package `Graphics`Animation`` is included in the *Mathematica* standard packages. These packages are an important collection of *Mathematica* code and were described in the previous chapter. This and all the packages are well documented in the *Guide to Standard Packages*.

The animation package can be loaded in the usual way.

```
In[1]:= Needs["Graphics`Animation`"]
```

▶ *Animate*

Animate is one of the main animation functions.

```
In[2]:= ?Animate
Animate[command, iterator, options...] uses the iterator to run
    the specified graphics command, and animates the results.
```

---

[5]The features of the front end are reviewed in the next chapter.

This is a simple animation. The `Plot` command is repeated for n from 0.2 to 1 in steps of 0.1.

In[3]:= **Animate[**
            Plot[Cos[x]^n, {x,-Pi/2, Pi/2}], {n,0.2,1,0.1}]

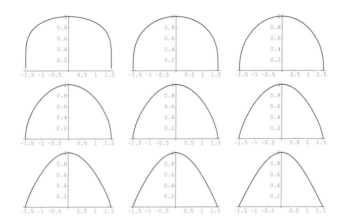

When the `Animate` command is executed the actual animation is presented in different ways depending on the interface being used. On non-notebook versions a new window is displayed containing the animation, which is already running. On a notebook version a sequence of images is generated; these must be selected and then animated with a special command. This is discussed in the next chapter, which describes the front end.

The animation shown above was especially simple. In particular, the range of coordinates for all the frames did not change. Normally this will not be so and special care must be taken to prevent the animation from looking uneven.

▶ *Frame Jump*

The animation here attempts to show a function as it develops. In fact it does a very poor job since the line in each frame automatically fills the same size in the image.

This is a bad animation. It shows a severe case of "frame jump".

`In[4]:= Animate[Plot[Sin[x], {x,0,n}], {n,.5,4.5,.5}]`

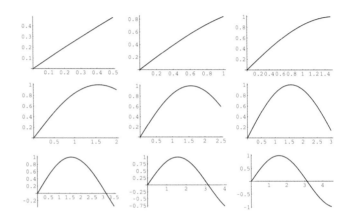

The solution to the problem is to set the same PlotRange for each image.

```
In[5]:= Animate[
          Plot[Sin[x], {x,0,n},
               PlotRange -> {{0,4}, {-1.2,1.2}}],
          {n,.5,4.5,.5}]
```

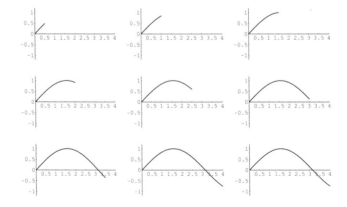

▶ *Animate Options*

The command `Animate` has a number of options. These control the number of frames that are seen and whether the sequence closes in on itself.

`Frames -> `*num*	an animation with *num* images
`Closed -> True`	first and last frames are identical, omit the last
`Closed -> False`	first and last frames are not identical, include both

Options of `Animate`.

Here the animation iterator, `{n, 0, 1}`, does not specify the step size. The number of frames is taken from the value of the `Frames` option. Here the ticks are removed since the picture is so small.

```
In[6]:= Animate[
         Plot[Cos[n x] Cos[x], {x, 0, 6 Pi},
           PlotRange -> {{0,6Pi}, {-1,1}},
         Ticks -> False, Frame -> True,
           FrameTicks -> None],
         {n, 0, 1}, Frames -> 9]
```

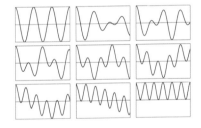

Setting the option `Closed` to be `True` specifies that the last frame of the animation should not be shown. This is useful when the last frame is equal to the first and prevents the animation from appearing to pause.

```
In[7]:= Animate[
         Plot3D[Sin[x y +n], {x, 0,Pi}, {y, 0, Pi},
                Axes -> False],
         {n, 0, 2Pi}, Frames -> 8, Closed -> True]
```

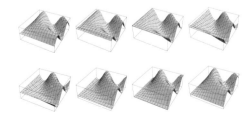

▶ *SpinShow*

Animation provides another dimension to use for visualization. This dimension is usually associated with time and is useful for demonstrating dynamical behavior. It is easy to use it to show a system moving from one state into another. Since it provides another dimension it can also be used to help to visualize objects that occupy more than two dimensions. One simple way to demonstrate this is to make an animation that spins a three-dimensional object. This can certainly be seen as a dynamical effect but the intent is to show the front, sides, and back of a three-dimensional object. This functionality is provided by the command SpinShow.

Here is an image to use.

```
In[8]:= a = Plot3D[Cos[x + Cos[y]],
                {x,-Pi,Pi}, {y,-Pi, Pi},
                Axes -> False]
```

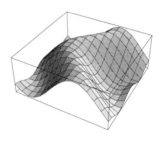

The image is spun. The number of frames that is normally shown is reduced for the sake of brevity.

```
In[9]:= SpinShow[a, Frames -> 10]
```

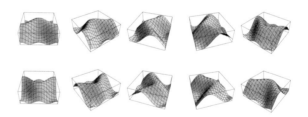

SpinShow has a number of options, many of which are used to determine how the rotation is arranged. The *Guide to Standard Packages* gives a description of these options.

```
In[10]:= Options[SpinShow]

Out[10]= {Frames -> 24, Closed -> True,
    SpinOrigin -> {0, 0, 1.5}, SpinTilt -> {0, 0},
    SpinDistance -> 2, SpinRange -> {0, 360 Degree},
    RotateLights -> False}
```

The rotation of a three-dimensional object tends to enhance the visual cues that are used to perceive the object as three-dimensional. Here the relevant cue is connected with the experience that as objects move, closer objects appear to move faster than objects farther away. This tends to make the image seem even more three-dimensional.

▶ *ShowAnimation*

Animate takes a plotting command and SpinShow takes a discrete object. However, sometimes it is useful to generate a list of graphical objects and animate them. This can be done with the command ShowAnimation.

This makes a table of images. Setting the DisplayFunction to Identity suppresses the display of any pictures at this stage.

```
In[11]:= tab =
            Table[Plot[Sin[x + n], {x,0,2Pi},
                DisplayFunction -> Identity], {n,0,Pi, Pi/5}]

Out[11]= {-Graphics-, -Graphics-, -Graphics-, -Graphics-,
          -Graphics-, -Graphics-}
```

This will animate the list of graphics objects.

```
In[12]:= ShowAnimation[tab]
```

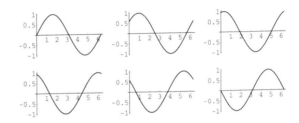

5.3 Summary

In this description of the use of *Mathematica* to carry out animations the commands provided by the package Graphics`Animation` have been reviewed. The most important of these are Animate, SpinShow, and ShowAnimation. Animations generated with these commands will be portable across all the *Mathematica* platforms that support animation. Some of the problems that can prevent effective animations have been discussed. The next chapter on the front end discusses some of the animation issues relevant to the front end.

x + Sin[x], {x,-10,10}]

In[1]:=
Plot[x + Sin[x], {x,-10,10}]

Graphics Demo

In[6]:=
Plot3D[Sin[x y], {x,0,2Pi},{y,0,Pi}]

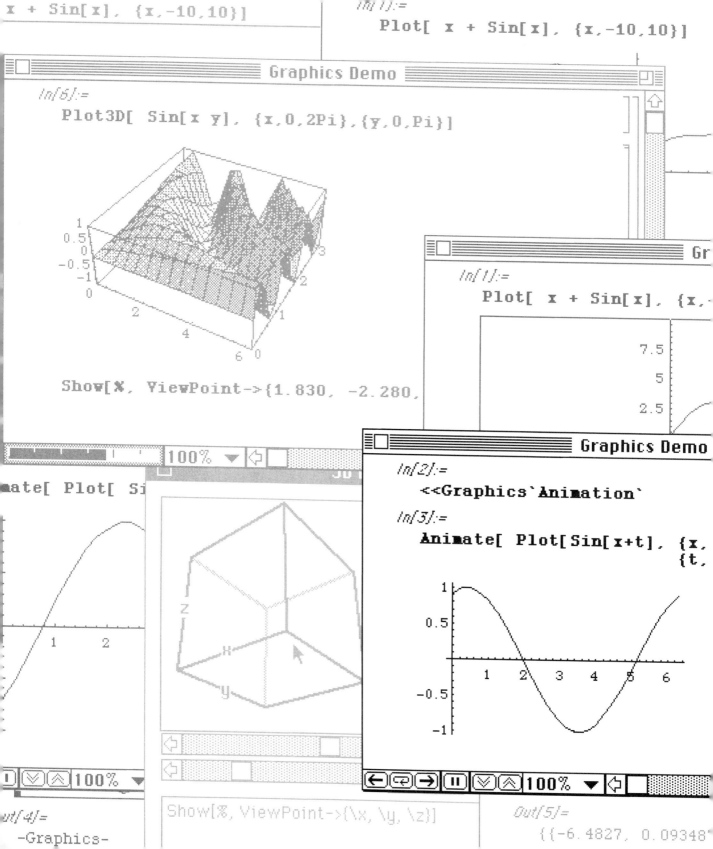

Show[%, ViewPoint->{1.830, -2.280,

Gr

In[1]:=
Plot[x + Sin[x], {x,

7.5

5

2.5

100% ▼

ate[Plot[Si

2

1

2

Z

H

y

Show[%, ViewPoint->{\x, \y, \z}]

Graphics Demo

In[2]:=
<<Graphics`Animation`

In[3]:=
Animate[Plot[Sin[x+t], {x,
                        {t,

1

0.5

1   2   3   4   5   6

-0.5

-1

100% ▼

Out[4]=
-Graphics-

Out[5]=
{{-6.4827, 0.09348

Chapter 6
The Mathematica Front End

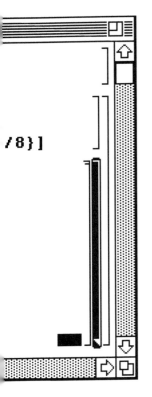

This chapter describes some of the facilities that are provided by the front end to work with images. This stands in contrast to the commands that are entered to the kernel to generate images. It will consider the two main types of front ends that are available to connect to the kernel: notebook front ends and non-notebook front ends. Notebook front ends provide many useful features for working with graphics and their features are described first. The non-notebook front end is a simpler application with fewer features. Nonetheless in certain circumstances it may be appropriate. It is described in the last section.

6.1 Notebook Front Ends

The notebook front end is a special *Mathematica* interface that allows the construction of sophisticated documents that mix text, computations, and graphics. When a picture is generated by the kernel it appears in the body of the current notebook. The picture is generated by first entering and then evaluating a graphics command in the notebook. When the evaluation is running, the cell bracket[6] expands, and then the picture is inserted below the command.

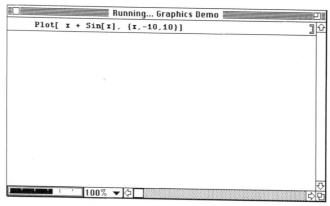

Evaluating a graphics command.

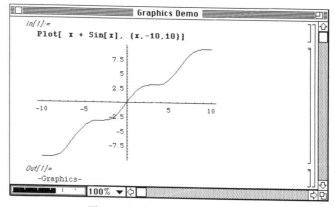

The result of a graphics command.

---

[6]A cell is the basic entity that holds all the information such as input, output, graphics, text, and groups of cells in the notebook. Its extent is displayed by means of brackets. The appropriate front end manual describes these features in detail.

When a picture has been generated in the notebook it can be manipulated in a number of ways. The picture can be moved by clicking the mouse in the picture and dragging. During this operation the distance that it moves is displayed in the lower-left corner of the notebook. When the mouse is released the picture appears in its new location.

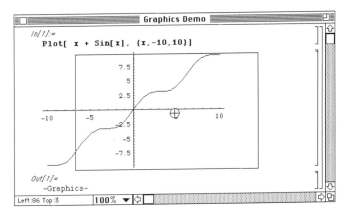

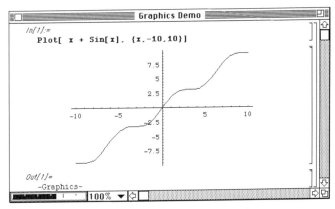

Moving a graphic in the front end.

In addition to moving the picture it can be resized. This is done by selecting the picture and clicking on one of the handles on its frame. Moving the mouse will cause the picture to change size. During this operation the current size is displayed in the lower-left corner.

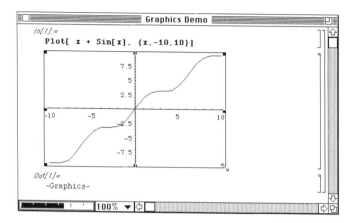

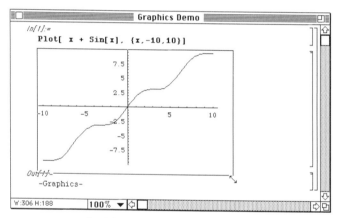

Resizing an image in the front end.

After a picture has been resized it can be returned to the default size with the **Make Standard Size** item from the **Graphics** menu.

There are certain other features of the front end relevant to graphics that are involved with lines. Various items from the **Graphics** menu allow lines to be redrawn thin or completely absent. The lines are actually drawn thin by making them one pixel wide. This means that their appearance depends upon the resolution of the rendering device and if the resolution is very high the line will be invisible. This defeats one advantage of PostScript as a resolution-independent page-description language: on one device the line is visible while on another it is not. For this reason it is much better to produce lines of the desired weight when the picture is generated.

6.2 Printing

The front end is an application that is designed in the typical fashion for applications of the system under which it runs; this applies to printing as other features. Thus printing on the Macintosh works in the normal Macintosh way and likewise for other versions. A problem is presented with printing from the X Windows front end. X Windows is only a window system and there is no native standard for printing to work. Despite this the X Windows front end contains special code to support printing in the obvious way. For all front ends printed output of a graphic is generated by choosing **Print** from the **File** menu. The selection of an individual printer and other details depend upon the type of system and are described in the documentation. The entire notebook including the text and the graphics can be printed. Alternatively, a portion of the notebook, such as one picture, can be selected and printed alone.

All front ends support printing to PostScript printers. Printing to non-PostScript printers is supported for certain types of printers. The front end documentation must be consulted to determine the supported printers. If problems are experienced in printing a graphic an alternative to using the front end is to generate a PostScript file and convert this into a format supported by the printer. This more advanced technique is described in Chapter 26.

6.3 Animation

Any sequence of graphics in a notebook can be animated. This is done by selecting a group of pictures and choosing **Animate Selected Graphics** from the **Graph** menu. While an animation is running, controls are made available to change the speed and direction of frames. The **Align Selected Graphics** item available under the **Graph** menu is available to align images. This is essential for a good animation, however, it is preferable to produce aligned images in the first place.

While any sequence of images can produce an animation it only makes sense to animate pictures that are related. For this reason it is likely that a single iterator type of command will generate them. In fact there is an animation package (this was described in Chapter 5 page 80) that provides a set of useful commands. It is not necessary to use this package for producing animations in a notebook front end but it is highly recommended. Chapter 5 describes this package and some other details necessary for good animations.

When one of the animation commands, such as `Animate`, has been executed a sequence of pictures will appear in the notebook. It is then common to group the pictures and close the group[7] so that only the first picture is seen. The **Animate Selected Graphics** command can then be chosen.

---

[7] A group of cells can be closed by clicking on the bracket.

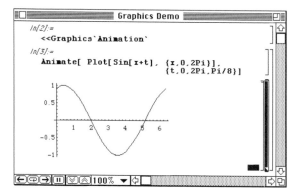

Generating frames for an animation in the front end.

Running an animation in the front end.

An interesting feature of the Macintosh front end is the capability to convert the animation to a QuickTime movie. This is done with the **Convert To QuickTime** item of the **Graph** menu.

So that the animation can run rapidly in the front end a bitmap must be kept in memory for each frame. If there are many frames and each one is in color this can consume a considerable amount of memory. If the animation does not show any color, such as a two-dimensional plot, it is highly beneficial to make sure that these bitmaps are not kept in color. This is done on the NeXT and Windows front ends by selecting monochrome bitmaps. On the Macintosh front end it is done by ensuring that the monitor is in monochrome mode. A full color bitmap may require 24 bits for each pixel while a monochrome bitmap requires 1 bit for each pixel, a significant saving in memory (a factor of 24). Of course, if the animation requires color, monochrome bitmaps are not suitable.

6.4 Saving and Restoring Notebooks

A notebook can contain a collection of inputs, outputs, pictures, and animations. It is easy to save with the **Save** item of the **File** menu. It can be reopened later with the **Open** item of the **File** menu. When it is reopened later it contains the same information. In this way an interesting body of work can be saved and passed around to other people. Since the data in a notebook consists of ASCII text it is very suitable to be sent by email. The front end manual should be consulted for more information on the structure of notebooks.

When a notebook is loaded back into the front end any pictures that were present will be restored. The actual *Mathematica* kernel expressions will not be restored. If the notebook contains the commands to create the pictures then the corresponding expressions can be re-created. In order to save and restore the actual kernel graphics objects kernel commands can be used. This was demonstrated in Chapter 4 page 58.

6.5 Displaying and Copying Coordinates

The coordinates in a two-dimensional picture can be displayed by selecting the graph and holding down the special key [8] while using the mouse to move the cursor inside the picture. As this is done the coordinates of the cursor are displayed in the lower-left corner. When the mouse is clicked a point is displayed on the graph and the coordinates saved. If **Copy** and **Paste** are then used following this procedure the points will be pasted into the notebook and they can be sent to the *Mathematica* kernel as an input.

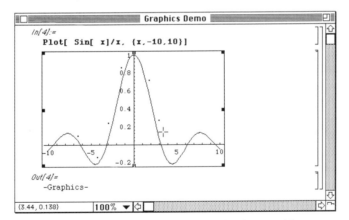

Finding coordinates and selecting points in a graphic.

---

[8]The special key is standard for each particular system but varies from one system to another. The details are described by the front end documentation.

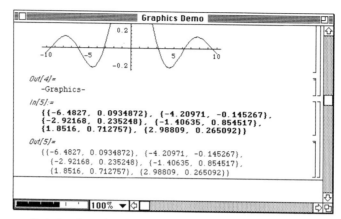

Entering the points from a graphic as input to Mathematica.

The same technique applies to a three-dimensional graphic. However, in this case the points that are displayed are given in the two-dimensional coordinate system after projection from three dimensions. Consequently, the feature is not very useful for three-dimensional graphics.

6.6 The Three-Dimensional ViewPoint Selector

Three-dimensional graphics are drawn by means of a projection from three to two dimensions. The details are described in Chapter 10. One important control is the actual position used to look at the object. In the *Mathematica* kernel this is set by the ViewPoint option of three-dimensional graphics objects. A value for this can be chosen with the three-dimensional ViewPoint selector, available from the **Prepare Input** submenu item of the **Action** menu[9]. When this is chosen a dialog box is displayed showing a three-dimensional box that can be manipulated with the mouse. Once an interesting view has been found then a template command changing the ViewPoint option can be prepared and pasted into the notebook. The command can then be evaluated and the new viewpoint displayed.

---

[9]The three-dimensional ViewPoint selector is not available in the Version 2.2 X Windows front end.

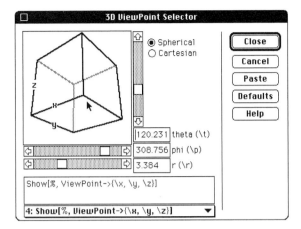

The three-dimensional `ViewPoint` selector.

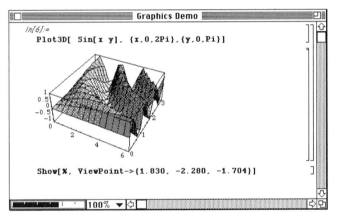

Pasting in a command built by the selector.

6.7 Non-Notebook Front Ends

The non-notebook front end is not a sophisticated application like the notebook front end. It does not provide as many facilities and those that are provided are not as convenient to use. However, the non-notebook front ends does support both graphics and animation. Entering the graphics commands described in *Mathematica Graphics* will cause a picture to appear. To make an animation the animation package must be loaded as described in Chapter 5 page 80.

A graphic can be printed by a command given to the kernel after a graphics object has been generated. The command that does this is usually called `PSPrint`; the exact details are found in the user manual for the particular system.

In[1]:= **?PSPrint**

PSPrint[-graphics-] sends graphics to a printer.

A picture is generated in the normal way.   *In[2]:=* **Plot[Sin[x] + x, {x,-10, 10}]**

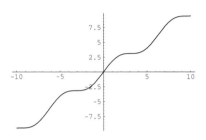

The plot will be printed on the default printer.

In[3]:= **PSPrint[%]**

Out[3]= -Graphics-

If problems are found with the PSPrint command it may be worth consulting Chapter 26, which covers exporting graphics from *Mathematica*.

Despite the fact that the non-notebook front end does not provide so many features as the notebook front end there are times when it can be very useful. It has a much lighter footprint on the computer and may be suitable for simple computations or experiments. When these become more complex the work can be switched to the notebook front end.

PART II
Graphics Programming

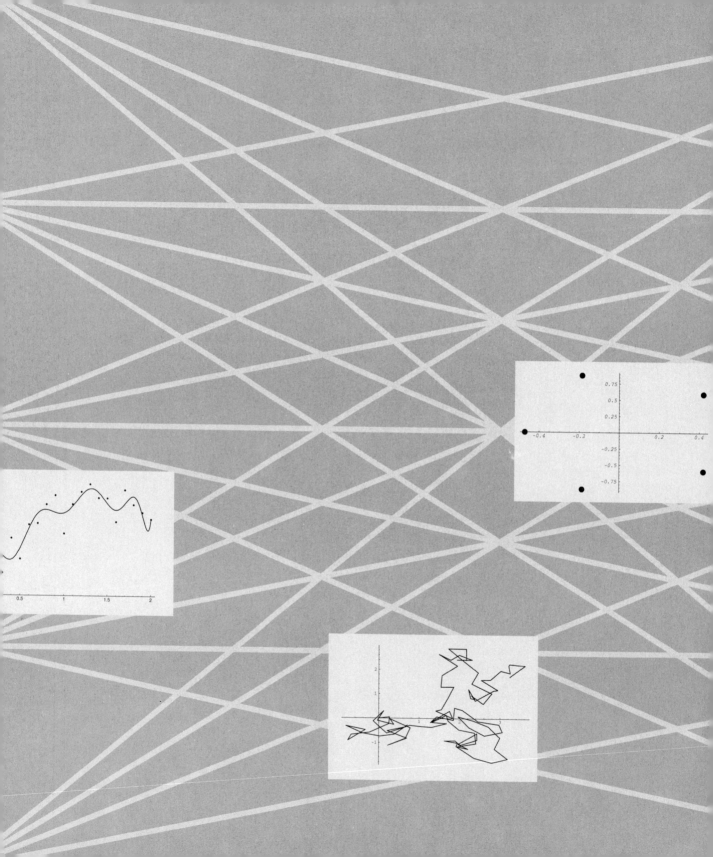

Chapter 7
Mathematica Programming

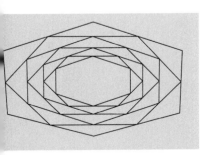

Part I of *Mathematica Graphics* examined the built-in functions of *Mathematica* graphics and detailed a variety of ways to use them to generate a wide array of graphical effects. Part II takes a more advanced look and aims to show how it is possible to construct new graphics functions. This is done by graphics programming, applying programming techniques to graphics: a powerful synthesis that forms one of the strengths and unique features of using *Mathematica* for graphics. Chapter 7 is intended as a summary of some of the important programming features that will be used in the rest of Part II. It is not intended as a detailed description of *Mathematica* programming. There are many other sources for this, such as the main *Mathematica* book. Nonetheless the examples will be useful to readers.

The first three sections of this chapter describe basic tools: defining functions, using replacement rules, and pure functions. These are fundamental programming constructs that will be used in the rest of Part II of *Mathematica Graphics*. This is followed by a description of some of the high-level *Mathematica* functions that are useful for implementing other functions.

This chapter presents a summary of some *Mathematica* programming techniques. It is not intended as a complete description but as a sample, something that readers can examine to see the types of programming tools that will be used. It can also be used as a simple reference.

7.1 Defining a New Function

It is easy to add a new function to *Mathematica*. This is done by one of the set commands such as `:=`, with the function, its arguments, as well as the body of the function. As an aside, it can be pointed out that `:=` is shorthand input for `SetDelayed`. An alternative setting command is `=`, which is shorthand input for `Set`. Their main difference is that `Set` evaluates its right-hand side whereas `SetDelayed` does not. As a general rule the former is useful for assigning a value to a symbol whereas the latter is useful for making a function. The *Mathematica* book discusses the difference between these in detail.

A function called `newfun` is defined. It takes one argument and returns a list containing the argument and its square.

```
In[1]:= newfun[x_] := {x, x^2}
```

`newfun` will work for an argument that is an integer expression.

```
In[2]:= newfun[5]
Out[2]= {5, 25}
```

`newfun` will work for an argument that is a symbol expression.

```
In[3]:= newfun[t]
Out[3]= {t, t }
```

`newfun` will accept any *Mathematica* expression as an argument.

```
In[4]:= newfun[Sin[4]]
                          2
Out[4]= {Sin[4], Sin[4] }
```

`newfun` can be used inside some other *Mathematica* construction; here it is used with a `Table` command.

```
In[5]:= Table[newfun[i], {i,10}]
Out[5]= {{1, 1}, {2, 4}, {3, 9}, {4, 16}, {5, 25}, {6, 36},
         {7, 49}, {8, 64}, {9, 81}, {10, 100}}
```

The result is just a *Mathematica* list that can be plotted with ListPlot.

In[6]:= **ListPlot[%]**

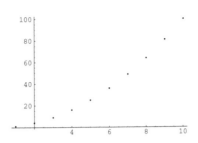

When two arguments are given newfun does not evaluate. The function has only been defined for one argument.

In[7]:= **newfun[a,b]**

Out[7]= newfun[a, b]

▸ *A Factorial Function*

The construction of a new function will now be illustrated by writing a factorial function. *Mathematica* has a built-in factorial function, but a version is implemented here as an example of *Mathematica* programming. This particular example demonstrates recursive programming, a program that calls itself, one of the many types of programming styles that *Mathematica* supports.

Factorial of n is defined as n times the factorial of (n − 1).

In[8]:= **fact[n_] := n fact[n-1]**

The factorial of 0 is defined to be 1. This could use = instead of :=. It does not to be consistent with the other function definitions.

In[9]:= **fact[0] := 1**

These are the definitions of the function fact. The definition of fact that will be used depends upon the actual input.

In[10]:= **??fact**

Global`fact

fact[0] := 1

fact[n_] := n*fact[n - 1]

This is the factorial of 10.

In[11]:= **fact[10]**

Out[11]= 3628800

The built-in factorial function agrees.

In[12]:= **10!**

Out[12]= 3628800

In this example, the function fact was defined for an unknown argument as well as a particular literal value. Defining it for a particular value allowed the function to stop the repeated application of its general definition. One of the important features of *Mathematica* programming is that a function can be defined to have different types of behavior for different types of input. For this function if an argument of 0 is never reached the function will continue to call itself. This will happen if the argument is not a positive integer (such as a negative integer or a symbol).

`fact[x]` is evaluated but will never reach 0. Eventually messages are generated because there is a limit on the depth of the recursion[1]. The evaluation stops and a short form of the result is printed.

```
In[13]:= Short[fact[x], 2]
```

$RecursionLimit::reclim: Recursion depth of 256 exceeded.

$RecursionLimit::reclim: Recursion depth of 256 exceeded.

$RecursionLimit::reclim: Recursion depth of 256 exceeded.

General::stop:
    Further output of $RecursionLimit::reclim
        will be suppressed during this calculation.

```
Out[13]//Short=

 (-251 + x) (-250 + x) (-249 + x) <<250>> Hold[<<1>>]

    Hold[Hold[Hold[-1 + Hold[Hold[-251 + x]] - 1]]]
```

`fact1` is an improved factorial function.

```
In[14]:= fact1[0] := 1
```

The argument of `fact1` is restricted to be a positive integer.

```
In[15]:= fact1[n_Integer /; Positive[n]] := n fact1[n - 1]
```

This works as before.

```
In[16]:= fact1[10]
Out[16]= 3628800
```

This does not evaluate since x is not a positive integer.

```
In[17]:= fact1[x]
Out[17]= fact1[x]
```

▸ *Module*

Usually a *Mathematica* program or function will be more complex than these examples. It may well have several steps with intermediate results to be kept. *Mathematica* provides `Module` for this purpose. This is an example that uses `Module` for a small program that combines a plot of some data with a plot of a fit to the data.

The details of this program will be discussed in the next few pages.

```
In[18]:= datafitPlot[data_ /; MatrixQ[data], n_Integer] :=
            Module[{p1, p2, fun, x},
                p1 = ListPlot[data,
                            DisplayFunction -> Identity] ;
                fun = Table[x^i,{ i, 0, n}] ;
                fun = Fit[data, fun, x] ;
                p2 = Plot[fun, {x, 0, 2},
                            DisplayFunction -> Identity] ;
                Show[p1, p2,
                        DisplayFunction -> $DisplayFunction]
                ]
```

This produces some data to be used by the `datafitPlot` function.

```
In[19]:= data = Table[{x, Sin[x] + Random[ ]}, {x,0,2,0.1}];
```

---

[1]The maximum depth of recursion is controlled by $RecursionLimit. Setting it to Infinity removes any limit on recursion.

When a polynomial of degree three is fitted through the points the result seems quite smooth.

In[20]:= **datafitPlot[data, 3]**

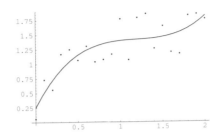

Increasing the degree of the polynomial can make a plot that wiggles around more.

In[21]:= **datafitPlot[data, 10]**

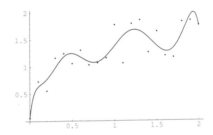

The function `datafitPlot` makes it very easy to fit different functions to the data and then examine the results visually. The two pictures here show that as the degree of the polynomial is increased the fit will wiggle more to try to pass closer to the data points. Of course if the data have a lot of scatter this may not be desirable.

Analysis of the Function

The individual parts of the program `datafitPlot` are now looked at and analyzed.

```
datafitPlot[data_ /; MatrixQ[data], n_Integer] :=
```

This is the definition of the function; it is called `datafitPlot` and takes two arguments. The first is a matrix of data to be fitted and the second an integer controlling the degree of the polynomial.

```
Module[{p1, p2, fun, x},
```

There are four local variables in the `Module`. `p1` and `p2` will hold the two plots that are generated. `fun` will first hold the basis functions to use to fit and then the resulting fitted function. `x` is the variable for the fit.

```
p1 = ListPlot[data, DisplayFunction -> Identity] ;
```

The data plot is made and assigned to the local variable p1. Graphics output is suppressed by setting the `DisplayFunction` option to `Identity`. This was demonstrated in Chapter 3 page 44.

```
fun = Table[x^i,{ i, 0, n}] ;
fun = Fit[data, fun, x] ;
```

A list of functions to use for the fit is generated with `Table`. The fit of the data to these functions is then carried out.

```
p2 = Plot[fun, {x, 0, 2}, DisplayFunction -> Identity] ;
```

A plot of the fitted function is made. The limits of this plot are arbitrarily from 0 to 2. It would be better to determine these limits from the data.

```
Show[p1, p2, DisplayFunction -> $DisplayFunction]
```

The combined plot is made and returned as the result. Since this is returned as the result `Show` could be used.

```
datafitPlot[data_ /; MatrixQ[data], n_Integer] :=
    Module[{p1, p2, fun, x, x0, x1},
        p1 = ListPlot[data, DisplayFunction -> Identity] ;
        fun = Table[x^i,{ i, 0, n}] ;
        fun = Fit[data, fun, x] ;
        x1 = Max[Map[First, data]] ;
        x0 = Min[Map[First, data]] ;
        p2 = Plot[fun, {x, x0, x1}, DisplayFunction -> Identity] ;
        Show[p1, p2, DisplayFunction -> $DisplayFunction]
        ]
```

This is an improved version of `datafitPlot` that determines the minimum and maximum x values of the data. These can be used in the `Plot` command. Other improvements could include argument checking. The data could be checked to confirm that they consist of real numbers and the degree could be checked that it is positive.

▶ *Patterns*

The functions demonstrated have taken arguments of any value, arguments with a particular value, or arguments that met some test. The functions that took arguments of any value employed a syntax _ (an underbar). This is referred to in *Mathematica* as a `Blank` and is an example of a pattern. Patterns in *Mathematica* are extremely powerful since they can be set up to match particular classes of expression. The table below shows some patterns and examples of expressions that they match.

`f[x_]`	f with one argument	`f[1],f[x],f[Sin[x]]`
`f[x_List]`	f with a list as argument	`f[{1,2}]`
`f[x_g]`	f with an expression of head g as argument	`f[g[1,2]]`
`f[x_ /; x > 4]`	f with an argument bigger than 4	`f[6],f[100.6]`
`f[x_, y_]`	f with two arguments	`f[a,b],f[{4,5}, 99.4]`
`f[g[x_, y_]]`	f with one argument of head g and two arguments	`f[g[a,b]],` `f[g[{4,5}, 99.4]]`
`f[x__]`	f with one or more arguments	`f[1],f[x, y]`
`f[x___]`	f with zero or more arguments	`f[ ],f[1],f[x, y]`

Examples of *Mathematica* patterns.

One simple way to check whether a pattern will match is to use the function `MatchQ`. This can test some of the examples in the table. This helps the writing of a function by testing the types of argument. It is also useful for understanding the types of expressions that match particular patterns.

This matches.

```
In[22]:= MatchQ[f[g[a,b]], f[g[x_, y_]]]
Out[22]= True
```

This does not match. `x__` matches one or more arguments.

```
In[23]:= MatchQ[f[ ], f[x__]]
Out[23]= False
```

This matches. `x___` can match zero or more arguments.

```
In[24]:= MatchQ[f[ ], f[x___]]
Out[24]= True
```

7.2 Replacement Rules

The previous section showed how a new function could be added to *Mathematica*. This was done by writing a pattern for the function combined with a result. This is one way to change an expression. Another way to change an expression is to use a replacement rule.

A rule that replaces a by c.

```
In[25]:= a -> c
Out[25]= a -> c
```

`->` is shorthand notation for `Rule`.

```
In[26]:= FullForm[%]
Out[26]//FullForm= Rule[a, c]
```

`/.` applies a rule to an object. It is shorthand notation for `ReplaceAll`. Since an a was found in the object the replacement was made.

```
In[27]:= a /. %
Out[27]= c
```

/. will descend to any level of an expression to find things to match.

```
In[28]:= f[x, y] /. x -> z
Out[28]= f[z, y]
```

/. can apply more than one rule at a time.

```
In[29]:= f[x, y] /. {x -> z1, y -> z2}
Out[29]= f[z1, z2]
```

Mathematica rules are obviously quite useful. What makes them very powerful is that they can use patterns. This allows them to match to particular classes of expression.

The rule will match every expression that has a head of Symbol.

```
In[30]:= f[arg1, arg2] /. x_Symbol -> new
Out[30]= new[new, new]
```

This rule removes the trailing False in a list.

```
In[31]:= rule = {x___, False} -> {x}
Out[31]= {x___, False} -> {x}
```

```
In[32]:= {a, b, False, False} /. rule
Out[32]= {a, b, False}
```

ReplaceRepeated, //., continues to apply its rule until the expression no longer changes. This returns a list that does not end in False.

```
In[33]:= {a, b, False, False} //. rule
Out[33]= {a, b}
```

▶ *Delayed Rules*

When a rule is defined with Rule the normal sequence of evaluation is followed. This means that the right-hand side is evaluated. To prevent this RuleDelayed is provided. This delays the evaluation of its right-hand side and is often essential for proper working of a rule.

The intent is to replace any expression with head f with its length. However, it does not work. The length of the expression of head f is 2 not 0.

```
In[34]:= {a, b, f[x, y], c} /. x_f -> Length[x]
Out[34]= {a, b, 0, c}
```

The previous example did not work because the rule evaluated its right-hand side before it was used.

```
In[35]:= x_f -> Length[x]
Out[35]= x_f -> 0
```

The solution is to use RuleDelayed, :>, which does not evaluate its argument.

```
In[36]:= x_f :> Length[x]
Out[36]= x_f :> Length[x]
```

Now the length of the expression of head f is inserted.

```
In[37]:= {a, b, f[x, y], c} /. %
Out[37]= {a, b, 2, c}
```

Mathematica rules can be used to go inside expressions and do very particular things. This is extremely powerful and will be used frequently throughout *Mathematica Graphics*.

▶ *Example: Plotting the Roots of a Polynomial*

An example of rules will now be shown that plots the roots of a polynomial. This will show how `Solve` returns replacement rules[2] and how the values can be extracted and plotted. The replacement rules returned by `Solve` are very useful since they indicate how many solutions were found and which solutions refer to which variables. They also allow individual solutions to be picked out.

This is a polynomial of degree five.

```
In[38]:= eqn = 5 x^5 + 4 x^3 + x + 1
                  3     5
Out[38]= 1 + x + 4 x  + 5 x
```

The roots of the polynomial are calculated by Solve. There are five different replacement rules signifying that there were five solutions to the equation. Since the equation involved floating-point numbers this is how the result appears.

```
In[39]:= Solve[eqn == 0.0, x]
Out[39]= {{x -> -0.470007}, {x -> -0.185633 - 0.877206 I},
   {x -> -0.185633 + 0.877206 I}, {x -> 0.420637 - 0.593597 I},
   {x -> 0.420637 + 0.593597 I}}
```

When the rules are substituted into x, a list of the actual numbers are returned.

```
In[40]:= x /. %
Out[40]= {-0.470007, -0.185633 - 0.877206 I,
   -0.185633 + 0.877206 I, 0.420637 - 0.593597 I,
   0.420637 + 0.593597 I}
```

The rule here converts the numbers to ordered pairs. The first element holds the real part and the second holds the imaginary part of each number.

```
In[41]:= % /. {a_Real -> {a,0}, Complex[r_, i_] -> {r,i}}
Out[41]= {{-0.470007, 0}, {-0.185633, -0.877206},
   {-0.185633, 0.877206}, {0.420637, -0.593597},
   {0.420637, 0.593597}}
```

ListPlot is the natural function to plot this set of numbers.

```
In[42]:= ListPlot[%, PlotStyle -> PointSize[0.03]]
```

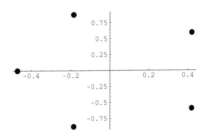

---

[2] All the solve functions such as `Solve`, `DSolve`, and `NDSolve` return replacement rules.

The steps shown previously can be combined into a short function. The local variable sols carries the intermediate result.

```
In[43]:= rootPlot[eqn_, var_, opts___] :=
            Module[{sols},
                sols = var /. Solve[ eqn == 0.0, var] ;
                sols = sols /. {a_Real -> {a,0},
                                   Complex[r_, i_] -> {r,i}} ;
                ListPlot[sols, opts,
                            PlotStyle -> PointSize[0.03]]
            ]
```

This sixth-degree polynomial has six roots.

```
In[44]:= rootPlot[5 x^6 + 4 x^3 + x + 1, x]
```

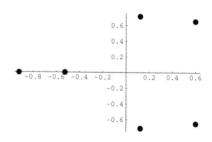

These steps show how the computations necessary to carry out a particular operation can each be tested individually. Once they have been determined to work properly they can be combined into a function.

7.3 Pure Functions

A function can be added to *Mathematica* by := with a pattern and a body, a left-hand and a right-hand side. This is somewhat cumbersome if the function is only to be used once or is to be generated by some other function. In this case a pure or anonymous function is appropriate. A common example of the use of pure functions is with commands like Map that take a function as their argument. In this example Map tests a list of numbers to see which are positive. This is done with the function Positive.

Map travels down the list building expressions Positive[*elem*], which evaluate to True or False.

```
In[45]:= Map[Positive, {1, -4, 7, 0.9, -2}]
Out[45]= {True, False, True, True, False}
```

This works for Positive, a function that only takes one argument. How can it work for a function that takes more than one argument? For example, how can Map test elements to see which are greater than 3? There is a function Greater but this takes two arguments. One solution is to write a new function; a better solution is to use a pure function.

greater3 takes one argument and compares it with 3.

```
In[46]:= greater3[x_] := Greater[x, 3]
```

greater3 can be used with Map.

```
In[47]:= Map[greater3, {1, -4, 7, 0.9, 3.1}]
Out[47]= {False, False, True, False, True}
```

A better solution is to use a pure function.

```
In[48]:= Map[Greater[#, 3]&, {1, -4, 7, 0.9, 3.1}]
Out[48]= {False, False, True, False, True}
```

The pure function is labeled by the & at the end. This example takes one argument which will be inserted for any #.

```
In[49]:= Greater[#, 3]&
Out[49]= #1 > 3 &
```

The pure function is applied to 2.

```
In[50]:= Greater[#, 3]& [2]
Out[50]= False
```

A pure function works as the head of an expression. It is important to realize that a head does not have to be a symbol, it can be any expression.

```
In[51]:= FullForm[Hold[Greater[#, 3]& [2]]]
Out[51]//FullForm= Hold[Function[Greater[Slot[1], 3]][2]]
```

The advantage of the pure function is that it can be built, used at the *actual* time it is needed, and then discarded. An ordinary function is slower to construct and will last after it has been used. If it will never be used again this is waste of system resources.

7.4 High-Level *Mathematica* Functions

Before attempting to solve some problem by developing a *Mathematica* program it is worth checking to see if *Mathematica* already possesses the functionality. It may exist in the *Mathematica* kernel or in one of the *Mathematica* standard packages. If it is necessary to write a program it is worth trying to use the high-level *Mathematica* functions as much as possible. Two such functions have already been introduced: Table and Map. When these are used then very efficient and compact programs can be written. There are other high-level functions that lend themselves to implementing an algorithm.

▶ *Apply*

Apply changes the head of an expression.

```
In[52]:= Apply[f, g[1,2,3]]
Out[52]= f[1, 2, 3]
```

With Apply it is easy to sum up the elements of a list and calculate the mean.

```
In[53]:= mean[data_] :=
            Apply[Plus, data]/Length[data]
```

```
In[54]:= mean[{1,5,6,4}]
Out[54]= 4
```

▶ *Nest and NestList*

The function fun is applied repeatedly.

```
In[55]:= fun[fun[fun[fun[x]]]]
Out[55]= fun[fun[fun[fun[x]]]]
```

It is much simpler just to use Nest.

```
In[56]:= Nest[fun, x, 4]
Out[56]= fun[fun[fun[fun[x]]]]
```

It is often natural to use a pure function for the function argument of Nest.

```
In[57]:= Nest[1/(1+#)&, x, 4]
```

$$Out[57]= \cfrac{1}{1 + \cfrac{1}{1 + \cfrac{1}{1 + \cfrac{1}{1 + x}}}}$$

Applying Cos repeatedly to a number converges to a fixed point. Even after 10 applications this is evident.

```
In[58]:= NestList[Cos, 0.5, 10]
Out[58]= {0.5, 0.877583, 0.639012, 0.802685, 0.694778,
   0.768196, 0.719165, 0.752356, 0.730081, 0.74512, 0.735006}
```

This convergence can be examined graphically.

```
In[59]:= ListPlot[%, PlotJoined -> True]
```

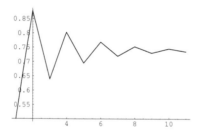

▶ *Fold and FoldList*

Fold and FoldList are extremely powerful commands. They apply a function repeatedly, as does Nest, but they also keep track of an intermediate result. Sometimes entire algorithms can be implemented using just these functions.

It seems abstract but it is very powerful.

```
In[60]:= ?FoldList
FoldList[f, x, {a, b, ...}] gives {x, f[x, a], f[f[x, a], b],
   ...}.
```

The result starts with x, adds in a, adds in b to that result, and so on, forming a cumulative sum.

```
In[61]:= FoldList[Plus, x, {a,b,c,d}]
Out[61]= {x, a + x, a + b + x, a + b + c + x, a + b + c + d + x}
```

This generates points in a random walk.

```
In[62]:= FoldList[Plus, {0,0}, Table[Random[ ]-0.5, {10}, {2}]]
Out[62]= {{0, 0}, {0.318071, -0.0814403}, {0.521185, 0.218597},
   {0.208956, -0.222738}, {0.540693, 0.218654},
   {0.643886, 0.0344133}, {0.584162, 0.118581},
   {0.30684, 0.00541874}, {0.0718683, 0.23117},
   {-0.0996339, -0.159888}, {0.0153974, -0.134382}}
```

Making a plot of the result often helps to understand what the function is doing.

```
In[63]:= ListPlot[
             FoldList[Plus, {0,0},
                 Table[Random[ ]-0.5, {100}, {2}]],
             PlotJoined -> True]
```

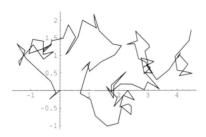

The example above, generating points in a random walk, is both concise and efficient. A program to carry out the same task in C or Fortran would be considerably larger and would take more time to develop.

It is not essential to write *Mathematica* programs using constructs like Nest and FoldList. They are presented here as examples of the types of things that can be done and are introduced to give a sense of a *Mathematica* style of programming.

7.5 Summary

This chapter has reviewed some of the ways *Mathematica* manipulates expressions to form functions and programs. Three types of construction were presented. First, the definition of a function was examined. This allows new functions to be added to *Mathematica*. Such functions can use *Mathematica* patterns to specify behavior for particular types of arguments. Secondly, the use of replacement rules to alter parts of *Mathematica* expressions was described. These can also make use of *Mathematica* patterns to act on particular parts of expressions. Thirdly, the use of pure functions was considered. These are functions that can be built as needed when they are used and are important for working with the many *Mathematica* commands that take functions as an argument. The last section considered some of the high-level programming constructs of *Mathematica*, constructs that allow the development of efficient and concise programs.

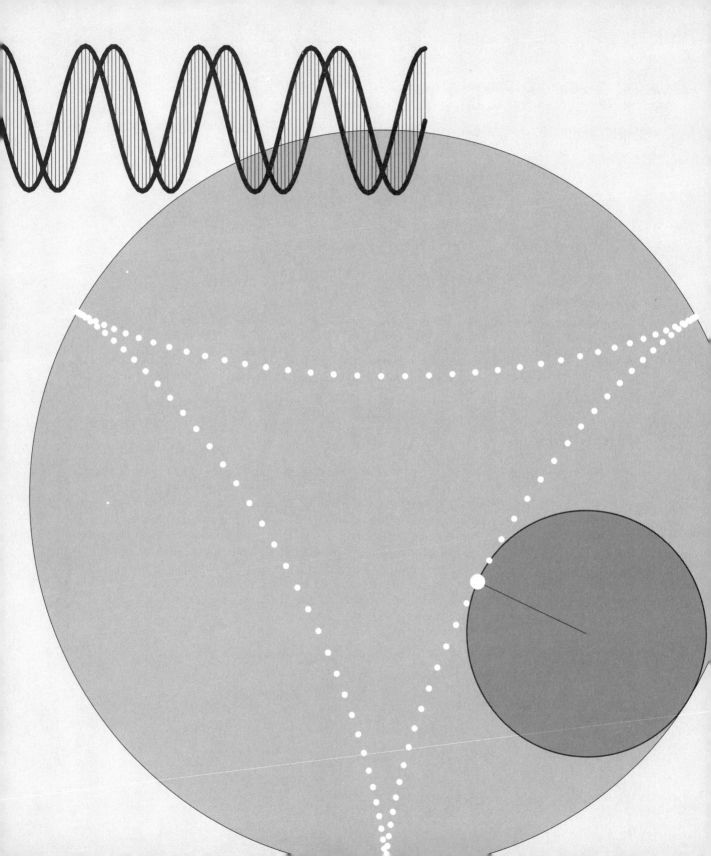

Chapter 8
Two-Dimensional Graphical Primitives

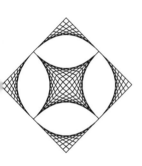

This chapter covers the building blocks that are available to construct two-dimensional graphical images. These will be studied in conjunction with programming methods introduced in the previous chapter. The chapter does not cover every detail of two-dimensional graphics. Such detail is provided in Part IV. The aim of this chapter is to give instruction in how to use the primitives, which will lay the foundations of the concept of graphics programming.

8.1 Primitives

A graphics command such as `Plot` accepts some input, builds a graphics object, displays it, and returns the object. This was demonstrated in Chapter 2 page 20.

A simple `Plot` command is evaluated. The `PlotPoints` option is altered to give a smaller output.

```
In[1]:= Plot[x, {x,0,1},PlotPoints -> 8]
```

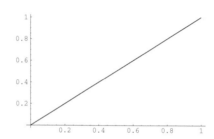

`InputForm[`*expr*`]` shows the input to *Mathematica* necessary to construct *expr*.

```
In[2]:= InputForm[%]

Out[2]//InputForm=
    Graphics[{{Line[{{1.428571428571428*10^-7,
        1.428571428571428*10^-7},
        {0.1374006284107128, 0.1374006284107128},
        {0.2846722997589262, 0.2846722997589262},
        {0.4237589851517804, 0.4237589851517804},
        {0.5601173418928481, 0.5601173418928481},
        {0.7008902271249863, 0.7008902271249863},
        {0.8389347837053382, 0.8389347837053382},
        {0.9813938687767606, 0.9813938687767606},
        {0.9999998571428571, 0.9999998571428571}}]}},
      {PlotRange -> Automatic, AspectRatio -> GoldenRatio^(-1),
       DisplayFunction :> $DisplayFunction,
       ColorOutput -> Automatic, Axes -> Automatic,
       AxesOrigin -> Automatic, PlotLabel -> None,
       AxesLabel -> None, Ticks -> Automatic, GridLines -> None,
       Prolog -> {}, Epilog -> {}, AxesStyle -> Automatic,
       Background -> Automatic, DefaultColor -> Automatic,
       DefaultFont :> $DefaultFont, RotateLabel -> True,
       Frame -> False, FrameStyle -> Automatic,
       FrameTicks -> Automatic, FrameLabel -> None,
       PlotRegion -> Automatic}]
```

The command `Plot` returns a result that contains `Line` primitives. These describe the loci of points of the original function. In addition to `Line` primitives there are other primitives that can be used in two-dimensional graphics.

`Point[`*pt*`]`	a single point
`Line[{`*pt1*`, `*pt2*`, `*pt3*`, ... }]`	a line through a set of points
`Polygon[{`*pt1*`, `*pt2*`, `*pt3*`, ... }]`	a polygon
`Circle[`*pt*`, `*r*`]`	a circle
`Disk[`*pt*`, `*r*`]`	a filled circle
`Raster[`*bitmap*`]`	a grayscale bitmap
`RasterArray[`*bitmap*`]`	a color bitmap
`Rectangle[`*pt1*`, `*pt2*`]`	a rectangle
`Text[`*expr*`, `*pt*`]`	a text primitive
`PostScript[`*string*`]`	a PostScript procedure

Graphics primitives.

A *Mathematica* graphics expression can be constructed from whatever primitives are desired. This Line primitive contains a list of the points to be connected.

```
In[3]:= Line[{{0,0}, {1,0}, {1,1}, {2,1},{2,0},{3,0}}]

Out[3]= Line[{{0, 0}, {1, 0}, {1, 1}, {2, 1}, {2, 0}, {3, 0}}]
```

Now an expression with a head of Graphics is built. It is printed with the special format of Graphics objects.

```
In[4]:= Graphics[%]

Out[4]= -Graphics-
```

The Graphics object can be displayed by making a call to Show.

```
In[5]:= Show[%]
```

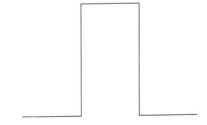

It would be very cumbersome if it were necessary to enter the explicit form of everything to be plotted. Instead, it is often preferable to use commands such as Table to build expressions. Usually, this provides for more concise input and allows a mathematical model to be used.

Table is a natural command to use to build a list of primitives.

```
In[6]:= Table[Line[{{i,0},{0,5-i}}], {i,0,5,0.5}];
```

This can be used to form part of a parabola.

In[7]:= **Show[Graphics[%]]**

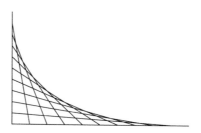

The expressions can be arbitrarily complicated. This combination of structural commands, like Table, with mathematical commands, like Sin, becomes very powerful.

In[8]:= **Table[**
             Line[{{i,0}, {i, Sin[Pi i/30]}}],
             {i, 60}];

The length of each line is governed by the Sin function.

In[9]:= **Show[Graphics[%]]**

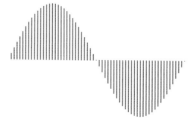

▶ *Defining a Graphics Function*

The previous chapter demonstrated how a new function could be introduced to *Mathematica*. Now these techniques can be applied to graphics to use *Mathematica* programming facilities to build a function. In this way a new primitive can be constructed.

Here the new primitive, poly, takes one argument which specifies the number of sides the figure should have. Floating-point numbers are used to make sure that the results are floating point.

In[10]:= **poly[n_] :=**
             Polygon[Table[{Cos[i 2.Pi/n],Sin[i 2.Pi/n]}, {i,n}]]

poly[*num*] returns a graphics primitive that can be plotted by *Mathematica*.

In[11]:= **poly[3]**

Out[11]= Polygon[{{-0.5, 0.866025}, {-0.5, -0.866025},
             {1., -2.44921 10^{-16}}}]

This new primitive will plot in the expected way. Here AspectRatio is set to Automatic to get the same scale in *x* and *y*.

```
In[12]:= Show[Graphics[poly[7]],
              AspectRatio -> Automatic]
```

This more complex version of poly sets the position of the center.

```
In[13]:= poly[{x_, y_}, n_] :=
             Polygon[
                 Table[{Cos[i 2.Pi/n] + x, Sin[i 2.Pi/n] + y},
                       {i,n}]]
```

In this picture the list of triangles forms a pattern. To make the triangles touch it was necessary to do some computations. Of course *Mathematica* is very well suited to such computations.

```
In[14]:= Show[
             Graphics[
                 Table[poly[{3/2 x, Sqrt[3] y}, 3],
                       {x, 10}, {y,10}],
             AspectRatio -> Automatic]]
```

Another example of a collection of primitives can be made by grouping a Circle, a Line, and a Point primitive. The line goes from the center of the circle to a point on the circumference. The arguments are the center of the circle, the orientation of the line, and the radius. The PointSize style directive makes the point larger. Style directives are described in the next section.

A collection of primitives.

```
In[15]:= markedCircle[{x_, y_}, t_, r_] :=
             {Circle[{x,y}, r],
              Line[{{x,y},r {Sin[t],Cos[t]}+{x,y}}],
              PointSize[0.02],Point[r {Sin[t],Cos[t]}+{x,y}]}
```

The primitive can be plotted. Setting AspectRatio to Automatic gives the same scale in *x* and *y*.

In[16]:= **Show[**
  Graphics[markedCircle[{1,1}, 0, 1]],
  AspectRatio -> Automatic]

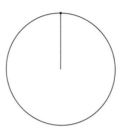

The markedCircle is placed inside a circle with a radius three times larger. This proportion is relevant to this example.

In[17]:= **Show[**
  Graphics[
    {markedCircle[{0,2}, 0, 1], Circle[{0,0},3]}],
  AspectRatio -> Automatic]

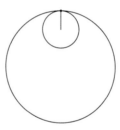

When the inner circle rolls by t radians its center moves -t/2 around the bigger circle (since the radii are 1 and 3 units respectively).

In[18]:= **markedCircle[2{Sin[-t/2],Cos[-t/2]}, t, 1];**

Cases picks out those parts of an expression that match a pattern. Here the Point primitive is extracted. This symbolic result could be plotted with ParametricPlot.

In[19]:= **pt = Cases[%, Point[_]]**

Out[19]= {Point[{-2 Sin[$\frac{t}{2}$] + Sin[t], 2 Cos[$\frac{t}{2}$] + Cos[t]}]}

These are some of the points traced out as the circle rolls around.

In[20]:= **newpts = Table[pt, {t,0,4Pi,0.1}];**

Everything is plotted together. The little circle is rotated by 2 radians[3].

```
In[21]:= Show[
            Graphics[
              {markedCircle[2{Sin[-1],Cos[-1]}, 2, 1],
                Circle[{0,0},3], newpts}],
            AspectRatio -> Automatic]
```

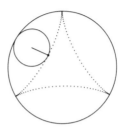

A final stage will generate an animation.

```
In[22]:= Needs["Graphics`Animation`"]
```

This will be used to hold a set of points.

```
In[23]:= total = {};
```

Since there is less space to show an animation in this book the number of frames is reduced and only half of the animation is shown.

```
In[24]:= Animate[
            AppendTo[total, pt];
            Show[
              Graphics[
                {markedCircle[2{Sin[-t/2],Cos[-t/2]}, t, 1],
                  Circle[{0,0},3], PointSize[0.06], total}],
            AspectRatio -> Automatic],
            {t,0,2Pi,Pi/3}]
```

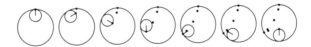

---

[3]The curve formed by the points is known as a deltoid.

In this example a function was defined that could be used for plotting as a new graphics primitive by passing it numeric arguments. A different use for the same function was to pass it symbolic arguments. In this case the primitive returned a symbolic form. It is very useful to be able to combine symbolic and numeric computations from the same function.

▶ *Using Replacement Rules*

Chapter 7, page 107, demonstrated how replacement rules provide a powerful mechanism to go inside an expression and alter specific parts. This chapter has started to describe the specifics of the structure of graphics expressions[4]. Understanding this structure allows replacement rules to be used to alter graphics objects, a technique that has many applications. One common example involves closing a set of points. If a set of points, a path, is to be filled then a `Polygon` primitive can be used, automatically closing the path when it is rendered. If a `Line` primitive is to be used to draw a line through the points it will not be closed automatically. In this case a replacement rule can be used to close the path.

These are a collection of points.

```
In[25]:= pts =
            Table[(3 + Random[ ]){Sin[t], Cos[t]},
                  {t,0,2Pi-Pi/3,Pi/3}]
Out[25]= {{0, 3.05607}, {3.14393, 1.81515},
         {2.90975, -1.67995}, {0, -3.87138}, {-3.34168, -1.92932},
         {-3.10434, 1.79229}}
```

A line can be drawn through them with a `Line` primitive.

```
In[26]:= Show[Graphics[Line[pts]]]
```

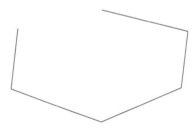

The path that the points form can be closed and filled by using a `Polygon` primitive.

```
In[27]:= Show[Graphics[Polygon[pts]]]
```

---

[4]These are described in detail in Chapter 20 page 538.

A replacement rule that closes the points is applied. This uses the pattern objects a_ and b__ to pick out the first and subsequent points.

In[28]:= **pts /. {a_, b__} :> {a,b,a}**

Out[28]= {{0, 3.05607}, {3.14393, 1.81515},

{2.90975, -1.67995}, {0, -3.87138}, {-3.34168, -1.92932},

{-3.10434, 1.79229}, {0, 3.05607}}

Now the line closes in on itself.

In[29]:= **Show[Graphics[Line[%]]]**

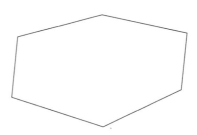

A replacement rule can be applied to the graphics object after it has been built. An example here is adapted from *The Penguin Dictionary of Curious and Interesting Geometry*, David Wells. Starting with a convex polygon with an even number of vertices a new polygon can be derived by joining the midpoints of each side. The process can be iterated, for example with NestList, to form a sequence of polygons.

NestList is well suited to generate the sequence of points.

In[30]:= **derived = NestList[(#+RotateLeft[#])/2&, pts, 6] ;**

Lines are formed from each set of points.

In[31]:= **lines = Map[Line, derived] ;**

The result looks strange since the lines are not closed.

In[32]:= **Show[Graphics[lines]]**

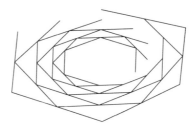

The replacement rule is applied to change Line primitives in the graphics object. The result is then displayed.

`In[33]:= Show[% /. Line[{a_, b__}] :> Line[{a,b,a}]]`

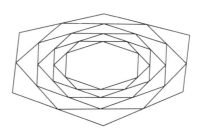

▶ *Understanding Mathematica Programming*

It is very useful to apply *Mathematica* programming to graphics. This can lead to the generation of many interesting pictures. A notable reverse is to use *Mathematica* graphics to understand *Mathematica* programming. Two examples of this will be presented; the first will look at the function Transpose and the second will look at the function Outer.

Transpose switches levels in a list.

`In[34]:= Transpose[{{p1, p2}, {q1,q2}}]`

`Out[34]= {{p1, q1}, {p2, q2}}`

This can be explored graphically by making some points.

`In[35]:= pts = {Table[{-1,i}, {i,5}] , Table[{1,i}, {i,5}]};`

This makes each element of the pts list into a line.

`In[36]:= Show[Graphics[Map[Line, pts]]]`

Now the elements of pts are transposed before being made into lines.

`In[37]:= Show[Graphics[Map[Line, Transpose[pts]]]]`

Outer forms the generalized outer product, in this case, of two lists.

```
In[38]:= Outer[List, {a,b}, {c,d}]
Out[38]= {{{a, c}, {a, d}}, {{b, c}, {b, d}}}

In[39]:= (p1 = Table[{-1,i}, {i,5}];
          p2 = Table[{1,i}, {i,5}])
Out[39]= {{1, 1}, {1, 2}, {1, 3}, {1, 4}, {1, 5}}
```

Each point in p1 is joined to each point in p2. The last argument of the Outer prevents it from going down into the sub-lists.

```
In[40]:= Show[Graphics[Outer[Line[{##}]&, p1, p2, 1]]]
```

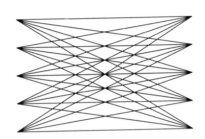

8.2 Style Directives

It is possible to build up and display complex collections of primitives. To do this effectively it may be necessary to alter the appearance of these primitives, to allow certain lines to be thicker and others to be dashed, and so on. This is done with the graphics style directives. These set the style in which primitives are rendered. In Part I they were used as settings for the PlotStyle option of functions like Plot and here they are applied to primitives.

Dashing[{d1, d2, ... }]	set dashing of line
AbsoluteDashing[{d1, d2, ... }]	set dashing of line (absolute units)
Thickness[t]	set thickness of line
AbsoluteThickness[t]	set thickness of line (absolute units)
PointSize[s]	set size of point
AbsolutePointSize[s]	set size of point (absolute units)
GrayLevel[g]	set color of object to gray
RGBColor[r, g, b]	set color of object to red, green, and blue
Hue[h]	set color of object to hue
Hue[h, s, b]	set color of object to hue, saturation, and brightness
CMYKColor[c, m, y, k]	set color of object to cyan, magenta, yellow, and black

Graphics style directives.

To use a style directive it is inserted in the graphics expression together with the primitives.

This line gets a different style due to the Dashing style directive that precedes it.

```
In[41]:= {Dashing[{0.02}],
            Line[{{0,0}, {2,0}, {2,1}, {0,1}, {0,0}}]}
Out[41]= {Dashing[{0.02}],
          Line[{{0, 0}, {2, 0}, {2, 1}, {0, 1}, {0, 0}}]}
```

The picture is displayed in the usual fashion.

```
In[42]:= Show[Graphics[%]]
```

There are directives to change the different style elements like thickness and color.

```
In[43]:= Show[
            Graphics[
              {GrayLevel[.5],
               Thickness[0.04],
               Line[{{0,0}, {1,1}, {2,0}, {0,0}}]}]]
```

Here the Table command builds a list; each element contains a PointSize directive, a Line, and a Point primitive.

```
In[44]:= Show[
           Graphics[
             Table[
               {PointSize[0.02 Abs[Cos[2 Pi i/50]]],
                Line[{{0,0},
                      {Cos[Pi i/50],Sin[Pi i/50]}}],
                Point[{Cos[Pi i/50], Sin[Pi i/50]}]},
               {i, 100}]]]
```

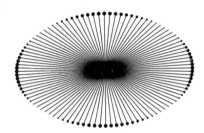

▶ Units for Dashing, Thickness, and PointSize

The style directives Dashing, Thickness, and PointSize all take size arguments. These are given as proportions of the size of the drawing area. Since they are defined in a relative system the lines get thinner when drawn in a smaller picture. The style directives AbsoluteDashing, AbsoluteThickness, and AbsolutePointSize all take size arguments specified in points. There are several definitions of a point; *Mathematica* uses that specified by PostScript in which there are 72 points to the inch[5].

The units of the arguments to Dashing and Thickness are set to proportions of the whole picture. A line of Thickness[1] drawn down the middle of the drawing area will fill it.

```
In[45]:= Show[
           Graphics[
             {Thickness[.006],
              Dashing[{0.02}],
              Table[
                Line[{{x,0},{x,1},{x+.2,1},{x+.2,0},{x+.4,0}}],
                {x,0,4,.4}]}]]
```

---

[5]More details on this and other features of PostScript are provided in the *PostScript Language Reference Manual*, Second Edition, Addison-Wesley.

Here the same picture is repeated in a `GraphicsArray` making each smaller. The thickness and dashing get correspondingly smaller.

In[46]:= `Show[GraphicsArray[{{%,%},{%,%}}]]`

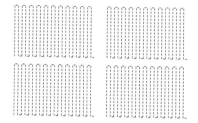

The dashing and thickness here are specified in absolute units, in points.

In[47]:= `Show[`
     `Graphics[`
       `{AbsoluteThickness[1],`
        `AbsoluteDashing[{3}],`
        `Table[`
          `Line[{{x,0},{x,1},{x+.2,1},{x+.2,0},{x+.4,0}}],`
          `{x,0,4,.4}]}]]`

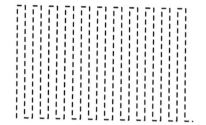

Now the sub-pictures do not look like a scaled down version of the larger picture.

In[48]:= `Show[GraphicsArray[{{%,%},{%,%}}]]`

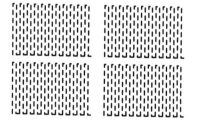

▸ *Scoping of Style Directives*

Style directives can be used to set the style for only some parts of a collection of primitives. Placing the style in the middle of a list of primitives will only affect those primitives that follow it. An alternative is to place the style and the relevant primitives inside a sub-list.

Here Thickness[0.01] appears inside a sub-list with the non-vertical lines. The vertical lines are not in the sub-list and are not affected.

```
In[49]:= Show[
          Graphics[
           {
            {Thickness[0.01],
             Line[Table[{i, Cos[Pi i/15]}, {i,60}]],
             Line[Table[{i, Sin[Pi i/15]}, {i,60}]]},
            Table[Line[{{i,Cos[Pi i/15]}, {i,Sin[Pi i/15]}}],
             {i,60}]}]]
```

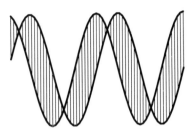

▸ *Changing Style Directives*

After a graphics object has been built it is possible to alter it and add different styles. There are several ways this can be done.

A basic plot.

```
In[50]:= p = Plot[Sin[x]/x, {x,-5,5}]
```

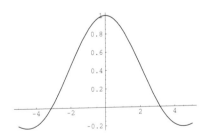

The Prolog option can be used to set the style.

In[51]:= **Show[p, Prolog -> Thickness[0.01]]**

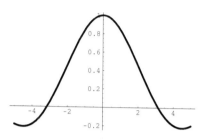

An alternative is to extract the primitives, the first argument, and to combine them with the new style. Notice that the axes disappear since the options were lost.

In[52]:= **Show[Graphics[{Thickness[0.01], First[p]}]]**

Insert can be used to enter the desired style. The argument {1,1} puts the new style in the first part of the first part.

In[53]:= **Show[Insert[p, Thickness[0.01], {1,1}]]**

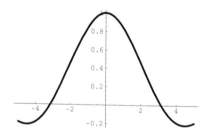

These three different methods have their strengths and weaknesses. The first, to use the Prolog option, is simple but the option may already be used by some other feature of the picture. The second is very simple but loses option settings. It is possible to insert these options but that makes it inconvenient. The last is probably the best if Prolog is already in use and it is important to keep all the options. It depends upon the exact structure of Graphics objects, which is described in Chapter 20 page 538.

▷ *Shading Style Directives*

The type of shading is set by style directives such as GrayLevel. These can be used in the same way as the other directives.

A collection of Rectangle primitives, each of which is shaded by GrayLevel, is shown.

```
In[54]:= rects =
            Table[
                {GrayLevel[Sin[i j]^2],
                 Rectangle[{i-.1, j-.1}, {i+.1, j+.1}]},
                {i,-2,2,.2}, {j,-2,2,.2}];
```

This displays the result.

```
In[55]:= Show[Graphics[rects]]
```

The same image can be constructed with Raster.

```
In[56]:= bitmap =
            Raster[
                Table[Sin[i j]^2,
                    {i,-2,2,.2}, {j,-2,2,.2}]];
```

The appearance of the Raster primitive is the same.

```
In[57]:= Show[Graphics[bitmap]]
```

The Raster primitive stores its data in a more economical manner.

```
In[58]:= {ByteCount[rects], ByteCount[bitmap]}
Out[58]= {88688, 9328}
```

The use of color style directives is explored in detail in Chapter 11 page 200. The rest of this chapter will look at some interesting examples of using graphics primitives. It will not give a detailed reference for each, which is done in Part IV.

8.3 Rectangle

`Rectangle[{`x_{min}`,`y_{min}`}, {`x_{max}`,`y_{max}`}]`   rectangle from {x_{min}, y_{min}} to {x_{max}, y_{max}} filled with the current drawing color

`Rectangle[{`x_{min}`,`y_{min}`}, {`x_{max}`,`y_{max}`},` *gobj*`]`

   rectangle from {x_{min}, y_{min}} to {x_{max}, y_{max}} filled with the graphics object *gobj*

Forms of the `Rectangle` primitive.

The two-argument form of `Rectangle` produces a result similar to that from a suitable `Polygon` primitive.

```
In[59]:= Show[
            Graphics[
                {Rectangle[{0,0}, {1,1}],
                 Polygon[{{2,2}, {2,3}, {3,3}, {3,2}}]}]]
```

The optional third argument takes an arbitrary graphics object to fill the rectangle. This example prepares a list of graphics objects, using `DisplayFunction` to suppress output.

```
In[60]:= plist =
            Table[Plot[Sin[x n], {x,0,2Pi},
                       DisplayFunction -> Identity],
                  {n,3}]
Out[60]= {-Graphics-, -Graphics-, -Graphics-}
```

The graphics objects are each drawn into a rectangle.

```
In[61]:= Show[
            Graphics[
                {Rectangle[{0,0}, {1,1}, Part[plist, 1]],
                 Rectangle[{1,1}, {2,2}, Part[plist, 2]],
                 Rectangle[{2,2}, {3,3}, Part[plist, 3]]}]]
```

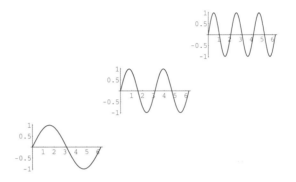

The scaling for a graphics object drawn in a rectangle can be demonstrated by changing the background drawing color.

```
In[62]:= p2 =
            Show[First[plist],
                 Background -> GrayLevel[0]]

Out[62]= -Graphics-
```

The same picture, p2, is drawn into two rectangles of different sizes. In each rectangle the picture scales to fill the available space preserving its AspectRatio.

```
In[63]:= Show[
            Graphics[
                {Rectangle[{0,0}, {1,1}, p2],
                 Rectangle[{1,1}, {2,4}, p2]}]]
```

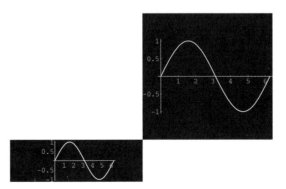

The way that an image expands to fill a Rectangle primitive is identical to the way that it would expand to fill a sheet of paper as described in Chapter 10 page 172. If a picture is completely to fill a rectangle its AspectRatio must match that of the shape of the Rectangle.

▶ *Inserting a Sub-Plot*

One use of filling a `Rectangle` primitive with a graphics object is to make an array of pictures such as is done by `GraphicsArray`. Another is to nest one picture inside another. To illustrate this an example described in the last chapter will be taken. This is the problem of displaying a least-squares fit to some data.

Here is a set of data.

```
In[64]:= data =
            Table[{i, Cos[i] + Random[ ]/2}, {i,0,4,.05}];
```

ListPlot makes a plot of the data.

```
In[65]:= dataplot = ListPlot[data]
```

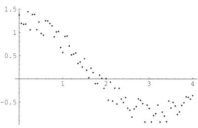

Fit fits a function to the data.

```
In[66]:= fun = Fit[data, {1,x,x^2},x]
```

$$Out[66]= 1.68941 - 1.24844\ x + 0.165104\ x^2$$

A plot of the function to the data.

```
In[67]:= funplot = Plot[fun, {x,0,4}]
```

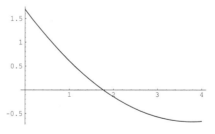

The combined plot.

```
In[68]:= Show[funplot, dataplot]
```

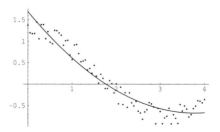

Fit works by minimizing the sum of the squares of the differences from the data point $\{x_i, y_i\}$ to the function $\{x_i, f[x_i]\}$. These differences are called residuals. One important way to examine the goodness of fit is to make a plot of these residuals. Such a plot can be made and added as a sub-picture. To do this the residuals must be calculated from the data and the function. It is natural to use Map with a suitable function.

<table>
<tr>
<td>The first datum will be used to test the function.</td>
<td>

```
In[69]:= test = First[data]
Out[69]= {0, 1.37145}
```

</td>
</tr>
<tr>
<td>A list is formed of the x value and the difference of the y value and the function. First and Last respectively extract the x and y values.</td>
<td>

```
In[70]:= {First[test], Last[test] - (fun /. x -> First[test])}
Out[70]= {0, -0.317957}
```

</td>
</tr>
<tr>
<td>Now a pure function can be defined that will compute the residuals.</td>
<td>

```
In[71]:= difference =
            {First[#], Last[#] - (fun /. x -> First[#])}&
Out[71]= {First[#1], Last[#1] - (fun /. x -> First[#1])} &
```

</td>
</tr>
<tr>
<td>Now the entire residual list is generated.</td>
<td>

```
In[72]:= residuals = Map[ difference, data];
```

</td>
</tr>
<tr>
<td>The sub-plot is put together. Some of the option settings are changed to help distinguish it from the main plot.</td>
<td>

```
In[73]:= residualplot =
            ListPlot[residuals,
                PlotStyle -> AbsolutePointSize[1],
                Frame -> True,
                FrameTicks -> {Automatic, None},
                PlotLabel -> "Residuals"]
```

</td>
</tr>
</table>

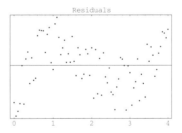

The sub-plot is inserted in a rectangle. Its frame is not exactly at the coordinates in the rectangle because of space left for the label.

```
In[74]:= Show[funplot, dataplot,
                Epilog -> Rectangle[{2,0.4},{4,1.6}, residualplot]]
```

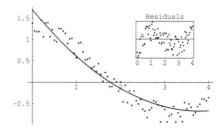

The plot of the residuals gives important information about the goodness of fit. In this example they are not very evenly distributed and this suggests that there are problems with the fit. The steps that were taken to form this plot could be combined into a program. This could be an extension of the `datafitPlot` function described in Chapter 7 page 104.

8.4 Text

Mathematica graphics provide a number of options for introducing labels. These include `AxesLabel`, `FrameLabel`, and `PlotLabel` and were discussed in Chapter 3 page 41. These options work by putting down labels at fixed positions. More flexibility is provided by the `Text` primitive, which can be used to place labels at any position in a picture.

`Text[expr, {x, y}]`	printed form of *expr* centered at {*x*, *y*}
`Text[expr, {x, y},{x_{off}, y_{off}}]`	printed form of *expr* with offset {x_{off}, y_{off}}
`Text[expr, {x, y},{x_{off}, y_{off}},{x_{vec}, y_{vec}}]`	
	printed form of *expr* rotated along vector {x_{vec}, y_{vec}}
`Text[FontForm[expr, {font, size}], {x, y}]`	
	printed form of *expr* in font {*font*, *size*}

Uses of the `Text` primitive.

The placement of text presents special problems since it will extend around the actual point at which it is placed. The default behavior is to place the center of the text at the rendering point. This can be changed by specifying a third argument so that, for example, the upper-right of the text bounding box appears at the rendering point. This is a very useful feature, if the actual textual content is changed the primitive still lines up in this specified way. The alignment of text is described in more detail in Chapter 20 page 541.

If the first argument of a Text primitive is not a string it is "stringified" by default into OutputForm. A different format can be achieved by converting into a string expression or by using the FormatType option[6].

```
In[75]:= Show[
            Graphics[
                {Text[Sin[x]^2, {0,1}],
                 Text[ToString[Sin[x]^2,
                        FormatType -> InputForm], {1,1}],
             Line[{{-1,0},{2,0},{2,2},{-1,2},{-1,0}}]}]]
```

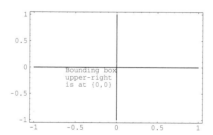

The offset argument aligns the bounding box of the text over the drawing position. If it is omitted the center of the text is placed at this point. The value {1,1} will position the upper-right of the bounding box at the drawing point.

```
In[76]:= Show[
            Graphics[
                {Line[{{0,-1},{0,1}}],
                 Line[{{-1,0},{1,0}}],
                 Text["Bounding box\nupper-right\nis at {0,0}",
                        {0,0},{1,1}]}],
             Frame -> True]
```

---

[6]The FormatType option of Text primitives was not available in Version 2.2 *Mathematica*.

The font in which *all* text is rendered can be changed with the `DefaultFont` option. Here the text is included with the `Epilog` option.

```
In[77]:= Plot[Exp[-x/3] Sin[x], {x,0,4Pi},
            Epilog -> Text["Damping Factor 3",{7.5,.2}],
            DefaultFont -> {"Helvetica", 6}]
```

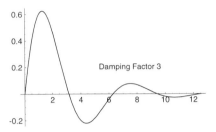

The font for individual text can be set by `FontForm`.

```
In[78]:= Show[%,
            Epilog ->
                Text[FontForm["Damping Factor 3",
                              {"Times-Roman", 9}],
                {7.5,.2}]]
```

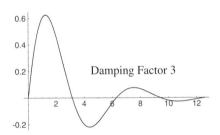

One practical use of the text primitive is to label a collection of points. This may be useful if the points are some data being processed by some algorithm. Making a little plot of the points can be helpful as a debugging tool, when the algorithm is being developed.

A collection of points.

```
In[79]:= pts = Table[{Random[ ], Random[ ]}, {10}] ;
```

This just plots out the points. `PlotRange` is set to make sure the points are not clipped. This is described in Chapter 10.

```
In[80]:= Show[
            Graphics[{PointSize[0.05], Map[Point, pts]}],
            PlotRange -> All]
```

Now the points are plotted in gray and with labels.

```
In[81]:= Show[
            Graphics[
              {{PointSize[0.05], GrayLevel[0.75],
                Map[Point, pts]},
               Table[Text[i, Part[pts, i]], {i,Length[pts]}]}],
            PlotRange -> All]
```

▶ *Options of the Text Primitive*

The Text primitive has three options to control the type of formatting, the font that is used, and a background box to prevent the text from colliding with other objects. The Text primitive in Version 2.2 (or earlier) *Mathematica* did not have any options and these examples will not work in these older versions.

Background	the color of a background box
DefaultFont	the font for the text
FormatType	the type of formatting for the text

Options of the Text primitive.

These are the options of the Text primitive.

```
In[82]:= Options[Text]
Out[82]= {Background -> None, DefaultFont -> Automatic,
          FormatType -> OutputForm}
```

Here the DefaultFont option sets the font and the Background option draws a box in the current background color around the text.

```
In[83]:= Show[
            Graphics[
                {Line[{{-1,0},{1,0}}],Line[{{0,-1},{0,1}}],
                Text["This is a label", {0,0},
                    DefaultFont -> {"Helvetica", 8},
                    Background -> Automatic]}]]
```

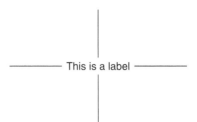

FormatType is the most important of the Text primitive options. It allows the use of typeset text in a plot. This example demonstrates labeling the solution of a differential equation.

This is the equation to be solved.

```
In[84]:= eqn = y''[x] + 0.3 y'[x] + y[x] == 0
Out[84]= y[x] + 0.3 y'[x] + y''[x] == 0
```

NDSolve will solve the equation.

```
In[85]:= sol =
            NDSolve[{eqn, y'[0] == 2,y[0] == 0},
                y[x], {x,0,20}]
Out[85]= {{y[x] -> InterpolatingFunction[{0., 20.}, <>][x]}}
```

Plot will plot the solution. The label here uses OutputForm, the default FormatType.

```
In[86]:= Plot[Evaluate[y[x] /. sol], {x,0,20},
            Epilog -> Text[eqn, {10, 1.25}]]
```

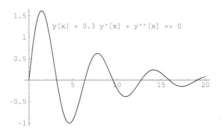

Now the label uses `TraditionalForm` to typeset the text into traditional mathematics notation.

```
In[87]:= Show[%,
           Epilog -> Text[eqn, {10, 1.25},
               FormatType -> TraditionalForm]]
```

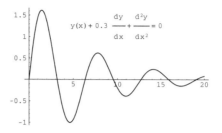

8.5 Summary

This chapter has reviewed the types of *Mathematica* expressions that can represent objects in a two-dimensional world. There are primitives that cause actual objects to be drawn and there are style directives that alter the appearance of the primitives. From these, graphics objects can be constructed with the many tools that *Mathematica* provides to generate expressions. For example, several primitives can be grouped to form a new graphics primitive. This primitive can be given numeric arguments and plotted. It can also be given symbolic arguments and return some useful result. This combination of interactive programming with graphics allows a wide range of phenomena to be exhibited and explored.

Chapter 9
Three-Dimensional Graphical Primitives

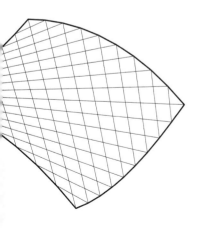

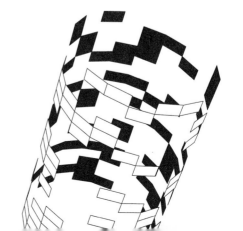

This chapter continues to look at the building blocks available to construct graphical images. Here the focus is on three-dimensional graphics. It will not review every detail of these primitives, which is done in Chapter 21. The purpose of this chapter is to show how manipulation of these components leads to a powerful synthesis of graphics and programming.

9.1 Primitives

There are several primitives that can be used in three-dimensional graphics. Three-dimensional plotting commands such as `ParametricPlot3D` return expressions built from these primitives. `Plot3D` returns a special result, a `SurfaceGraphics` object, the structure of which is described in Chapter 22 page 620.

Point[*pt*]	a point
Line[{*pt1*, *pt2*, *pt3*, ... }]	a line through a set of points
Polygon[{*pt1*, *pt2*, *pt3*, ... }]	a polygon defined by its vertices
Cuboid[*pt*]	a cuboid
Text[*expr*, *pt*]	a text primitive

Graphics3D primitives.

Collections of primitives can be built in ways equivalent to two-dimensional graphics.

```
In[1]:= Table[
            Line[{{0,0,0},
                    {Cos[t], Sin[t], 0},
                  {Cos[t], Sin[t], Sin[t]}}],
                  {t,0,3,.25}];
```

The group of primitives is turned into a Graphics3D object and displayed with a call to Show.

```
In[2]:= Show[Graphics3D[%]]
```

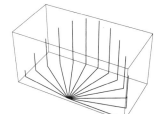

In this example a list of Polygon primitives representing a cone is constructed.

```
In[3]:= cone =
            Table[
              Polygon[
                {{Sin[t], Cos[t], 0},
                 {Sin[t+.25], Cos[t+.25],0},
                 {0,0,2}}],
              {t,.25,2Pi,.25}];
```

The cone is displayed. The polygons that form this cone are shaded by a simulated lighting model. Lighting is discussed in detail in Chapter 11 page 213.

In[4]:= **Show[Graphics3D[cone]]**

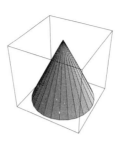

Now the cone is drawn with another polygon. The primitives intersect and when they are drawn they are broken up so that the picture appears properly.

In[5]:= **Show[**
            Graphics3D[
              {cone, Polygon[{{-1.2,-1.2,0}, {1.2,-1,1},
                  {1.2,1.2,1},{-1.2,1.2,0}}]}]]

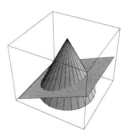

The Cuboid primitive represents a three-dimensional cuboid oriented parallel to the axes. Here a collection of Cuboid primitives is made. Flatten is used to remove the empty lists.

In[6]:= **octa =**
            Flatten[
              Table[
                If[Abs[x]+ Abs[y]+ Abs[z] > 8 &&
                    Abs[x]+ Abs[y]+ Abs[z] < 10,
                  Cuboid[{x,y,z}],{}],
                  {x,-10,10},{y,-10,10},{z,-10,10}]] ;

The Cuboid can be used as a three-dimensional pixel. Here they are used to display an octahedron. The ViewPoint option is altered to get a more interesting view.

```
In[7]:= Show[
           Graphics3D[octa],
           ViewPoint -> {0.6, -2, 0.6}];
```

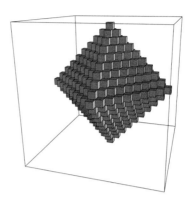

▶ *Replacement Rules*

Mathematica replacement rules were introduced in Chapter 7 page 107 and used on two-dimensional graphics in Chapter 8 page 122. They provide a powerful tool for *Mathematica* programming since they can descend inside an object and change particular parts. This can be very useful when applied to three-dimensional primitives. In this example several different styles for plotting a three-dimensional shape will be demonstrated. The shape is a torus loaded from the package Graphics`Shapes`. *Mathematica* packages were discussed in Chapter 4 page 63.

The package Graphics`Shapes` also contains definitions for a variety of different shapes, including a torus.

```
In[8]:= Needs["Graphics`Shapes`"]
```

The usage message describes the function.

```
In[9]:= ?Torus
```

Torus[(r1:1, r2:0.5, (n:20r1, m:20r2))] is a list of n*m
    polygons approximating a torus centered around the z-axis
    with radii r1 and r2.

The torus is turned into a Graphics3D object and plotted.

```
In[10]:= torus = Show[Graphics3D[Torus[ ]]]
```

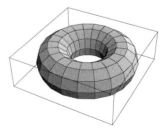

Now each Polygon is split into two Polygons. This introduces a different style that might be useful for identification.

```
In[11]:= Show[torus /. Polygon[{a_,b_,c_,d_}] :>
                    {Polygon[{a,b,c}],Polygon[{a,c,d}]}]
```

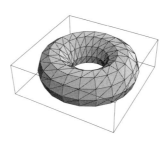

Instead of plotting surfaces it is easy to draw the figure as a wire frame. It is hard to see this as a three-dimensional object. Spinning the wire frame in an animation would strengthen its three-dimensional appearance.

```
In[12]:= Show[torus /. Polygon[p_] :> Line[p]]
```

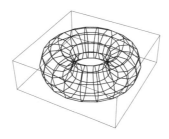

▶ *Introducing a Graphics Function*

In the last two chapters many examples of defining new functions have been given. These can provide a wide variety of graphics functionality. They can produce collections of primitives to form some shape, such as the torus above, or they could represent some collection of points. The example here shows the use of two functions that generate points on parabolae. These points will then be used to represent a hyperbolic paraboloid.

This is a definition for a parabola in a plane with specified y coordinate. The start and end points are defined and so is the height.

```
In[13]:= yParabola[{x_, y_}, h_] :=
            Table[{ xi, y, h-h xi^2/x^2},{ xi,-x,x,2x/9}]
```

A definition for a parabola in a plane with specified x coordinate is given.

```
In[14]:= xParabola[{x_, y_}, h_] :=
            Table[{ x, yi, h-h yi^2/y^2},{ yi,-y,y,2y/9}]
```

Here a collection of parabolae are built.

```
In[15]:= (x1 = xParabola[{2,2},-0.5];
          x2 = xParabola[{-2,-2},-0.5];
          y1 = yParabola[{2,2},0.5];
          y2 = yParabola[{-2,-2},0.5]);
```

The points are formed into four line primitives.

```
In[16]:= frame = Map[Line, {x1, y1, x2, y2}];
```

The curves generated in the previous computation can be plotted.

In[17]:= **Show[Graphics3D[frame]]**

The individual points on the curves can be displayed by converting the components of the Line primitives to Point primitives.

In[18]:= **Show[% /. Line[pts_] :> Map[Point, pts]]**

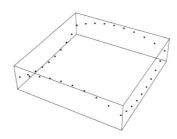

The previous picture shows four sets of parabolae. If corresponding points on adjacent curves are joined then a surface known as a hyperbolic paraboloid is formed. One way to join corresponding points like this is to use Transpose.

Transpose joins corresponding points. Line primitives are then formed from the result.

In[19]:= **lines =**
            Map[Line, Transpose[{x1, y1}]];

This plots out the frame and the lines across one corner.

In[20]:= **Show[**
            Graphics3D[{frame, lines}]]

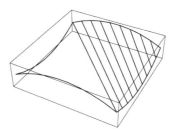

Now the process is repeated for all the sides. This could be made compact but this is a direct extension of the previous method.

```
In[21]:= lines =
            Map[Map[Line, Transpose[#]]&,
                {{x1, y1},{x1, y2},{x2,y1},{x2,y2}}];
```

Now the lines along the hyperbolic paraboloid are shown along with the parabolae from which they were constructed.

```
In[22]:= Show[
            Graphics3D[{frame, Thickness[0.001], lines}]]
```

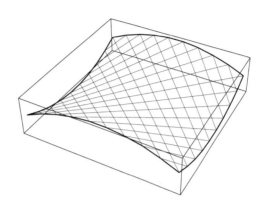

9.2 Style Directives

All the two-dimensional style directives of Graphics work for Graphics3D primitives. In addition, there are some extra types of style directives special to three-dimensional graphics.

Style directives alter the appearance of three-dimensional primitives.

```
In[23]:= Show[
            Graphics3D[
                {Thickness[0.05],
                GrayLevel[0.5],
                Line[{{0,0,0}, {1,1,1}}]}]]
```

`Thickness[`*t*`]`	set thickness of line
`AbsoluteThickness[`*t*`]`	set thickness of line (absolute units)
`Dashing[{`*d1*`, `*d2*`, ... }]`	set dashing of line
`AbsoluteDashing[{`*d1*`, `*d2*`, ... }]`	set dashing of line (absolute units)
`PointSize[`*s*`]`	size of point
`AbsolutePointSize[`*s*`]`	size of point (absolute units)
`GrayLevel[`*g*`]`	set color of object to gray
`RGBColor[`*r*`, `*g*`, `*b*`]`	color of object to red, green, and blue
`Hue[`*h*`]`	color of object to hue
`Hue[`*h*`, `*s*`, `*b*`]`	color of object to hue, saturation, and brightness
`CMYKColor[`*c*`, `*m*`, `*y*`, `*k*`]`	color of object to cyan, magenta, yellow, and black
`FaceForm[`*style*`]`	style for the face of a polygon
`EdgeForm[`*style*`]`	style for the edge of a polygon
`SurfaceColor[`*spec*`]`	complex lighting for a polygon

`Graphics3D` style directives.

There are several style directives in this table that set the color for polygon faces and interact with the simulated lighting. These are discussed in more detail in Chapter 11 page 222.

▸ *EdgeForm*

`EdgeForm` is a style directive that is special to three-dimensional graphics. Any style that is placed inside `EdgeForm` will only apply to polygons and consequently it allows the edges of polygons to be given a special style.

These are two intersecting polygons.

```
In[24]:= polys =
    {Polygon[Table[{0,Sin[2Pi t/6],Cos[2Pi t/6]},{t,6}]],
     Polygon[Table[{Sin[2Pi t/6], 0,Cos[2Pi
t/6]},{t,6}]]};
```

This sets a distinct style for the polygon edges. In this example it helps to identify where the polygons intersect.

```
In[25]:= Show[
            Graphics3D[
               {EdgeForm[Thickness[0.01]], polys}]]
```

▶ *Changing Style Directives*

The style of an existing `Graphics3D` object can be changed with some of the techniques that were introduced for two-dimensional graphics. The `Prolog` option cannot be used for style directives since it specifies two-dimensional primitives. It is possible to use `Insert` to add style directives to a `Graphics3D` object. This depends upon the `Graphics3D` structure, which is described in Chapter 21 page 590.

The edges of the polygons are drawn in the default style.

```
In[26]:= sphere =
            ParametricPlot3D[
               {Sin[t] Sin[p], Sin[t] Cos[p], Cos[t]},
               {t,0,Pi}, {p,0,2Pi}]
```

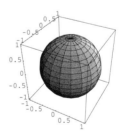

The polygon edges are made thicker. `Insert` at {1,1} places the style in the first part of the first part.

```
In[27]:= Show[
            Insert[sphere, EdgeForm[Thickness[0.01]], {1,1}]]
```

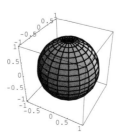

The primitives are pulled out using First, combined with the new style, and redisplayed. The effect of EdgeForm[ ] is to hide the polygon edges.

In[28]:= **Show[Graphics3D[{EdgeForm[ ], First[sphere]}]]**

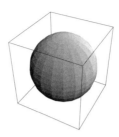

In this last picture the edges of the polygon have been removed. The result has been to make the picture harder to understand as a three-dimensional object. This is because the edges play an important role in the process by which the picture is understood as being three-dimensional.

▸ *FaceForm*

Like EdgeForm, FaceForm is a style directive that is special to three-dimensional graphics. It is used to set the style for polygon faces. Since a three-dimensional polygon has two sides, FaceForm has a one- and a two-argument form. The latter can distinguish between the inside and outside of a collection of polygons.

FaceForm[*style*]	style for both faces of a polygon
FaceForm[*style₁*, *style₂*]	different styles for each face of a polygon

Uses of FaceForm.

A cylinder that will demonstrate FaceForm.

In[29]:= **ParametricPlot3D[{Sin[t], Cos[t], z},**
{t,0,2Pi}, {z,0,3}]

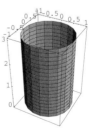

Some of the faces of the cylinder are dropped.

In[30]:= **Select[First[%], (Random[ ] > 0.7)&];**

The chopped-up cylinder.

In[31]:= **Show[Graphics3D[%]]**

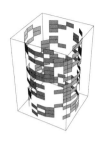

The inner faces are GrayLevel[0] and the outer faces GrayLevel[1]. For this to work it is necessary to switch off the simulated lighting as discussed in Chapter 11 page 213.

In[32]:= **Show[**
  Insert[%,
    FaceForm[GrayLevel[0], GrayLevel[1]],
    {1,1}],
  Lighting -> False]

9.3 Polygon Triangulation

When a two-dimensional object is generalized to a three-dimensional form there are often special issues that arise. This is the case with the Polygon primitive. In two dimensions a Polygon primitive is defined by a path of points and the interior of this path is filled. When the path intersects itself *Mathematica* graphics rendered on a true PostScript device will follow what is called the non-zero winding rule[7]. In three dimensions the situation is more complex. When the polygon is displayed it must be turned into triangular components, a process called triangulation. As this happens certain decisions have to be made because there is usually more than one way that it can be done.

This is a Polygon primitive to be used for demonstration. Its vertices do not all lie in the same plane.

In[33]:= **poly = Polygon[{{-1,-1,0}, {-1,1,1}, {1,1,0},{1,-1,1}}]**

Out[33]= Polygon[{{-1, -1, 0}, {-1, 1, 1}, {1, 1, 0},
  {1, -1, 1}}]

[7]More details on this and other features of PostScript are provided in the *PostScript Language Reference Manual*, Second Edition, Addison-Wesley.

The primitive can be plotted in the normal way.

In[34]:= **Show[Graphics3D[poly]]**

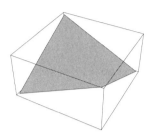

Here the Polygon primitive is split in two. This is one way that poly can be triangulated.

```
In[35]:= Show[
           Graphics3D[poly /.
             Polygon[{a_,b_,c_,d_}] ->
                {Polygon[{a,b,c}], Polygon[{a,c,d}]}]]
```

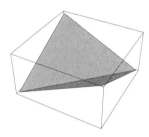

This is another way to triangulate poly.

```
In[36]:= Show[
           Graphics3D[poly /.
             Polygon[{a_,b_,c_,d_}] ->
                {Polygon[{a,b,d}], Polygon[{b,c,d}]}]]
```

▶ *The Triangulation Method of Mathematica*

There is more than one method that *Mathematica* can choose to triangulate polygons. Two different triangulations were just demonstrated, each as valid as the other. Since there are several methods, *Mathematica* chooses one that is simple and easy to understand. It joins the first vertex to successive pairs of vertices around the edge. This can be demonstrated in the following function.

The first point is taken with pairs of points along the point list.

```
In[37]:= triMake[Polygon[a_List] /; Length[a] > 2] :=
            Table[
              Polygon[{First[a], Part[a, i-1], Part[a,i]}],
              {i,3, Length[a]}]
```

The triangulation of a polygon.

```
In[38]:= triMake[Polygon[{a,b,c,d}]]

Out[38]= {Polygon[{a, b, c}], Polygon[{a, c, d}]}
```

triMake is applied to poly.

```
In[39]:= Show[Graphics3D[triMake[poly]]]
```

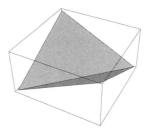

The result of `triMake` does not look quite the same as the rendering of the original polygon. There is an edge drawn across the middle of the polygon and the shading of each triangle is different. It is possible to remove these differences and such a version of `triMake` is demonstrated on page 157. The triangulation of the polygon becomes even more complicated when the outline of the polygon is not convex[8]; this can be demonstrated with another example.

A two-dimensional polygon.

```
In[40]:= poly = Polygon[{{-1,-1}, {1,-1}, {-1,1}, {1,1}}]

Out[40]= Polygon[{{-1, -1}, {1, -1}, {-1, 1}, {1, 1}}]
```

The polygon is defined by a path and this path intersects itself. This is not a simple polygon.

```
In[41]:= Show[Graphics[poly]]
```

---

[8]The concept of a convex set of points is discussed in more detail in Chapter 16 page 399.

A replacement rule is used to form a three-dimensional polygon.

```
In[42]:= poly3d = poly /. {x_, y_} -> {x, y, 0}

Out[42]= Polygon[{{-1, -1, 0}, {1, -1, 0}, {-1, 1, 0},
    {1, 1, 0}}]
```

The three-dimensional polygon is plotted but it looks very different from the two-dimensional form.

```
In[43]:= Show[Graphics3D[poly3d]]
```

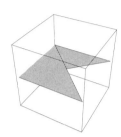

The result looks strange. It can be explained by the following sequence of pictures. This takes a polygon and moves one of the vertices to end with something similar to the example above. It could be demonstrated by an animation, but here the pictures will be plotted in a GraphicsArray.

Three vertices of the polygon are fixed. The other moves across starting and ending in the plane formed by the fixed points.

```
In[44]:= plist =
    Table[
        Polygon[{{-1,-1,0}, {2 Sin[t] -1,1,Cos[t]},
                {-1,1,0}, {1,-1,0}}],
        {t,-Pi/2,Pi/2,Pi/5}] ;
```

Each element is made into a Graphics3D object. The resulting list is partitioned in two.

```
In[45]:= Partition[
    Map[
        Graphics3D[#, PlotRange -> {{-3,1}, {-1,1}, {-1,1}},
            ViewPoint -> {0.3,-2,1.0}]&,
        plist], 3]

Out[45]= {{-Graphics3D-, -Graphics3D-, -Graphics3D-},
    {-Graphics3D-, -Graphics3D-, -Graphics3D-}}
```

These pictures show that one vertex is moving over. The final polygon is one that has been folded over.

```
In[46]:= Show[GraphicsArray[%]]
```

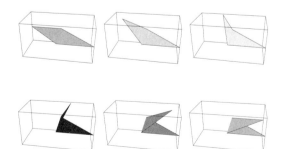

In these examples the polygon triangulation is consistent as it is folded over. This is a desirable property of the triangulation. It would be very strange if the polygon had a different arrangement when it was planar than when it was non-planar. If a polygon suddenly rearranged itself just as a vertex moved into the plane of the others this would be highly unusual. Due to this constraint and due to the ambiguity of triangulation *Mathematica* takes the simple triangulation scheme described earlier.

▶ *Polygon Normal and Edge Specification*

The `Polygon` primitive has features that allow the specification of the normal vector and the style for the edges. These features were not present in Version 2.2 (or earlier) *Mathematica*.

`Polygon[pts, norm]`	use *norm* as the normal to the polygon
`Polygon[pts, Automatic]`	use the default normal
`Polygon[pts, Automatic, {True, False, ... }]`	
	whether edges are to be drawn

Arguments of the `Polygon` primitive.

The specification of the normal will be covered in Chapter 11 page 214 when color and the lighting model are discussed. Here the discussion will demonstrate how control over the edge form can specify the triangulation. In Chapter 17 page 448 this topic is revisited and code presented that allows more complex triangulation.

In this example the first and third edges of the polygon are drawn.

```
In[47]:= Show[
            Graphics3D[
                Polygon[{{-1,-1,0},{-1,1,0},{1,1,0},{1,-1,0}},
                    Automatic, {True, False, True, False}]]]
```

Now a new version of `triMake` that does not draw edges in the middle of the polygon can be made.

```
In[48]:= triMake[Polygon[a_List] /; Length[a] > 2] :=
            Table[
                Polygon[{First[a], Part[a, i-1], Part[a,i]},
                    Automatic, {i==3, True, i==Length[a]}],
                {i,3, Length[a]}]
```

The triangulation of a polygon.

```
In[49]:= triMake[Polygon[{a,b,c,d}]]

Out[49]= {Polygon[{a, b, c}, Automatic, {True, True, False}],
    Polygon[{a, c, d}, Automatic, {False, True, True}]}
```

triMake is applied to the non-planar polygon. Now there is no edge drawn down the center.

```
In[50]:= Show[
            Graphics3D[
              triMake[
                Polygon[{{-1,-1,0}, {-1,1,1},
              {1,1,0},{1,-1,1}}]]]]
```

9.4 Three-Dimensional Realism

In this last section of the chapter the discussion will focus on issues of three-dimensional realism. It will look at what it means to view objects in three dimensions. This will start with an example.

Here three-dimensional Text and Line primitives are drawn.

```
In[51]:= Show[
            Graphics3D[
              {Line[{{0,2,2}, {4,2,2}}],
               Text["Label", {2,2,2},{-1,-1}]}]]
```

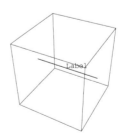

Now a `Polygon` primitive is included.   *In[52]:=* `Show[`
                                                    `Graphics3D[`
                                                      `{Line[{{0,2,2}, {4,2,2}}],`
                                                       `Polygon[{{0,0,0},{3.5,0,0},{3.5,0,4},{0,0,4}}],`
                                                       `Text["Label", {2,2,2},{-1,-1}]}]]`

In the second picture a polygon is drawn that is closer to the viewpoint than the line or the label. It obscures part of the picture. The line is broken but the text label is not. This is because a three-dimensional `Text` primitive does not really put down a three-dimensional object. It is only three-dimensional in that its point consists of three numbers. If it were three-dimensional it would need more parameters (to describe the three-dimensional plane in which it lived and so on).

The fact that it is possible to place something that is not three-dimensional in a `Graphics3D` object may seem strange. In fact it is very sensible. Two-dimensional text can be drawn with a huge range of beautiful fonts and special typeset layout; these features are all available in three-dimensional pictures. If text was to be fully three-dimensional much of this would be sacrificed and the labeling process would be considerably more complex. The compromise has been made to favor practicality over three-dimensional realism.

This type of problem is fundamental to all three-dimensional drawing systems. Some systems strongly favor three-dimensional realism. Taken to extremes, this means that a system may not be capable of drawing a line since it can only draw three-dimensional solid objects. This is perfectly acceptable if the aim is to produce computer-generated animations for rock videos or films. The *Mathematica* three-dimensional renderer is intended to produce diagrams and visualizations of functions and data. As a consequence it favors practicality over realism. Of course, if a different renderer is used then a different balance may be struck. There is a clear distinction in *Mathematica* between the creation of primitives to be rendered and the actual renderer that is used. Chapter 26 discusses the possibility of using different renderers.

Another example of the practicality of *Mathematica* three-dimensional graphics is concerned with lines and with line thickness. The thickness is added to help distinguish different lines. It is not a three-dimensional effect and the thickness is not drawn in perspective. Again, this has sacrificed realism for practicality. It is very useful to have thick lines and dashed lines. In a system that was strongly realistic neither of these would be possible. This is not to say that *Mathematica* is right and other systems are wrong. It merely indicates that *Mathematica* is well suited to what it does.

Mathematica is a programmable system and it is possible to change this behavior. It is possible to construct text from lines and polygons. It is also possible to draw the thickness in perspective. An example is now presented that draws the edges of polygons in perspective. This can be done by representing them with other polygons. The vertices of these are fixed though it would be quite possible to write a *Mathematica* function to do this automatically.

This uses other polygons for edges. To make them black the SurfaceColor directive is used. SurfaceColor is described in Chapter 11 page 222.

```
In[53]:= Show[
    Graphics3D[
      {{SurfaceColor[RGBColor[0,0,0]],
        Polygon[{{1,0,0},{0.9,0.1,0},{0.1,0.1,0},{0,0,0}}],
        Polygon[{{1,1,0},{0.9,0.9,0},{0.9,0.1,0},{1,0,0}}],
        Polygon[{{0,1,0},{0.1,0.9,0},{0.9,0.9,0},{1,1,0}}],
        Polygon[{{0,0,0},{0.1,0.1,0},{0.1,0.9,0},{0,1,0}}]
        },
      Polygon[{{0.1,0.1,0},{0.9,0.1,0},
               {0.9,0.9,0},{0.1,0.9,0}}]}]]
```

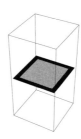

Changing the ViewPoint option demonstrates the perspective for the polygon edges.

```
In[54]:=   Show[ %, ViewPoint ->{0.1, -1, 0.3}]
```

9.5 Summary

This chapter has shown the types of *Mathematica* expressions that represent objects in a three-dimensional world. There are primitives that have an actual appearance and there are style directives that modify the primitives. Knowing the structure of these primitives it is possible to use *Mathematica* programming techniques to write functions to generate new collections of primitives and to modify existing ones. The chapter ended with a discussion of polygon triangulation and three-dimensional realism.

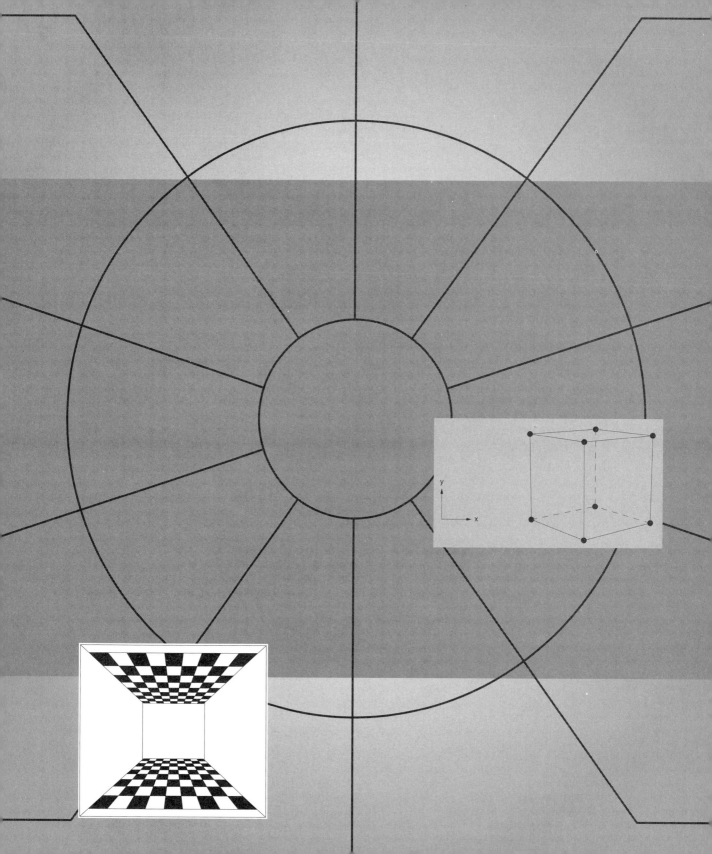

Chapter 10
Coordinate Systems

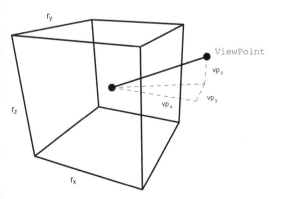

This chapter explains the types of coordinate systems that are available in *Mathematica* graphics, as well as the scaling and other calculations carried out as graphics expressions are rendered into pictures. It will do this by concentrating on Graphics and Graphics3D objects. These are designed for flexibility and are very useful for graphics programming. The other types of graphics objects, such as ContourGraphics or SurfaceGraphics, are not the focus of this chapter. Their behavior, which is very similar to either Graphics or Graphics3D, is discussed in the appropriate chapters of Part IV. These objects can only be displayed in one particular way and must be converted to Graphics or Graphics3D objects to be altered; this is the topic of Chapter 12.

10.1 Two Dimensions

This section concentrates on two-dimensional graphics. It will first describe the types of coordinate system that can be used. It will then define PlotRange and AspectRatio, basic concepts that determine how objects are displayed.

▶ *Coordinates*

There are several types of coordinates that can be used by two-dimensional graphics primitives. In addition to ordinary coordinates there are Scaled and Offset coordinates. Offset was not available in Version 2.2 (or earlier) *Mathematica*. Both Scaled and Offset are useful for constructing elements of a picture such as making special symbols or placing labels.

{x, y}	point given in ordinary coordinates
Scaled[{x, y}]	point given in scaled coordinates
Scaled[{x_s, y_s}, {x, y}]	point in both scaled and ordinary coordinates
Offset[{x_p, y_p}, {x, y}]	point in both absolute and ordinary coordinates

Coordinate specifications in two-dimensional graphics.

Here is a line that goes from {-10, -1} to {1,10}. These points are given in ordinary coordinates and the values are confirmed by the axes.

```
In[1]:= Show[
          Graphics[
            Line[{{-10, -1}, {1,10}}],
            Frame -> True]]
```

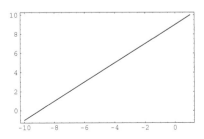

Now a thicker line with `Scaled`
coordinates is added. `Scaled[{0,0.5}]`
is halfway up the left and
`Scaled[{0.5,1}]` is halfway across the
top.

```
In[2]:= Show[
          Graphics[
            {Line[{{-10,-1}, {1,10}}],
             Thickness[0.02],
             Line[{Scaled[{0, 0.5}], Scaled[{0.5,1}]}]}],
          Frame -> True]
```

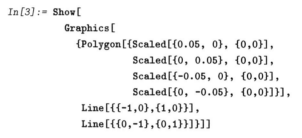

The two-argument version of `Scaled`
moves to a particular point and then
moves a scaled amount. Here the first
point is formed by moving to ordinary
coordinates {0,0} and then by the scaled
amount {0.05,0}.

```
In[3]:= Show[
          Graphics[
            {Polygon[{Scaled[{0.05, 0}, {0,0}],
                      Scaled[{0, 0.05}, {0,0}],
                      Scaled[{-0.05, 0}, {0,0}],
                      Scaled[{0, -0.05}, {0,0}]}],
             Line[{{-1,0},{1,0}}],
             Line[{{0,-1},{0,1}}]}]]
```

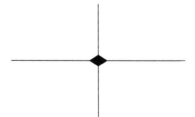

Offset is very similar to the two-argument version of Scaled. Here the first point is formed by moving to ordinary coordinates {0,0} and then by {15,0} points[9].

```
In[4]:= Show[
          Graphics[
            {Polygon[{Offset[{15, 0}, {0,0}],
                      Offset[{0, 15}, {0,0}],
                      Offset[{-15, 0}, {0,0}],
                      Offset[{0, -15}, {0,0}]}],
             Line[{{-1,0},{1,0}}],
             Line[{{0,-1},{0,1}}]}]]
```

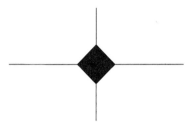

Each of the two-dimensional graphics primitives that were described in Chapter 8 can be built from any of these coordinates.

```
In[5]:= Show[
          Graphics[
            Table[Circle[{Random[ ], Random[ ]},
                          Scaled[{0.02,0.02},{0,0}]], {10}]]]
```

When a graphics object is constructed from primitives these exist in an abstract space that will be called the user space. Ordinary coordinates of these primitives are interpreted in a system that will be called the user coordinate system. When *Mathematica* displays the graphics object it does so by choosing a rectangular region of the user space. This region is transformed to fit on a display device such as a printed page or in a window on the screen.

Scaled coordinates are described in terms of this rectangular region itself. For example, Scaled[{0.5, 0.5}] will always come out in the middle of this region. Offset coordinates are specified in terms of absolute distances relative to some point in user coordinates. Offset[{10,10},{1,1}] is 10 points above and 10 points to the right of the point {1,1} in ordinary coordinates. The details of the mapping of primitives

---

[9] A point is a basic unit of size. *Mathematica* uses the definition of 72 points to the inch that is specified by PostScript.

from the user space onto the output device are controlled by the values of two options, `PlotRange` and `AspectRatio`.

▶ *PlotRange*

The `PlotRange` of a graphics object describes the rectangular region chosen by *Mathematica* when the object is displayed. When this happens the region is mapped onto the output device and only those parts of primitives inside the region will become visible. Since it is a rectangular region oriented with the axes it can be specified by two points $\{x_{min}, y_{min}\}$ and $\{x_{max}, y_{max}\}$. The `PlotRange` specifies this pair and its value is determined from the setting of the graphics option `PlotRange`.

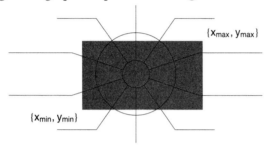

Choosing primitives with the `PlotRange`**.**

The picture above demonstrates the selection of primitives with the `PlotRange`. Only those primitives that fall inside the gray rectangle will be rendered when the graphics object to which they belong is displayed. The actual choice of primitives that would be made is shown in the picture below. Here the dotted line represents the boundary of the `PlotRange`. None of the parts of the primitives that fall outside this rectangular region are visible.

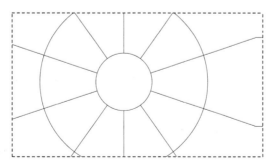

Primitives selected by the `PlotRange`**.**

`PlotRange -> Automatic`	display a representative sample of points
`PlotRange -> All`	display all points
`PlotRange -> {`y_{min}`, `y_{max}`}`	display points with y coordinates between y_{min} and y_{max}
`PlotRange -> {{`x_{min}`, `x_{max}`}, {`y_{min}`, `y_{max}`}}`	
	display points in the region {x_{min}, y_{min}} to {x_{max}, y_{max}}
`PlotRange -> {`x_{spec}`, `y_{spec}`}`	different `PlotRange` specifications in x and y

Settings for the `PlotRange` option in two dimensions.

These lines and text are shown with the default `PlotRange` of `Automatic`. This is calculated by scanning the coordinates and taking a representative sample. The point {30,10}, which is located further from the other primitives, is not included in the `PlotRange` and is not visible.

```
In[6]:= testp =
          Show[
            Graphics[
              {Line[{{0,10}, {0,0}, {10,0}}],
               Table[Text[i, {i, .5}], {i,10}],
               Table[Text[i, {.5, i}], {i,10}],
               PointSize[0.03], Point[{30, 10}]}]]
```

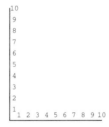

`FullOptions` returns the actual setting of the `PlotRange` option. It was described in Chapter 3 page 35.

```
In[7]:= FullOptions[%, PlotRange]
Out[7]= {{-0.48125, 19.7313}, {-0.25, 10.25}}
```

When the `PlotRange` setting is `All` the coordinates of all the primitives are scanned to find the smallest and the largest. The setting is then chosen to extend slightly beyond both.

```
In[8]:= Show[testp, PlotRange -> All]
```

Now the setting in the x direction has changed.

```
In[9]:= FullOptions[%, PlotRange]
Out[9]= {{-0.75, 30.75}, {-0.25, 10.25}}
```

This changes PlotRange in the y direction and causes the line parallel to the x axis to be outside of the PlotRange and thus not visible.

```
In[10]:= Show[testp, PlotRange -> {1.5,5.5}]
```

The PlotRange in the y direction was changed but not that in the x direction.

```
In[11]:= FullOptions[%, PlotRange]
Out[11]= {{-0.48125, 19.7313}, {1.5, 5.5}}
```

This changes PlotRange in both y and x directions. It shows a close view of the lower-left corner of the original picture.

```
In[12]:= Show[testp, PlotRange -> {{-1,5.5}, {-1, 4.5}}]
```

A combination of different specifications can be given to PlotRange.

```
In[13]:= Show[testp, PlotRange -> {All, {5, 12}}]
```

▷ *AspectRatio*

The PlotRange describes the coordinates of the rectangular region that is used to view primitives. The AspectRatio describes the observed shape of this region. It is concerned with the scaling of user coordinates onto the page. It is set by the value of the option AspectRatio.

AspectRatio -> *fact*   scale x and y so that the height is *fact* times the width

AspectRatio -> Automatic   scale x and y the same

Settings of the option AspectRatio.

This is the default setting for the AspectRatio option of Graphics.

```
In[14]:= Options[Graphics, AspectRatio]

                                 1
Out[14]= {AspectRatio ->  ------------}
                           GoldenRatio
```

This is the numeric value.

```
In[15]:= N[%]
Out[15]= {AspectRatio -> 0.618034}
```

This random line function will help to examine things further.

```
In[16]:= ranline :=
             Line[{{Random[ ], Random[ ]},
                   {Random[ ], Random[ ]}}]
```

Here are some random lines. A frame with no ticks is drawn so that the shape of the image is clearly shown.

```
In[17]:= Show[
             Graphics[
                {ranline, ranline, ranline}],
             Frame -> True,
             FrameTicks -> None]
```

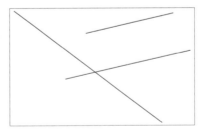

No matter what points are actually plotted the picture has the same rectangular shape. This shape is the AspectRatio.

```
In[18]:= Show[
            Graphics[Table[ranline, {20}]],
                Frame -> True,
                FrameTicks -> None]
```

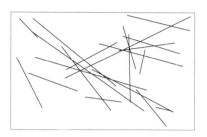

This is the setting of the AspectRatio option that was used. The value was set by the defaults for Graphics.

```
In[19]:= FullOptions[%, AspectRatio]
Out[19]= 0.618034
```

The AspectRatio is the ratio of the picture's height to its width and sets the shape of the final image. It is related to the scaling in the x and y directions as they are transformed from user coordinates onto the page. With the same scale in x and y this ratio would be $(y_{max} - y_{min}) : (x_{max} - x_{min})$. To obtain this particular scale it would be possible to determine the PlotRange setting, perhaps using FullOptions, and calculate the appropriate value for AspectRatio. In fact these calculations are unnecessary since the setting Automatic is provided for exactly this purpose.

This picture is drawn with the golden-ratio AspectRatio. Three circles were drawn but each came out looking compressed.

```
In[20]:= ParametricPlot[
            {{Cos[t], Sin[t]},{2+Cos[t],Sin[t]},
             {4+Cos[t],Sin[t]}}, {t,0,2Pi}]
```

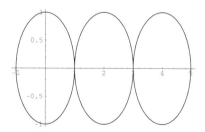

Now the scale in both x and y is the same and the circles look like circles.

`In[21]:= Show[%, AspectRatio -> Automatic]`

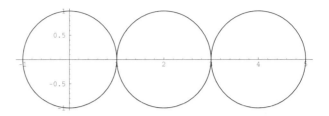

This is the random line picture with `AspectRatio` set to be `Automatic`. Since the points are chosen randomly the result is close to a square.

```
In[22]:= Show[
            Graphics[Table[ranline, {20}]],
            Frame -> True,
            FrameTicks -> None,
            AspectRatio -> Automatic]
```

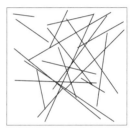

10.2 The Transformation in Two Dimensions

This section will describe the full transformation from primitives, which are arguments in `Graphics` objects, to an actual drawing on the page. The transformation will be divided into two parts. This is appropriate since there are two parts to rendering a *Mathematica* graphical image. In the first a set of *Mathematica* graphics primitives are converted into a stream of PostScript primitives. This stream may be saved in a file or it may be sent directly to a PostScript interpreter. When it is finally interpreted another procedure is enacted that involves rendering the PostScript on an actual display device.

The first process concerns the transformation between the coordinate system of the primitives, the user coordinate system, and the coordinate system of the emitted PostScript, which will be referred to as PostScript coordinates. This transformation is set into effect when the graphic is rendered into PostScript by the command `Display`. The details of `Display` are described in Chapter 26 page 668.

The second process is involved with the transformation from the PostScript coordinate system to the display coordinate system. This takes place when an interpreter is invoked, as happens when the PostScript stream arrives at the *Mathematica* front end or is sent to a PostScript printer.

▶ *User Coordinates to PostScript Coordinates*

The transformation from user to PostScript coordinates depends upon the values of the PlotRange and AspectRatio so that:

$$\{x_{min}, y_{min}\} \rightarrow \{0, 0\}$$
$$\{x_{max}, y_{max}\} \rightarrow \{1, asp\}$$

The transformation is thus:

$$x_{ps} = (x_{user} - x_{min}) / (x_{max} - x_{min})$$
$$y_{ps} = (y_{user} - y_{min}) \, asp / (y_{max} - y_{min})$$

where $\{x_{min}, y_{min}\}$ and $\{x_{min}, y_{min}\}$ are the lower-left and upper-right of the PlotRange respectively, asp is the AspectRatio, and c_{user} and c_{ps} are coordinates in the user and PostScript systems.

This function will calculate PostScript coordinates from user coordinates and particular settings of PlotRange and AspectRatio.

```
In[23]:= transform[{x_, y_}, {{x0_, x1_}, {y0_, y1_}}, asp_] :=
            {(x - x0)/(x1-x0),
             (y - y0) asp /(y1-y0)}
```

Here the transformation is invoked for symbolic values of x and y. Particular values for the PlotRange and AspectRatio are substituted in and the result expanded.

```
In[24]:= transform[{x, y}, {{3.2, 20}, {-5, 30}}, 1.9]//Expand

Out[24]= {-0.190476 + 0.0595238 x, 0.271429 + 0.0542857 y}
```

The transformation here is one that will translate and scale an object in two dimensions. It is a sub-set of a class of transformations known as affine. Chapter 16 page 376 and Chapter 17 page 418 contain detailed descriptions of affine transformations with a number of examples.

▶ *PostScript Coordinates to Display Coordinates*

The transformation from PostScript coordinates to display coodinates is more complex than the previous transformation. This is due to special considerations for scaling text. These will be set aside for the moment and an example analyzed. For this example the PostScript primitives extend from $(0, 0)$ to $(1, asp)$. It is desired to print this picture onto a page which is 8.5 by 11 inches[10]. The coordinate system of the output device is a typical initial PostScript rendering coordinate system with the origin, $(0, 0)$, on the lower-left corner and 72 points to the inch in both x and y. Of course the size of the page and the initial coordinate system are quite arbitrary; these values are chosen for the purposes of illustration.

Now the transformation that maps the image on the paper must be determined. This requires two questions to be answered: where on the page and what size is the image to be? A reasonable solution is to center the image on the page, maintain the AspectRatio, and make the result as big as possible. This is shown in the figure on the following page.

---

[10]Of course metric or any other units could be substituted for inches in this example.

Fitting a picture onto the page.

The transformation can be summarized as:

$$x_{page} = s\, x_{ps} + t_x$$
$$y_{page} = s\, y_{ps}\, asp + t_y$$

where s, t_x, and t_y are given by

$$s = min\left(\, width,\ height/asp\,\right)$$
$$t_x = (width - s)\, /2$$
$$t_y = \left(height - s\right)\, /2$$

Here *width* and *height* are respectively the width and height of the paper and *asp* is the `AspectRatio` of the image to be printed.

▶ *Text Scaling*

The description just given of the scaling calculations to draw a *Mathematica* graphical image left out an important factor: the necessity to scale the image so that complete text strings are drawn on the page. For example, it is desirable to ensure that axes labels are drawn completely and do not protrude off the page and become chopped up.

There are two complications that text introduces into the scale calculation. The first is that when text is rendered into PostScript, the *Mathematica* kernel has no knowledge of how large this text actually is. The second complication is that text is given in an absolute size. The font that is to be used to render text is specified in points and the size of this text will not change if the drawing is done onto a large or a small sheet of paper.

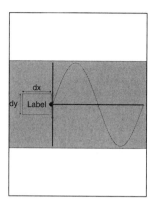

Scaling for text.

The problem is demonstrated in the figure, which shows an 8.5 by 11 inch sheet of paper onto which the figure will be drawn. The coordinates of the primitives to be drawn are known but the size of the text is not. In the figure the text is given sizes dx, dy and these numbers are not known. The only information that is available about the label are the coordinates of the point at the right edge.

This problem with text is solved when the PostScript is rendered. When this takes place the size of the text is known and a calculation is made to adjust for the values dx, dy. This is demonstrated in the picture below.

When a picture is drawn with a large label, shown here somewhat exaggerated, the picture scales so that the label is visible.

```
In[25]:= Plot[Sin[x], {x,0,2Pi},
            AxesLabel ->
              "This is really a very very long label"]
```

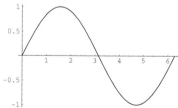

However, when the long label is included in a text primitive the picture does not rescale. Here the label is lost.

```
In[26]:= Plot[Sin[x], {x,0,2Pi},
           Epilog ->
             Text["This is really a very very long label",
               {0,1.3}]]
```

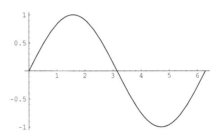

These two examples demonstrate one case where text is included in the PostScript to display scaling and one where it is not. In general, any text that is part of an embellishment option such as Axes, AxesLabel, or PlotLabel is used for scaling. Any text that is part of a Text primitive included in the main body, in Prolog, or in Epilog is not included in the scaling. There is one way that Text included in a Text primitive can be used for scaling and that is to set the PlotRange option to All.

Setting PlotRange to All includes the Text primitive in the scaling calculations and it is all visible in the resulting picture.

```
In[27]:= Show[%, PlotRange -> All]
```

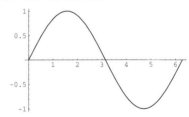

Setting PlotRange to All to include text in the scaling calculations is somewhat strange since this option also selects the size of the region from which primitives will be displayed, a different use. A problem can arise if one wants to scale for text using some specific PlotRange other than All. A partial solution to this problem is presented in the extended labeling package described in Chapter 13 page 267.

Thus *Mathematica* scales pictures to work with text when the PostScript is displayed. The advantage of a scaling like this is that the picture looks right. When a picture is made there is no need to ensure that enough space is left for labels. The disadvantage is that it is not possible to set the mapping of the graphic onto the page from within *Mathematica*. This would make it possible to do things like line up sub-pictures in a GraphicsArray, something that is hard to do at present. It is hoped that a future version of *Mathematica* will add this capability, taking care to maintain the existing functionality.

10.3 Three Dimensions

For three-dimensional graphics the transformation from user coordinates to the page has much in common with that for two dimensions. However, an extra level of complexity is the conversion of the three-dimensional form into two dimensions. This conversion from three to two dimensions is called a projection. Before looking at the mechanism of a projection the coordinates used in three-dimensional graphics will be reviewed.

▸ *Coordinates*

There are two types of coordinates that can be used by three-dimensional graphics primitives. The main type of coordinates are ordinary coordinates. In addition, primitives can be specified by `Scaled` coordinates.

`{x, y, z}`	point given in ordinary coordinates
`Scaled[{x, y, z}]`	point given in scaled coordinates

Coordinate specifications in three-dimensional graphics.

Here is a line from `{-10, -1, 1}` to `{1,10, -5}`. The axes confirm these values.

```
In[28]:= Show[
           Graphics3D[
             Line[{{-10, -1, 1}, {1,10, -5}}],
             Axes -> True, AxesLabel -> {"x","y","z"}]]
```

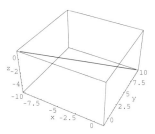

Now a thicker line with coordinates given with Scaled is added. Scaled[{0,0.5,0}] is halfway across the left edge of the bottom face. Scaled[{1,0.5,1}] is halfway across the right edge of the top face.

```
In[29]:= Show[
            Graphics3D[
              {Line[{{-10,-1, 1}, {1,10, -5}}],
               Thickness[0.02],
               Line[{Scaled[{0, 0.5, 0}],
                     Scaled[{1, 0.5,1}]}]}],
            Axes -> True]
```

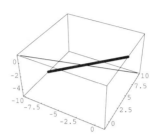

When a three-dimensional graphics object is entered to *Mathematica* the primitives exist in the user space. Ordinary coordinates of these primitives are interpreted in a coordinate system called the user coordinate system. When *Mathematica* displays this graphics object it does so by choosing a box from this space. This box is transformed to fit on a printed page or a window on the screen. The region can be thought of as a bounding box. Scaled coordinates are described in terms of this bounding box. Thus the scaled coordinate, Scaled[{0,0,0}], will always come out at the lower-left-bottom of the box.

▶ *PlotRange*

The PlotRange of a three-dimensional graphics object describes the bounding box that is chosen by *Mathematica*. When the object is displayed this region is mapped onto the display device and only primitives inside will become visible. Since this is a box oriented with the axes it can be specified by the coordinates $\{x_{min}, y_{min}, z_{min}\}$ and $\{x_{max}, y_{max}, z_{max}\}$. The PlotRange in three dimensions specifies this pair of coordinates. The value of the PlotRange is set by the option PlotRange. The use of a box oriented with the axes is a direct extention from the rectanglular region that was the two-dimensional PlotRange.

PlotRange -> Automatic	display a representative sample of points
PlotRange -> All	display all points
PlotRange -> $\{z_{min}, z_{max}\}$	display points with z coordinates between z_{min} and z_{max}
PlotRange -> $\{\{x_{min}, x_{max}\}, \{y_{min}, y_{max}\}, \{z_{min}, z_{max}\}\}$	display points in the region $\{x_{min}, y_{min}, z_{min}\}$ to $\{x_{max}, y_{max}, z_{max}\}$
PlotRange -> $\{x_{spec}, y_{spec}, z_{spec}\}$	different PlotRange specifications in x, y, and z

Settings for the PlotRange option in three dimensions.

These lines and text are shown with the default setting of the PlotRange option of Automatic. In this case all the coordinates are shown.

```
In[30]:= testp =
           Show[
             Graphics3D[
               {Line[{{10,0,0}, {-10,0,0}}],
                Line[{{0,10,0}, {0,-10,0}}],
                Line[{{0,0,10}, {0,0,-10}}]},
               Axes -> True,
               AxesLabel -> {"x", "y", "z"}]]
```

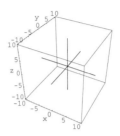

FullOptions returns the actual value of the PlotRange. It was described in Chapter 3 page 35.

```
In[31]:= FullOptions[%, PlotRange]
Out[31]= {{-10.5, 10.5}, {-10.5, 10.5}, {-10.5, 10.5}}
```

This changes the PlotRange in the z direction.

```
In[32]:= Show[testp, PlotRange -> {-5,5}]
```

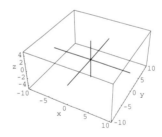

The z component of the PlotRange has been changed but not the x or y components.

```
In[33]:= FullOptions[%, PlotRange]
Out[33]= {{-10.5, 10.5}, {-10.5, 10.5}, {-5., 5.}}
```

This changes the x, y, and z components of the PlotRange. It is important to remember that all three components can be changed.

In[34]:= **Show[testp, PlotRange -> {{-5,5},{-5,5},{-5,5}}]**

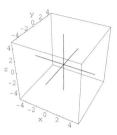

▶ *BoxRatios*

In two dimensions the PlotRange describes a rectangular region that determines the primitives that will be visible. The observed shape of the region when it was plotted was set by the AspectRatio. In three dimensions the PlotRange specifies a box that determines the primitives that will be visible. The observed shape of this box is determined by the BoxRatios and these are set by the BoxRatios option. This is the three-dimensional analogue of AspectRatio.

BoxRatios -> $\{b_x, b_y, b_z\}$	scale x, y, and z so the sides of the bounding box are in ratios $\{b_x, b_y, b_z\}$
BoxRatios -> Automatic	scale x, y, and z the same

Settings of the option BoxRatios.

This is the default setting for the BoxRatios option of Graphics3D. This gives the same scale in x, y, and z.

In[35]:= **Options[Graphics3D, BoxRatios]**

Out[35]= {BoxRatios -> Automatic}

A picture with the default setting is made.

In[36]:= **p =**
      Show[
        Graphics3D[
          Line[Table[{Sin[t], Cos[t], t},
          {t,0,4Pi, 0.1}]]]]

These are the actual numeric settings.

```
In[37]:= FullOptions[%, BoxRatios]
Out[37]= {0.159965, 0.159975, 1.}
```

Now a different setting for BoxRatios is used. The shape is identical to that of a picture generated by Plot3D.

```
In[38]:= Show[p, BoxRatios -> {1,1,0.4}]
```

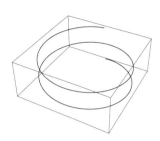

This is the default value for SurfaceGraphics.

```
In[39]:= Options[SurfaceGraphics, BoxRatios]
Out[39]= {BoxRatios -> {1, 1, 0.4}}
```

10.4 The Transformation in Three Dimensions

In the last section it was demonstrated how a three-dimensional box was constructed and used to show primitives on the display device. The coordinates of this box were set by the PlotRange and its relative dimensions by the BoxRatios. This section describes the transformation to draw the box and its contents. The details of this are more complex than for two-dimensional graphics. This is because the three-dimensional objects must be transformed into two dimensions by a projection.

▶ *Forming a Projection*

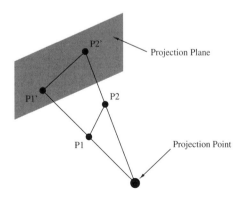

Projecting three-dimensional points onto a plane.

The figure shows how a projection from three dimensions to two dimensions can be carried out. Here the three-dimensional points P1 and P2 are projected into a plane to form the image points P1′ and P2′. To do this a plane, into which to project, and a point, from which to project, must be specified. These will be labeled respectively the projection plane and projection point. A point P is projected by forming the line that passes through P and the projection point. The point where this line intersects the projection plane, P', is the projection of P.

It is important when a projection is used that it give a sense of three-dimensional form. The sense of perspective that a projection can generate is a powerful tool to make this happen. This can be demonstrated with some pictures.

A grid is created that will be used for demonstration.

```
In[40]:= grid =
          Table[{GrayLevel[If[Mod[i,2] === Mod[j,2],0,1]],
               Polygon[{{i, j, 0}, {i+1, j, 0},
                        {i+1, j+1, 0}, {i, j+1, 0}}]},
               {i, 0,8},{j, 0,8}] ;
```

When the grid is looked at from above with a viewpoint far away it is clearly composed of squares.

```
In[41]:= Show[
          Graphics3D[grid,
          Lighting -> False, ViewPoint -> {0,0,100}]]
```

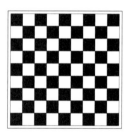

Now another grid is placed on top, by using a simple replacement rule, and both are viewed from the side. The result gives a strong perspective effect that demonstrates many important features.

```
In[42]:= Show[
          Graphics3D[{grid, grid /. {x_, y_, z_} :> {x,y,8}},
          Lighting -> False, ViewPoint -> {0,-1,0}]]
```

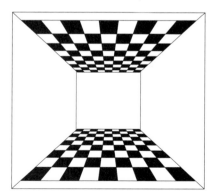

This picture demonstrates many details of perspective. Interpreted literally, neither of the grids are composed of squares. However, this picture and the picture preceding it seem quite consistent. It is easy to perceive the grid as composed of squares that diminish with distance. This reduction in size is called foreshortening and is a powerful three-dimensional effect. Another powerful effect is the grid lines that fall along the line of sight. In three-dimensional space these are parallel. In the picture they appear to get closer and in fact they converge to a single point, known as the vanishing point, as demonstrated in the picture below.

The vanishing point.

The picture above was generated by *Mathematica*, as was every picture in this book. The code that produces it is slightly complex and is not provided here in the text.

The use of three-dimensional effects is quite old. By the 13th century artists used both geometric grids and architectural structures to give their work a strong three-dimensional appearance. Later, during the renaissance, the mathematics of perspective was developed and the empirical tools already developed were put on a mathematical basis. Artists would sometimes combine the vanishing point with a compositional focus to make particular points about the subject matter.

Today with modern computer graphics it is easy to make images of three-dimensional objects. These tools will not necessarily make good or effective pictures. That is still up to the person, user or artist, who must choose the individual composition of a picture. This includes creating the right balance of perspective; if the viewpoint is too far away the perspective will be too weak and if the viewpoint is too close the image will appear distorted and unnatural. The various embellishments that can be added to a picture can help considerably, the grid being one of the most important of these. The pictures below demonstrate this.

By default Plot3D will put down a grid on the surface it generates.

In[43]:= **Plot3D[Sin[x Sin[y]], {x,0,2Pi}, {y,0,Pi}]**

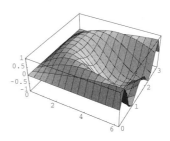

When the grid is removed the picture does not appear so three-dimensional.

In[44]:= **Show[%, Mesh -> False]**

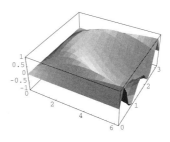

The box is another feature that helps the three-dimensional appearance.

In[45]:= **Show[%, Boxed -> False, Axes -> False]**

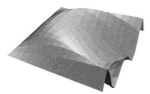

A more dramatic way to draw a grid on a surface is provided in the package CheckPlot3D[11].

In[46]:= **Needs["ExtendGraphics`CheckPlot3D`"]**

---

[11]The ExtendGraphics packages are a collection of packages that are described in the appendix. For this example to work they must be installed properly.

The result is similar to Plot3D except that the surface is colored with black and white polygons.

In[47]:= **CheckPlot3D[Sin[x y], {x,0,2Pi}, {y,0,Pi}]**

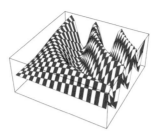

There are other tools that can help improve three-dimensional appearance, such as color and lighting. These are described in the next chapter. Another powerful technique is animation, which is connected with the experience that closer objects move faster than more distant ones. Yet another is stereoscopic viewing, a tool supported by a few computer systems.

These are some of the important ways that a picture can be composed to give a strong three-dimensional effect. If this is done well the message contained in the picture will be transmitted successfully. If the picture is arranged poorly its strange appearance will dominate and it will not be successful. Following the ideas here can help to avoid this. The rest of Chapter 10 will describe in detail how *Mathematica* controls the projection that is used to make three-dimensional images. It is these controls that must be applied to produce good pictures.

▶ *The Projection Point*

In *Mathematica* the projection point is set by the option ViewPoint. This is given in terms of a special scaled coordinate system described by the bounding box.

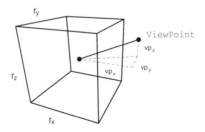

The ViewPoint **coordinate system.**

This coordinate system has origin at the center of the box and is scaled so that the longest side of the box has unit length. Thus if the BoxRatios are {1,1,1}, then the ViewPoint, {0.501, 0.501, 0.501} will sit just outside of the box top-right-back corner.

This shows a picture using the default ViewPoint.

```
In[48]:= Show[
            Graphics3D[
              {PointSize[0.05],
               Point[{0,0,0}]},
              BoxRatios -> {1,1,1}]]
```

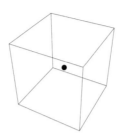

This puts the ViewPoint just outside a corner of the bounding box. A projection from this close to the box looks unnatural.

```
In[49]:= Show[%, ViewPoint -> {0.501, 0.501, 0.501}]
```

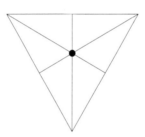

The ViewPoint is given in a special coordinate system so that a default setting is likely to produce an interesting view of a surface. Sometimes, however, it is desired to specify a ViewPoint in the user coordinate system. This can be done quite easily if the BoxRatios and the PlotRange are known. These can be determined by using FullOptions, which was described in Chapter 3 page 35. This is the mapping to calculate the x component specified in user coordinates.

$$ x_{user} = vp_x (x_{max} - x_{min}) b_{max}/b_{min} + (x_{max} - x_{min})/2 $$

Here b_x and vp_x are the x component of the BoxRatios and ViewPoint, b_{max} is the maximum component of the BoxRatios, and x_{min} and x_{max} are respectively the lower and upper bounds of the x coordinate of the bounding box. The transformation in y and z is similar. A *Mathematica* function that implements the transformation is quite easy to write. Functions to convert ViewPoint to and from user coordinates are available in the package ExtendGraphics`View3D`[12].

---

[12]The package ExtendGraphics`View3D` contains many useful functions for working with three-dimensional graphics.

`ViewPointFromUser[`*pnt, prng, box*`]`	`ViewPoint` corresponding to a point in user coordinates for particular `PlotRange` and `BoxRatios`
`ViewPointToUser[`*view, prng, box*`]`	point in user coordinates corresponding to a `ViewPoint` for particular `PlotRange` and `BoxRatios`

`ViewPoint` functions defined in `ExtendGraphics`View3D``.

The `ExtendGraphics`View3D`` package is loaded.

```
In[50]:= Needs["ExtendGraphics`View3D`"]
```

A `ViewPoint` on a corner of the bounding box.

```
In[51]:= ViewPointFromUser[
            {5., 10., 10.},
            {{2,5}, {5,10}, {-6, 10}},
            {1,5,2}]
```
```
Out[51]= {0.1, 0.5, 0.2}
```

This `ViewPoint` is on a corner of the box and the corresponding point in user coordinates is generated.

```
In[52]:= ViewPointToUser[
            {0.1, 0.5, 0.2},
            {{2,5}, {5,10}, {-6, 10}},
            {1,5,2}]
```
```
Out[52]= {5., 10., 10.}
```

In order to demonstrate this function an actual plot is generated.

```
In[53]:= s = Plot3D[Sin[x Sin[y]], {x, 0,Pi}, {y,0,Pi}]
```

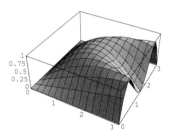

The necessary information is extracted from the plot with `FullOptions` and used to return the `ViewPoint` specified in user coordinates.

```
In[54]:= ViewPointToUser[
            ViewPoint /. Last[s],
            FullOptions[s, PlotRange],
            FullOptions[s, BoxRatios]]
```
```
Out[54]= {5.65487, -5.96903, 5.75}
```

Now the `ViewPoint` is set to be at the point {6,6,2}, specified in user coordinates.

```
In[55]:= Show[s,
            ViewPoint ->
                ViewPointFromUser[{6,6,2},
                    FullOptions[s, PlotRange],
                    FullOptions[s, BoxRatios]]]
```

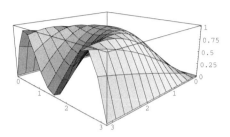

▷ *The Projection Plane*

The projection plane is derived from the option `ViewCenter`. The projection plane is defined as the plane containing the `ViewCenter` that is perpendicular to the vector from the `ViewPoint` to the `ViewCenter`. This vector is sometimes referred to as the line-of-sight vector.

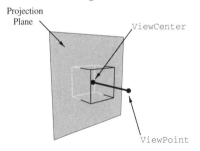

The projection plane.

The `ViewPoint`, `ViewCenter`, and the projection plane are all demonstrated in this figure. The plane is defined by the `ViewCenter` and the vector from the `ViewPoint` to the `ViewCenter`. To assist in the illustration a three-dimensional box has been drawn. The parts of the box behind the plane are white and those in front are black.

The `ViewCenter` is given in a special coordinate system with origin at the bottom-left-front of the bounding box and unit length for each edge of the box, irrespective of the `BoxRatios`. Thus a `ViewCenter` of {1,1,1} will refer to the top-right-back corner of the bounding box.

This is the default setting for
ViewCenter.

In[56]:= **Options[Graphics3D, ViewCenter]**

Out[56]= {ViewCenter -> Automatic}

The default setting of ViewCenter is used
in this picture.

In[57]:= **Show[**
            Graphics3D[
              {PointSize[0.05],
                Point[{0,0,0}]}]]

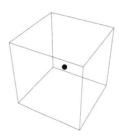

This moves the ViewCenter to the
top-right-back corner of the bounding
box.

In[58]:= **Show[%, ViewCenter -> {1,1,1}]**

The ViewCenter can be thought of as the point that is viewed; the center of the field of view. The ViewPoint can be thought of as the point that is viewed from. Since the ViewCenter is looked at it appears in the center of the image. This of course can lead to empty space in the resulting image. To reduce this empty space the default setting of Automatic is provided. This forms the projection plane from the center of the box. However, unlike a setting for ViewCenter of {0.5,0.5,0.5}, it expands the picture to fill the output device. This issue of exanding to fill the page will be considered in more detail at the end of the chapter.

▸ *Viewing the Image*

When the `ViewPoint` and `ViewCenter` are defined the projection is completely specified. Every point in three-dimensional space can now be projected into a plane. However, if a two-dimensional image is to be formed then two-dimensional points must be generated from the three-dimensional points in the projection plane.

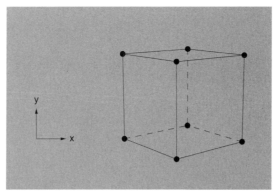

Two-dimensional coordinates in the projection plane.

This is demonstrated in the picture. Here the projection plane is shown together with several points that have been projected into it. A possible two-dimensional coordinate system is shown by the arrows on the left. This coordinate system is defined by its origin, its orientation, and its scale. The relative scale between the x and y directions can be fixed immediately since they must be identical in order for the projection not to be affected. A consequence of this is that three-dimensional graphics all have an `AspectRatio` option set to `Automatic`. If this is altered the results are not be very useful since the projection will be affected in some strange way.

▸ *Orientation in the Projection Plane*

The actual orientation of this two-dimensional coordinate system is fixed by a three-dimensional vector that is taken to point "up". This vector is refered to as the `ViewVertical` and is set by the `ViewVertical` option.

The `ViewVertical` has a value that is an "imaginary" vector drawn from the `ViewCenter`. The plane is rotated so that the image of this vector in the projection plane points up when viewed on the display device. It is an "imaginary" vector since it is not actually visible. Furthermore, it only sets a direction and its absolute magnitude is not relevant.

This is the default setting.	`In[59]:= Options[Graphics3D, ViewVertical]`
	`Out[59]= {ViewVertical -> {0., 0., 1.}}`

These polygons will be used for illustration purposes.

```
In[60]:= prims =
         {Polygon[{{0,0,1}, {0,1,0},{0,0,-1},{0,-1,0}}],
          Polygon[{{0,0,1}, {1,0,0},{0,0,-1},{-1,0,0}}],
          Polygon[{{1,0,0}, {0,1,0},{-1,0,0},{0,-1,0}}]};
```

The default setting of `ViewVertical` makes the *z* direction point up.

```
In[61]:= (vv = {0,0,1.5};
          Show[
          Graphics3D[
            {prims, Line[{{0,0,0}, vv}],
             Text["Up", vv, {0, -1.4}]},
            ViewVertical -> vv,
            PlotRange -> {{-2,2}, {-2,2}, {-2,2}}]])
```

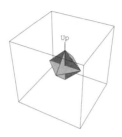

A different setting for `ViewVertical` produces a different picture. The projection of the polygons is identical but they have rotated in the projection plane.

```
In[62]:= (vv = {1.5,1.5,1.5};
          Show[
          Graphics3D[
            {prims,Line[{{0,0,0}, vv}],
             Text["Up", vv, {0, -1.4}]},
            ViewVertical -> vv,
            PlotRange -> {{-2,2}, {-2,2}, {-2,2}}]])
```

▸ *Scaling and Translating in the Projection Plane*

The two-dimensional coordinate system in the projection plane is not yet completely determined. It still must be given an origin and it must have a scale. The same problem is encountered in two-dimensional graphics and hinges on the questions of where on the output device to place the image and what size to make it. Since the bounding box has the broadest extent in any direction and encloses all the visible primitives the discussion can be limited to how the projection of the bounding box should be viewed. The same transformation will be applied to all the primitives. Since they are enclosed in the bounding box they must fit inside the projection of the bounding box.

In two-dimensional graphics a rectangular image was placed onto a rectangular device. For this a transformation was chosen which centered the image, maintained the `AspectRatio`, and made the result as big as possible. Now things are more complex since the projection of the bounding box is not rectangular. As was described earlier in the discussion on the projection plane if the `ViewCenter` option is set to `Automatic` the picture is expanded to fill the output device. However, if it is set to some explicit value then the projection of that point is placed in the center of the output and then the picture is maximized. Whatever the setting of `ViewCenter` the picture should be maximized on the output device. There are two ways this can be done. The first is to expand the projection of the bounding box so that it fills as much of the page as possible, which is shown in the diagram below.

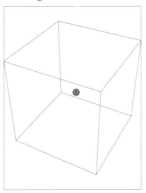

Drawing the bounding box: Method 1.

This method of drawing the bounding box will use as much space as possible. The edges of the box touch the edges of the page. However, as the box is rotated in three-dimensional space by changing the `ViewPoint`, the scaling will change and the box may increase or decrease in size.

An alternative way to arrange the transformation is to consider the imaginary sphere that surrounds the bounding box. If the projection of this sphere is made to fill the output device then as the `ViewPoint` is changed there will be no alteration in the size of the image. However, the picture may not fill the output device for all views. This transformation is represented in the diagram below.

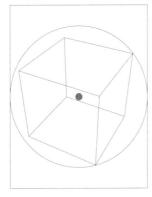

Drawing the bounding box: Method 2.

These two diagrams were made by applying the real transformations implemented in *Mathematica* code to an actual sequence of three-dimensional primitives. The package `ExtendGraphics'View3D'` contains all the code necessary to make the three-dimensional transformations and the text in *Mathematica Graphics* explains the two-dimensional transformations.

Mathematica provides both methods of carrying out projections. The selection between them is made by setting the option `SphericalRegion`. A setting of `SphericalRegion -> True` will make the sphere surrounding the bounding box fill the output device while a setting of `SphericalRegion -> False` will make the actual bounding box fill the output. For this reason when making an animation of objects rotating by changing the `ViewPoint` it is a good idea to set `SphericalRegion -> True`.

`SphericalRegion` can be demonstrated with an image that uses the same `ViewPoint` and has been rotated with `ViewVertical`. Since neither the projection point nor the projection plane have changed there can be no difference due to any projection effect.

This three-dimensional graphics object will demonstrate two different views with SphericalRegion set to False.	```
In[63]:= g1 =
    Graphics3D[
        Polygon[{{0,0,0}, {1,0,0}, {1,1,0}, {0,1,0}}],
        ViewPoint -> {0,0,2},
        SphericalRegion -> False]
```
*Out[63]=* -Graphics3D- |
| The picture on the left fits better into the rectangular output and is scaled larger than the one on the right. | ```
In[64]:= Show[
    GraphicsArray[
        {g1, Append[g1, ViewVertical -> {1,1,0}]}]]
``` |

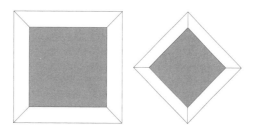

This three-dimensional graphics object will demonstrate two different views with SphericalRegion set to True.	```
In[65]:= g2 =
    Graphics3D[
        Polygon[{{0,0,0}, {1,0,0}, {1,1,0}, {0,1,0}}],
        ViewPoint -> {0,0,2},
        SphericalRegion -> True]
```
*Out[65]=* -Graphics3D- |
```

Now the sphere containing the bounding box is used for scaling and the sizes of the two pictures are identical.

```
In[66]:= Show[
           GraphicsArray[
             {g2, Append[g2, ViewVertical -> {1,1,0}]}]]
```

▶ *Plot3Matrix*

The transformations described in the previous sections are used to generate a two-dimensional representation of a collection of three-dimensional objects. These transformations can be described by the application of a single four-dimensional matrix. Matrix techniques used to represent transformations like these are discussed in Chapter 17 page 418 and in other computer graphics texts such as *Computer Graphics: Principles and Practice*, Second Edition, J. Foley, A. van Dam, S. Feiner, and J. Hughes and *Graphics Gems*, ed. A.S. Glassner.

In *Mathematica* this transformation matrix is called the Plot3Matrix and this is a three-dimensional graphics option. In practice this option is not very easy to use because of the complexity of scaling the image onto the output device. Also, since the options for setting the projection are quite powerful, there is little need to set Plot3Matrix. However, if the value of the Plot3Matrix option is known it is possible to mix two- and three-dimensional coordinates to insert primitives into three-dimensional graphics that are available in two dimensions. A package is provided in the ExtendGraphics directory that defines functions to calculate this matrix.

Plot3Matrix[*obj*]	the transformation matrix used to view Graphics3D or SurfaceGraphics object *obj*
ProjectVector[*mat*, *vec*]	apply *mat* to *vec* and return the two-dimensional result

Projection matrix functions defined in ExtendGraphics`View3D`.

The package is loaded.

```
In[67]:= Needs["ExtendGraphics`View3D`"]
```

This makes a simple picture.

```
In[68]:= p =
         Plot3D[Sin[x y], {x,0,2Pi}, {y,0,Pi}]
```

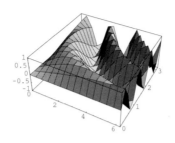

This returns the 4 × 4 transformation matrix.

```
In[69]:= mat = Plot3Matrix[%]
Out[69]= {{0.289771, 0.459922, -0.0563869, 0.0592014},
   {-0.133132, 0.491564, 0.295919, 1.33749},
   {-0.0413639, 0.152728, -0.0762902, -0.109826},
   {-0.061145, 0.225766, -0.112774, 3.22144}}
```

The function ProjectVector takes a three-dimensional vector and a 4 × 4 matrix and returns the two-dimensional projection of the vector.

```
In[70]:= pos = ProjectVector[mat, {0.5,0.5,1}]
Out[70]= {0.118353, 0.568047}
```

Here the Epilog option is used to draw a Raster primitive with the lower-left corner at {0.5,0.5,1} and sides of 15 points. Neither Raster nor Offset are available for primitives in three-dimensional graphics. Nonetheless here they are used and located at a specific three-dimensional position.

```
In[71]:= Show[p,
            Epilog ->
              Raster[Table[Random[ ], {5},{5}],
                     {pos, Offset[{15,15}, pos]}]]
```

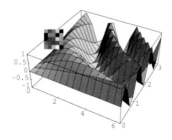

▶ *Final Scaling*

The previous steps have described how the image is rendered into PostScript coordinates. At this point the image is essentially two-dimensional and the process is identical to that for two-dimensional graphics. There is a final stage of scaling that takes place when the PostScript is rendered on the output device. This is identical to that described for two-dimensional graphics.

Similar considerations for scaling text apply as in the case for two-dimensional graphics. Text that is part of a label added by an option is included in the scaling calculation. One difference with two-dimensional graphics is that text included by `Text` primitives is not scaled for when the `PlotRange` is `All`.

Text that is part of a plot label is automatically included in the scaling calculations.

```
In[72]:= Plot3D[Sin[x Sin[y]], {x,0,Pi}, {y,0,Pi},
              AxesLabel -> "This is a long label   "]
```

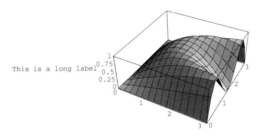

10.5 Summary

This chapter has reviewed the coordinate systems used to describe *Mathematica* graphics primitives and the transformations that are used to render images on an output device. In two-dimensional graphics it was shown how a rectangular region, the `PlotRange`, selected a group of primitives. The coordinate system of these primitives was described as the user coordinate system. These primitives were rendered into PostScript in the PostScript coordinate system. In a subsequent stage the PostScript was rendered onto a display device.

Three-dimensional graphics work in a similar fashion to two-dimensional graphics. The process has an extra conversion, which is necessary to project the three-dimensional objects into two dimensions. The projection is controlled by the `ViewPoint`, `ViewCenter`, and `ViewVertical` options.

The discussion in this chapter has concentrated on `Graphics` and `Graphics3D`. There is in fact no need to discuss other types of graphics objects since they follow similar arguments. Thus `ContourGraphics`, `DensityGraphics`, and `GraphicsArray` use similar rendering technology as `Graphics` while `Surface-Graphics` is analogous to `Graphics3D`. The manner in which these objects are rendered into two- or three-dimensional primitives is covered in the relevant chapters of Part IV.

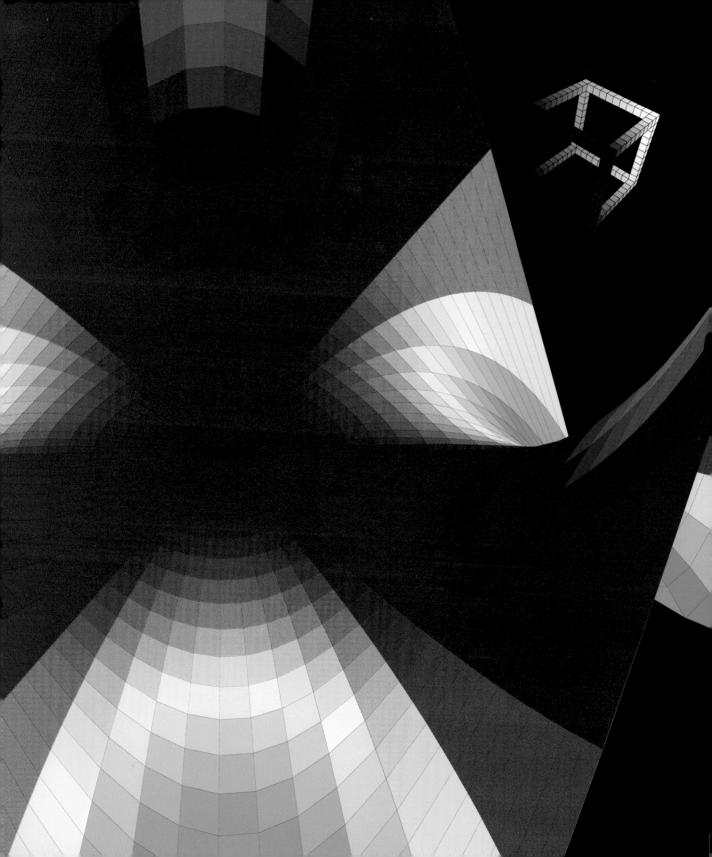

Chapter 11
Color

There are several ways that color can be introduced to *Mathematica* graphics. This chapter provides an overview of these and other color-related issues. It will start by looking at the style directives and graphics programming using color. It will then look at the built-in functions that can introduce color into plots. The next part will look at three-dimensional lighting, a topic that continues on from the last chapter. The chapter ends with a discussion of ways in which colors can be altered as graphics output is generated.

11.1 Style Directives

A simple and direct way to add color to a picture is with color style directives. These work in a fashion typical of all graphics style directives.

GrayLevel[*g*]	set color of object to gray
RGBColor[*r*, *g*, *b*]	set color of object to red, green, and blue
Hue[*h*]	set color of object to hue
Hue[*h*, *s*, *b*]	set color of object to hue, saturation, and brightness
CMYKColor[*c*, *m*, *y*, *k*]	set color of object to cyan, magenta, yellow, and black

Color style directives.

▸ *GrayLevel*

The shades of these `Rectangle` primitives range from `GrayLevel[0]` (black) to `GrayLevel[1]` (white).

```
In[1]:= Show[
          Graphics[
            {Table[
              {GrayLevel[i/39],
                Rectangle[{ i, 0}, { i+1, 8}]},
              { i, 0, 39}],
            Line[{{0,0},{40,0},{40,8},{0,8},{0,0}}]},
          AspectRatio -> Automatic]]
```

The shading that `GrayLevel` provides takes one argument that can vary from zero to one. It can be useful when a one-dimensional shading function is desired and is also appropriate for a monochrome monitor or printer.

▶ *RGBColor*

Color shading is provided by the `RGBColor` style directive. This takes three arguments to set the *red*, *green*, and *blue* components of a color. It is well matched to the way that most computer screens generate colors with a combination of red, green, and blue phosphors.

Here an array made with `RasterArray` shows a range of colors with a blue component of zero. The lower-left has color black and the upper-right yellow.

```
In[2]:= Show[
          Graphics[
            RasterArray[
              Table[RGBColor[i, j, 0], {i,0,1,.1},
                {j,0,1,.1}]]]]
```

One way to look at the color space of `RGBColor` is as a cube. A disadvantage of this approach is that parts of the color space are obscured.

```
In[3]:= Show[
          Graphics3D[
            Table[
              {RGBColor[i,j,k], Cuboid[10 {i,j,k}]},
              {i,0,1,.2},{j,0,1,.2},{k,0,1,.2}]],
            Lighting -> False,
            Boxed -> False]
```

To see the color cube more clearly the interior of the cube will not be plotted. Here a list of edge specifications is generated.

```
In[4]:= Join[
          Permutations[{0, 0, k}],
          Permutations[{0, 1, k}], Permutations[{1, 1, k}]]
Out[4]= {{0, 0, k}, {0, k, 0}, {k, 0, 0}, {0, 1, k}, {0, k, 1},
     {1, 0, k}, {1, k, 0}, {k, 0, 1}, {k, 1, 0}, {1, 1, k},
     {1, k, 1}, {k, 1, 1}}
```

The above edge specifications can now be used in a Table command. Each one sets both the color and the position of a Cuboid primitive.

```
In[5]:= Show[
          Graphics3D[
            Map[
              Table[{RGBColor @@ #, Cuboid[10 #]},
                    {k, 0, 1, 0.1}]&, %]],
            Lighting -> False,
            Boxed -> False]
```

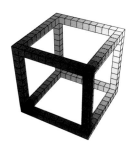

▷ *Hue*

Hue[*h*] specifies a color with a particular hue; Hue[*h*, *s*, *b*] additionally specifies the saturation and brightness so that Hue[*h*, 1, 1] is equivalent to Hue[*h*]. Hue is circular in its first argument and provides a cylindrical color space. This is in contrast to RGBColor, which provides a rectilinear color space naturally represented by a cube.

This makes a strip colored from Hue[0] to Hue[1]. Notice that Hue is cyclical: the ends of the strip have the same color.

```
In[6]:= Show[
          Graphics[
            {Table[
              {Hue[i/39],
                Rectangle[{i, 0}, {i+1, 8}]},
              {i, 0, 39}],
              Line[{{0, 0},{40, 0},{40, 8}, {0, 8}, {0, 0}}]}],
            AspectRatio -> Automatic]]
```

⟩ *CMYKColor*

The style directives, RGBColor and Hue, form colors from additive primaries. Since most color monitors do so by radiating mixtures of these primaries it is simple to map these additive primaries to the display. An alternative method for generating color is using subtractive primaries. These are cyan, magenta, and yellow, the complements of the additive primaries. This type of color system is similar to the manner in which color printing works. These primaries can be thought of as ink which will be placed on paper. Color is generated on printed material by removing components from the ambient light, usually white, leaving the desired shade. A fourth component, black, is added to reduce the total amount of ink that is put down and to obtain a true black. The CMYKColor style directive specifies colors with this subtractive scheme by stating the components of cyan, magenta, yellow, and black.

When CMYKColor is displayed on the screen it is translated into a color the monitor can display. When rendered on a printer it specifies how much and what type of ink should be put down.

```
In[7]:= Show[
          Graphics[
            {CMYKColor[1,0,0,0],
             Rectangle[{0,0}, {1,1}]}]]
```

⟩ *Example: Coloring a Map*

One of the famous theorems from mathematics is the four color map theorem. This is concerned with the minimum number of colors necessary to color any map in the plane so that no two adjacent regions have the same color. The theorem states that the minimum number of colors is four. A related, though simpler problem, will now be studied. This is concerned with coloring a triangular map, a map composed of triangles. For such a map it is believed that three colors are always sufficient. This is only a supposition and no mathematical proof is offered here.

A triangular map that requires two colors.

```
In[8]:= Show[
          Graphics[
            Table[{Hue[0], Polygon[{{i,j},{i+1,j},{i,j+1}}],
                  Hue[1/3],
                    Polygon[{{i+1,j+1},{i+1,j},{i,j+1}}]},
                {i,3},{j,3}]]]
```

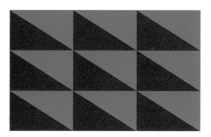

A triangular map that requires three colors.

```
In[9]:= Show[
          Graphics[
            {Hue[0], Polygon[{{0,0},{1,0},{1,1}}],
             Hue[1/3], Polygon[{{0,0},{0,1},{1,1}}],
             Hue[1/3], Polygon[{{1,0},{1,1},{2,1}}],
             Hue[0], Polygon[{{0,1},{1,1},{1,2}}],
             Hue[2/3], Polygon[{{1,1},{2,1},{1,2}}]}]]
```

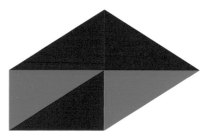

One basic way to apply the color scheme automatically from a given set of points and triangles is to use the Random[ ] function.

Here are some points and the triangles that compose a map from them.

```
In[10]:= (pts = {{0,0},{1,0},{1,1},{0,1},{2,1},{1,2}};
         tri = {{1,2,3},{1,3,4},{2,3,5},{3,4,6},{3,5,6}};)
```

Random[ ] is used to generate a color so that each triangle can be distinguished.

```
In[11]:= Show[
          Graphics[
            Map[{RGBColor[Random[ ], Random[ ],1],
                 Polygon[Part[pts,#]]}&, tri]]]
```

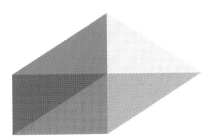

In this example more colors were used than necessary. The exact same color will not be used twice since Random[ ] does not repeat itself until something in excess of 10^{460} calls. This means that even on the fastest computers it would take many times the lifetime of the universe for Random[ ] to repeat itself. Of course, in a shorter time it will generate colors that are numerically different but appear similar.

The ideal would be to be more exact and selective in the assignment of colors. This can be done by checking each triangle's neighbors to see if they have been assigned colors. If they have, then a different color should be chosen. This is done in the two functions applyColor and colorTris.

The neighbors of {a,b,c} are found and then tested to see if they have colors assigned. The new color is then calculated. The color of each triangle is stored by triColor.

```
In[12]:= applyColor[{a_,b_,c_}, trilist_] :=
          Module[{next},
            next = Apply[Cases[trilist, triH[#1, #2,_]]&,
                         {{a,b}, {b,c},{c,a}}, {1}] ;
            next = Flatten[next] ;
            next = DeleteCases[next, triH[a,b,c]] ;
            cols = Apply[triColor, next, {1}] ;
            new = Map[MemberQ[cols, #]&, {0,1,2}] ;
            new = Part[Position[new, False],1,1] ;
            triColor[a,b,c] = new-1
          ]
```

The main driving function colorTris takes a list of triangles. It initializes triColor, used to keep the colors of the triangles. This is made Orderless since the order of the vertices is not important. triH is a holder for the triangles, and again must be Orderless to help select neighbors.

```
In[13]:= colorTris[tris_List] :=
          Module[{trilist, res},
            Clear[triColor] ;
            triColor[___] := {} ;
            SetAttributes[triH, Orderless] ;
            SetAttributes[triColor, Orderless] ;
            trilist = Apply[triH, tris, {1}] ;
            res = Flatten[Map[applyColor[#, trilist]&,tris]];
            Clear[triColor] ;
            res
          ]
```

These are the different colors that are necessary with the triangles shown above.

```
In[14]:= cols = colorTris[tri]
Out[14]= {0, 1, 1, 0, 2}
```

The colors can be combined with the triangles and plotted.

```
In[15]:= Show[
           Graphics[
             Table[{Hue[Part[cols,i]/3],
                    Polygon[Part[pts,Part[tri,i]]]},
             {i,Length[tri]}]]]
```

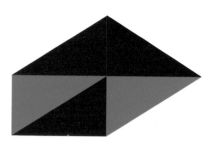

To demonstrate a larger example a more powerful triangulation must be employed. One possible method is a Delaunay triangulation, which is discussed in more detail in Chapter 16 page 401. A package that implements Delaunay triangulation is available in the ExtendGraphics packages. For the examples that follow to work the ExtendGraphics packages must be installed properly as described in the appendix.

This loads the package for Delaunay triangulation.

```
In[16]:= Needs["ExtendGraphics`Delaunay`"]
```

These points will be used for an example.

```
In[17]:= pts = Table[{Random[ ], Random[ ]}, {40}];
```

The command TrianglePlot forms and plots triangles from a set of points. These are the triangles that will be colored.

```
In[18]:= TrianglePlot[pts]
```

DelaunayVertices returns the indices of the triangles.

```
In[19]:= tri = DelaunayVertices[pts];
```

The color indices are generated.

```
In[20]:= cols = colorTris[tri];
```

This is the larger triangulation filled in and colored.

```
In[21]:= Show[
           Graphics[
             Table[{Hue[Part[cols,i]/3],
                 Polygon[Part[pts,Part[tri,i]]]},
               {i,Length[tri]}]], AspectRatio -> Automatic]
```

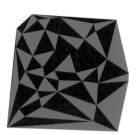

11.2 Function Evaluation

Plot3D[{$f[x,y]$, $s[x,y]$}, x_{rng}, y_{rng}]   draw a surface of height f and shading s

Plot3D[$f[x\ y]$, x_{rng}, y_{rng}, ColorFunction -> $colfun$]

draw a surface of height f and shading $colfun[f]$

ParametricPlot3D[{$x[u,v]$, $y[u,v]$, $z[u,v]$, $s[u,v]$}, u_{rng}, v_{rng}]

draw the parametrized surface shaded by $s[u,v]$

Introducing color into three-dimensional plotting routines.

Some of the plotting commands support the evaluation of a function that introduces color into their output. The equivalent list plotting commands accept an array of colors to produce analogous results. Color can be used in this way to introduce an extra dimension for visualization.

▶ *Function Plotting Commands*

Plot3D takes a function that is evaluated to determine the height of the surface at each point in a rectangular grid. When a pair of functions is given the first one sets the height of the surface and the second is used to color it. This ability to color the surface by function evaluation allows extra information to be added to a plot. In the first two of these examples this functionality is used to show the behavior of a function in the complex plane.

The height is determined by the real part of the result and the color by the argument of the result.

```
In[22]:= Plot3D[{Re[Sin[x + I y]],
             Hue[Arg[Sin[x + I y]]/2/Pi]},
         {x, -2Pi, 2Pi},{y, -2, 2},
         PlotPoints -> 40]
```

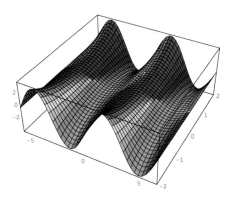

Now the height is determined by the imaginary part of the result.

```
In[23]:= Plot3D[{Im[Sin[x + I y]],
             Hue[Arg[Sin[x+ I y]]/2/Pi]},
         {x,-2Pi, 2Pi},{y,-2., 2.},
         PlotPoints -> 40]
```

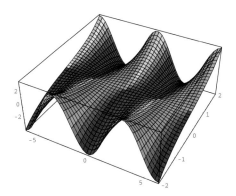

In these two pictures the color describes the mixture of real and imaginary parts of the picture. When the surface is positive or negative real the color is red or cyan respectively; for these points the first picture carries all the information. When it is positive or negative purely imaginary the color is green or blue respectively and the second picture shows this.

ParametricPlot3D can include coloring in its results. Here a surface known as the monkey saddle surface is colored according to its curvature[1]. This surface could be generated with Plot3D. Using ParametricPlot3D allows a polar form to be plotted.

The monkey saddle function is converted to a polar representation.

```
In[24]:= x (x^2-3y^2) /.
              {x -> r Sin[t], y -> r Cos[t]}//Simplify
```

$$Out[24]= -(r^3 \; Sin[3 \; t])$$

Here the monkey saddle is colored according to its curvature.

```
In[25]:= ParametricPlot3D[
             {r Sin[t], r Cos[t], -r^3 Sin[3t],
              Hue[27 r^5 Sin[3t]/(1+9r^4)^(3/2)/2]},
             {r,0,1},{t,0,2Pi}, Lighting -> False,
                PlotPoints -> {25,65}]
```

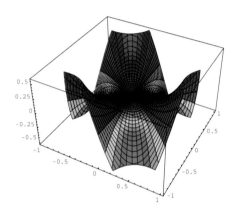

▶ *Data Plotting Commands*

Plot3D can accept a function to be used to color the surface. ListPlot3D also accepts an array of color data that can be used for coloring. The first example replicates the surface generated above.

These are the data from which the height of the surface is constructed.

```
In[26]:= data =
             Table[Re[Sin[N[x +I y]]],
                   {y,-2,2,4/39},{x,-2Pi,2Pi,4Pi/39}];
```

These colors will be used to shade the surface.

```
In[27]:= colors =
             Table[Hue[Arg[Sin[N[x +I y]]]/2/Pi],
                   {y,-2,2,4/39},{x,-2Pi,2Pi,4Pi/39}];
```

---

[1]These examples come from *Modern Differential Geometry of Curves and Surfaces*, Alfred Gray. This book, which contains many examples plotted with *Mathematica*, describes how to calculate the curvature of a surface.

ListPlot3D uses the color array to shade the surface[2]. The MeshRange option is set to make the *x* and *y* axes come out properly.

```
In[28]:= ListPlot3D[data, colors,
            MeshRange -> {{-2Pi,2Pi}, {-2,2}}]
```

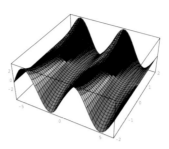

The color array that was given to ListPlot3D was of identical dimensions as the data. This means that the color is specified at each grid point at which the data are specified. An alternative form of the color array is to have it specify the color in the center of each surface quadrilateral. In this case the length of the color array in each dimension is one less than that of the data array. Version 2.2 *Mathematica* only accepted the second form of color array. To generate this form is possible to write a function that will average the four colors at each grid point. Such a function is not very complex. A simpler solution, demonstrated here, is to use the color at one grid point.

This reduces the size of the color array.

```
In[29]:= colors1 = Rest[Map[Rest, colors]];
```

These are the dimensions of the data.

```
In[30]:= Dimensions[data]
Out[30]= {40, 40}
```

These are the lengths of each dimension for the colors. They are one shorter in each dimension.

```
In[31]:= Dimensions[colors1]
Out[31]= {39, 39}
```

ListPlot3D also accepts this form of color data.

```
In[32]:= ListPlot3D[data, colors1,
            MeshRange -> {{-2Pi,2Pi}, {-2,2}}]
```

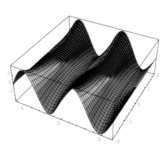

---

[2]This example did not work in Version 2.2 *Mathematica*. The text explains why and what can be done to make it work.

◈ *ColorFunction*

An alternative scheme for shading is provided by the option ColorFunction. This shades according to height and works with both function and data plotting commands. ColorFunction is an option not only of Plot3D and ListPlot3D but also of the contour and density plotting commands.

The value of the ColorFunction option is used as a function and is passed the height of the array at each point. The height is scaled so that the minimum and maximum values of the *z* component of the PlotRange are 0 and 1 respectively. The function must then return a valid color.

This is the electric potential that surrounds a positive and negative charge pair.

```
In[33]:= pot =
            1/Sqrt[(1 - x)^2 + y^2] -1/Sqrt[(-1 - x)^2 + y^2];
```

Hue is very useful as a ColorFunction since it has a convenient one-argument form.

```
In[34]:= g = Plot3D[pot,
               {x,-3.5,3.5},{y,-3.5,3.5},
               PlotPoints -> 30, MeshStyle -> Thickness[0.001],
               ColorFunction -> Hue]
```

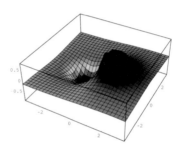

Here a named function of one argument is defined to use with the ColorFunction option.

```
In[35]:= colfun[z_] :=
            Hue[If[z < 0.57735,  z^2, -0.122008 + 0.788675 z]]
```

ColorFuntion is an option of SurfaceGraphics and can be reset with a call to Show.

```
In[36]:= Show[g, ColorFunction -> colfun]
```

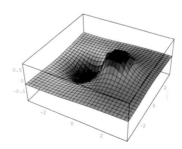

The actual range of values that are passed to ColorFunction can be demonstrated by using a function that prints its argument before returning a color. This is demonstrated for ListPlot3D. The minimum and maximum values of the *z* component value of the PlotRange are 0 and 4 respectively. In the example below, the second value comes from averaging the four numbers {0,0,1,2} and then applying the linear transformation that maps 0 to 0 and 4 to 1. The result is 0.1875.

These are the values that are passed to ColorFunction. This setting displays the value with a Print command and then returns a color.

```
In[37]:= ListPlot3D[
                {{0,0,1,2}, {0,0,2,3},{1,2,4,4}, {2,2,4,4}},
                PlotRange -> {0,4},
                DisplayFunction -> (Display["tmp.ps", #]&),
                ColorFunction ->
                        ((Print[#]; RGBColor[#,1,1])&)]

0.
0.1875
0.4375
0.1875
0.5
0.75
0.5
0.8125
1.

Out[37]= -SurfaceGraphics-
```

The ColorFunction option can be used to shade contour plots. Here a pure function with RGBColor is used. The parentheses are necessary due to the precedence of &.

```
In[38]:= ContourPlot[Sin[x] Sin[y], {x,-Pi,Pi},{y,-Pi,Pi},
                    ColorFunction ->
                        (RGBColor[#, 1-#,0]&),
                    PlotPoints -> 30]
```

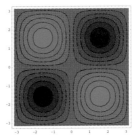

The ColorFunction option can be used to shade density plots.

```
In[39]:= DensityPlot[
                Sin[x /Sin[y]], {x, -Pi,Pi},{y,-Pi,Pi},
                ColorFunction -> Hue,
                PlotPoints -> 40,
                Mesh -> False]
```

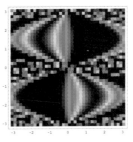

11.3 Lighting

Mathematica three-dimensional graphics can make use of a system of simulated lighting for illumination. These are controlled through a number of options of the three-dimensional graphics objects `Graphics3D` and `SurfaceGraphics`. By lighting different parts of an object the three-dimensional appearance can be improved.

`Lighting`	whether simulated light sources should be used
`LightSources`	the simulated light sources
`AmbientLight`	non-directional shading

Options to control simulated lighting.

The lighting options of `Graphics3D` are extracted.

```
In[40]:= Options[Graphics3D,
                {AmbientLight, LightSources, Lighting}]

Out[40]= {AmbientLight -> GrayLevel[0], Lighting -> True,
    LightSources ->
      {{{1., 0., 1.}, RGBColor[1, 0, 0]},
       {{1., 1., 1.}, RGBColor[0, 1, 0]},
       {{0., 1., 1.}, RGBColor[0, 0, 1]}}}
```

▸ *Switching Lighting On and Off*

The option `Lighting` determines whether or not simulated lighting is used. If color style directives have been included with the three-dimensional primitives, lighting must be off for them to have an effect on `Polygon` primitives.

This polygon and color will be used for demonstration.

```
In[41]:= prims =
            {RGBColor[1,0,0],
             Polygon[{{0,0,0}, {0,1,0}, {0,0,1}}]};
```

Even though a color style is included the polygon is not affected. This is because the simulated lighting is used.

```
In[42]:= Show[Graphics3D[prims], Lighting -> True]
```

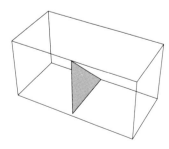

Now the polygon is displayed with lighting off and it uses the color style directive.

In[43]:= **Show[%, Lighting -> False]**

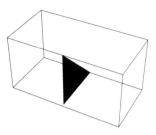

If no color directive is included the polygon is rendered in the default color of black.

In[44]:= **Show[**
Graphics3D[
Polygon[{{0,0,0}, {0,1,0}, {0,0,1}}]],
Lighting -> False]

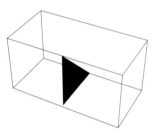

▷ *The Light Source Calculation*

The light sources that are used by the *Mathematica* three-dimensional graphics renderer provide a simulated lighting model. The light emitted by these sources does not diverge and does not cast shadows. Lighting serves to distinguish different parts of a surface and to enhance its three-dimensional appearance. It does not provide photo-realistic rendering but is consistent with the aims of the *Mathematica* three-dimensional renderer as described in Chapter 9 page 158.

The actual computation that is carried out to determine the color given to a particular part of the surface is quite simple:

$$a + \sum_i c_i\, \hat{n} \cdot \hat{l}_i$$

Here the sum is over each light source, $\hat{n}$ is the unit normal vector to the polygon, c_i and $\hat{l}_i$ are the color of and direction vector to, the ith light source and a is the ambient light. This calculation is carried out to determine the shading for each of the *red*, *green*, and *blue* components. For each color component the ambient light a and the color of a particular light source c_i may differ.

The light source calculation will now be illustrated by an example. First a function that computes the unit normal to a polygon will be defined. The normal is a vector perpendicular to the plane of the polygon. Here a formula involving the cross product will be used with no explanation. For a fuller discussion of normals including a variety of graphical representations the reader is referred to Chapter 17 page 417.

The normal is calculated with a cross product. Here the package that defines the cross product is loaded.

```
In[45]:= Needs["LinearAlgebra`CrossProduct`"]
```

polygonNormal will take a Polygon primitive and return its normal.

```
In[46]:= polygonNormal[Polygon[{a_, b_, c_, d___}]] :=
            Module[{norm},
                norm = Cross[a-b, c-b] ;
                norm/Sqrt[norm.norm]
            ]
```

A polygon to use for demonstration.

```
In[47]:= poly = Polygon[{{1.,0,0},{0,0,1.},{0,1.,0}}]

Out[47]= Polygon[{{1., 0, 0}, {0, 0, 1.}, {0, 1., 0}}]
```

Here is the normal to the polygon. The calculation of the normal used by the default lighting model is described below.

```
In[48]:= polygonNormal[poly]

Out[48]= {0.57735, 0.57735, 0.57735}
```

These are the default light sources for Graphics3D objects.

```
In[49]:= LightSources /. Options[Graphics3D]

Out[49]= {{{1., 0., 1.}, RGBColor[1, 0, 0]},
    {{1., 1., 1.}, RGBColor[0, 1, 0]},
    {{0., 1., 1.}, RGBColor[0, 0, 1]}}
```

The lights are scaled so that each direction vector has unit length.

```
In[50]:= Map[# /. {x_,y_,z_} :>
                    {x,y,z}/Sqrt[{x,y,z}.{x,y,z}]&,%]

Out[50]= {{{0.707107, 0., 0.707107}, RGBColor[1, 0, 0]},
    {{0.57735, 0.57735, 0.57735}, RGBColor[0, 1, 0]},
    {{0., 0.707107, 0.707107}, RGBColor[0, 0, 1]}}
```

Here the actual light source calculation is carried out. The result is the coefficient for the color of each source.

```
In[51]:= cols =
            Map[First[#].polygonNormal[poly] Last[#]&, %]

Out[51]= {0.816497 RGBColor[1, 0, 0], 1. RGBColor[0, 1, 0],
    0.816497 RGBColor[0, 0, 1]}
```

The AmbientLight option makes no contribution to the color of the polygon. If it was not zero it would have to be added in as well.

```
In[52]:= AmbientLight /. Options[Graphics3D]

Out[52]= GrayLevel[0]
```

The coefficients for each color are expanded out to generate the color that the polygon will take.

```
In[53]:= RGBColor @@ (Plus @@ cols /. RGBColor -> List)

Out[53]= RGBColor[0.816497, 1., 0.816497]
```

The color of each polygon thus depends upon the ambient light, the light source positions, the light source colors, and the polygon normal. The first is set by the AmbientLight option, and the second two by the LightSources option. The value used for the polygon normal requires some explanation. The normal to the polygon that is used is calculated from the polygon after the projective transformation has been applied. The details of this projection are described in detail in Chapter 10 page **??** in the discussion on coordinate systems. The result of this transformation is to place objects into the coordinate system shown in the picture below, with the z axis coming directly out of the diagram.

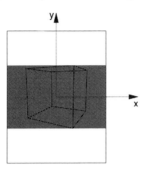

Coordinate system for three-dimensional objects.

This is the coordinate system used to calculate the normals for the polygons and this is the coordinate system in which the light sources are defined. With this system a light source at {0,0,1} will give light propagating directly down on the screen as though it came from the ViewPoint.

This list of polygons will be used in an example.

```
In[54]:= polys =
            {Polygon[{{0,0,1}, {1,0,0},{0,1,0}}],
             Polygon[{{0,0,1}, {0,1,0},{-1,0,0}}],
             Polygon[{{0,0,1}, {-1,0,0},{0,-1,0}}],
             Polygon[{{0,0,1}, {0,-1,0},{1,0,0}}]};
```

The polygons are now oriented to be viewed from on top. It can be seen that one of the facets is only shaded by the AmbientLight option.

```
In[55]:= Show[
            Graphics3D[
               polys, ViewPoint -> {0,0,1}]]
```

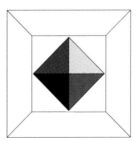

This makes a more distributed set of light sources that lights all the polygons.

```
In[56]:= Show[%,
            LightSources ->
              {{{1,0,1}, RGBColor[1,0,0]},
               {{-1,1,1}, RGBColor[0,1,0]},
               {{-1,-1,1}, RGBColor[0,0,1]}}]
```

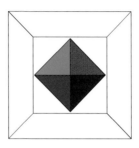

This method of calculating the normals to the polygons has some advantages but also has some disadvantages. The main advantage is that the default setting for the LightSources produces attractive graphics for both Plot3D and ParametricPlot3D. The main disadvantage is that as the ViewPoint (used to look at an object) is changed, so is the effect of lighting. This can be demonstrated in the following pictures.

Here the default ViewPoint is extracted from the options list.

```
In[57]:= view = ViewPoint /. Options[Plot3D, ViewPoint]
Out[57]= {1.3, -2.4, 2.}
```

This uses the default viewing options.

```
In[58]:= Plot3D[Sin[x y], {x,0,2Pi},{y,0,Pi},
            ViewPoint -> view]
```

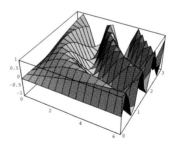

Now the ViewPoint is moved out by a factor of 100. Notice how the color changes.

```
In[59]:= Show[%, ViewPoint -> 100 view]
```

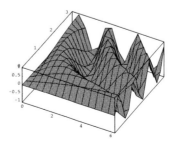

Thus when the normals that are used in the color calculation are computed *after* the projective transformation the actual normal is very sensitive to the details of this transformation.

▷ *Polygon and Normal Specification*

As was described in Chapter 9 page 157 the polygon primitive in three dimensions can accept a specification of the normal vector. It can also accept a specification of the style in which edges should be drawn. This functionality was not available in Version 2.2 (or earlier) *Mathematica*.

`Polygon[pts, norm]`	use *norm* as the normal to the polygon
`Polygon[pts, Automatic]`	use the default normal
`Polygon[pts, Automatic, {True, False, ... }]`	
	whether edges are to be drawn

Arguments of the `Polygon` primitive.

This is very useful when it comes to lighting calculations. If a normal is found in the `Polygon` arguments the lighting calculations will use this normal *directly*. It will not transform it or modify it in any way. The light sources are kept in the same coordinate system as before; they are rotated so that a light at {0,0,1} would come from the `ViewPoint` and a light at {0,1,0} would come down the projection of the `ViewVertical` in the projection plane. These terms are defined in Chapter 10 page 185. This coordinate system is more complex to use since normals must be inserted into the `Polygon` primitives, but the results can be quite pleasing.

Two polygons are displayed. The one on the left specifies its own normal.

```
In[60]:= Show[
            Graphics3D[{Polygon[{{2,0,0},{3,0,0},{2,1,0}}],
                Polygon[{{0,0,0},{1,0,0},{0,1,0}}, {0,0,1}]}],
            ViewPoint -> view]
```

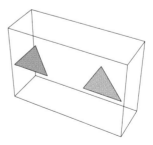

Now when the ViewPoint is moved out the polygon on the left, shaded with its own normal, does not change color.

`In[61]:= `**`Show[%, ViewPoint -> 100 view]`**

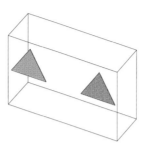

    Normally it would not make much sense to have two polygons with two different lighting models. They are included here for the purpose of comparison. In certain cases it is useful to calculate the normal from the actual polygon vertices. This is of course easy to do with *Mathematica*. The polygonNormal function that was defined previously can be used for this.

An old style sphere.

`In[62]:= `**`ParametricPlot3D[`**
           `{Sin[t] Sin[p], Sin[t] Cos[p], Cos[t]},`
           `{t,0,Pi}, {p,0,2Pi}, PlotPoints -> 25]`

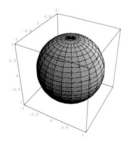

Now the sphere is changed to specify the normals directly. It looks strange due to the light sources.

`In[63]:= `**`Show[% /. p_Polygon :> Append[p, polygonNormal[p]]]`**

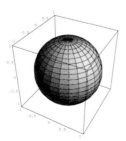

The light sources are altered to make them more distributed. The result is more colorful.

```
In[64]:= Show[%, LightSources ->
              {{{1, 0, 1}, RGBColor[1, 0, 0]},
               {{-1, 1, 1}, RGBColor[0, 1, 0]},
               {{-1, -1, 1}, RGBColor[0, 0, 1]}}}]
```

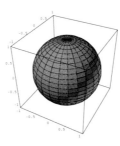

Since it is very useful to insert the normals into Polygon primitives a package has been provided that does this automatically. ExtendGraphics`View3D` provides functions that set and restore the DisplayFunction and LightSources options.

SetNormalDisplayFunction	set $DisplayFunction to insert normals in polygons
SetOldDisplayFunction	restore $DisplayFunction
SetColorLights	set the LightSources options of ParametricPlot3D and Graphics3D to use colored lights
SetWhiteLights	set the LightSources options of ParametricPlot3D and Graphics3D to use white lights
SetOldLights	restore the LightSources options of ParametricPlot3D and Graphics3D

Functions in the package ExtendGraphics`View3D`.

The package is loaded.

```
In[65]:= Needs["ExtendGraphics`View3D`"]
```

$DisplayFunction is set so that normals are inserted into Polygon primitives. The LightSources options of Graphics3D and ParametricPlot3D are altered to use evenly distributed light sources.

```
In[66]:= (SetNormalDisplayFunction[ ];SetColorLights[ ])
```

The new settings are used.

In[67]:= **ParametricPlot3D[**
        {Sin[t] Sin[p], Sin[t] Cos[p], Cos[t]},
        {t,0,Pi}, {p,0,2Pi}, PlotPoints -> 25]

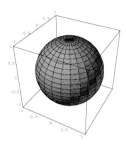

Plot3D does not use the new system.

In[68]:= **Plot3D[Sin[x] Sin[y], {x, -Pi,Pi},{y,-Pi,Pi},**
        PlotPoints -> 25]

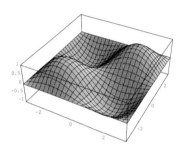

The picture can be converted to
Graphics3D and then it will have
normals inserted into the polygons.

In[69]:= **Show[Graphics3D[%],**
        LightSources -> ColorLights]

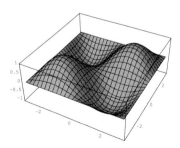

$DisplayFunction and the
LightSources options are restored to
their old values.

In[70]:= **(SetOldDisplayFunction[ ]; SetOldLights[ ])**

❯ *SurfaceColor*

SurfaceColor[d]	set diffuse color
SurfaceColor[d, s]	set diffuse and specular color; specular exponent is 1
SurfaceColor[d, s, n]	set diffuse color, specular color, and specular exponent

The uses of SurfaceColor.

SurfaceColor provides a more sophisticated model of lighting known as the Phong illumination model[3]. This takes account of both diffuse and specular properties of a surface. The actual calculation is given by the expression:

$$a + \sum_i c_i \left(k_d \, \hat{n} \cdot \hat{l}_i + k_s \, (\hat{r} \cdot \hat{v})^n \right)$$

where now k_d denotes the diffuse and k_s the specular components of the surface, n is the specular exponent, $\hat{r}$ is the reflected light vector, $\hat{v}$ is the vector to the viewpoint. a is the ambient light, c_i and $\hat{l}_i$ are the color and direction vector of the ith light source. As before the calculation is repeated for each color with a, c_i, k_d, and k_s changing for each color component.

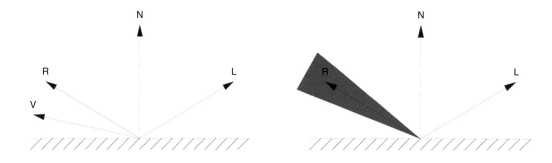

Specular reflection.

The vectors are demonstrated in the diagram on the left. The diagram on the right shows the cone of light that is generated by a particular specular reflection. The larger the specular exponent the narrower this cone will be. The examples of SurfaceColor that are given here will make use of the normal specification as described in the previous section. This is done because the results are more pleasing than with the older light source system. The package ExtendGraphics`View3D` will be used to switch between the different systems.

---

[3] A full description of this and other illumination models is given in *Computer Graphics: Principles and Practice*, Second Edition, J. Foley, A. van Dam, S. Feiner, and J. Hughes

The package that allows the resetting of the DisplayFunction and LightSources options is loaded.

In[71]:= **Needs["ExtendGraphics`View3D`"]**

$DisplayFunction is set to insert normals into Polygon primitives.

In[72]:= **SetNormalDisplayFunction[ ]**

The LightSources options are reset.

In[73]:= **SetWhiteLights[ ]**

This will form the bowl of a glass.

In[74]:= **bowl =**
First[ParametricPlot3D[
          {Sin[t] Sin[p], Sin[t] Cos[p], Cos[t]},
          {t,Pi/2,Pi},{p,0,2Pi},PlotPoints -> 40,
          DisplayFunction -> Identity]];

This will form the stem of a glass.

In[75]:= **stem =**
First[ParametricPlot3D[
          {Sin[p]/8, Cos[p]/8, z},
          {z,-1,-4},{p,0,2Pi},PlotPoints -> {9, 41},
          DisplayFunction -> Identity]];

Here the diffuse component of SurfaceColor is given. This gives the object a matte-like appearance.

In[76]:= **Show[**
   Graphics3D[
      {EdgeForm[ ], SurfaceColor[RGBColor[0.45,0.45,0]],
      bowl, stem}]]

Now a specular component is added. This gives the object a shiny, metallic appearance.

```
In[77]:= Show[
            Graphics3D[
              {EdgeForm[ ],
               SurfaceColor[RGBColor[0.45,0.45,0],
                            RGBColor[0.2,0.2,0.4], 10],
               bowl, stem}]]
```

The options are set back to their default values.

```
In[78]:= (SetOldDisplayFunction[ ]; SetOldLights[ ])
```

11.4 Color Output

The last section in this chapter is concerned with the output of colors as *Mathematica* graphics are rendered into PostScript. When this happens color style directives are translated directly into PostScript color operators. The option ColorOutput provides a method by which colors can be intercepted just before they are emitted so that they can be changed.

GrayLevel	produce gray colors
RGBColor	produce colors defined in red, green, blue
CMYKColor	produce colors defined in cyan, magenta, yellow, black
fun	use *fun* to determine the actual color

Settings for the ColorOutput option.

This colored primitive will be used to demonstrate ColorOutput.

```
In[79]:= test =
            Graphics[{RGBColor[1,0,0], Rectangle[{0,0},{1,1}]}]

Out[79]= -Graphics-
```

When the graphics object test is emitted the result is a red rectangle.

In[80]:= **Show[test]**

When ColorOutput is set to GrayLevel the colors are all converted to gray.

In[81]:= **Show[test, ColorOutput -> GrayLevel]**

colfun makes a simple conversion from RGBColor to CMYKColor.

In[82]:= **colfun[RGBColor[r_, g_, b_]] :=**
            Module[{k},
              k = 1- Max[{r,g,b}] ;
              CMYKColor[1-r-k, 1-g-k, 1-b-k, k]
              ]

colfun will leave GrayLevel unchanged.

In[83]:= **colfun[GrayLevel[g_]] := GrayLevel[g]**

Now colfun is applied to change the colors as they are emitted.

In[84]:= **Show[test, ColorOutput -> colfun]**

Another use for the `ColorFunction` option is to change the contrast in a picture. This can be done by applying a function to the gray values. Generally it is more convenient to export the picture with the original color specifications and to use some other specialized application to alter the colors. Methods for exporting pictures from *Mathematica* are discussed in Chapter 26.

11.5 Summary

This chapter has reviewed the main tools that *Mathematica* provides to work with color. Color style directives can be used in two- and three-dimensional graphics to alter the appearance of the primitives. These directives are *Mathematica* expressions and can be constructed by *Mathematica* programs just like any other expression. Another way to introduce color into pictures is by function evaluation and this was demonstrated for `Plot3D`, `ParametricPlot3D`, and by the `ColorFunction` option. The simulated lighting model was then covered. It was shown how the basic lighting model produces a good appearance for default settings but that it suffered from some deficiencies. A solution to this involved inserting normals into the `Polygon` primitive itself. The final section discussed the use of `ColorOutput` to alter colors as graphics output is produced.

Chapter 12
Combining and Converting Graphics

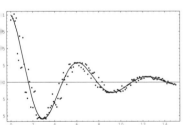

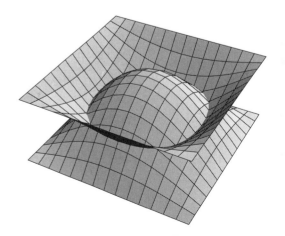

Part II of *Mathematica Graphics* is intended to show how to combine graphics with programming. There are many graphics problems that can be solved by writing some *Mathematica* code. Of course, it would be preferable to avoid writing any code, if existing functions could be used or adapted in some way. This chapter shows how to do this, how to use the graphics functions and convert and combine their results. In this way many interesting pictures can be generated without having to write any code at all.

12.1 Combining Objects with Show

A particularly clean and simple way to combine pictures is to use Show. This has been demonstrated repeatedly throughout previous sections. For example, the results of Plot and ListPlot can easily be combined.

Plot generates one picture to be combined.

In[1]:= **p1 = Plot[Cos[x] Exp[-x/5], {x,0,15}]**

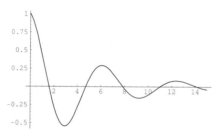

ListPlot builds the other.

In[2]:= **p2 =**
      ListPlot[
         Table[{i, i+= Random[ ]-0.5; Cos[i] Exp[-i/5]},
            {i, 0, 15, 0.1}]]

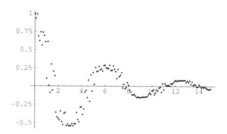

When both pictures are used as arguments to Show the combined result is displayed.

In[3]:= **Show[p1, p2]**

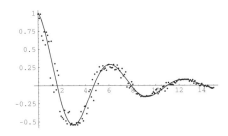

It is straightforward to combine these graphics objects since they are both Graphics objects. Both Plot and ListPlot result in expressions with the same head. Combining them means that the primitives in both expressions should be collected in one Graphics expression and Show called again. It is more complex to combine the results of Plot3D. The result of a Plot3D command is a SurfaceGraphics object, a surface with only one z value for a given $\{x, y\}$ point.

One surface is generated with Plot3D. The result of this evaluation is a SurfaceGraphics object.

In[4]:= **sur1 = Plot3D[Sin[x] Sin[y], {x,0,Pi}, {y,0,Pi}]**

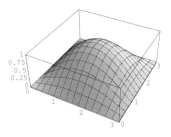

Another surface is built. The result is also a SurfaceGraphics object.

In[5]:= **sur2 = Plot3D[1-Sin[x] Sin[y], {x,0,Pi}, {y,0,Pi}]**

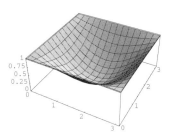

The Head of each graphics object is SurfaceGraphics.

In[6]:= **{Head[sur1], Head[sur2]}**

Out[6]= {SurfaceGraphics, SurfaceGraphics}

Both are passed to Show and the combined picture is generated. Note that the result is a Graphics3D object.

In[7]:= **Show[sur1, sur2]**

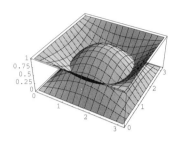

The Head of the resulting combined object is Graphics3D.

In[8]:= **Head[%]**

Out[8]= Graphics3D

Show combined these SurfaceGraphics objects with two steps. First each object was converted to the collection of Graphics3D primitives that represented the surface. Representing an object with Graphics3D primitives means that a broader class of objects can be displayed at the expense of efficiency. The primitives that can build Graphics3D objects were described in Chapter 9 and are covered in detail in Chapter 21. Chapter 22 contains a full description of SurfaceGraphics objects. After conversion, the two Graphics3D objects that result can then be combined in a way similar to the combining of Graphics objects demonstrated earlier.

▶ *Options and Show*

When several graphics objects are combined by Show the primitives and directives are simply merged. A question arises as to how the options should be combined. There may be a conflict between the settings, one object may give one value and another a different value. Show reconciles this problem by using the options of the first object.

A plot with a specific setting for the PlotRange option.

In[9]:= **p1 =**
        Plot[Sin[x], {x,0,2Pi},
            PlotRange -> {{0,2Pi}, {0,1}}]

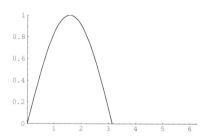

A plot with a different setting for its
PlotRange option.

In[10]:= **p2 =**
    Plot[Cos[x], {x,0,2Pi},
       PlotRange -> {{0,2Pi}, {-1,1}}]

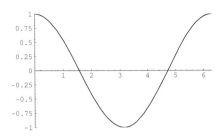

When they are combined with **p1** first the
options of **p1** are used.

In[11]:= **Show[p1, p2]**

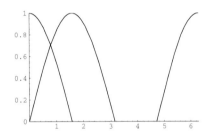

Now **p2** is first and its options are used.

In[12]:= **Show[p2, p1]**

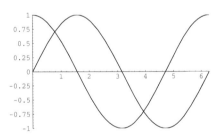

Of course it is possible to set a new value
for the option with the call to Show.

In[13]:= **Show[p1, p2,**
    PlotRange -> {{0,2Pi}, {-1.5,1.5}}]

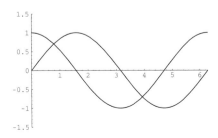

▶ *FilledPlot Example*

Many of the graphics commands that are built in and defined in the standard packages provide the ability to plot several functions. An example is the function FilledPlot, defined in the package Graphics`FilledPlot. This plots different functions while shading between the curves.

The package must be loaded, as was described in Chapter 4 page 65.

In[14]:= **Needs["Graphics`FilledPlot`"]**

FilledPlot shades the area between the two functions.

In[15]:= **FilledPlot[{Sin[x], Cos[x]}, {x,0,2Pi}]**

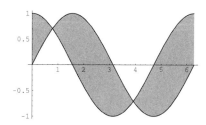

An interesting variant on FilledPlot is to shade only parts of the region between the functions. For example, with two functions only shading those parts where one function is lower in value than the other. This new functionality could be created by examining the code for FilledPlot and modifying it. A much simpler way to add the functionality is to make several plots and display them together.

Two functions are plotted here, one being the parabola x^2-1. The other function is the lesser in value of 4 Sin[4 x] and x^2-1.

In[16]:= **FilledPlot[**
{If[4 Sin[4 x] > x^2-1, x^2-1, 4 Sin[4 x]],
x^2 -1}, {x, -3,3}]

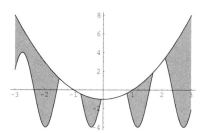

These are the parts of the plot that were omitted in the previous picture.

In[17]:= **Plot[4 Sin[4 x], {x, -3,3}]**

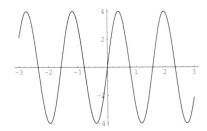

Now a call to Show combines the two pictures. A function to make this picture automatically would be quite simple.

In[18]:= **Show[%%, %]**

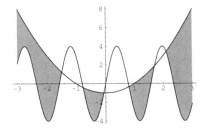

This example makes an important point. It started with existing functionality that was close to some desired result. It then generated this result by making use of existing functions. When this approach can be followed successfully the amount of development required to add some new functionality is at an absolute minimum. Most of the work was done when the functions like Plot or FilledPlot were written.

12.2 How Objects Are Converted

When two graphics objects are to be combined it may be necessary to convert them to a more general type. For example, SurfaceGraphics may be converted to Graphics3D. The way this is done by *Mathematica* is simple and often very powerful. The table here demonstrates how these conversions are carried out.

Graphics3D[SurfaceGraphics[*obj*]]	convert SurfaceGraphics to Graphics3D
Graphics[SurfaceGraphics[*obj*]]	convert SurfaceGraphics to Graphics
Graphics[ContourGraphics[*obj*]]	convert ContourGraphics to Graphics
Graphics[DensityGraphics[*obj*]]	convert DensityGraphics to Graphics
Graphics[Graphics3D[*obj*]]	convert Graphics3D to Graphics

Converting between different graphics objects.

Plot3D generates this simple SurfaceGraphics expression that will show the results of conversion.

```
In[19]:= surf =
           Plot3D[Sin[x y], {x,0,1}, {y,0,1}, PlotPoints -> 3]
```

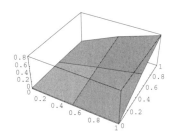

The SurfaceGraphics objects keeps its data in a special compact representation. This is described in Chapter 22 page 620.

```
In[20]:= First[surf]
Out[20]= {{0., 0., 0.}, {0., 0.247404, 0.479426},
    {0., 0.479426, 0.841471}}
```

Now the SurfaceGraphics object is converted to Graphics3D. Because of the special output format it does not look very interesting.

```
In[21]:= Graphics3D[surf]
Out[21]= -Graphics3D-
```

This is the InputForm of the converted expression. It contains a list of the Polygon primitives that form the surface and a collection of options. Previously there was only a grid of z values.

```
In[22]:= InputForm[%]

Out[22]//InputForm=
  Graphics3D[{Polygon[{{0., 0.5, 0.}, {0., 0., 0.},
      {0.5, 0., 0.}, {0.5, 0.5, 0.2474039592545229}}],
    Polygon[{{0.5, 0.5, 0.2474039592545229}, {0.5, 0., 0.},
      {1., 0., 0.}, {1., 0.5, 0.479425538604203}}],
    Polygon[{{0., 1., 0.}, {0., 0.5, 0.},
      {0.5, 0.5, 0.2474039592545229},
      {0.5, 1., 0.479425538604203}}],
    Polygon[{{0.5, 1., 0.479425538604203},
      {0.5, 0.5, 0.2474039592545229},
      {1., 0.5, 0.479425538604203},
      {1., 1., 0.8414709848078965}}]},
   {PlotRange -> Automatic,
    DisplayFunction -> (Display[$Display, #1] & ),
    ColorOutput -> Automatic, Axes -> True, PlotLabel -> None,
    AxesLabel -> None, Ticks -> Automatic, Prolog -> {},
    Epilog -> {}, AxesStyle -> Automatic,
    Background -> Automatic, DefaultColor -> Automatic,
    DefaultFont -> {"Courier", 5.5}, AspectRatio -> Automatic,
    ViewPoint -> {1.3, -2.4, 2.}, Boxed -> True,
    BoxRatios -> {1, 1, 0.4}, Plot3Matrix -> Automatic,
    Lighting -> True, AmbientLight -> GrayLevel[0],
    LightSources ->
     {{{1., 0., 1.}, RGBColor[1, 0, 0]},
      {{1., 1., 1.}, RGBColor[0, 1, 0]},
      {{0., 1., 1.}, RGBColor[0, 0, 1]}},
    ViewCenter -> Automatic, PlotRegion -> Automatic,
    ViewVertical -> {0., 0., 1.}, FaceGrids -> None,
    Shading -> True, AxesEdge -> Automatic,
    BoxStyle -> Automatic, SphericalRegion -> False}]
```

Another example demonstrates the conversion applied to a ContourGraphics object.

```
In[23]:= ContourPlot[Sin[x y], {x,0,1}, {y,0,1},
            Contours -> 2,
            PlotPoints -> 3]
```

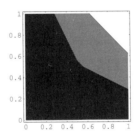

When the ContourGraphics object is
converted a collection of shaded
polygons is returned. If the
ContourGraphics was not shaded the
result would be a sequence of lines.

```
In[24]:= First[Graphics[%]]
Out[24]= {{GrayLevel[0.],
    Polygon[{{0., 1.}, {1., 1.}, {1., 0.}, {0., 0.}}]}},
   {GrayLevel[0.5], Polygon[{{1., 0.285214}, {0.556189, 0.5},
      {0.5, 0.556189}, {0.285214, 1.}, {1., 1.}}]},
   {GrayLevel[0.], Thickness[0.001],
    Line[{{1., 0.285214}, {0.556189, 0.5}, {0.5, 0.556189},
      {0.285214, 1.}}]}},
   {GrayLevel[1.], Polygon[{{1., 0.622315}, {0.622315, 1.},
      {1., 1.}}]}, {GrayLevel[0.], Thickness[0.001],
    Line[{{1., 0.622315}, {0.622315, 1.}}]}]}}
```

12.3 Surface, Contour, and Density Plots

Each of these plots displays essentially the same type of information, three-dimensional data, in different
ways. Since the information being displayed is the same it is possible to interconvert the pictures so that the
data can be visualized in the three different formats. The interconversion works because of the similarity in
the way that SurfaceGraphics, ContourGraphics, and DensityGraphics store their data. The details
of how they store data are described in Chapters 22, 23, and 24 respectively.

SurfaceGraphics [*plot*]	convert to SurfaceGraphics
ContourGraphics [*plot*]	convert to ContourGraphics
DensityGraphics [*plot*]	convert to DensityGraphics

Interconversion of surface, contour, and density plots.

A simple plot to demonstrate conversion
of a ContourGraphics object.

```
In[25]:= ContourPlot[Sin[x y], {x,0,1}, {y,0,1},
                    Contours -> 2,
                    PlotPoints -> 3]
```

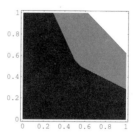

The contour plot is converted to a
density plot.

```
In[26]:= DensityGraphics[%]
Out[26]= -DensityGraphics-
```

The density plot can be displayed with a call to Show.

In[27]:= **Show[%]**

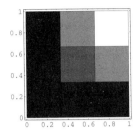

For a demonstration of the use of this type of conversion a contour plot with no shading is constructed.

In[28]:= **plot1 =**
ContourPlot[x y, {x,-2,2}, {y,-2,2},
PlotPoints -> 30,
ContourShading -> False]

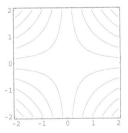

The picture is converted to a density plot and then displayed. The Mesh option is set to False to prevent the mesh from being displayed.

In[29]:= **plot2 = Show[DensityGraphics[plot1], Mesh -> False]**

The two plots are converted to Graphics objects and combined.

In[30]:= Show[plot2, plot1]

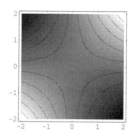

ContourDensityPlot will make a combined contour and density plot. The DisplayFunction option is used to prevent intermediate pictures being displayed[16].

```
In[31]:= ContourDensityPlot[fun_, xrng_, yrng_, opts___] :=
            Module[{p1, p2},
                p1 = ContourPlot[fun, xrng, yrng,
                    ContourShading -> False,
                    DisplayFunction -> Identity,
                    opts] ;
                p2 = Show[DensityGraphics[p1],
                    DisplayFunction -> Identity,
                    Mesh -> False] ;
                Show[p2, p1, DisplayFunction -> $DisplayFunction]]
```

This invokes the function. Note that the function does no checking of any of the arguments.

```
In[32]:= ContourDensityPlot[
            Sin[x] Sin[y], {x, -Pi,Pi},{y,-Pi,Pi},
            PlotPoints -> 30]
```

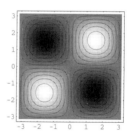

Another interesting picture combines a surface and a contour representation of the same function. Here the contours will be drawn on one of the faces of the box that surrounds the surface.

---

[16]The use of the DisplayFunction option to supress graphics output was described in Chapter 3 page 44.

A representation of a function plotted as a surface.

```
In[33]:= s1 =
            Plot3D[x y (x^2 - y^2)/(x^2 + y^2),
                {x, -2,2}, {y,-2,2},
                PlotPoints -> 30]
```

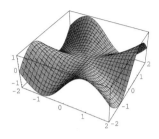

Here the surface is converted to a contour plot with a call to ContourGraphics. Show is then used to add an option.

```
In[34]:= c1 =
            Show[ContourGraphics[s1], ContourShading -> False]
```

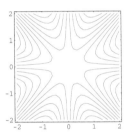

Now a call to Graphics makes a two-dimensional graphics object. The primitives are then extracted with a call to First.

```
In[35]:= g1 = First[Graphics[c1]] ;
```

In this step every two-dimensional line primitive is converted to a three-dimensional primitive by inserting a height. The value of the height is chosen to be that of the bottom of the bounding box.

```
In[36]:= g1 =
            Graphics3D[g1 /. Line[x_] :>
                        Line[Map[Append[#, -2]&, x]]]
Out[36]= -Graphics3D-
```

This combines the surface and the three-dimensional object that was generated from the contour plot. The latter goes on the bottom of the box since a value of −2 for the z value was used in the previous step.

```
In[37]:= Show[s1, g1,
              ViewPoint -> {1.3, -2.4, 1}]
```

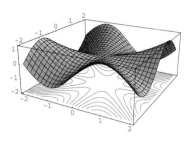

12.4 Summary

The chapter has shown how to combine and convert different graphics objects. This is a simple but powerful aspect of *Mathematica* graphics. It means that many of the existing *Mathematica* tools can be used and applied to new problems. When the ideas in this chapter are applied successfully, new graphics functionality can be introduced with very little effort.

Chapter 13
Programming Examples

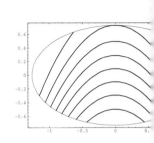

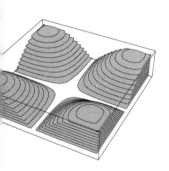

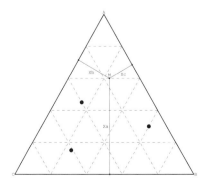

This is the last chapter of Part II of *Mathematica Graphics*. The theme of Part II has been the manner in which *Mathematica* programming and graphics can be combined. This chapter will summarize by presenting a number of examples, each of which tackles a realistic graphics problem. The problems will be described and solutions will be presented. Each solution will then be analyzed to explain how it works and to highlight any particularly interesting features. Many of these examples tackle complicated problems and require a significant amount of code to solve them. It is not necessary to solve every problem by writing large amounts of *Mathematica* code. Often the amount of code can be very small, a consequence of the power of *Mathematica* programming. However, for complicated problems there is sometimes no choice other than to write code. A number of the problems presented in this chapter fall into this category.

13.1 Avoiding Asymptotes in Plot

When the `Plot` command is used for functions discontinuous at a point, a line is drawn at the discontinuity. Here is an example for the `Tan` function.

The discontinuities in `Tan[x]`, for x values of n Pi/2 for integral values of n, are clearly seen.

`In[1]:= Plot[Tan[x], {x,0,2Pi}]`

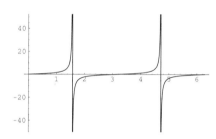

While these can be thought of as asymptotes sometimes it would be desirable to avoid drawing them. This example shows how to avoid these asymptotes.

▶ *Solution to the Problem*

The solution to this problem is to extend the `Plot` command.

$$Plot[f, \{x, x_{start}, x_1, x_2, \ldots x_i, x_{end}\}]$$

$$\text{plot } f \text{ over } x \text{ ranges } \{x_{start}, x_1\}, \{x_1, x_2\} \ldots$$

Extension to `Plot` defined in the package `ExtendGraphics`Plot``.

The package is loaded. If this does not work the packages that go with *Mathematica Graphics* have not been installed properly. The appendix describes how this should be done.

`In[2]:= Needs["ExtendGraphics`Plot`"]`

Now Plot uses the new functionality. $In[3]:=$ **Plot[Tan[x], {x, 0, Pi/2, Pi, 3Pi/2, 2Pi}]**

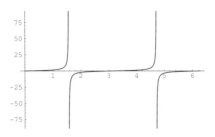

▶ *Explanation of the Solution*

```
Unprotect[Plot]

Plot[f_, {x_, a_, lims__, b_}, opts___] :=
    Module[{ dfun, tmp, d},
        dfun = DisplayFunction /. {opts} /. Options[Plot] ;
        d = (a + b) $MachineEpsilon 10 ;
        tmp = Partition[{ a, lims, b}, 2,1] ;
        tmp = Map[# + {d, d})&, tmp] ;
        tmp = Map[Plot[f, Evaluate[Prepend[#,x]],
                    DisplayFunction -> Identity, opts]&, tmp] ;
        Show[tmp, DisplayFunction -> dfun]
    ]
```

Avoiding singularities in Plot.

This problem may be conveniently divided in two. The first problem is concerned with the detection of discontinuities of the values of function f in variable x over the range $\{x_{start},\ x_{end}\}$. The second problem begins with the use of this knowledge by Plot. This example does not attempt to solve the first problem, this would involve some mathematical programming to analyze the function being plotted. Only a solution to the second problem will be presented.

User Interface

Determining the interface to a solution is an important part of its design that should be settled as early as possible. Here there is a function f in a variable x with a set of points $\{x_{start}, x_1, x_2, \dots x_{end}\}$. The implementation of the solution will generate the sequence of plots over $\{x_{start}, x_1\}, \{x_1, x_2\}, \dots \{x_i, x_{end}\}$. To determine this implementation and its user interface it is worth searching for a precedent. The function NIntegrate, which is closely related to Plot, does have a solution to exactly this problem. As described in the reference guide section of the main *Mathematica* book NIntegrate[f, $\{x, x_{start}, x_1, x_2, \dots x_i, x_{end}\}$] will break up the range of quadrature to the sub-intervals $\{x_{start}, x_1\}, \{x_1, x_2\}, \dots \{x_i, x_{end}\}$.

The application of this syntax will mean overloading the Plot function. There is no need to invent some new command as an existing command is extended. This implementation will be quite straightforward since the new syntax is clearly distinguished from the old by the length of the iterator list.

Implementation

Now the implementation will be considered and explained:

```
Unprotect[Plot]

Plot[f_, {x_, a_, lims__, b_}, opts___] :=
```

Unprotect must be used since a rule is being attached to Plot which is an internal symbol.

The second line gives the rule to attach to Plot and contains three patterns. The first, f_, describes the function to be plotted. This pattern will match the first argument. The second part, {x_, a_, lims__, b_}, will match a list of four or more elements. x_, a_, and b_ describe the variable, start, and endpoints and will all match single elements. The repeated pattern, lims__, describes the intermediate points and will match one or more objects. This whole pattern will only match if the iterator has a length of four or more and therefore it will not match a normal use of Plot. The last part, opts___, describes any options, such as those to control axes or scaling. This will match zero or more arguments.

```
Module[{ dfun, tmp, d},
```

This code is encapsulated inside a Module statement with three local variables, dfun, tmp, and d.

```
    dfun = DisplayFunction /. {opts} /. Options[Plot] ;
```

This line saves the DisplayFunction value set for the plot. This will display the result.

```
    d = (a + b) $MachineEpsilon 10 ;
```

The start and endpoints are averaged and from this a reduction factor for each interval determined. This reduction will shrink each sub-plot back from its endpoints avoiding any special problems at these points. Such problems are clearly possible since these points can represent singularities.

```
    tmp = Partition[{ a, lims, b}, 2,1] ;
```

In this line the different intervals are constructed. The symbol lims will be replaced by the match from the pattern object lims__. Since it came from a repeated pattern object, lims will hold a Sequence expression. These have various special properties when used to build expressions:

A Sequence object on its own evaluates normally.

```
In[4]:= lims = Sequence[s1, s2, s3]

Out[4]= Sequence[s1, s2, s3]
```

A Sequence object, placed as an argument in another expression, places its arguments directly in the top object. The original Sequence object disappears and leaves only its arguments.

```
In[5]:= f[a, lims, b]

Out[5]= f[a, s1, s2, s3, b]
```

Partition divides up the range. Here the expression being partitioned has head f.

```
In[6]:= tmp = Partition[%, 2,1]

Out[6]= f[f[a, s1], f[s1, s2], f[s2, s3], f[s3, b]]
```

The head of the expression being partitioned can just as well be List.

```
In[7]:= tmp = Partition[{a, lims, b}, 2,1]

Out[7]= {{a, s1}, {s1, s2}, {s2, s3}, {s3, b}}
```

```
tmp = Map[# + {d, -d})&, tmp] ;
```

Now the list is traversed and a pure function is applied to each element. For every element, each a list of length two, d is added to the first and subtracted from the second parts. The result is returned to be held by tmp. This operation relies on the listablity of Plus.

Here the attributes of Plus are seen to include Listable.

```
In[8]:= Attributes[Plus]

Out[8]= {Flat, Listable, NumericFunction, OneIdentity,
         Orderless, Protected}
```

Since Plus is listable each element of the list is added.

```
In[9]:= {a,b} + {c,d}

Out[9]= {a + c, b + d}
```

The function takes each element of the list tmp. Each element is a list of two parts; the first part has d added and the second has it subtracted.

```
In[10]:= tmp = Map[(# + {d, -d})&, tmp]

Out[10]= {{a + d, -d + s1}, {d + s1, -d + s2},
          {d + s2, -d + s3}, {d + s3, b - d}}
```

```
tmp = Map[Plot[f, Evaluate[Prepend[#,x]],
             DisplayFunction -> Identity, opts]&, tmp] ;
```

This line of code uses Plot to generate a list of the sub-plots. Evaluate is necessary since Plot has the Attribute HoldAll. If Evaluate was not used Prepend would not evaluate properly. The DisplayFunction option is set to Identity to prevent the display of pictures at this point. The result is returned in a list to be held by tmp.

```
Show[tmp, DisplayFunction -> dfun]
```

This last command passes the list of graphics objects to Show, which combines them. The Display-Function option is reset to the value saved earlier. For the default a picture will appear and the combined graphics primitives will be returned.

13.2 Plotting Smooth Contours

When *Mathematica* draws contour lines it is presented with an array of data points that represent the heights of the function over a rectangular grid. This is the output of the function `ContourPlot`. When the contours are drawn it takes each rectangular element and checks if the contour crosses or not. If it does then either linear or cubic interpolation is used to determine the crossing points[17]. This generates accurate contours but they are also sometimes rather jagged. Obviously the best solution is to increase the number of grid points. For `ContourPlot` this can be done easily with the `PlotPoints` option. A larger setting will increase the number of points at which the function is sampled and generate a smoother result.

This strategy may not be possible in all cases. The data may have come from outside of *Mathematica* and the number of data points may not be under user control. This example shows how it is possible to make smoother pictures even in this circumstance. The details of the solution depend upon the way that `ContourGraphics` objects store their information, as a grid of data points; this is described in Chapter 23 page 632.

▹ *Solution to the Problem*

The solution to the problem is to provide a function that will interpolate between the data points. This solution works not only for `ContourGraphics` objects but also for `SurfaceGraphics` and `DensityGraphics`.

`SmoothGraphics[obj[data, opts], num]`   generate a smoothed `SurfaceGraphics`, `ContourGraphics`, or `DensityGraphics` object using interpolation between data points

---

Function defined in the package `ExtendGraphics`SmoothGraphics`.

The package is loaded.

`In[11]:= Needs["ExtendGraphics`SmoothGraphics`"]`

A contour plot that uses the default setting of `PlotPoints`.

`In[12]:= cont =`
`        ContourPlot[Sin[x] Cos[y], {x, -Pi, Pi}, {y,-Pi, Pi}]`

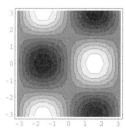

---

[17]The algorithm for drawing contour lines is described in Chapter 23 page 633.

Dimensions returns the number of data points in the grid. ContourGraphics uses this data to form contour lines. This is described in Chapter 23 page 632.

```
In[13]:= Dimensions[First[cont]]
Out[13]= {15, 15}
```

Now the number of data points is increased and a smoother result is produced.

```
In[14]:= Show[SmoothGraphics[cont, 3]]
```

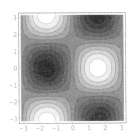

The result of SmoothGraphics applied to a ContourGraphics object is a new ContourGraphics object with more grid points.

```
In[15]:= Head[%]
Out[15]= ContourGraphics
```

SmoothGraphics has tripled the number of grid points in both the x and y directions.

```
In[16]:= Dimensions[First[%%]]
Out[16]= {45, 45}
```

The same function can be applied to surface and density plots. This is an unsmoothed SurfaceGraphics object.

```
In[17]:= Plot3D[Sin[x y], {x,-Pi,Pi}, {y,-Pi,Pi}]
```

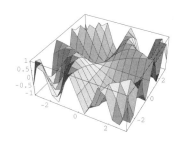

Again a smoother picture is produced. $In[18]:=$ **Show[SmoothGraphics[%, 3]]**

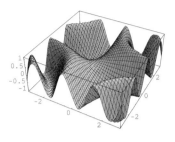

▷ *Explanation of the Solution*

```
SmoothGraphics[
   head_[data_, opts___] /;  MemberQ[
                    {
                    ContourGraphics,
                    SurfaceGraphics,
                    DensityGraphics
                    }, head], smooth_Integer?Positive] :=
   Module[{mesh, xn, yn, x0, x1, y0, y1, ndata},
       mesh = MeshRange /. Flatten[{opts}] /. Options[head] ;
       {xn, yn} = N[Dimensions[data]] ;
       {{x0, x1}, {y0, y1}} =
               If[mesh === Automatic, {{1,xn}, {1, yn}}, mesh] ;
       ndata = Table[
                    {
                    x0 + (i-1) (x1 - x0)/(xn - 1),
                    y0 + (j-1) (y1 - y0)/(yn - 1),
                    Part[data, i, j]
                    }, {i, xn}, {j,yn}] ;
       ndata = Interpolation[Flatten[ndata, 1]] ;
       ndata = Table[
                    ndata[x, y],
                    { x, x0, x1, (x1 - x0)/(xn smooth -1)},
                    { y, y0, y1, (y1 - y0)/(yn smooth -1)}] ;
       head[ndata, opts]
       ]
```

User Interface

There is no obvious solution such as existed in the previous example. One good solution would be to add a new option to Plot3D, ContourPlot, and related commands. Another is to provide a new function. Adding a new option requires attaching rules to a number of internal functions so is more complex and it still requires a function to do the smoothing. The example on changing the PlotLabel command later in this chapter page 267 gives some idea of how to add rules to existing functions. Here the example will demonstrate a new function, SmoothGraphics.

Implementation

```
SmoothGraphics[
   head_[data_, opts___] /;  MemberQ[
                 {
                 ContourGraphics,
                 SurfaceGraphics,
                 DensityGraphics
                 }, head], smooth_Integer?Positive] :=
```

This is the declaration of the function SmoothGraphics. The first argument is a conditional pattern with a test on a pattern head_[data_, opts___]. This pattern will match any expression that has a first argument, to be called data, and zero or more subsequent arguments, to be called opts. The first argument will represent the data and the second options. The test of the conditional pattern will only return True when head is SurfaceGraphics, ContourGraphics, or DensityGraphics. The conditional pattern will only match when its test returns True and hence the entire pattern will only match one of these heads.

The second argument, smooth_Integer?Positive, will match any positive integer.

```
   Module[{mesh, xn, yn, x0, x1, y0, y1, ndata},
```

This declares a Module with a number of local variables.

```
      mesh = MeshRange /. Flatten[{opts}] /. Options[head] ;
```

In this line the setting of the MeshRange option is saved in the local variable mesh. This is necessary so that the *x* and *y* ranges can be set properly. The options, represented here by the sequence opts, are applied before the default options of head, which are generated by Options[head].

```
      {xn, yn} = N[Dimensions[data]] ;
```

This determines the dimensionality of the data to be interpolated. It converts the pair of integers, returned by Dimensions, into real numbers and saves them in local variables, xn and yn.

Here is an assignment with a list on the left-hand and right-hand sides. The assignment is made for each component of the lists.

In[19]:= **{point1, point2} = {1,2}**

Out[19]= {1, 2}

The symbol point1 has been given the value specified in the previous input.

In[20]:= **point1**

Out[20]= 1

```
      {{x0, x1}, {y0, y1}} =
               If[mesh === Automatic, {{1,xn}, {1, yn}}, mesh] ;
```

This command extracts the values of minumum and maximum x and y values and saves them in local variables. It checks the `mesh` local variable to see if the value is `Automatic`. This is the default value for list plotting commands such as `ListContourPlot`.

```
ndata = Table[
           {
             x0 + (i-1) (x1 - x0)/(xn - 1),
             y0 + (j-1) (y1 - y0)/(yn - 1),
             Part[data, i, j]
           }, {i, xn}, {j,yn}] ;
```

Here a list is built that contains the x, y, and z data points. x starts at x0 and increments by `(x1 - x0)/(xn - 1)` to result in xn equally spaced points between x0 and x1. An equivalent iteration applies to the y values. The relevant z point is extracted from `data`. The result is saved in the local variable `ndata`.

```
ndata = Interpolation[Flatten[ndata, 1]] ;
```

This line actually does the interpolation. First the data are flattened by one level to the form $\{\{x_1,y_1,z_1\},\dots\}$ which is suitable for the `Interpolation` function. This flattening is necessary because `ndata` was generated by a `Table` command of two iterators.

A data set to be used as an example is constructed.

```
In[21]:= data = Table[i^2, {i,5}]
Out[21]= {1, 4, 9, 16, 25}
```

Now an interpolation function is built. The data to be interpolated had the form $\{y_1,y_2,\dots\}$. The x points were inferred to be $1,2,\dots$ respectively.

```
In[22]:= ifun = Interpolation[data]
Out[22]= InterpolatingFunction[{1, 5}, <>]
```

The `InterpolationFunction` works as a function. This one takes a single argument and returns an interpolation of the original data.

```
In[23]:= ifun[3.1]
Out[23]= 9.61
```

The interpolation function will work as a function in any of the *Mathematica* commands that require numeric input.

```
In[24]:= Plot[ifun[x], {x,1,5}]
```

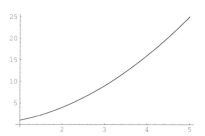

This is the original data that were used to generate the InterpolationFunction.

$In[25]:=$ **ListPlot[data]**

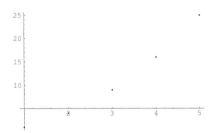

This is a higher dimensional set of data.

$In[26]:=$ **data = Flatten[Table[{x, y, x y}, {x,5}, {y,5}], 1];**

Interpolation is called in exactly the same way.

$In[27]:=$ **ifun = Interpolation[data]**

$Out[27]=$ InterpolatingFunction[{{1, 5}, {1, 5}}, <>]

This InterpolationFunction was derived from data with two independent variables and it must be given *two* arguments for it to evaluate.

$In[28]:=$ **ifun[1.5, 4.2]**

$Out[28]=$ 6.3

```
ndata = Table[
            ndata[x, y],
            { x, x0, x1, (x1 - x0)/(xn smooth -1)},
            { y, y0, y1, (y1 - y0)/(yn smooth -1)}] ;
```

Now the InterpolationFunction can be used to generate a new set of data. This has respectively {xn smooth, yn smooth} points in the *x* and *y* directions. The result is saved by the variable ndata.

```
head[ndata, opts]
```

The final step constructs the result with the original head and options, but with data points built from ndata instead of data. This example works because the data in the graphics objects are arranged in a regular grid. Interpolation can only interpolate data that are arranged in this fashion. The interpolation of irregular data is discussed in Chapter 16 page 404.

13.3 Constraining Contour Plots

Mathematica provides the contour plot function that will plot the loci of points {x, y} that solve equations of the form f[x, y] == a. These solutions are plotted for all values of *x* and *y* within a given range. Sometimes, however, it is interesting to see only that part of the solution that obeys some constraint on *x* and *y*.

▶ *Solution to the Problem*

This problem is solved by a new function `ConstrainedContourPlot`. This will be a new function but it will be made to look as much like `ContourPlot` as possible.

> `ConstrainedContourPlot[`*fun*, *cons*, `{`*x*, x_1, x_2`}`, `{`*y*, y_1, y_2`}]`
>
> make the contour plot of *fun* over the range,
> `{`*x*, x_1, x_2`}`,`{`*y*, y_1, y_2`}` subject to the constraint *cons*

Function defined in the package `ExtendGraphics`ConstrainedContour``.

This will load the package.

`In[29]:= Needs["ExtendGraphics`ConstrainedContour`"]`

Here the usage message is displayed.

`In[30]:= ?ConstrainedContourPlot`

ConstrainedContourPlot[f, c, x-rng, y-rng] plots contours of f
    over x-rng and y-rng subject to the constraint c.

Here the contour plot of `Sin[x^2 + y]` is constructed but only those parts that are inside the ellipse `x^2 + 3 y^2 == 1.6` are drawn.

`In[31]:= ConstrainedContourPlot[`
          `Sin[x^2 + y], x^2 + 3 y^2 < 1.6,`
          `{x, -1.5, 1.5}, {y,-1.5, 1.5}]`

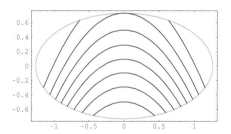

The plot here shows lines which are below the parabola y = x^2 − 1.1.

`In[32]:= ConstrainedContourPlot[Abs[x y], y < x^2 - 1.1,`
          `{x, -1.5, 1.5}, {y,-1.5, 1.5}]`

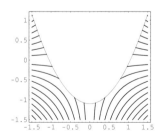

In this picture, with the same function as the previous one, the parts above the parabola are visible.

$In[33]:=$ **ConstrainedContourPlot[Abs[x y], y > x^2 - 1.1,**
{x, -1.5, 1.5}, {y,-1.5, 1.5}]

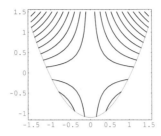

When they are combined the individual parts line up.

$In[34]:=$ **Show[%, %%]**

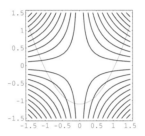

▶ *Explanation of the Solution*

The package that provides the solution for this is quite large and only part of it will be examined. The first part of the package is quite obvious, the contour plot is made and converted into a `Graphics` object that consists of a set of line objects. The crucial part of the package is carried out when the constraint is applied to show only those parts of the lines that meet the constraint. This is done with the function `ApplyConstraint`.

```
ApplyConstraint[pts_, f_, c_, x_, y_] :=
   Module[{res, len},
      res = Map[((c /. {x -> #[[1]], y -> #[[2]]}) > 0.0)&, pts] ;
      len = Length[pts] ;
      res =
         Table[
            If[
               res[[i]],
               {pts[[i]]},
               {
               If[
                  (i =!= 1    && res[[i-1]]),
                  GetRoot[f, c, x, y, pts[[i]], pts[[i-1]]], False],
               If[
                  (i =!= len    && res[[i+1]]),
```

```
                    GetRoot[f, c, x, y, pts[[i]], pts[[i+1]]], False]
                }],
                {i,len}] ;
    res = Flatten[res, 1] ;
    res =
        Which[
            FreeQ[res, False], {res},
            Union[res] === {False}, {},
            True,
                res = res //. {a___, False, False, b___} -> {a, False, b} ;
                res = Fold[
                        If[#2 === False,
                                Append[#1, {}],
                                Insert[#1, #2, {-1,-1}]]&,{{}}, res] ;
                        res = DeleteCases[res, {}]];
        Map[Line, res]
        ]
```

ApplyConstraint accepts five arguments. The first is a list of points, pts_. These are from the line primitives that must be clipped. f_ is the function that corresponds to these points. This will be written so that for every point in the line f will equal zero. c_ represents the constraint that must be met; this will be written so that only points for which c is greater than zero should be returned. Finally x_ and y_ are the variables in which the functions are defined.

```
    res = Map[((c /. {x -> #[[1]], y -> #[[2]]}) > 0.0)&, pts] ;
```

Here it is determined whether the points meet the constraint, in which case True is inserted into the list res, or if they do not, in which case False is inserted. At the end of this command the variable res points to a list of True or False.

Of course it would be possible to use this test to select appropriate points and simply return them. This would not be satisfactory since it would not show any intersections of the contour line with the constraint line. The remaining parts of the code are concerned with finding such intersections.

```
    len = Length[pts] ;
    res =
        Table[
            If[
              res[[i]],
                {pts[[i]]},
                {
                If[
                (i =!= 1    && res[[i-1]]),
                    GetRoot[f, c, x, y, pts[[i]], pts[[i-1]]], False],
                If[
                (i =!= len    && res[[i+1]]),
                    GetRoot[f, c, x, y, pts[[i]], pts[[i+1]]], False]
                }],
                {i,len}] ;
```

In these commands a list is generated by looking at the list `res`. If the ith element is `True` then the ith element of `pts` is put into the solution. If the ith element is `False` and either the previous or the next elements are `True` then an intersection is taking place. In this case the function `GetRoot` is called to determine the exact point of intersection. If none of these criteria is fullfilled the point cannot contribute to the solution and `False` will be inserted in the solution.

This result uses the command `Table` to travel down and examine every element of a list. Normally `Map` is a more compact way to do this. In this instance `Table` must be used since each element and its neighbors may be looked at.

The function `GetRoot`, defined in the package, proceeds to use `f`, the constraint `c`, the names of the variables `x` and `y`, and the two points that straddle the intersection. It then uses the `FindRoot` internal function to find the points that satisfy both `f` and `c`. This is the point of intersection. `FindRoot` can use the points that straddle this intersection as starting values and in most cases will converge rapidly on the solution.

```
res = Flatten[res, 1] ;
res =
    Which[
        FreeQ[res, False], {res},
        Union[res] === {False}, {},
```

After the solution list is flattened it will consist either of points or `False`. This must be processed to construct line primitives from these points. These evaluations deal with the two extreme cases. If there is no `False` present the list consists of points to be returned. If the list consists only of `False` there are no points to be returned.

```
    res = res //. {a___, False, False, b___} -> {a, False, b} ;
    res = Fold[
        If[#2 === False,
            Append[#1, {}],
            Insert[#1, #2, {-1,-1}]]&,{{}}, res] ;
    res = DeleteCases[res, {}]];
```

These steps break up the list of points and `False` into sub-lists of points.

This is a possible set of points.	`In[35]:= res = {p1, p2, p3, False, False, p4, p5, False}`
	
	`Out[35]= {p1, p2, p3, False, False, p4, p5, False}`

This step applies a rule to remove consecutive instances of False. The rule must be applied repeatedly until no more pairs are found.	`In[36]:= res =`
	`          res //. {a___, False, False, b___} -> {a, False, b}`
	
	`Out[36]= {p1, p2, p3, False, p4, p5, False}`

Now Fold visits each element of res applying a function while building up the result. If the function encounters False a new sub-list is started. If not the point is inserted at the end of the last sub-list.

```
In[37]:= res = Fold[
                If[#2 === False,
                    Append[#1, {}],
                    Insert[#1, #2, {-1,-1}]]&,{{}}, res]
Out[37]= {{p1, p2, p3}, {p4, p5}, {}}
```

Finally any empty lists are eliminated.

```
In[38]:= res = DeleteCases[res, {}]
Out[38]= {{p1, p2, p3}, {p4, p5}}
```

```
Map[Line, res]
```

The last line of ApplyConstraint takes a list of the lists of points from which line segments are to be constructed. It places Line around each and returns the result.

This makes the list of line segments that are to be returned.

```
In[39]:= Map[Line, res]
Out[39]= {Line[{p1, p2, p3}], Line[{p4, p5}]}
```

13.4 Choosing Tick Mark Positions

Mathematica provides a variety of different styles of axes. These can only provide some of the many styles that may be desired. A basic ingredient for drawing axes is choosing sensible positions for the tick marks. This example shows how this may be done.

▶ *Solution of the Problem*

A completely new function TickPosition is provided.

TickPosition[x_{lower}, x_{upper}, *num*]	return a list of "nice" positions between x_{lower} and x_{upper}

Function defined in the package ExtendGraphics`Ticks`.

This will load the axes package.

```
In[40]:= Needs["ExtendGraphics`Ticks`"]
```

This shows the usage message for the function TickPosition.

```
In[41]:= ?TickPosition
TickPosition[ min, max, num] returns a list of at most num
    nicely rounded positions between min and max.  These can be
    used for tick mark positions.
```

These are the positions for at most 8 tick marks between -24.4 and 100.5. This would be suitable for major tick marks.

```
In[42]:= TickPosition[-24.4, 100.5, 8]
Out[42]= {-20., 0, 20., 40., 60., 80., 100.}
```

These are the positions for at most 40 tick marks between -24.4 and 100.5. This would be suitable for minor tick marks.

```
In[43]:= TickPosition[-24.4, 100.5, 40]
Out[43]= {-20., -15., -10., -5., 0, 5., 10., 15., 20., 25.,
       30., 35., 40., 45., 50., 55., 60., 65., 70., 75., 80., 85.,
       90., 95., 100.}
```

The tick marks on this plot use the default internal algorithm to select their position.

```
In[44]:= Plot[x^4-x^3, {x,-2,2}]
```

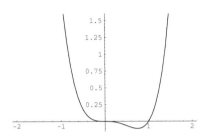

Now the picture is redisplayed with the TickPosition function choosing at most 10 tick marks. Since no instructions are given to draw the minor tick marks they are not drawn.

```
In[45]:= Show[%,
         Ticks ->
           {
           TickPosition[#1, #2, 10]&,
           TickPosition[#1, #2, 10]&
           }]
```

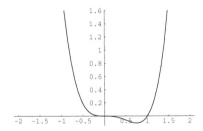

▶ *Explanation of the Solution*

```
TickPosition[x0_Real, x1_Real, num_Integer?Positive] :=
  Module[{ dist, scale, min, max, i, delta, space},
      space = {1., 2., 2.5, 5., 10.} ;
      dist = (x1 - x0)/(num - 1) ;
      scale = 10.^Floor[Log[10, dist]] ;
      dist = dist / scale ;
      If[dist < 1., dist *= 10.; scale /= 10.] ;
      If[dist >= 10., dist /= 10.; scale *= 10.] ;
      delta = First[Select[space, (# >= dist)&]] scale;
      min = Ceiling[x0/delta]*delta ;
```

```
Table[Floor[x/delta + 0.5]*delta, {x, min, x1, delta}]
]
```

User Interface

This is completely new functionality and therefore a new function is required. The name `TickPosition` is a good description of the functionality that is provided. The arguments must include the minimum and maximum values of the range and the desired number of tick marks. It *could* take the possible spacings between tick marks as an argument. However, it is not expected that these should change from one invocation to another and they are held as local data.

Implementation

```
TickPosition[x0_Real, x1_Real, num_Integer?Positive] :=
    Module[{ dist, scale, min, max, i, delta, space},
    space = {1., 2., 2.5, 5., 10.} ;
```

`TickPosition` takes three arguments: `x0` and `x1` represent the minimum and maximum positions while `num` represents the maximum number of tick marks. The positions must be real numbers and the number of tick marks must be a positive integer.

The code is contained in a `Module` with a number of local variables. The `space` local variable holds the desired spacings between the tick marks. It would be possible to have this data as a local variable in the whole package and only have its value set once. This would be more efficient but in practice it would not make any difference to the actual time for execution of the function. It is neater simply to tuck it away in the body of the function.

```
dist = (x1 - x0)/(num - 1) ;
scale = 10.^Floor[Log[10, dist]] ;
dist = dist / scale ;
If[dist < 1., dist *= 10.; scale /= 10.] ;
If[dist >= 10., dist /= 10.; scale *= 10.] ;
```

These steps determine the distance between consecutive tick positions to achieve the stated number of tick marks. The actual distance may be more than this but it won't be less. This distance is held as two numbers, `dist` and `scale`, such that the true distance is `dist * scale`. Such a decomposition is necessary so that comparison can be made with the ideal spacings.

```
delta = First[Select[space, (# >= dist)&]] scale;
```

Here the actual distance between tick marks is computed. Each element of the `space` list is compared with the ideal distance, `dist`. The first element of `space` that is greater or equal to `dist` will be used. This is multiplied by `scale` to generate a number of the correct magnitude.

```
min = Ceiling[x0/delta]*delta ;
Table[Floor[x/delta + 0.5]*delta, {x, min, x1, delta}]
```

In these steps the actual positions are chosen. The minimum position is first chosen by rounding up, then the positions are calculated by incrementing from the minimum. Further rounding is done to ensure that the increment process itself does not introduce any extra digits. The list of these positions is returned as the result.

13.5 Setting the Style of Tick Marks

Mathematica provides an internal algorithm to draw axes on its plots. While it is clearly useful to have a default setting that is simple, sometimes it is desirable to change these settings. This example shows how the style of tick marks can be altered.

These axes are drawn with the default style.

$In[46]:=$ **Plot[Cos[x] Sin[x]^2, {x,0,2Pi}]**

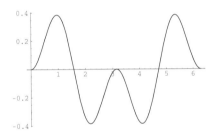

It would be useful to be able to control the style of the tick marks on this picture. For example, suppose the minor tick marks, the ones without labels, are not necessary. Alternatively, it may be that the weight of the lines should be changed.

▶ *Solution to the Problem*

The solution demonstrated here is to provide a function `TickFunction` that can be used with the `Ticks` and `FrameTicks` options.

| `TickFunction[`x_{min}`, `x_{max}`, opts]` | return a list of ticks suitable for the `Ticks` or `FrameTicks` options |

Function defined in the package `ExtendGraphics`'`Ticks`'.

MajorLength	length of major tick marks
MinorLength	length of minor tick marks
MajorStyle	style of major tick marks
MinorStyle	style of minor tick marks
TextFunction	function to calculate the text label for major tick marks

Options of `TickFunction`.

This loads the package.

```
In[47]:= Needs["ExtendGraphics`Ticks`"]
```

The default settings of `TickFunction` are close to the internal methods.

```
In[48]:= Plot[Cos[x] Sin[x]^2, {x,0,2Pi},
              Ticks -> {TickFunction, TickFunction}]
```

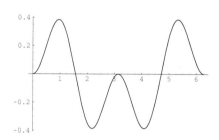

An option of `TickFunction` is set and this is done by constructing a pure function. This example suppresses the *x* axis minor tick marks by drawing them with zero length.

```
In[49]:= Plot[Sin[x], {x,0,2Pi},
              Ticks -> {
                  TickFunction[#1, #2,
                      MinorLength -> {0,0}]&,
                  TickFunction}]
```

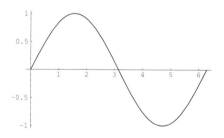

SetOptions can be used for
TickFunction.

```
In[50]:= SetOptions[
               TickFunction,
                       MajorLength -> {0.00625, 0.00625},
                       MinorLength -> {0,0}]
Out[50]= {MajorLength -> {0.00625, 0.00625},
   MinorLength -> {0, 0}, MajorStyle -> {Thickness[0.002]},
   MinorStyle -> {Thickness[0.001]}, TextFunction -> Automatic,
   TickLabels -> Automatic, TickNumbers -> {8, 32}}
```

This omits the minor tick marks and sets
the major tick marks to straddle the axis.
This is the style that was used for tick
marks in *Mathematica* before Version 2.0.

```
In[51]:= Plot[Sin[x], {x,0,2Pi},
                Ticks -> {
                        TickFunction,
                        TickFunction
                        }]
```

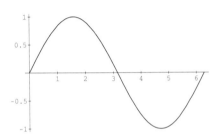

▶ *Explanation of the Solution*

```
Options[TickFunction] =
        {
        MajorLength -> {0.00625, 0},
        MinorLength -> {0.003125, 0},
        MajorStyle -> {Thickness[0.002]},
        MinorStyle -> {Thickness[0.001]},
        TextFunction -> Identity
        }

TickFunction[x0_, x1_, opts___] :=
   Module[{maj, min, majlen, minlen, majstyle, minstyle, textfun},
        majlen = MajorLength /. {opts} /. Options[TickFunction] ;
        minlen = MinorLength /. {opts} /. Options[TickFunction] ;
        majstyle = MajorStyle /. {opts} /. Options[TickFunction] ;
        mainstyle = MinorStyle /. {opts} /. Options[TickFunction] ;
        textfun = TextFunction /. {opts} /. Options[TickFunction] ;
        maj = TickPosition[x0, x1, 8] ;
        min = TickPosition[x0, x1, 40] ;
        min = Complement[min, maj] ;
        maj = Transpose[{maj, Map[textfun, maj]}] ;
        maj = Map[{#[[1]], #[[2]], majlen, majstyle}&, maj] ;
```

```
If[Apply[Plus, minlen] =!= 0,
    min = Map[{#, "", minlen, minstyle}&, min] ;
    maj = Join[maj, min]] ;
maj
]
```

User Interface

The method of controlling tick marks presented here works by setting a function as the value of the `Ticks` option. This function will receive the minimum and maximum values of the `PlotRange` as arguments and return a list {{x_1, *label$_1$*, {*plen*, *nlen*}, *style*}, ... }. In this result x_1 describes the position of the tick, *label$_1$* its text label, {*plen*, *nlen*} its lengths in the positive and negative directions, and *style* its style.

Of course, it is possible to draw axes and tick marks without using this built-in functionality, but to do so is quite complex. This solution extends the built-in functionality.

Implementation

```
Options[TickFunction] =
    {
    MajorLength -> {0.00625, 0},
    MinorLength -> {0.003125, 0},
    MajorStyle -> {Thickness[0.002]},
    MinorStyle -> {Thickness[0.001]},
    TextFunction -> Identity
    }
```

The function `TickFunction` is given five options and these are their default values.

```
TickFunction[x0_, x1_, opts___] :=
    Module[{maj, min, majlen, minlen, majstyle, minstyle, textfun},
```

The definition of `TickFunction` is given. It will take the minimum and maximum values of the `PlotRange` in addition to any options. A `Module` is set up with local variables to hold the major and minor tick marks and the values of the various options.

```
    majlen = MajorLength /. {opts} /. Options[TickFunction] ;
    minlen = MinorLength /. {opts} /. Options[TickFunction] ;
    majstyle = MajorStyle /. {opts} /. Options[TickFunction] ;
    minstyle = MinorStyle /. {opts} /. Options[TickFunction] ;
    textfun = TextFunction /. {opts} /. Options[TickFunction] ;
```

These evaluations will extract the option settings.

```
maj = TickPosition[x0, x1, 8] ;
min = TickPosition[x0, x1, 40] ;
min = Complement[min, maj] ;
```

The function `TickPosition` is used to return the major and minor tick mark positions. Any elements of the list of minor tick marks that are also present in the major tick marks are removed.

```
maj = Transpose[{maj, textfun[maj]}] ;
maj = Map[{#[[1]], #[[2]], majlen, majstyle}&, maj] ;
```

The `TextFunction` is applied to the list of positions of the major tick marks. It is applied to the *whole* list since the label in one position may depend upon the label in another. The length and style fields are then filled in.

```
If[Apply[Plus, minlen] =!= 0,
    min = Map[{#, "", minlen, minstyle}&, min] ;
    maj = Join[maj, min]] ;
maj
```

The length of the minor tick marks is tested and if non-zero a minor tick mark list is generated. This is joined to the major list and the result returned.

13.6 Adding Labels to a Plot

There are many options that draw labels on two-dimensional graphics. These include `PlotLabel`, `AxesLabel`, and `FrameLabel`. However, these labeling options all have specified positions for their labels. This example shows how the position of these labels can be altered. This is done by extending one of the existing options of a graphics object by attaching rules to describe how the object should be displayed. The new behavior will be generated by using a `Rectangle` primitive to combine different graphics objects. This solution requires detailed knowledge of the internals of graphics.

▶ *Solution to the Problem*

The solution to this problem is to add new functionality to the `PlotLabel` option. Code to implement this is in the package `ExtendGraphics`Label``.

```
Show[g, PlotLabel -> Text[label, pos]]
                              display g with text label at pos
```

Functionality defined in the package `ExtendGraphics`Label``.

This loads the package.

In[52]:= `Needs["ExtendGraphics`Label`"]`

The plot is shown here with three labels. Each label is a text primitive specifying its position in the plot.

In[53]:= `Plot[Sin[x], {x,0,2Pi},`
        `PlotLabel ->`
            `{Text["Left Label", Scaled[{0.0, 0.5}], {1,0},`
    `{0,1}],`
                `Text["X-axis Label", {6.5,0.0 }, {-1, 0}],`
                `Text["Corner Label", {6.5,1}, {-1,-1}]}]`

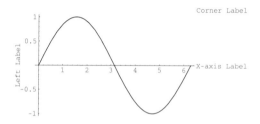

This shows labels as embellishments on frame axes.

In[54]:= `Show[%,`
        `Frame -> True,`
        `PlotLabel ->`
            `{Text["Main Label", Scaled[{0.5, 1.0}], {0, -1}],`
                `Text["Bottom Label", Scaled[{0.5, 0.0}], {0, 1}],`
                `Text["Left Label", Scaled[{0.0, 0.5}], {1, 0},`
    `{0,1}]}]`

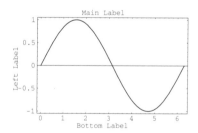

▶ *Explanation of the Solution*

The explanation of the workings of the code in ExtendGraphics will not look at every part in detail. It will only look at the parts that attach new behavior to a graphics option and carry out scaling calculations.

```
Unprotect[Graphics];

Graphics /:
Display[
    stm_,
    obj:Graphics[g_, opts___] /; LabelTest[Graphics, Flatten[{opts}]]] :=
    (
    Display[stm, InsertLabel[obj]];
        obj
    );
```

These statements are concerned with detecting the presence of the special setting for the PlotLabel option when a Graphics object is displayed by Display. Display is the command that generates PostScript and is used by the DisplayFunction option as described in Chapter 26 page 668. The special setting for PlotLabel is detected by putting a rule on Graphics that matches Display[*stream*, Graphics[*objects*]] when a test function, LabelTest, returns True. The function LabelTest will be called when a Graphics object with the new version of PlotLabel is actually displayed with a call to Show[18].

The rule is attached to Graphics by using /:. This is the shorthand notation for TagSet, which attaches a rule to a specific symbol rather than to the head of the expression, in this case Display. Since the symbol to which the rule is attached is an argument to the main expression the rule is called upcode. TagSet and upcode are both described in detail in the main *Mathematica* book.

Any expression with head of Display and a Graphics object for a second argument is a potential match for this pattern. When such an expression is encountered the pattern matcher will call the function LabelTest and if this returns True the pattern matches. In this case the function InsertLabel will be called and the result of this passed to Display. It is necessary for InsertLabel to disable the features that caused the rule to apply in the first place. If this were not the case infinite recursion would result. Upon completion the original and not the modified Graphics object is returned as the result. This is done quite deliberately to allow the PlotLabel option to be changed by a call to Show in the normal way.

```
LabelTest[head_, opts_] :=
        !FreeQ[PlotLabel /. opts /. Options[head], Text];
```

LabelTest will return True if the PlotLabel option has a value that contains the symbol Text. If it does not the function will return False and PlotLabel will work in the original way. There will be a problem if the label actually contains the symbol Text with the old mechanism. This is considered to be an acceptable limitation, since the symbol could be made into a string expression.

---

[18] As explained in Chapter 26 page 666, Show calls the DisplayFunction option. If this is set to render the picture into PostScript it will use Display and this code will be used.

```
InsertLabel[Graphics[g_, opts___]] :=
   Module[{newp, x1, x2, y1, y2, asp, labs},
      newp = Show[Graphics[g, opts],
               PlotLabel -> None,
                  DisplayFunction -> Identity] ;
      {{x1, x2}, {y1, y2}} =
            FullOptions[newp, PlotRange] ;
      asp = FullOptions[newp, AspectRatio] ;
      labs = PlotLabel /. Flatten[{opts}] /. Options[Graphics] ;
      labs = labs /.
               Scaled[{x_, y_}] :> {x (x2-x1) + x1, y (y2-y1) + y1} ;
      Graphics[
            {
            Rectangle[{x1,y1}, {x2, y2}, newp],
            labs
            },
            PlotRange -> All,
            AspectRatio -> asp]
      ]
```

InsertLabel will match g with the primitives of the Graphics object and opts to the sequence of options. It will return a modified Graphics object with the labels in place and the necessary scaling established. This is done by generating the Graphics object to be displayed with a call to Show at the same time clearing the PlotLabel function and setting the DisplayFunction not to actually display any pictures. The result is stored by the symbol newp.

The next step is to calculate the actual PlotRange and AspectRatio of the Graphics object with suitable calls to FullOptions. These are used to calculate the actual text primitives that will hold the labels. When the actual PlotRange is known the Scaled coordinates can be replaced with real coordinates by the mapping:

$$x = x_{scaled} \left(x_{max} - x_{min} \right) + x_{min}$$
$$y = y_{scaled} \left(y_{max} - y_{min} \right) + y_{min}$$

The last step is to construct the final Graphics object. The option AspectRatio is set to maintain the AspectRatio of the picture to which labels are being added. This is necessary to maintain the proper scaling of the labels which are being added. The option PlotRange is given the setting All. This makes sure that the text labels are accounted for in the scaling calculations as was described in Chapter 10 page 174. The graphics object contains two arguments, a Rectangle primitive containing the original graphics object and the text primitives that made up the PlotLabel. The Rectangle is given coordinates calculated from the PlotRange of the graphics object. This example shows how the Rectangle primitive can be used to mix different graphics objects with different scalings.

In fact the package does not work perfectly. This is because the picture placed inside the Rectangle primitive does not quite match the coordinates of the Rectangle primitive as demonstrated in the following example.

The "Corner Label" matches its coordinates, but the "Left Label" does not.

```
In[55]:= Plot[Sin[x], {x,0,2Pi},
            PlotLabel ->
               {Text["Left Label", {0,0}, {1,0}],
                Text["Corner Label", {6.5,1}, {-1,-1}]}]
```

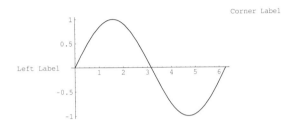

In the picture one of the labels fits its coordinates well but the other does not appear to be at its coordinates. The reason for this is that the picture in the Rectangle shrinks back from the boundary of the Rectangle to leave space for the tick mark labels. This problem would be solved if the tick marks were placed manually by the InsertLabel function. Despite this limitation the package is still useful; when Scaled coordinates are used it is quite exact about the placement of labels.

13.7 Defining a New Graphics Object

The simplest way to write a new graphics function is to have the function return some existing graphics object such as a Graphics or a Graphics3D object. Many of the graphics functions in the standard packages are written in this way. An alternative is to define a new graphics object. This is more complicated but presents many advantages. One major advantage is that Show can handle objects with special options or options that must be treated in special ways. For example, the object may use unusual scaling and a call to change PlotRange must be treated in a non-standard way. If a new graphics object was not used the only way such a special option could be changed would be to re-create the entire object.

An example of the definition of a new graphics object will be given for functions to plot ternary component mixtures. A ternary mixture can be plotted with three coordinates that are constrained to sum to 1. Since the coordinates are constrained a plot can be made with a two-dimensional picture rather than a three-dimensional picture. The standard form is a two-dimensional triangular picture.

ComponentGraphics	object representing a ternary component plot
ComponentListPlot	plot the list of ternary component points

Functionality defined in the package ExtendGraphics`ComponentPlot`.

The package is loaded.

```
In[56]:= Needs["ExtendGraphics`ComponentPlot`"]
```

ComponentListPlot will plot a list of ternary components.

In[57]:= **?ComponentListPlot**

ComponentListPlot[data] plots a three-dimensional data set in a ternary component plot.

ComponentListPlot takes a list of three-dimensional points.

In[58]:= **ComponentListPlot[**
    {{0.15,0.24,0.61},
     {0.3, 0.6, 0.1},
     {0.45, 0.15, 0.4}}]

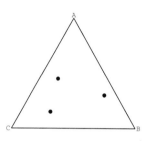

A grid can be added to the picture which can help identify points.

In[59]:= **p = Show[%, Grid -> Automatic]**

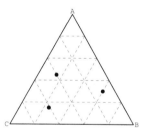

The Head of the result is a ComponentGraphics object. This is why Show is able to change the Grid option.

In[60]:= **Head[p]**

Out[60]= ComponentGraphics

The points must each lie between 0 and 1 and all add up to 1. When they don't an error is generated.

```
In[61]:= ComponentListPlot[{{2, 2, 2}}]
```

```
ComponentGraphics::baddata:
    The data point 2, 2, 2
        does not consist of three components which sum to 1 and
        each lie between 0 and 1 inclusive.
```

These are some points that will be used to add some extra embellishments to the picture.

```
In[62]:= (m = {0.6,0.23,0.17};
         a = {0,0.53,0.47};
         b = {0.715,0,0.285};
         c = {0.685,0.315,0};)
```

Here some extra primitives are added to the picture. The options like `Epilog` can be used to add more primitives in this way.

```
In[63]:= Show[p, Epilog -> {Text[M, m, {0,-2.5}], Point[m],
             Map[Point, {a,b,c}],
             Text[Xa, (m+a)/2.,{1.5,0}],
             Text[Xb, (m+b)/2.,{1,2}],
             Text[Xc, (m+c)/2.,{-1,2}],
             Thickness[0.001],
             Map[Line[{m,#}]&, {a,b,c}]}]
```

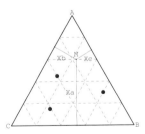

▸ *Explanation of the Solution*

The package will not be examined in detail; only those parts that add the new graphics object will be described. This can be divided into two steps; converting a `ComponentGraphics` object into ordinary primitives, and making this conversion work when `Show` and `Display` of `ComponentGraphics` are invoked.

```
ComponentGraphics /:
Show[ComponentGraphics[p_, opts___], nopts___] :=
    (Show[Graphics[ComponentGraphics[p, nopts, opts]]];
     ComponentGraphics[p, nopts, opts])

ComponentGraphics /:
Display[stm_, c:ComponentGraphics[stuff___]] :=
    (Display[stm, Graphics[c]]; c)
```

Here rules that describe how Show and Display should behave are given. The rules are actually attached to ComponentGraphics as upcode thereby making sure that there is no impact on the efficiency for other plots. Upcode was also used in the last example and is described in detail in the main *Mathematica* book. The two rules each convert ComponentGraphics to Graphics and the result of this is used in Show or Display. However, it is a ComponentGraphics object that is returned as the result.

It is necessary to attach rules to Show as well as Display because this is an entirely new object. If new functionality is added to an option of Graphics it is only necessary to change the behavior of Display, as in the previous example, since Show already knows about Graphics objects. In this example, Show does not know about ComponentGraphics and a rule must be added.

```
ComponentGraphics /:
Graphics[ComponentGraphics[prims_, opts___]] :=
    Module[{ndata, axes, grid, gstyle,
            axstyle, opt, nprims, prol,epil},
        opt = Join[Flatten[{opts}], Options[ComponentGraphics]] ;
        axstyle = AxesStyle /. opt ;
        grid    = Grid /. opt ;
        gstyle  = GridStyle /. opt ;
        prol    = BuildPrimitives[Prolog /. opt] ;
        epil    = BuildPrimitives[Epilog /. opt] ;
        nprims  = BuildPrimitives[prims] ;
        axes = JoinStyle[axstyle, TriangularAxes[ ]] ;
        grid = If[grid === Automatic,
                    JoinStyle[gstyle, Map[Grid, Range[0.2,0.8,0.2]]], {}] ;
        Graphics[{axes, nprims, grid},
            Prolog -> prol, Epilog -> epil,
            FilterOptions[Graphics, Sequence @@ opt]]
    ]
```

This function specifies how ComponentGraphics are to be converted to Graphics objects. This could be done with a function with some special name. Instead it is preferable to do this by a rule involving Graphics. This makes it consistent with the way that the conversions, described in Chapter 12, work. Consistency permits ease of system extension.

The function works by doing the usual option processing to extract all the options that will work in a different way from Graphics. It then builds all primitives with a function BuildPrimitives. The next lines build axes and the grid. The final step is to build the resulting Graphics object. This is quite simple;

the converted primitives are collected together with options. `FilterOptions` is used to ensure that only options of `Graphics` are used.

```
BuildPrimitives[Point[pt_]] :=
    Point[ConvertCoordinates[pt]]

BuildPrimitives[obj_] :=
    obj
```

This is a sample of some of the rules for the `BuildPrimitives` function. It must be defined for all primitives and style directives. The first rule is for `Point` primitives; these have coordinates that must be converted from ternary form to two-dimensional form. This is done with the function `ConvertCoordinates`. When `BuildPrimitives` receives an expression for which it has no special rule then the expression is passed through unaltered. This is how style directives work.

```
ConvertCoordinates[{h_, k_, l_}] :=
    If[N[h+k+l] == 1. && SizeQ[h] && SizeQ[k] && SizeQ[l],
        {h/2 + k, h Tan[Pi/3]/2},
        Message[ComponentGraphics::baddata, {h,k,l}];
        {0,0}]
```

The `ConvertCoordinates` takes a list of three numbers that represents a ternary coordinate. The numbers must all sum to 1 and lie between 0 and 1. If this is so then the appropriate two-dimensional coordinates are generated. When illegal coordinates are encountered an error is issued and {0,0} (as good a result as any) is returned.

```
Format[ComponentGraphics[___]] = "-ComponentGraphics-"
```

This line sets up a `Format` rule to give the object a special print form that is typical of other graphics objects.

ComponentGraphics objects print out with the typical special format of graphics.

```
In[64]:= ComponentListPlot[{{0.15,0.24,0.61}},
                    DisplayFunction -> Identity]

Out[64]= -ComponentGraphics-
```

When the result is viewed in
InputForm the structure is exposed.

```
In[65]:= InputForm[%]

Out[65]//InputForm=
  ComponentGraphics[{AbsolutePointSize[3],
    {Point[{0.15, 0.24, 0.61}]}}, DisplayFunction -> Identity,
  AspectRatio -> Automatic, Axes -> False, AxesLabel -> None,
  AxesOrigin -> Automatic, AxesStyle -> {},
  Background -> Automatic, ColorOutput -> Automatic,
  DefaultColor -> Automatic, Epilog -> {}, Frame -> False,
  FrameLabel -> None, FrameStyle -> Automatic,
  FrameTicks -> Automatic, GridLines -> None,
  PlotLabel -> None, PlotRange -> All,
  PlotRegion -> Automatic, Prolog -> {}, RotateLabel -> True,
  Ticks -> Automatic, DefaultFont :> $DefaultFont,
  DisplayFunction :> $DisplayFunction, Grid -> False,
  GridStyle -> {AbsoluteThickness[0.1], AbsoluteDashing[{2}]}}]
```

13.8 Forming Contour Lines in Three Dimensions

A contour plot of some function $f[x, y]$ shows lines of equal value of the function in a two-dimensional plot. It is thus a useful way to show a three-dimensional object, a surface, by a two-dimensional picture. This removes any artifacts that arise from perspective. However, the contour lines carry different information from the surface plot and it would be interesting if the two pictures could be combined in some way. Chapter 12 page 242 presented an example of drawing a contour plot on the base of the bounding box. This example shows how to draw the contour lines as three-dimensional objects.

The function to be plotted is defined as a *Mathematica* function. This will be useful later on and will help to try this example with different functions.

```
In[66]:= fun[x_,y_] := x y
```

A contour plot of the function is made.

```
In[67]:= c = ContourPlot[fun[x, y], {x, -2,2},{y, -2,2},
              ContourShading -> False]
```

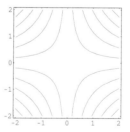

Here is the surface plot of the same function. It would be good to combine the surface and contour plot in the same picture.

```
In[68]:= s = Show[SurfaceGraphics[c]]
```

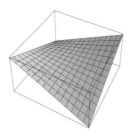

Now the contour plot is converted to a Graphics object. The lines are converted to three-dimensional lines by inserting the value of the function at that point.

```
In[69]:= c3d =
            First[Graphics[c]] /.
              Line[pts_] :>
                (val = Apply[fun,First[pts]];
                Line[Map[Append[#, val]&, pts]]) ;
```

The lines can be plotted as a Graphics3D object.

```
In[70]:= Show[Graphics3D[c3d]]
```

Using a call to Show will plot the surface and the lines together.

```
In[71]:= Show[s, %]
```

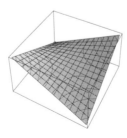

This technique can be made into a function and enhanced in a number of ways. One enhancement is to lift the lines slightly off the surface. This prevents problems when they pass behind the surface and are not visible. Another enhancement would be to use a different style for the contour lines thereby helping to distinguish them. A quite different way to make the same type of plot is to slice up the surface with horizontal planes. This is demonstrated in Chapter 17 page 444.

An alternative way to use a contour plot in three dimensions is to plot polygons formed by the contour lines. This can be done by choosing `ContourShading` to be `True` and then working with the polygons that this generates.

Now a different function will be plotted.

```
In[72]:= fun[x_,y_] := Abs[Sin[x] Sin[y]]
```

The contour plot can be generated.

```
In[73]:= c = ContourPlot[fun[x,y], {x, -2,2},{y, -2,2},
             PlotPoints -> 30]
```

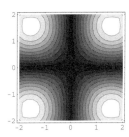

Now the `Polygon` primitives are converted to three dimensions and the `Line` primitives are thrown away.

```
In[74]:= c3d =
           First[Graphics[c]] /.
             {Polygon[pts_] :>
                (val = Apply[fun,First[pts]];
                 Polygon[Map[Append[#, val]&, pts]]),
              Line[_] -> {}} ;
```

The three-dimensional polygons are displayed. The large polygon that `ContourGraphics` puts out interferes with the picture. This polygon makes sure that every region of the contour plot is shaded.

```
In[75]:= Show[Graphics3D[c3d]]
```

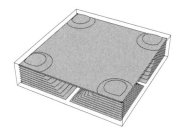

Now the main surface can be plotted. The `Drop` is necessary to remove the large region.

In[76]:= `Show[Graphics3D[Drop[c3d, 1]]]`

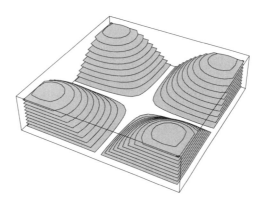

This picture has a powerful three-dimensional appearance. If a ball were released on some part of the surface it is quite obvious how it would move. One reason for the strong three-dimensional effect is that this is how a surface would probably look if an actual physical version were assembled in a workshop.

This example is based upon using the shading of `ContourGraphics`, as described in Chapter 23 page 633. The shading is made to produce good contour plots. It does this by first putting out one region to shade properly the entire picture. Subsequent regions are then put out and drawn on top. This is the region that caused the problems shown above since the boundary is not a contour but is there to make the shading look correct. It is easy to drop this region, but other problems may also be faced. The regions that are created may not be convex and may convert in a strange way in three dimensions. This problem can be solved with the triangulation techniques described in Chapter 17 page 446. A last problem is that when the function has a minimum near a corner `ContourGraphics` will build this as a solid region. This is perfectly acceptable for constructing contour plots but will create artifacts in a plot like this.

13.9 Using Three-Dimensional Symbols

Several packages contain functions that plot points in three-dimensional space. A basic example is the function `ScatterPlot3D` defined in the package `Graphics`Graphics3D``.

The package `Graphics`Graphics3D`` is loaded.

In[77]:= `Needs["Graphics`Graphics3D`"]`

In[78]:= `?ScatterPlot3D`

```
ScatterPlot3D[{{x1, y1, z1}, ...}, (options)] plots points in
    three  dimensions as a scatter plot.
```

A set of three-dimensional data is constructed.

In[79]:= `d = Table[{t, Sin[t], Cos[t]}, {t,0,4Pi,.25}];`

Now the data are plotted. In some ways ScatterPlot3D is the three-dimensional analog of ListPlot.

$In[80]:=$ **ScatterPlot3D[d]**

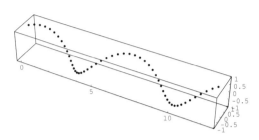

These points are shown with the three-dimensional primitive Point. They are not really three-dimensional objects but instead two-dimensional filled circles drawn at a particular location. This is an example of the compromise between three-dimensional realism and practicality that was described in Chapter 9 page 158. This example shows how it is possible to draw these points with three-dimensional primitives. One advantage of this is the fact that the graphics object may be exported to an alternative renderer that can only render points as single pixels. An example of this is the Live program distributed with *Mathematica* for the SGI and IBM RS6000 that uses the GL library. Another reason for this change is that using different objects to represent points will allow different sets of data to be distinguished.

▶ *Solution of the Problem*

Mathematica contains code to draw a number of three-dimensional shapes such as tetrahedra, cubes, and octahedra. The solution to the problem will work by replacing Point primitives with one of these objects. A related function will place objects at the control points of Line primitives.

PointSubstitute[*obj*, *shape*]	replace Point primitives with *shape* in Graphics3D object obj
PointSubstitute[*obj*, *shape*, *size*]	scale the *shape* object by factor *size*
LineSubstitute[*obj*, *shape*]	include *shape* at the points of Line primitives in Graphics3D object obj
LineSubstitute[*obj*, *shape*, *size*]	scale the *shape* object by factor *size*

Functions defined in ExtendGraphics`PointSubstitute3D`.

The package is loaded.

$In[81]:=$ **Needs["ExtendGraphics`PointSubstitute3D`"]**

A data set to be used for demonstration is constructed.

$In[82]:=$ **d = Table[{Sin[t Pi], Cos[t Pi],t}, {t,0,2,.1}];**

ScatterPlot3D is defined in the package
Graphics`Graphics3D`.

In[83]:= **ScatterPlot3D[d]**

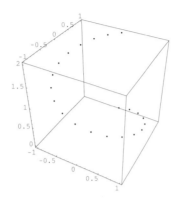

PointSubstitute will replace every
point in the original object with an
octahedron.

In[84]:= **Show[PointSubstitute[%, Octahedron[ ]]]**

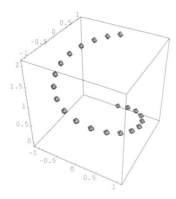

The PlotJoined options will draw lines
instead of points.

In[85]:= **ScatterPlot3D[d, PlotJoined -> True]**

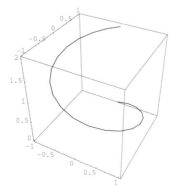

Now the control points of the lines are replaced by the objects.

In[86]:= `Show[LineSubstitute[%, Octahedron[ ]]]`

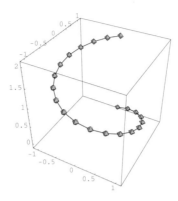

▶ *Explanation of the Solution*

The explanation of the solution here will concentrate on the function `PointSubstitute`.

```
PointSubstitute[obj_Graphics3D,
        shape_ /; VectorQ[shape, (Head[#] === Polygon)&],
        size_:Automatic] :=
    Module[{rng, nsize},
        nsize =
          If[!NumberQ[size],
                rng = FullOptions[obj, PlotRange] ;
                rng = Min[Map[(Last[#] - First[#])&, rng]] ;
                rng/40.,
                size] ;
        obj /. Point[pt_] :>
        Map[
            Polygon[Map[Function[{p1}, pt + nsize p1], First[#]]]&,
              shape]
        ]
```

The function `PointSubstitute` will accept two or three arguments. The first two arguments must both have head of `Graphics3D`. The first argument, `obj`, is the object in which `Point` primitives will be replaced. The second argument, `shape`, must be a list of `Polygon` primitives and will form the new symbol. The optional third argument, `size`, will be given a value of `Automatic` if it is not present. This will control the size of the new shapes.

```
    If[!NumberQ[size],
        rng = FullOptions[obj, PlotRange] ;
        rng = Min[Map[(Last[#] - First[#])&, rng]] ;
        rng/40.,
        size] ;
```

Here the setting of the `size` argument is examined. If it is not a number, as is the case if it was set to `Automatic`, then the `PlotRange` of the `obj` is used to calculate the scale factor for the replacement symbol as 1/40 of the minimum distance across the bounding box. If `size` is a number it will be used as the scale factor.

```
obj /. Point[pt_] :>
    Map[
        Polygon[Map[Function[{p1}, pt + nsize p1], First[#]]]&,
        shape]
```

The actual substitution for `Point` primitives is done here. Every such primitive is found and replaced by the `shape`. This is done with a `RuleDelayed` to prevent `Map` from evaluating too early. Note how a pure function is placed inside of another pure function by defining one in an explicit form with `Function`. The result of this evaluation is then returned.

13.10 *MathLink* and **Fractal Images**

There are a number of ways that *Mathematica* can display bitmap images. These include `DensityGraphics` objects and the two-dimensional primitives `Raster` and `RasterArray`. These can represent a variety of different types of bitmap images. One important type of image are those that result from some photographic process. Another type of image that a bitmap is very suited to displaying is a fractal image. One of the most famous images involving fractals is the Mandelbrot set. This can be generated by the process $z \rightarrow z^2 + k$. For different complex numbers k the values of the sequence tends to infinity, to a fixed point or oscillate around. Numbers that do not tend to infinity are members of the Mandelbrot set. These can be explored by *Mathematica* in a number of ways.

NestList is a very compact way to generate repeated application of a function. This shows the process for k of 2 + 2I. The value increases rapidly.

```
In[87]:= NestList[(#^2 + 2.+ 2.I)&, 0, 10]
```

$Out[87]= \{0, 2. + 2. I, 2. + 10. I, -94. + 42. I,$

$7074. - 7894. I, -1.22738\ 10^{7} - 1.11684\ 10^{8}\ I,$

$-1.23227\ 10^{16} + 2.74157\ 10^{15}\ I,$

$1.44334\ 10^{32} - 6.75674\ 10^{31}\ I,\ 1.62669\ 10^{64} - 1.95045\ 10^{64}\ I,$

$-1.15814\ 10^{128} - 6.34554\ 10^{128}\ I,$

$-3.89246\ 10^{257} + 1.46981\ 10^{257}\ I\}$

This function generates the number of iterations that were required for the absolute value to exceed 100. It does this for a maximum of 100 iterations.

```
In[88]:= mandelbrot[k_] :=
            Module[{val = 0, cnt = 0},
                While[Re[val]^2+Im[val]^2 < 10000 && cnt < 100,
                    val = val^2 + k;
                    cnt++] ;
                cnt]
```

For *k* of 2.+ 2.I only 3 iterations are required for the result to exceed the size bound. This will reach infinity quickly.

```
In[89]:= mandelbrot[2.+ 2.I]
Out[89]= 3
```

For *k* of 0.252 the result reaches infinity somewhat more slowly.

```
In[90]:= mandelbrot[0.252]
Out[90]= 71
```

For *k* of -0.5 + 0.1 I the absolute value does not exceed 100 in 100 iterations.

```
In[91]:= mandelbrot[-0.5 + 0.1 I]
Out[91]= 100
```

These are iterations 90 to 100 of the sequence for -0.5 + 0.1 I. They have converged to a fixed value.

```
In[92]:= Take[NestList[(#^2 + -0.5 + 0.1 I)&, 0, 100], -10]
Out[92]= {-0.367939 + 0.0576077 I, -0.367939 + 0.0576077 I,
    -0.367939 + 0.0576077 I, -0.367939 + 0.0576077 I,
    -0.367939 + 0.0576077 I, -0.367939 + 0.0576077 I,
    -0.367939 + 0.0576077 I, -0.367939 + 0.0576077 I,
    -0.367939 + 0.0576077 I, -0.367939 + 0.0576077 I}
```

Another way to explore $z \to z^2 + k$ is by some graphical method. Before starting to do this the time taken by the function will be examined.

This measures the time to carry out a number of computations.

```
In[93]:= Table[mandelbrot[x + I y],
             {x,-2,2,.2}, {y,-2,2,.2}];//Timing
Out[93]= {15.1 Second, Null}
```

In an attempt to make the function faster the internal compiler is used. It is very important to use Set so that Compile is evaluated only once.

```
In[94]:= mandelbrot =
            Compile[{{k, _Complex}},
              Module[{val = 0+0I, cnt = 0},
                While[Re[val]^2+Im[val]^2 < 10000 && cnt < 100,
                   val = val^2 + k;
                   cnt++] ;
                cnt]];
```

The compiled version runs much faster.

```
In[95]:= Table[mandelbrot[x + I y],
             {x,-2,2,.2}, {y,-2,2,.2}];//Timing
Out[95]= {1.36667 Second, Null}
```

Now that the function has been optimized it can be used to make a bitmap plot. This is the typical picture showing the Mandelbrot set in white.

```
In[96]:= DensityPlot[mandelbrot[x + I y], {x,-3,1}, {y,-2,2},
             PlotPoints -> 50, Mesh -> False]
```

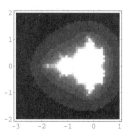

This last picture shows 50 by 50 samples. If a picture with many more samples is desired then a faster way to produce it would be very useful. After the internal compiler has been tried the next solution is to use C code and *MathLink*. The rest of this example will demonstrate a *MathLink* program that generates images of the Mandelbrot set. It will actually return to *Mathematica* not the array of data that would be used for a normal bitmap representation by `DensityGraphics` but a more compact encoding of the data. As described in Chapter 24 page 646, the way that a `DensityGraphics` object holds its data is very general. The images in these examples are very specific and it is possible to make a significant saving of space and time by representing them in a special compact method.

▶ *Solution to the Problem*

The *MathLink* program to generate bitmaps of the Mandelbrot set is installed by loading the package `ExtendGraphics`Mandelbrot``. This package installs the binary `mandelbrot` and sets up *Mathematica* functions to generate `Graphics` objects that represent the image. The appendix describes how this is done.

`GetMandelbrot[{`x_{min}`, `y_{min}`}, {`x_{min}`, `y_{min}`}, `*n*`, `*cont*`]`
                                return an image of the Mandelbrot set
`MandelbrotImage[{`x_{min}`, `y_{min}`}, {`x_{min}`, `y_{min}`}, `*n*`, `*cont*`]`
                                return a `Graphics` object with an imported image

---

Functions defined in the package `ExtendGraphics`Mandelbrot``.

This loads the package and carries out the necessary installation.	`In[97]:= Needs["ExtendGraphics`Mandelbrot`"]`
The `LinkObject` that connects to the compiled C program `mandelbrot` is listed here.	`In[98]:= Links[ ]` `Out[98]= {LinkObject[mandelbrot, 1, 1]}`

	`In[99]:= ?MandelbrotImage`
	
	`MandelbrotImage[ {x0,y0},{x1,y1},n,cont] returns a Graphics`
	`    object  containing an image of the Mandelbrot set generated`
	`    by GetMandelbrot. The image contains n by n samples from`
	`    {x0,y0} to {x1,y1}. The argument cont changes the contrast of`
	`    the image.`

`MandelbrotImage` returns a `Graphics` object.	`In[100]:= MandelbrotImage[{-3,-2}, {1,2}, 50, 10]` `Out[100]= -Graphics-`

The Graphics object can be displayed with the usual call to Show. This picture is similar to that generated earlier.

In[101]:= **Show[%]**

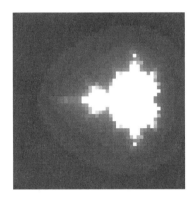

Now a much higher resolution picture is made. This image has 500 by 500 samples.

In[102]:= **Show[MandelbrotImage[{-2,-1.5}, {1,1.5}, 500, 10]]**

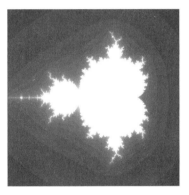

A frame placed around the picture displays the numbers involved.

In[103]:= **Show[%, Frame -> True]**

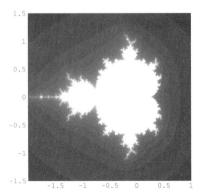

This details the tiny circular region on the left of the previous picture. Again the image has 500 by 500 samples.

```
In[104]:= Show[
              MandelbrotImage[{-1.49, -0.01},
                              {-1.47, 0.01}, 500, 2]]
```

These pictures demonstrate an interesting feature that makes this a fractal image. As the picture is looked at in higher and higher resolution more and more detail appears. The detail never decreases and parts of the picture at high resolution look similar to parts at lower resolution. The function `MandelbrotImage` makes it easy to explore and experiment with different parts of the Mandelbrot set.

▶ *Explanation of the Solution*

There are two parts to the solution. The first is contained in the package `Mandelbrot.m`. The second is the template file `mandelbrot.tm` that is used to build the *MathLink* binary `mandelbrot`. When the package is loaded the binary is installed automatically. The author prefers this way of arranging *MathLink* programs, to have a binary that is as minimal as possible connected to top-level *Mathematica* code that uses the C code in a variety of ways. The aim is to keep those parts of the code that are written in C to an absolute minimum. Anything that can be done by a *Mathematica* function without losing efficiency should be done by *Mathematica*. This maintains the efficiency for development and flexibility offered by the *Mathematica* programming language without losing computational efficiency.

```
MandelbrotImage[{x0_, y0_}, {x1_, y1_}, n_, fact_] :=
    Module[{image, str},
        image = GetMandelbrot[N[{x0,y0}], N[{x1,y1}], n, N[fact]] ;
        str = ToString[n] ;
        Graphics[
            PostScript[
                "0 0 translate",
                "1 1 scale",
                str <> " string",
                StringReplace["xx xx 8 [xx 0 0 xx 0 0]", "xx" -> str],
                "{ currentfile 1 index readhexstring pop } image",
                image,
                "pop"],
            PlotRange -> {{x0,x1}, {y0,y1}},
```

```
        AspectRatio -> 1]
    ]
```

Mathematica package.

The function `MandelbrotImage` generates a `Graphics` object containing a `PostScript` primitive. The primitive is filled with raw PostScript that will display the image data generated by `GetMandelbrot`. It will scale the picture to fill the region in PostScript coordinates {0,0} to {1,1}. The `PlotRange` and `AspectRatio` options of the enclosing `Graphics` object are set accordingly. The description of coordinate systems used by *Mathematica* graphics in Chapter 10 page 173 will help to explain the values used here. The PostScript image operator is documented fully in the PostScript reference manual. In this example, each datum for the image is encoded with a pair of hexadecimal digits and can therefore have a value between 0 and 255.

The contents of the `Graphics` object returned by `MandelbrotImage` can be seen in `InputForm`.

```
In[105]:= MandelbrotImage[{-1.5,-.125}, {-1.25,.125}, 5,
              1.]//InputForm

Out[105]//InputForm=
  Graphics[PostScript["0 0 translate", "1 1 scale",
     "5 string", "5 5 8 [5 0 0 5 0 0]",
     "{ currentfile 1 index readhexstring pop } image",
     "090B0D0E15\n0B0C14FF57\nFFFFFFFFFF\n0B0C14FF57\n090B0D0E1\
5\n", "pop"], PlotRange -> {{-1.5, -1.25}, {-0.125, 0.125}},
     AspectRatio -> 1]
```

The hexadecimal encoding is generated by `GetMandelbrot`.

```
In[106]:= GetMandelbrot[{-1.5,-.125}, {-1.25,.125}, 5, 1.]

Out[106]= 090B0D0E15
          0B0C14FF57
          FFFFFFFFFF
          0B0C14FF57
          090B0D0E15
```

The result is a string expression, an extremely compact way to represent this data.

```
In[107]:= InputForm[%]

Out[107]//InputForm= "090B0D0E15\n0B0C14FF57\nFFFFFFFFFF\n0B0C1\
4FF57\n090B0D0E15\n"
```

The method of representing the image data with a string is more compact than the normal *Mathematica* method, which would represent the data with an array of numbers. This can be demonstrated by using the function `MemoryInUse[ ]` to return the amount of memory that is currently being used by *Mathematica*.

The amount of memory used to hold the result of `MandelbrotImage`.

```
In[108]:= (t = MemoryInUse[ ];
           MandelbrotImage[{-2,-2}, {2,2}, 50, 10];
           MemoryInUse[ ] - t)

Out[108]= 5336
```

The memory necessary for a conventional plot.

```
In[109]:= (t = MemoryInUse[ ];
            DensityPlot[mandelbrot[x + I y], {x, -2, 2}, {y,-2, 2},
                Mesh -> False,
                PlotPoints -> 50,
                DisplayFunction -> Identity];
            MemoryInUse[ ] - t)

Out[109]= 152824
```

There is a large saving in the amount of memory used to store the image with the hexadecimal encoding. *Mathematica* could not always do this since a general image requires a general way of representing data.

Now the code that generates the binary `mandelbrot` will be looked at. The description given here is not intended as a detailed introduction to using *MathLink* with *Mathematica*. It is provided to suggest the power of *MathLink*. There are many Wolfram Research publications such as the *MathLink Reference Guide* that describe *MathLink* in addition to a number of items on `MathSource`. Of these the tutorial notes on *MathLink* written for the 1994 *Mathematica* Developers Conference are particularly useful.

The file `mandelbrot.tm` that generates the binary `mandelbrot` contains two parts. At the beginning is a template that contains information about how the function should interact with *Mathematica*. The rest of the file contains C code. Templates are a very useful feature of *MathLink*, they are automatically expanded out by tools provided with *MathLink* to insert a significant amount of code that makes it very easy to connect the binary to *Mathematica*. For the details of how these tools are invoked the documentation for particular versions of *Mathematica* should be consulted.

```
:Begin:
:Function:        sendimage
:Pattern:         ExtendGraphics`Mandelbrot`GetMandelbrot[
                        {x0_Real, y0_Real},
                        {x1_Real, y1_Real},
                        n_Integer, fact_Real]
:Arguments:       {{x0,x1},{y0,y1},n,fact}
:ArgumentTypes:   {Manual}
:ReturnType:      Manual
:End:

#include <math.h>
#include "mathlink.h"


void sendimage()
{
    char * tmp, * res, str[16];
    int n, len, cnt;
    double *xlim, *ylim, x, y, xinc,
            yinc, vx, vy, vox, fact;
    long ix, iy;

    MLGetRealList( stdlink, &xlim, &ix);
    MLGetRealList( stdlink, &ylim, &iy);
```

```
    MLGetInteger( stdlink, &n);
    MLGetDouble( stdlink, &fact);

/* C code to generate C string of result here... */

    MLPutString( stdlink, res);
    MLDisownRealList( stdlink, xlim, ix);
    MLDisownRealList( stdlink, ylim, iy);
    free( res);
        return;
}

int main(argc, argv)
        int argc; char* argv[ ];
{
        return MLMain(argc, argv);
}
```

The template appears at the top of the file, it starts with :Begin: and ends with :End:. It declares that there will be one function in the external C program, sendimage, to be invoked by the *Mathematica* function GetMandelbrot. The definition of GetMandelbrot shows how it calls the binary mandelbrot.

This shows the definition of GetMandelbrot.

```
In[110]:= ??GetMandelbrot
```

GetMandelbrot[{x0,y0},{x1,y1},n,cont] returns a string
    expression containing a PostScript image of the Mandelbrot
    set.   It contains n by n samples from {x0,y0} to {x1,y1}.
    The argument cont changes the contrast of the image.

```
GetMandelbrot[{x0_Real, y0_Real}, {x1_Real, y1_Real},
    n_Integer, fact_Real] :=
    ExternalCall[LinkObject["mandelbrot", 1, 1],
        CallPacket[0, {{x0, x1}, {y0, y1}, n, fact}]]
```

This definition for GetMandelbrot is entered to *Mathematica* when mandelbrot is installed. When *Mathematica* evaluates GetMandelbrot and the arguments match the patterns then these arguments are transmitted from *Mathematica* to the binary. At this point *Mathematica* waits until a result has come back. In the binary mandelbrot the function sendimage is entered, the arguments are read, computations carried out and a result returned to *Mathematica*. The template in the source code sets the :Arguments: and :ReturnType: fields to Manual. This means that sendimage must make *MathLink* calls to collect arguments and return the result. If the arguments were simpler it would be possible to allow the template to take care of collecting arguments and returning a result as well.

After the template description comes the C source code. This consists of two functions, main and sendimage. The latter is entered when the *Mathematica* kernel evaluates GetMandelbrot. It uses MLGetRealList to read the *x* and *y* limits, MLGetInteger to read the number of samples, and MLGetReal to get the contrast factor. These read commands were all carried out explicitly since the argument type in the template was Manual. The details of these functions are documented in the *MathLink Reference Guide*.

The actual computation of the image is then carried out with some conventional C code. It constructs a C string that contains a hexadecimal encoding of the image data. After this is done the string is returned to *Mathematica* by the *MathLink* function MLPutString. At this point *Mathematica*, which has been waiting for a result, will continue and use this result. In sendimage the memory used to hold the string and the

x and y limits is freed, the former by a call to `free` and the latter with a call to the *MathLink* function `MLDisownRealList`. The function then exits and the binary `mandelbrot` waits until it is sent another computation from *Mathematica*. The various steps in the execution of the *MathLink* binary `mandelbrot` are summarized in the diagram below.

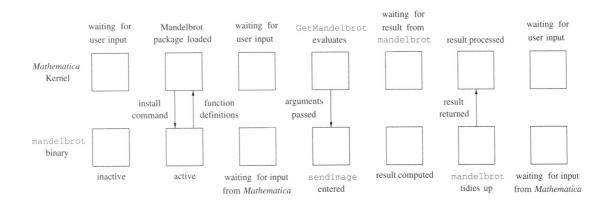

Steps in the execution of the binary `mandelbrot`.

The advantage of using a template program is quite clear. All the interaction between *Mathematica* and the *MathLink* binary is taken care of: functions defined, arguments sent, *Mathematica* set to wait for an answer while the binary carries out computations, and the binary set to wait for *Mathematica* to send a new computation. The code for all of this is generated automatically when the template is expanded. This means that C code development can concentrate on implementing the algorithm of interest while details of communicating with *Mathematica* are taken care of by the template. In the diagram above the only step that must have code specially created is the computation of the result. Everything else is done automatically.

This is a simple example of a *MathLink* program that provides a powerful way to experiment with the Mandelbrot set. It saved time and memory by computing the data with a *MathLink* program and holding the result with a hexadecimal string suitable for use by PostScript. Cases like this, where special advantage can be made of PostScript, are quite rare but this raises some interesting points. Holding the result as a string rather than as a *Mathematica* `DensityGraphics` object decreased the computation time but lost functionality. If the image is to be rescaled or if color is to be introduced then more C code must be written. With a `DensityGraphics` object this is much easier since the `PlotRange` and `ColorFunction` options can be used. This demonstrates a tradeoff between functionality and efficiency, one that is often encountered.

13.11 Summary

The problems and solutions examined in this chapter have highlighted a wide selection of *Mathematica* graphics functionality. Problems in many areas have been tackled and a variety of solutions have been presented. These examples are furnished to show some of the power of graphics programming with *Mathematica* and to stimulate further development by the reader.

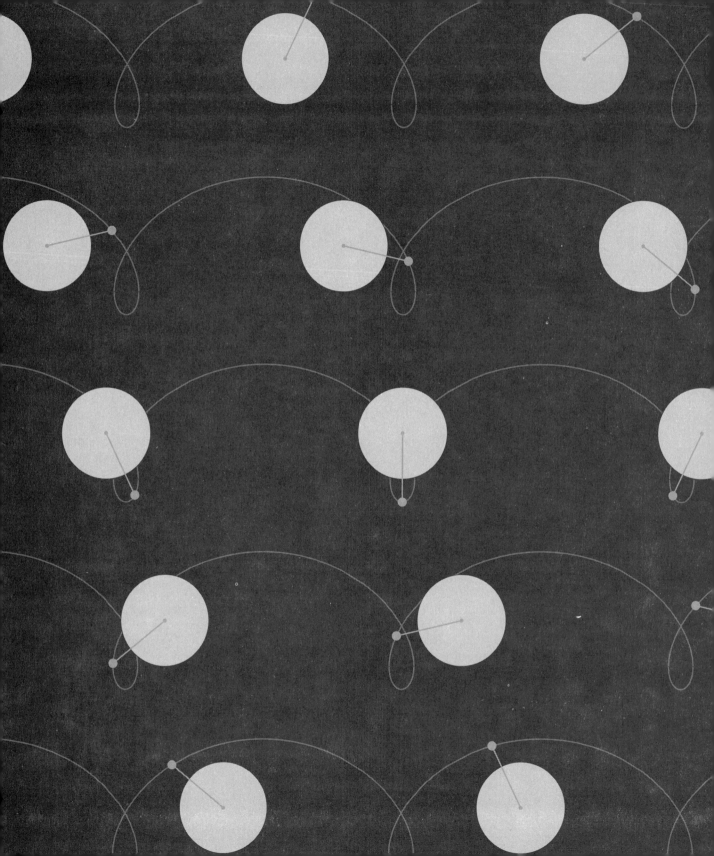

PART III
Applications in Visualization and Computer Graphics

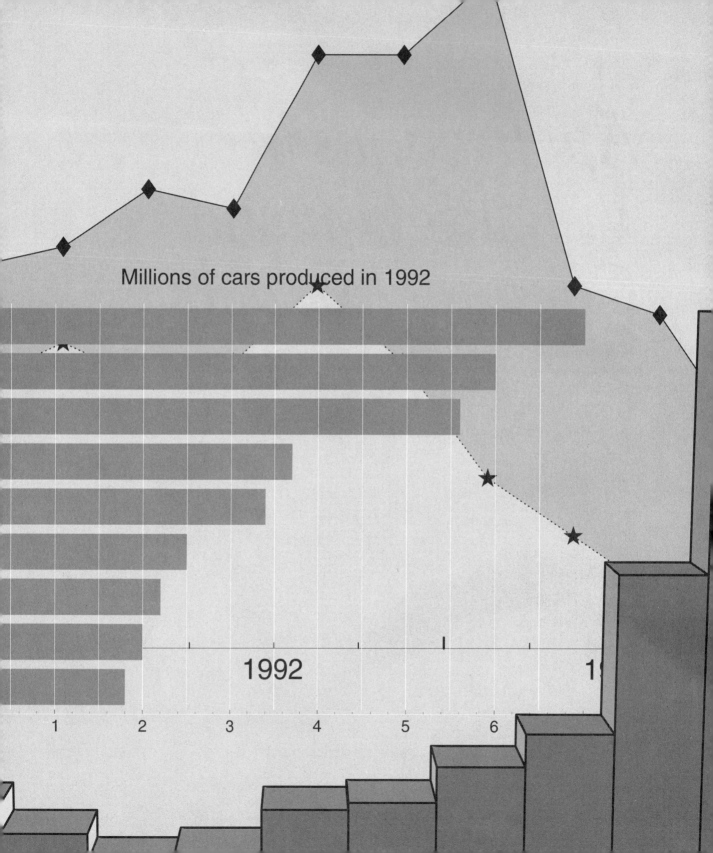

Millions of cars produced in 1992

1992

1   2   3   4   5   6

Chapter 14
The Design of Effective Graphics

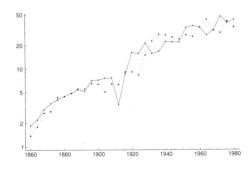

Part III of *Mathematica Graphics* is concerned with applications of *Mathematica*. Each chapter will address different areas of graphics and show how *Mathematica* provides powerful functionality to solve problems in these areas. Techniques will vary from straightforward to advanced, as appropriate. The primary aim will be to solve particular graphics problems, which is in contrast to Part II, where the primary aim was to understand how to combine *Mathematica* programming with graphics.

This first chapter of Part III will tackle a fundamental problem in graphics: that of making effective data pictures, concentrating on two dimensions. This problem has become increasingly significant over the past decade as there has been a rapid increase in the ease with which people can use computers to make pictures that represent numerical data. However, the fact that it is easy does not mean that the pictures will be effective in presenting their information. Often the ease with which pictures can be put together and with which extraneous colors and features can be added conspire to make a poorly designed picture that does not do a good job of getting ideas across.

What are the aims of a well-designed graph? A well-designed graph should communicate quantitive arguments to a broad audience. It should show a truthful representation of the numbers and be capable of highlighting unexpected trends. Different graphs may be combined to show different aspects of the same data. The process of making a graph involves important decisions about the data.

The design of data pictures has been extensively studied and discussed. Among these studies one that stands out is *The Visual Display of Quantitive Information*, E.R. Tufte. In this seminal work various principles are put forward that help to improve the design and layout of a picture. Another powerful book is *Exploratory Data Analysis*, J. Tukey. Like these studies this chapter will make a variety of different pictures and discuss those features that make them effective though on a somewhat narrower scale. In addition, unlike the publications by Tufte and Tukey, there is information on exactly how the pictures can be produced.

In designing a picture one cardinal principle is the importance of avoiding unnecessary elements. For example, do not use a three-dimensional picture where two dimensions will suffice, do not add color unnecessarily, and do not employ extra devices in a picture that do not convey any additional data content. In extreme cases, for example the three-dimensional pie chart, the extra complication actually detracts from the picture, since the result is harder to comprehend. It is a poor bargain that expends effort to make something worse. It may be easy to introduce all kinds of embellishments to a picture but any that do not enhance getting the message across must be resisted.

14.1　The Basic Graph of Data

This chapter will demonstrate examples of pictures. It will do this by presenting a basic picture and then working to improve it. This method will be demonstrated first for some data taken from *Nature*, vol. 368, p. 746, April 21, 1994. The data represent the severity of experimental allergic encephalomyelitis (EAE), a disease related to multiple sclerosis in rats. Some of the rats are treated with an inhibitor and some are not; the data will demonstrate the differences between these two groups.

The data are available in the file ExtendGraphics`EAEdata`. Chapter 4 page 54 discussed the *Mathematica* commands that read data.

```
In[1]:= data =
        ReadList["ExtendGraphics`EAEdata`", Number,
                RecordLists -> True];
```

The first number represents the number of days after treatment, the second and third the severity index in the untreated and treated rats, respectively.

```
In[2]:= Part[data, 15]
Out[2]= {24, 1.35, 0.2}
```

A data set is formed for the untreated rats.

```
In[3]:= untreated = Map[Part[#, {1,2}]&, data];
```

This is a two-dimensional data set.

```
In[4]:= Part[untreated, 15]
Out[4]= {24, 1.35}
```

A data set is formed for the treated rats.

```
In[5]:= treated = Map[Part[#, {1,3}]&, data];
```

MultipleListPlot is the function that makes general data plots. It must be loaded from a package.

```
In[6]:= Needs["Graphics`MultipleListPlot`"]
```

The basic plot is made by MultipleListPlot. This can be improved by adding some labels and adjusting the type of axes.

```
In[7]:= MultipleListPlot[untreated, treated]
```

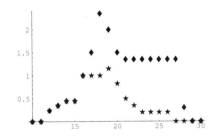

Now a line through the points and labels are added while the axes are labeled.

```
In[8]:= MultipleListPlot[untreated, treated,
            PlotJoined -> True,
            Frame -> {True, True, False, False},
            FrameLabel -> {"Days", "EAE severity index"}]
```

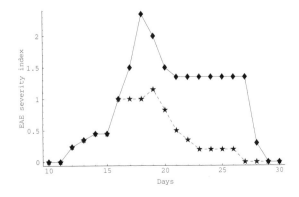

Including a legend helps to identify the data sets[1].

```
In[9]:= MultipleListPlot[untreated, treated,
            PlotJoined -> True,
            PlotLegend -> {"Untreated", "Treated"},
            Frame -> {True, True, False, False},
            FrameLabel -> {"Days", "EAE severity index"}]
```

These commands demonstrate the minimum amount of work that is necessary to generate a data picture. The data are read in and manipulated to generate two data sets. Then `MultipleListPlot` was used to make a general data plot. The first picture that was made was not suitable and a number of options had to be altered to make an acceptable picture.

Why it is necessary to set all these options? Why can't *Mathematica* set them automatically? The answer is that there are too many things only the person making the picture can decide upon. How could *Mathematica* decide what label should be put on the axes or in the legend? How could *Mathematica* know whether it is better to join the points or not to join the points? If certain types of pictures are generated repeatedly it is quite possible to set the default options of a command like `MultipleListPlot` to use these defaults. Maybe an even better solution is to use the programming techniques described in Part II to define a new function that will use `MultipleListPlot` with various options. This is one of the first things described in Chapter 7 page 102, the chapter that covers *Mathematica* programming. Defining a new function is a good solution since a number of different plotting routines can be used at the same.

`TrialPlot` takes two data sets and calls `MultipleListPlot` with various options set.

```
In[10]:= TrialPlot[untreat_, treat_, opts___] :=
            MultipleListPlot[untreat, treat,
                PlotJoined -> True,
                PlotLegend -> {"Untreated", "Treated"},
                Frame -> {True, True, False, False},
                FrameLabel -> {"Days", "EAE severity index"},
                opts]
```

Now the command that generates the plot is very simple.

```
In[11]:= TrialPlot[untreated, treated]
```

---

[1]`MultipleListPlot` did not have a legend in Version 2.2 (or earlier) *Mathematica*.

This example shows how to combine the commands that form a picture into a short program. In this way it is straightforward to make simple commands that generate a particular style of picture. The rest of this chapter will demonstrate various techniques that produce two-dimensional pictures. Often a step-by-step approach will be used that experiments with different styles to generate a final picture. For each of these examples the final picture can easily be generated by using a simple function, as in the example here.

14.2 Changing the Style

This example will look at some of the styles that can be added to a data graph. Some of these styles will make a strong picture and some will make a weak picture. One convenient source for data is from the standard package `Miscellaneous`ChemicalElements`` that contains a variety of data such as atomic weights and numbers of chemical elements. In the *Mathematica Graphics* packages a supplement to the chemical elements package is `ExtendGraphics`Ionization``. This adds data for the first ionization energy of chemical elements.

A variety of data on the chemical elements is now loaded.	`In[12]:= Needs["Miscellaneous`ChemicalElements`"]`
The atomic number of potassium is returned.	`In[13]:= AtomicNumber[Potassium]` `Out[13]= 19`
This is the atomic weight of oxygen.	`In[14]:= AtomicWeight[Oxygen]` `Out[14]= 15.9994`
`ExtendGraphics`Ionization`` contains data for the first ionization energy of the elements.	`In[15]:= Needs["ExtendGraphics`Ionization`"]`
A list is made of the atomic number and the ionization energy of every element. The latter information is not available for every element.	`In[16]:= ion = Transpose[{AtomicNumber[Elements],` `                Ionization[Elements]}];`

The first data element; the units of the ionization energy are in Kilo Joule/Mole.

```
In[17]:= First[ion]
```

$$Out[17]= \{1, \frac{1312. \text{ Joule Kilo}}{\text{Mole}}\}$$

The last data element; the ionization energy for this is not known.

```
In[18]:= Last[ion]
Out[18]= {106, Unknown}
```

Unknown ionization energies are filtered out and the units cast to one.

```
In[19]:= ion =
            Select[ion, #[[2]] =!= Unknown&] /.
                Kilo Joule/Mole -> 1 ;
```

MultipleListPlot is the natural function to construct a data picture.

```
In[20]:= Needs["Graphics`MultipleListPlot`"]


In[21]:= MultipleListPlot[ion]
```

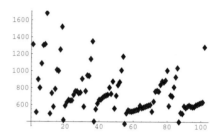

Joining the points with a line helps to show how the points are organized. Making the lines thin and dashed prevents them from being too prominent.

```
In[22]:= MultipleListPlot[ion,
            PlotJoined -> True,
            PlotStyle -> {{AbsoluteThickness[0.25],
                            AbsoluteDashing[{2}]}}]
```

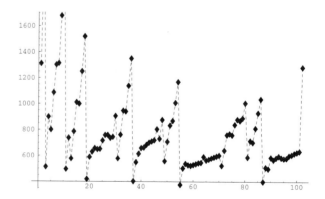

The axes are changed to frame axes, avoiding interference with the data, and the `PlotRange` is adjusted to include all the data.

```
In[23]:= good =
            Show[%, PlotRange -> All,
                Frame -> {True, True, False, False}]
```

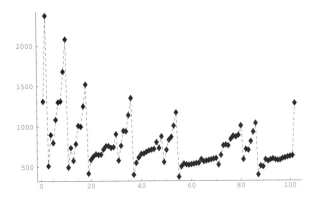

As an experiment gridlines are added to the picture. Here they overburden the plot, adding no new information. They are irrelevant to the purpose of displaying data.

```
In[24]:= Show[good, GridLines -> Automatic]
```

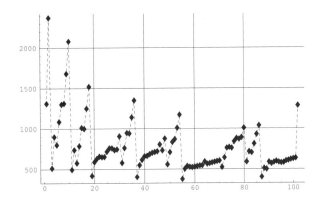

In these pictures adding lines to join the points definitely helped the picture. They showed how the points were organized and drew attention to various peaks and dips that otherwise might not have been so obvious. Adding the grid did not help; it just made the picture messier. It added graphical elements that did not convey any actual information.

The next stage in working on this picture will add labels. These are necessary for the axes and also for some of the data elements. It is important that each label be clearly attached to an individual point without obscuring any of the data. This can be done conveniently by placing labels above the peaks.

Mathematica has a number of ways to add labels and adjust their position. One way is to set the alignment argument of the *Mathematica* `Text` primitive, as is described in Chapter 20 page 541. An alternative is to use the `Offset` coordinate specification. The example here will not use `Offset` (it is used in later examples).

Certain peaks in the plot, which correspond to the inert gases, are labeled. The alignment vector is {0,3}, this makes sure that each text label is lifted up from the point it describes.

The text labels are added and so are labels around the frame.

```
In[25]:= text =
        Map[
          Text[
            FontForm[#, {"Helvetica", 6}],
            {AtomicNumber[#], Ionization[#] /.
                Kilo Joule/Mole -> 1},
            {0,-3}]&,
          {He, Ne, Ar, Kr, Xe, Rn}];
In[26]:= final =
        Show[good,
          Epilog -> text,
          FrameLabel -> {"Atomic Number",
                "Ionization Energy"}]
```

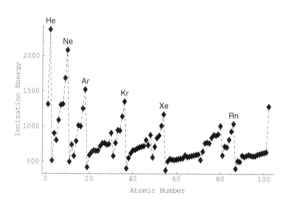

As an experiment the frame lines are hidden by making them white. While this concentrates on the data, the frame is useful to hold the picture together[2].

```
In[27]:= Show[%, FrameStyle -> GrayLevel[1]]
```

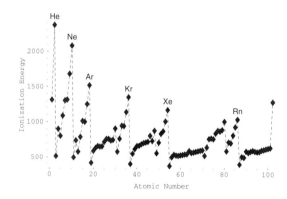

---

[2]The style of the tick marks is unaffected by the AxesStyle or FrameStyle options. Their style can be changed with the Ticks package.

Finally frame axes labels are added
and the font for the tick mark labels is
specified. This is the final picture.

```
In[28]:= Show[final,
            DefaultFont -> {"Times-Roman", 8},
            FrameLabel ->
               {FontForm["Atomic Number", {"Helvetica", 11}],
                FontForm["Ionization Energy  kJ/mol",
                                              {"Helvetica", 11}]}]
```

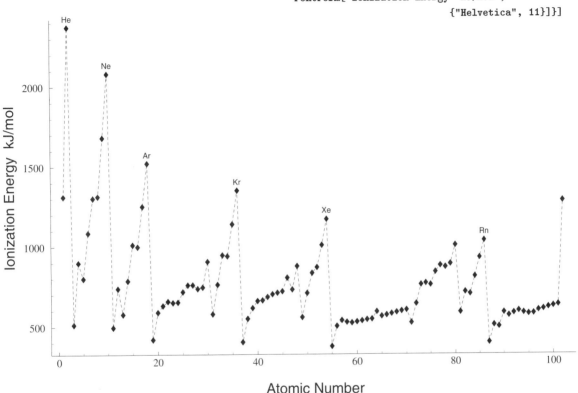

This final picture displays a considerable amount of data in an economical way. It clearly demonstrates the various trends in ionization energies of the elements, the peaks at the inert gases together with smaller intermediate features. Other elements that could be added to the picture include showing the numeric value with each inert gas label. This would be a better way to include numbers than adding grid lines would be. However, it is not clear that this would improve anything. This picture is fine for showing trends and strange features. It is not the most appropriate way to depict actual numeric values. A better way to achieve the latter would be with a table of numbers. Another point to note from this picture is that the vertical scale does not start at zero. This can be seen as rescaling the data to concentrate attention on the relative differences between each element rather than on their absolute values. The decisions that must be made when pictures are created often involve a compromise such as this.

14.3 Adding Lines to Organize the Data

A line is a useful feature in a data plot that helps to show how the data are organized. For both of the previous examples a line was included by the simple expedient method of joining the points. This is a simple form of interpolation (linear interpolation). It would be possible to use higher-order interpolation with the `Interpolation` function and this might generate a smoother line. When interpolation is used there is an implicit assumption that all the data are valid, that there is not uncertainty in the data, a good assumption for the first ionization energy of chemical elements.

An alternative to interpolation is fitting. Fitting assumes that there is uncertainty in the data and finds a line of best fit by minimizing the difference between the data values and the fitted curve. This will avoid the suggestion of features that may be formed by joining the dots. It is more complex since certain decisions must be made about the nature of the function to be fitted and the method by which this should happen.

There have been a number of examples of plotting a fit to some data in *Mathematica Graphics* that used a linear fitting technique. Now an example will be given where the data contain uncertainty and a more complex non-linear fitting technique will be used. The data for this example are taken from *Science* vol. 260, p. 1490, June 4, 1993. It describes the change of streaking intensity in a transmission electron microscope study.

The data are available in the file ExtendGraphics`Streakdata`. It can easily be read with `ReadList`.

```
In[29]:= data =
            ReadList["ExtendGraphics`Streakdata`",
                Number, RecordLists ->True];
```

The `MultipleListPlot` command will be used.

```
In[30]:= Needs["Graphics`MultipleListPlot`"]
```

The data is plotted with MultipleListPlot[3].

```
In[31]:= graph =
            MultipleListPlot[data,
                SymbolShape -> PlotSymbol[Box],
                PlotRange -> {20,100}]
```

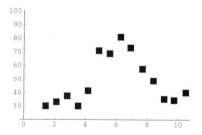

---

[3]The `SymbolShape` was not present in `MultipleListPlot` for Version 2.2 *Mathematica*.

Now the points are joined together. Since the data are noisy the line is a distraction suggesting features that do not exist.

```
In[32]:= MultipleListPlot[data,
              PlotJoined -> True,
              SymbolShape -> PlotSymbol[Box],
              PlotRange -> {20,100}]
```

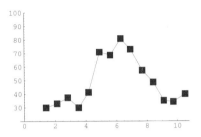

In an attempt to get a smoother line a fit to the data is made.

```
In[33]:= fitfun = Fit[data, {1,x,x^2,x^3,x^4}, x]
```

$$Out[33]= 130.957 - 116.321\ x + 41.4073\ x^2 - 5.22604\ x^3 + 0.21509\ x^4$$

A line representing the fit can be generated with Plot.

```
In[34]:= Plot[fitfun, {x, 1.4, 10.5}]
```

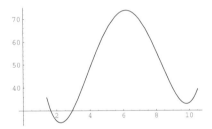

The original data plot and the line can be combined. This result is not very satisfactory since the lines bend around at each end.

```
In[35]:= Show[graph, %]
```

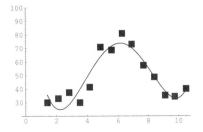

Both methods to form a line through the points exhibit problems. The data were noisy so that the points could not be joined. However, the shape of the data, with a peak, was such that a fit with a polynomial would not work unless high-order terms were included. When these were included the line curved up at the ends.

Some knowledge about the phenomenon can now be used. If the general functional form is known it can be used for the fit. A Gaussian is often appropriate for a peak, and here a linearly shifted Gaussian of the form $a\ e^{-c(x-b)^2} + d\ x + e$, where a, b, c, d, and e are the coefficients that will be varied to form the fit. This function cannot be used with the `Fit` command since that will only fit functions that are linear in their coefficients. This function must be fitted with `NonlinearFit`, a command defined in the package `Statistics`NonlinearFit``.

A more satisfactory line could be obtained by fitting a more complicated function. To do this the `NonlinearFit` package will be used.

```
In[36]:= Needs["Statistics`NonlinearFit`"]
```

The data are fitted with a linearly shifted Gaussian peak. The starting values for the parameters can be derived from examining the data picture[4].

```
In[37]:= NonlinearFit[data,
              a Exp[-c(x-b)^2] + d x + e, x,
              {{a,50.},{b, 6.0},{c,1.},{d,1.},{e,30}}]
```

$$Out[37]= 29.4706 + \frac{46.4267}{E^{0.304982\ (-6.17558\ +\ x)^2}} + 0.657178\ x$$

Now the fitted function can be plotted.

```
In[38]:= Plot[%, {x, 1.4, 10.5}]
```

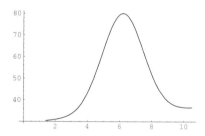

---

[4]`NonlinearFit` in Version 2.2 *Mathematica* returned replacement rules for the coefficients of the model. These had to be substitued back into the orginal function. This was changed to make `NonlinearFit` work like `Fit`.

When the fitted line is plotted with the data the line is a good approximation to the data.

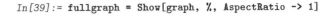

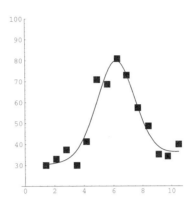

The key to making this picture was generating the line to pass through the points with `NonlinearFit`. In order for this to be successful good starting values were given for the coefficients being fitted. They were determined by visual inspection of the data. If the data are known to have some particular shape, such as consisting of a single peak, then these coefficients can be determined algorithmically. A crude and simple way to do this is given below.

A crude function that will attempt to fit a peak to a set of data.

```
In[40]:= PeakFit[data_] :=
            Module[{a,b,c,d,e,ai,bi,ci,di,ei},
              {bi, ai} = Last[Sort[data, #1[[2]] < #2[[2]]&]] ;
              ei = Fit[Drop[data, {3,-3}], {1,x}, x] ;
              di = Coefficient[ei, x, 1] ;
              ei = Coefficient[ei, x, 0] ;
              ai -= ei ;
              ci = (Part[data,-1,1] - Part[data,1,1]) ;
              NonlinearFit[data,
                  a Exp[-c(x-b)^2] + d x + e, x,
                  {{a,ai},{b, bi},{c,ci},{d,di},{e,ei}}]]
```

The `PeakFit` function automatically carries out a fit to the data.

```
In[41]:= PeakFit[data]
```

$$Out[41]= 29.4706 + \frac{46.4267}{E^{0.304984 \, (-6.17558 + x)^{2}}} + 0.657178 \, x$$

The `PeakFit` function described here is crude and not at all robust. It is given as an example to be expanded upon. It could be improved by picking out parts of the data and carrying out linear fits to different parts to determine the starting points for the non-linear fit.

Now in returning to the original picture as a final effect some labels will be added. These will use the typesetting capabilities; the way that these could be used in plot labels was described in Chapter 3 page 42. The format type `StandardForm` is used for these labels since they do not require any special mathematical notation. Typesetting was not available in Version 2.2 (or earlier) *Mathematica*.

These will be used as labels on the full picture. One of the labels is wrapped in StandardForm and will come out formated in a typeset notation.

```
In[42]:= labs =
            {StandardForm[
                SequenceForm["Electron dose J (", 10^"-5",
                    " C ", cm^"-2",")"]],
                "Streaking Intensity (a.u.)"};
```

The final picture is made.

```
In[43]:= Show[fullgraph,
            Frame -> {True,True, False, False},
            FrameLabel -> labs,
            DefaultFont -> {"Helvetica", 7}]
```

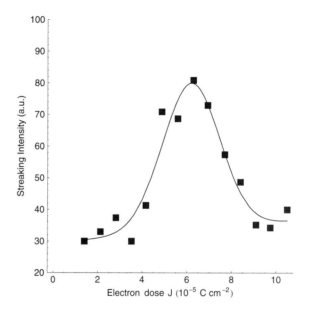

The purpose of this section has been to demonstrate how a line can be generated that passes through a set of points when those points are noisy. This can be done by fitting a function to the data. When the form of the data is simple then a linear fit can be used with a power series. When the data are more complicated, for example if it contains a peak, then a non-linear fitting procedure may be required. To do this successfully required some knowledge of the type of process going on and some visual inspection of the data. This allowed a function representing a peak to be fitted to the data and the line was generated. The line is a useful element that makes a point about how the data are arranged.

In this example the line was formed to improve the picture. The coefficients that formed the line may be useful in themselves. These form numeric values that have been extracted from the data and represent quantities such as the position and width of the peak. A further embellishment is to generate some statistical analysis to obtain confidence limits on this numeric information.

14.4 Changing the Shape

The shape of a picture drawn with *Mathematica* is determined by the `AspectRatio` option. The default value is the golden ratio, a division of a line in two so that the length of the shorter to the longer part equals the length of the longer to the whole, $a/b = b/(a + b)$. A rectangle constructed with sides in the golden ratio is called a golden rectangle. Whenever a square is removed from a golden rectangle the remaining rectangle is also a golden rectangle.

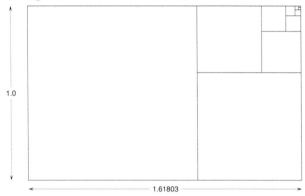

The golden rectangle.

The main reason why this shape is appropriate for data plots is that it is wider than it is long. Some simple experiments will demonstrate this by using *Mathematica* to make pictures with different settings for the `AspectRatio` option. These examples use the picture generated from the ionization data in the preceding section.

The picture is made to be twice as tall as it is wide. The result is very cluttered. Even if the plotting symbols were smaller the peaks would run into each other.

```
In[44]:= Show[final,
            AspectRatio -> 2]
```

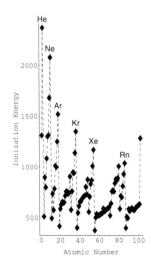

Here x and y are reversed and the picture is redrawn. The picture is improved, but it is still difficult to comprehend.

```
In[45]:= Show[
            % /. {x_?NumberQ, y_?NumberQ} -> {y,x},
            FrameLabel -> {"Ionization Energy", "Atomic Number"}]
```

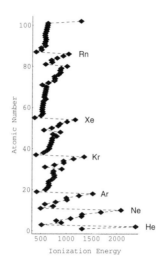

This is clearly a good shape for the data. The organization is very similar to the previous picture but improved.

```
In[46]:= Show[final,
            AspectRatio -> 0.5]
```

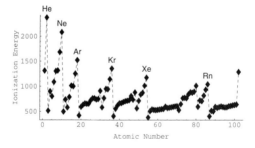

The wider picture is clearly more effective than either of the tall pictures. It is just easier to scan across the picture from left to right to see what is happening. Making the picture tall does not help and reversing x and y does not help either. Looking at these the eye tends to start at the bottom and move upwards scanning left and right. This seems to require more movement of the eye than with the wide picture. For this the eye can start at one side and scan to the other, the peaks are readily identified as the eye scans. It is these peaks, the local extrema, that cause a problem. If the data were monotonic the situation could well be different. The next example will show exactly this: monotonic data where the shape does not have to be constrained. The data just seen here are not monotonic, they show a number of local maxima and minima and are better shown in a wide picture. This phenomenon is noted by Tukey who states that "smoothly-changing curves can stand being taller than wide, but a wiggly curve needs to be wider than tall".

There are a number of reasons why the more complex data require a wider picture. Tufte suggests that people find this easier since they are used to reading left to right and the eye is tuned to scanning the horizon and optimized to detect deviations from the horizontal rather than the vertical. When text is included in a picture this may fit with the wider shape as well. This will not apply to text that is written vertically. For example, Japanese contains elements that are written vertically. However, technical Japanese, more likely to be included in a graph, is written left to right. Other languages are written right to left and text in these will fit with a wide picture.

▶ *Using the Shape*

When the data to be plotted are simple, for example if it is monotonic, the requirement that the picture be wider than tall does not apply. In this situation the shape becomes another graphical element to be exploited to get the message across. An example will now be presented that does exactly that. It presents the transition temperature of a set of superconductors as a function of the year in which they were discovered. The data are taken from *Science at the Frontier: Volume 1*, Addison Greenwood. One of the key points to be made is that in very recent years the maximum temperature at which superconductors operate has increased dramatically. A tall thin picture will be used to make this point effectively.

The data are loaded from a file.

```
In[47]:= data =
           ReadList["ExtendGraphics`SuperConductor1`",
                    {{Number, Number},{Number, Number},
                     Expression}];
```

The data are organized by the year and temperature, a text offset, and the name of the compound.

```
In[48]:= First[%]
Out[48]= {{1913, 4}, {-1, -2}, {Hg}}
```

ListPlot makes a plot of the data.

```
In[49]:= plot =
           ListPlot[Map[First, data],
             PlotStyle -> AbsolutePointSize[3],
             Frame -> True, Axes -> False]
```

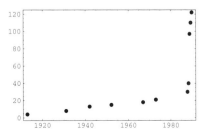

A line through the points can be drawn with these primitives. The numbers are determined by visual inspection, a simple way to form a line.

```
In[50]:= line =
            {AbsoluteDashing[{5}],
             AbsoluteThickness[0.5],
             Line[{{1913, 4}, {1988, 25}, {1990, 120}}]};
```

Prolog is used to include the line.

```
In[51]:= graph = Show[plot, Prolog -> line]
```

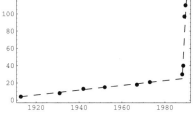

Now labels will be added to the picture. The labels represent chemical compounds and the text for these was present in the data file. The actual contents of the file will require processing to generate a formatted text label. The steps that produce these labels are expanded to explain how they work. In a real version they would be compressed, or perhaps the data in the file would be pre-processed to reduce this effort.

This is the label that goes with the last datum. The whole thing is kept in a list; subscripts are kept in sub-lists.

```
In[52]:= Part[data, -1,-1]
Out[52]= {Tl, {2}, Ba, {2}, Ca, {2}, Cu, {3}, O, {y}}
```

Now the sub-lists are converted into subscripts.

```
In[53]:= Map[If[ListQ[#], Subscript[First[#]], #]&, %]
Out[53]= {Tl,  , Ba,  , Ca,  , Cu,  , O,  }
              2       2       2       3      y
```

Putting everything into SequenceForm makes it print joined together.

```
In[54]:= Apply[SequenceForm, %]
Out[54]= Tl Ba Ca Cu O
            2  2  2  3 y
```

The steps can be put together in a little program.

```
In[55]:= fixLabel[lab_] :=
             Apply[SequenceForm,
                Map[If[ListQ[#], Subscript[First[#]], #]&, lab]]
```

The fixLabel function converts the label automatically.

```
In[56]:= fixLabel[Part[data, -1,-1]]
Out[56]= Tl Ba Ca Cu O
            2  2  2  3 y
```

Now all the text labels are constructed. The second entry in each data element states how the label is to be rendered relative to the point.

```
In[57]:= labels =
             Map[Text[fixLabel[Last[#]], First[#], Part[#,2]]&,
                data];
```

The labels are added and the result displayed. The result is very congested.

In[58]:= **Show[graph, Epilog -> labels]**

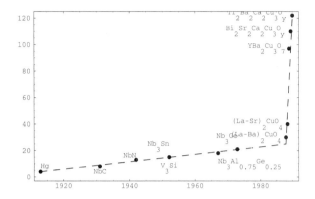

The picture here is very congested and must be redrawn at a larger size. In addition, some changes to the fonts will be made. As this is done the whole purpose of the picture should be considered. The aim of the picture is to show the dramatic rise in temperatures at which superconductors work. The shape of this picture, being short and wide, does not make this point effectively. It will be made taller by changing the AspectRatio. This will get the message across much more effectively.

Labels on the frame axes will be drawn with this font.

In[59]:= **framefont = {"Helvetica", 12};**

The final picture is put together. The AspectRatio is changed to make a taller and narrower picture.

In[60]:= **Show[graph,**
    Epilog -> labels,
    FrameLabel ->
       {FontForm["Year", framefont],
        FontForm["Transition Temperature (K)",
                    framefont]},
    DefaultFont -> {"Courier", 8},
    AspectRatio -> 1.5]

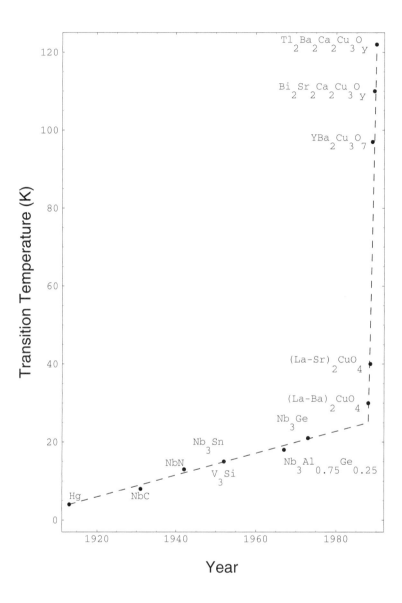

The picture here is quite effective. The tall size makes a dramatic statement about the data. However, the labels on the picture are unsatisfactory for several reasons. They all use a fixed width font, Courier, which spreads them out. The subscripts use the same size of text as the main label, which gives them as much prominence as the text they are subscripting. Another, more subtle, problem with the labels is their alignment with the points. This is done with the third argument of the Text primitive. A much better way to make this picture would be with typeset labels and by moving the text labels a distance in points from their anchor. The next section describes how this can be done.

14.5 Advanced Labeling Features

Mathematica provides certain features that are extremely valuable for producing high-quality graphs and diagrams. Two features that are relevant to the picture introduced in the last section are typeset text and the `Offset` coordinate specification. This section will reproduce the last picture making use of these features. Neither of these features were available in Version 2.2 (or earlier) *Mathematica*.

▶ *Typesetting with Mathematica*

Typeset text labels can be introduced into graphics by using a typesetting formatter. The two main typesetting formatters are `StandardForm` and `TraditionalForm`. The former generates standard *Mathematica* notation while the latter approximates traditional mathematics. All of the ordinary *Mathematica* formatting constructs such as `SequenceForm` or `Subscripted` will automatically be converted in a typeset representation. It is therefore easy to introduce typeset labels into graphics. This can be done by using the formatting constructs to generate labels, as was done in the last section, and then formatting them with `StandardForm` or `TraditionalForm`.

A label defined in terms of *Mathematica* formatting constructs, SequenceForm and Subscript.

```
In[61]:= label =
            SequenceForm[Nb,Subscript[3],Al,Subscript[0.75],
                Ge,Subscript[0.25]]

Out[61]= Nb Al    Ge
            3  0.75  0.25
```

A Text primitive that uses formatting techniques available in Version 2.2 *Mathematica*.

```
In[62]:= txt1 =
            Text[label, {0,0}];
```

A Text primitive that formats its contents with `StandardForm`.

```
In[63]:= txt2 =
            Text[label, {0,1},
                FormatType -> StandardForm];
```

The two labels are displayed in Courier; the upper label is much more compact than the lower.

```
In[64]:= Show[Graphics[{txt1, txt2},
            PlotRange -> All,
            DefaultFont -> {"Courier", 10}]]
```

$$Nb_3Al_{0.75}Ge_{0.25}$$

$$Nb\ Al\quad Ge$$
$$3\quad 0.75\quad 0.25$$

Now the font is changed to Helvetica, a nonfixed-width font. The Version 2.2 label is hopeless while the typeset label works well.

```
In[65]:= Show[
            Graphics[{txt1, txt2},
            PlotRange -> All,
            DefaultFont -> {"Helvetica", 8}]]
```

$Nb_3Al_{0.75}Ge_{0.25}$

```
Nb Al   Ge
3 0.75  0.25
```

Typeset labels in *Mathematica* can be generated by using the existing formatting constructs such as ColumnForm or SequenceForm with a typesetting formatter. This produces a pleasing result that is visually more compact. In Version 2.2 subscripts were rendered in the same font on the line below the main text. The typeset labels use subscripts in a smaller font that are tucked in underneath the main text. In addition the Version 2.2 labels had to use a fixed-width font when they extended over several lines. There is no such restriction for the typeset labels.

▷ *Offset*

The careful placement of labels is extremely important to make a well-balanced graph. The Offset coordinate specification allows labels and other primitives to be placed in a very specific way by specifying distances involving printers points. These were defined in Chapter 8 page 127.

A text label with a long text segment.

```
In[66]:= label1 =
            Text["This is a long label", {0,0}, {-1,0}];
```

A label that is shorter.

```
In[67]:= label2 =
            Text["Short", {0,1}, {-1,0}];
```

Both labels can be placed exactly on the right of the line.

```
In[68]:= Show[
            Graphics[
               {label1, label2, Line[{{0,-1},{0,2}}]},
            PlotRange -> All]]
```

Short

This is a long label

In an attempt to move the label away from the line the alignment vector is altered.

```
In[69]:= label1 =
            Text["This is a long label", {0,0}, {-1.5,0}];
```

```
In[70]:= label2 =
            Text["Short", {0,1}, {-1.5,0}];
```

Now both labels are moved from the line but the longer label has moved further[5].

```
In[71]:= Show[
            Graphics[
              {label1, label2, Line[{{0,-1},{0,2}}]},
            PlotRange -> All]]
```

```
                          Short



                             This is a long label
```

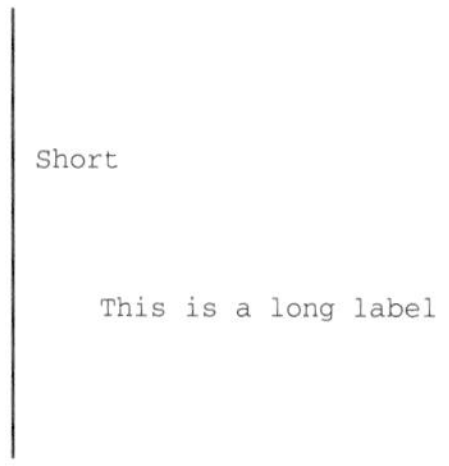

Now the labels are made using the coordinate specification Offset.

```
In[72]:= label1 =
            Text["This is a long label",
                 Offset[{5,0},{0,0}], {-1,0}];
```

This text will appear to the right of the point that is 5 points to the right of {0,1}.

```
In[73]:= label2 =
            Text["Short", Offset[{5,0},{0,1}], {-1,0}];
```

Now the two text labels are the same distance from the line.

```
In[74]:= Show[
            Graphics[{label1, label2, Line[{{0,-1},{0,2}}]},
            PlotRange -> All]]
```

```
                          Short



                          This is a long label
```

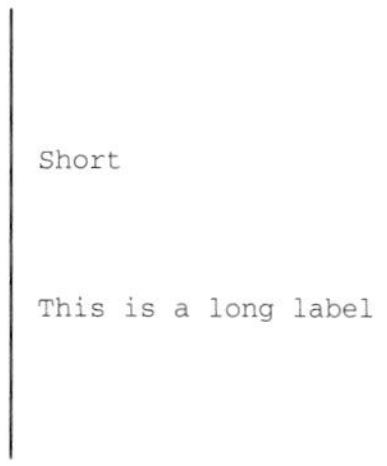

Thus Offset provides a powerful yet simple way to line up text and other graphical objects some fixed amount that does not change with the size, scale, or shape of the picture.

---

[5]This is because the coordinate system of the alignment vector is described in terms of the size of the bounding box of the text.

▶ *Using Typeset and Offset*

Now the picture on high-temperature superconductors that was produced in the previous section will be re-created using both `Offset` and typeset labels. A new data file has been written that contains the offset distances to be used.

A new data file set up to allow more careful positioning of text labels.

```
In[75]:= data =
            ReadList["ExtendGraphics`SuperConductor2`",
                    {{Number, Number}, {Number, Number},
                        {Number, Number}, Expression}];
```

The second element is the alignment vector and the third is the offset in points.

```
In[76]:= Part[data, 5]
```

$Out[76]= \{\{1954, 16\}, \{1, -1\}, \{0, 2\}, \{Nb, \{3\}, Sn\}\}$

The `fixLabel` function will produce labels formatted with `SequenceForm` and `Subscript`.

```
In[77]:= fixLabel[lab_] :=
            Apply[SequenceForm,
                Map[If[ListQ[#], Subscript[First[#]], #]&, lab]]
```

```
In[78]:= fixLabel[Part[data, -1,-1]]
```

$Out[78]= Tl_2 Ba_2 Ca_2 Cu_3 O_y$

Text labels are constructed that will be formatted in `StandardForm` and use the font Helvetica.

```
In[79]:= labels =
            Map[Text[fixLabel[Last[#]],
                        Offset[Part[#,3],First[#]], Part[#,2],
                        FormatType -> StandardForm,
                        DefaultFont -> {"Helvetica", 7}]&,
                data];
```

This is how one of the labels looks as a *Mathematica* expression.

```
In[80]:= Part[labels, 5]
```

$Out[80]= Text[Nb_3 Sn, Offset[\{0, 2\}, \{1954, 16\}], \{1, -1\},$

   $FormatType -> StandardForm, DefaultFont -> \{Helvetica, 7\}]$

`ListPlot` makes a plot of the data.

```
In[81]:= plot =
            ListPlot[Map[First, data],
                PlotStyle -> AbsolutePointSize[3],
                Frame -> True, Axes -> False]
```

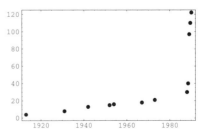

This line through the points will help to organize them. The numbers are determined by visual inspection.

```
In[82]:= line =
            {AbsoluteDashing[{5}],
            AbsoluteThickness[0.5],
            Line[{{1913, 4}, {1988, 25}, {1990, 120}}]]};
```

The line is added as a Prolog and the labels are added as an Epilog.

```
In[83]:= graph = Show[plot, Prolog -> line, Epilog -> labels]
```

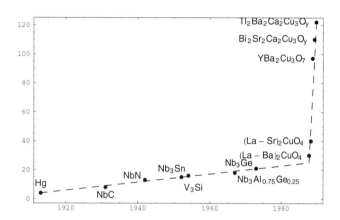

Labels on the frame axes will be drawn with this font.

```
In[84]:= framefont = {"Helvetica", 12};
```

Now the final picture is generated, the AspectRatio is adjusted to make a tall thin picture, more labels are added, and the fonts are altered.

```
In[85]:= Show[graph,
            FrameLabel ->
            {FontForm["Year", framefont],
             FontForm["Transition Temperature (K)",
                                    framefont]},
            DefaultFont -> {"Times-Roman", 8},
            AspectRatio -> 1.5]
```

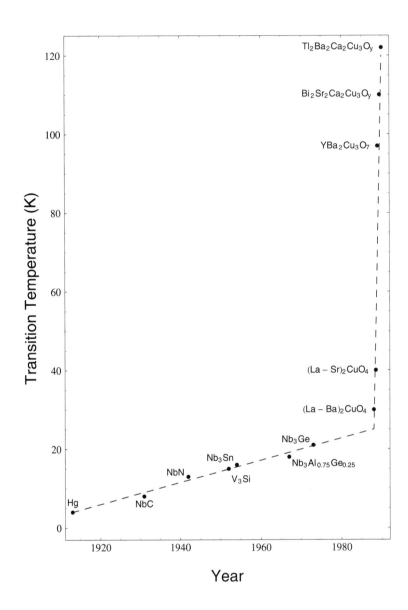

The picture is improved with the typeset labels. These are more compact and this conforms with the rules for a well-designed picture. The use of `Offset` to position the labels also improves the picture and will lessen the need to adjust the layout if the labels are changed or the size of the picture is altered.

14.6 Multiple Data Sets

The example in this section will look at techniques that can be used to make a plot from more than one set of data. This will be explored with data taken from *The Economist*, February 5, 1994. The data show interest rates adjusted for inflation measured in the middle of each quarter from 1991 to the beginning of 1994 for France and Germany. If the data represented averages for each quarter they would be better displayed in a bar chart. Here they represent samples taken at intervals and a point and line plot is the appropriate format.

The interest rate data to be plotted. The first element of each datum is the French data and the second is the German.

```
In[88]:= data =
          {{6.0,5.8},{5.6,5.6},{4.8,6.0},{5.2,6.2},
           {4.8,6.8},{5.0,6.6},{5.8,8.2},{5.0,8.2},
           {3.8,9.0},{3.2,5.8},{2.6,5.5},{2.4,4.2},
           {2.2,4.0}};
```

MultipleListPlot can be loaded to plot the data.

```
In[89]:= Needs["Graphics`MultipleListPlot`"]
```

The data are measured at the middle of each quarter; this computes the *x* values.

```
In[90]:= year = Table[1991.125 + i 0.25, {i,0,12}];
```

Two data sets can be built up, one for the French data and one for the German data.

```
In[91]:= (fdata = Transpose[{year, Map[First, data]}];
          gdata = Transpose[{year, Map[Last, data]}];)
```

MultipleListPlot will make the plot but the *x* axis tick marks come out looking rather strange.

```
In[92]:= MultipleListPlot[gdata, fdata,
            PlotJoined -> True,
            Axes -> False,
            Frame -> {True,True,False,False}]
```

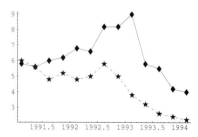

The tick package allows the labels to be controlled.

```
In[93]:= Needs["ExtendGraphics`Ticks`"]
```

A new tick function is defined that sets the options of TickFunction to reduce the number of tick marks and to set the positions and text of the labels.

```
In[94]:= tickfun[x0_, x1_] :=
            TickFunction[x0, x1,
               MajorLength -> {0.01, 0},
               MinorLength -> {0.005, 0},
               TickNumbers -> {4, 15},
               TickLabels -> {{1991.5, 1991},
                              {1992.5,1992},{1993.5,1993}}]
```

These settings will be used for subsequent plots.

```
In[95]:= axes =
            {PlotJoined -> True,
             Axes -> False,
             Frame -> {True, True,False,False},
             FrameTicks -> {tickfun, Automatic}};
```

Now the altered *x* axis ticks are used. The year label comes in the middle of each year.

```
In[96]:= MultipleListPlot[gdata, fdata, axes]
```

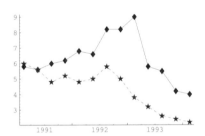

This function constructs the option settings for the legend.

```
In[97]:= legend[pt_] :=
            {PlotLegend -> {"Germany", "France"},
             LegendPosition -> pt,
             LegendShadow -> None};
```

The legend is added to the picture.

```
In[98]:= p1 =
            MultipleListPlot[gdata, fdata,
                             axes, legend[{0.7,0.2}]]
```

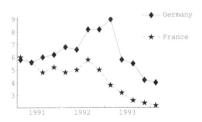

The final picture is made by adjusting the fonts and adding a label to the top of the picture.

```
In[99]:= Show[p1,
             PlotLabel -> FontForm["Real Interest Rates",
                           {"Helvetica", 10}],
             DefaultFont -> {"Helvetica", 7}]
```

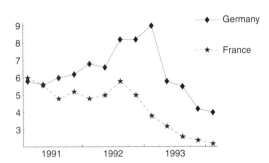

It may seem that there are many steps that must be taken to adjust the various options. All of these options can be set as the default options for `MultipleListPlot` or a small concise function can be written as demonstrated in the first section of this chapter. When this approach is followed the steps are programmed in once and then can be used many times.

This is the simplest way to present several data sets in the same picture. The approach uses `MultipleListPlot` and sets options to put down a legend to identify the data, add labels, and change the fonts.

▶ *Separate Pictures*

An alternative to plotting all the sets of data in the same picture is to make separate pictures and arrange them together. This approach may be useful if the data sets overlap each other. The individual plots are generated with `ListPlot` and these are arranged with `GraphicsArray`.

A list of two graphics objects is constructed.

```
In[100]:= Map[
              ListPlot[#,
                  DisplayFunction -> Identity]&,
              {fdata, gdata}]
Out[100]= {-Graphics-, -Graphics-}
```

GraphicsArray plots the two pictures side by side.

In[101]:= Show[GraphicsArray[%]]

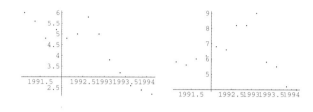

It can immediately be seen that the *y* axis in the two pictures does not have the same scale. Other problems with the picture include the lack of labels and the positions of the axes. These can be improved by supplying more options to the ListPlot.

Now the two pictures are generated with the same PlotRange. In addition, various options to put down labels, set the axes and ticks, and adjust fonts are included.

```
In[102]:= p1 =
            Map[
              ListPlot[First[#],
                DisplayFunction -> Identity,
                PlotJoined -> True,
                PlotLabel -> Last[#],
                Axes -> False, PlotRange ->{2.1,9.2},
                Frame -> True,
                DefaultFont -> {"Helvetica", 7},
                FrameTicks -> {tickfun,TickFunction,None,None}]&,
              {{fdata, "France"}, {gdata, "Germany"}}]

Out[102]= {-Graphics-, -Graphics-}
```

The GraphicsArray is plotted with its PlotLabel option to label both pictures.

```
In[103]:= Show[
            GraphicsArray[p1],
            PlotLabel -> FontForm["Real Interest Rates",
                                   {"Helvetica", 10}]]
```

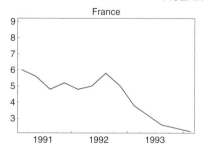
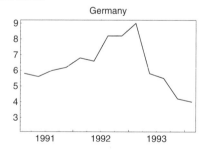

The GraphicsArray method of plotting the data sets is quite successful. An alternative to this picture is to plot the pictures one on top of the other. A disadvantage of the picture is the difficulty with which the data sets are compared point by point, while its strength is the simplicity. If the message to be derived from the data is that one increased while others fell this arrangement could be appropriate.

▶ *The Filled Plot*

When two sets of data are to be compared a special way to do this is to shade the area between each plot. This can make it easier to see not only each data set but also how the difference between them evolves. The functionality to do this shading is provided by the function ListFilledPlot defined in the standard package Graphics`FilledPlot`.

In[104]:= **Needs["Graphics`FilledPlot`"]**

This makes the filled plot. One problem with this picture is that it is hard to distinguish the two data sets.

In[105]:= **ListFilledPlot[fdata, gdata]**

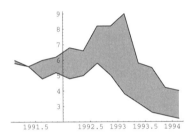

It is possible to combine the data plot with the shaded plot. This is done by extracting the primitives that make the shading. The replacement rule removes the Line primitives.

In[106]:= **prims = First[% /. Line[_] -> {}];**

These primitives can be displayed in the usual way.

In[107]:= **Show[Graphics[prims]]**

The data plot now includes the shading by means of the Prolog option. gdata and fdata were generated earlier.

In[108]:= **MultipleListPlot[gdata, fdata,**
        PlotJoined -> True,
        Prolog -> prims]

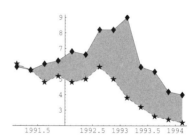

This function constructs the option settings for the legend.

In[109]:= **legend[pt_] :=**
        {PlotLegend -> {"Germany", "France"},
        LegendPosition -> pt,
        LegendShadow -> None};

These are the options that set the axes.

In[110]:= **axes =**
        {PlotJoined -> True,
        Axes -> False,
        Frame -> {True, True,False,False},
        FrameTicks -> {tickfun, TickFunction}};

These are the options that set the fonts and the main label.

In[111]:= **label =**
        {PlotLabel -> FontForm["Real Interest Rates\n",
                        {"Helvetica", 10}],
        DefaultFont -> {"Helvetica", 7}};

Now the picture is put together with the lists of options that were generated earlier.

```
In[112]:= MultipleListPlot[gdata, fdata,
            Prolog -> prims,
            PlotJoined -> True,
            legend[{0.6,0.0}], axes, label]
```

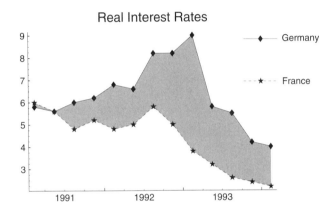

In order to generate this picture it was necessary to combine the results of two different plotting functions, `ListFilledPlot` and `MultipleListPlot`. The ease with which the results of different commands can be combined is a strength of *Mathematica*. It means that each command does not just stand alone to do one fixed set of operations. Each command can be combined and tailored by a program to generate results beyond those originally envisaged when the command was developed.

In the picture here the shading between the lines helps to show the changing relationship between the data sets. It stands in contrast to the `GraphicsArray` method that plotted two separate pictures. This picture draws attention to the relationship between the two data sets. For example it is easy to see when the difference between interest rates in the two countries was large and when it was small. This is seen in combination with the individual trend in each country.

14.7 Rescaling the Data

The scale of a picture is concerned with the way that each datum is mapped to a point in the plot. The typical scale is linear, a scale that is easy to comprehend visually. When the data cover a narrow range of values this scale is quite adequate. However when the data cover a wide range of values the linear scale introduces problems. If some values are many times larger than the smallest these small values may be poorly displayed. An example of this can be demonstrated with data showing voting for the Republican and Democratic parties in U.S. presidential elections. The data exist in the file `ExtendGraphics`‘`USVotingData`‘[6].

---

[6]The data is taken from *The Limits of Liberty: American History 1607-1980*, Maldwyn A. Jones.

The data are read with ReadList. They are read in as string expressions so that the descriptive text at the beginning can be removed.

```
In[113]:= data =
              ReadList["ExtendGraphics`USVotingData`",
                  Word, RecordLists -> True];
```

The first element is some identifying text, the rest is the data.

```
In[114]:= Short[data,3]
Out[114]//Short=
  {{Year, Rep, Dem}, {1860, 1.866, 1.383}, {1864, 2.214, 1.805},
    {1868, 3.013, 2.703}, <<26>>, {1976, 39.148, 40.829},
    {1980, 42.797, 34.434}}
```

The identifying text is dropped. The remaining strings are turned into number expressions.

```
In[115]:= ndata = ToExpression[Rest[data]];
```

ListPlot will plot one part of the data.

```
In[116]:= ListPlot[Map[Part[#, {1,2}]&, ndata]]
```

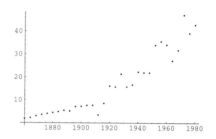

The relevant data can be extracted to be used further on.

```
In[117]:= (rvotes = Map[Part[#, {1,2}]&, ndata];
              dvotes = Map[Part[#, {1,3}]&, ndata];)
```

MultipleListPlot will plot both sets of data.

```
In[118]:= Needs["Graphics`MultipleListPlot`"] ;
```

A problem with this picture is that data from early years are compressed.

```
In[119]:= MultipleListPlot[rvotes, dvotes,
              PlotJoined -> True,
              PlotLegend -> {"Republican", "Democrat"}]
```

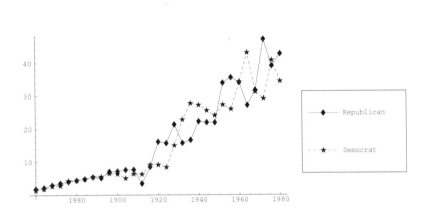

It is hard to understand the results of the earliest elections from this picture. Nonetheless, it does portray some interesting information. For example, the sharp increases between the 1910s and the 1920s and then again in the 1950s reflect changes in electoral law that enfranchised a larger section of the population. However, if the aim of the picture is to show how well the two parties did relative to each other it does a poor job until after about 1920.

The solution is to use a different scale. The way to expand out small values is to use a logarithmic scale. Since only one component of the data, the y values, will be scaled the result will be a semilogarithmic plot. A logarithmic picture can be made with the `LogListPlot` function defined in the standard package `Graphics`Graphics``.

This graphics package defines logarithmic plots.

```
In[120]:= Needs["Graphics`Graphics`"] ;
```

```
In[121]:= ?LogListPlot
```
```
LogListPlot[{y1, y2, ...}] or LogListPlot[{{x1, y1}, {x2, y2},
    ...}] generates a plot of Log[yi] against the xi.
```

The small values are now expanded but it would be good if `MultipleListPlot` could be used.

```
In[122]:= LogListPlot[rvotes]
```

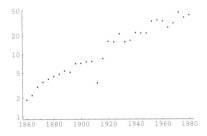

The data can be rescaled by taking the logarithm of the y values.

```
In[123]:= {rlog, dlog} =
            {rvotes, dvotes} /.
            {x_?NumberQ, y_?NumberQ} :> {x, Log[10, y]} ;
```

It would be better if the tick marks on the y axis were logarithmically scaled.

In[124]:= **MultipleListPlot[rlog, dlog,**
  PlotJoined -> True]

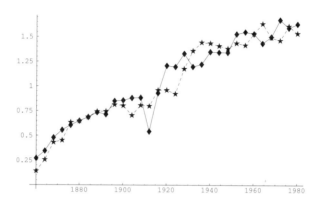

The LogScale function, loaded from Graphics`Graphics`, will do this.

In[125]:= **?LogScale**

LogScale[xmin, xmax] gives a list of "nice" values between xmin
   and xmax suitable for use as tick mark positions on a
   logarithmic scale. LogScale[xmin, xmax, n] attempts to find n
   such values.

The y axis ticks are now properly scaled.

In[126]:= **MultipleListPlot[rlog, dlog,**
  Ticks -> {Automatic, LogScale},
  PlotJoined -> True]

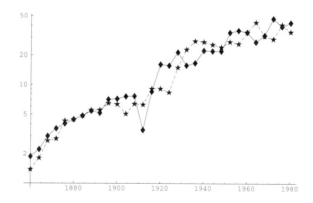

The steps to make log plots with MultipleListPlot can be combined to make a new function. One change is to alter the symbol shape (not to use a star).

```
In[127]:= MultipleLogListPlot[data__, opts___?OptionQ] :=
              Module[{ldata},
                 ldata = Apply[{#1,Log[10,#2]}&, {data}, {2}] ;
                 MultipleListPlot[Sequence @@ ldata, opts,
                     Axes -> False, PlotJoined -> True,
                     Frame -> {True, True, False, False},
                     FrameTicks -> {Automatic, LogScale},
                     LegendShadow -> None,
                     LegendPosition -> {0.6, -0.3},
                     SymbolShape ->
                             {PlotSymbol[Diamond,Filled->False],
                              PlotSymbol[Box, 1.5,Filled->False]}]]
```

The new function works in the expected way.

```
In[128]:= MultipleLogListPlot[rvotes, dvotes]
```

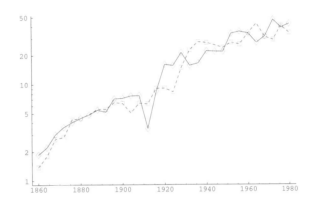

Now the final picture is made. The fonts are adjusted and some more labeling is added.

```
In[129]:= MultipleLogListPlot[rvotes, dvotes,
              PlotLegend -> {"Republicans", "Democrats"},
              FrameLabel -> {"Year", "Millions of Votes"},
              PlotLabel ->
                      "Presidental Elections: 1860-1980\n",
              DefaultFont -> {"Helvetica", 8}]
```

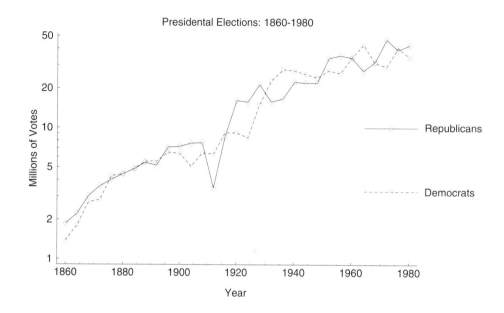

This picture clearly shows trends in voting patterns in U.S. presidential elections. The early dominance of Republicans followed by the extremely close elections of 1876, 1880, 1884, and 1888 are clearly displayed. The election of 1912, where much of the Republican vote was lost to Theodore Roosevelt, is shown. After this comes alternating cycles of victories by one party and the other. In the middle of these the four victories of Franklin D. Roosevelt are clearly shown. Another point that can be found from the graph is its nearly linear form, representing an exponential growth in the number of people exercising their right to vote. However, the logarithmic scale tends to hide certain details. The most notable are sudden changes in the number of people voting as a result of electoral legislation. If this was an important point a linear scale would be more appropriate.

This picture is yet another example of combining functionality from different plotting packages. This functionality was easily combined to form a new plotting command similar to `MultipleListPlot` but with logarithmic scaling. When this picture was made one of the default plotting symbols, a star, was changed to a box. This was necessary due to a special connotation of the star in the context of the subject matter. It is important to avoid making inadvertent and unfortunate points like this.

14.8 The Bar Chart

The bar chart portrays a set of data with vertical or horizontal columns. It is most appropriate for displaying data for which it is not meaningful to interpolate between each datum. In this example some data have been taken from *The Economist*, April 23, 1994. The data represent the percentage of new loans in Japan made by state institutions. In *Mathematica* bar charts are produced by the function `BarChart`, which is defined in the standard package `Graphics`Graphics`.

In[130]:= **Needs["Graphics`Graphics`"]**

The BarChart primitive was defined when the package Graphics`Graphics` was loaded.

In[131]:= **?BarChart**

BarChart[list1, list2, ...] generates a bar chart of the data in
    the lists.

The data to be plotted.

In[132]:= **data =**
            {17.51, 13.5, 9.9, 6.3, 7.6, 13.0, 13.9,
                        18.4, 22.5, 42.2, 73.7};

The basic bar chart is made. One serious problem with this is the *x* axis tick labels.

In[133]:= **BarChart[data]**

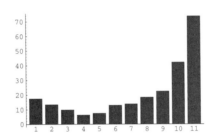

The positions and labels for the *x* axis tick labels can easily be constructed.

In[134]:= **ticks =**
                Transpose[{Range[11],
                Prepend[Range[84,93], 1983]}]

Out[134]= {{1, 1983}, {2, 84}, {3, 85}, {4, 86}, {5, 87},
    {6, 88}, {7, 89}, {8, 90}, {9, 91}, {10, 92}, {11, 93}}

The new ticks are added to the picture.

In[135]:= **BarChart[data,**
                Ticks -> {ticks, Automatic}]

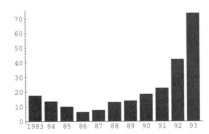

Now the axes are drawn in white so they are hidden. The picture already contains strong horizontal and vertical components and the axes lines are unnecessary. Of course, this is a matter of taste.

```
In[136]:= bar =
            BarChart[data,
                Ticks -> {ticks, Automatic},
                AxesStyle -> GrayLevel[1]]
```

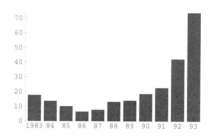

The bar chart picture above could be improved if some elements were added that helped to show how bars on one side of the picture compared with those on the other. One way that this can be achieved would be to draw horizontal gridlines across the picture.

This is not successful. The GridLines are much too strong. The most prominent parts of the picture are those where there are no data.

```
In[137]:= Show[bar, GridLines -> {None, Automatic}]
```

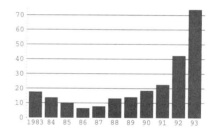

An alternative is to draw white rulings on top of the bars.

```
In[138]:= rules =
            {GrayLevel[1], AbsoluteThickness[0.25],
                Table[Line[{{0.5,i}, {11.5, i}}], {i,10,80,10}]};
```

The rulings are combined with the picture.

```
In[139]:= Show[bar, Epilog -> rules]
```

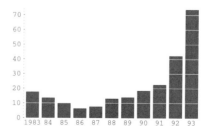

The final result is assembled.

In[140]:= **Show[bar, Epilog -> rules,**
                 AxesLabel -> "%",
                 DefaultFont -> {"Helvetica", 5}]

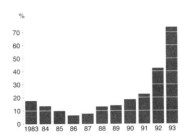

The final picture appears above. Such a picture is an alternative to printing data in a table. One of the features of a bar chart is that it can be plotted with a small size. These data represent the value of some quantity each year and it is not meaningful to interpolate between the samples. Consequently it is suitable to be visualized by a bar chart.

▷ *Three-Dimensional Bar Chart*

Another type of bar chart that is very popular is a three-dimensional bar chart. This can be constructed with BarChart3D, defined in the standard package Graphics`Graphics3D`.

The graphics package that defines the three-dimensional bar chart.

In[141]:= **Needs["Graphics`Graphics3D`"] ;**

BarChart3D accepts a rectangular array of data.

In[142]:= **?BarChart3D**

BarChart3D[list, opts] creates a three-dimensional bar graph of
     the   rectangular matrix list.   BarChart3D[{{{z,
     style},...}...},opts] creates a bar graph with a specific
     style for each bar.   BarChart3D[{{{x, y, z}, style}...}]
     creates a bar graph of bars scattered at specific x and y
     coordinates with height z and a specific style.

The data are made into an array by putting them into a list.

In[143]:= **BarChart3D[{data}]**

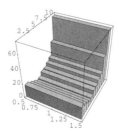

By altering the BoxRatios and ViewPoint options the appearance is improved.

```
In[144]:= Show[%,
               BoxRatios -> {.1, 1, .6},
               ViewPoint -> {2, 0, .3}]
```

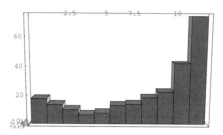

Finally the ticks and axes are altered.

```
In[145]:= Show[%,
               Ticks -> {None,ticks,Automatic},
               AxesEdge -> {{1,-1}, {1,-1},{1,1}},
               Boxed -> False]
```

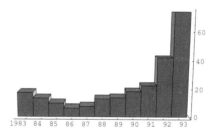

This type of picture can be developed further but it is deficient in some fundamental respects. It is a three-dimensional picture drawn with a perspective transformation. This means that distances across the picture are not uniform and it will be harder to take measurements from the picture than for a two-dimensional bar chart. Despite this the three-dimensional bar chart remains highly popular even though it is not as effective a tool for displaying data as a two-dimensional bar chart.

▶ *The Horizontal Bar Chart*

A different style of bar chart is one in which the bars are arranged horizontally. One type of data to which this is suited is the measurement of some quantity from a series of different samples. One advantage of the horizontal bar chart is that the bars are oriented in the same direction as the text labels. An example of this type of picture can be produced from this data describing 1992 car production from *The Economist*, September 11, 1993.

```
In[146]:= Needs["Graphics`Graphics`"]
```

Here is the basic data, taken from *The Economist*, September 11, 1993.

```
In[147]:= data =
            {{1.8, "Honda"}, {2., "Peugot-Citroen"},
             {2.2, "Chrysler"}, {2.5, "Fiat"},
             {3.4, "Nissan"},
             {3.7, "Volkswagen"}, {5.6, "Toyota"},
             {6., "Ford"}, {7., "General Motors"}};
```

The numeric and textual data are separated.

```
In[148]:= (number = Map[First, data] ;
            names  = Map[Last, data];)
```

The text will be used to put down tick marks.

```
In[149]:= names = Transpose[{Range[Length[names]], names}];
```

The BarOrientation option makes this bar chart horizontal.

```
In[150]:= bar =
            BarChart[number,
              BarOrientation -> Horizontal,
              BarEdges -> False,
              BarStyle -> (GrayLevel[0.5]&),
              Ticks -> {Automatic, names}]
```

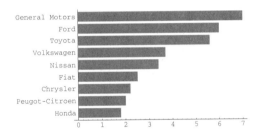

The basic bar chart can be combined with some white rules across the bars.

```
In[151]:= Show[bar,
             Epilog -> {GrayLevel[1], AbsoluteThickness[0.25],
               Table[Line[{{i,0.5}, {i,9.5}}],
                 {i,0.5,6.5,0.5}]}]
```

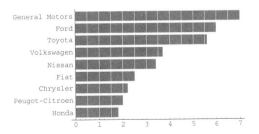

Now more labels are added and the chart is complete.

```
In[152]:= Show[%,
              AxesStyle -> GrayLevel[1],
              PlotLabel ->
                FontForm["Millions of cars produced in 1992",
                         {"Helvetica", 8}],
              DefaultFont -> {"Helvetica", 6}]
```

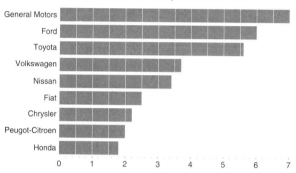

Adding a frame around a picture like this can help to hold it together. This is easily done using `GraphicsArray`.

```
In[153]:= Show[GraphicsArray[{%}, Frame -> True]]
```

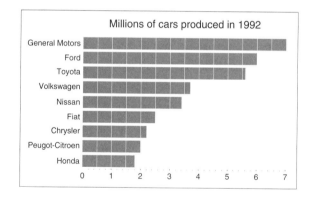

14.9 The Pie Chart

The pie chart can be used to display the component parts of some object showing the relationship of each part to the whole. It will not be effective unless the number of parts is small, certainly no larger than ten. As a mechanism for displaying data the pie chart can be criticized, for example, Tufte states, "Given their low data-density and failure to order numbers along a visual dimension, pie charts should never be used." Nonetheless, the pie chart can be an appropriate tool to display the proper type of data. In *Mathematica* a pie chart is created by the function `PieChart` defined in the standard package `Graphics`Graphics`.

In[154]:= **Needs["Graphics`Graphics`"]**

A data set taken from *The Economist*,
October 23, 1993. It describes spending
on hospitals in the U.S. in 1992.

In[155]:= **data = {33, 15, 18, 25, 9};**

The basic pie chart is produced.

In[156]:= **PieChart[data]**

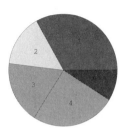

The data are converted to percentage
labels. This conversion is rather crude
since it does not check that they sum to
100.

In[157]:= **labels =**
       Map[ToString[Round[#]] <> "%"&,
          data 100 / Apply[Plus, N[data]]]

Out[157]= {33%, 15%, 18%, 25%, 9%}

The coloring of the slices is changed to be
grayscale and the slices are labeled
according to their percentage size.

In[158]:= **pie =**
       PieChart[data,
          PieLabels -> labels,
          PieStyle -> Table[GrayLevel[i], {i,.25,1,.175}]]]

This picture would be considerably improved by labeling it with some text that described the meaning of each slice. One way to do this is with Text primitive placed around the perimeter of the pie. There is no neat way to do this other than by manually entering the coordinates of these points. Putting the diagram in a drawing program and placing the labels interactively would be much easier. An alternative is to place a legend beside the chart that describes the slices. This can be done with the package Graphics`Legend`".

The legend package is loaded.   *In[159]:=* **Needs["Graphics`Legend`"]**

These strings identify the slices.

```
In[160]:= txt =
              {"Health\nInsurers 33%",
               "Veterans\nAdministration 15%", "Medicaid 18%",
               "Medicare 25%","Private\nPatients 9%"};
```

This forms the information for the legend.

```
In[161]:= leg =
              Table[{GrayLevel[i 0.175 + 0.075], Part[txt,i]},
              {i,5}];
```

The ShowLegend command plots the legend with the graphic.

```
In[162]:= pleg =
              ShowLegend[pie, {leg, LegendShadow -> None,
                 LegendSize -> {1.6,1.3}, LegendPosition ->
              {1,-0.5}}]
```

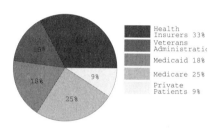

$DefaultFont is altered so that the legend font will change.

```
In[163]:= (oldFont = $DefaultFont;
              $DefaultFont = {"Helvetica", 5})

Out[163]= {Helvetica, 5}
```

The ShowLegend command plots the legend with the graphic.

```
In[164]:= Show[pleg,
              PlotLabel -> "Spending on hospitals: 1992",
              DefaultFont -> {"Helvetica", 8}]
```

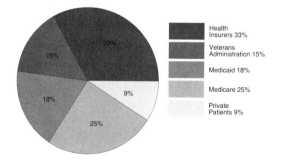

As a final result a frame is put around the whole picture.

`In[165]:= Show[GraphicsArray[{%}, Frame -> True]]`

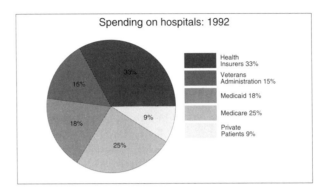

$DefaultFont is restored to its original value.

`In[166]:= $DefaultFont = oldFont`

`Out[166]= {Courier, 5.5}`

This final result is minimal in terms of graphical elements used. It clearly achieves the primary purpose of a pie chart: to show the relationship between the component parts. For example, it can immediately be seen that slightly over half of the spending on hospitals is undertaken by the federal government. A linear type of picture such as a bar chart would not show this so easily.

There are variants on a pie chart such as drawing it in three dimensions. This is a very dubious thing to do. Under projection its shape is not circular and the advantage of the pie chart, seeing how parts add up, becomes lost. A three-dimensional pie chart is an example of excessive use of graphics. Nonetheless, it remains widely used in publications and the ability to produce a three-dimensional pie chart is sometimes used to demonstrate the prowess of some graphics package. The reason for this popularity is probably a confusion with the primary purpose of the picture. The purpose should be to use the data to make specific points, instead of demonstrating the plotting process itself.

14.10 Primitive Styles and Summary

This chapter has discussed various principles that can be used to make a well-designed picture. It has been done by considering a variety of sample pictures. Now, this last section will look at the styles with which the component parts of these pictures are rendered.

▶ *If Nothing Else!*

If nothing else is to be changed then at the very least some consideration should be given to the font that is used. This needs to be thought of in conjunction with the size of the final picture. It is an extremely simple process to use $DefaultFont to change the font. Despite this, pictures are often seen generated with *Mathematica* with completely inappropriate fonts, usually with fonts that are too large for the picture. This happens in publications with graphics made by *Mathematica* and it even happens in books that people write about *Mathematica*. If nothing else is to be changed, at least adjust the font to be appropriate for the final picture.

▸ *Output Device*

If the appearance of the picture is important then the first thing to be considered is the output device that will be used. Two important ways that the output device has an influence are the way that color is represented and the resolution of the device. Obviously a picture designed to use different colors to distinguish different elements may not work well when printed on a gray-scale printer. The number of different colors or shades that can be displayed is also important. A monochrome output device can display different levels of gray only by sacrificing spatial resolution through mechanisms such as halftoning or dithering. In fact, on low-resolution devices, the effective use of non-saturated colors such as RGBColor[0.5,0,0] or GrayLevel[0.5] may be limited. In these cases saturated colors such as RGBColor[1,0,0], Hue[0.5], or GrayLevel[0] may be more powerful. The influence of the resolution of the output device is described in the following sections.

▸ *Lines*

In general the thickness of lines should be reduced to some minimum value. If they are reduced too much they will become one pixel wide on most output devices. This is acceptable on a 70-dpi screen or a 300-dpi printer but on a 1200-dpi printer the line will be hard to observe. A minumum size is probably 0.25 points for an absolute thickness and 0.001 for relative thickness. For a picture 4 inches in width these two are roughly equivalent. This size will give a line that is 1 pixel thick on all except the highest resolution output devices.

In addition to thinning out lines some hierarchy of styles may be necessary. There are various alternatives to the thinning of a line that achieve the same result of reducing its impact. These include dashing and drawing it in a gray shading. On a low- or medium-resolution output device a mixture of dashing and grayscale will often produce artifacts and should be avoided. In fact on a low-resolution device dashing on its own can look strange.

When a picture is made in *Mathematica* the thickness, color, and dashing of line primitives can be controlled easily by the various directives. When lines represent tick marks this is more complex but they can be altered by means of the package ExtendGraphics`Ticks`. An example of this is shown later in this section.

▸ *Text*

The choice of the font in which text is rendered is of prime importance. Courier is often good for output on a low-resolution device and especially at small sizes. This is because the typeface is mostly vertical or horizontal with few diagonal strokes. Consequently it makes effective bitmaps for small sizes on low-resolution screens. Since it is a fixed-width font each character occupies the same space in the output and they tend to be well spaced. On a low-resolution device this will promote the ease with which the text can be read.

At higher resolutions the fixed-width nature of Courier presents a disadvantage. It means that any text built from Courier tends to take up more space than would a nonfixed-width font. The requirement that a well-designed picture have few elements and be compact suggests that fixed-width fonts should be avoided at higher resolutions.

Fonts such as Times-Roman or Helvetica are not fixed-width. The Times-Roman font is very popular but the preference for the pictures in this book is Helvetica. The main difference between them is the lack of serifs, little embellishments at the extrema of the characters, with Helvetica. Its characters are quite minimal and this is consistent with the graphical design principles of avoiding unneccessary elements in the picture. For example, it might be tempting to use some highly stylized gothic font in a picture. The result would be to draw attention away from the data in the picture and concentrate it on the text. This would hinder the process of using the data to convey a message.

In *Mathematica* graphics the font is altered by the use of `DefaultFont` and `FontForm`. It must be noted that in Version 2.2 (or earlier) *Mathematica* a fixed-width font was required to make text layout and it was not possible to mix fonts within a text label. Now the typesetting capabilities overcome these limitations. Typeset text is more economical in its size and the ability to mix different fonts is clearly essential (for example placing greek and roman letters in the same label).

A last problem to consider with text is that it may be important to ensure that a group of text labels have consistent formats.

The tick labels include a "1" and a "0.5". It would be better to have both "1.0" and "0.5".

In[167]:= **Plot[Sin[x], {x,0,2}]**

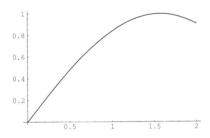

This loads the axes package discussed in Chapter 13 page 264.

In[168]:= **Needs["ExtendGraphics`Ticks`"]**

`TickFunction` will replicate the default tick marks.

In[169]:= **Plot[x, {x,0,100},**
          Ticks -> TickFunction]

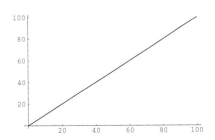

The TextFunction option is set to TrimText, which trims all text labels to the same length.

```
In[170]:= Plot[Sin[x], {x,0,2},
              Ticks ->
                  (TickFunction[#1, #2,
                      TextFunction -> TrimText]&)]
```

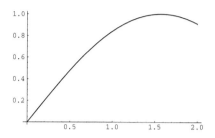

The style of the ticks are changed as well as the label.

```
In[171]:= Plot[Sin[x], {x,0,2},
              Ticks ->
                  (TickFunction[#1, #2,
                      MajorStyle -> {Thickness[0.001]},
                      MajorLength -> {0.006, 0.006},
                      MinorLength -> {0,0},
                      TextFunction -> TrimText]&)]
```

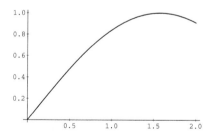

▸ *Fills*

Mathematica graphics provide many ways to fill a region including Polygon, Rectangle, or Disk primitives. In general, on a low resolution output device if the fill region is a non-saturated color there will be a loss of spatial resolution. This will be very noticeable if the region is complex. In this case saturated colors such as GrayLevel[1] and RGBColor[0,0,1] are very suitable as is any color made with the one argument form of Hue, which will be fully saturated by definition.

▶ *Summary*

This section has discussed the ways that design principles influence the use of *Mathematica* graphics at the level of the primitives. Many of the difficulties that can arise were traced to problems related to the resolution of the output device and the size of the final picture. These can be summarized in the table that follows.

	Low Resolution	Medium Resolution	High Resolution
Example Device	1–8 bit monitor	24-bit monitor laser printer	Phototypesetter
Text: font	Courier font looks best	All fonts look good	All fonts look good
Text: color	Non-saturated color is bad	Non-saturated color is bad	Non-saturated color is acceptable
Lines: dashing	Small dashes have artifacts	Small dashes are good	Small dashes are good
Lines: color	Dashing and non-saturated color mix poorly	Dashing and non-saturated color mix poorly	Dashing and non-saturated color mix well
Fills: color	Non-saturated color can look strange	Non-saturated color looks acceptable	Non-saturated color is good

Summary of primitive styles and device resolution.

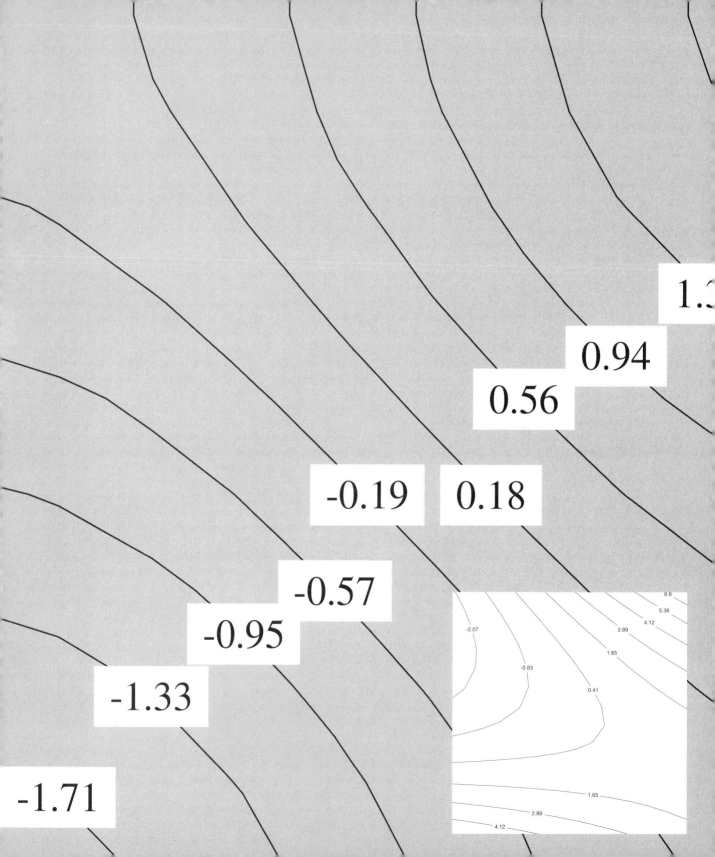

Chapter 15
Labeling Contour Plots

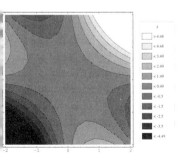

Part III of *Mathematica Graphics* is concerned with applying *Mathematica* to various graphics problems. The problems discussed in the last chapter concentrated on ways to generate effective pictures. It demonstrated how lines and points could be arranged to form a clear and concise picture. Labels often must be added to aid in this process. When the picture is a contour plot it becomes more important to produce a clear label since there are no axes describing the value of each contour line. At the same time the actual placement of labels is more challenging. This chapter discusses how the problem of labeling contour plots can be solved.

In the case of *Mathematica* graphics, options such as `ColorFunction` and `ContourStyle` provide simple ways to label contour plots. However, these do not provide a numeric scale and it can be rather difficult to determine which lines belong to which values. The approach in this chapter is to use numeric labels to display the values of the contour lines.

There are two solutions presented in this chapter. The first uses an automatic technique to place labels on the contour lines themselves, which works well for unshaded contour plots. The second places a legend at the side of the whole picture and is more appropriate for shaded plots.

15.1 Labeling Contour Lines

The ability to label the contour lines is provided by the package `ExtendGraphics`LabelContourLines`. In this text many examples of contour plots will be given. The font that is used to label them is set quite small so that it fits in a relatively small number of pages. Normally the number of contour plots will be fewer and the size at which they appear will be larger.

Load the package which defines the function to label the contour lines.

```
In[1]:= Needs["ExtendGraphics`LabelContour`"]
```

The font for the labels is set to be quite small because of the small size of the pictures in this book. The options are described later.

```
In[2]:= SetOptions[LabelContourLines,
            LabelFont -> {"Times-Roman", 3}]

Out[2]= {LabelFont -> {Times-Roman, 3},
    LabelPlacement -> Center, PointFactor -> 1, PointSkip -> 4}
```

The function LabelContourLines is the central function.

```
In[3]:= ?LabelContourLines
```

LabelContourLines[cont, opts] displays the contour plot cont
    with a label on each contour line giving its height.

Here is a contour plot without labeled contour lines.

In[4]:= **ContourPlot[Sin[x] Sin[y], {x,0,Pi},{y,0,Pi},
                ContourShading -> False]**

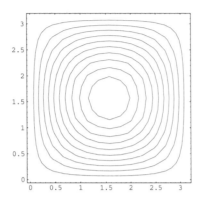

The contour lines are now labeled according to their heights.

In[5]:= **LabelContourLines[%]**

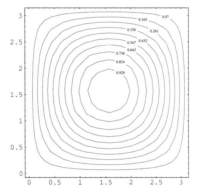

Another example is of an unlabeled contour plot.

In[6]:= **ContourPlot[x y, {x, -2,2}, {y,-2,2},
                ContourShading -> False]**

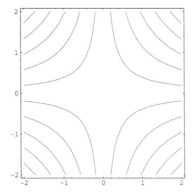

The labels increase the ease with which
the contour plot can be understood.

In[7]:= **LabelContourLines[%]**

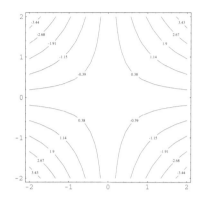

The function LabelContourLines takes a ContourGraphics object and places labels on the lines. It can therefore be used to label the result of ContourPlot as in these examples and also the result of ListContourPlot. In Chapter 18 page 484 it is used to label an extension of ListContourPlot that generates contour plots for irregular data sets.

LabelContourLines[*contour*]	display a Graphics object with numeric values for the contours
LabelFont	an option of LabelContourLines to set the font for labels
LabelPlacement	an option of LabelContourLines to set the method used to place labels
PointFactor	an option of LabelContourLines that works with automatic LabelPlacement
PointSkip	an option of LabelContourLines that works with automatic LabelPlacement

Labeling contour lines.

▷ *Placement of the Labels*

The default operation of LabelContourLines is to place labels at the midpoint of each line segment that represents a contour line. This simple method usually produces pleasing results. On occasion the positions are rather strange. This may be because the labels are too close to each other or because they line up in some unusual fashion. This section shows how the problem can be avoided.

This is a very symmetric contour plot.

In[8]:= **c1 =**
        ContourPlot[x^2 - y^2, {x,-2,2},{y,-2,2},
          ContourShading -> False]

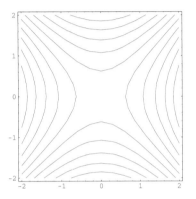

These labels line up so strongly that they produce a visual effect that rivals the actual contour plot.

In[9]:= **LabelContourLines[c1]**

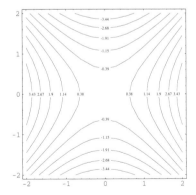

The labels are now distributed evenly
around the picture.

In[10]:= **LabelContourLines[c1,**

    LabelPlacement -> Automatic]

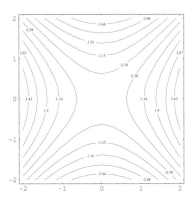

In the previous picture some of the labels
hit the edge and caused holes to appear
in the frame. A small expansion of the
PlotRange option will remove this effect.

In[11]:= **Show[%,**

    PlotRange -> FullOptions[%, PlotRange] 1.02]

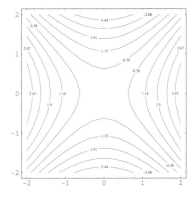

In this contour plot the lines all approach very close together at certain points.

```
In[12]:= c2 =
           ContourPlot[
             Exp[-Sqrt[x^2+y^2]] Cos[ArcTan[x, y]],
               {x,-2,2},{y,-2,2},
             PlotPoints -> 30,
             ContourShading -> False]
```

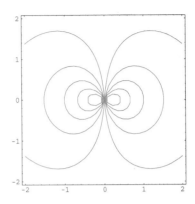

This is just a bad way to place these labels. They should be spaced further apart.

```
In[13]:= LabelContourLines[c2]
```

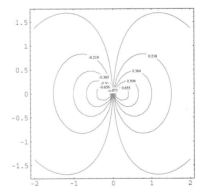

Setting the LabelPlacement option to Automatic allows the function to try and place the labels to avoid each other.

In[14]:= **LabelContourLines[c2, LabelPlacement -> Automatic]**

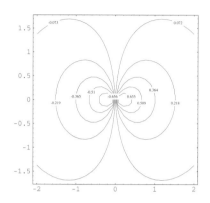

Setting PointFactor to 0.1 tends to spread out the labels in the *x* direction.

In[15]:= **LabelContourLines[c2,**
      LabelPlacement ->Automatic, PointFactor -> 0.1]

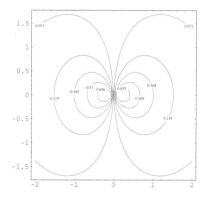

Setting PointFactor to 10 tends to spread out the labels in the *y* direction. In this case the picture is not improved.

In[16]:= **LabelContourLines[c2,**
      LabelPlacement ->Automatic, PointFactor -> 10]

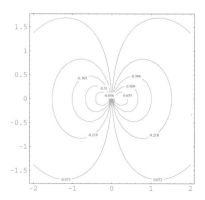

Automatic label placement uses an algorithm to find the position on each contour line furthest from the nearest position on the two contours on either side. A relative weight is given to the x and y directions determined by the setting of the `PointFactor` option. Changing this setting can improve the appearance of the picture by spreading the labels in the x or y direction.

In order to make the algorithm run faster it does not examine every point on each contour. The actual points that are used is controlled by the `PointSkip` option. This should be set to a positive non-zero integer. A setting of 1 means that every point is looked at but the algorithm will take longer to run. A setting of 5 means that every fifth point is tested and the algorithm runs faster. There is a choice between appearance and execution time.

Every point is looked at and a pleasing result generated.

```
In[17]:= LabelContourLines[c2,
              LabelPlacement -> Automatic,
              PointSkip -> 1]
```

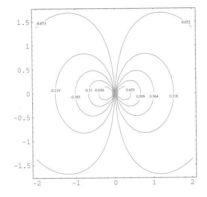

▶ *Setting the Font*

The option LabelFont provides a mechanism to alter the type and size of fonts used to label the contour lines.

In[18]:= **Options[LabelContourLines, LabelFont]**

Out[18]= {LabelFont -> {Times-Roman, 3}}

This is another contour plot to be labeled.

In[19]:= **cont =**
ContourPlot[x y + x + y^2, {x, -2,2}, {y,-2,2},
ContourShading -> False]

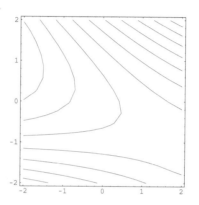

Now Helvetica with a point size of 3 is used for the labels.

In[20]:= **LabelContourLines[cont,**
LabelFont -> {"Helvetica", 3}]

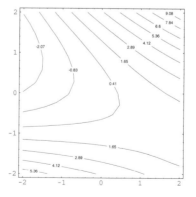

Now Times-Roman with a point size of 5 is used. The result is quite congested because of the small size of the picture. Normally the picture will be larger.

In[21]:= **LabelContourLines[cont,**
        LabelFont -> {"Times-Roman", 5}]

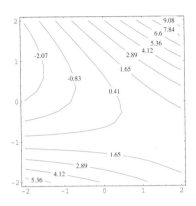

▶ *Shaded Contour Plots*

When the contour plot is shaded the lines can also be labeled with LabelContourLines.

This is a shaded contour plot. The output is suppressed by resetting the DisplayFunction.

In[22]:= **ContourPlot[x^2 y + x y^2, {x, -2,2}, {y,-2,2},**
        DisplayFunction -> Identity]

Out[22]= -ContourGraphics-

The labels still appear on the contour lines.

In[23]:= **LabelContourLines[%]**

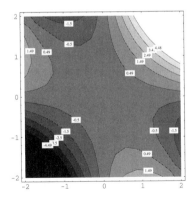

     The method of labeling a shaded contour plot by placing labels on the contour lines makes unsuitable pictures since the labels look strange. There are other methods more suitable for labeling these pictures. One involves placing a legend beside the plot.

15.2 Labeling ContourPlots with a Legend

The levels of a shaded contour plot can be displayed by means of a legend beside the picture. This functionality is provided by the package ExtendGraphics`LabelContour`.

Needs will load the package if it has not already been loaded.

In[24]:= **Needs["ExtendGraphics`LabelContour`"]**

In[25]:= **?LabelContourLegend**

LabelContourLegend[cont, opts] displays the contour plot cont with a legend containing the values of the heights of the contours.

In[26]:= **cont = ContourPlot[x^2 y + x y^2, {x, -2,2}, {y,-2,2}]**

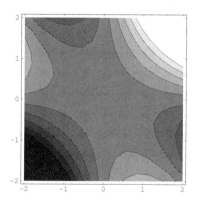

This shows the contour plot with a legend describing the contours.

In[27]:= **LabelContourLegend[cont]**

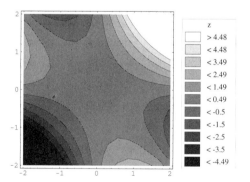

LabelContourLegend[*contour*]	display a Graphics object with a legend of the numeric values of the contours
HeightName	an option of LabelContourLegend setting the text to use for the label; default is z
LegendSize	an option of LabelContourLegend setting the size of the legend
LegendPosition	an option of LabelContourLegend setting the position for the legend
LabelFont	an option of LabelContourLegend setting the font for the labels

Placing a legend beside a contour plot.

The graphics output is suppressed.

```
In[28]:= cont =
            ContourPlot[Sin[x] Sin[y], {x,-Pi,Pi},{y,-Pi,Pi},
                    DisplayFunction -> Identity]
```

Out[28]= -ContourGraphics-

The HeightName option specifies the text to use for the height.

```
In[29]:= LabelContourLegend[cont, HeightName -> "T"]
```

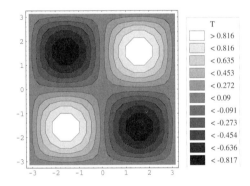

If a blank string is given then no name is used.

In[30]:= **LabelContourLegend[cont, HeightName -> ""]**

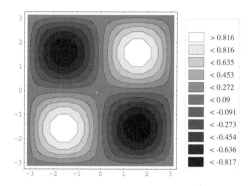

▸ *Legend Position and Size*

The options LegendPosition` and LegendSize` set the position and size of the legend. The default values of these, Automatic, attempt to take into account the number of levels and the size of the font.

This produces a contour plot with only four contour lines.

In[31]:= **cont1 =**
        Show[cont,
            Contours -> {-0.75, -0.25, 0.0001, 0.25, 0.75},
            DisplayFunction -> Identity]

Out[31]= -ContourGraphics-

The legend adjusts its size to account for the number of contour lines.

In[32]:= **LabelContourLegend[cont1]**

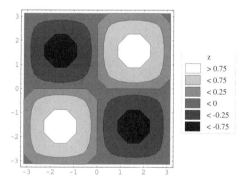

If the font is made bigger the legend will also adjust.

In[33]:= **LabelContourLegend[cont1, LabelFont -> 9]**

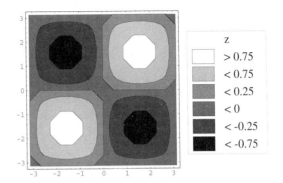

However, the legend does not take into account the overall size of the picture or the size of the HeightName setting. In these cases it may be necessary to alter the setting of the LegendSize' option.

Here the HeightName is made bigger and the legend misses some of the numeric labels.

In[34]:= **LabelContourLegend[cont,**
HeightName -> "Driving Force/N"]

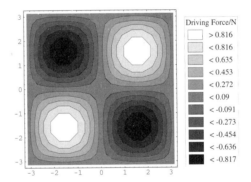

The legend placed by LabelContourLegend is generated by the standard package Graphics'Legend'. The options for legend placement are thus passed into the functions in Graphics'Legend'. To understand how they work the documentation for Graphics'Legend' in the *Guide to Standard Packages* can be studied. However, they are quite complex and a trial-by-error method may be necessary.

Changing the LegendSize option allows the legend to display the longer labels.

```
In[35]:= LabelContourLegend[cont,
              HeightName -> "Driving Force/N",
              LegendSize -> {0.8, 1.7}]
```

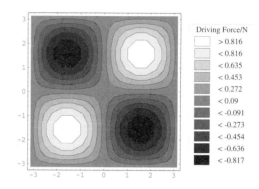

Here the legend is moved to the other side of the picture.

```
In[36]:= LabelContourLegend[cont,
              LegendPosition -> {-2.0, -0.84}]
```

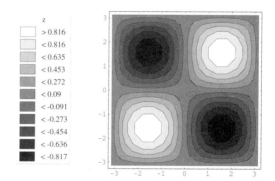

▸ *Setting the Font*

The option `LabelFont` provides a mechanism to alter the type and size of fonts in which the labels appear.

The `LabelFont` option can set the font name.

```
In[37]:= LabelContourLegend[cont,
            LabelFont -> "Helvetica"]
```

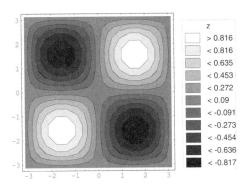

`LabelFont` can set both the font name and size. The legend adjusts to account for the font size.

```
In[38]:= LabelContourLegend[cont,
            LabelFont -> {"Helvetica", 4}]
```

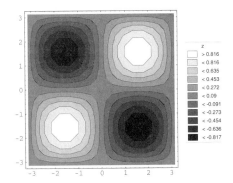

15.3 Labeling in Version 2.2 *Mathematica*

The method of labeling contour lines places text primitives on top of the lines. Normally if a text primitive is put down on top of a line it will be hard to read. This is solved by using the `Background` option of the text primitive to make sure that space is left around the text. This feature was not available in Version 2.2 (or earlier) *Mathematica*. These must move the text to the side to avoid the interaction of text and lines. The package tests which version of *Mathematica* is being used and makes the appropriate choice.

The labeling package must be loaded.   `In[39]:= Needs["ExtendGraphics`LabelContour`"]`

A typical contour plot.

In[40] := c = **ContourPlot[x y, {x,-2,2}, {y,-2,2},**
                       ContourShading -> False]

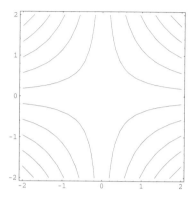

This is how the contour lines are labeled.

In[41] := **LabelContourLines[c]**

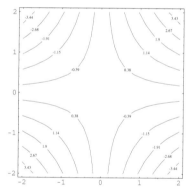

This is how the labels appeared in Version 2.2 *Mathematica*. The result is not so pleasing but still valuable.

In[42] := **LabelContourLines[c]**

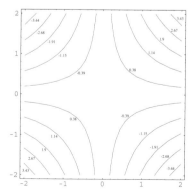

▶ *Legend*

The drawing of a legend beside a contour plot does not use any new features of *Mathematica* and hence works in Version 2.2 *Mathematica*.

15.4 Automatic Placement of Labels

The labeling functions described in this chapter can be used automatically whenever a contour plot is made.   This is done with the `ContourDisplayFunction`, a function also defined in the package `ExtendGraphics`LabelContour`.   When this is set as the `DisplayFunction` option for the contour plotting routines the appropriate labeling routine is invoked.

The labeling package must be loaded.

In[43]:= **Needs["ExtendGraphics`LabelContour`"]**

In[44]:= **?ContourDisplayFunction**

ContourDisplayFunction is a display function for contour plots
    that causes automatic label placement.

`ContourDisplayFunction` is set to be the default `DisplayFunction` for `ContourPlot`.

In[45]:= **SetOptions[ContourPlot,**
               DisplayFunction -> ContourDisplayFunction];

The labeling function is called automatically.

In[46]:= **c = ContourPlot[Sin[x] + Sin[y], {x,-2,2}, {y,-2,2},**
               ContourShading -> False]

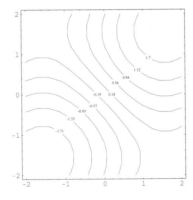

Options are passed automatically to the appropriate labeling routine.

In[47]:= **Show[c, LabelPlacement -> 1]**

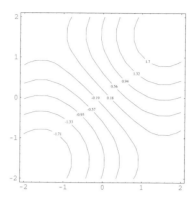

When a shaded contour plot is made the label uses a legend.

In[48]:= **Show[c, ContourShading -> True]**

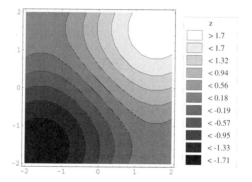

15.5 Summary

This chapter demonstrated how to label contour plots. It presented two methods. One was suited to unshaded contour plots and involved placing labels on the contour lines. The other was appropriate for shaded contour plots and placed a legend beside the picture. A variety of controls was provided to allow tweaking of the positions of the labels and alteration of the font that they used. The first method, labeling the actual lines, has some restrictions when applied in Version 2.2 (or earlier) *Mathematica*. The second works in these older versions. Finally, a method for invoking these routines automatically as contour plots are constructed was presented.

Chapter 16
Two-Dimensional Geometry

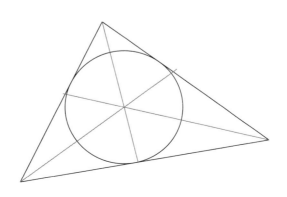

This chapter explores basic mathematical applications of *Mathematica* graphics. It does this by concentrating on two-dimensional geometry. The combination of symbolic and numerical mathematics with graphics makes *Mathematica* a powerful tool for such work. This study will prove to be very valuable for several reasons.

The first reason is that the material here will help the reader to learn, to understand, and to experiment with geometry. This is useful not only for geometry but for the many areas of mathematics that have a geometric interpretation. *"L'algebre n'est qu'une geometrie ecrite; la geometrie n'est qu'une algebre figuree"*[7]. It is often the case that constructing a picture to explain and understand some concept proves to be incisive. This applies as much in mathematics as in other disciplines.

Another reason that makes the material in this chapter valuable is that it covers some of the mathematical foundations of computer graphics. While it does not provide a complete description of computer graphics as does a book such as *Computer Graphics: Principles and Practice*, Second Edition, J. Foley, A. van Dam, S. Feiner, and J. Hughes, it is still of considerable interest to the computer graphics programmer. The wide collection of results that are given here are not just formulae to be copied but live interactive programs that can be modified and used. The collection of results here is somewhat inspired by the series of books starting with *Graphics Gems*, ed. A.S. Glassner. These provide a powerful and broad collection of methods, ideas, and results.

A last reason for the chapter is that it will prove to be useful later. Many of the techniques that are introduced here will prove to have visualization applications utilized in Chapters 18 and 19. For example, the computational geometry techniques that are described at the end of the chapter will be used in Chapter 18 page 475 to form surfaces from three-dimensional data. Giving some explanation of the underlying techniques will make it easier to use the applications into which they are built. Some of the results here are used in later sections of *Mathematica Graphics* but *all* of them can be useful for building some particular type of picture.

In this chapter results are developed and their workings explained. It is not necessary to enter the code that is demonstrated here since it is all collected into a variety of packages and distributed with *Mathematica Graphics*. The main package is the geometry package `ExtendGraphics`Geometry``, which contains the bulk of the results.

▶ *Setting the Mathematica Scale*

Since the topic of the chapter is two-dimensional geometry it is important to make the scale in the x and y directions the same. This is done by setting the `AspectRatio` option of `Graphics` to be `Automatic`. If this is not done some of the examples will not come out properly, for example things that are perpendicular will not appear so and circles will appear as ellipses. The default value of the `AspectRatio` is set to give a rectangular picture irrespective of the scale in x and y. The coordinate systems used by *Mathematica* were described in Chapter 10 page 164.

The scale in x and y is set the same. It is very important that this is done.

```
In[1]:= SetOptions[Graphics,
            AspectRatio -> Automatic];
```

---

[7] Algebra is nothing but written geometry; geometry is nothing but drawn algebra: Sophie Germain.

16.1 Basic Geometric Objects

The study of two-dimensional geometry in this chapter will start by defining basic geometric objects. It is the study of the properties and relations of these fundamental primitives that forms the geometry covered here.

▶ *Vector*

In this chapter a vector will be understood to represent an ordered pair of numbers $\{x, y\}$. Such an entity can describe a point in a two-dimensional space. In general, vectors can consist of more than two numbers and describe points in multidimensional spaces. Some of the results given here can be generalized to higher dimensions and some cannot. For example, the method given here for calculating the length of a vector works for any dimensionality. However, the method in this chapter that finds the circle inscribing a triangle does not generalize to higher dimensions. Vectors can be manipulated by *Mathematica* both as numeric and as symbolic entities. This makes it straightforward to demonstrate vector operations such as addition and multiplication.

```
In[2]:= (p = {px, py};
         q = {qx, qy};)
```

The addition of two vectors adds the corresponding components.

```
In[3]:= p + q
Out[3]= {px + qx, py + qy}
```

Multiplication of a vector by a scalar multiplies each component by the scalar.

```
In[4]:= 3 p
Out[4]= {3 px, 3 py}
```

Dot Product

The dot product of two vectors is defined as the sum of the product of corresponding components.

The dot or scalar product of the vectors $\{px, py\}$ and $\{qx, qy\}$.

```
In[5]:= {px, py}.{qx, qy}
Out[5]= px qx + py qy
```

A vector can be thought of as having a magnitude and a direction. These are exposed by the dot product for two vectors since it is equal to the length of each multiplied by the cosine of the angle between them, $|p||q| \cos \theta$. As a consequence of this definition the dot product of a vector with itself determines the magnitude or length of the vector.

Vector Length

The length of a vector.

```
In[6]:= VectorLength[p_] := Sqrt[p.p]
```

The length of the vector $\{1,1\}$.

```
In[7]:= VectorLength[{1,1}]
Out[7]= Sqrt[2]
```

The length of the vector $\{a,b\}$.

```
In[8]:= VectorLength[{a,b}]
Out[8]= Sqrt[a  + b ]
```
$$Out[8]= \text{Sqrt}[a^2 + b^2]$$

Normal Vectors

In two dimensions the normal is a vector perpendicular to the original vector.

In[9]:= **NormalVector[{px_, py_}] := {py, -px}**

The vectors are perpendicular and the result is zero.

In[10]:= **{2,3}.NormalVector[{2,3}]**

Out[10]= 0

There are two choices for the normal vector. It can be on the right or the left of a vector corresponding to a clockwise movement or a counterclockwise movement. The convention taken by NormalVector is for a normal to be a 90 deg clockwise rotation of the given vector.

The normal (dashed line) is seen to be on the right-hand side of the vector (solid line).

In[11]:= **Show[**
　　　　Graphics[
　　　　　　{Line[{{0,0}, {2,3}}],
　　　　　　　Dashing[{0.05}],
　　　　　　　Line[{{0,0}, NormalVector[{2,3}]}]}]]

Cross Product

Finally, the cross product of two vectors is introduced. This is a concept peculiar to three dimensions but is useful for certain results in two-dimensional geometry. The cross product is a vector perpendicular to the original vectors with a length equal to the area of the parallelogram they generate.

This loads the cross product package.

In[12]:= **Needs["LinearAlgebra`CrossProduct`"]**

The cross product of two two-dimensional vectors can be taken by embedding them in some plane in a three-dimensional space. The plane z == 0 is particularly convenient.

In[13]:= **Cross[{px, py, 0}, {qx, qy, 0}]**

Out[13]= {0, 0, -(py qx) + px qy}

▶ *Point*

A point describes a location in two-dimensional space. It can be described by a vector and can be plotted with the *Mathematica* primitive `Point`. In this chapter the term point can describe both a location in space and a `Point` primitive. The primitive is specific to *Mathematica* and is something that can be used as part of a `Graphics` object. When this is rendered, `Point[{x,y}]` will cause an actual dot to be drawn by *Mathematica* at the point {x,y}. The context in which the term appears will make clear the specific meaning being used.

▶ *Line*

A line can be generated from two distinct points. It forms the shortest path between the points and extends infinitely in either direction. A line like this can be parametrized by the loci of point $\mathbf{p_1} + (\mathbf{p_2} - \mathbf{p_1})\, t$. Here $\mathbf{p_1}$ and $\mathbf{p_2}$ are two points on the line and t is a parameter that describes progress down the line. When t is 0 the point on the line will be at $\mathbf{p_1}$ and when t is 1 it will be at $\mathbf{p_2}$. The `Line` primitive that *Mathematica* provides is closely related to this explicit form for a line. `Line[{p1,p2}]` refers to the segment of the line between the points p1 and p2.

An alternative way to describe a line in two dimensions is an implicit specification. This is the loci of points $\mathbf{p}$ that satisfy the equation $(\mathbf{p} - \mathbf{c}) \cdot \vec{\mathbf{n}} = 0$. Here $\mathbf{c}$ is a point on the line and $\vec{\mathbf{n}}$ is the normal to the line. This generates a line as demonstrated by the `ContourPlot` command, a natural way to plot an implicit equation.

The loci of points {x,y} satisfying ({x,y} - {1,2}).{-1,1} == 0 inside the domain $(-2 \le x \le 2, -2 \le y \le 2)$.

```
In[14]:= ContourPlot[({x,y} - {1,2}).{-1,1},
              {x,-2,2}, {y,-2,2},
              Contours -> {0},
              ContourShading -> False]
```

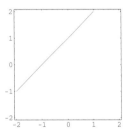

This expression represents an implicit line. The next function converts it to a `Line` primitive.

```
In[15]:= ImplicitLine[{cx, cy}, {nx, ny}]

Out[15]= ImplicitLine[{cx, cy}, {nx, ny}]
```

To plot the `ImplicitLine` this function, which converts it into a `Line` primitive, is required.

```
In[16]:= ToLine[ImplicitLine[{cx_, cy_}, {nx_, ny_}]] :=
              Line[{{cx, cy}, {cx, cy} + {-ny, nx}}]
```

It would be possible to make this happen automatically. Since the implicit form is useful it will be converted only when necessary.

```
In[17]:= ToLine[ImplicitLine[{x0, y0}, {x1, y1}]]
Out[17]= Line[{{x0, y0}, {x0 - y1, x1 + y0}}]
```

The ImplicitLine primitive can be plotted.

```
In[18]:= Show[
           Graphics[
             ToLine[ImplicitLine[{5,5}, {1,1}]]]]
```

An explicit line can be converted into an implicit line.

```
In[19]:= ToImplicit[Line[{p1_, p2_}]] :=
              ImplicitLine[p1, NormalVector[p2-p1]]
```

Here is a symbolic example.

```
In[20]:= ToImplicit[Line[{{a,b}, {c,d}}]]
Out[20]= ImplicitLine[{a, b}, {-b + d, a - c}]
```

ToLine will convert the implicit line back to the original explicit line.

```
In[21]:= ToLine[%]
Out[21]= Line[{{a, b}, {c, d}}]
```

The length of a line segment can be defined as the length of the vector between the two points.

```
In[22]:= LineLength[Line[{p1_, p2_}]] :=
              VectorLength[p2-p1]
```

This is the length of the line segment between the points {2.5, 9} and {2, 7}.

```
In[23]:= LineLength[Line[{{2.5, 9}, {2, 7}}]]
Out[23]= 2.06155
```

The implicit line representation will prove very useful in later results. In fact it is quite distinct from the explicit line. The explicit line lies on the shortest path between two points. The implicit line divides the space into two regions. The fact that when plotted they both look the same and they can be interconverted is a unique feature of two-dimensional space. When the *Mathematica* representation of an implicit line is converted to a *Mathematica* Line primitive, as is done here, decisions must be made for its length and direction. These are made so that ToImplicit and ToLine applied one after the other will regenerate the original expression. In other words they are inverse functions to each other.

▶ *Triangle*

A triangle can be represented in *Mathematica* with the Polygon primitive.

A representation of a triangle.	*In[24]:=* **tri = Polygon[{{4,6}, {9,1}, {-5, 2}}]**
	Out[24]= Polygon[{{4, 6}, {9, 1}, {-5, 2}}]
The triangle can be plotted.	*In[25]:=* **Show[Graphics[tri]]**

Boundary makes it easier to see how a triangle interacts with other geometric elements.	*In[26]:=* **Boundary[Polygon[{a_, b__}]] := Line[{a,b,a}]**
Drawing the triangle in this outline form makes it easier to see.	*In[27]:=* **Show[Graphics[Boundary[tri]]]**

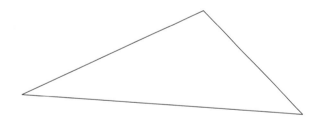

Graphics options such as Frame are often useful to estimate the range of coordinates.

In[28]:= **Show[%, Frame -> True]**

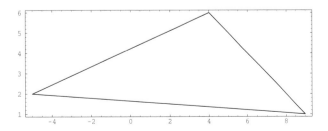

▶ *Circle*

The *Mathematica* primitive `Circle` is quite suitable to represent a circle. The basic form of the circle specifies the center and radius. The *Mathematica* primitive can also represent ellipses and arcs.

If this does not look circular it may be that the `AspectRatio` option has not been set to `Automatic` as described at the beginning of the chapter.

In[29]:= `Show[Graphics[Circle[{6,2}, 2]]]`

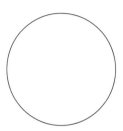

16.2 Geometric Transformations

The vectors that make up the geometric primitives can undergo a variety of transformations. Here a simple but important class of transformations known as affine transformations will be looked at. Such transformations can be represented by matrices and generate translations, rotations, and scalings.

There are several *Mathematica* packages containing functions that carry out these transformations. An example is the package `Graphics`GraphicsOperations`` that is available on *MathSource*. This section looks at the workings of geometric transformations and how they can be understood with the help of *Mathematica*.

▶ *Translation*

A translation of a vector $\{v_x, v_y\}$ by $\{t_x, t_y\}$ will take it to $\{v_x + t_x, v_y + t_y\}$. It is easy to apply a translation in *Mathematica* by making use of a replacement rule to go inside an expression and alter every pair of coordinates. The use of replacement rules was introduced in Chapter 7 page 107.

The point {x,y} is translated by {ta, tb}.

In[30]:= `{x, y} + {ta, tb}`

Out[30]= `{ta + x, tb + y}`

A test graphics object.

In[31]:= `p =`
`            Plot[Sin[x], {x,0,2Pi},AspectRatio -> Automatic]`

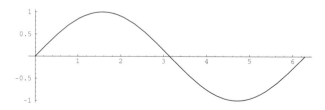

This function will test expressions to see if they are points to be transformed.

In[32]:= **PointQ[p_] := VectorQ[p, NumberQ] && Length[p] == 2**

The vectors are all translated by {2, -0.5} and the result displayed.

In[33]:= **Show[p /. pt_?PointQ :> pt + {2, -0.5}]**

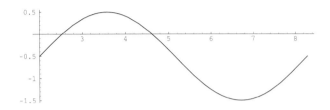

Using a replacement rule like this to apply a transformation is quite crude since there may be pairs of numbers that do not represent points. It is shown here because of its simplicity. A better way to apply the transformation would be to make functions that operated on specific parts of specific primitives.

▸ *Rotation*

A rotation in two dimensions is defined by a single angle of rotation. This can generate a rotation matrix that can be multiplied into vectors thereby generating the rotated result. There already is a *Mathematica* package that generates this two-dimensional rotation matrix for a clockwise rotation.

This package defines the rotation matrix.

In[34]:= **Needs["Geometry`Rotations`"]**

The rotation matrix for clockwise rotation by t radians.

In[35]:= **RotationMatrix2D[t]**

Out[35]= **{{Cos[t], Sin[t]}, {-Sin[t], Cos[t]}}**

The rotation matrix for rotation by Pi/2 radians.

In[36]:= **rot = RotationMatrix2D[Pi/2]**

Out[36]= **{{0, 1}, {-1, 0}}**

All vectors are rotated by Pi/2 around the origin.

In[37]:= **Show[p /. pt_?PointQ :> rot.pt]**

Sometimes the rotation is defined in terms of two vectors, one of which is to be rotated to lie along the other. In this case the rotation matrix is defined by the difference in angle between them.

The rotation matrix that rotates the vector {1.5,1} to lie along {-1,-1.5}.

```
In[38]:= rot =
             RotationMatrix2D[ArcTan[1.5, 1]- ArcTan[-1, -1.5]]

Out[38]= {{-0.923077, 0.384615}, {-0.384615, -0.923077}}
```

The rotation matrix does indeed do its job.

```
In[39]:= rot.{1.5, 1}

Out[39]= {-1., -1.5}
```

An important feature of rotation is that it takes place around a point. The examples here all rotate their objects around the origin {0,0}.

▸ *Scale*

A scale in two dimensions involves increasing or decreasing the scale in the x and y directions. It is represented by a matrix of the form $\{\{s_x,0\},\{0,s_y\}\}$.

A scale of sx in the x and sy in the y direction.

```
In[40]:= scale = {{sx,0}, {0,sy}}

Out[40]= {{sx, 0}, {0, sy}}
```

It is easy to see the effect of the scale.

```
In[41]:= scale.{x, y}

Out[41]= {sx x, sy y}
```

The scale matrix {{2,0},{0,1}} is applied to the plot generated earlier.

```
In[42]:= Show[p /. pt_?PointQ :> {{2,0},{0,1}}.pt]
```

If one of the scale parameters is negative a reflection is generated.

```
In[43]:= Show[p /. pt_?PointQ :> {{2,0},{0,-1}}.pt]
```

As with rotation transformations, scale transformations scale around a point. The examples here scale around the origin {0,0}.

▶ *Shear*

Another type of transformation is a shear transformation. This also has a simple matrix representation. A shear along the x axis has a transformation matrix {{1,sh_x},{0,1}} while along the y axis the matrix is {{1,0},{sh_y,1}}.

This box will demonstrate a shear transformation.	In[44]:= **box = Line[{{0,0}, {1,0}, {1,1},{0,1},{0,0}}];**
A matrix representation of a shear along the x axis.	In[45]:= **xshear = {{1,2}, {0,1}};**
The original box.	In[46]:= **Show[Graphics[box]]**

The box is transformed. Note that lines parallel before are still parallel after the transformation.

In[47]:= **Show[% /. pt_?PointQ :> xshear.pt]**

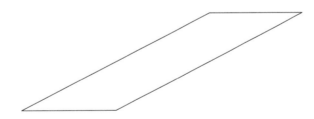

As with rotation and scale transformations shear transformations shear around a point. The examples here shear around the origin {0,0}.

The transformations described here can be referred to as affine transformations. This important class maintains parallelism and collinearity of lines. Lines parallel before the transformation are still parallel after the transformation. Points that fall on a line before the transformation will fall on a line after the transformation.

▸ *Homogeneous Transformations*

Affine transformations can all be represented by two-dimensional matrices. However, they fall in two categories: the translation transformation is applied by matrix addition and the others are applied by matrix multiplication. It would be very convenient if all transformations had a uniform application. This is clearly not possible with two-dimensional matrices but is possible with three-dimensional matrices.

A three-dimensional representation of a two-dimensional translation.	`In[48]:= trans = {{1,0,1}, {0,1,1}, {0,0,1}}`
	
	`Out[48]= {{1, 0, 1}, {0, 1, 1}, {0, 0, 1}}`

The two-dimensional point {x,y} is embedded in the three-dimensional plane z == 1. The effect of the matrix trans is a translation in this plane.	`In[49]:= trans.{x,y,1}`
	
	`Out[49]= {1 + x, 1 + y, 1}`

Therefore, by embedding a two-dimensional point in a three-dimensional plane (the plane z == 1 is convenient) a matrix multiplication method of generating a two-dimensional translation is obtained. In fact the transformation in three dimensions is a shear but looked at in the appropriate plane it is a translation.

A function to generate a homogeneous translation matrix.	`In[50]:= HomogeneousTranslation[{tx_, ty_}] :=` `            {{1,0,tx}, {0,1,ty}, {0,0,1}}`
This function will apply a homogeneous transformation to a two-dimensional point.	`In[51]:= HomogeneousMultiply[mat_, vec_] :=` `            Drop[mat.Append[vec,1], -1]`

A translation of {a,b} can be applied to the point {x,y}.	`In[52]:= HomogeneousMultiply[`
	`              HomogeneousTranslation[{a, b}], {x, y}]`
	
	`Out[52]= {a + x, b + y}`

The other affine transformations can be generated with similar functions.

A homogeneous rotation matrix.	`In[53]:= HomogeneousRotation[t_] :=`
	`            Append[`
	`              Map[Append[#, 0]&, RotationMatrix2D[t]],`
	`              {0,0,1}]`

A homogeneous scale matrix.	`In[54]:= HomogeneousScale[{sx_, sy_}] :=` `            {{sx,0,0}, {0,sy,0}, {0,0,1}}`
Homogeneous shear matrix.	`In[55]:= HomogeneousShear[{sx_, sy_}] :=` `            {{1,sx,0}, {sy,1,0}, {0,0,1}}`

These transformations can all be applied with the function HomogeneousMultiply.	`In[56]:= HomogeneousMultiply[`
	`              HomogeneousShear[{a, b}], {x, y}]`
	
	`Out[56]= {x + a y, b x + y}`

▶ *Composition*

A uniform description of affine transformations allows sequences or compositions of transformations. These are made by multiplying the relevant matrices to form one transformation matrix:

$$M_{comp} = M_n \cdot M_{n-1} \ldots M_2 \cdot M_1$$

M_{comp} is the transformation obtained by first applying M_1 then M_2 and so on. An example of the use of composition of transformations is the construction of a matrix for rotation around some point other than the origin. This is done by translating to place that point at the origin, rotating, and then reversing the translation.

Translate to put {Pi/2,1} at the origin, rotate by Pi, and translate to restore the original origin.

```
In[57]:= mat =
           HomogeneousTranslation[{Pi/2,1}].
           HomogeneousRotation[Pi].
           HomogeneousTranslation[{-Pi/2, -1}]
Out[57]= {{-1, 0, Pi}, {0, -1, 2}, {0, 0, 1}}
```

The plot is rotated around the point {Pi/2,1}.

```
In[58]:= Show[p,
           p /. pt_?PointQ :> HomogeneousMultiply[mat, pt]]
```

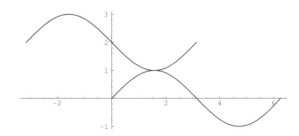

▶ *Transformation Package*

These functions for transforming objects are collected into the package `ExtendGraphics`Transform``. In addition is a utility function that descends down into a `Graphics` object applying a transformation to each primitive. One of the interesting aspects of this package is that much of the code works both for two- and three-dimensional transformations. In fact the package could be adapted with little effort to represent affine transformations in spaces of arbitrary dimension.

`HomogeneousTranslation[{`t_x`, `t_y`}]`	matrix for the translation {t_x, t_y}
`HomogeneousRotation[t]`	matrix for rotation by t
`HomogeneousScale[{`s_x`, `s_y`}]`	matrix for the scale {s_x, s_y}
`HomogeneousShear[{`sh_x`, `sh_y`}]`	matrix for the shear {sh_x, sh_y}
`HomogeneousTransform[mat, gobj]`	transform the graphics object *gobj* by *mat*

Functions defined in `ExtendGraphics`Transform``.

The graphics transformation package is loaded.

In[59]:= **Needs["ExtendGraphics`Transform`"]**

The main transformation function.

In[60]:= **?HomogeneousTransform**

HomogeneousTransform[mat, g] applies the transformation specified by mat to the graphics object g.

mat represents a shear in the *xy* plane.

In[61]:= **mat = HomogeneousShear[{1,0}]**

Out[61]= {{1, 1, 0}, {0, 1, 0}, {0, 0, 1}}

A graphics object can be built with ParametricPlot.

In[62]:= **rose =**
   ParametricPlot[Sin[2t] {Sin[t], Cos[t]},
      {t,0,2Pi}, AspectRatio -> Automatic]

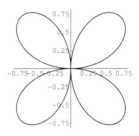

The transformation can easily be applied to the graphics object.

In[63]:= **Show[HomogeneousTransform[mat, rose]]**

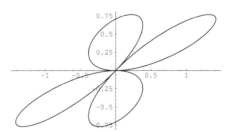

16.3 Geometric Results

A collection of basic geometric objects has been described. The previous section illustrated how the coordinates that make up these objects could be transformed. This section will look at the interactions of these geometric objects. A variety of results describing these interactions will be presented.

▶ *The Intersection of Two Lines*

Two lines intersect when the same point exists on both lines. This point will satisfy the equation of each line. Writing one equation explicitly and the other implicitly gives $\mathbf{p} = \mathbf{p_1} + (\mathbf{p_2} - \mathbf{p_1})\,t$ and $(\mathbf{p} - \mathbf{c}) \cdot \vec{\mathbf{n}} = 0$.

The explicit form of a line is assigned to pe.

```
In[64]:= pe = p1 + (p2-p1) t
Out[64]= p1 + (-p1 + p2) t
```

The implicit form of a line is written as an equation.

```
In[65]:= (pi - c).n == 0
Out[65]= -c . n + pi . n == 0
```

The implicit point pi is replaced with the explicit point pe.

```
In[66]:= % /. pi -> pe
Out[66]= -c . n + p1 . n + ((-p1 + p2) t) . n == 0
```

After some expansion of dot products this can be solved for t. The denominator here will be zero if the lines are parallel.

```
In[67]:= Solve[t (p2 -p1).n + (p1-c).n == 0, t]
```
$$Out[67]= \left\{\left\{t \to \frac{-c \cdot n + p1 \cdot n}{p1 \cdot n - p2 \cdot n}\right\}\right\}$$

Substituting the result for t into the original expression for pe returns the coordinates of the intersection.

```
In[68]:= pe /. First[%]
```
$$Out[68]= p1 + \frac{(-p1 + p2)\,(-c \cdot n + p1 \cdot n)}{p1 \cdot n - p2 \cdot n}$$

IntersectionPoint returns the point of intersection of two lines. The first is an explicit line defined by p1 and p2 while the second is defined implicitly by c and n.

```
In[69]:= IntersectionPoint[Line[{p1_, p2_}],
                           ImplicitLine[c_, n_]] :=
           Module[{tst},
             tst = Chop[(p2 - p1).n] ;
             If[tst === 0,
                 Print["Parallel Lines"];
                 {Infinity, Infinity},
                 p1 - (p2 - p1) (p1 - c).n/tst
             ]
           ]
```

When symbolic arguments are given a symbolic result is returned.

```
In[70]:= IntersectionPoint[Line[{p1, p2}], ImplicitLine[c, n]]
```
$$Out[70]= p1 - \frac{(-p1 + p2)\,(-c \cdot n + p1 \cdot n)}{-p1 \cdot n + p2 \cdot n}$$

Some lines for an example.

```
In[71]:= (l1 = Line[{{3,2}, {1,-1}}];
         l2 = ImplicitLine[{3,1}, {0,2}];)
```

With numeric arguments a numeric result is returned, and this can be plotted.

```
In[72]:= Show[
            Graphics[
              {l1, ToLine[l2],
                AbsolutePointSize[3],
                Point[IntersectionPoint[l1, l2]]
              }]]
```

▶ *Point on a Line*

To test if a point falls on a line requires the substitution of the point into the equation of the line. For this the implicit form of the line is the appropriate version to use.

The point p is substituted into the implicit line defined by c and n. The result of this is compared with zero.

```
In[73]:= PointOnLineQ[p_, ImplicitLine[c_, n_]] :=
            Chop[(p-c).n] === 0
```

The point {2,2} is not on the line defined by
$\big(\{x,y\} - \{2,3\}\big) \cdot \{1,1\} = 0.$

```
In[74]:= PointOnLineQ[{2,2}, ImplicitLine[{2,3}, {1,1}]]

Out[74]= False
```

▶ *Point on a Line Closest to a Point*

The point **q** on a line l closest to some other fixed point **p** will occur when the line between **p** and **q** is perpendicular to l.

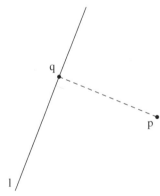

Minimum distance from a point to a line.

Let **p** be the fixed point and $(\mathbf{v} - \mathbf{c}) \cdot \vec{\mathbf{n}} = 0$ be the equation of the line. Let **q** be the point on the line closest to **p**. Then:

$$(\mathbf{q} - \mathbf{c}) \cdot \vec{\mathbf{n}} = 0$$

$$\mathbf{p} = \mathbf{q} + t\vec{\mathbf{n}}$$

which can be solved first for parameter t and then point **q**. This is the closest point to **p**.

$$t = \frac{(\mathbf{p} - \mathbf{c}) \cdot \vec{\mathbf{n}}}{\vec{\mathbf{n}} \cdot \vec{\mathbf{n}}}$$

$$\mathbf{q} = \mathbf{p} - \frac{(\mathbf{p} - \mathbf{c}) \cdot \vec{\mathbf{n}}}{\vec{\mathbf{n}} \cdot \vec{\mathbf{n}}} \vec{\mathbf{n}}$$

This function finds the point on a line nearest to an external point.

```
In[75]:= ClosestPointOnLine[p_, ImplicitLine[c_, n_]] :=
            p - (p-c).n/n.n n
```

These will be useful to demonstrate the workings of ClosestPointOnLine.

```
In[76]:= (p = {1,2};
            l = ImplicitLine[{2, -2}, {5,4}];)
```

The closest point on l to p.

```
In[77]:= ClosestPointOnLine[p, l]//N

Out[77]= {-0.341463, 0.926829}
```

ClosestPointOnLine demonstrated graphically.

```
In[78]:= Show[
            Graphics[
              {AbsolutePointSize[3],
               Point[p],
               ToLine[l],
               Point[ClosestPointOnLine[p, l]]}],
            Frame -> True]
```

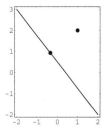

▶ *Minimum Distance from a Point to a Line*

The previous example found the point on a line nearest to another. This can be used to find the minimum distance from some point to a line. The distance will be the distance to the closest point.

This is a symbolic point and line.

$In[79]:=$ `(p = {px, py};`
`l = ImplicitLine[{cx, cy}, {nx, ny}];)`

q is the point on l nearest to p.

$In[80]:=$ `q = ClosestPointOnLine[p, l]`

$Out[80]=$ $\{px - \dfrac{nx\ (nx\ (-cx + px) + ny\ (-cy + py))}{nx^2 + ny^2},$

$py - \dfrac{ny\ (nx\ (-cx + px) + ny\ (-cy + py))}{nx^2 + ny^2}\}$

The distance from p to q.

$In[81]:=$ `LineLength[Line[{p, q}]]`

$Out[81]=$ $Sqrt[\dfrac{nx^2\ (nx\ (-cx + px) + ny\ (-cy + py))^2}{(nx^2 + ny^2)^2} +$

$\dfrac{ny^2\ (nx\ (-cx + px) + ny\ (-cy + py))^2}{(nx^2 + ny^2)^2}]$

Simplification results in a more compact answer.

$In[82]:=$ `Simplify[%]`

$Out[82]=$ $Sqrt[\dfrac{(-(cx\ nx) - cy\ ny + nx\ px + ny\ py)^2}{nx^2 + ny^2}]$

This separates out the powers in the numerator and denominator.

$In[83]:=$ `% /. Sqrt[a_/b_] :> Sqrt[a]/Sqrt[b]`

$Out[83]=$ $\dfrac{Sqrt[(-(cx\ nx) - cy\ ny + nx\ px + ny\ py)^2]}{Sqrt[nx^2 + ny^2]}$

This simplification only holds for a being positive, which it is in this case.

$In[84]:=$ `% /. Sqrt[a_^2] :> a`

$Out[84]=$ $\dfrac{-(cx\ nx) - cy\ ny + nx\ px + ny\ py}{Sqrt[nx^2 + ny^2]}$

Symbolic points are substituted into the implicit equation for a line. The result has the same form as the numerator of the previous result.

$In[85]:=$ `(pt-c).n /.`
`{pt -> {ptx, pty},`
`c -> {cx, cy}, n -> {nx, ny}}//Expand`

$Out[85]=$ $-(cx\ nx) - cy\ ny + nx\ ptx + ny\ pty$

The expression, $(\mathbf{p} - \mathbf{c}) \cdot \vec{\mathbf{n}}$, is thus the distance from $\mathbf{p}$ to the line when $\vec{\mathbf{n}}$ is normalized. The implicit form of a line is thus a set of points for which the distance to the line is zero.

▷ *Which Side of a Line*

In two dimensions a line divides the plane into two regions. Therefore it is possible to ask into which region a given point falls. This can be deduced from the implicit equation of the line. It depends upon the sign of $(\mathbf{p} - \mathbf{c}) \cdot \vec{\mathbf{n}}$ though the question of which sign denotes which side has to be fixed. This is an arbitrary choice and the practice here is to start from an explicit line, a line which goes from one point to another.

RightOfLineQ takes a point and a line. It converts the line to an implicit form and substitues in the point. If the result is positive the point is on the right of the line.

```
In[86]:= RightOfLineQ[p_, Line[{p1_, p2_}]] :=
             (p - First[#]).
             Last[#]&[ToImplicit[Line[{p1, p2}]]] > 0
```

These points will be used in this example.

```
In[87]:= (r = {2,3};
           s = {5,6};
           t = {1,5};)
```

The point t is not right of the line from r to s.

```
In[88]:= RightOfLineQ[t, Line[{r,s}]]
```

Out[88]= False

The test used in RightOfLineQ is quite naive. It does not take into account the magnitude of the coordinates of the vectors nor of the possibility that the point may be collinear with the line. A much improved version is presented next.

The vectors from p1 to p2 and from p1 to p are normalized. Then the dot product of the first with the normal vector to the second is taken.

```
In[89]:= SideOfLine[p_, Line[{p1_, p2_}]] :=
             Module[{u, v, test},
                u = (p2 - p1) ;
                u = u/VectorLength[u] ;
                v = (p - p1) ;
                v = v/VectorLength[v] ;
                test = u.NormalVector[v] ;
                If[test > 10^(-15.),
                    Left,
                    If[test < -10^(-15.),
                        Right,
                        Collinear]]]
```

The function SideOfLine is more sophisticated. It will return Left, Right, or Collinear according to the arrangement of the points.

t is left of the line from r to s.

```
In[90]:= SideOfLine[t, Line[{r, s}]]
```

Out[90]= Left

That t is left of Line[{r,s}] is
confirmed. A point has been drawn at s
to show the direction of the line segment.

```
In[91]:= Show[
             Graphics[
                {AbsolutePointSize[3],
                 Line[{r,s}], Point[s],
                 Point[t]}]]
```

Of course when the line is reversed, t
is on the right-hand side.

```
In[92]:= SideOfLine[t, Line[{s,r}]]
Out[92]= Right
```

The point {11.5,12.5} is collinear
with the points s and r.

```
In[93]:= SideOfLine[{11.5, 12.5}, Line[{s,r}]]
Out[93]= Collinear
```

The function ToImplicit was arranged so that the expression $(\mathbf{p} - \mathbf{c}) \cdot \vec{\mathbf{n}}$ would be positive when the
p is on the right side of the line.

▶ *Point in a Triangle*

Since it is possible to test which side of a line a point falls it is possible to test whether it falls inside a
triangle. A triangle is defined by its three vertices $\{\mathbf{v}_1, \mathbf{v}_2, \mathbf{v}_3\}$. The test involves the three line segments
$\mathbf{v}_1 \rightarrow \mathbf{v}_2$, $\mathbf{v}_2 \rightarrow \mathbf{v}_3$, and $\mathbf{v}_3 \rightarrow \mathbf{v}_1$. If the point is on the right of all or if it is on the left of all it must be inside
the triangle. This test is made in the function PointInTriangle. If the point is collinear with one edge but
is inside the other edges a special case occurs and the routine returns Collinear.

A polygon primitive of three vertices is
used to represent a triangle.

```
In[94]:= PointInTriangle[p_, Polygon[{p1_, p2_, p3_}]] :=
             Module[{test},
                test =
                   Map[SideOfLine[p,Line[#]]&,
                           {{p1,p2},{p2,p3},{p3,p1}}] ;
                If[MemberQ[test, Collinear],
                    test = DeleteCases[test, Collinear] ;
                    If[Apply[SameQ, test],
                        Collinear,
                        False]
                    ,
                    Apply[SameQ, test]]
                ]
```

These primitives will make an example.

```
In[95]:= (tri = Polygon[{{4,5}, {2,1}, {9,5}}];
          pt = {6,4};)
```

The point is inside the triangle.

```
In[96]:= PointInTriangle[pt, tri]
Out[96]= True
```

A picture demonstrates that this is indeed the case.

```
In[97]:= Show[
          Graphics[
            {AbsolutePointSize[8],
             tri, GrayLevel[0.5],
             Point[pt]}]]
```

A different test point.

```
In[98]:= pt1 = {3,3};
```

This point is inside the triangle but collinear with one of the edges.

```
In[99]:= PointInTriangle[pt1, tri]
Out[99]= Collinear
```

The point lies on one of the edges.

```
In[100]:= Show[
           Graphics[
             {AbsolutePointSize[8],
              tri, GrayLevel[0.5],
              Point[pt1]}]]
```

This can be generalized to a polygon with more than three vertices. However, for this simple version to work the polygon must be convex. Convex polygons are defined later in the chapter when computational geometry is discussed.

▸ *Center of Gravity of a Triangle*

The center of gravity of a triangle is given by the average of the vertices.

Take the average of the vertices.

```
In[101]:= CenterOfGravity[
              Polygon[{p1_, p2_, p3_}]] := (p1+p2+p3)/3
```

A triangle for an example.

```
In[102]:= tri = Polygon[{{4,5}, {2,1}, {9,5}}];
```

The center of gravity of tri is drawn along with the boundary of tri.

```
In[103]:= Show[
              Graphics[
                {AbsolutePointSize[8],
                 Boundary[tri],
                 GrayLevel[0.5],
                 Point[CenterOfGravity[tri]]}]]
```

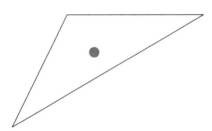

Medians draws lines from each vertex to the middle of the opposite edge.

```
In[104]:= Medians[Polygon[{p1_, p2_, p3_}]] :=
              {Line[{p1, (p2+p3)/2}],
               Line[{p2, (p3+p1)/2}],
               Line[{p3, (p1+p2)/2}]}
```

Now the coincidence of the center of gravity and the intersection of the medians is demonstrated.

```
In[105]:= Show[
              Graphics[
                {Boundary[tri],
                 AbsoluteDashing[{3}],
                 Medians[tri],
                 AbsolutePointSize[8],
                 GrayLevel[0.5],
                 Point[CenterOfGravity[tri]]}]]
```

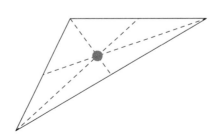

▶ *The Perimeter of a Triangle*

The perimeter of a triangle is the sum of the lengths of each side. This is given by a simple formula:

$$Perimeter\ (\triangle \mathbf{p_1 p_2 p_3}) = |\mathbf{p_2} - \mathbf{p_1}| + |\mathbf{p_3} - \mathbf{p_2}| + |\mathbf{p_1} - \mathbf{p_3}|$$

The formula can easily be written as a *Mathematica* function.

```
In[106]:= Perimeter[Polygon[p_List]] :=
              Apply[Plus, Map[VectorLength, p - RotateLeft[p]]]

In[107]:= tri = Polygon[{{4,5}, {2,1}, {9,5}}];
```

The perimeter of `tri`.

```
In[108]:= Perimeter[tri]
Out[108]= 5 + 2 Sqrt[5] + Sqrt[65]
```

▶ *Area of a Triangle*

The area of a triangle can be determined from the cross product function. This is because the magnitude of the cross product of two vectors, $\vec{\mathbf{p}}_1 \times \vec{\mathbf{p}}_2$, is equal to the area of the parallelogram the two vectors form. The area of a triangle is exactly one-half of this:

$$|(\vec{\mathbf{p}}_2 - \vec{\mathbf{p}}_1) \times (\vec{\mathbf{p}}_2 - \vec{\mathbf{p}}_1)|/2$$

which can be rearranged to give this formula for the area of a triangle:

$$Area\ (\triangle \mathbf{p_1 p_1 p_1}) = |\mathbf{p_1} \times \mathbf{p_2} + \mathbf{p_2} \times \mathbf{p_3} + \mathbf{p_3} \times \mathbf{p_1}|/2$$

This can be implemented with a *Mathematica* function.

One problem with this definition is that the cross product is only defined for three-dimensional vectors.

```
In[109]:= Area[Polygon[{p1_, p2_, p3_}]] :=
              Module[{res},
                  res = Partition[{p1, p2, p3, p1}, 2,1] ;
                  res = Map[Cross[#[[1]], #[[2]]]&, res] ;
                  VectorLength[Apply[Plus, res]]/2
              ]
```

The area of a triangle in two dimensions is derived from that of a three-dimensional triangle in the `z == 0` plane.

```
In[110]:= Area[
              Polygon[{{x1_, y1_}, {x2_, y2_}, {x3_, y3_}}]] :=
              Area[Polygon[{{x1,y1,0}, {x2,y2,0},{x3,y3,0}}]]
```

The area of the triangle in the previous example.

```
In[111]:= Area[tri]
Out[111]= 10
```

For this simple triangle the area is clearly seen to be the familiar result of half the base times the height.

```
In[112]:= Area[Polygon[{{0,0}, {5,0}, {5,5}}]]

Out[112]= 25
         ──
          2
```

▶ *Circle inside a Triangle*

The circle inscribed in a given triangle is defined by radius r_{in} and center c_{in}:

$$r_{in} = 2\,Area\,(\triangle \mathbf{p_1 p_2 p_3})/Perimeter\,(\triangle \mathbf{p_1 p_2 p_3})$$

$$c_{in} = (|\mathbf{p_2} - \mathbf{p_3}|\mathbf{p_1} + |\mathbf{p_3} - \mathbf{p_1}|\mathbf{p_2} + |\mathbf{p_1} - \mathbf{p_2}|\mathbf{p_3})/Perimeter\,(\triangle \mathbf{p_1 p_2 p_3})$$

InCircle returns the circle inscribed in a given triangle.

```
In[113]:= InCircle[t:Polygon[{p1_, p2_, p3_}]] :=
            Module[{per, rad, cent},
                per = Perimeter[t] ;
                rad = 2 Area[t]/per ;
                cent =  VectorLength[p2 - p3] p1 +
                        VectorLength[p3 - p1] p2 +
                        VectorLength[p1 - p2] p3 ;
                cent = cent / per ;
                Circle[cent, rad]]
```

The circle is indeed inside the triangle.

```
In[114]:= Show[
            Graphics[
             {Boundary[tri],
              InCircle[tri]}]]
```

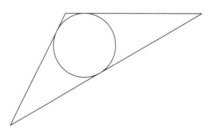

In fact the center of this circle is at the point of intersection of the bisectors of each angle of the triangle.

Bisector finds the bisector line of pairs of intersecting lines by marking points at equal lengths down each line, finding the middle of the line between these points and joining to the intersection.

```
In[115]:= Bisector[Line[{p_, p1_}], Line[{p_, p2_}]] :=
            Module[{pn1, pn2, vl1, vl2},
                pn1 = p1 - p ;
                pn2 = p2 - p ;
                vl1 = VectorLength[pn1] ;
                vl2 = VectorLength[pn2] ;
                pn1 = pn1 * (vl1+vl2)/2/vl1 ;
                pn2 = pn2 * (vl1+vl2)/2/vl2 ;
                Line[{p, p+(pn1+pn2)/2}]
                ]
In[116]:= (p = {4,5};
            p1 = {8,2};
            p2 = {2,1};)
```

The bisecting line is drawn in a lighter shade of gray.

```
In[117]:= Show[
            Graphics[
              {Line[{p, p1}],
               Line[{p, p2}],
               GrayLevel[0.5],
               Bisector[Line[{p, p1}], Line[{p, p2}]]}]]
```

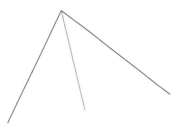

The center of the inscribed circle is at the intersection of the bisectors of each angle.

```
In[118]:= Show[
            Graphics[
              {Boundary[Polygon[{p, p1, p2}]],
               InCircle[Polygon[{p, p1, p2}]],
               GrayLevel[0.5],
               Bisector[Line[{p, p1}], Line[{p, p2}]],
               Bisector[Line[{p1, p}], Line[{p1, p2}]],
               Bisector[Line[{p2, p}], Line[{p2, p1}]]}]]
```

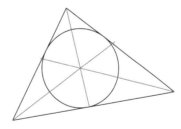

The problem of finding the circle inside a triangle is equivalent to finding the circle that is tangent to three lines. The triangle is formed from the intersection of the successive pairs of lines.

▶ *Circle outside a Triangle*

The circle that circumscribes a given triangle can be defined[8] by radius r_{out} and center c_{out}:

$$d_1 = (\mathbf{p_3} - \mathbf{p_1}) \cdot (\mathbf{p_2} - \mathbf{p_1})$$
$$d_2 = (\mathbf{p_1} - \mathbf{p_2}) \cdot (\mathbf{p_3} - \mathbf{p_2})$$
$$d_3 = (\mathbf{p_2} - \mathbf{p_3}) \cdot (\mathbf{p_1} - \mathbf{p_3})$$

$$c_1 = d_2 d_3 \quad c_2 = d_3 d_1 \quad c_3 = d_1 d_2$$
$$c = c_1 + c_2 + c_3$$

$$r_{out} = \frac{\sqrt{(d_1 + d_2)(d_2 + d_3)(d_3 + d_1)/c}}{2}$$
$$c_{out} = \frac{(c_2 + c_3)\mathbf{p_1} + (c_3 + c_1)\mathbf{p_2} + (c_1 + c_2)\mathbf{p_3}}{2c}$$

The circle is generated by the *Mathematica* function OutCircle.

OutCircle returns the circle that circumscribes a triangle.

```
In[119]:= OutCircle[t:Polygon[{p1_, p2_, p3_}]] :=
            Module[{d1, d2, d3, c1, c2, c3, c, rad, cent},
              d1 = (p3 - p1).(p2 - p1) ;
              d2 = (p1 - p2).(p3 - p2) ;
              d3 = (p2 - p3).(p1 - p3) ;
              c1 = d2 d3 ;
              c2 = d3 d1 ;
              c3 = d1 d2 ;
              c = c1 + c2 + c3 ;
              rad = Sqrt[(d1+d2)(d2+d3)(d3+d1)/c]/2 ;
              cent = (c2+c3)p1 + (c3+c1)p2 + (c1+c2)p3 ;
              cent = cent/2/c;
              Circle[cent, rad]
            ]
```

---

[8]This result and several others in this section have been adapted from *Graphics Gems*, ed. A.S. Glassner.

The vertices of the triangle lie on the circle.

```
In[120]:= Show[
              Graphics[
                {Boundary[tri],
                 OutCircle[tri]}]]
```

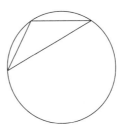

Solving this problem is equivalent to solving the problem of the circle that passes through three points. This will be a useful result for the computational geometry tools that are introduced later.

▸ *Point in a Circle*

The last result is to test whether or not a point falls inside a given circle defined by three points. This could be solved by forming the circumscribing circle and comparing the distance from the test point to the center with the radius. A more efficient method places the points into the complex plane by making the x coordinate the real part and the y coordinate the imaginary part. The cross-ratio, $((x - a)(b - c))/((x - c)(b - a))$, is then calculated. This will be real if x lies on the circle through a, b, and c. The sign of the imaginary part distinguishes inside from outside. If the points are in counterclockwise order a positive imaginary part means x is inside.

A simple implementation of PointInCircleQ.

```
In[121]:= PointInCircleQ[x_, a_, b_, c_] :=
              Module[{xi, ai, bi, ci},
                xi = x /. {r_, i_} :> r + I i ;
                ai = a /. {r_, i_} :> r + I i ;
                bi = b /. {r_, i_} :> r + I i ;
                ci = c /. {r_, i_} :> r + I i ;
                Im[((xi-ai)(bi-ci))/((xi-ci)(bi-ai))] > 0
              ]
```

These are some points to use for demonstration.

```
In[122]:= (a = {9,1};
           b = {5,4};
           c = {8,5};
           x = {6,4};)
```

The point marked by x falls in the circle.

```
In[123]:= Show[
            Graphics[
              {AbsolutePointSize[3],
               Text["x", x],
               Text["a", a, {-2.0, 2.0}],
               Text["b", b, {1.5, -1.5}],
               Text["c", c, {-1.5, -2.0}],
               Boundary[Polygon[{a,b,c}]],
               OutCircle[Polygon[{a,b,c}]]}]]
```

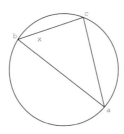

The PointInCircleQ predicate reports that the position is *not* in the circle. This is wrong!

```
In[124]:= PointInCircleQ[x, a, b, c]
Out[124]= False
```

The problem here is that the points are not ordered counterclockwise. This is quite easy to test with the RightOfLineQ predicate.

Since b is not right of the line from a to c the points are not arranged in a counterclockwise fashion.

```
In[125]:= RightOfLineQ[b, Line[{a, c}]]
Out[125]= False
```

This is very similar to the previous version except that now the points a, b, and c are tested for orientation.

```
In[126]:= PointInCircleQ[x_, a_, b_, c_] /;
              RightOfLineQ[
                b,
                Line[{a, c}]] :=
            Module[{xi, ai, bi, ci},
              xi = x /. {r_, i_} :> r + I i ;
              ai = a /. {r_, i_} :> r + I i ;
              bi = b /. {r_, i_} :> r + I i ;
              ci = c /. {r_, i_} :> r + I i ;
              Im[((xi-ai)(bi-ci))/((xi-ci)(bi-ai))] > 0
            ]
```

This takes care of the case when the points are arranged clockwise.

```
In[127]:= PointInCircleQ[x_, a_, b_, c_] :=
            PointInCircleQ[x, a, c, b]
```

PointInCircleQ now correctly reports that x is in the circle.

```
In[128]:= PointInCircleQ[x, a, b, c]
Out[128]= True
```

This version of the predicate, `PointInCircleQ`, will work properly but it can be optimized. It uses complex arithmetic to generate the cross-ratio. This will calculate both the real and imaginary parts when in fact all it needs is the latter. Furthermore, it might be difficult to implement the function in languages, such as C, which do not support complex arithmetic. For these reasons a version that has expanded out the complex arithmetic into the underlying real arithmetic will be made. This is quite straightforward to do with *Mathematica*. It must be stressed that this is an unusal thing to do that is normally unnecessary. It is done here to minimize the number of calculations that will be done when a point is tested.

Expand with the assumption that all variables are real.

```
In[129]:= ComplexExpand[(numr + I numi)/(denr + I deni)]
```

$$Out[129]= \frac{deni\ numi}{deni^2 + denr^2} + \frac{denr\ numr}{deni^2 + denr^2} +$$

$$I\ (\frac{denr\ numi}{deni^2 + denr^2} - \frac{deni\ numr}{deni^2 + denr^2})$$

The required result is the imaginary part. `ComplexExpand` is necessary to make sure that all variables are assumed to be real.

```
In[130]:= Together[ComplexExpand[Im[%]]]
```

$$Out[130]= \frac{denr\ numi - deni\ numr}{deni^2 + denr^2}$$

The denominator of the previous result will never be negative. Thus the only thing to calculate is the numerator. The sign of this will determine the result.

```
In[131]:= Numerator[%]
```

$$Out[131]= denr\ numi - deni\ numr$$

This expression represents the numerator.

```
In[132]:= num =
            ((xr + I xi) - (ar + I ai))*
                ((br + I bi) - (cr + I ci))
```

$$Out[132]= (I\ bi + br - I\ ci - cr)\ (-I\ ai - ar + I\ xi + xr)$$

This expression represents the denominator.

```
In[133]:= den =
            ((xr + I xi) - (cr + I ci))*
                ((br + I bi) - (ar + I ai))
```

$$Out[133]= (-I\ ai - ar + I\ bi + br)\ (-I\ ci - cr + I\ xi + xr)$$

The real and imaginary parts of the numerator and denominator are extracted and expanded.

```
In[134]:= (numr = ComplexExpand[Re[num]];
            numi = ComplexExpand[Im[num]];
            denr = ComplexExpand[Re[den]];
            deni = ComplexExpand[Im[den]];)
```

`TableForm` prints out a nicely formated result.

```
In[135]:= TableForm[{numr, numi, denr, deni},
                TableHeadings ->
                    {{"numr", "numi", "denr", "deni"}, None}]
```

```
Out[135]//TableForm=
```

numr	-((bi - ci) (-ai + xi)) + (br - cr) (-ar + xr)
numi	(br - cr) (-ai + xi) + (bi - ci) (-ar + xr)
denr	-((-ai + bi) (-ci + xi)) + (-ar + br) (-cr + xr)
deni	(-ar + br) (-ci + xi) + (-ai + bi) (-cr + xr)

A new version can now be written down. First the old definitions are cleared away.

```
In[136]:= Clear[PointInCircleQ]
```

The optimized version of PointInCircleQ.

```
In[137]:= PointInCircleQ[
                {xr_,xi_},{ar_,ai_},
                {br_,bi_},{cr_,ci_}] /;
                        RightOfLineQ[
                            {br,bi},
                            Line[{{ar,ai}, {cr,ci}}]] :=
           Module[{numr, numi, denr, deni},
               numr = (br - cr)(xr - ar) - (bi - ci)(xi - ai);
               numi = (br - cr)(xi - ai) + (bi - ci)(xr - ar);
               denr = (br - ar)(xr - cr) - (bi - ai)(xi - ci);
               deni = (br - ar)(xi - ci) + (bi - ai)(xr - cr);
               denr numi - deni numr > 0
               ]
```

The function for when the points are arranged clockwise.

```
In[138]:= PointInCircleQ[x_, a_, b_, c_] :=
              PointInCircleQ[x, a, c, b]
```

The PointInCircleQ predicate correctly reports that the position is in the circle.

```
In[139]:= PointInCircleQ[x, a, b, c]
Out[139]= True
```

16.4 Computational Geometry

Computational geometry can be defined as the application of algorithms to solve geometric problems. So far in this chapter many geometric results have been presented that can be efficiently computed by the application of some formula. As the problems become more complex it may be necessary to apply some algorithm.

   The presentation here will pose some simple problems in computational geometry and then solve these problems. It will not present any analysis of how the algorithms actually work. To do this would require a significant expansion of the material in this book and thus it is left to a future publication. *Mathematica*, with a combination of pictures and animations, makes a powerful tool to aid in understanding how these computational geometry algorithms work.

   In *Mathematica* there is a standard package DiscreteMath`CompuationalGeometry` which contains many functions for calculating convex hulls, forming triangulations, and making special diagrams. The algorithmic solutions presented in this chapter do not use this package since for large problems it runs quite slowly. Some of the solutions make use of a *MathLink* binary that is much faster. On top of this *MathLink* method a variety of small *Mathematica* functions are available that solve particular tasks.

▶ *Convex Hull*

A polygon is convex when the line segment between any two points inside the polygon also lies completely inside the polygon. If this is not true the polygon is non-convex. The convex hull of an arbitrary collection of points is the smallest convex polygon containing all the points. The convex hull can be formed by stretching an elastic band around the points. The band will shrink down to form the convex hull.

The outline of a regular convex polygon.

```
In[140]:= Show[
            Graphics[
              Line[Table[{Sin[i], Cos[i]}, {i,0,2Pi,Pi/6}]]]]
```

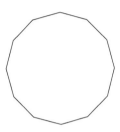

A data set that incorporates some randomness.

```
In[141]:= points =
            Table[Random[ ] {Sin[i], Cos[i]}, {i,0,2Pi,Pi/6}]
Out[141]= {{0, 0.584579}, {0.371453, 0.643375},
    {0.339015, 0.19573}, {0.357224, 0}, {0.329535, -0.190257},
    {0.464461, -0.80447}, {0, -0.175248}, {-0.429209, -0.743411},
    {-0.774383, -0.44709}, {-0.277896, 0}, {-0.562914, 0.324998},
    {-0.100122, 0.173417}, {0, 0.17906}}
```

The outline of a non-convex polygon.

```
In[142]:= Show[
            Graphics[
              Line[points /. {a_, b__} :> {a,b,a}]]]
```

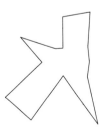

One way to calculate a convex hull is to use the package `ExtendGraphics`SimpleHull``. This is a small *Mathematica* package that provides a function to calculate the convex hull. It does not use *MathLink* and is thus appropriate for small collections of points.

The simple hull package is loaded.

```
In[143]:= Needs["ExtendGraphics`SimpleHull`"]
```

```
In[144]:= ?ConvexHull
```

ConvexHull[pts] will take a list of two-dimensional points and
    return the vertices of the convex hull.

These are the indices of the points that form the convex hull.

```
In[145]:= hull = ConvexHull[points]
```

```
Out[145]= {11, 9, 8, 6, 2, 1}
```

A graphical representation of the hull.

```
In[146]:= Show[
            Graphics[
              {AbsolutePointSize[3], Map[Point, points],
               Line[Part[points, hull]] /.
                 {a_, b__} :> {a,b,a}}]]
```

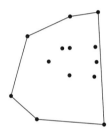

A function to make this plot, ConvexHullPlot, is provided.

```
In[147]:= ?ConvexHullPlot
```

ConvexHullPlot[pts] will plot the convex hull of a list of
    two-dimensonal points.

```
In[148]:= ConvexHullPlot[points]
```

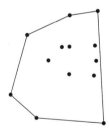

This package will work well when the number of points to be worked with is small. When the number is large the program becomes very slow. In this case a *MathLink* method is available. The package ExtendGraphics`Delaunay` launches a *MathLink* binary when it is loaded. The main functionality defined in this package is to form a triangulation from a set of points.

▸ *Delaunay Triangulation*

A triangulation of a set of points involves composing triangles from the points so that each point is at the vertex of at least one triangle.

A random set of points.

```
In[149]:= pts = Table[{Random[ ], Random[ ]}, {15}];
```

The points can be displayed in a plot.

```
In[150]:= Show[
               Graphics[
                  {AbsolutePointSize[3], Map[Point, pts]}]]
```

A naive triangulation method would sort them according to increasing *x* value.

```
In[151]:= Sort[pts];
```

Each point is joined to the following two.

```
In[152]:= Table[Take[%, {i, i+2}], {i, Length[%]-2}];
```

Line primitives that form the perimeter of triangles are generated.

```
In[153]:= Map[# /. {a_, b__} :> Line[{a,b,a}]&, %];
```

Finally the triangles are displayed. The result is hopeless.

```
In[154]:= Show[Graphics[%]]
```

The resulting triangulation is highly unsatisfactory. The triangles tend to be long and thin. Many regions that might be considered falling inside the area of triangulation are not in triangles at all (the method can also have overlapping triangles). The result is non-convex in a rather arbitrary way. A more complex sorting method may work better, but it is not clear that this will work efficiently or produce good results.

A good solution to this problem is to form a Delaunay triangulation. The specification of the Delaunay triangulation is that it maximizes the minimum angle of the triangles. Each triangle is as close to equilateral as possible. In geometric terms this can be shown to mean that for each triangle the circumscribing circle contains no other points, a problem solved earlier in this chapter. In order to calculate the Delaunay triangulation rapidly a *MathLink* binary is used. This binary is loaded automatically when the package ExtendGraphics`Delaunay` is loaded.

$$In[155]:= \textbf{Needs["ExtendGraphics`Delaunay`"]}$$

The package uses a *MathLink* binary to provide the core function. This is the link object connecting to the binary when this book was generated.

$$In[156]:= \textbf{Links[ ]}$$
$$Out[156]= \{LinkObject[delaunay, 1, 1]\}$$

One of the functions in the Delaunay package.

$$In[157]:= \textbf{?DelaunayVertices}$$

DelaunayVertices[pts] will take a list of points, {x, y, ...}, and return the list of vertices which forms the Delaunay triangulation in the xy plane.

The vertices of the triangles for the Delaunay triangulation are calculated.

$$In[158]:= \textbf{verts = DelaunayVertices[pts]}$$
$$Out[158]= \{\{5, 11, 13\}, \{5, 13, 3\}, \{5, 3, 1\}, \{11, 9, 7\},$$
$$\{11, 7, 13\}, \{13, 7, 3\}, \{7, 9, 14\}, \{7, 14, 3\}, \{9, 12, 8\},$$
$$\{9, 8, 14\}, \{3, 2, 1\}, \{3, 14, 6\}, \{3, 6, 2\}, \{12, 4, 8\},$$
$$\{12, 15, 4\}, \{8, 10, 14\}, \{8, 4, 10\}, \{14, 10, 6\},$$
$$\{10, 4, 6\}, \{4, 15, 6\}, \{1, 2, 6\}\}$$

The triangles can easily be plotted.

```
In[159]:= Show[
              Graphics[
                {AbsoluteThickness[0.25],
                 Map[(Line[Part[pts, #]] /.
               {a_, b__} :> {a,b,a})&, verts]}]]
```

TrianglePlot does this automatically.

$$In[160]:= \textbf{?TrianglePlot}$$

TrianglePlot[pts, opts] will take a list of points. Each point of the form {x, y}. It will plot the triangles which form the Delaunay triangulation.

Making a plot like this is often very useful. Consequently a special function is provided to make an easy task even easier.

```
In[161]:= triplot = TrianglePlot[pts]
```

The circumscribing circles of each triangle can be calculated.

```
In[162]:= circles =
              Map[OutCircle[Polygon[Part[pts, #]]]&, verts];
```

The triangle plot is combined with some of the circumscribing circles. Some of the circles are quite large and are omitted.

```
In[163]:= Show[triplot,
              Epilog -> {AbsoluteThickness[0.25],
                  Select[circles, (#[[2]] < 0.16)&]}]
```

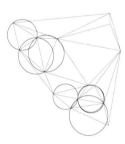

The package also calculates the convex hull.

```
In[164]:= ConvexHull[pts]
```

```
Out[164]= {12, 15, 6, 1, 5, 11, 9}
```

Here is a much larger data set. It is also a challenging data set since so many points are collinear.

```
In[165]:= pts =
              Flatten[
                  Table[{x, y}, {x,30}, {y,30}], 1];
```

The Delaunay triangulation of the data set is generated with no problems.

```
In[166]:= TrianglePlot[pts]
```

There are many applications of Delaunay triangulation. Two applications will be reviewed briefly. Chapter 18 page 474, which discusses the visualization of numeric data, contains more examples of applications of Delaunay triangulation. The examples are more complicated and interesting than the simple versions given here.

Surface Construction

A three-dimensional data set consists of a vector of points {x,y,z}. One way to construct a surface over these points builds triangles by means of a Delaunay triangulation. This is an extremely useful way to build a surface since it can do so without the data being organized in some special way.

A random data set of the form {x,y,xy},... is generated.

```
In[167]:= data =
            Table[{xvar = Random[ ], yvar = Random[ ], xvar
          yvar},
                  {50}];
```

These are the data points that form the Delaunay triangulation.

```
In[168]:= tris = DelaunayVertices[data];
```

Now polygons are formed from the triangulation data and plotted. This plots a surface over the data set.

```
In[169]:= Show[
            Graphics3D[
              Map[Polygon[Part[data, #]]&, tris]]]
```

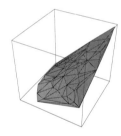

Chapter 18 covers the visualization of numeric data and has much more to say about the construction of surfaces from numeric data. It presents a variety of different tools to do this as well as many examples.

It may seem strange that the result was a three-dimensional plot. The topic of this chapter is two-dimensional geometry and it is reasonable to ask what this has to do with three-dimensional plotting. The answer is that the basis was a triangulation in the *xy* plane, the triangulation was a a two-dimensional process. Triangulations can be carried out in dimensions higher than two and they can be carried out in curved spaces such as on the surface of a sphere. The triangulation functions presented here are two-dimensional and only work in the plane.

Irregular Interpolation

A region filled by a set of points can be broken into sets of triangles. Each point forms the vertex of one or more triangles. This can be used as the basis of an interpolation method. Given a new point the surrounding points from the original data can be determined and this information used in an interpolation process. This is the basis of the package `ExtendGraphics`TriangularInterpolation`, which makes a linear interpolation of an irregular three-dimensional data set.

In[170]:= **Needs["ExtendGraphics`TriangularInterpolate`"]**

In[171]:= **?TriangularInterpolate**

TriangularInterpolate[pts] constructs a TriangularInterpolation
    function which represents an approximate function that
    interpolates the data. The data must have the form {x,y,z}
    and do not have to be regularly spaced.

A three-dimensional data set.

In[172]:= **data =**
             Table[{xvar = Random[ ], yvar = Random[ ], xvar
        yvar},
                     {50}];

The domain can be plotted by extracting
the *x* and *y* values and making a
TrianglePlot.

In[173]:= **TrianglePlot[Map[Take[#, 2]&, data]]**

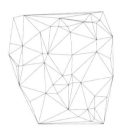

The triangular interpolation function is
generated.

In[174]:= **fun = TriangularInterpolate[data]**

Out[174]= TriangularInterpolating[<>]

This returns the value. The function
x y gives 0.15.

In[175]:= **fun[0.5, 0.3]**

Out[175]= 0.151276

The interpolation function can be used
to generate an array of heights of the
functions. The error messages arise
when x or y fall outside the domain of
the original data.

In[176]:= **new = Table[fun[x, y], {x, 0,1,0.1}, {y,0,1,0.1}] ;**

TriangularInterpolating::dmval:
    Input value {0, 0} lies outside domain of the interpolating
      function.

TriangularInterpolating::dmval:
    Input value {0, 0.1} lies outside domain of the interpolating
      function.

TriangularInterpolating::dmval:
    Input value {0, 0.2} lies outside domain of the interpolating
      function.

General::stop:
    Further output of TriangularInterpolating::dmval
      will be suppressed during this calculation.

The resampled data, new, can be plotted
with ListPlot3D.

In[177]:= **ListPlot3D[new]**

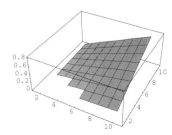

▷ *Non-Convex Triangulation*

The triangulation generated by the Delaunay package fills the convex hull of the points. In fact the convex hull is generated at the same time as the triangulation. If the points represent some outline this triangulation will loose the structure of the outline if it is not convex. To avoid this a non-convex triangulation must be applied.

A set of points.

```
In[178]:= hpts =
            {{1,0.5},{1,4},{2,4},{2,-4},
             {1,-4},{1,-0.5},{-1,-0.5},{-1,-4},
             {-2,-4},{-2,4},{-1,4},{-1,0.5}};
```

The outline formed by these points can be plotted.

```
In[179]:= Show[
            Graphics[
              Line[hpts /. {a_, b__} :> {a,b,a}]]]
```

When the points are triangulated with the Delaunay package this is done to fill the convex hull. The original shape is lost.

```
In[180]:= TrianglePlot[hpts]
```

A non-convex triangulation can be carried out with this package.

```
In[181]:= Needs["ExtendGraphics`NonConvexTriangulate`"]
```

```
In[182]:= ?NonConvexTriangulate
```

NonConvexTriangulate[pts] returns a triangulation of the points pts that maintains the outline.

```
In[183]:= nverts = NonConvexTriangulate[hpts]

Out[183]= {{1, 2, 3}, {1, 3, 4}, {4, 5, 6}, {7, 8, 9},
           {7, 9, 10}, {10, 11, 12}, {1, 4, 6}, {1, 6, 7}, {7, 10, 12},
           {7, 12, 1}}
```

The new triangulation preserves the original shape.

```
In[184]:= Show[
            Graphics[
              {AbsoluteThickness[0.1],
               Map[Line[Part[hpts,#]] /.
                     {a_,b__} :> {a,b,a}&,
                 nverts]}]]
```

The triangulation of a set of points to preserve the outline is behavior that will prove to be very useful when the problems of visualizing polygons in three dimensions is discussed in the next chapter.

▶ *Computational Geometry Functions*

This is a summary of the computational geometry packages and their functions that were introduced in this section. The packages are organized so that there is one *MathLink* function used. The core functionality provided by this is distributed among a variety of functions for such tasks as making triangulations, constructing convex hulls, and interpolation over irregular data. This combines computational efficiency with the ease of programming provided by top-level *Mathematica* code.

```
ConvexHull[{{x₁, y₁}, {x₂, y₂}, ... } ]
```
$\qquad$ generate the convex hull of the points (without *MathLink*)

```
ConvexHullPlot[{{x₁, y₁}, {x₂, y₂}, ... } ]
```
$\qquad$ plot the convex hull of the points (without *MathLink*)

`ExtendGraphics`SimpleHull`.`

```
Delaunay[{{x₁, y₁, ... }, {x₂, y₂, ... }, ... } ]
```
generate the convex hull and Delaunay triangulation in the xy plane

```
ConvexHull[{{x₁, y₁, ... }, {x₂, y₂, ... }, ... } ]
```
generate the convex hull in the xy plane

```
DelaunayVertices[{{x₁, y₁, ... }, {x₂, y₂, ... }, ... } ]
```
generate the vertices of the Delaunay triangulation in the xy plane

```
TriangulatePoints[{{x₁, y₁, ... }, {x₂, y₂, ... }, ... } ]
```
generate Delaunay triangles in the xy plane

```
TrianglePlot[{{x₁, y₁}, {x₂, y₂}, ... } ]
```
plot the Delaunay triangles in the xy plane

ExtendGraphics`Delaunay`.

```
TriangularInterpolate[{{x₁, y₁, z₁}, {x₂, y₂, z₂}, ... } ]
```
generate the triangular interpolation from the points

```
TriangularInterpolating[data][x, y]
```
return the interpolated value for the point {x, y}

ExtendGraphics`TriangularInterpolate`.

```
NonConvexTriangulate[{{x₁, y₁}, {x₂, y₂}, ... } ]
```
generate the non-convex triangulation that preserves the outline

ExtendGraphics`NonConvexTriangulate`.

16.5 Summary

This chapter has looked at two-dimensional geometry. It started with basic objects in a geometrical system and the manner in which they could be represented, both mathematical and visually, by *Mathematica*. Affine transformations of these objects were then discussed. This presented a uniform representation based upon the multiplication of three-dimensional homogeneous matrices that allowed the composition of collections of transformations.

This was followed by a collection of results for the interactions of the geometric objects. These considered such things as the intersection of lines and testing points to see if they were inside a triangle. These results are very useful when complicated pictures are formed.

The last topic gave a brief introduction to some computational geometry problems and to their solutions in *Mathematica*. Included here were topics such as the convex hull, generating a Delaunay triangulation, and triangulating a non-convex outline, techniques which have many applications in the field of visualization. Later chapters of *Mathematica Graphics* will utilize these and other techniques.

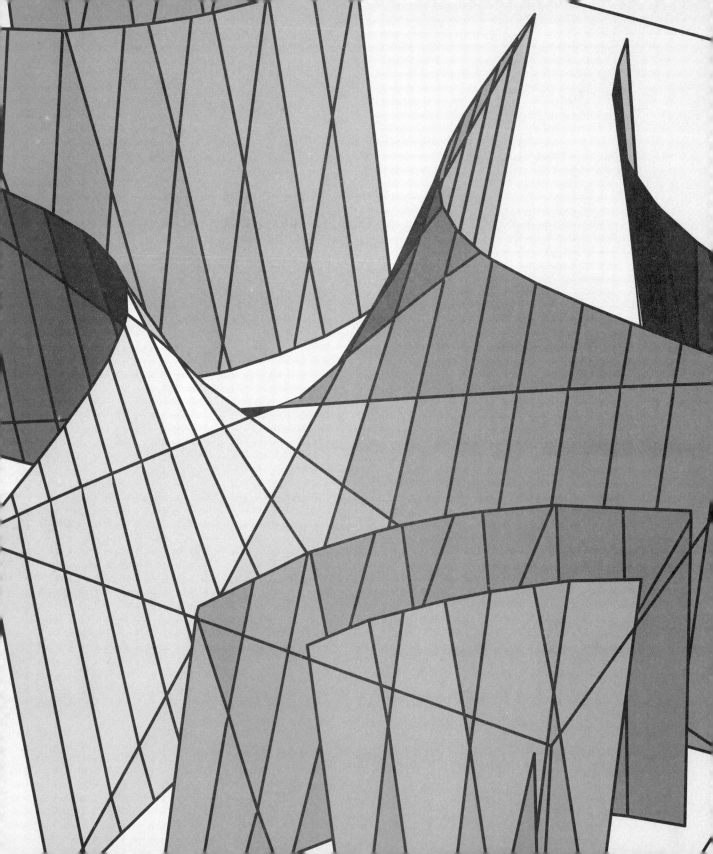

Chapter 17
Three-Dimensional Geometry

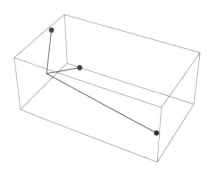

This chapter is an extension of the previous chapter. It works with the geometry of three-dimensional objects to look at mathematical applications of *Mathematica* graphics and is useful for several reasons. First the study is useful for itself; the combination of symbolic and numerical mathematics with graphics makes a powerful system for visualizing these and related parts of mathematics. Secondly, the material has many applications in computer graphics programming. Finally, the chapter will generate many results that will be used in later parts of *Mathematica Graphics*.

An indication of the value of this chapter is to consider the simple but important example of the derivation of the matrix that rotates two perpendicular vectors into two other perpendicular vectors. It is very useful to demonstrate this not just by some formula or even with some pictures but by providing the short code examples that readers can use with *Mathematica*. It is possible to make little interactive experiments to really understand how it works and to check that the matrices do what they are expected to. The ability to apply interactive programs like this is extremely useful, both for understanding how things work and for checking that some algorithm is producing the correct answer. The alternative, to write some program in Fortran or C, is a considerable amount of effort to go through just to check some matrix.

All the functions presented in this chapter are collected into the package `ExtendGraphics`Geometry3D``. The results from the last chapter were collected into the package `ExtendGraphics`Geometry``. The results presented in these chapters can be obtained by loading these packages. An alternative to loading these packages is to load the master package, `ExtendGrahics`Master``, which will load a package automatically when any of its functions are used.

▸ *Setting Up Mathematica*

In the previous chapter the `AspectRatio` option of `Graphics` was set to be `Automatic` so that when *Mathematica* made pictures the scale in x was the same as that in y. `BoxRatios` is the equivalent option of `Graphics3D` and this has a default value of `Automatic` giving the same scale in x, y, and z. Therefore the option does not need to be changed. However it will be necessary to load the two-dimensional geometry package, which is done automatically when `ExtendGraphics`Geometry3D`` is loaded.

The geometry package developed in the previous chapter is required for many of the results in this chapter.

```
In[1]:= Needs["ExtendGraphics`Geometry`"]
```

17.1 Basic Geometric Objects

This section will define the basic objects that are used in this examination of three-dimensional geometry. When they have been defined their properties and interactions can be studied.

▸ *Vector*

A three-dimensional vector is represented by a triple of numbers $\{x, y, z\}$. Such an entity can describe a point in a three-dimensional space. Many properties of three-dimensional vectors are direct extensions from two-dimensional vectors. For example three-dimensional vectors can be added and subtracted, and multiplied by a scalar. The dot product of two three-dimensional vectors can be taken in a way analogous to two-dimensional vectors.

```
In[2]:= (p = {px, py, pz};
         q = {qx, qy, qz};)
```

The addition of three-dimensional vectors.

```
In[3]:= p + q
Out[3]= {px + qx, py + qy, pz + qz}
```

Multiplication by a scalar.

```
In[4]:= 3 p
Out[4]= {3 px, 3 py, 3 pz}
```

The definition of the dot product in three dimensions is an extension of that in two dimensions.

```
In[5]:= p.q
Out[5]= px qx + py qy + pz qz
```

The VectorLength function defined in the previous chapter will work for vectors of any dimension.

```
In[6]:= ?VectorLength
VectorLength[ v] returns the length of the vector v.
```

The length of p.

```
In[7]:= VectorLength[p]
```
$$Out[7]= \mathrm{Sqrt}[px^2 + py^2 + pz^2]$$

Dividing through by the length of a vector normalizes it.

```
In[8]:= pnorm = p/VectorLength[p]
```
$$Out[8]= \left\{ \frac{px}{\mathrm{Sqrt}[px^2 + py^2 + pz^2]}, \frac{py}{\mathrm{Sqrt}[px^2 + py^2 + pz^2]}, \right.$$
$$\left. \frac{pz}{\mathrm{Sqrt}[px^2 + py^2 + pz^2]} \right\}$$

The length of a normalized vector is 1.

```
In[9]:= VectorLength[pnorm]//Simplify
Out[9]= 1
```

Cross Product

In three dimensions there are infinitely many vectors perpendicular to a given vector. For two non-parallel vectors a third vector perpendicular to both is generated by the cross product.

Load the cross product package.

```
In[10]:= Needs["LinearAlgebra`CrossProduct`"]
```

```
In[11]:= r = Cross[p, q]
```

```
Out[11]= {-(pz qy) + py qz, pz qx - px qz, -(py qx) + px qy}
```

The dot product of r with p and q is zero since it is perpendicular to each.

```
In[12]:= {r.p, r.q}//Simplify
```

```
Out[12]= {0, 0}
```

The length of the cross product is equal to twice the area of the triangle formed by the two vectors.

```
In[13]:= VectorLength[r] - 2 Area[Polygon[{{0,0,0}, p, q}]]
```

```
Out[13]= 0
```

There are two possible directions for the cross product. It could point above the plane formed by the two vectors or below. In fact the cross product has a right-handed definition. This means that when the right hand is arranged with the fingers curled to go from the first vector to the second the thumb points along the cross product. The first and second vectors are ordered so that the angle between them is less than π.

```
In[14]:= v1 = {1,0,0}; v2 = {0,1,0}; v3 = Cross[v1, v2];
```

The right hand is curled as though it holds a pole. The palm is placed at v1 and the fingers curl past v2. The thumb points along the cross product.

```
In[15]:= Show[
            Graphics3D[
              {Text["palm", v1 1.2],
               Text["thumb", v3 1.1],
               Line[{{0,0,0}, 0.9 v1}],
               Line[{{0,0,0}, 0.9 v2}],
               Line[{{0,0,0}, 0.9 v3}],
               Line[{{0.1,0.9,0},v2,{0.1,1.1,0}}],
               Line[Table[{Cos[t], Sin[t], 0},
                          {t,0.1,Pi/2,0.05}]]}],
            PlotRange -> {{-0.4, 1.2},{-0.4,1.2},{-0.4,1.2}}]
```

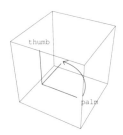

Orthogonal Vectors

Given two vectors, a third vector perpendicular to both can be generated. Given one vector it would be useful to find two new vectors so that all three are mutually perpendicular. In this case the three vectors form an orthogonal set. The main problem is to find the first perpendicular vector; once that is found the second can be determined from the cross product.

A vector perpendicular to $\{x, y, z\}$ can easily be found. The vector $\{-y, x, 0\}$ is perpendicular, as are $\{z, 0, -x\}$ and $\{0, -z, y\}$. When the components are all numeric the component with the smallest absolute value should be dropped for reasons of numerical stability. When the components are symbolic there is no obvious choice.

When the vector is numeric the two largest components are used to form the vector v1. The vector v2 is then determined from the cross product.

```
In[16]:= OrthogonalVectors[norm:{_,_,_}] :=
            Module[{pos, a, b, v1, v2},
                pos = If[VectorQ[norm, NumberQ],
                        Abs[N[norm]], norm] ;
                pos = Sort[Transpose[{pos, Range[3]}]] ;
                {pos, a,b} = Map[Last, pos] ;
                v1 = ReplacePart[{0,0,0}, -Part[norm, a], b] ;
                v1 = ReplacePart[v1, Part[norm, b], a] ;
                v2 = Cross[norm, v1] ;
                {v1, v2}
                ]
In[17]:= p = {a,b,c};
```

These are two vectors orthogonal to p.

```
In[18]:= {p1, p2} = OrthogonalVectors[p]
```

$Out[18]= \{\{0, c, -b\}, \{-b^2 - c^2, a\,b, a\,c\}\}$

The three vectors, p, p1, and p2, form an orthogonal set.

```
In[19]:= {p1.p, p2.p, p1.p2}//Simplify
Out[19]= {0, 0, 0}

In[20]:= (p = {1,3,-1};
          {p1, p2} = OrthogonalVectors[p];)
```

A graphical representation demonstrates the relationships between the vectors.

```
In[21]:= Show[
            Graphics3D[
                {AbsolutePointSize[4],
                Map[Point, {p, p1, p2}],
                Map[Line[{{0,0,0}, #}]&, {p, p1, p2}]}]]
```

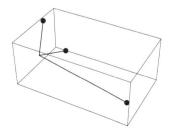

▶ *Point*

Many of the representations for geometric entities from two dimensions are very similar in three dimensions. For example, a point in three-dimensional space can be plotted with the Point primitive.

▶ *Line*

A line in three-dimensional space can be generated from two distinct points. The line is the shortest path between the points and extends infinitely in either direction. Such a line can be parametrized by the loci of points $\mathbf{p}_1 + (\mathbf{p}_2 - \mathbf{p}_1)t$ where $\mathbf{p}_1$ and $\mathbf{p}_2$ are two points on the line and t is a parameter that describes progress down the line. When t is 0 the point on the line is at $\mathbf{p}_1$ and when t is 1 the point is at $\mathbf{p}_2$. The Line primitive provided by *Mathematica* is closely related to this explicit form for a line. Line[{p1,p2}] describes the segment of the line between the points p1 and p2.

This is of course closely related to the definition of a line in two dimensions. However, in two dimensions an implicit representation of a line was also presented. Plotting the implicit equation, $(\mathbf{p}-\mathbf{c})\cdot\vec{n} = 0$, in three dimensions does not generate a line as can be seen from the ContourPlot3D command.

ContourPlot3D is defined in the package Graphics`ContourPlot3D`.

```
In[22]:= Needs["Graphics`ContourPlot3D`"]
```

This draws the implicitly defined surface. It is a plane.

```
In[23]:= ContourPlot3D[({x,y,z} - {1,2,-1}).{-1,1,1},
             {x,-2,2}, {y,-2,2}, {z,-2,2}]
```

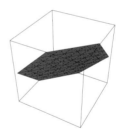

Thus the implicit equation, $(\mathbf{p} - \mathbf{c}) \cdot \vec{n} = 0$, defines a plane in three dimensions. In general it defines a hyperplane, in two dimensions this is a line and in three dimensions this is a plane.

▶ *Plane*

As shown in the last example a three-dimensional plane can be defined as the set of points that satisfy the implicit equation $(\mathbf{p} - \mathbf{c}) \cdot \vec{n} = 0$. Here $\mathbf{c}$ and $\vec{n}$ are a point in and the normal to the plane respectively. A plane divides the space into two regions just as in two dimensions a line divides the space. It will be possible to determine on which side of a plane a particular point falls. It would be quite meaningless to determine which side of a line a given point fell.

An expression representing a plane in three-dimensional space.

```
In[24]:= Plane[{5,6,2}, {6,1,3}]

Out[24]= Plane[{5, 6, 2}, {6, 1, 3}]
```

ToPolygon converts a Plane to a Polygon primitive. Vectors orthogonal to the normal are used to determine the polygon. The extent of the polygon is set by an optional second argument.

```
In[25]:= ToPolygon[Plane[c:{_,_,_}, n:{_,_,_}], size_:1] :=
            Module[{v1, v2},
                {v1, v2} = OrthogonalVectors[n] ;
                v1 = v1/VectorLength[v1] ;
                v2 = v2/VectorLength[v2] ;
                Polygon[
                    {c + size v1, c + size v2,
                        c - size v1, c - size v2}]
            ]
```

A Plane object is converted to a Polygon that represents part of it.

```
In[26]:= ToPolygon[Plane[{1.5,1,1}, {-1,-2,1.5}]]

Out[26]= Polygon[{{1.5, 0.4, 0.2},
    {2.42848, 0.702887, 1.22283}, {1.5, 1.6, 1.8},
    {0.571523, 1.29711, 0.777166}}]
```

A Graphics3D object can be formed and plotted.

```
In[27]:= Show[Graphics3D[%]]
```

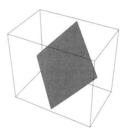

PlaneComponents shows a representative polygon and the center point and normal vector.

```
In[28]:= PlaneComponents[Plane[c:{_,_,_},n:{_,_,_}],size_:1] :=
            Module[{v1, v2},
                poly = ToPolygon[Plane[c, n], size] ;
                {AbsolutePointSize[4],
                 Point[c],
                 Line[{c, c+size n/VectorLength[n]}],
                 poly}
            ]
```

This a useful way to visualize a plane.

```
In[29]:= Show[
            Graphics3D[
                PlaneComponents[Plane[{1.5,1,1}, {-1,-2,1.5}]]]]
```

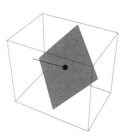

By a strict analogy with the two-dimensional geometry covered in Chapter 16 this should be called `ImplicitPlane` and there should be a `Plane` object that is defined by three points. This would correspond to the objects `Line` and `ImplicitLine` used in Chapter 16 page 373. In practice in this chapter only the implicit form will be used and there will be no special object `ImplicitPlane`.

▶ *Triangle*

A triangle can be represented in three dimensions by a *Mathematica* `Polygon` primitive. It is defined by the vertices of the triangle. Many of the results that were determined for a triangle in two dimensions such as area or perimeter will also hold in three dimensions. The triangle in three dimensions is closely related to a plane; for a given triangle there is a unique plane in which that triangle resides.

17.2 Geometric Transformations

The vectors that make up three-dimensional geometric primitives can undergo a variety of transformations. In the previous chapter, on two-dimensional geometry, affine transformations were studied. Now three-dimensional affine transformations will be studied. These include translations, rotations, and scalings.

▶ *Translation*

A vector $\{v_x, v_y, v_z\}$ can be translated by adding a vector, $\{t_x, t_y, t_z\}$, representing the translation. The result will be $\{v_x + t_x, v_y + t_y, v_z + t_z\}$.

A `Graphics3D` object.

```
In[30]:= p =
   Take[ParametricPlot3D[{x, y, Sin[x y]},
                {x,0,Pi}, {y,0,Pi}], 1]
```

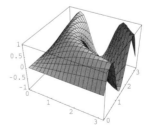

The Polygon primitives are translated by {2,1,-2}. The effect is noticeable from the change in the axes.

```
In[31]:= Show[p /.
            {x_?NumberQ, y_?NumberQ, z_?NumberQ} :>
               {x,y,z} + {2,1,-2}, Axes -> True]
```

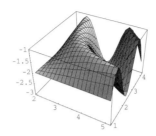

The transformation was applied by a rule that matched triples of numbers. This is quite a crude way to make a transformation since it may affect other sets of numbers that do not represent points, for example lighting options. This is why only the primitives were taken from the result of `ParametricPlot3D` above. A much better way to make these transformations would be to operate on actual primitives. This will be demonstrated later in this section.

▸ *Rotation*

A rotation in three dimensions is more complex than in two dimensions. One way to generate a rotation matrix is to specify the three Euler angles of rotation. The standard *Mathematica* package `Geometry`Rotations` contains code to generate a three-dimensional rotation matrix defined in terms of the Euler angles.

The code for the rotation matrix is loaded.

```
In[32]:= Needs["Geometry`Rotations`"]
```

```
In[33]:= ?RotationMatrix3D
RotationMatrix3D[phi,theta,psi] gives the matrix for rotation by
    the specified Euler angles in three dimensions.
```

The actual definitions for these are in terms of three Euler angles. The first specifies a rotation around the *z* axis, then around the *x* axis, and finally around the *z* axis again.

A rotation of t radians around the *z* axis.

```
In[34]:= RotationMatrix3D[t,0,0]
Out[34]= {{Cos[t], Sin[t], 0}, {-Sin[t], Cos[t], 0}, {0, 0, 1}}
```

The rotation defined by `RotationMatrix3D` is such that a positive rotation around an axis will appear clockwise when looking along the axis from a positive value to the origin.

To save on the amount of code to be entered a pure function that returns a replacement rule that applies a transformation to a point is defined. This is a simple but effective way to carry out the transformations demonstrated here. An animation would be a powerful way to demonstrate the rotations; here they are shown as individual steps.

`ApplyMatrix` returns a pure function that takes one argument.

```
In[35]:= ApplyMatrix =
            ({x_?NumberQ, y_?NumberQ, z_?NumberQ} :> #.{x,y,z})& ;
```

ApplyMatrix applied to a transformation matrix returns a rule that can transform points.

```
In[36]:= ApplyMatrix[mat]

Out[36]= {(x_)?NumberQ, (y_)?NumberQ, (z_)?NumberQ} :>
    mat . {x, y, z}
```

The Graphics3D object p is shown before and after it has been rotated by Pi around the *z* and the *x* axes.

```
In[37]:= Show[
            GraphicsArray[
              {p,
               p /. ApplyMatrix[RotationMatrix3D[Pi, Pi, 0]]}]]
```

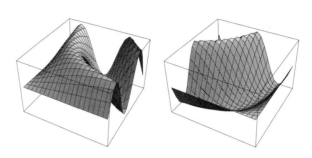

These axes will help identify the rotations.

```
In[38]:= axes =
            Graphics3D[
              {Text["X", {1.1,0,0}], Line[{{0,0,0}, {1,0,0}}],
               Text["Y", {0,1.1,0}], Line[{{0,0,0}, {0,1,0}}],
               Text["Z", {0,0,1.1}], Line[{{0,0,0}, {0,0,1}}]
              }, PlotRange -> {{-1.2,1.2},{-1.2,1.2}, {-1.2,1.2}}]

Out[38]= -Graphics3D-

In[39]:= Show[axes]
```

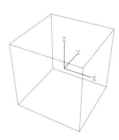

The original axes are kept to be drawn in gray.

```
In[40]:= oldaxes = Insert[axes, GrayLevel[0.5], {1,1}];
```

This shows a first rotation around the *z* axis by −Pi/2. This is a negative rotation so the result is counterclockwise looking down the axis.

```
In[41]:= Show[oldaxes,
             axes /. ApplyMatrix[
                     RotationMatrix3D[-Pi/2, 0,0]]]
```

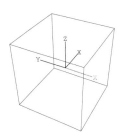

Now a rotation around the *x* axis is added.

```
In[42]:= Show[oldaxes,
             axes /. ApplyMatrix[
                     RotationMatrix3D[-Pi/2, Pi/4,0]]]
```

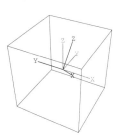

The last component is another rotation around the *z* axis.

```
In[43]:= Show[oldaxes,
             axes /.
               ApplyMatrix[
                     RotationMatrix3D[-Pi/2, Pi/4,Pi/2]]]
```

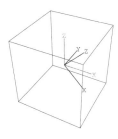

There are many other ways to parametrize a three-dimensional rotation. One alternative method is to define the rotation in terms of two pairs of perpendicular vectors. The first pair are rotated into the second. In two dimensions the task was to rotate one vector into another. This was much easier since the angle between the two vectors was used to parametrize the rotation. The three-dimensional problem is solved by dividing it into two steps. The first rotates both vectors, assumed to be normalized, into two of the axes. This is done by a matrix M:

$$\begin{pmatrix} M_{11} & M_{12} & M_{13} \\ M_{21} & M_{22} & M_{23} \\ M_{31} & M_{32} & M_{33} \end{pmatrix} \cdot \begin{pmatrix} a_x \\ a_y \\ a_z \end{pmatrix} = \begin{pmatrix} 1 \\ 0 \\ 0 \end{pmatrix}$$

and $M \cdot \{b_x, b_y, b_z\} = \{0, 1, 0\}$ and $M \cdot \{c_x, c_y, c_z\} = \{0, 0, 1\}$. Where $\vec{a}$ and $\vec{b}$ are the original vectors and $\vec{c}$ is equal to $\vec{a} \times \vec{b}$. The matrix that does this is:

$$\begin{pmatrix} a_x & a_y & a_z \\ b_x & b_y & b_z \\ c_x & c_y & c_z \end{pmatrix}$$

a result that follows from the orthonormality of the vectors $\vec{a}, \vec{b}$, and $\vec{c}$. For example $\{a_x, a_y, a_z\} \cdot \{a_x, a_y, a_z\} = 1$ since $\vec{a}$ is normalized and $\{a_x, a_y, a_z\} \cdot \{b_x, b_y, b_z\} = 0$ since $\vec{a}$ and $\vec{b}$ are orthogonal. A *Mathematica* function to do this can be defined.

The input vectors are normalized, the cross product is formed, and the resulting matrix returned.

```
In[44]:= RotateVectorsToAxes[
              a:{_,_,_}, b:{_,_,_}] /; a.b == 0 :=
           Module[{ad, bd, c},
             ad = a/VectorLength[a] ;
             bd = b/VectorLength[b];
             c = Cross[ad, bd];
             {ad, bd, c}
           ]
```

A matrix that rotates {0.5,0.5,0.5} to lie along the *x* axis and {-1.,0.5,0.5} to the *y* axis is calculated.

```
In[45]:= rot1 =
           RotateVectorsToAxes[{0.5,0.5,0.5}, {-1.,0.5,0.5}]
Out[45]= {{0.57735, 0.57735, 0.57735},
         {-0.816497, 0.408248, 0.408248}, {0., -0.707107, 0.707107}}
```

A collection of primitives to demonstrate the application of rotation by `rot1`.

```
In[46] := vecs =
            Show[
              Graphics3D[
                {Text["A", {0.6,0.6,0.6}],
                 Text["B", {-1.1,0.55,0.55}],
                 Line[{{0,0,0}, {0.5,0.5,0.5}}],
                 Line[{{0,0,0}, {-1,0.5,0.5}}]},
                 PlotRange ->
                   {{-1.2,1.2},{-1.2,1.2},{-1.2,1.2}}]]
```

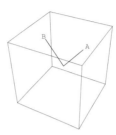

Transform A to lie along the *x* axis and B to the *y* axis.

```
In[47] := Show[vecs /. ApplyMatrix[rot1]]
```

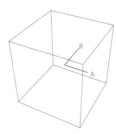

The second part of the problem is to rotate from these axes to another pair of perpendicular vectors. This is the reverse of the problem just solved and requires that the inverse transform be found. The inverse is given by the transpose of the rotation matrix:

$$\begin{pmatrix} a_x & a_y & a_z \\ b_x & b_y & b_z \\ c_x & c_y & c_z \end{pmatrix} \cdot \begin{pmatrix} a_x & b_x & c_x \\ a_y & b_y & c_y \\ a_z & b_z & c_z \end{pmatrix} = \begin{pmatrix} 1 & 0 & 0 \\ 0 & 1 & 0 \\ 0 & 0 & 1 \end{pmatrix}$$

again a result of the orthonormality of the vectors $\vec{a}$, $\vec{b}$, and $\vec{c}$.

The axes primitives, introduced earlier, are transformed back to lie along the test vectors. The two pictures are plotted side by side in a `GraphicsArray`.

```
In[48]:= Show[
            GraphicsArray[
               {vecs, axes /. ApplyMatrix[Transpose[rot1]]}]]
```

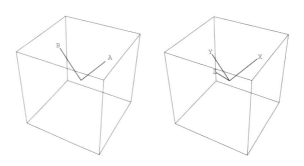

`RotateVectorsToVectors` takes two pairs of perpendicular vectors and returns the rotation that transforms the first to the second.

```
In[49]:= RotateVectorsToVectors[
               a:{_,_,_}, b:{_,_,_}, an:{_,_,_}, bn:{_,_,_}] /;
                  a.b == an.bn == 0 :=
            Transpose[RotateVectorsToAxes[an, bn]].
               RotateVectorsToAxes[a,b]
```

This matrix rotates {0.5,0.5,0.5} to {-1,1,1} and {-1.,0.5,0.5} to {0,-1,1}.

```
In[50]:= rot2 =
            RotateVectorsToVectors[
               {0.5,0.5,0.5}, {-1.,0.5, 0.5},
               {-1, 1, 1}, {0,-1,1}]

Out[50]= {{-0.333333, -0.910684, 0.244017},
          {0.910684, -0.244017, 0.333333},
          {-0.244017, 0.333333, 0.910684}}
```

A graphical representation of the vectors before and after the rotation.

```
In[51]:= Show[Insert[vecs, GrayLevel[0.5], {1,1}],
            vecs /. ApplyMatrix[rot2],
            Axes -> True]
```

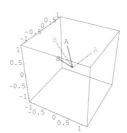

▶ *Scale and Shear*

A transformation matrix that represents a scale can be written as $\{\{s_x,0,0\},\{0,s_y,0\},\{0,0,s_z\}\}$. Such a transformation expands or contracts the scale by the specified amount along each coordinate. It is very similar to the two-dimensional scale. Shear transformations can be classified according to the plane in which they are carried out. A shear in the xy plane is represented by $\{\{1,0,sh_x\},\{0,1,sh_y\},\{0,0,1\}\}$.

p is transformed by a shear in the xy plane of $\{-0.4,-0.4\}$.

```
In[52]:= Show[p /.
            ApplyMatrix[{{1,0,-0.4}, {0,1,-0.4}, {0,0,1}}]]
```

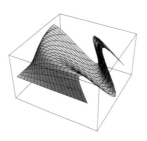

▶ *Homogeneous Transformations*

A uniform matrix representation of affine transformations can be attained by using homogeneous transformation matrices. These are four-dimensional transformations that allow the three-dimensional translation to be represented by matrix multiplication. The translation is represented by a shear in the xyz hyperplane.

The point vec is embedded in the four-dimensional hyperplane $x_4 == 1$, the transformation is carried out and the three-dimensional result is returned.

```
In[53]:= HomogeneousMultiply[tmat_, vec_] :=
            Drop[tmat.Append[vec, 1], -1]
```

ApplyHomogeneousMatrix will work with homogeneous matrices.

```
In[54]:= ApplyHomogeneousMatrix =
            ({x_?NumberQ, y_?NumberQ, z_?NumberQ} :>
                HomogeneousMultiply[#, {x,y,z}])&
```
```
Out[54]= {(x_)?NumberQ, (y_)?NumberQ, (z_)?NumberQ} :>
            HomogeneousMultiply[#1, {x, y, z}] &
```

The rule is returned that uses HomogeneousMultiply instead of the normal matrix multiplication provided by Dot.

```
In[55]:= ApplyHomogeneousMatrix[mat]
```
```
Out[55]= {(x_)?NumberQ, (y_)?NumberQ, (z_)?NumberQ} :>
            HomogeneousMultiply[mat, {x, y, z}]
```

This homogeneous matrix represents a three-dimensional translation.

```
In[56]:= HomogeneousTranslation[{tx_, ty_, tz_}] :=
            {{1,0,0,tx},{0,1,0,ty},{0,0,1,tx},{0,0,0,1}}
```

The point {x,y,z} can be translated by {tx,ty,tz}.

```
In[57]:= HomogeneousMultiply[
               HomogeneousTranslation[{tx, ty, tz}], {x,y,z}]
Out[57]= {tx + x, ty + y, tx + z}
```

HomogeneousMatrix will turn a three-dimensional matrix into a homogeneous four-dimensional matrix.

```
In[58]:= HomogeneousMatrix[mat_] :=
               Append[Map[Append[#, 0]&, mat], {0,0,0,1}]
```

The rotation matrix generated earlier is converted to a four-dimensional matrix.

```
In[59]:= rotmat = HomogeneousMatrix[rot2]
Out[59]= {{-0.333333, -0.910684, 0.244017, 0},
          {0.910684, -0.244017, 0.333333, 0},
          {-0.244017, 0.333333, 0.910684, 0}, {0, 0, 0, 1}}
```

The homogeneous transformation is applied.

```
In[60]:= Show[p /. ApplyHomogeneousMatrix[rotmat]]
```

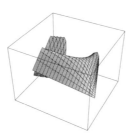

The matrix multiplication function HomogeneousMultiply defined here makes the assumption that the transformation will never move the object out of the four-dimensional hyperplane $x_4 == 1$. For affine transformations this will always be the case. More general four-dimensional transformations can be constructed and for these the transformation back to the $x_4 == 1$ hyperplane must be considered. The result of such a transformation in three dimensions can be non-affine, for example it may be a perspective projection. The Plot3Matrix, that was described in Chapter 10 page 194, refers to the four-dimensional homogeneous matrix that *Mathematica* uses to project three-dimensional graphics when they are plotted.

▶ *Composition of Transformations*

A uniform description of affine transformations allows sequences or compositions of transformations. These are made by multiplying the relevant matrices to form one transformation matrix.

$$M_{comp} = M_n \cdot M_{n-1} \ldots M_2 \cdot M_1$$

M_{comp} is the transformation obtained by first applying M_1 then M_2 and so on. An example of the use of composition of transformations is the construction of a matrix for rotation around some point other than the origin. This is done by translating that point to the origin, rotating, and then reversing the translation.

Translate {Pi,1,1} to the origin, rotate by Pi around the new z axes, and then translate to restore the original origin.

```
In[61]:= mat =
            HomogeneousTranslation[{Pi,Pi, 0}].
            HomogeneousMatrix[RotationMatrix3D[Pi,0,0]].
            HomogeneousTranslation[{-Pi, -Pi, 0}]

Out[61]= {{-1, 0, 0, 2 Pi}, {0, -1, 0, 2 Pi}, {0, 0, 1, 0},
         {0, 0, 0, 1}}
```

p is rotated around the point {Pi, Pi, 0}.

```
In[62]:= Show[p /. ApplyHomogeneousMatrix[mat]]
```

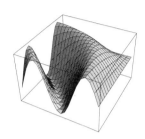

▷ *Transformation Package*

The transformation functions demonstrated here and some more utilities are collected into the package `ExtendGraphics`Transform`.

```
HomogeneousTranslation[{t_x, t_y, t_z}]
                                matrix for the translation {t_x, t_y, t_z}
HomogeneousRotation[{r_phi, t_theta, t_psi}]
                                matrix for the rotation {r_phi, t_theta, t_psi}
HomogeneousScale[{s_x, s_y, s_z}]       matrix for the scale {s_x, s_y, s_z}
HomogeneousShear[{{sh_Xy, sh_Xz}, {sh_Yx, sh_Yz}, {sh_Zx, sh_Zy}}]
                                matrix for the shear
                                  {{sh_Xy, sh_Xz}, {sh_Yx, sh_Yz}, {sh_Zx, sh_Zy}}
HomogeneousTransform[mat, g]         transform the graphics object g by mat
```

Functions defined in `ExtendGraphics`Transform`.

The graphics transformation package is loaded.

```
In[63]:= Needs["ExtendGraphics`Transform`"]
```

The main transformation function.

```
In[64]:= ?HomogeneousTransform

HomogeneousTransform[ mat, g] applies the transformation
      specified  by mat to the graphics object g.
```

mat represents a shear in the *xy* plane.

```
In[65]:= mat = HomogeneousShear[{{0,0},{0,0}, {1,1}}]

Out[65]= {{1, 0, 1, 0}, {0, 1, 1, 0}, {0, 0, 1, 0},
    {0, 0, 0, 1}}
```

A three-dimensional object that can be transformed.

```
In[66]:= sphere =
            ParametricPlot3D[
                {Sin[t] Sin[p], Sin[t] Cos[p], Cos[t]},
                    {t,0,Pi},{p,0,2Pi}]
```

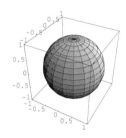

The transformation can easily be applied to the Graphics3D object. HomogeneousTransform only applies the transformation to coordinates of primitives.

```
In[67]:= Show[HomogeneousTransform[mat, sphere]]
```

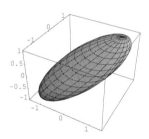

17.3 Geometric Results

Some basic primitives of three-dimensional geometry have been introduced. Some of the ways in which transformations can be applied to these primitives were demonstrated in the previous section. Now the interactions of these primitives will be examined.

▸ *Intersection of Two Lines*

Two lines interesect when the same point is found on both lines. This point will satisfy the equation of both lines. Writing both equations in a parametric form:

$$\mathbf{a} = \mathbf{a}_1 + (\mathbf{a}_2 - \mathbf{a}_1)t$$
$$\mathbf{b} = \mathbf{b}_1 + (\mathbf{b}_2 - \mathbf{b}_1)s$$

The intersection occurs when **a** is equal to **b**:

$$\mathbf{a_1} + (\mathbf{a_2} - \mathbf{a_1})t = \mathbf{b_1} + (\mathbf{b_2} - \mathbf{b_1})s$$

This can be solved for *s* and *t* as follows. First subtract $\mathbf{a_1}$ from both sides and take the cross product with $(\mathbf{b_2} - \mathbf{b_1})$:

$$(\mathbf{a_2} - \mathbf{a_1}) \times (\mathbf{b_2} - \mathbf{b_1})t = (\mathbf{b_1} - \mathbf{a_1}) \times (\mathbf{b_2} - \mathbf{b_1})$$

Now dotting with $(\mathbf{a_2} - \mathbf{a_1}) \times (\mathbf{b_2} - \mathbf{b_1})$ and dividing by $|(\mathbf{a_2} - \mathbf{a_1}) \times (\mathbf{b_2} - \mathbf{b_1})|^2$ gives:

$$t = \frac{((\mathbf{b_1} - \mathbf{a_1}) \times (\mathbf{b_2} - \mathbf{b_1})) \cdot ((\mathbf{a_2} - \mathbf{a_1}) \times (\mathbf{b_2} - \mathbf{b_1}))}{|(\mathbf{a_2} - \mathbf{a_1}) \times (\mathbf{b_2} - \mathbf{b_1})|^2}$$

and solving for s:

$$s = \frac{((\mathbf{b_1} - \mathbf{a_1}) \times (\mathbf{a_2} - \mathbf{a_1})) \cdot ((\mathbf{a_2} - \mathbf{a_1}) \times (\mathbf{b_2} - \mathbf{b_1}))}{|(\mathbf{a_2} - \mathbf{a_1}) \times (\mathbf{b_2} - \mathbf{b_1})|^2}$$

In this expression the triple product term $\vec{a} \times \vec{b} \cdot \vec{c}$ is equal to the determinant of the matrix $\{\vec{a}, \vec{b}, \vec{c}\}$. This can be confirmed by *Mathematica*.

The identity can be confirmed by *Mathematica*.

```
In[68]:= Det[{{ax,ay,az}, {bx,by,bz},{cx,cy,cz}}] ==
            Cross[{ax, ay, az},
                {bx, by, bz}].{cx,cy,cz}//Simplify

Out[68]= True
```

Now a *Mathematica* function for finding the intersection of two three-dimensional lines can be defined.

IntersectionPoint returns the points of intersection of the two lines.

```
In[69]:= IntersectionPoint[
            Line[{a1_, a2_}], Line[{b1_, b2_}]] :=
         Module[{v1, v2, cross, len},
            v1 = (a2-a1) ;
            v2 = (b2-b1) ;
            cross = Cross[v1,v2] ;
            len = Chop[VectorLength[cross]^2] ;
            If[len === 0,
                Print["Parallel Lines"];
                Return[{Infinity, Infinity}]] ;
            {a1 + (a2 - a1) *
                    Det[{b1-a1, v2, cross}]/len,
            b1 + (b2 - b1) *
                    Det[{b1-a1, v1, cross}]/len}
            ]
```

Some lines to demonstrate intersection.

```
In[70]:= (l1 = Line[{{0,-1,2}, {5,1,2.}}] ;
         l2 = Line[{{-1,1,2}, {4,0,2.}}];)
```

The two points are equal, since the lines cross.

```
In[71]:= {t, s} = IntersectionPoint[l1, l2]

Out[71]= {{3., 0.2, 2.}, {3., 0.2, 2.}}
```

The points are confirmed to be the point of intersection of the lines.

```
In[72]:= Show[
            Graphics3D[
              {AbsolutePointSize[4],
               Point[t], Point[s], l1, l2}]]
```

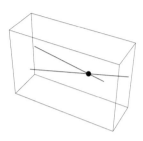

A different set of lines.

```
In[73]:= (l1 = Line[{{0,-1,1.5}, {2,1,1.5}}];
          l2 = Line[{{0.5,1,0}, {2.5,-2,1}}];)
```

The two points are not coincident since the lines do not cross.

```
In[74]:= {t, s} = IntersectionPoint[l1, l2]

Out[74]= {{1.05556, 0.0555556, 1.5},
          {1.27778, -0.166667, 0.388889}}
```

The points mark the points of closest approach on each line.

```
In[75]:= Show[
            Graphics3D[
              {AbsolutePointSize[4],
               Point[t], Point[s], l1, l2}]]
```

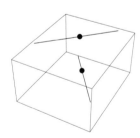

▶ *Point in a Plane*

To test if a point falls in a plane requires substitution into the equation of the plane, $(\mathbf{p} - \mathbf{c}) \cdot \vec{\mathbf{n}} = 0$.

p is substituted into the equation of the plane defined by **c** and **n̄**. The result of this is compared with zero.

```
In[76]:= PointInPlaneQ[p_, Plane[c_, n_]] :=
             Chop[(p-c).n] === 0
```

The point {1,0,1} is not in the plane Plane[{0,0,0}, {0,0,1}].

```
In[77]:= PointInPlaneQ[{1,0,1}, Plane[{0,0,0}, {0,0,1}]]
Out[77]= False
```

The picture demonstrates that this is so.

```
In[78]:= Show[
            Graphics3D[
              {AbsolutePointSize[3],
               Point[{1,0,1}],
               ToPolygon[Plane[{0,0,0}, {0,0,1}],2]},
              ViewPoint -> {1,-1.2,.2}]]
```

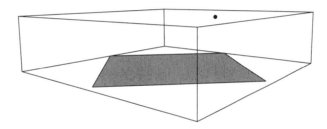

▶ *Point in a Plane Closest to a Point*

This result is identical to that in two dimensions, which is used here. The point **q** in a plane, defined by **c** and **n̄**, closest to a point **p** is given by:

$$q = p - \frac{(\mathbf{p} - \mathbf{c}) \cdot \vec{\mathbf{n}}}{\vec{\mathbf{n}} \cdot \vec{\mathbf{n}}} \; \vec{\mathbf{n}}$$

ClosestPointInPlane finds the point in a plane closest to another point.

```
In[79]:= ClosestPointInPlane[p_, Plane[c_, n_]] :=
             p - (p-c).n/n.n n
```

This is the closest point in Plane[{0,0,0}, {0,0,1}] to the point {1,0,1}.

```
In[80]:= ClosestPointInPlane[{1,0,1}, Plane[{0,0,0}, {0,0,1}]]
Out[80]= {1, 0, 0}
```

```
In[81] := Show[
            Graphics3D[
              {AbsolutePointSize[3],
               Point[{1,0,1}],
               ToPolygon[Plane[{0,0,0}, {0,0,1}], 2],
               Point[
              ClosestPointInPlane[{1,0,1},
                  Plane[{0,0,0}, {0,0,1}]]]},
              ViewPoint -> {1,-1.2,.2}]]
```

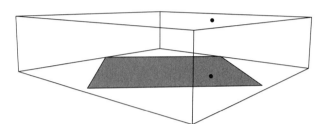

This result can be used to determine the minimum distance from a plane to a point.

▶ *Which Side of a Plane*

A plane divides a three-dimensional space into two regions. Therefore it is possible to determine the region in which a given point is found. The answer can be deduced from the equation of the plane where it depends upon the sign of $(\mathbf{p} - \mathbf{c}) \cdot \vec{\mathbf{n}}$. The question of which sign denotes which side has to be fixed. Unlike the two-dimensional analogue to this problem there is no readily available standard and it is actually necessary to think about the direction in which the normal vector $\vec{\mathbf{n}}$ points.

SideOfPlaneQ takes a point and a plane. It substitutes the former into the latter and tests the sign of the result.

```
In[82] := SideOfPlaneQ[p_, Plane[c_, n_]] :=
            (p - c).n > 0
```

These will be useful for an example.

```
In[83] := (p = {6,3,2};
           c = {5,6,1};
           n = {1,1,1};)
```

The point t is not on the side of the plane to which n points.

```
In[84] := SideOfPlaneQ[p, Plane[c, n]]

Out[84] = False
```

The plane is drawn with the output of PlaneComponents, which draws the center and normal to the plane.

```
In[85]:= Show[
            Graphics3D[
                {PlaneComponents[Plane[c, n]],
                AbsolutePointSize[4],
                Point[p]}]]
```

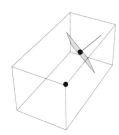

▶ *Intersection of a Line with a Plane*

This is the equivalent to the problem of the intersection of a pair of two-dimensional lines. The solution is found by substituting the equation for the line into the equation of the plane.

A definition is added to IntersectionPoint for the case of a line and a plane.

```
In[86]:= IntersectionPoint[
                Line[{p1_, p2_}], Plane[c_, n_]] :=
            Module[{tst},
                tst = Chop[(p2 - p1).n] ;
                If[tst === 0,
                    Print["Parallel Primitives"];
                    Table[Infinity, {Length[p1]}],
                    p1 - (p2 - p1) (p1 - c).n/tst]
                ]
In[87]:= (p = Plane[{5,4,3}, {1,0.5,1}];
            l = Line[{{4,2.5,2}, {6,5,4}}];)
```

The point is drawn at the intersection of line with the plane.

```
In[88]:= Show[
            Graphics3D[
                {ToPolygon[p],l,
                AbsolutePointSize[4],
                Point[IntersectionPoint[l, p]]}]]
```

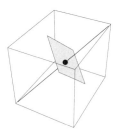

The last two results, deciding which side of a plane points fall and calculating the intersection of a line with a plane, will be used to clip geometric objects by a plane.

▶ *Plane through a Set of Points*

In a three-dimensional space there is a unique plane that passes through any three distinct non-collinear points. The equation of the plane could be determined by taking one of the points as the "point in the plane" **c** and calculating the normal **n̄** from the cross product of the vectors from this point to the other two. For more than three points it would be better to use some averaging method. The values **c** and **n̄** can be calculated for each point and the resulting collection averaged. This avoids any artifacts from choosing one particular point. For the case of three points it is also better to use an averaging technique.

These are three test points.

```
In[89]:= (p1 = {x1, y1, z1};
          p2 = {x2, y2, z2};
          p3 = {x3, y3, z3};)
```

The cross product of each point with the others is calculated. This forms the three normal vectors.

```
In[90]:= (n1 = Cross[p2-p1, p3-p1];
          n2 = Cross[p3-p2, p1-p2];
          n3 = Cross[p1-p3, p2-p3];)
```

The centroid is calculated by averaging the points.

```
In[91]:= (p1+p2+p3)/3
```

$$Out[91]= \{\frac{x1 + x2 + x3}{3}, \frac{y1 + y2 + y3}{3}, \frac{z1 + z2 + z3}{3}\}$$

The normal is calculated by averaging the three normals.

```
In[92]:= Simplify[(n1+n2+n3)/3]
```

```
Out[92]= {-(y2 z1) + y3 z1 + y1 z2 - y3 z2 - y1 z3 + y2 z3,

          x2 z1 - x3 z1 - x1 z2 + x3 z2 + x1 z3 - x2 z3,

          -(x2 y1) + x3 y1 + x1 y2 - x3 y2 - x1 y3 + x2 y3}
```

ToPlane repeats the calculation for a set of points in three-dimensional space. It averages the normals and center, returning the corresponding equation of a plane.

```
In[93]:= ToPlane[pts_ /; MatrixQ[pts] &&
                          Length[pts] > 2 &&
                          Length[First[pts]] === 3] :=
         Module[{x,y,z,x1,y1,z1, norm},
             {x,y,z} = Transpose[pts] ;
             {x1,y1,z1} = Map[RotateLeft, {x,y,z}] ;
             norm = {Dot[y-y1, z+z1],
                     Dot[z-z1, x+x1],
                     Dot[x-x1, y+y1]} ;
             If[norm == {0,0,0},
                 norm = Cross[Part[pts, 2]-First[pts],
                              Part[pts, 3]-First[pts]]];
             Plane[Apply[Plus, pts]/Length[pts], norm]
             ]
```

The result here uses the **c** and $\vec{n}$ which were derived previously.

```
In[94]:= ToPlane[{p1,p2,p3}]
```

$$Out[94]= \text{Plane}[\{\frac{x1 + x2 + x3}{3}, \frac{y1 + y2 + y3}{3}, \frac{z1 + z2 + z3}{3}\},$$

$$\{(y1 - y2) (z1 + z2) + (-y1 + y3) (z1 + z3) +$$
$$(y2 - y3) (z2 + z3), (x1 + x2) (z1 - z2) +$$
$$(x2 + x3) (z2 - z3) + (x1 + x3) (-z1 + z3),$$
$$(x1 - x2) (y1 + y2) + (-x1 + x3) (y1 + y3) +$$
$$(x2 - x3) (y2 + y3)\}]$$

A collection of points from which the plane of best fit can be calculated.

```
In[95]:= tst =
            Table[{x=Sin[t], y=Cos[t], x+y+2+Random[ ]/2},
                  {t,0,2Pi-Pi/5,Pi/5}]//N ;
```

The plane of best fit.

```
In[96]:= p = ToPlane[tst]
```

$$Out[96]= \text{Plane}[\{2.22045\ 10^{-17}, 0., 2.26165\},$$
$$\{6.27391, 5.18717, -5.87785\}]$$

A picture shows the plane with the points.

```
In[97]:= Show[
            Graphics3D[
                {ToPolygon[p, 2],
                 AbsolutePointSize[4],
                 Map[Point, tst]}]]
```

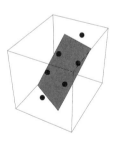

Adjusting the ViewPoint helps to show that the plane makes a good fit to the points.

```
In[98]:= Show[%, ViewPoint -> {5, -2, 3}]
```

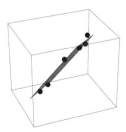

17.4 Projection and Embedding

A projection can be defined as a linear transformation that takes a linear space into a subspace of itself. A particularly simple type of projection is a parallel projection. Lines joining corresponding parts of a figure with its projection are formed. If the lines are all found to be parallel the projection is a parallel projection. In the rest of this section the term projection will mean a parallel projection.

▶ *Parallel Projection into a Plane*

Each point is mapped to the closest point in the plane.	```In[99]:= ParallelProject[pts_ /;` ` MatrixQ[pts] && Length[First[pts]] === 3,` ` Plane[c_, n_]] :=` ` Map[ClosestPointInPlane[#, Plane[c,n]]&, pts]```
These points will demonstrate parallel projection into a plane.	```In[100]:= (pts = Table[{Random[ ], Random[ ], Random[ ]}, {10}] ;` ` plane = Plane[{-1,-2,0}, {1,-1,1}];)```
The points are projected into the plane.	```In[101]:= proj = ParallelProject[pts, plane] ;```
The projected points can be tested to see if they lie in the plane.	```In[102]:= Map[PointInPlaneQ[#, plane]&, proj]` `Out[102]= {True, True, True, True, True, True, True, True,` ` True, True}```
The lines from each point to its projection are all parallel.	```In[103]:= Show[` ` Graphics3D[` ` {ToPolygon[plane,3],` ` Map[Line, Transpose[{pts, proj}]]},` ` ViewPoint -> {-1,-1,0}]]```

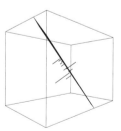

▶ *Parallel Plane Projection into Two Dimensions*

The function `ParallelProject` projected points in a three-dimensional space into a plane forming the three-dimensional results. One purpose of a projection into a plane is to lower the dimensionality of the points, to move them to a space of lower dimensions. Projecting into a plane can do this by returning the coordinates of the projected point in the plane.

Two orthonormal basis vectors, v1 and v2 are found in the plane. The points are projected into the plane and the extent along the basis vectors gives the two-dimensional result.

```
In[104]:= ParallelProjectTo2D[pts_ /;
                MatrixQ[pts] && Length[First[pts]] === 3,
                Plane[c_, n_]] :=
             Module[{npts},
                {v1, v2} = N[OrthogonalVectors[n]] ;
                v1 = v1/VectorLength[v1] ;
                v2 = v2/VectorLength[v2] ;
                npts = ParallelProject[pts, Plane[c, n]] ;
                npts = Map[(#-c)&, npts] ;
                Map[{#.v1, #.v2}&, npts]
             ]
```

pts are projected into a two-dimensional space formed by plane.

```
In[105]:= ParallelProjectTo2D[pts, plane]

Out[105]= {{2.14512, -2.11255}, {2.07033, -2.21118},
   {2.14466, -1.52097}, {2.59804, -2.38567}, {2.4771, -1.93518},
   {2.04382, -1.4707}, {2.06401, -2.51898}, {1.98474, -2.14005},
   {2.1148, -1.76076}, {1.92614, -1.6946}}
```

As an example three-dimensional line primitives forming a space curve are generated.

```
In[106]:= First[
             ParametricPlot3D[{t Sin[t], t Cos[t], t},
                             {t,0,6Pi}]];
```

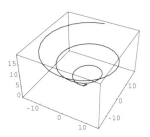

The points of each line primitive are projected into a two-dimensional space defined by plane.

```
In[107]:= % /. Line[pts_] :>
                Line[ParallelProjectTo2D[pts, plane]];
```

The two-dimensional line primitives can now be displayed.

```
In[108]:= Show[Graphics[%]]
```

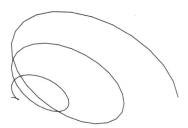

▶ *Embedding*

The functions that carry out projection, such as `ParallelProjectTo2D`, take points in three dimensions and project them to two-dimensional space. The reverse process, taking points in two dimensions and placing them in three dimensions, can be referred to as embedding. This is not the inverse of the original projective mapping since points are only returned to the plane in three-dimensional from which they were originally projected. The projective mapping itself cannot be inverted.

`EmbedIn3D` takes points in two dimensions and a plane in three dimensions. The points are embedded in the plane.

```
In[109]:= EmbedIn3D[pts_ /;
                 MatrixQ[pts] && Length[First[pts]] === 2,
                 Plane[c_, n_]] :=
          Module[{npts},
                 {v1, v2} = N[OrthogonalVectors[n]] ;
                 v1 = v1/VectorLength[v1] ;
                 v2 = v2/VectorLength[v2] ;
                 Map[(c + #.{v1, v2})&, pts]
                 ]
```

These points are embedded in three-dimensional space. The `Plane` plane was defined previously.

```
In[110]:= EmbedIn3D[{{3., 2.}, {6., 1.}}, plane]
Out[110]= {{-2.63299, -0.695176, 2.93782},
           {-1.8165, 1.83439, 4.65089}}
```

Complete two-dimensional primitives can be embedded. These are constructed from `ParametricPlot`.

```
In[111]:= prims =
             First[
               ParametricPlot[
                 LegendreP[3, Cos[t]] {Sin[t], Cos[t]},
                 {t,0,2Pi}]];
```

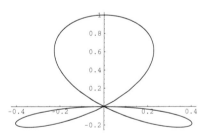

The points of the line primitives are embedded in the plane.

```
In[112]:= prims /. Line[pts_] :> Line[EmbedIn3D[pts, plane]] ;
```

The result is made into a
three-dimensional graphics object and
displayed.

In[113]:= **Show[Graphics3D[%]]**

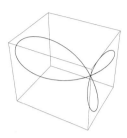

Orientation in the Plane

When the points are embedded in the three-dimensional space the center of the two-dimensional coordinate system is translated to the center of the plane. Orientation in the plane must also be determined. This can be specified by a third argument to EmbedIn3D defining a vector that will be projected to point up in the three-dimensional space.

A rotation is applied to the
two-dimensional points to make sure
that the projection of the vector $\{x,y\}$
on the z axis is maximized.

In[114]:= **EmbedIn3D[pts_ /;**
   MatrixQ[pts] && Length[First[pts]] === 2,
   Plane[c_, n_], {x_, y_}] :=
   Module[{npts, v1, v2, st, ct, xh, yh, z1, z2, tst},
     {v1, v2} = N[OrthogonalVectors[n]] ;
     v1 = v1/VectorLength[v1] ;
     v2 = v2/VectorLength[v2] ;
     z = Map[Last, {v1, v2}] ;
     z = z/VectorLength[z] ;
     {xh, yh} = {-y, x}/VectorLength[{x, y}] ;
     {st, ct} = {{-xh, -yh}, {yh, -xh}}.z ;
     If[({{ct, st}, {-st, ct}}.{x, y}).z < 0,
             ct = -ct ; st = -st] ;
     npts = Map[{{ct, st}, {-st, ct}}.#&, pts] ;
     Map[(c + #.{v1, v2})&, npts]
     ]

These points are embedded in
three-dimensional space. One will
form a horizontal line in the plane and
the other will form a vertical line.

In[115]:= **EmbedIn3D[**
        {{1,0}, {0,1}}, Plane[{0,0,0}, {1,1,1}], {0,1}]
Out[115]= {{-0.707107, 0.707107, 1.43657 10^{-17}},
    {-0.408248, -0.408248, 0.816497}}

In[116]:= `Show[Graphics3D[Map[Line[{{0,0,0},#}]&, %]],`
`ViewPoint -> {1,1,1}]`

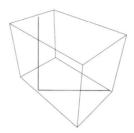

The points of the line primitives are embedded in the plane in three dimensions. The object prims was generated with ParametricPlot several inputs previously.

In[117]:= `prims /.`
`Line[pts_] :> Line[EmbedIn3D[pts, plane, {0,1}]];`

The result is made into a three-dimensional object and displayed. Now the loop points up.

In[118]:= `Show[Graphics3D[%]]`

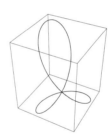

17.5 Clipping

On occasion it is useful to take a slice through geometric primitives, allowing some interior detail to be exposed. This process is called clipping and the results that have been obtained in previous examples allow a clipping function to be written.

A plane and a collection of random points.

In[119]:= `(plane = Plane[{0,0,0}, {1,-1,1}];`
`pts =`
`Table[Point[{Random[ ], Random[ ], Random[ ]} -0.5],`
`{10}] ;)`

It is easy to clip point primitives with a plane.

In[120]:= **Select[pts, SideOfPlaneQ[First[#], plane]&]**

Out[120]= {Point[{0.0255067, -0.350562, -0.245008}],

  Point[{0.336433, -0.490898, 0.369362}],

  Point[{0.42797, 0.0404019, -0.0379924}],

  Point[{0.23709, -0.156198, -0.182277}],

  Point[{0.489225, 0.466228, 0.357031}]}

Clipping Line primitives is more challenging since some of the points may be on one side of the plane and others on the other side. In this case the point of intersection must be found.

The function Clip3D tests all the points. If there are any intersections the function (as yet undefined) ComplexClip3D is called.

In[121]:= **Clip3D[(head:Line|Polygon)[pts_], Plane[c_, n_]] :=**
        Module[{tst},
           tst = Map[SideOfPlaneQ[#,Plane[c,n]]&,pts] ;
           If[Apply[SameQ, tst],
              If[First[tst],
                 head[pts],
                 {}],
              ComplexClip3D[head, pts, tst, Plane[c, n]]]
           ]

A line primitive.

In[122]:= **lines =**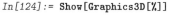
        Line[Table[{x=Sin[t],y=Cos[t],x y},
              {t,0,2Pi,Pi/30}]];

In[123]:= **Clip3D[lines, Plane[{0,0,-3}, {0,0,1}]];**

All the points of the line are on the positive side of the plane and hence none of them are clipped.

In[124]:= **Show[Graphics3D[%]]**

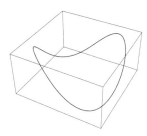

If the plane intersects with any of the line segments the function ComplexClip3D, referred to in Clip3D, will be used.

Each pair of points is tested by
TestPairs. The result of these is fed
into Fold, which is good for moving
down a list building up a result.

```
In[125]:= ComplexClip3D[head_, pts_, test_, plane_] :=
              Module[{work, len},
                 work = Transpose[{pts, test}] ;
                 work = Transpose[{work, RotateLeft[work]}] ;
                 work = Map[TestPairs[#, plane]&, work] ;
                 If[head === Line && Last[test],
                   work =
                     ReplacePart[work,
                               {Last[pts]},Length[pts]]];
                 work =
                   Fold[If[#2 === {},
                          Append[#1, {}],
                          Append[Drop[#1,-1],Join[Last[#1],#2]]]&,
                        {{}}, work] ;
                 work = DeleteCases[work, {}] ;
                 If[head === Line,
                      Map[Line, work],Polygon[Flatten[work, 1]]]
                 ]
```

TestPairs takes a pair of points and a
test. If the segment between the points
is cut then the intersection is
calculated.

```
In[126]:= TestPairs[{{p1_, t1_}, {p2_, t2_}}, plane_] :=
              Which[
                 t1  && t2 , {p1},
                 !t1 && !t2 , {},
                 t1  && !t2 ,
                     {p1,IntersectionPoint[Line[{p2,p1}],plane]},
                 !t1 && t2 ,
                     {IntersectionPoint[Line[{p1, p2}], plane]}
              ]
```

The line is clipped by this plane.

```
In[127]:= Show[Graphics3D[Clip3D[lines, Plane[{0,0,0},
              {0,1,1}]]]]
```

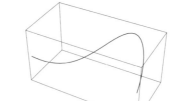

Clip3D is extended to work with
Point primitives.

```
In[128]:= Clip3D[Point[pt_], Plane[c_, n_]] :=
                 If[SideOfPlaneQ[pt, Plane[c, n]],
                    Point[pt], {}]
```

Clip3D is extended to work with lists
of primitives.

```
In[129]:= Clip3D[prims_List, Plane[c_, n_]] :=
              Map[Clip3D[#, Plane[c, n]]&, prims]
```

Clip3D will now descend down through the primitives in a Graphics3D object.

In[130]:= **Clip3D[Graphics3D[prims_, opts___],Plane[c_, n_]]:=**
                Graphics3D[Clip3D[prims, Plane[c, n]], opts]

When the object is unknown it just passes through.

In[131]:= **Clip3D[unknown_, Plane[c_, n_]] := unknown**

A polygon primitive for demonstration.

In[132]:= **poly =**
                Polygon[Table[{Sin[t],Cos[t],0},
                {t,0,2Pi-Pi/3,Pi/3}]];

These primitives have been introduced for demonstration.

In[133]:= **Show[Graphics3D[{pts, lines, poly}]]**

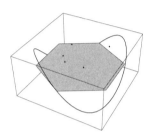

The primitives are now clipped by plane.

In[134]:= **Show[Clip3D[%, plane]]**

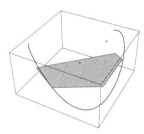

Being able to cut up objects with planes allows some interesting surfaces to be constructed. One type of surface is to make horizontal cuts to form equipotential surfaces.

Another three-dimensional object to
demonstrate clipping.

```
In[135]:= surf =
            Graphics3D[Plot3D[Sin[x y],{x,-Pi,Pi},{y,-Pi,Pi},
                PlotPoints -> 20]];
```

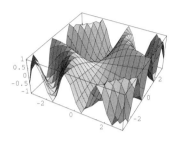

The object is clipped by two horizontal
planes. Fold is a convenient way to
make successive applications of
Clip3D.

```
In[136]:= Fold[Clip3D[#1, #2]&, surf,
                {Plane[{0,0,0.5}, {0,0,-1}],
                 Plane[{0,0,-0.5},{0,0,1}]}]

Out[136]= -Graphics3D-
```

The clipped surface can now be viewed.

```
In[137]:= Show[%]
```

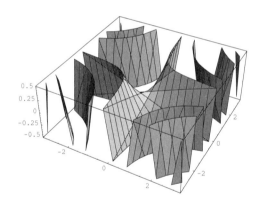

This is an interesting way to view the surface that seems to draw attention to the saddle point in the
center. The cutting of the surface by horizontal planes is a good way to superimpose contours on a surface.
This topic was discussed in Chapter 13 page 276, which showed how to plot three-dimensional forms of
contour lines. Here in a different method, the surface is formed and then sliced up with horizontal planes.

The primitives are extracted.

```
In[138]:= prims = First[surf];
```

The surface is sliced up to form a list of
the segments which, put together, form
the surface.

```
In[139]:= slist =
            Map[Function[h,
                Fold[Clip3D[#1, #2]&, prims,
                {Plane[{0,0,h}, {0,0,1}],
                 Plane[{0,0,h+0.4},{0,0,-1}]}]],
                Range[-1.2, 0.8, .4]];
```

In[140]:= **Show[Graphics3D[slist]]**

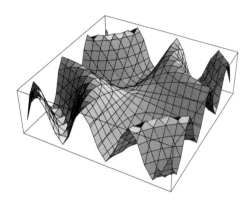

This drops every other segment.

In[141]:= **Show[**
　　　　　　Graphics3D[Part[slist,
　　　　　　　　　　　　　Range[1, Length[slist],2]]]]

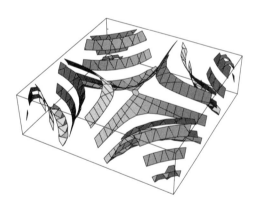

Now a list of color specifications and segments is formed.

In[142]:= **Transpose[**
　　　　　{Table[Hue[i], {i,0,1,1/(Length[slist-1]-1)}],
　　　　　slist}];

The surface is plotted with the different segments colored differently.

`In[143]:= Show[Graphics3D[Flatten[%], Lighting -> False]]`

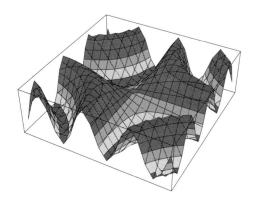

17.6 Polygon Triangulation

When the *Mathematica* primitive `Polygon` is rendered with the command `Display` it must be broken into a collection of triangles, a process known as triangulation. Chapter 9 page 153, which discussed three-dimensional primitives, described how this was done. It pointed out that there were different triangulation schemes that could be used. Some alternative methods and how they can be applied are the topic of this section.

`Polygon` primitives can be triangulated by forming the two-dimensional coordinates that result from projecting the vertices into a plane. A triangulation can then be calculated from the two-dimensional coordinates. The resulting triangulation states which vertices should be joined together and in what order. This information can then be applied to the three-dimensional coordinates.

▸ *Convex Triangulation*

Triangulating to form the convex hull of the vertices is one simple triangulation scheme. This is accomplished with the function `ConvexPolygon`, based on a function `ConvexHull` that calculates the convex hull of a set of points. In Chapter 16 page 401 a package that used a *MathLink* binary was introduced. This method was very good for working with large sets of points. In this case it is unnecessary since the number of vertices is usually small and a *Mathematica* package can be used.

A top-level package to calculate the convex hull of a set of points.

`In[144]:= Needs["ExtendGraphics`SimpleHull`"]`

The points are projected into the plane of best fit. The convex hull of the projected points is then determined. This is used to form vertices of the resulting polygon.

```
In[145]:= ConvexPolygon[Polygon[pts_]] :=
            Module[{plane, pts2d},
              plane = ToPlane[pts] ;
              pts2d = ParallelProjectTo2D[pts, plane] ;
              Polygon[Part[pts, ConvexHull[pts2d]]]
            ]
```

A polygon with vertices not ordered around the convex hull.

```
In[146]:= poly =
             Polygon[{{-1, -1,0}, {1,-1,0},{-1,1,0},{1,1,0}}];
```

The polygon is drawn with the default triangulation.

```
In[147]:= Show[Graphics3D[poly]]
```

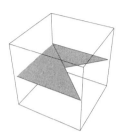

Now the polygon is triangulated to its convex hull.

```
In[148]:= ConvexPolygon[poly]

Out[148]= Polygon[{{-1, -1, 0}, {1, -1, 0}, {1, 1, 0},
    {-1, 1, 0}}]

In[149]:= Show[Graphics3D[%]]
```

This polygon is non-planar and non-convex.

```
In[150]:= poly1 =
             Polygon[
               {{-1, -1, Random[ ]}, {1,-1,Random[ ]},
                {-1,1,Random[ ]}, {1,1,Random[ ]}}]

Out[150]= Polygon[{{-1, -1, 0.874803}, {1, -1, 0.135713},
    {-1, 1, 0.553784}, {1, 1, 0.364827}}]
```

It will be drawn with a folded-over appearance.

In[151]:= **Show[Graphics3D[poly1]]**

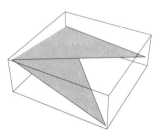

Now the polygon is triangulated to its convex hull.

In[152]:= **ConvexPolygon[poly1]**

Out[152]= Polygon[{{1, -1, 0.135713}, {1, 1, 0.364827},
   {-1, 1, 0.553784}, {-1, -1, 0.874803}}]

The convex polygon is displayed correctly.

In[153]:= **Show[Graphics3D[%]]**

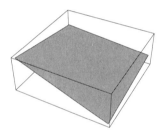

▶ *Non-Convex Triangulation*

In certain cases a non-convex triangulation that preserves the outline is appropriate. As was explained in Chapter 9 page 153 the basic triangulation method of Polygon primitives does not do this. This section shows how a function that preserves a non-convex outline can be used in three-dimensional graphics.

A sequence of points in two-dimensional space.

In[154]:= **pts2d =**
   {{0,0},{1,-2},{1.5,-2},{4,4},{2.5,4},
   {1,0},{.5,1},{-.5,1},{-1,0},{-2.5,4},
   {-4,4},{-1.5,-2},{-1,-2}};

The points can be plotted in a two-dimensional polygon. The result is a "W".

```
In[155]:= Show[
            Graphics[Polygon[pts2d]],
            AspectRatio -> Automatic]
```

The points can be embedded in a plane in three-dimensional space.

```
In[156]:= pts =
            EmbedIn3D[pts2d, Plane[{0,0,0}, {1,-2,.2}], {0,1}];
```

A Line primitive will display the same outline.

```
In[157]:= Show[
            Graphics3D[Line[pts /. {a_, b__} -> {a,b,a}]]]
```

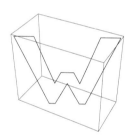

The Polygon version looks strange.

```
In[158]:= Show[
            Graphics3D[Polygon[pts]]]
```

Rotating the points of the polygon will not improve the picture.

In[159]:= **Show[**
    Graphics3D[Polygon[RotateLeft[pts, 5]]]]

The convex triangulation will not display the letter.

In[160]:= **Show[**
    Graphics3D[ConvexPolygon[Polygon[pts]]]]

    In this case the outline is non-convex and neither the basic triangulation scheme nor triangulating to the convex hull is appropriate. The solution is to use the function NonConvexTriangulate defined in the package ExtendGraphics`NonConvexTriangulate`. This travels around the perimeter of the polygon forming triangles that will maintain the original shape.

In[161]:= **Needs["ExtendGraphics`NonConvexTriangulate`"]**

The sets of vertices that form the shape are returned.

In[162]:= **NonConvexTriangulate[pts2d]**

Out[162]= {{1, 2, 3}, {3, 4, 5}, {3, 5, 6}, {3, 6, 7},
  {3, 7, 8}, {9, 10, 11}, {9, 11, 12}, {9, 12, 13}, {9, 13, 1},
  {1, 3, 8}, {1, 8, 9}}

It is easy to use these sets of vertices to draw the triangles from the original points.

```
In[163]:= Show[
              Graphics[
                Map[Line[Part[pts2d, #] /.
                    {a_,b__} -> {a,b,a}]&, %]]]
```

NonConvexPolygon does all these steps. It projects points into the plane of best fit and forms a non-convex triangulation. This is used to form polygons.

```
In[164]:= NonConvexPolygon[Polygon[pts_]] :=
              Module[{plane, pts2d},
                plane = ToPlane[pts] ;
                pts2d = ParallelProjectTo2D[pts, plane] ;
                Map[Polygon[Part[pts, #]]&,
                    NonConvexTriangulate[pts2d]]
              ]
```

This shows the outline properly but edges in the interior are still visible.

```
In[165]:= Show[
              Graphics3D[NonConvexPolygon[Polygon[pts]]]]
```

Now the interior lines are removed.

```
In[166]:= NonConvexPolygon[Polygon[pts_]] :=
            Module[{plane, pts2d, tri, t},
              plane = ToPlane[pts] ;
              pts2d = ParallelProjectTo2D[pts, plane] ;
              tri = NonConvexTriangulate[pts2d] ;
              sides =
                Map[Transpose[{#, RotateLeft[#]}]&, tri];
              sides = Map[(t = Abs[Apply[Subtract, #]];
                t === 1 || t === Length[pts]-1)&,sides,{2}];
              tri = Transpose[{tri, sides}] ;
              Map[Polygon[Part[pts, First[#]],
                  Automatic, Last[#]]&, tri]
            ]
```

Now the three-dimensional letter is drawn properly.

```
In[167]:= Show[
            Graphics3D[NonConvexPolygon[Polygon[pts]]]]
```

The specification of whether or not the edges of a `Polygon` primitive should be drawn allows the interior lines of the composite polygon to be hidden. This feature was not available in Version 2.2 (or earlier) *Mathematica*.

17.7 Extruding Solids

The material in this chapter on three-dimensional geometry has concentrated on primitives such as lines and planes and so far has not worked with solid objects. Of course *Mathematica* is a powerful tool with which to build and study three-dimensional solids. The standard packages `Graphics`Shapes`` and `Graphics`SurfaceOfRevolution`` are examples of packages that build solid objects. Another way to build a solid object is to extrude a two-dimensional polygon. The idea originates from pushing some viscous material through a stencil. A solid object results, the cross-section of which is determined by the stencil.

The Extrude function takes a three-dimensional polygon and generates further polygons that represent the solid object formed by extrusion. The parameter d controls the length of extrusion.

```
In[168]:= Extrude[Polygon[pts_] /;
                  MatrixQ[pts] && Length[First[pts]] === 3,
              d_] :=
          Module[{poly, side, add},
            poly = NonConvexPolygon[Polygon[pts]] ;
            poly = Map[SplitPolygon[#, {0,0,d}]&, poly] ;
            side = Transpose[{pts, RotateLeft[pts]}] ;
            add = {{0,0,d}, {0,0,d}} ;
            side = Map[Polygon[Join[# + add,
                            Reverse[#] - add]]&, side] ;
            {side, poly}
          ]
```

An auxiliary function necessary to deal with faces of the polygon[9].

```
In[169]:= SplitPolygon[Polygon[pts_, norm_, side_], d_] :=
            Module[{ext},
              ext = Table[d, {Length[pts]}] ;
              {Polygon[pts + ext, norm, side],
               Polygon[pts - ext, norm, side]}
            ]
```

A simple polygon.

```
In[170]:= poly =
            Polygon[Table[{Sin[t],Cos[t]},
                    {t,0,2Pi-Pi/3,Pi/3}]];
```

The polygon can be plotted.

```
In[171]:= Show[
            Graphics[{GrayLevel[0.5],poly}],
            AspectRatio -> Automatic]
```

A three-dimensional form of poly is formed.

```
In[172]:= poly3d =
            poly /.
              Polygon[pts_] :>
                Polygon[Map[Append[#,0]&, pts]];
```

---

[9]This function will not work in Version 2.2 *Mathematica*. For this version a one-argument version of Polygon should be used.

The three-dimensional polygon can be extruded and the result plotted.

```
In[173]:= Show[
              Graphics3D[Extrude[poly3d, .1]]]
```

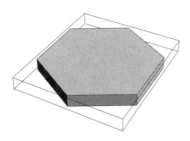

A more interesting example can be made from a cogwheel.

```
In[174]:= Cog[r_, num_] :=
            Module[{ang, angi, ang1, ang2,
                   rf = 1.15, id = 0.4, od = 0.4},
               ang = N[2Pi/num] ;
               angi = ang*id ;
               ang1 = ang*(1+id-od)/2. ;
               ang2 = ang*(1+id+od)/2. ;
               pts =
                 Table[{r { Cos[t], Sin[t]},
                         r {Cos[t+angi],Sin[t+angi]},
                         r rf { Cos[t+ang1], Sin[t+ang1]},
                         r rf {Cos[t+ang2],Sin[t+ang2]}
                        }, {t,0,2Pi-ang,ang}] ;
               Polygon[Flatten[pts, 1]]
               ]
```

A sample cog.

```
In[175]:= cog = Cog[3, 15];
```

The cog can be plotted in two dimensions.

```
In[176]:= Show[
              Graphics[{GrayLevel[0.5], cog}],
              AspectRatio -> Automatic]
```

It is easy to embed the points of the Cog in the *xy* plane of three-dimensional space.

```
In[177]:= cog3d =
              cog /.
                Polygon[pts_] :>
                    Polygon[Map[Append[#,0]&, pts]];
```

To plot the three-dimensional form it must be triangulated.

```
In[178]:= Show[
              Graphics3D[NonConvexPolygon[cog3d]]]
```

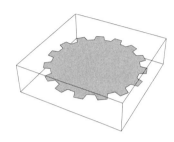

The result is a solid object, the cross-section determined by the original cog.

```
In[179]:= Show[
              Graphics3D[Extrude[cog3d, 0.2]]]
```

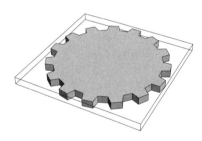

This Extrude function allows many interesting shapes and objects to be constructed.

17.8 Summary

This chapter has presented a variety of results and functions relevant to three-dimensional geometry. First, basic forms such as lines and planes were presented. Then ways in which these objects could be transformed and moved around three-dimensional space were studied. This culminated with the use of four-dimensional homogeneous transformation matrices that could compose affine and other transformations via a uniform matrix multiplication representation.

The next part built up a variety of results from the basic objects to find intersections and to test points. These results were then used for projection and embedding that allowed transformation between two- and three-dimensional spaces. This transformation was very useful for forming convex and non-convex triangulations of polygons. Finally a method of constructing solid objects by extrusion was introduced.

All of the material in this chapter can be applied in many areas. Some example applications, such as visualizing three-dimensional rotations, slicing up a surface, or extruding solids, were shown. This material forms basic building blocks from which complex pictures can be constructed with *Mathematica*.

Chapter 18
Visualizing Numeric Data

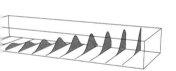

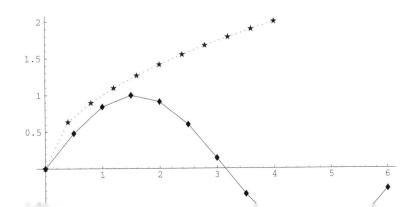

This chapter is concerned with the visualization of numeric data. It can be seen as an extension of Chapter 14, since it will strive to construct effective pictures that use the data to make specific points. However, Chapter 14 concentrated on two-dimensional pictures representing two-dimensional data, a task that is much simpler and better understood. This chapter will look at techniques that can work for data of different dimensions. Since this task is more complicated more attention will be paid to explaining the details of how these techniques work. This process was started in Chapters 16 and 17, which laid some of the foundations.

In order to review the different techniques that can be used to visualize numeric data it is necessary to develop a classification system. One basic measure of a set of data is its dimensionality, the number of items that comprise each datum. Another basic measure concerns how many entries in a datum represent independent variables and how many represent dependent variables. If each datum contains only one dependent item it can be said to be scalar. With more than one dependent item the data can be said to be vector data. The number of entries representing independent variables can be used to determine the graphical structure that is appropriate for visualization. For example three-dimensional data with one independent dimension are best represented by a line while a surface is appropriate when there are two independent variables.

Vector data can be visualized with certain specialized methods that involve actually drawing vector arrows and lines. These particular techniques will be considered in the following chapter.

18.1 One-Dimensional Data

One-dimensional data can be represented in the form $\{p_1, p_2, p_3, \dots\}$ where each p_i is a single number. This type of data could be generated by a number of measurements of some variable, which must be a dependent variable. While the data do not explicitly refer to any independent variable there is an implicit reference. A one-dimensional data set can be recast as a two-dimensional set by using the index into the set as the value of independent variable, $\{\{1, p_1\}, \{2, p_2\}, \{3, p_3\}, \dots\}$. Once it has been coerced in this way techniques for visualizing two-dimensional data sets can be used. In *Mathematica* this casting to two dimensions is often unnecessary, as it is done automatically by functions such as `ListPlot`.

Here `Table` has a scalar first argument and one iterator. This returns a one-dimensional data set.

In[1]:= `data = Table[i^2 - 4 i, {i, 10}]`

Out[1]= `{-3, -4, -3, 0, 5, 12, 21, 32, 45, 60}`

It is straightforward to visualize a one-dimensional data set with `ListPlot`.

In[2]:= `ListPlot[data]`

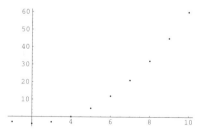

Transpose and Range will generate an indexed two-dimensional set. This could be used for other visualization techniques.

```
In[3]:= Transpose[{Range[Length[data]], data}]

Out[3]= {{1, -3}, {2, -4}, {3, -3}, {4, 0}, {5, 5}, {6, 12},
   {7, 21}, {8, 32}, {9, 45}, {10, 60}}
```

18.2 Two-Dimensional Data

Two-dimensional data can be represented in the form $\{\{x_1,y_1\},\{x_2,y_2\},\{x_3,y_3\},\dots\}$. A data set of this form often represents one independent and one dependent variable. It can be visualized by plotting a line showing how y depends upon x though of course the data may be plotted in a variety of other ways and present other information. A plot of this type can be thought of as the locus of points $\{x,f(x)\}$ showing a plot of $y = f(x)$. The data can be thought of as representing samples of $\{x,f(x)\}$. ListPlot is the basic tool provided by *Mathematica* to visualize two-dimensional data.

Here Table has one iterator and a first argument that returns a pair of numbers, thereby generating a two-dimensional data set.

```
In[4]:= data = Table[{i, Cos[i]}, {i, 0., 6}]

Out[4]= {{0., 1.}, {1., 0.540302}, {2., -0.416147},
   {3., -0.989992}, {4., -0.653644}, {5., 0.283662},
   {6., 0.96017}}
```

The data are plotted by joining the points together.

```
In[5]:= ListPlot[data, PlotJoined -> True]
```

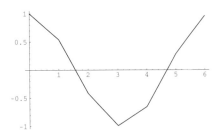

▶ *Ordering*

The data set just plotted had points ordered according to the x value, which increased monotonically. It is quite possible that the data points are not all ordered in this way. If the data is to be ordered it must be sorted.

These points are not ordered with increasing x coordinate.

```
In[6]:= data = Table[{xvar = 6 Random[ ], Cos[xvar]}, {i, 10}]

Out[6]= {{0.336425, 0.943941}, {3.7818, -0.801973},
   {2.15937, -0.555172}, {5.22826, 0.493295},
   {5.15187, 0.425471}, {3.50747, -0.93381},
   {4.45743, -0.252202}, {2.34877, -0.701834},
   {2.14334, -0.541773}, {2.28309, -0.653568}}
```

It is clear that the points are not ordered.

In[7]:= `ListPlot[data, PlotJoined -> True]`

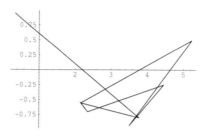

The function `Sort` will order the points. Since no ordering function is given they are sorted by their *x* value.

In[8]:= `data1 = Sort[data]`

Out[8]= {{0.336425, 0.943941}, {2.14334, -0.541773},

{2.15937, -0.555172}, {2.28309, -0.653568},

{2.34877, -0.701834}, {3.50747, -0.93381},

{3.7818, -0.801973}, {4.45743, -0.252202},

{5.15187, 0.425471}, {5.22826, 0.493295}}

Now the points are ordered.

In[9]:= `ListPlot[data1, PlotJoined -> True]`

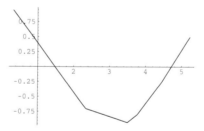

This sorting of points should not be carried out if the original order is important. Only if the order is unimportant can they be sorted. Then a decision of whether or not to sort can be taken according to other criteria. For example, sorting will allow the points to be joined by a line and this may improve the design of the picture. Chapter 14 page 304 discussed reasons why this might be desirable.

▸ *Resampling*

Just as the data may not be ordered they may not be regularly spaced in the independent variable. If data samples are required on a regular grid these must be generated by resampling. This issue is extremely important for three-dimensional visualization but is still relevant in two-dimensional visualization where it is easier to discuss. Resampling of data requires that a representative mathematical function be derived. This can be done by following either of two different approaches.

The first approach is appropriate when the data are accurate, when each datum does not contain any significant uncertainty. In this case an interpolation technique is the method that should be used. The simplest form of interpolation is generated by joining the points, as is done in many pictures. Interpolation assumes that the data points are all good and attempts to fill in the regions between them.

The second approach is appropriate when the data are known to be inaccurate. In this case a fitting technique can be used. Visually this will produce a line of best-fit to the data. To carry this out the form of the function to be fitted must be known. With this knowledge one of the fitting methods that *Mathematica* provides can be applied. After this, one of the function plotting commands can be used. An example of making a non-linear fit to some data was presented in Chapter 14 page 306.

In general it may not be known if the data contain errors until after some visual inspection. In this case if resampling is required by the visualization technique this must be done with interpolation. After a measure of the shape of the data has been obtained, it may be apparent that it is inaccurate and then a fitting technique can be applied. However, interpolation methods should be applied first and the rest of this chapter will concentrate on how they can be used to resample data. In *Mathematica* this is done by the command `Interpolation`.

The data from the previous example can be used to generate an InterpolatingFunction.

```
In[10]:= fun = Interpolation[data]
Out[10]= InterpolatingFunction[{0.336425, 5.22826}, <>]
```

This interpolating function takes one argument that is used to return an estimate of the original data set.

```
In[11]:= fun[2.5]
Out[11]= -0.799493
```

Here Table returns a list of regularly spaced resampled points that could be plotted with ListPlot.

```
In[12]:= Table[{i, fun[i]}, {i, 5}]
Out[12]= {{1, 0.539589}, {2, -0.41624}, {3, -0.982597},
          {4, -0.652476}, {5, 0.283651}}
```

Plot can use the InterpolatingFunction to draw a curve representing the data.

```
In[13]:= Plot[fun[t], {t,1,5}]
```

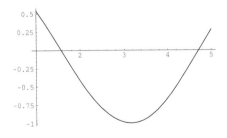

▶ *Multiple Data Sets*

There are several techniques for displaying a plot of a collection of two-dimensional data sets. The data will be organized as $\{d_1, d_2, d_3, \ldots\}$ where each d_i is a two-dimensional data set. It is simple to plot this type of data in a `GraphicsArray`.

A pair of two-dimensional data sets.

```
In[14]:= data = {Table[{i,Sin[i]}, {i,0,2Pi,0.5}],
                  Table[{i,Sqrt[i]},{i,0,4,0.4}]};
```

It is simple to make two separate pictures.

```
In[15]:= plots =
             Map[
                 ListPlot[#, DisplayFunction -> Identity]&,
                 data]
Out[15]= {-Graphics-, -Graphics-}
```

`GraphicsArray` will display the two pictures in an array.

```
In[16]:= Show[GraphicsArray[plots]]
```

`MultipleListPlot` is an alternative way to display the data. It was described in Chapter 4 page 64.

```
In[17]:= Needs["Graphics`MultipleListPlot`"]
```

`Apply` and `MultipleListPlot` will plot the data.

```
In[18]:= Apply[MultipleListPlot, data]
```

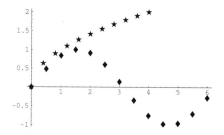

If an option of MultipleListPlot is to be set a pure function can be used with Apply. This was demonstrated in Chapter 4 page 69.

In[19]:= **Apply[MultipleListPlot[##, PlotJoined -> True]&, data]**

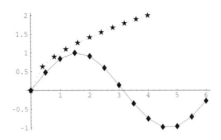

Another way to display multiple sets of two-dimensional data is to arrange them in a three-dimensional plot. This is conveniently done with the function StackGraphics, defined in the package Graphics-`Graphics3D`.

The package is loaded in the usual way.

In[20]:= **Needs["Graphics`Graphics3D`"]**

A set of data to show a stacked plot.

In[21]:= **data =**
                Table[{i, t Exp[-(i-t)^2/4]},
                      {t,0,10},
                      {i,0,10,.2}];

This list of graphics objects is constructed with Map and ListPlot.

In[22]:= **plots =**
                Map[ListPlot[#,
                        DisplayFunction -> Identity,
                        PlotJoined -> True]&, data]

Out[22]= {-Graphics-, -Graphics-, -Graphics-, -Graphics-,
   -Graphics-, -Graphics-, -Graphics-, -Graphics-, -Graphics-,
   -Graphics-, -Graphics-}

The pictures are put together in three dimensions.

In[23]:= **Show[StackGraphics[Reverse[plots]]]**

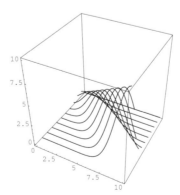

The picture is improved by altering the viewing parameters.

```
In[24]:= Show[%,
               BoxRatios -> {1,3,.4},
               ViewPoint -> {-2,-1,.5},
               Lighting -> False]
```

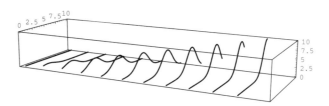

A different way to make this picture is to show solid plots instead of curves. This can be done by using ListFilledPlot instead of ListPlot. ListFilledPlot is defined in a package that must first be loaded.

```
In[25]:= Needs["Graphics`FilledPlot`"]
```

ListFilledPlot is applied to one of the data sets.

```
In[26]:= ListFilledPlot[Last[data]]
```

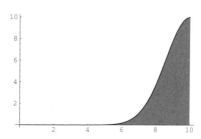

ListFilledPlot and Map build a list of graphics objects.

```
In[27]:= plots =
           Map[ListFilledPlot[#,
               DisplayFunction -> Identity]&, data];
```

The three-dimensional picture is constructed with StackGraphics[10].

In[28]:= **Show[StackGraphics[Reverse[plots]]]**

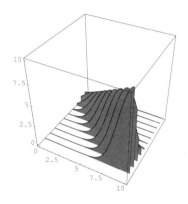

As before, altering the viewing parameters improves the picture.

In[29]:= **Show[%,**
        BoxRatios -> {1,3,.4},
        ViewPoint -> {-2,-1,.5},
        Lighting -> False]

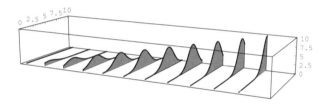

The lines can be thinned out and the picture improved still more.

In[30]:= **Show[Insert[%, Thickness[0.001], {1,1}]]**

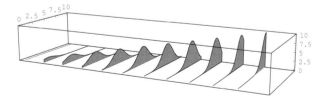

18.3 Three-Dimensional Data

Three-dimensional data consist of a collection of points, each of which contains three numbers. Each point may represent a measurement of one or two independent variables. For one independent variable line plotting techniques similar to those for two-dimensional data can be used. For two independent variables different techniques are appropriate. One visualization method is to generate a surface plot; alternatively a contour plot or a density plot can be used. With two independent variables the problems of ordering and resampling become considerably more complex.

Three-dimensional data can in general be taken as a collection of points of the form of triples $\{x_i, y_i, z_i\}$. One simple way to plot such data is to use a three-dimensional analogue of `ListPlot`. Such a function is `ScatterPlot3D`, defined in the package `Graphics`Graphics3D``. By default this shows a plot made up of discrete points. This leaves it up to the observer to decide how to view the points.

▶ *One Independent Variable*

A data set with one independent variable.

```
In[31]:= data = Table[{Sin[i], Cos[i], i}, {i, 0., 6., .2}];
```

`Short` will print a concise form of the expression.

```
In[32]:= Short[data, 5]
Out[32]//Short=
 {{0., 1., 0.}, {0.198669, 0.980067, 0.2},
   {0.389418, 0.921061, 0.4}, {0.564642, 0.825336, 0.6},
   {0.717356, 0.696707, 0.8}, {0.841471, 0.540302, 1.}, <<22>>,
   {-0.631267, 0.775566, 5.6}, {-0.464602, 0.88552, 5.8},
   {-0.279415, 0.96017, 6.}}
```

The package that defines `ScatterPlot3D` is loaded.

```
In[33]:= Needs["Graphics`Graphics3D`"]
```

It is natural to collect these points and form a line.

```
In[34]:= ScatterPlot3D[data]
```

The PlotJoined option will actually join the dots in the order they appear in the list.

`In[35]:= ScatterPlot3D[data, PlotJoined -> True]`

When the points are joined the plot can be thought of as representing the locus of points $\{f_1(t), f_2(t), t\}$ where t is the independent variable. With one independent variable the resulting plot uses a one-dimensional structure, a line.

▶ *Sorting and Resampling*

Three-dimensional data with one independent variable can be sorted and resampled with techniques similar to those applied in two dimensions. The basic method is to order along the independent variable.

Some data with one independent variable.

```
In[36]:= data =
            Table[
                zvar = 6 Random[ ];
                {Sin[zvar], Cos[zvar], zvar},
                {i, 50}];
```

A very poor view of the data.

`In[37]:= ScatterPlot3D[data, PlotJoined -> True]`

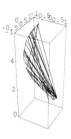

Sorting the data on its third, independent, variable will help.

`In[38]:= data = Sort[data, #1[[3]] < #2[[3]]&];`

A much better view of the data.

In[39]:= `ScatterPlot3D[data, PlotJoined -> True]`

The data can be resampled by
constructing two separate
interpolating functions.

```
In[40]:= {fun1, fun2} =
            Map[Interpolation,
              {
                Map[Part[#, {3,1}]&, data],
                Map[Part[#, {3,2}]&, data]
              }]
Out[40]= {InterpolatingFunction[{0.0546132, 5.64835}, <>],
          InterpolatingFunction[{0.0546132, 5.64835}, <>]}
```

The resampled data can then be used
with ScatterPlot3D.

```
In[41]:= ScatterPlot3D[
            Table[{fun1[z], fun2[z], z}, {z,0.1, 5.6,.25}],
            PlotJoined -> True]
```

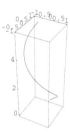

▶ *Two Independent Variables*

When the three-dimensional data have two independent variables things are considerably more complex. One useful way to display such data is to plot a surface over them. The height of the surface shows the dependent variable changing with the independent variables. A plot of this type is the locus of points $\{x, y, f(x,y)\}$. Here x and y are the independent variables. There are two of them and the result is a two-dimensional structure, a surface.

When it actually comes to drawing the surface there are certain problems that must be faced concerning how the points are to be joined. The simplest way that *Mathematica* provides to plot a surface from three-dimensional data is from data in the form $\{\{z_{11}, z_{12}, \dots \}, \{z_{21}, z_{22}, \dots \}, \dots \}$ where each z_{ij} is a number representing the height of respectively the ith and jth components of the independent variables. Data in this form are said to be rectangularly ordered and can easily be plotted with the built-in function `ListPlot3D`.

An array of heights.

```
In[42]:= data = Table[x y, {x, -1,2}, {y, -1, 2}]
Out[42]= {{1, 0, -1, -2}, {0, 0, 0, 0}, {-1, 0, 1, 2},
     {-2, 0, 2, 4}}
```

This plots the surface but the axes are wrong. They can be fixed by setting the `MeshRange` option.

```
In[43]:= ListPlot3D[data]
```

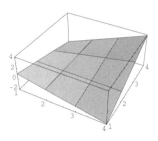

Looking at the surface from above demonstrates how it is constructed from a regular grid of points.

```
In[44]:= Show[%, ViewPoint -> {0,0,200}]
```

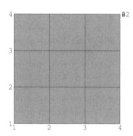

By the definition of data given in this chapter, this array of heights could be considered to be a collection of two-dimensional data sets. In fact it is used by `ListPlot3D` to plot a surface in three-dimensional space, a three-dimensional data plotting technique for two-independent variables. The organization of the data shows how the surface should be connected and the independent variables are implicit.

If the data set is organized in a rectangular array with each datum of the form $\{x, y, z\}$ with regularly spaced x and y values it can still be plotted with `ListPlot3D`. In order to do this the z values must first be extracted.

Now the x and y values are present with the z value.

```
In[45]:= data = Table[{x, y, x y}, {x, -1,2}, {y, -1, 2}];
```

TableForm shows how the data set is organized.

```
In[46]:= TableForm[data, TableDepth -> 2]

Out[46]//TableForm=
{-1, -1, 1}    {-1, 0, 0}    {-1, 1, -1}    {-1, 2, -2}
{0, -1, 0}     {0, 0, 0}     {0, 1, 0}      {0, 2, 0}
{1, -1, -1}    {1, 0, 0}     {1, 1, 1}      {1, 2, 2}
{2, -1, -2}    {2, 0, 0}     {2, 1, 2}      {2, 2, 4}
```

In order to use ListPlot3D the heights are extracted from the data.

```
In[47]:= dataz = Map[Last, data, {2}]

Out[47]= {{1, 0, -1, -2}, {0, 0, 0, 0}, {-1, 0, 1, 2},
   {-2, 0, 2, 4}}
```

This plots the surface. Now the axes are set properly by using the MeshRange option.

```
In[48]:= ListPlot3D[dataz,
            MeshRange -> {{-1,2},{-1,2}}]
```

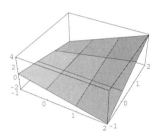

The same data can be plotted as a contour plot.

```
In[49]:= ListContourPlot[dataz,
            MeshRange -> {{-1,2},{-1,2}}]
```

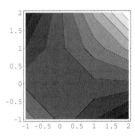

Now a density plot is made.

```
In[50]:= ListDensityPlot[dataz,
            MeshRange -> {{-1,2},{-1,2}}]
```

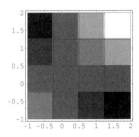

These types of pictures are closely related. A contour plot shows a representation of a surface by drawing lines of equal height on the surface. In this sense it can be thought of as plotting solutions of the implicit equation $f(x, y) = c_i$, where c_i is the value of the contour line. This was described in the definition of contour plots given in Chapter 2 page 15.

ListPlot3D can only plot a simple surface. The x and y values must be laid out on a regular rectangular grid and the surface cannot fold over itself. If the spacings between x and/or y were different the data may still be on a rectangular grid but ListPlot3D could not work. The data may be even more complicated and represent a surface that has more than one height for a given coordinate in the xy plane. This happens when the surface intersects itself. In this case ListPlot3D cannot draw the surface.

▸ *Plotting Complicated Surfaces*

If the data are rectangularly ordered, but not regularly spaced or represent a complicated surface that intersects itself, the function ListSurfacePlot3D can be used to plot the surface. This is the list plotting analogue to ParametricPlot3D. If the latter can generate a surface, ListSurfacePlot3D will be able to take a set of data and generate the same surface.

The package was already loaded previously in this session but Needs can be executed again with no harm.

```
In[51]:= Needs["Graphics`Graphics3D`"]
```

```
In[52]:= ?ListSurfacePlot3D
ListSurfacePlot3D[{{{x11, y11, z11}, ...},{{x12, y12, z12},
    ...}, (options)] plots a matrix of points in three dimensions
    as a surface.
```

Here is a data set suitable to be used by ListSurfacePlot3D. Note the similarity to ParametricPlot3D.

```
In[53]:= data =
            Table[{Sin[z] Sin[t], Sin[z] Cos[t], z},
                  {t,0,2Pi,Pi/10}, {z,-Pi, Pi, Pi/10}] ;
```

Now a surface can be generated from the data set.

```
In[54]:= ListSurfacePlot3D[data]
```

ListSurfacePlot3D accepts data points in the form $\{\{p_{11}, p_{12}, \ldots \}, \{p_{21}, p_{22}, \ldots \}, \ldots \}$. It then plots the surface constructed from patches of the form Polygon[$\{p_{ij}, \ p_{ij+1}, \ p_{i+1j+1}, \ p_{i+1j}\}$]. Connecting points in this way to form patches on the surface requires that the neighbors to a given point are known. Here the data set itself was organized to describe how points should be joined to form the surface.

▶ *Summary of ListPlot3D, ListContourPlot, and ListDensityPlot*

To use ListPlot3D to plot three-dimensional data the data must be arranged into a rectangular grid. The same holds for ListContourPlot or ListDensityPlot. If the data come from some measurement with two independent variables it may be possible to arrange that the values of these variables fit into the regular grid. The data processing tools that are part of *Mathematica* can be used to manipulate the data to be in the correct form for ListPlot3D.

In general the data may not be organized in this convenient way. For data with only one independent variable it was straightforward to organize it by sorting along the independent variable. For two independent variables this cannot be done so easily. Along which variable is the sorting to be done? How can this be done efficiently? These are basic visualization problems that are investigated in the next section.

18.4 Triangulation and Resampling

This section will solve the problem of constructing a surface over a three-dimensional data set that is not organized. To solve this the independent variables x and y will be taken and formed into components that can be used to construct a surface. The obvious type of component to form is a triangle. Thus the problem will be solved by forming triangles in the xy plane. This problem was solved in Chapter 16 page 401 as part of the introduction to computational geometry. It described and solved some of the basic problems such as finding a convex hull and triangulating a collection of points. The latter was solved by forming a Delaunay triangulation.

▶ *Delaunay Triangulation*

The Delaunay triangulation constructs triangles from a set of points so the minimum angle of each triangle is maximized. Each triangle is as close to equilateral as possible. The package ExtendGraphics`Delaunay` loads a package that calculates the Delaunay triangulation.

$In[55]:=$ **Needs["ExtendGraphics`Delaunay`"]**

The package uses a *MathLink* binary to provide the core function. This shows the link to the binary.

$In[56]:=$ **Links[ ]**

$Out[56]=$ {LinkObject[delaunay, 1, 1]}

A random set of points.

$In[57]:=$ **pts = Table[{Random[ ], Random[ ]}, {20}];**

The Delaunay triangulation of the data set is displayed.

$In[58]:=$ **TrianglePlot[pts]**

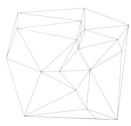

Now that triangles can be formed from the independent variables it is possible to form a surface over the data. This can be demonstrated for a simple data set.

A set of random data over which a surface will be constructed.

```
In[59]:= data =
           Table[{xvar = Random[ ], yvar = Random[ ], xvar yvar},
               {10}];
```

These are the indices into the data set of the Delaunay triangulation.

```
In[60]:= tris = DelaunayVertices[data]
```

```
Out[60]= {{5, 8, 10}, {5, 10, 6}, {5, 6, 4}, {5, 4, 1},
           {6, 10, 2}, {6, 2, 4}, {10, 8, 9}, {10, 9, 2}, {8, 3, 9},
           {2, 3, 4}, {2, 9, 7}, {2, 7, 3}, {9, 3, 7}, {3, 1, 4}}
```

Now polygons are formed from the triangulation data and plotted.

```
In[61]:= Show[
           Graphics3D[
               Map[Polygon[Part[data, #]]&, tris]]]
```

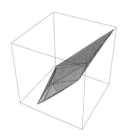

It is easy to carry out these steps, to form the triangulation and use it to generate and plot a surface. Since this is such important functionality a new version of ListSurfacePlot3D has been written that does this automatically. It makes data plotting work in a similar way to the way that ListPlot3D and related functions work. The new functionality is available in the new package ExtendGraphics`SurfaceGraphics3D`. The new version of ListSurfacePlot3D preserves all of the old functionality while adding important new capabilities.

The package for the new version of ListSurfacePlot3D is loaded.

```
In[62]:= Needs["ExtendGraphics`SurfaceGraphics3D`"]
```

A data set to demonstrate ListSurfacePlot3D.

```
In[63]:= data =
           Table[
               Table[{r Sin[t], r Cos[t],
                           Cos[2t] BesselJ[1, 7 r]},
                   {t, 0, 2Pi-2Pi/( 10 r),2Pi/ (10 r)}],
               {r,10}];
```

This data cannot readily be organized since it consists of a number of parts each with a different length.

```
In[64]:= {Length[First[data]], Length[Last[data]]}
```

```
Out[64]= {10, 100}
```

Now it is a three-dimensional data set.

```
In[65]:= data = Flatten[data, 1];
```

ListSurfacePlot3D projects the data into the *xy* plane, triangulates, and plots the resulting surface.

In[66]:= **surf = ListSurfacePlot3D[data]**

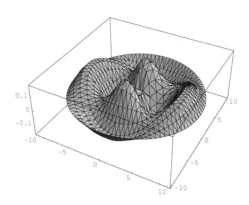

The result of ListSurfacePlot3D is a SurfaceGraphics3D object that represents the surface. This allows special options of SurfaceGraphics3D to be changed.

In[67]:= **Head[surf]**

Out[67]= SurfaceGraphics3D

These are options of SurfaceGraphics objects and they work for SurfaceGraphics3D.

In[68]:= **Show[surf,**
            MeshStyle -> GrayLevel[0.25],
            ColorFunction -> Hue]

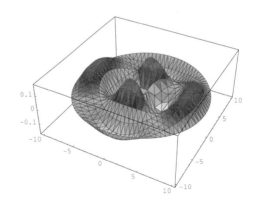

Here is the grid of points used for the surface.

In[69]:= TrianglePlot[Map[Take[#, 2]&, data]]

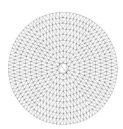

The surface generated in this example demonstrates an interesting feature. It was a surface defined with cylindrical coordinates, r, θ, and z. As r increased the number of points that were sampled also increased. Thus the surface demonstrated its features more effectively.

▶ *Resampling*

The triangulation of data for three-dimensional visualization is equivalent to the sorting of data for two-dimensional visualization. Just as sorting was one important process so was resampling to obtain values defined on a more regular grid. The reason why this might be desirable can be demonstrated.

These data are randomly distributed in the xy plane.

In[70]:= data =
         Table[{xvar = Random[Real, {-2,2}],
                yvar = Random[Real, {-2,2}],
                Exp[-Sqrt[xvar^2+yvar^2]]}, {250}];

The correct surface is plotted but it looks very messy.

In[71]:= ListSurfacePlot3D[data]

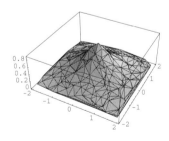

The plot is messy. It would be much better if it was cleaned up somewhat. One way to do this is to average the data into a set of bins and plot those. A function to do this, GridSort, is defined in ExtendGraphics`SurfaceGraphics3D`. Since the GridSort function is quite simple the code is shown here.

```
GridSort[data_ /;
    MatrixQ[data] &&
    Length[First[data]] === 3, n_] :=
  Module[{tmp, x0, x1, y0, y1, xi, yi, d, res},
```

```
{x0, x1} = Map[#[Map[First, data]]&, {Min, Max}] ;
tmp = Map[Part[#,2]&, data] ;
{y0, y1} = Map[#[tmp]&, {Min, Max}] ;
res = Table[{0,0}, {n}, {n}] ;
Do[
    d = Part[data, i] ;
    xi = Round[(n-1)( Part[d,1]-x0)/(x1-x0)]+1;
    yi = Round[(n-1)( Part[d,2]-y0)/(y1-y0)]+1;
    res[[xi,yi,1]] += Part[d,3];
    res[[xi,yi,2]]++,
    {i,Length[data]}] ;
res = res /. {0,0} -> Indeterminate ;
Map[Apply[Divide, #]&, res, {2}]
    ]
```

GridSort takes a three-dimensional array of data and sorts it out into n by n rectangular bins. The contents of each bin is the average of the original data.

```
In[72]:= ?GridSort
```

GridSort[data, n] takes a three-dimensional array of data and
    sort it into n by n rectangular bins containing an average
    of the original data. The matrix of values is returned.
    Bins which remain empty are returned with Indeterminate.

When there are only three bins all the bins are filled.

```
In[73]:= GridSort[data, 3]
```

```
Out[73]= {{0.113065, 0.202311, 0.120315},
    {0.192451, 0.494631, 0.231028},
    {0.125844, 0.209319, 0.111404}}
```

```
In[74]:= sort = GridSort[data, 10];
```

For 100 bins some will be empty. They are represented by Indeterminate.

```
In[75]:= Short[sort, 6]
```

```
Out[75]//Short=
 {{0.0700175, 0.0882683, 0.0987424, 0.147009, 0.151519,
    Indeterminate, 0.13706, 0.0990172, 0.0894346, 0.0753049},
    <<8>>, {0.0665777, 0.0873887, 0.117648, Indeterminate,
    0.146035, 0.149744, 0.140532, 0.114115, 0.0924412,
    Indeterminate}}
```

ListPlot3D will plot the bins that contain numbers.

```
In[76]:= ListPlot3D[sort,
            MeshRange -> {{-2,2},{-2,2}}]
```

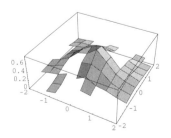

ListDensityPlot is an alternative that may be effective to view the contents of the sorted grid.

In[77]:= **ListDensityPlot[sort,**
           MeshRange -> {{-2,2},{-2,2}}]

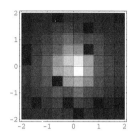

Instead of sorting to form an array of heights suitable for plotting with ListPlot3D an alternative is to form the {x,y,z} points from the sorted data. The values that are Indeterminate can then be filtered out. This way the whole surface is plotted with ListSurfacePlot3D but with more organization than when the raw data was plotted. This type of sorting can be done with the TriangleSort function, also defined in the package ExtendGraphics`ListSurfacePlot3D`.

The TriangleSort function takes a three-dimensional array of data and generates another three-dimensional array determined by averaging the data into rectangular bins.

In[78]:= **?TriangleSort**

TriangleSort[data, n] takes a three-dimensional array of data
    and sort it into n by n rectangular bins containing an
    average of the original data. The data is combined with its
    {x,y} values, empty bins dropped and the result returned as
    a new three-dimensional set.

TriangleSort averages the original data into a new three-dimensional set.

In[79]:= **TriangleSort[data, 3]**

Out[79]= {{-1.32179, -1.33315, 0.113065},
    {-1.32179, -0.0225499, 0.202311},
    {-1.32179, 1.28805, 0.120315},
    {0.00278158, -1.33315, 0.192451},
    {0.00278158, -0.0225499, 0.494631},
    {0.00278158, 1.28805, 0.231028},
    {1.32735, -1.33315, 0.125844},
    {1.32735, -0.0225499, 0.209319}, {1.32735, 1.28805, 0.111404}}

The surface plotted by ListSurfacePlot3D has more organization than the original data.

In[80]:= **ListSurfacePlot3D[TriangleSort[data, 10]]**

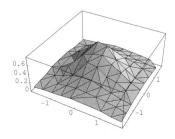

The technique of averaging into bins will be more successful as the number of data points increases compared with the desired number of bins. It is very suitable for visualizing large amounts of data.

Another technique of resampling is to use an interpolation method. For two-dimensional data this was done with the function Interpolation which is only effective for rectangularly ordered data. When the data are irregularly ordered it is still possible to carry out an interpolation with the function TriangularInterpolation defined in the package ExtendGraphics`TriangularInterpolate`. This package makes use of the same triangulation techniques that are used by ListSurfacePlot3D.

In[81]:= **Needs["ExtendGraphics`TriangularInterpolate`"]**

A small three-dimensional data set.

In[82]:= **data =**
    Table[{xvar = Random[ ], yvar = Random[ ], xvar yvar},
        {20}];

The triangular interpolation function is generated.

In[83]:= **fun = TriangularInterpolate[data]**

Out[83]= TriangularInterpolating[<>]

This returns the value. The accurate result is 0.15.

In[84]:= **fun[0.5, 0.3]**

Out[84]= 0.14874

The interpolation function can be used to generate an array of heights of the functions. The error messages arise when x or y fall outside the domain of the original data.

In[85]:= **new = Table[fun[x, y], {x, 0,1,.2}, {y,0,1,.2}] ;**

TriangularInterpolating::dmval:
  Input value {0, 0} lies outside domain of the interpolating
    function.

TriangularInterpolating::dmval:
  Input value {0, 0.2} lies outside domain of the interpolating
    function.

TriangularInterpolating::dmval:
  Input value {0, 0.4} lies outside domain of the interpolating
    function.

General::stop:
  Further output of TriangularInterpolating::dmval
    will be suppressed during this calculation.

The original data can be plotted with ListSurfacePlot3D.

In[86]:= **orig = ListSurfacePlot3D[data]**

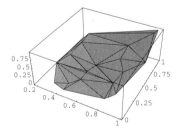

ListPlot3D will plot the interpolated data.

In[87]:= **ListPlot3D[new,**
          MeshRange -> {{0,1}, {0,1}}]

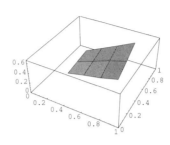

The triangular interpolation provides a useful method to plot a surface. Consequently, a function to do this, InterpolateSurface, is provided in ExtendGraphics`TriangularInterpolation`.

In[88]:= **?InterpolateSurface**

InterpolateSurface[SurfaceGraphics3D[data]] returns a new
     SurfaceGraphics3D object in which the data has been resampled
     with regular points.

InterpolateSurface takes the SurfaceGraphics3D result from ListSurfacePlot3D and generates a new one.

In[89]:= **InterpolateSurface[orig]**

Out[89]= -SurfaceGraphics3D-

The result can be plotted with Show.

In[90]:= **Show[%]**

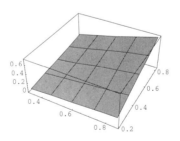

Here is a much larger data set.

In[91]:= **data =**
          Table[
               t = N[2 Pi Random[ ]]; r = Random[ ]/1.5;
               {r Sin[t], r Cos[t], Exp[-r]}, {250}];

ListSurfacePlot3D generates the messy plot.

In[92]:= **ListSurfacePlot3D[data]**

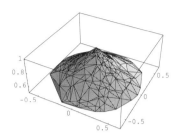

InterpolateSurface takes the messy surface and produces a cleaner surface.

In[93]:= **Show[InterpolateSurface[%]]**

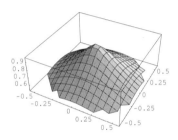

▶ *Contour Plots*

The package ExtendGraphics`SurfaceGraphics3D` provides functions to construct a surface from irregularly spaced three-dimensional data. A contour plot is an alternative way to view three-dimensional data. In *Mathematica* the built-in contour plotting functions only work for rectangularly ordered data.

The package ExtendGraphics`Contour` extends the function ListContourPlot and generates contour plots from irregularly spaced data. Since the contour plot, in the plane, can never represent a surface that intersects itself this package just extends the existing function. There is no need to provide a new function as was the case for surface plotting. It was not possible to extend ListPlot3D but a new function ListSurfacePlot3D was added. There is no problem with using the extended version of ListContourPlot, it is just used when necessary.

This loads the package.

In[94]:= **Needs["ExtendGraphics`Contour`"]**

These are the links that are open. One is for Delaunay triangulation and the other for contour construction.

In[95]:= **Links[ ]**

Out[95]= {LinkObject[delaunay, 1, 1], LinkObject[contour, 2, 2]}

Some data to be plotted are generated.

```
In[96]:= d1 =
            Flatten[
              Table[
                Table[{r Sin[t], r Cos[t], r^2 Cos[t] Sin[t]},
                      {t, 0, 2Pi-2Pi/( 10 r),2Pi/ (10 r)}],
                {r,10}], 1];
```

The underlying grid is shown to be quite irregular. The normal version of ListContourPlot would not be able to draw contours from this data.

```
In[97]:= TrianglePlot[Map[Take[#,2]&, d1]]
```

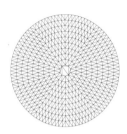

This uses the extended contour plot.

```
In[98]:= c = ListContourPlot[d1]
```

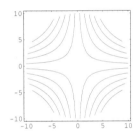

A ContourGraphics object is still returned and it can be altered with Show in the normal way.

```
In[99]:= Show[c, Contours -> 4]
```

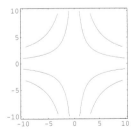

```
In[100]:= Needs["ExtendGraphics`LabelContour`"]
```

Other functions that work with contour plots such as labeling the contour lines will work in the normal way.

In[101]:= `LabelContourLines[c, LabelFont -> 4]`

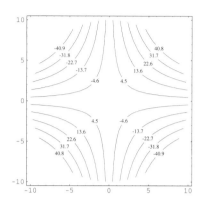

18.5 Summary of Three-Dimensional Visualization

Many techniques have been presented for plotting three-dimensional data sets. A quick review and summary of these will now be given. In this summary p_i refers to a three-dimensional point.

▶ *One Independent Variable*

With one independent variable the function `ScatterPlot3D` defined in the package `Graphics`Graphics3D`` can be used.

```
Graphics`Graphics3D`                    package defining ScatterPlot3D
ScatterPlot3D[{p_1, p_2, p_i, ... }]    plot the points p_i
ScatterPlot3D[{p_1, p_2, p_i, ... }, PlotJoined -> True]
                                        join the points p_i
```

Visualization functions for three-dimensional data with one independent variable.

▷ *Two Independent Variables, Regular Data*

With two independent variables and regular data the built-in function `ListPlot3D` will plot a surface, the built-in function `ListContourPlot` will draw a contour plot, and the built-in function `ListDensityPlot` will generate a density plot.

`ListPlot3D[{{`z_{11}`, `z_{12}`, ... }, {`z_{21}`, `z_{22}`, ... }, ... }]`

                   plot the surface defined by the heights z_{ij}

`ListContourPlot[{{`z_{11}`, `z_{12}`, ... }, {`z_{21}`, `z_{22}`, ... }, ... }]`

                   draw the contour plot defined by the heights z_{ij}

`ListDensityPlot[{{`z_{11}`, `z_{12}`, ... }, {`z_{21}`, `z_{22}`, ... }, ... }]`

                   draw the density plot defined by the heights z_{ij}

Visualization functions for regular three-dimensional data with two independent variables.

▷ *Two Independent Variables, Irregular Data*

When there are two independent variables and irregular data the function `ListSurfacePlot3D` defined in the package `ExtendGraphics`SurfaceGraphics3D`` will plot a surface. A contour plot can be drawn with an extension of `ListContourPlot` defined in `ExtendGraphics`Contour``.

`ExtendGraphics`SurfaceGraphics3D``   package for `ListSurfacePlot3D`

`ListSurfacePlot3D[{`p_1`, `p_2`, `p_i`, ... }]`

                   plot the surface over the points p_i

`ListSurfacePlot3D[{{`p_{11}`, `p_{12}`, ... },{`p_{21}`, `p_{22}`, ... },... }]`

                   plot the surface over the points p_{ij}

`SurfaceGraphics3D`   object returned by `ListSurfacePlot3D`

Visualization functions for irregular three-dimensional data with two independent variables.

`ExtendGraphics`Contour``   package for extending contour drawing functions

`ListContourPlot[{`p_1`, `p_2`, `p_i`, ... }]`   construct a contour plot from the points p_i

---

Contour plotting for irregular three-dimensional data.

▶ *Resampling Data*

To resample three-dimensional data use the functions `GridSort` and `TriangleSort`, defined in the package `ExtendGraphics‘SurfaceGraphics3D‘`. To resample a `SurfaceGraphics3D` surface use the function `InterpolateSurface` defined in the package `ExtendGraphics‘TriangularInterpolate‘`.

`ExtendGraphics‘SurfaceGraphics3D‘`	package for `GridSort` and `TriangleSort`
`GridSort[{`p_1`, `p_2`, `p_i`, ... }, `n`]`	sort the points p_i into an n by n rectangular array
`TriangleSort[{`p_1`, `p_2`, `p_i`, ... }, `n`]`	sort the vector of points p_i into an n by n rectangular array and then flatten it

Resampling irregular three-dimensional data.

`ExtendGraphics‘TriangularInterpolate‘`	
	package for triangular interpolation
`InterpolateSurface[`*surf*`]`	resample `SurfaceGraphics3D` object *surf*
`InterpolateSurface[`*surf*`, `n`]`	resample `SurfaceGraphics3D` object *surf* on an n by n grid

Resampling to generate a smooth surface.

18.6 Four-Dimensional Data

A four-dimensional data set consists of a collection of four-tuples, of points of the form $\{x_1,x_2,x_3,x_4\}$. Such data can be interpreted in several ways. One is to see them as a set of scalar data values in a three-dimensional space. Here each datum is of the form $\{x,y,z,f[x,y,z]\}$, $f[x,y,z]$ is the value of a scalar function at the point $\{x,y,z\}$. An alternative way to view the data is as a set of vector data in a two-dimensional space. Here each datum is of the form $\{x,y,f[x,y],g[x,y]\}$ where $\{f[x,y],g[x,y]\}$ is the value of a two-dimensional vector function at the point $\{x,y\}$. Such data could be visualized by plotting vectors in the plane. These methods will be explored in Chapter 19 page 500; this chapter will concentrate on scalar visualization methods.

The three-dimensional methods demonstrated in this chapter can be extended to higher dimensionality data. For example, some kind of four-dimensional plotting function could be used. Data with three independent variables could be plotted with a `ListPlot4D` function that would generate three-dimensional structures in a four-dimensional space. There is of course a basic problem in that it is hard to visualize four-dimensional space with the visualization tools generally available. However, there are applications that can explore spaces of higher dimensions. These will not be explored in this text.

▶ *General Plotting*

One technique that will always work for plotting four-dimensional data is to make a point plot. Points are plotted in three-dimensional space with coordinates defined by three values, for example $\{x_1, x_2, x_3\}$, and the point is colored according to the coordinate x_4. This technique can provide information on four-dimensional data with one, two, or three independent variables. It is simple to make a *Mathematica* function to make this type of plot.

This is a simple four-dimensional plotting function. The last coordinate is passed to the function fun scaled to have the smallest value map to 0 and the largest to 1.

```
In[102]:= ScatterPlot4D[data_ /;
            MatrixQ[data, NumberQ] &&
            Length[First[data]] === 4,
                    fun_, opts___] :=
          Module[{res, coord},
          coord = Map[Last, data] ;
          min = Min[coord] ;
          max = Max[coord] ;
          Show[Graphics3D[
              Map[
                {
                fun[(Last[#] - min)/(max-min)],
                Point[Take[#, 3]]
                }&, data], opts]]
            ]
```

A random data set is generated.

```
In[103]:= (
          rnd := 2 Random[ ] - 1;
          data = Table[{xvar = rnd, yvar = rnd, zvar = rnd,
          Abs[xvar yvar zvar]},
           {100}];
          )
```

The point plot is created by shading with GrayLevel.

```
In[104]:= ScatterPlot4D[data, GrayLevel]
```

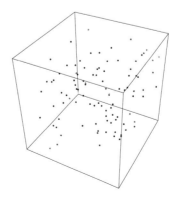

Now a pure function based on RGBColor is used to color the points.

In[105]:= **ScatterPlot4D[data, RGBColor[#, 1-#,1]&]**

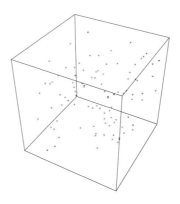

Instead of plotting points Cuboid primitives can be plotted. This is related to a density plot.

In[106]:= **Show[% /.**
     Point[pt_] :> Cuboid[pt, pt+{0.1,0.1,0.1}],
        Lighting -> False]

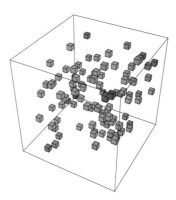

This type of plot is simple to make and can be used for a quick grasp of the data. The technique can be seen as an extension of a density plot to higher dimensions. It is closely related to volume rendering.

▷ *Animation Techniques*

Mathematica provides simple tools to make animations and these can be employed to visualize four-dimensional data. From each datum $\{x_1,\ x_2,\ x_3,\ x_4\}$ one variable, say x_3, is assigned to be the animation variable. Then a sequence of surfaces in three-dimensional space is formed. To generate each surface all of the problems of generating surfaces discussed in the previous example must be faced. The first demonstration of this technique will use Plot3D to generate surfaces.

It is necessary to load the animation package.

```
In[107]:= Needs["Graphics`Animation`"]
```

On a computer screen this would be an animated sequence.

```
In[108]:= Animate[
              Plot3D[Sin[x y + z], {x,0,Pi},{y,0,Pi},
                  PlotRange -> {-1,1}],
              {z,0,Pi,Pi/5}];
```

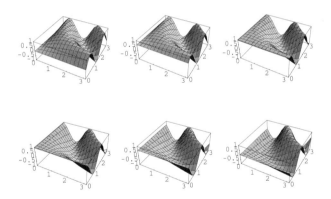

The sequence of pictures above can be understood as representing slices through a three-dimensional solid structure in a four-dimensional space. Of course, it is not always easy to imagine how a four-dimensional space should look. Now the animation above will be generated from a set of data.

The data set for the animation.

```
In[109]:= data = Table[N[Sin[x y + z]],
              {z,0,Pi,Pi/5},
              {y,0,Pi,Pi/15},
              {x,0,Pi,Pi/15}] ;
```

The data has six different *z* values.

```
In[110]:= Length[data]
Out[110]= 6
```

Each set is suitable for plotting with ListPlot3D.

```
In[111]:= Dimensions[First[data]]
Out[111]= {16, 16}
```

The animation shown earlier is generated
again but this time from a set of data.

```
In[112]:= Animate[ListPlot3D[Part[data, i]],
              {i,1,Length[data],1}];
```

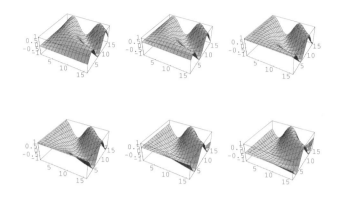

        For this type of technique to work the data must be well sorted in the variable in which the animation
will be carried out. It must be capable of being formed into distinct sets each of which will form a frame of the
animation. If this is not so then a resampling technique can be applied. If there are very many data points a
bin sorting technique could be applied. It would not be difficult to adapt the GridSort function, introduced
earlier, to higher dimensions. An alternative is resampling with triangular interpolation; however, for four-
dimensional data this would be rather complex and is not demonstrated here.

▸ *Three-Dimensional Contours*

The contour plot is one of the methods that is commonly used to visualize three-dimensional data. One
of its attractions is that it generates a two-dimensional result that conveniently fits into a two-dimensional
plot. In an analogous way four-dimensional data can be examined with a three-dimensional contour plot.
This type of plot is sometimes called an iso-surface. What is actually plotted is the values of x, y, and
z for which the implicit function $g(x, y, z)$ is equal to some value c_i. This can be plotted as a surface in
three-dimensional space. *Mathematica* provides the functions ContourPlot3D and ListContourPlot3D,
defined in the package Graphics`ContourPlot3D` to make this type of plot.

The package must be loaded.

```
In[113]:= Needs["Graphics`ContourPlot3D`"]
```

This is the surface of {x,y,z} points that satisfies the equation x^2 + y^2 + z^2 == 0.5.

```
In[114]:= ContourPlot3D[
              x^2 + y^2 + z^2,
              {x, -1,1}, {y, -1,1}, {z, -1,1},
              Contours -> {0.5}]
```

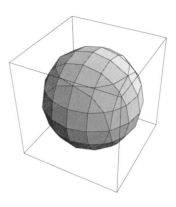

These are the {x,y} points of the intersection of the surface x^2 + y^2 + z^2 == 0.5 with the plane z == 0.3.

```
In[115]:= ContourPlot[x^2 + y^2 + 0.3,
              {x, -1,1}, {y,-1,1},
              Contours -> {0.5},
              ContourShading -> False]
```

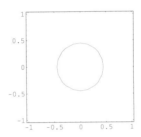

The surface above was generated from a function. `ListContourPlot3D` will generate it from a data set. The data must be in the form of a rank 3 tensor, each element of which represents the value of the function over the grid of points in *x*, *y*, and *z*. This is an extension of the form of data required by `ListContourPlot`, `ListPlot3D`, and `ListDensityPlot`.

This generates the data set.

```
In[116]:= data =
              Table[x^2 + y^2 + z^2,
              {z,-1,1,0.25},
              {y,-1,1,0.25},
              {x,-1,1,0.25}];
```

A similar plot is generated. For this example the box is omitted.

```
In[117]:= ListContourPlot3D[data,
              Contours -> {0.5}, Boxed -> False]
```

Of course, to make this plot it is necessary that the data be ordered on a rectangular grid. If the data are not ordered it would be possible to carry out a triangulation process extending that shown earlier in this chapter on page 475. Such a triangulation requires a complicated algorithm and no example of implementing it is presented in this text.

▶ *Surface Coloring*

The last method that will be considered for the plotting of four-dimensional data is to use the first three elements of data to construct a surface and the last element to color it. This would be suitable when there are two independent and two dependent variables. ListSurfacePlot3D provides a mechanism for this through the ColorFunction option. When the data are three-dimensional the ColorFunction is applied to the third argument, which sets both the height and the color. When a fourth argument is present it is used with ColorFunction.

It is necessary to ensure that the package is loaded to define ListSurfacePlot3D.

```
In[118]:= Needs["ExtendGraphics`SurfaceGraphics3D`"]
```

A four-dimensional data set.

```
In[119]:= data =
              Table[
                {r Sin[t], r Cos[t],
                 Sin[t] Exp[-r^2], (1+ Cos[t])/2.},
                   {r, 0, 3,.15}, {t,0,2Pi,Pi/8}];
```

The surface is shaded with the default light sources.

In[120]:= **ListSurfacePlot3D[data]**

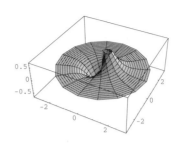

The ColorFunction option when set is applied to the fourth argument and the result used to shade the surface.

In[121]:= **Show[%, ColorFunction -> Hue]**

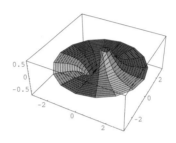

In this data set the fourth element is a list of two elements.

```
In[122]:= data =
            Table[
              {r Sin[t], r Cos[t],
               Sin[t] Exp[-r^2], {r/3, t/(2Pi)}},
                {r, 0., 3,.15}, {t,0.,2Pi,Pi/8}];
```

In this sample datum the first three elements give the *x*, *y*, and *z* values respectively. The last element will be used as an argument in the ColorFunction.

```
In[123]:= Part[data,3,14]
Out[123]= {-0.277164, 0.114805, -0.844362, {0.1, 0.8125}}
```

Now the surface is colored using the data stored in the last element.

```
In[124]:= ListSurfacePlot3D[data,
            ColorFunction -> (RGBColor[#[[1]], #[[2]], 0]&)]
```

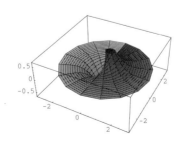

18.7 Multidimensional Data

As the dimensionality of the data increases the methods presented in this chapter lose effectiveness. It is possible to keep using clever rendering methods to construct sequences of hypersurfaces of higher and higher dimensionality. However, the information that these pictures convey steadily decreases as they become more complicated. At this point much simpler techniques are required that can answer basic questions about the data. The simplest type of plot is a two-dimensional picture, and this type will be utilized. One basic measure of information that can be generated from a multidimensional data set is the correlation of the information in each dimension with the other dimensions. Such a plot can be called a correlation plot and a package that builds these is available.

A two-dimensional data set.

```
In[125]:= data = Table[{x, x^2}, {x,5}]
Out[125]= {{1, 1}, {2, 4}, {3, 9}, {4, 16}, {5, 25}}
```

Now four data sets are formed from the original two-dimensional set.

```
In[126]:= res =
           Table[Map[{Part[#, i], Part[#, j]}&, data],
               {i, 2}, {j, 2}] ;
```

A GraphicsArray of the four plots is displayed. The individual pictures are not very informative, it is the method that is demonstrated.

```
In[127]:= Show[
           GraphicsArray[
             Map[ListPlot[#,
                 Frame -> True,
                 PlotJoined -> True,
                 DisplayFunction -> Identity]&,
                 res, {2}]]]
```

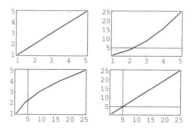

An *n*-dimensional data set can be split up into n^2 two-dimensional sets. Each two-dimensional set will plot one of the original dimensions against another. A function to make plots like this from data sets of any dimensionality is quite short.

The n^2 data sets are formed and then reversed so the diagonal goes from lower-left to upper-right. The individual plots are then made.

```
In[128]:= CorrelationPlot[data_] :=
              Module[{i, j, res, len = Length[First[data]]},
                res =
                Table[Map[{Part[#, i], Part[#, j]}&, data],
                        {j, len}, {i, len}] ;
                res = Reverse[res] ;
                res = Map[ListPlot[#, Frame -> True,
                    Axes -> False,
                    FrameTicks -> None,
                    AspectRatio -> 1,
                    DisplayFunction -> Identity]&,
                    res, {2}] ;
                Show[GraphicsArray[res]]
              ]
```

A more complex data set.

```
In[129]:= data = Table[{x, Random[ ], -x^2, x^3}, {x,-1,2,.05}];
```

The correlation plot neatly shows the relationships between different coordinates.

```
In[130]:= CorrelationPlot[data]
```

A more sophisticated version is available in the package ExtendGraphics`CorrelationPlot`.

```
In[131]:= Needs["ExtendGraphics`CorrelationPlot`"]
```

The new version can include labels.

In[132]:= `CorrelationPlot[data,`
`          Labels -> {x, Random, -x^2, x^3}]`

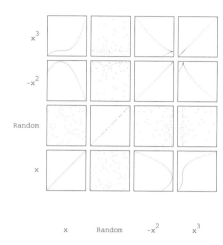

It can also include axes.

In[133]:= `CorrelationPlot[data,`
`          Labels -> {x, Rnd, -x^2, x^3},`
`          Axes -> True,`
`          TickFont -> 3]`

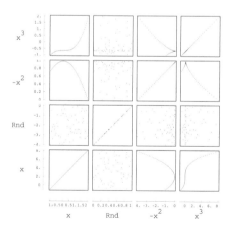

18.8 Summary

This chapter has looked at the problem of visualizing data. The data were classified according to the dimensionality and the number of dependent variables of each datum. First the techniques that worked for two-dimensional data were examined. These involved the plotting of lines in a two-dimensional picture. If the data needed to be sorted or resampled this was straightforward.

For three-dimensional data the plotting of curves was shown to be a simple extension of two-dimensional plotting. However, when surfaces were plotted certain new problems arose. These were related to the ordering of the data and how it could be resampled. A variety of solutions for plotting surfaces and contours for regular and irregular data were demonstrated. When irregular data were plotted it was first necessary to order them by a process of triangulation. These same triangulation methods could be used to resample data. Resampling could also be done by sorting the data into various groups or bins. Functions that carried out all of these different processes were demonstrated.

A number of methods for visualizing four-dimensional data were explored. These involved generalizations from the previous techniques making point plots and drawing contours. Finally, the correlation plot, a technique for understanding data of very high dimensionality, was introduced.

Chapter 19
Visualizing Vectors

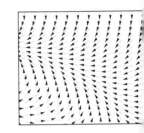

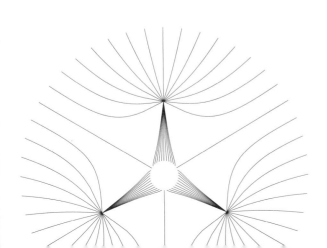

The previous chapter examined a variety of techniques for visualizing numeric data. This chapter extends the discussion to consider ways that vector data can be visualized. It will look at the plotting of two-dimensional vectors in a two-dimensional space and at three-dimensional vectors in a three-dimensional space. With the classifications of data made in the previous chapter these can be described as a four-dimensional data set with two dependent variables and a six-dimensional data set with three dependent variables.

Two visualization techniques will be demonstrated. The first will draw discrete vectors for each datum and is related to the point plotting methods. The second technique will form vector field lines that will give a more global view of the data and is related to the line plotting visualization techniques in Chapter 18 page 461 and page 469. The first method is much simpler; it plots discrete items and there are no issues of sorting, triangulation, or resampling to be faced. When vector field lines are plotted these issues may be relevant.

▶ *What are Vectors?*

Chapter 16 page 371 and Chapter 17 page 413 defined vectors as ordered groups of numbers. A two-dimensional vector consists of two numbers and a three-dimensional vector consists of three numbers. A vector can be seen as having a magnitude and a direction and stand in contrast to a scalar, which only has a magnitude. There are many areas in which vectors arise. For example, they naturally represent measurements of fluid flow such as a collection of wind velocity measurements at different locations. Any measurement that can be thought of as having a direction may be suitable to be visualized as vector data.

Another way to generate a vector field is to take the gradient of a scalar function. For a function f of two variables, x and y, the gradient is {D[f,x],D[f,y]}, a two-dimensional vector. The gradient points in the direction of maximum increase of the function.

19.1 Two-Dimensional Vectors

Mathematica provides the standard package Graphics`PlotField` to make two-dimensional vector plots. As is typical with *Mathematica* plotting utilities there are function and list plotting versions. These commands visualize vector information at certain points by drawing arrows. This means that the coordinate system is used for two purposes, one is to locate the points and the second is to show the magnitude of the arrows. Of course these will probably be quite unrelated. For example, the data may represent force vectors at various positions in some object. In this case the units of each component of the position may be centimeters while the units of the force may be newtons. Including them both in the same picture may be visually compact but can complicate the plotting process.

The vector plotting package is loaded.   *In[1]:=* **Needs["Graphics`PlotField`"]**

The basic vector plotting function is
PlotVectorField.

In[2]:= **?PlotVectorField**

PlotVectorField[f, {x, x0, x1, (xu)}, {y, y0, y1, (yu)},
    (options)] produces a vector field plot of the
    two-dimensional vector function f.

The vectors are determined by the *x* and
y coordinates and thus radiate out from
the origin.

In[3]:= `PlotVectorField[{x, y}, {x,-2,2},{y,-2,2}]`

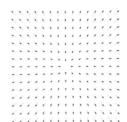

These vectors have a Sin function
applied to each component.

In[4]:= `PlotVectorField[Sin[{x, y}],`
                  `{x,-2Pi,2Pi},`
                  `{y,-2Pi,2Pi}, PlotPoints -> 20]`

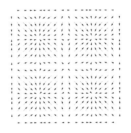

As with many *Mathematica* commands there are function and list versions of vector plotting. The list
plotting version is called `ListPlotVectorField`.

```
Graphics`PlotField`                    package for ListPlotVectorField
ListPlotVectorField[{{p₁, v₁}, {p₂, v₂}, ... }]
                                 plot the vectors vᵢ at positions pᵢ
ListPlotVectorField[{{v₁₁, v₁₂, ... }, {v₂₁, v₂₂, ... }, ... }]
                                 plot the vectors vᵢⱼ at positions ij
```

Plotting two-dimensional vector data.

There are two types of data that can be accepted by `ListPlotVectorField`. One type of data includes
the {x,y} values explicitly. In the other a two-dimensional array of vectors is given without {x,y} values.
The values are taken implicitly from the indices in the array. Other list plotting routines such as `ListPlot`
and `ListPlot3D` can specify the independent variables in this implicit way.

The usage message provides some basic information.

In[5]:= **?ListPlotVectorField**

ListPlotVectorField[{{vec11,vec12,..},...}] accepts a
    rectangular array of two-dimensional vectors (larger than
    2x2) and displays them, with each vector positioned in the
    same location graphically as the matrix would be (ie, vector
    1,1 in the upper left corner).
ListPlotVectorField[{{pt,vec},{pt,vec},...}] displays a list
    of vectors, each based at the corresponding point.

The Table command generates a set of data.

In[6]:= **data =**
        Table[{{x, y}, {x, y}}, {x,-2,2,.5}, {y,-2,2,.5}];

This data must be flattened to the first level to be passed to ListPlotVectorField.

In[7]:= **data = Flatten[data, 1];**

Each data element consists of $\{\{x,y\},\{v_1,v_2\}\}$. The vector $\{v_1,v_2\}$ is to be drawn at the point $\{x,y\}$.

In[8]:= **First[data]**

Out[8]= {{-2, -2}, {-2, -2}}

The picture can be improved upon since the vectors are too long.

In[9]:= **ListPlotVectorField[data]**

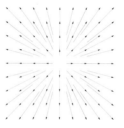

Now the ScaleFactor option is altered. The longest vector is scaled to be 0.5 units long. The other vectors are scaled linearly.

In[10]:= **ListPlotVectorField[data,**
          ScaleFactor -> 0.5]

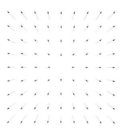

An alternative method of encoding the data is to give an array of vectors.

In[11]:= **data = Table[Tan[{x,y}], {x,-5,5},{y,-5,5}];**

The *x* and *y* values of the ijth vector are
{i,j}.

```
In[12]:= ListPlotVectorField[data,
              ScaleFactor -> 0.75]
```

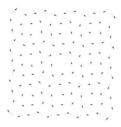

In these examples of ListPlotVectorField it was necessary to set ScaleFactor to make sure that the arrows came out to be a size appropriate for the picture. This is because the coordinate system in the picture is used both to locate the base of each vector and to show its components. The function plotting routines such as PlotVectorField produce output on a rectangular grid and can scale the vectors to fit into this grid. The list plotting routines accept data that does not have to be arranged on a grid. In this case it is necessary to set options like ScaleFactor to make the arrows fit into the picture.

▶ *Altering the Vector*

In *Mathematica* the arrows drawn to represent vectors make use of the package Graphics`Arrow`. This package allows sophisticated arrow shapes to be constructed. The package was introduced with Version 2.2 *Mathematica*. Older versions of Graphics`PlotField` used a less sophisticated arrow drawing mechanism.

ColorFunction	set the color according to vector length
MaxArrowLength	upper limit for vector length
ScaleFactor	scale vector length with factor
ScaleFunction	scale vector length with function

Options of ListPlotVectorField that set the style of vectors.

A data set of normalized vectors to demonstrate the use of arrow options.

```
In[13]:= data =
             Flatten[
              Table[{{x, y},
                     {x/Sqrt[x^2+y^2], y/Sqrt[x^2+y^2]}},
                   {x,-2,2,4/9.}, {y,-2,2,4/9.}], 1];
```

The vectors all have a length of 1 unit.

In[14]:= **ListPlotVectorField[data,**
Frame -> True]

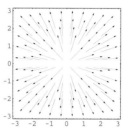

Now the length of each vector is halved.

In[15]:= **ListPlotVectorField[data,**
ScaleFunction -> (0.5 # &),
Frame -> True]

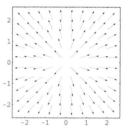

An alternative method halves the length of each vector. This works since the original vectors were all one unit long.

In[16]:= **ListPlotVectorField[data,**
ScaleFactor -> 0.5,
Frame -> True]

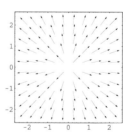

Both ScaleFactor and ScaleFunction alter the lengths of the vectors. Of these ScaleFactor is simpler and is preferable if a linear rescaling is required. In addition to these options the options MaxArrowLength and ColorFunction also work to change the vector style.

```
In[17]:= data =
            Flatten[
              Table[{{x, y}, {y/4, - x/4}},
                    {x,-4,4,1}, {y,-4,4,1}], 1];
```

This is a basic plot of the data set. The twisted appearance is because the base of the vector starts at the drawing point. With a crowded picture like this a strange effect is produced.

```
In[18]:= ListPlotVectorField[data,
            Frame -> True]
```

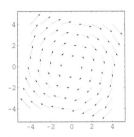

Now vectors with a length of more than 1 are omitted. This picture is less crowded and the tilted effect is significantly reduced.

```
In[19]:= ListPlotVectorField[data,
            MaxArrowLength -> 1,
            Frame -> True]
```

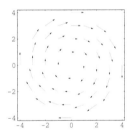

The vectors are colored by the ColorFunction option applied to their lengths.

```
In[20]:= ListPlotVectorField[data,
            ColorFunction -> Hue,
            Frame -> True]
```

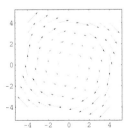

Now the vectors are all drawn with
length 0.5 but different colors. The
ColorFunction option is applied before
the vectors are scaled.

```
In[21]:= ListPlotVectorField[data,
            ScaleFunction -> (0.5&),
            ColorFunction -> (RGBColor[#,1-#,0]&),
            Frame -> True]
```

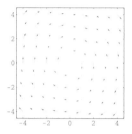

The examples here have demonstrated options of vector plotting commands such as ListPlotVec-torField. These options altered the length and color of arrows. The arrow is actually drawn by the Arrow primitive, which is defined in the standard package Graphics`Arrow`. This is loaded automatically when Graphics`PlotField` is loaded. There are several options of the Arrow primitive that can be passed through the vector plotting commands. These offer further control of the appearance of individual arrows.

HeadScaling	coordinate system for arrow head
HeadShape	shape of arrow head
HeadLength	length of arrow head (when HeadShape is Automatic)
HeadCenter	location of center of arrow base (when HeadShape is Automatic)
HeadWidth	width of arrow head (when HeadShape is Automatic)
ZeroShape	shape of zero length arrows

Options of the Arrow primitive used by ListPlotVectorField.

With these options it is possible to alter the way that the vectors are rendered. The default options usually work well so there is little need for this. Two options that may be of use are the HeadScaling and HeadLength options. The first can be set to scale the heads of the arrows along with their lengths.

```
In[22]:= data =
          Flatten[
            Table[{{x,y}, {x^2 y, x y^2}},
              {x,-2,2,0.5},{y,-2,2,0.5}], 1];
```

Here the ScaleFactor has been set to make the longest vector 0.6 units.

```
In[23]:= ListPlotVectorField[data,
            ScaleFactor -> 0.6]
```

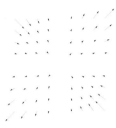

Now HeadScaling of Relative is set. The heads of the vectors scale with the lengths but they are much too small.

```
In[24]:= ListPlotVectorField[data,
            ScaleFactor -> 0.6,
            HeadScaling -> Relative]
```

Finally the length of the head is set to be 0.3 of the length of the arrow.

```
In[25]:= ListPlotVectorField[data,
            ScaleFactor -> 0.6,
            HeadScaling -> Relative,
            HeadLength -> 0.3]
```

19.2 Flow around an Object

This section will present an example of using vectors to represent the flow of a fluid around an object. It will use an animation to give an impression of movement. The vector field plotting commands that are given in this chapter will adjust many of the options to produce interesting pictures.

This example needs the vector field package and the animation package.

```
In[26]:= (Needs["Graphics`PlotField`"];
          Needs["Graphics`Animation`"]);
```

A function that represents steady flow. At every point the flow is in the *x* direction.

```
In[27]:= steady[{x_, y_}] := {{x,y}, {1,0}}
```

This is a data set that represents flow.

```
In[28]:= data = Table[steady[{x,y}], {x, -5, 5,2}, {y,-4,4,1}];
```

The first data element shows the flow through the line x == -5.

```
In[29]:= testdata = First[data]
Out[29]= {{{-5, -4}, {1, 0}}, {{-5, -3}, {1, 0}},
  {{-5, -2}, {1, 0}}, {{-5, -1}, {1, 0}}, {{-5, 0}, {1, 0}},
  {{-5, 1}, {1, 0}}, {{-5, 2}, {1, 0}}, {{-5, 3}, {1, 0}},
  {{-5, 4}, {1, 0}}}
```

The flow through x == -5 is plotted. It is necessary to adjust the options of ListPlotVectorField to obtain a good picture.

```
In[30]:= ListPlotVectorField[testdata,
              ScaleFactor -> 0.75,
              HeadScaling -> Relative,
              HeadLength -> 0.25,
              Frame -> True,
              FrameTicks -> None,
              PlotRange -> {{-6,6}, {-4.5,4.5}}]
```

Now an animation is constructed from the data.

```
In[31]:= Animate[
            ListPlotVectorField[Part[data, i],
                ScaleFactor -> 0.75,
                HeadScaling -> Relative,
                HeadLength -> .5,
                Frame -> True,
                FrameTicks -> None,
                PlotRange -> {{-6,6}, {-4.5,4.5}}],
            {i,1,Length[data],1}];
```

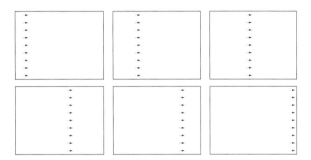

The sequence of pictures above shows how a set of flow vectors propagates through the system. However, since it only shows one set at a time it does not give much global information. A much better way would be to show more vectors and at the same time reduce the number of frames. This can be done since it is only necessary for each vector to catch up with the one in front.

Instead of making one row of vectors a collection is made.

```
In[32]:= data1 =
            Table[
              Flatten[
                Table[steady[{x+d/4.,y}], {x,-7,5,2},{y,-4,4}],
                    1], {d,0,7,2}];
```

Now the animation has fewer frames but has a stronger sensation of movement. This is much more apparent in a real animation.

```
In[33]:= Animate[
           ListPlotVectorField[Part[data1, i],
               ScaleFactor -> 0.75,
               HeadScaling -> Relative,
               HeadLength -> 0.25,
               Frame -> True,
               FrameTicks -> None,
               PlotRange -> {{-6,6}, {-4.5,4.5}}],
           {i,1,Length[data1],1}];
```

This example shows vectors representing fluid movement through space free from any interference. A new function representing flow around an object is now introduced. The use of complex functions to describe flow is covered in texts on complex variables such as *Complex Variables and Applications*, R.V. Churchill and J.W. Brown.

This function represents restricted flow around an object.

```
In[34]:= restrict[{x_, y_}] :=
           Module[{z},
             z = 1-1/(x+ I y)^2;
             {{x,y}, {Re[z], -Im[z]}}]
```

Two different calculations are joined together to avoid flow for y == 0.

```
In[35]:= data =
           Table[
             Flatten[
               Table[
                 {restrict[N[{x+d/4.,y}]],
                  restrict[N[{x+d/4.,-y}]]},
                     {x,-7,5,1},{y,0.5,3,2.5/4.}],
                 2], {d,0,3-3/8.,3/8.}];
```

There is an obstruction at the origin and the flow is distorted to pass around it.

```
In[36]:= ListPlotVectorField[First[data],
             ScaleFunction -> (If[# > 1.5, 0.75, 0.5 #]&),
             HeadScaling -> Relative,
             HeadLength -> 0.25,
             Frame -> True,
             FrameTicks -> None,
             PlotRange -> {{-5,5}, {-3.5,3.5}},
             Epilog -> Disk[{0,0},0.5]]
```

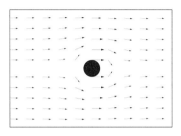

This is the restricted flow animation. The sense of movement here is quite strong.

```
In[37]:= Animate[
             ListPlotVectorField[Part[data, i],
             ScaleFunction -> (If[# > 1.5, 0.75, 0.5 #]&),
             HeadScaling -> Relative,
             HeadLength -> 0.25,
             Frame -> True,
             FrameTicks -> None,
             PlotRange -> {{-5,5}, {-3.5,3.5}},
             Epilog -> Disk[{0,0},0.5]],
             {i,1,Length[data],1}];
```

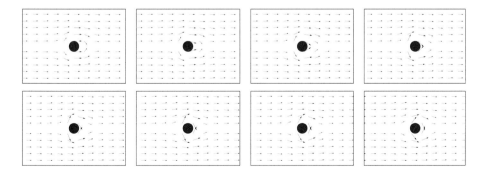

The way that this process has been represented is quite simple. It would be possible to make a more complete model that might give an even stronger idea of movement. One way to do this would be to construct the flow lines and move arrows along these. A later section in this chapter explains how flow lines can be calculated.

19.3 Three-Dimensional Vectors

Mathematica provides tools to plot three-dimensional vectors in a three-dimensional space. As is typical with vector drawing functions the space is used to show both the positions of the data points and the actual vectors. These three-dimensional vector plots can be made with the functions in the package Graphics`PlotField3D`[11]. One problem, typical of three-dimensional visualization, is that the actual picture can quickly become very cluttered.

Here the package is loaded.

```
In[38]:= Needs["Graphics`PlotField3D`"]
```

The basic vector plotting function is PlotVectorField3D.

```
In[39]:= ?PlotVectorField3D
```

```
PlotVectorField3D[{xfunc,yfunc,zfunc},xrange,yrange,zrange]
    plots a vector field designated by the given functions, over
    the given ranges, where a range is described as
    {variable,min,max,(increment)}.  Also accepts options like
    those of ListPlotVectorField3D.
```

Even for a simple example this type of plot quickly becomes quite cluttered.

```
In[40]:= PlotVectorField3D[{y, -x, 0},
          {x,-1,1},{y,-1,1}, {z,0,2}]
```

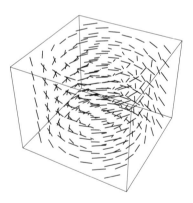

There is of course a list plotting version as well.

```
In[41]:= ?ListPlotVectorField3D
```

```
ListPlotVectorField3D[{{pt,vec},...},(options)] plots a list of
    vectors in three dimensions, each vector based at a
    corresponding point pt.
```

---

[11]In *Mathematica* Version 2.2 (and earlier) there was a shadowing conflict between certain symbols in the two- and three-dimensional vector plotting packages. This problem has now been rectified. In these older versions it can be overcome either by restarting *Mathematica* or by assigning each of the newer symbols to evaluate to the older.

Flatten is necessary to generate data of the form $\{\{p_1,\ v_1\},\ \{p_2,\ v_2\},\ \ldots\}$.

```
In[42]:= data =
            Flatten[
                Table[{{x, y, z}, {y, -x, 0}},
                {x,-1,1,1/3.}, {y,-1,1,1/3.},{z,-1,1,1/3.}], 2];
```

It is often necessary to adjust the ScaleFactor option to get vectors of a suitable size.

```
In[43]:= ListPlotVectorField3D[data,
            ScaleFactor -> 0.2]
```

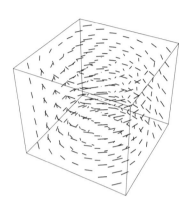

By default the arrow heads are not drawn. Setting the VectorHeads option causes them to appear.

```
In[44]:= ListPlotVectorField3D[data,
            ScaleFactor -> 0.2,
            VectorHeads -> True]
```

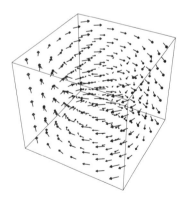

The clutter in this type of picture is quite apparent. The reason is that in these examples the vectors are drawn throughout the space. One solution is to show only some of the vectors at any time. For example, it is possible to make a collection of pictures each of which shows vectors in a different plane.

This can be illustrated with this new data set.

```
In[45]:= data = Flatten[Table[{{x,y,z}, {y z, x z, x y}},
                {x, -1,1,0.25},{y,-1,1,0.25}, {z,-1,1,0.4}], 2];
```

A list is formed of the z coordinate values.

```
In[46]:= zvals = Union[Map[Part[#, 1, 3]&, data]]
Out[46]= {-1, -0.6, -0.2, 0.2, 0.6, 1.}
```

Now data elements with *z* coordinate equal to the first of zvals are collected.

```
In[47]:= data1 =
            Select[data, Part[#, 1, 3] === First[zvals]&] ;
```

The slice of vectors can now be plotted.

```
In[48]:= ListPlotVectorField3D[data1,
            ScaleFactor -> 0.2]
```

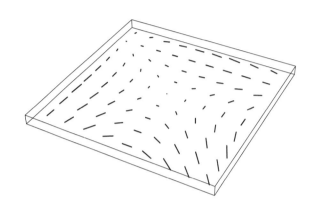

A list of each element in the zvals list is made. Here one pure function is used inside another. This is done by using the full notation Function.

```
In[49]:= ndata =
            Map[
              Function[arg, Select[data, Part[#,1,3] === arg&]],
              zvals] ;
```

Now a list of Graphics3D objects is built.

```
In[50]:= plots =
            Map[
              ListPlotVectorField3D[#,
                DisplayFunction -> Identity,
                ScaleFactor -> 0.4,
                PlotRange -> {{-1.2,1.2},{-1.2,1.2},{-1.2,1.2}},
                ViewPoint -> {.4,-2,1.2},
                BoxRatios -> {1,1,1}]&,
              ndata]

Out[50]= {-Graphics3D-, -Graphics3D-, -Graphics3D-,
           -Graphics3D-, -Graphics3D-, -Graphics3D-}
```

The list of Graphics3D objects can be broken up and displayed in a GraphicsArray.

```
In[51]:= Show[GraphicsArray[Partition[plots, 3]]]
```

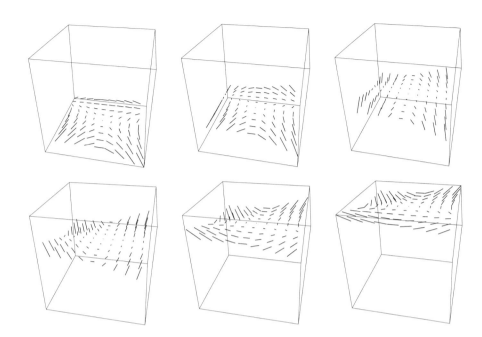

The picture here gives a good idea of how the vector data varies as different slices are looked at. It could be improved by adding a label to each picture describing the z value of the plane being plotted. A further improvement would be to make an animation. This could be done by applying the command ShowAnimation to the list of Graphics3D objects.

The technique used here, plotting only a sub-set of vectors, is often successful for three-dimensional vector plots. It will enhance the picture when there is one particular set of vectors that are of interest. For example the data may represent flow around a body. In this case the picture will be improved by plotting only some vectors, maybe those at a special distance from the body. Alternatively several pictures can be generated while this distance is varied. The collection of pictures may be more effective than one picture where everything is thrown together.

▶ *Setting the Vector Style*

Since these are three-dimensional vectors the tools that *Mathematica* provides to render them are not as sophisticated as those for two-dimensional vectors. In particular the arrows that are used in two dimensions are not available in three dimensions. This is because, as was discussed in Chapter 9 page 153, the requirement that three-dimensional objects be projected into two dimensions places certain constraints on the type of primitives that can be used. However there are some options that set the style of the three-dimensional vectors. These work in similar ways to the two-dimensional versions of the options.

ColorFunction	set the color according to vector length
MaxArrowLength	upper limit for vector length
ScaleFactor	scale vector length with factor
ScaleFunction	scale vector length with function
VectorArrowHeads	whether or not to draw heads on vectors

Options of three-dimensional vector plotting commands that set the style of vectors.

19.4 Field Lines

The last section of this chapter looks at a different technique for visualizing vectors. Instead of plotting vectors as discrete arrows they are joined to form field lines. This is a complex task that is more difficult to automate and can take longer to compute. The first examples will demonstrate how to generate field lines from mathematical functions. After this the technique will be used for vectors defined by numeric data. The basic functions that calculate field lines are not very complicated but since they are useful they are collected into the package `ExtendGraphics`FieldLines`.

Here the basic package is loaded.

In[52]:= `Needs["Graphics`PlotField`"]`

The potential at {x,y} around a point charge at {x1,y1}.

In[53]:= `potential[{x1_, y1_}] =`
         `1/Sqrt[(x1-x)^2 + (y1-y)^2]`

$$Out[53] = \frac{1}{Sqrt[(-x + x1)^2 + (-y + y1)^2]}$$

The potential can be plotted by ContourPlot.

In[54]:= `ContourPlot[potential[{1,1}],`
         `{x, 0,2}, {y, 0,2}, PlotPoints -> 16]`

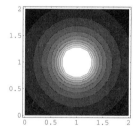

An alternative way to visualize the potential is to plot the vector field it generates.

```
In[55]:= PlotGradientField[potential[{1,1}],
              {x, 0,2}, {y, 0,2},
              ScaleFactor -> 5,
              MaxArrowLength -> 6,
              PlotPoints -> 12]
```

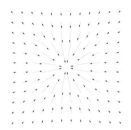

PlotGradientField takes the gradient of a scalar function, $f[x,y]$, and plots the resulting vector field, {D[f[x,y],x],D[f[x,y],y]}. The picture here shows discrete samples of this vector field. It gives little idea of how the vectors in one part of the picture compare with vectors in another. Plotting vector field lines provides this information. The field line can be thought of as the trajectory of a particle of infinitesimal mass under the influence of the field. It can be calculated by solving a differential equation:

$$\frac{dx}{dt} = E_x \quad \frac{dy}{dt} = E_y$$

where t represents progress down the trajectory and E_x and E_y are the field components in x and y respectively. A more rigorous definition of the field line is generated by writing it in parametric form $c[t] = \{x[t], y[t]\}$. The tangent to this is $c'[t] = \{x'[t], y'[t]\}$. The field line is parallel to the field and hence $c'[t] = \{E_x, E_y\}$, which gives the equations above. These differential equations can be solved numerically with the *Mathematica* function NDSolve.

These are the x and y components of the field.

```
In[56]:= {ex, ey} =
            -{D[potential[{1,1}], x], D[potential[{1,1}], y]}
```

$$Out[56]= \{-(\frac{1 - x}{((1 - x)^2 + (1 - y)^2)^{3/2}}),$$

$$-(\frac{1 - y}{((1 - x)^2 + (1 - y)^2)^{3/2}})\}$$

NDSolve requires that x and y be made into functions of the independent variable.

```
In[57]:= {exf, eyf} = {ex, ey} /. {x -> x[t], y -> y[t]}
```

$$Out[57]= \{-(\frac{1 - x[t]}{((1 - x[t])^2 + (1 - y[t])^2)^{3/2}}),$$

$$-(\frac{1 - y[t]}{((1 - x[t])^2 + (1 - y[t])^2)^{3/2}})\}$$

Starting from the point {1.1,1.1} the trajectory is followed out. ex and ey are made negative to make sure it moves away from {1,1}.

```
In[58]:= NDSolve[
             {x'[t] == exf, y'[t] == eyf,
              x[0] == 1.1, y[0] == 1.1},
             {x[t], y[t]}, {t,0,5}]

Out[58]= {{x[t] -> InterpolatingFunction[{0., 5.}, <>][t],
           y[t] -> InterpolatingFunction[{0., 5.}, <>][t]}}
```

ParametricPlot can then plot the resulting trajectory.

```
In[59]:= ParametricPlot[Evaluate[{x[t], y[t]} /. %], {t,0,5}]
```

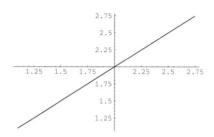

Making a picture of just one single field line is not very useful. It would be preferable to make a plot of a whole sequence of lines. To do this it will be convenient to define a function that combines all the steps together.

FieldLine will calculate a length t1 of the field line from the field {ex,ey} starting at {x0,y0}.

```
In[60]:= FieldLine[{x_, ex_, x0_},
                   {y_, ey_, y0_}, {t_, t1_}] :=
         Module[{exf, eyf, sol, t2},
           {exf, eyf} = {ex, ey} /. {x -> x[t], y -> y[t]} ;
           sol = NDSolve[
                   {x'[t] == exf, y'[t] == eyf,
                    x[0] == x0, y[0] == y0
                   }, {x[t], y[t]}, {t,0,t1}] ;
           sol = {x[t], y[t]} /. First[sol] ;
           If[VectorQ[sol /. t -> 0, NumberQ],
             t2 = Part[sol, 1, 0, 1, 2] ;
             sol =
                 ParametricPlot[Evaluate[sol], {t,0,t2},
                     DisplayFunction -> Identity] ;
           First[Cases[sol, Line[_], Infinity]],
           Line[{{x0, y0}}]]
           ]
```

The FieldLine function solves a
differential equation and returns a
Line primitive.

```
In[61]:= FieldLine[{x, ex, 1.1}, {y, ey, 1.1}, {t, 5}]

Out[61]= Line[{{1.10001, 1.10001}, {1.59771, 1.59771},
        {1.76136, 1.76136}, {1.86911, 1.86911}, {1.95369, 1.95369},
        {2.02761, 2.02761}, {2.09102, 2.09102}, {2.14954, 2.14954},
        {2.20166, 2.20166}, {2.24871, 2.24871}, {2.29383, 2.29383},
        {2.33521, 2.33521}, {2.37342, 2.37342}, {2.41077, 2.41077},
        {2.44556, 2.44556}, {2.4798, 2.4798}, {2.5119, 2.5119},
        {2.54211, 2.54211}, {2.5721, 2.5721}, {2.60043, 2.60043},
        {2.62866, 2.62866}, {2.65543, 2.65543}, {2.68086, 2.68086},
        {2.70632, 2.70632}, {2.73058, 2.73058}, {2.74399, 2.74399}}]
```

A collection of field lines is made.

```
In[62]:= lines =
            Table[
                FieldLine[
                    {x, ex, 1 + 0.2 Sin[i]},
                    {y, ey, 1 + 0.2 Cos[i]},{t, 50}],
                        {i,0,2Pi-Pi/16,Pi/16}];
```

These lines can now be plotted. The
AspectRatio option is set to Automatic
to get the same scale in x as y.

```
In[63]:= Show[
            Graphics[lines,
                AspectRatio -> Automatic,
                Frame -> True]]
```

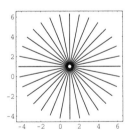

The picture seen here is that of field lines radiating from the point charge. It is interesting to compare this with the discrete vector plot or with the contour plot of the potential. In the discrete vector plot the magnitude of the field is shown by the size of the arrows. In the field line plot the magnitude of the field is shown by how closely the lines are packed together.

This picture shows a single charge. A more complex type of field results when a second charge of equal negative charge is positioned close by. This arrangment of charges is called a dipole.

These field components represent the
negative end of the dipole.

```
In[64]:= {enx, eny} =
            {D[potential[{-1,1}], x],
            D[potential[{-1,1}], y]};
```

Now an error message is generated. This is because the trajectory is very close to the negative charge where the potential is singular.

```
In[65]:= FieldLine[{x, ex + enx, 0.9},
                   {y, ey + eny, 0.9}, {t, 5}];
NDSolve::ndsz:
    At t = 0.887086, step size is effectively zero; singularity
      suspected.
```

The field line can be plotted.

```
In[66]:= Show[Graphics[%], Frame -> True]
```

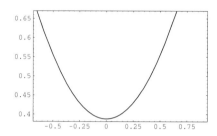

The error message can be turned off since it appears when the solution has already been constructed.

```
In[67]:= Off[NDSolve::ndsz];
```

This generates a collection of field lines.

```
In[68]:= lines =
             Table[
               FieldLine[
                 {x, ex + enx, 1 + 0.1 Sin[ti]},
                 {y, ey + eny, 1 + 0.1 Cos[ti]}, {t, 9}],
               {ti,0,2Pi-Pi/16,Pi/16}];
```

The plot is close to the typical appearance of the field around a dipole.

```
In[69]:= Show[
             Graphics[lines,
               AspectRatio -> Automatic, Frame -> True]]
```

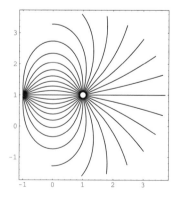

There are several problems with this picture of the field lines around a dipole. The main problem is that certain lines leave the positive charge but do not arrive at the other charge. In this case equivalent lines should be calculated starting at the negative charge. In addition there is no sense of direction in the picture. The trajectories actually depict movement but it is hard to tell in which direction.

The picture will be improved by looking at the last point of each line when it is calculated. If the x value has crossed the y axis a new line will be started at this point, which should reach the negative charge. If the line has not crossed the y axis then a line should be started from the negative charge. When this is done arrows will be added to the lines.

DipoleFieldLine calculates field lines around a dipole.

```
In[70]:= DipoleFieldLine[{x_, ex_, x0_},
                          {y_, ey_, y0_}, {t_, t1_}] :=
        Module[{line, xl, yl, test},
          line = FieldLine[{x, ex,x0}, {y, ey,y0}, {t,t1}] ;
          {xl, yl} = Part[line, 1, -1] ;
          If[xl > 0,
              {line,
               Map[Reverse,
                     FieldLine[{x,-ex,-x0},{y,-ey,y0},{t,t1}]]},
              test = Abs[xl+x0]/(Abs[xl]+Abs[x0]) +
                      Abs[yl-1]/(Abs[yl]+Abs[1]) ;
              If[xl < -x0 || test < 0.01,
                  line,
                  Line[
                    Join[First[line],
                          First[
                            FieldLine[{x,ex,xl},
                                       {y,ey,yl},{t,t1}]]]]]
          ]]]
```

When a field line leaves one charge but does not approach the other, a second line will be calculated.

```
In[71]:= DipoleFieldLine[{x, ex + enx, 1.1},
                          {y, ey + eny, 1.1}, {t, 5}];
```

```
In[72]:= Show[Graphics[%,
                AspectRatio -> Automatic,
                Frame -> True]]
```

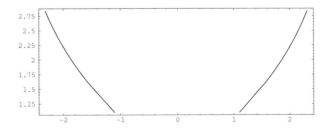

A collection of field lines is generated.

```
In[73]:= lines =
            Table[
              DipoleFieldLine[
                {x, ex + enx, N[1 + 0.1 Sin[ti]]},
                {y, ey + eny, N[1 + 0.1 Cos[ti]]}, {t, 5}],
                {ti,0.,2Pi-Pi/16,Pi/16}];
In[74]:= Show[
            Graphics[lines,
                AspectRatio -> Automatic, Frame -> True]]
```

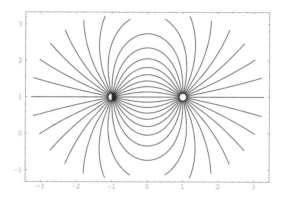

As a final effect arrows should be added to the picture. This can be done with the Graphics`Arrow` package.

The arrow package must be loaded.

```
In[75]:= Needs["Graphics`Arrow`"]
```

The AddArrow function travels down a line primitive and adds an arrow every d units. A maximum of num arrows will be drawn.

```
In[76]:= AddArrow[Line[pts_], d_, num_:5] :=
            Module[{arrow = {}, n = 0},
              Fold[
                If[First[#1] >= d && n < num,
                  n++;
                  AppendTo[arrow,
                          Arrow[Last[#1], #2,
                                HeadScaling -> Absolute,
                                HeadCenter -> 0.5,
                                HeadLength -> 4]];
                  {0, #2},
                  {First[#1] +
                    Sqrt[Apply[Plus, (Last[#1]-#2)^2]], #2}]&,
                  {0, First[pts]}, Rest[pts]] ;
              arrow]
```

The function is applied to the first line primitive.

```
In[77]:= AddArrow[First[lines], 1];
```

The line is plotted with the arrows. The AspectRatio option is set to give the same scale in x and y.

```
In[78]:= Show[
            Graphics[{%, First[lines]},
                AspectRatio -> Automatic]]
```

The AddArrow will be mapped to the list of lines. The list is flattened to make sure that every element is a line primitive.

```
In[79]:= lines = Flatten[lines];
```

Arrows are added to all the field lines.

```
In[80]:= arrows = Map[AddArrow[#, 1]&, lines];
```

The final picture is generated. The lines are thinned out and a disk added around the negative charge to make the picture symmetric.

```
In[81]:= Show[
            Graphics[
                {Thickness[0.001], arrows, lines},
                AspectRatio -> Automatic,
                Epilog -> {GrayLevel[1], Disk[{-1,1}, 0.1]},
                Frame -> True]]
```

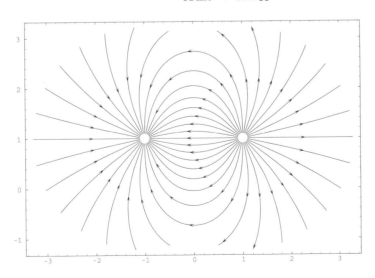

▸ *Field Lines from Numeric Data*

When the field is expressed as a mathematical function the function `FieldLine` will return a field line. If the field is available as numeric vector data this must be used to construct a mathematical function. This can be done either by fitting or interpolation and was discussed in Chapter 18 page 462. The examples here will all use interpolation techniques. As was discussed in Chapter 18 the way that this is done depends upon whether or not the data are regular or irregular.

Regular Data

When the data are regular, that is, available on a rectangular grid, it is quite straightforward to use the *Mathematica* function `Interpolation` to generate a mathematical function that will interpolate the data.

A regular vector data set to be used as an example.

```
In[82]:= data =
            Flatten[
              Table[{{x, y}, {Sin[x y], Cos[x y]}},
                {x, 0.,Pi,Pi/19}, {y, 0.,1.75,1.75/19}],1];
```

The vector plot of the field data is made. Each point fits in a rectangular grid in the *xy* plane.

```
In[83]:= ListPlotVectorField[data, ScaleFactor -> 0.15]
```

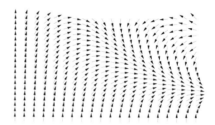

In this picture discrete samples of the field are plotted. This makes it the vector analogue of the point plotting techniques available from functions such as `ScatterPlot3D` that were discussed in the previous chapter. The picture is made up from individual samples and it is up to the observer to group them together. This technique does not need to consider issues of data ordering or resampling.

When field lines are plotted these discrete points are joined together. This is actually done by solving a differential equation with `NDSolve`. To do this the data must be turned into a mathematical function with an interpolation method. The way that this is done depends upon the ordering of the data. When the data are rectangularly arranged the `Interpolation` command can be used.

The *x* component of the field.

```
In[84]:= e1x =
            Interpolation[
              Map[Part[Flatten[#], {1,2,3}]&, data]] ;
```

The *y* component of the field.

```
In[85]:= e1y =
            Interpolation[
              Map[Part[Flatten[#], {1,2,4}]&, data]] ;
```

The interpolated and original values are compared. The two are close.

```
In[86]:= {{e1x[1,1], e1y[1,1]}, {Sin[1.], Cos[1.]}}

Out[86]= {{0.841468, 0.5403}, {0.841471, 0.540302}}
```

Another version of FieldLine is made that works with InterpolatingFunction objects.

```
In[87]:= FieldLine[{x_, ex_InterpolatingFunction, x0_},
                   {y_, ey_InterpolatingFunction, y0_},
                   {t_, t1_}] :=
         Module[{exf, eyf, x1, y1, sol, t2},
            exf[x1_, y1_] := ex[x1, y1] ;
            eyf[x1_, y1_] := ey[x1, y1] ;
            sol =
              NDSolve[
                 {x'[t] == exf[x[t],y[t]],
                  y'[t] == eyf[x[t],y[t]],
                  x[0] == x0, y[0] == y0
                 }, {x[t], y[t]}, {t,0,t1}] ;
            sol = {x[t], y[t]} /. First[sol] ;
            If[VectorQ[sol /. t -> 0, NumberQ],
               t2 = Part[sol, 1, 0, 1, 2] ;
               sol =
                     ParametricPlot[Evaluate[sol], {t,0,t2},
                        DisplayFunction -> Identity] ;
               First[Cases[sol, Line[_], Infinity]],
               Line[{{x0, y0}}]]
            ]
```

Error messages arise because eventually the field line leaves the domain of the interpolating function.

```
In[88]:= FieldLine[{x, e1x, 0.2}, {y, e1y, 0.}, {t, 4.36}];

InterpolatingFunction::dmwarn:
    Warning: Input value lies outside domain of the interpolating
      function.

InterpolatingFunction::dmwarn:
    Warning: Input value lies outside domain of the interpolating
      function.

InterpolatingFunction::dmwarn:
    Warning: Input value lies outside domain of the interpolating
      function.

General::stop:
    Further output of InterpolatingFunction::dmwarn
      will be suppressed during this calculation.
```

The field line can be plotted.

```
In[89]:= Show[
            Graphics[%,
               AspectRatio -> Automatic]]
```

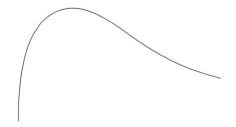

Since the messages are produced when the important parts of the line have been calculated they can be turned off.

```
In[90]:= (Off[InterpolatingFunction::dmwarn];
          Off[InterpolatingFunction::dmval];
          Off[NDSolve::ndnum];)
```

Now a collection of field lines can be made.

```
In[91]:= lines =
          Table[
            FieldLine[{x, e1x, i}, {y, e1y, 0.}, {t, 4}],
            {i, 0,Pi,0.25}];
```

These lines all started at points along the *x* axis.

```
In[92]:= Show[
          Graphics[lines,
            AspectRatio -> Automatic]]
```

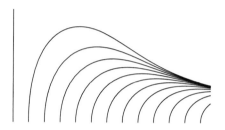

Arrows are generated for the field lines. Since the lines come sharply together only one arrow on each line will be drawn.

```
In[93]:= arrows =
          Map[AddArrow[#, 1, 1]&, lines];
```

This is the final picture. It is interesting to compare this with the discrete vector plot.

```
In[94]:= Show[
          Graphics[
            {Thickness[0.001], arrows, lines},
            AspectRatio -> Automatic,
            Frame -> True]]
```

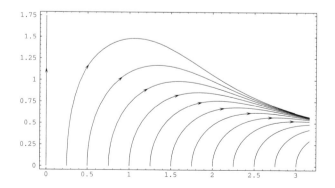

The key to these plots was the use of interpolation to generate a mathematical function representing the data that would work inside NDSolve. This function was obtained with the command Interpolation and for this to work the data had to be arranged on a rectangular grid.

The rectangular arrangement of the data in the *xy* plane can be seen in this plot.

```
In[95]:= Show[
            Graphics[Map[Point[First[#]]&, data]],
            AspectRatio -> Automatic]
```

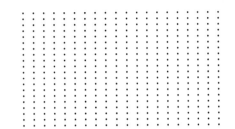

Irregular Data

When the data are not rectangularly arranged the *Mathematica* command Interpolation cannot be used and a triangular interpolation technique must be used instead. This was used in Chapter 18 page 480 for three-dimensional visualization. The TriangularInterpolate command is defined in the package ExtendGraphics`TriangularInterpolate`. At the present the triangular interpolation is too slow for a collection of field lines to be calculated in a reasonable time.

▷ *Three-Dimensional Field Lines*

Three-dimensional field lines can be generated with similar techniques to those used for two-dimensional field lines.

```
In[96]:= Needs["Graphics`PlotField3D`"]
```

The three-dimensional vector field plot.

```
In[97]:= PlotVectorField3D[
            {y, -x, 0.1}, {x,-1,1},{y,-1,1},{z,1,4}]
```

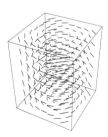

The three-dimensional version is
closely related to the two-dimensional
counterparts.

```
In[98]:= FieldLine3D[{x_, ex_, x0_}, {y_, ey_, y0_},
                     {z_, ez_, z0_}, {t_, t1_}] :=
         Module[{exf, eyf, ezf, sol, t2},
           {exf, eyf, ezf} = {ex, ey, ez} /.
                          {x -> x[t], y -> y[t], z -> z[t]} ;
           sol =
             NDSolve[
               {x'[t] == exf, y'[t] == eyf, z'[t] == ezf,
                x[0] == x0, y[0] == y0, z[0] == z0
               }, {x[t], y[t], z[t]}, {t,0,t1}] ;
           sol = {x[t], y[t], z[t]} /. First[sol] ;
           If[VectorQ[sol /. t -> 0, NumberQ],
             t2 = Part[sol, 1, 0, 1, 2] ;
             sol =
                 ParametricPlot3D[Evaluate[sol], {t,0,t2},
                     DisplayFunction -> Identity] ;
             Cases[sol, Line[_], Infinity],
               Line[{{x0, y0, z0}}]]
         ]
```

A field line can be generated for the
field shown above. If error messages
are generated they should be switched
off as described in the section on
two-dimensional field lines.

```
In[99]:= FieldLine3D[{x, y, 0.1}, {y, -x, 0.1},
                     {z, 0.1, 1}, {t,5}];
```

The field line can be plotted.

```
In[100]:= Show[Graphics3D[%], Axes -> True]
```

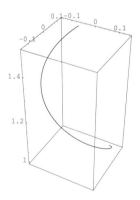

A collection of field lines can be generated. Each is given a different color to assist distinguishing between them.

```
In[101]:= lines =
             Table[
               {Hue[i/(2Pi)],
                FieldLine3D[{x, y, 0.1 Sin[i]},
                            {y, -x, 0.1 Cos[i]},
                            {z, 0.1, 1}, {t,5}]},
               {i,0,2Pi-Pi/2,Pi/2}];
```

It is hard to separate the different lines since they lie on top of each other. Plotting them with different colors helps to distinuish them.

```
In[102]:= Show[Graphics3D[lines], Axes -> True]
```

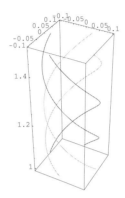

▷ *The FieldLine Package*

The routines that calculate field lines are provided in the package `ExtendGraphics`FieldLines``. A summary and some examples of using this package will now be given.

`FieldLine[{x,E_x,x_0}, {y,E_y,y_0},{t,t_{len}}]`	
	calculate the field line from $\{E_x, E_y\}$ starting at $\{x_0, y_0\}$
`FieldLine3D[{x,E_x,x_0}, {y,E_y,y_0}, {z,E_z,z_0},{t,t_{len}}]`	
	calculate the field line from $\{E_x, E_y, E_z\}$ starting at $\{x_0, y_0, z_0\}$
`AddArrow[line, dist]`	generate arrows every *dist* down the line *line*

Functions in `ExtendGraphics`FieldLines``.

The package is loaded.

```
In[103]:= Needs["ExtendGraphics`FieldLines`"]
```

The vector plotting package is loaded.

```
In[104]:= Needs["Graphics`PlotField`"]
```

The $1/r$ potential can generate some interesting pictures.

```
In[105]:= potential[{x1_, y1_}]  =
              1/Sqrt[(x1-x)^2 + (y1-y)^2]
```

$$Out[105]= \frac{1}{Sqrt[(-x + x1)^2 + (-y + y1)^2]}$$

Here a triangular arrangement of charges is specified.

```
In[106]:= tri =
              Sum[potential[{Sin[t], Cos[t]}],
                 {t,0,2Pi-2Pi/3,2Pi/3}]
```

$$Out[106]= \frac{1}{Sqrt[(\frac{-Sqrt[3]}{2} - x)^2 + (-(-\frac{1}{2}) - y)^2]} +$$

$$\frac{1}{Sqrt[(\frac{Sqrt[3]}{2} - x)^2 + (-(-\frac{1}{2}) - y)^2]} + \frac{1}{Sqrt[x^2 + (1 - y)^2]}$$

The discrete vector plot shows the three charges. A more interesting picture arises from plotting field lines.

```
In[107]:= PlotGradientField[tri, {x, -2,2}, {y, -2,2},
                            ScaleFactor -> 8,
                            MaxArrowLength -> 3,
                            PlotPoints -> 11]
```

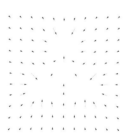

The field components are calculated. These are for negative charges so that the positively charged massless particle travels toward them.

```
In[108]:= {ex, ey} = Simplify[N[{D[tri, x], D[tri, y]}]];
```

A group of lines on the outside of the triangle is made.

```
In[109]:= lines1 =
              Table[FieldLine[{x, ex, 2 Sin[t]},
                              {y,ey,2 Cos[t]}, {s, 5}],
                              {t,0,2. Pi-Pi/24,Pi/24.}];
```

Arrows are generated to be placed on the lines.

```
In[110]:= arrows = Map[AddArrow[#, 0.5, 1]&, lines1];
```

The picture is plotted. The three charges act as attractors for the field lines.

```
In[111]:= Show[
              Graphics[{Thickness[0.001],arrows, lines1},
                  Frame -> True, AspectRatio -> Automatic]]
```

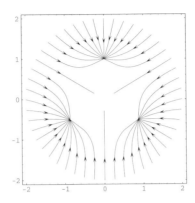

The picture here shows that lines that start on the boundary travel in to reach one of the charges. There are three lines that are equally spaced between pairs of charges that make a straight trajectory toward the center. This picture shows how the field behaves when it is outside the group of charges but it does not show the behavior inside the charges. A different picture can provide this information.

A different group of lines are started in the center of the picture.

```
In[112]:= lines2 =
              Table[FieldLine[{x, ex, 0.2 Sin[t]},
                  {y,ey,0.2 Cos[t]}, {s, 5}],
                  {t,0,2. Pi-Pi/18,Pi/18. }];
```

The inner set of lines are plotted. These travel out to reach the charges.

```
In[113]:= Show[
              Graphics[{Thickness[0.001],lines2},
                  Frame -> True, AspectRatio -> Automatic]]
```

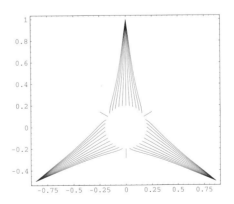

Both sets of lines can be included in the same picture.

```
In[114]:= Show[Graphics[{Thickness[0.001],lines1, lines2},
                  Frame -> True, AspectRatio -> Automatic]]
```

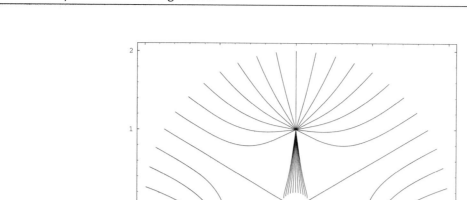

Showing both sets of lines in the same picture is visually attractive but somewhat misleading since the scale of the two sets is different. The scale is determined by the initial density of field lines, which is different in the two pictures. One way to demonstrate that the lines are different would be to use a shading technique.

Finally a demonstration will given of combining field lines with a contour plot. The original potential can be plotted with a contour plot and this can be compared with the field line plots. The field lines will be perpendicular to the contours.

The contour plot of the potential.

```
In[115]:= cont = ContourPlot[ tri,
              {x,-2,2},{y,-2,2},
              ContourShading -> False,
              PlotPoints -> 50]
```

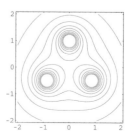

The contour plot and the field line plot are combined. The field lines are perpendicular to the contours.

In[116]:= **Show[cont, Graphics[lines1], Frame -> True]**

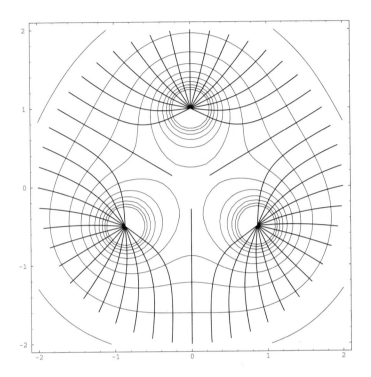

19.5 Summary

This chapter has demonstrated how numeric vector data can be visualized. The first sections looked at the *Mathematica* functions that plotted arrows for both two- and three-dimensional vector data. This is a simple and often intuitive way to understand this data. The last section of the chapter looked at a more complicated visualization method. This involved calculating actual field lines and gave a more global picture of the data.

PART IV
A Reference to Graphics in Mathematica

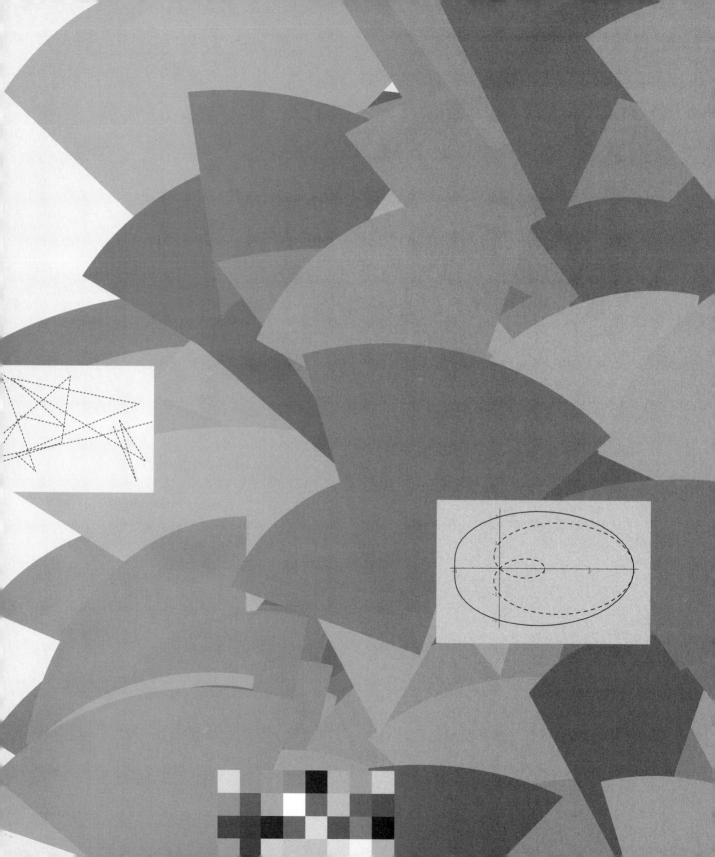

Chapter 20
Graphics Reference

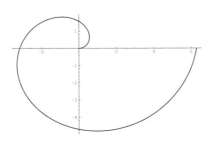

This chapter is intended to be a reference to Graphics objects and is intended to give a description of all the functionality, as well as examples. It is not intended to provide instruction in how Graphics objects should be used. This is provided by Parts I, II, and III of *Mathematica Graphics*.

20.1 Basic Structure

Graphics[*prims*, *opt₁*, *opt₂*, ...]   Graphics object with primitives and options

The structure of Graphics objects.

Graphics objects are provided to represent two-dimensional graphical structures. The basic structure is that the first argument holds two-dimensional graphics primitives. This is followed by zero or more arguments that must be options or lists of options. These are some examples of Graphics objects. Any one of these could be displayed with a call to Show.

A Graphics object with one primitive and no options.

```
In[1]:= Graphics[Line[{{0,0}, {1,1}}]]
Out[1]= -Graphics-
```

A Graphics object with a list of two primitives and one option.

```
In[2]:= Graphics[
            {Line[{{0,0}, {1,1}}],Point[{2,2}]},
            Axes -> True]
Out[2]= -Graphics-
```

A Graphics object with a style directive and a primitive followed by two options.

```
In[3]:= Graphics[
            {Dashing[{0.01}], Line[{{0,0}, {1,1}}]},
            Axes -> True, AxesLabel -> "Plot"]
Out[3]= -Graphics-
```

A Graphics object with a style directive and a primitive followed by a list containing two options.

```
In[4]:= Graphics[
            {Dashing[{0.01}], Line[{{0,0}, {1,1}}]},
            {Axes -> True, AxesLabel -> "Plot"}]
Out[4]= -Graphics-
```

Any of these Graphics objects can be displayed with a call to Show.

```
In[5]:= Show[%]
```

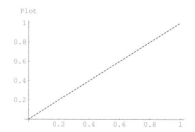

A `Graphics` object must consist of at least one argument if it is to be displayed. The first argument must contain the primitives; if there is more than one primitive then they must be collected in a list. The subsequent arguments must be options or lists of options.

Graphics objects can be constructed directly, as in these examples, or by using one of the other commands, such as `Plot`. There are situations for which either method is appropriate.

20.2 Primitives

There are many primitives that can be used inside `Graphics` objects. This section describes the basic operation and features of each primitive. Examples are given as often as possible. Chapter 8 also discusses two-dimensional graphics primitives. It shows how they can be generated with the tools that are provided by the rest of *Mathematica*.

▷ *Point, Line, and Polygon*

`Point[p]`	a point drawn at p
`Line[{`p_1`, `p_2`, `p_3`, ... }]`	a line through $p_1, p_2, p_3, \ldots$
`Polygon[{`p_1`, `p_2`, `p_3`, ... }]`	a polygon with vertices $p_1, p_2, p_3, \ldots$

`Point`, `Line`, and `Polygon` primitives.

A `Point` primitive can be constructed.

```
In[6]:= Point[{5,5}]
Out[6]= Point[{5, 5}]

In[7]:= Show[Graphics[{PointSize[0.02], %}]]
```

The points for a `Line` primitive can be built with a `Table` command.

```
In[8]:= Line[Table[{x,Sin[x]^2/x}, {x,-5,5,.1}]];
```

An alternative way to make this picture would be with Plot.

In[9]:= **Show[Graphics[%]]**

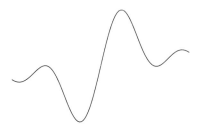

A random walk can be constructed with FoldList.

In[10]:= **Line[FoldList[Plus, {0,0},**
            Table[Random[ ]-0.5, {100},{2}]]];

In[11]:= **Show[Graphics[%]]**

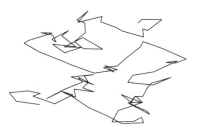

A Polygon primitive is similar to a Line primitive except that endpoints are joined and the interior is filled in.

In[12]:= **Polygon[Table[{Sin[t], Cos[t]}, {t,0,2Pi-Pi/3,Pi/3}]];**

In[13]:= **Show[Graphics[%]]**

▶ *Text*

The Text primitive allows text to be placed in pictures. A variety of controls allow the alignment, orientation, and font to be set.

Text[*expr*, *pt*]	text form of *expr* centered at *pt*
Text[*expr*, *pt*,{x_{off}, y_{off}}]	text form of *expr* with offset {x_{off}, y_{off}}
Text[*expr*, *pt*, {x_{off}, y_{off}},{x_{vec}, y_{vec}}]	text form of *expr* rotated along vector {x_{vec}, y_{vec}}
Text[FontForm[*expr*, {*font*, *size*}], *pt*]	
	text form of *expr* in font {*font*, *size*}

Arguments of the Text primitive.

A basic text label.

In[14]:= **Text["This is some text", {2,2}]**

Out[14]= Text[This is some text, {2, 2}]

The Frame is displayed to demonstrate that this is a Graphics object.

In[15]:= **Show[Graphics[%],Frame -> True]**

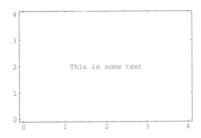

Alignment

The Text primitive contains a coordinate that specifies where the text is to appear. The entire text object is then aligned with this point. By default this alignment is done so that the middle of the bounding box of the text coincides with this anchor point.

In[16]:= **{Text["This is some text", {2,2}],**
          Line[{{1,2},{3,2}}],Line[{{2,1},{2,3}}]}

Out[16]= {Text[This is some text, {2, 2}],
    Line[{{1, 2}, {3, 2}}], Line[{{2, 1}, {2, 3}}]}

The center of the bounding box of the text is at {2,2}.

In[17]:= **Show[Graphics[%]]**

The alignment of the text to the anchor position can be set with a third argument. This third argument must be a pair of numbers. A specification of {1,1} means that the upper-right corner of the bounding box should coincide with the anchor point. Alternatively {-1,-1} means that the lower-left coincides with the anchor.

```
In[18]:= {Text["This is some text", {2,2}, {1,1}],
            Line[{{1,2},{3,2}}],Line[{{2,1},{2,3}}]]}
Out[18]= {Text[This is some text, {2, 2}, {1, 1}],
         Line[{{1, 2}, {3, 2}}], Line[{{2, 1}, {2, 3}}]]}
```

The upper-right of the bounding box of the text is at {2,2}.

```
In[19]:= Show[Graphics[%]]
```

```
In[20]:= {Text["This is some text", {2,2}, {-1,-1}],
            Line[{{1,2},{3,2}}],Line[{{2,1},{2,3}}]]}
Out[20]= {Text[This is some text, {2, 2}, {-1, -1}],
         Line[{{1, 2}, {3, 2}}], Line[{{2, 1}, {2, 3}}]]}
```

The lower-left of the bounding box of the text is at {2,2}.

```
In[21]:= Show[Graphics[%]]
```

The alignment of the Text primitive is summarized in the following diagram. It shows a text bounding box with various settings for the alignment vector. Using one of these settings will place the rendering point at the indicated position. If no third argument is given the center of the bounding box appears at the anchor point. This is equivalent to an alignment specification of {0,0}.

The alignment of the Text **primitive.**

Orientation

The orientation of a Text primitive is set by specifying a fourth argument. This fourth argument must be a pair of numbers that represents the vector along which the text will be drawn.

In[22]:= **Text["This is some text", {2,2}, {0,0}, {0,1}]**

Out[22]= Text[This is some text, {2, 2}, {0, 0}, {0, 1}]

The text is drawn along the vector {0,1}.   *In[23]:=* **Show[Graphics[%]]**

This is some text

Font

The font of a Text primitive can be set with FontForm. The font specification must be a list of a string, interpreted as the font name, and a positive number, interpreted as the font size.

A font specification.   *In[24]:=* **font = {"Helvetica", 8}**

Out[24]= {Helvetica, 8}

In[25]:= **Text[FontForm["This is some text", font], {2,2}]**

Out[25]= Text[FontForm[This is some text, {Helvetica, 8}],

{2, 2}]

The text is now drawn in Helvetica font
in size 8.

In[26]:= **Show[Graphics[%]]**

This is some text

▶ *Text Primitive Options*

The Text primitive has three options. These allow the setting of a background, the font, and the type of formatting to be used. In Version 2.2 (or earlier) *Mathematica* the Text primitive did not possess these options.

Background	background shading
DefaultFont	font
FormatType	formatting style

Options of the Text primitive.

Options of the Text primitive.

In[27]:= **Options[Text]**

Out[27]= {Background -> None, DefaultFont -> Automatic,
   FormatType -> OutputForm}

Background

When a Text primitive is drawn on top of a Line primitive it is hard to read. The Background option draws a box of a particular color underneath the text so that it is not obscured by other primitives.

The text here is difficult to read due to the lines.

In[28]:= **Show[**
   Graphics[
     {Line[{{1,2},{3,2}}],Line[{{2,1},{2,3}}],
      Text["This is some text", {2,2}]}]]

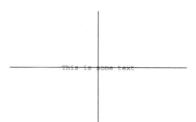

Setting the Background option to be
Automatic allows the text to be
understood more easily.

```
In[29]:= Show[
            Graphics[
                {Line[{{1,2},{3,2}}],Line[{{2,1},{2,3}}],
                Text["This is some text", {2,2},
                    Background -> Automatic]}]]
```

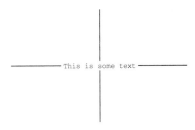

Setting the Background option to be a
color specification draws a box
underneath the text with that color.

```
In[30]:= Show[
            Graphics[
                {Line[{{1,2},{3,2}}],Line[{{2,1},{2,3}}],
                Text["This is some text", {2,2},
                    Background -> GrayLevel[0.75]]}]]
```

Background -> Automatic causes a box to be drawn underneath the text with the background color
of the graphics object. Background -> *color* causes a box shaded by *color* to be drawn underneath the text.

DefaultFont

The DefaultFont option allows the font of a text primitive to be set. This is a cleaner way to specify the
font than FontForm.

The text is drawn in Helvetica size 8.

```
In[31]:= Show[
            Graphics[
                Text["This is some text", {2,2},
                    DefaultFont -> {"Helvetica", 8}]]]
```

This is some text

FormatType

The FormatType option sets the format style for a Text primitive. This is especially useful with the typesetting capabilities which are available in *Mathematica*. This provides a considerable amount of functionality such as compact output with different fonts so that superscripts and subscripts appear in smaller fonts, greek and roman lettering can be mixed, and mathematical symbols such as radical signs and integral signs can be included in text. These typesetting capabilities were not available in *Mathematica* Version 2.2 (or earlier).

The default format type of OutputForm. This cannot display greek characters in graphics.

```
In[32]:= Show[
          Graphics[Text[Sin[\[Alpha]]^2, {2,2}]]]
```

$$Sin[00\overset{2}{3}-]$$

StandardForm is a typeset format type designed to be close to *Mathematica* syntax.

```
In[33]:= Show[
          Graphics[Text[Sin[\[Alpha]]^2, {2,2},
                   FormatType -> StandardForm]]]
```

$$Sin\,[\alpha]^2$$

TraditionalForm is a typeset format type designed to be close to traditional mathematics syntax.

```
In[34]:= Show[
          Graphics[Text[Sin[\[Alpha]]^2, {2,2},
                   FormatType -> TraditionalForm]]]
```

$$\sin^2(\alpha)$$

If a nonfixed-width font is used the layout of the text works properly.

```
In[35]:= Show[
            Graphics[Text[Sin[\[Alpha]]^2, {2,2},
                FormatType -> TraditionalForm,
                DefaultFont -> {"Helvetica", 7}]]]
```

$$\sin^2(\alpha)$$

Chapter 3 page 42 and Chapter 14 page 315 also discuss the typesetting capabilities of *Mathematica*. It provides a number of examples of how it can be utilized.

▸ *Circle and Disk*

`Circle[pt, r]`	circle centered at *pt* of radius *r*
`Disk[pt, r]`	filled circle centered at *pt* of radius *r*
`Circle[pt, {`r_x`, `r_y`}]`	ellipse centered at *pt* with radii r_x and r_x
`Disk[pt, {`r_x`, `r_y`}]`	filled ellipse centered at *pt* with radii r_x and r_x
`Circle[pt, r, {`$theta_1$`, `$theta_2$`}]`	circular arc starting at *theta₁* and ending at *theta₂* centered at *pt* of radius *r*
`Disk[pt, r, {`$theta_1$`, `$theta_2$`}]`	filled circular arc starting at *theta₁* and ending at *theta₂* centered at *pt* of radius *r*

`Circle` and `Disk` primitives.

A `Circle` primitive.

```
In[36]:= circle = Circle[{1,1}, 0.5]
Out[36]= Circle[{1, 1}, 0.5]
```

When the picture is displayed it is an ellipse due to the setting of the `AspectRatio` option.

```
In[37]:= Show[Graphics[circle]]
```

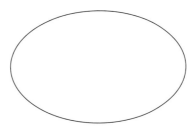

Setting the AspectRatio to Automatic uses the same scale in *x* and *y* and a circle results.

In[38]:= **Show[Graphics[circle], AspectRatio -> Automatic]**

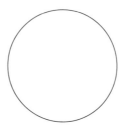

An ellipse.

In[39]:= **Show[**
        Graphics[
            Circle[{1,1}, {0.25, 0.5}]],
            AspectRatio -> Automatic]

A filled circle.

In[40]:= **Show[**
        Graphics[
            Disk[{1,1}, 0.5]],
            AspectRatio -> Automatic]

A filled ellipse.

```
In[41]:= Show[
           Graphics[
             Disk[{1,1}, {0.25, 0.5}]],
           AspectRatio -> Automatic]
```

A circular arc.

```
In[42]:= Show[
           Graphics[
             Circle[{1,1}, 0.5, {Pi/4,3Pi/4}]],
           AspectRatio -> Automatic]
```

A filled circular arc.

```
In[43]:= Show[
           Graphics[
             Disk[{1,1}, 0.5, {Pi/4,3Pi/4}]],
           AspectRatio -> Automatic]
```

Scaled

The coordinate specification `Scaled` can be used to specify the position of the `Circle` or `Disk` primitive. It can also be used to specify the radius.

<table>
<tr>
<td>A circle with a radius scaled to 5% of the width of the picture.</td>
<td>

```
In[44]:= Show[
            Graphics[
               Circle[{0.5,0.5}, Scaled[{0.05, 0.05}]]],
            AspectRatio -> Automatic]
```

</td>
</tr>
</table>

Offset

In *Mathematica* the coordinate specification `Offset` can be used to specify the position of the `Circle` or `Disk` primitive. It can also be used to specify the radius. This allows the construction of a circle with a radius specified in points. Points were defined in Chapter 8 page 127 to be a unit of length with 72 points to the inch. `Offset` was not available in *Mathematica* Version 2.2 (or earlier).

<table>
<tr>
<td>A circle with a radius of 5 points.</td>
<td>

```
In[45]:= Show[
            Graphics[
               Circle[{1,1}, Offset[{5, 5}, {0,0}]]],
            AspectRatio -> Automatic]
```

</td>
</tr>
</table>

▶ *Raster and RasterArray*

The primitives `Raster` and `RasterArray` represent raster or bitmap images. `Raster` takes an array of numbers, which by default it will represent as a gray bitmap. `RasterArray` takes an array of colors, which it will display as a color bitmap.

There are two ways that color images can be represented with Graphics primitives. One way is with an array of the color specifications inside RasterArray. The other is with an array of numbers inside Raster with a suitable ColorFunction.

Raster[{{z_{11}, z_{12}, ... }, {z_{21}, z_{22}, ... }, ... }]

                  a raster image with values determined by z_{11}, ...

Raster[*array*, {{x_{min}, y_{min}},{x_{max}, y_{max}}}]

                  a raster image extending from {x_{min}, y_{min}} to {x_{max}, y_{max}}

Raster[*array*, *coords*, {z_{min}, z_{max}}]   a raster image with values scaled to run from z_{min} to z_{max}

Raster[*array*, ColorFunction -> *fun*]   a raster image with *fun* applied to values

---

Uses of the Raster primitive.

In[46]:= **d = Table[Random[ ], {5}, {8}];**

A basic use of the Raster primitive.   *In[47]:=* **Show[Graphics[Raster[d]]]**

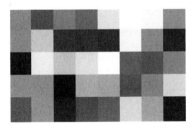

Specification of the rectangle into which the Raster is drawn.   *In[48]:=* **Show[**
                Graphics[Raster[d, {{-1,-1},{1,1}}], Frame -> True]]

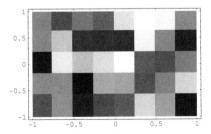

The image is lightened by making the z values run from -1 to 1.

$In[49]:=$ **Show[Graphics[Raster[d, {{-1,-1},{1,1}}, {-1,1}]]]**

The use of a `ColorFunction` can change the contrast in the data in a non-linear way. The `ColorFunction` could have made a color image instead.

$In[50]:=$ **Show[**
    Graphics[
      Raster[d,
        ColorFunction -> (GrayLevel[Sqrt[#]]&)]]]

`RasterArray[{{`col_{11}`, `col_{12}`, ... }, {`col_{21}`, `col_{22}`, ... }, ... }]`
                              a raster image with values $col_{11}, \ldots$
`RasterArray[`*array*`, {{`x_{min}`, `y_{min}`},{`x_{max}`, `y_{max}`}}]`
                              a raster image extending from $\{x_{min}, y_{min}\}$ to $\{x_{max}, y_{max}\}$

Uses of the `RasterArray` primitive.

$In[51]:=$ **cols = Table[Hue[Random[ ]], {5}, {8}];**

A basic use of the `RasterArray` primitive.

`In[52]:= Show[Graphics[RasterArray[cols]]]`

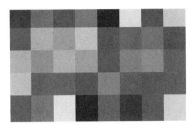

Specification of the rectangle into which the `RasterArray` is drawn.

```
In[53]:= Show[
          Graphics[
            RasterArray[cols, {{-1,-1},{1,1}}], Frame -> True]]
```

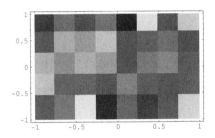

There is no three-argument form of the `RasterArray` primitive.

▶ *Rectangle*

The `Rectangle` graphics primitive draws a filled rectangular region parallel to the axes. Normally the fill is carried out in the current drawing color, however, if a graphics object is given as third argument to `Rectangle` this is used as the fill.

`Rectangle[{`x_{min}`, `y_{min}`}, {`x_{max}`, `y_{max}`}]`	rectangle from {x_{min}, y_{min}}, to {x_{max}, y_{max}} filled with the current drawing color
`Rectangle[{`x_{min}`, `y_{min}`}, {`x_{max}`, `y_{max}`}, `*obj*`]`	rectangle from {x_{min}, y_{min}}, to {x_{max}, y_{max}} filled with the graphics object *obj*

The `Rectangle` primitive.

The rectangle is filled in the current drawing color.

In[54]:= **Show[Graphics[Rectangle[{-1,1}, {4,6}]]]**

A Graphics object is constructed.

In[55]:= **p1 =**
      Plot[Sin[x], {x,0,Pi}, DisplayFunction -> Identity]

Out[55]= -Graphics-

A Graphics3D object is constructed.

In[56]:= **p2 =**
      Plot3D[Sin[x y], {x,0,Pi}, {y,0,Pi},
          DisplayFunction -> Identity]

Out[56]= -SurfaceGraphics-

Two rectangles are drawn, one filled with a Graphics object, the other with a Graphics3D object.

In[57]:= **Show[**
    Graphics[
      {Rectangle[{-1,-1}, {0,1}, p1],
      Rectangle[{0, -1}, {1,1}, p2]}]]

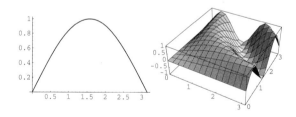

This last example makes a point about how the options of graphics objects in Rectangle primitives are handled. Both p1 and p2 had their DisplayFunction option set to Identity. However, this had no effect on the Graphics object in which they were contained. This outer Graphics object had its own DisplayFunction option that used the default value, $DisplayFunction. In general, option settings inside Rectangle primitives do not affect the outer Graphics object.

▶ *PostScript*

The PostScript primitive allows custom PostScript code to be included in the output from *Mathematica*. In general there are very few areas where it is of use, an exception to this is the Mandelbrot example in Chapter 13 page 287. It is preferable if *Mathematica* graphics provide all the facilities necessary to construct pictures without having to use PostScript at all. Using the PostScript primitive makes graphics which are not portable to other rendering methods and requires careful work to ensure that the PostScript is scaled properly.

20.3 Style Directives

In *Mathematica* graphics style directives cause a change in the style in which primitives are rendered. They change the size of points and lines, make lines dashed, and alter the color.

▶ *Size Directives*

PointSize[s]	size for points
AbsolutePointSize[s]	absolute size for points
Thickness[t]	thickness for lines
AbsoluteThickness[t]	absolute thickness for lines
Dashing[{d}]	dashing for lines
AbsoluteDashing[{d}]	absolute dashing for lines

Size style directives.

▶ *PointSize and AbsolutePointSize*

The size of Point primitives can be set by PointSize and AbsolutePointSize. They are unaffected by Thickness and Dashing.

A point with a width 5% of the width of the picture.

```
In[58]:= Show[
            Graphics[{PointSize[0.05], Point[{1,1}]}]]
```

●

A point with a 10-point width.

In[59]:= **Show[**
    Graphics[{AbsolutePointSize[10], Point[{1,1}]}]]

▶ *Thickness and AbsoluteThickness*

The thickness of primitives that involve lines, such as Line and Circle, can be altered with Thickness and AbsoluteThickness.

A line with a thickness 5% of the width of the picture.

In[60]:= **Show[**
    Graphics[{Thickness[0.05], Line[{{1,1}, {2,2}}]}],
    PlotRange -> {{0,3},{0,3}}]

A circle drawn with a line 5 points wide.

In[61]:= **Show[**
    Graphics[{AbsoluteThickness[5], Circle[{1,1}, 1]}]]

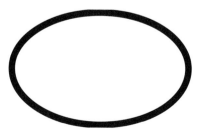

    In addition to setting the thickness of lines in primitives Thickness and AbsoluteThickness can also be used as a style specification for options such as AxesStyle which involve the drawing of lines.

▶ *Dashing and AbsoluteDashing*

Primitives which involve lines such as Line and Circle can be drawn in a dashed mode with Dashing
and AbsoluteDashing.

A line with a dashing 5% of the width of
the picture.

```
In[62]:= Show[
            Graphics[{Dashing[{0.05}], Line[{{1,1}, {2,2}}]}]]
```

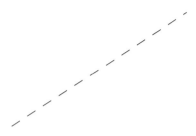

A more complex dashing pattern, on for
5% of the width and then off for 2%.

```
In[63]:= Show[
            Graphics[{Dashing[{0.05, 0.02}],
                      Line[{{1,1}, {2,2}}]}]]
```

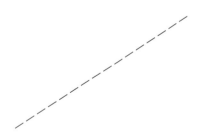

A circle drawn with a dashed line. Each
dash is 3 points long.

```
In[64]:= Show[
            Graphics[{AbsoluteDashing[{3}], Circle[{1,1}, 1]}]]
```

In addition to dashing the lines in primitives, Dashing and AbsoluteDashing can also be used as a
style specification for options such as AxesStyle.

▶ *Color Directives*

GrayLevel[*g*]	gray
RGBColor[*r*, *g*, *b*]	*red, green, blue* color
Hue[*h*]	*hue* color
Hue[*h*, *s*, *b*]	*hue, saturation, brightness* color
CMYKColor[*c*, *m*, *y*, *k*]	*cyan, magenta, yellow, black* color

Color directives.

▶ *GrayLevel*

GrayLevel is a color specification that sets the current drawing color to be gray. An argument of 0 generates black, while 1 is white.

A gray rectangle.   *In[65]:=* **Show[**
                    Graphics[{GrayLevel[0.5], Rectangle[{1,1}, {2,2}]}]]

▶ *RGBColor*

RGBColor is a color specification that sets the current drawing color to be a color obtained by mixing the specified amounts of red, green, and blue.

A red rectangle. This example requires a   *In[66]:=* **Show[**
color output device to appear in color.   **Graphics[{RGBColor[1,0,0], Rectangle[{1,1}, {2,2}]}]]**

▶ *Hue*

Hue is a color specification that sets the current drawing color to a specific hue. The one argument of Hue is circular in nature since Hue[0] is the same color as Hue[1].

A circle demonstrates the characteristic nature of Hue. This example requires a color output device to appear in color.

```
In[67]:= Show[
            Graphics[
              Table[
                {Hue[t/(2Pi-Pi/10)],
                  Polygon[{{0,0}, {Sin[t], Cos[t]},
                            {Sin[t+Pi/10], Cos[t+Pi/10]}}]},
                {t,0,2Pi-Pi/10,Pi/10}]],
            AspectRatio -> Automatic]
```

The three-argument version of Hue specifies the color by allowing control of the saturation and brightness as well as the hue.

In this strip the saturation of a red color is varied. Here the unsaturated color, on the left, is white while the fully saturated color, on the right, is bright red.

```
In[68]:= Show[
            Graphics[
              {Table[
                {Hue[0, i/39, 1],
                  Rectangle[{i, 0}, {i+1, 8}]},
                {i, 0, 39}],
              Line[{{0,0},{40,0},{40,8},{0,8},{0,0}}]},
              AspectRatio -> Automatic]]
```

The brightness of a fully saturated color is varied here. The least bright, on the left, is black while the brightest, on the right, is green.

```
In[69]:= Show[
            Graphics[
              {Table[
                {Hue[1/3, 1, i/39],
                  Rectangle[{i, 0}, {i+1, 8}]},
                {i, 0, 39}],
              Line[{{0,0},{40,0},{40,8},{0,8},{0,0}}]},
              AspectRatio -> Automatic]]
```

▶ *CMYKColor*

CMYKColor is a color specification that sets the current drawing color to a color obtained by mixing the specified amounts of cyan, magenta, yellow, and black.

A magenta rectangle. This example requires a color output device to appear in color.

```
In[70]:= Show[
            Graphics[
              {CMYKColor[0,1,0,0],Rectangle[{1,1},{2,2}]}]]
```

20.4 Graphics Options

There are many options that affect the way that graphics appear. This is a list of the options of Graphics objects together with examples of their important uses.

▶ *AspectRatio*

The AspectRatio option sets the shape of the frame drawn around the picture.

```
In[71]:= Show[
            Graphics[Circle[{1,1}, 1]],
            AspectRatio -> 0.5,
            Frame -> True]
```

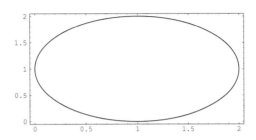

A setting of Automatic will use the same scale in *x* and *y*.

```
In[72]:= Show[
            Graphics[Circle[{1,1}, 1]],
            AspectRatio -> Automatic,
            Frame -> True]
```

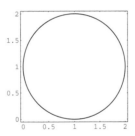

▶ *Axes*

Setting the Axes option to be False causes no axes to appear.

```
In[73]:= Show[
            Graphics[Line[{{0,0}, {1,1}}]],
            Axes -> False]
```

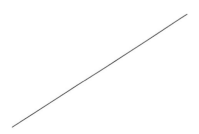

Setting the Axes option to be True draws axes.

```
In[74]:= Show[
          Graphics[Line[{{0,0}, {1,1}}]],
          Axes -> True]
```

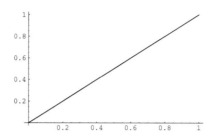

Setting the Axes option to be Automatic draws axes with no ticks when Frame axes are present and the axes do not fall near the edge of the picture.

```
In[75]:= Show[
          Graphics[Line[{{-1,-1}, {1,1}}]],
          Frame -> True,
          Axes -> Automatic]
```

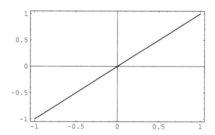

▶ *AxesLabel*

The AxesLabel option adds a label to the axes. Here only one axis is labeled.

```
In[76]:= Show[
          Graphics[Line[{{0,0}, {1,1}}]],
          Axes -> True,
          AxesLabel -> "The y-axis"]
```

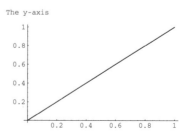

Both axes can be labeled.

```
In[77]:= Show[
            Graphics[Line[{{0,0}, {1,1}}]],
            Axes -> True,
            AxesLabel -> {"The x-axis", "The y-axis"}]
```

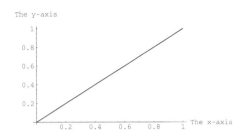

The font of the labels can be controlled with either FontForm or DefaultFont. A typeset label can be generated by using one of a typesetting format type.

A label to demonstrate typeset labels. Greek letters can be entered with the \[*char*] notation.

```
In[78]:= label =
            Sin[\[Alpha]]^2/ (\[Gamma]^2 + x^2) ;
```

StandardForm reproduces *Mathematica* notation.

```
In[79]:= Show[
            Graphics[Line[{{0,0}, {1,1}}]],
            Axes -> True,
            AxesLabel -> StandardForm[label]]
```

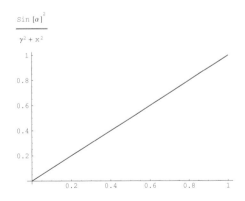

TraditionalForm reproduces traditional mathematical notation.

```
In[80]:= Show[
            Graphics[Line[{{0,0}, {1,1}}]],
            Axes -> True,
            AxesLabel -> TraditionalForm[label]]
```

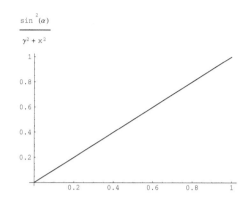

▶ *AxesOrigin*

The point at which the axes cross is set by AxesOrigin.

```
In[81]:= Show[
            Graphics[Line[{{0,0}, {1,1}}]],
            Axes -> True,
            AxesOrigin -> {0.5,0.5}]
```

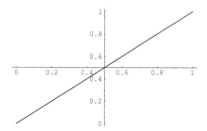

When the AxesOrigin is outside the PlotRange setting the axes do not cross.

```
In[82]:= Show[
            Graphics[Line[{{0,0}, {1,1}}]],
            Axes -> True,
            AxesOrigin -> {-0.1, -0.1}]
```

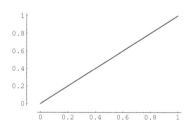

▷ *AxesStyle*

AxesStyle sets the style of the axes. Here they are drawn in white matching the background color.

```
In[83]:= Show[
            Graphics[Line[{{0,0}, {1,1}}]],
            Axes -> True,
            AxesStyle -> GrayLevel[1]]
```

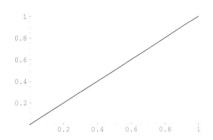

▷ *Background*

Background sets the background color for the picture. The drawing color adjusts automatically.

```
In[84]:= Show[
            Graphics[Line[{{0,0}, {1,1}}]],
            Background -> GrayLevel[0]]
```

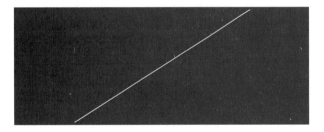

▷ *ColorOutput*

Here ColorOutput forces the output to come out in gray.

```
In[85]:= Show[
            Graphics[{RGBColor[1,0,0],Line[{{0,0}, {1,1}}]}],
            ColorOutput -> GrayLevel]
```

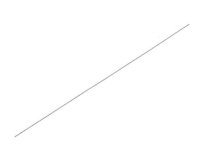

Setting ColorOutput to be a function can be used to alter the contrast of an image.

```
In[86]:= Show[
           Graphics[Raster[Table[i j/100, {i,10},{j,10}]]],
           ColorOutput -> (GrayLevel[Sqrt[First[#]]]&)]
```

▶ *DefaultColor*

DefaultColor sets the default drawing color.

```
In[87]:= Show[
           Graphics[Rectangle[{0,0}, {1,1}]],
           DefaultColor -> GrayLevel[0.5]]
```

▶ *DefaultFont*

The font used for text in *Mathematica* graphics is controlled by the DefaultFont option.

```
In[88]:= Show[
           Graphics[
             Table[Text[i, {i,i}],{i,4}]],
           Frame -> True,
           DefaultFont -> {"Helvetica", 7}]
```

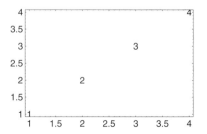

The default value of the DefaultFont option is the global variable $DefaultFont.

```
In[89]:= Options[Graphics, DefaultFont]
Out[89]= {DefaultFont :> $DefaultFont}
```

In this book $DefaultFont has a special value. On a computer screen this would be too small to be clearly visible.

```
In[90]:= $DefaultFont
Out[90]= {Courier, 5.5}
```

▶ *DisplayFunction*

The DisplayFunction option determines what is done with graphics objects when they have been assembled. Chapter 26 page 666 discusses how the DisplayFunction works.

The default value of the DisplayFunction option is the global variable $DisplayFunction.

```
In[91]:= Options[Graphics, DisplayFunction]
Out[91]= {DisplayFunction :> $DisplayFunction}
```

The value of $DisplayFunction. Display is the command that generates PostScript and is described in Chapter 26 page 666.

```
In[92]:= $DisplayFunction
Out[92]= Display[$Display, #1] &
```

Setting DisplayFunction to Identity causes no graphics output to be generated. The graphics object is returned as the result.

```
In[93]:= Show[
            Graphics[
              Line[Table[Random[ ], {20},{2}]]],
              DisplayFunction -> Identity]
Out[93]= -Graphics-
```

▶ *Epilog*

The Epilog option specifies graphics primitives to be rendered after the main graphics object.

```
In[94]:= Show[
            Graphics[Line[{{0,0}, {2,2}}]],
            Epilog -> Text["Label", {0.5,1}]]
```

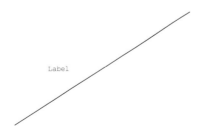

▷ *Frame*

The Frame axes are drawn around the outer edge of the PlotRange.

```
In[95]:= Show[
          Graphics[Circle[{-1,-1}, {2,1}]],
          Frame -> True]
```

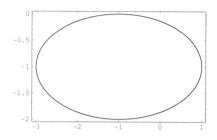

The setting of the Frame option can be some combination of True and False. The order is {*bottom*, *left*, *top*, *right*}.

```
In[96]:= Show[
          Graphics[Circle[{-1,-1}, {2,1}]],
          Frame -> {True, False, False, True}]
```

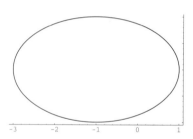

▷ *FrameLabel*

FrameLabel adds labels to Frame axes.

```
In[97]:= Show[
          Graphics[Circle[{-1,-1}, {2,1}]],
          Frame -> True,
          FrameLabel -> {"Bottom", "Left", "Top", "Right"}]
```

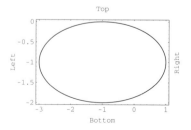

The font of the labels can be controlled with either FontForm or DefaultFont.

▶ *FrameStyle*

FrameStyle sets the style of Frame axes.

```
In[98]:= Show[
            Graphics[Circle[{-1,-1}, {2,1}]],
            Frame -> True,
            FrameStyle -> GrayLevel[1]]
```

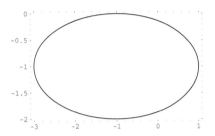

▶ *FrameTicks*

Setting FrameTicks to Automatic causes ticks to be drawn on Frame axes.

```
In[99]:= Show[
            Graphics[Circle[{-1,-1}, {2,1}]],
            Frame -> True,
            FrameTicks -> Automatic]
```

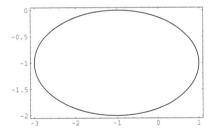

Setting FrameTicks to None causes no ticks to be drawn. This is a convenient way to surround a picture with a box.

```
In[100]:= Show[
             Graphics[Circle[{-1,-1}, {2,1}]],
             Frame -> True,
             FrameTicks -> None]
```

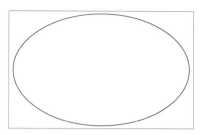

Instead of setting FrameTicks to Automatic or None it can be set in more complex ways. These include using a *Mathematica* function to allow extensive control of the positions and styles. There are examples of this in the description of the Ticks option which is similar to FrameTicks.

▶ *GridLines*

The GridLines option can be set to Automatic to draw a grid on the picture.

```
In[101]:= Show[
             Graphics[Circle[{-1,-1}, {2,1}]],
             GridLines -> Automatic]
```

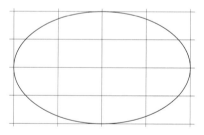

The GridLines option can be set to a list of numbers. These are used to specify the positions in *x* and *y*.

```
In[102]:= Show[
             Graphics[Circle[{-1,-1}, {2,1}]],
             GridLines -> {Range[-3,1,.5],Range[-2,0,.5]}]
```

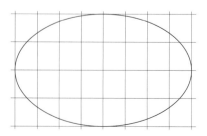

The GridLines option can be set to a list
of number and style specifications.

```
In[103]:= Show[
            Graphics[Circle[{-1,-1}, {2,1}]],
            GridLines ->
              {Table[{x,{GrayLevel[0], Dashing[{0.01}]}},
            {x,-3,1,.5}],None}]
```

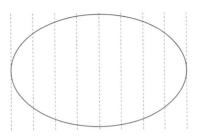

▶ *PlotLabel*

PlotLabel specifies a label to place at the
top of a picture.

```
In[104]:= Show[
            Graphics[Line[Table[Random[ ], {10}, {2}]]],
            PlotLabel -> "A Random Line"]
```

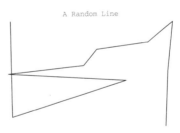

The font used for the PlotLabel can be set with FontForm. If FontForm is not used then the font will
be specified by the DefaultFont option.

▶ *PlotRange*

PlotRange of Automatic specifies that a representative sample of coordinates will be shown. The point which lies away from the line is not shown.

```
In[105]:= Show[
              Graphics[{Line[Table[Random[ ], {20}, {2}]],
                       Point[{10,10}]}],
              PlotRange -> Automatic]
```

PlotRange of All specifies that all coordinates will be included.

```
In[106]:= Show[
              Graphics[{Line[Table[Random[ ], {20}, {2}]],
                       Point[{10,10}]}],
              PlotRange -> All]
```

.

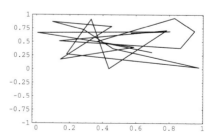

PlotRange of {*num₁* , *num₂*} specifies the range in the y direction.

```
In[107]:= Show[
              Graphics[Line[Table[Random[ ], {20}, {2}]]],
              PlotRange -> {-1,1},
              Frame -> True]
```

PlotRange of {*spec₁* , *spec₂*} specifies the range in both the *x* and the *y* directions. *spec_i* can be any valid specification.

```
In[108]:= Show[
            Graphics[Line[Table[Random[ ], {20}, {2}]]],
            PlotRange -> {{-1,1}, Automatic},
            Frame -> True]
```

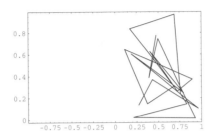

A specification of {0,Automatic} can be used.

```
In[109]:= Show[
            Graphics[Line[Table[Random[ ]+1, {20}, {2}]]],
            PlotRange -> {{0,Automatic}, {0,Automatic}},
            Frame -> True]
```

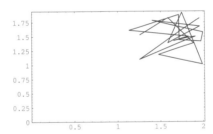

▶ *PlotRegion*

PlotRegion specifies a sub-region inside of which the picture will be displayed.

```
In[110]:= Show[
            Graphics[Line[Table[Random[ ], {20}, {2}]]],
            PlotRegion -> {{0,0.5},{0,0.5}},
            Background -> GrayLevel[0],
            Frame -> True]
```

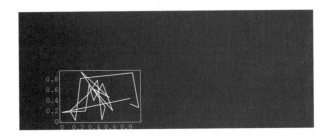

▶ *Prolog*

The Prolog option specifies graphics primitives and style directives to be rendered before the main graphics object.

```
In[111]:=  Show[
              Graphics[Line[Table[Random[ ], {20},{2}]]],
              Prolog -> Dashing[{0.01}]]
```

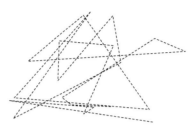

▶ *RotateLabel*

The RotateLabel option specifies whether or not a label on Frame axes is to be rotated.

```
In[112]:=  Show[
              Graphics[Raster[Table[Random[ ], {5},{5}]]],
              Frame -> True, FrameLabel -> "This is a label",
              RotateLabel -> False]
```

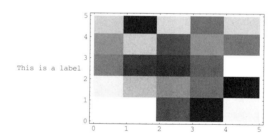

▶ *Ticks*

Ticks -> Automatic states that tick marks should be drawn on axes.

```
In[113]:=  Show[
              Graphics[
                Table[Circle[{Random[ ], Random[ ]},0.05],{10}]],
              Axes -> True, Ticks -> Automatic]
```

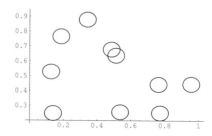

Ticks -> None states that tick marks
should not be drawn on axes.

```
In[114]:= Show[
            Graphics[
              Table[Circle[{Random[ ], Random[ ]},0.05],{10}]],
            Axes -> True, Ticks -> None]
```

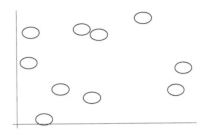

Ticks can be set to a list of positions to
be used.

```
In[115]:= Show[
            Graphics[
              Table[Circle[{Random[ ], Random[ ]},0.05],{10}]],
            Axes -> True, Ticks -> {{0.2,0.4,0.8},None}]
```

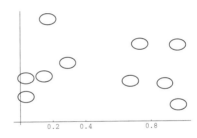

Ticks can be set to a list of positions and
labels.

```
In[116]:= Show[
            Graphics[
              Table[Circle[{Random[ ], Random[ ]},0.05],{10}]],
            Axes -> True,
            Ticks -> {{{0.2, a},{0.4,b},{0.8,c}},None}]
```

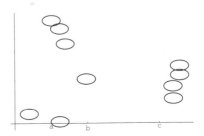

A more complicated setting for the `Ticks` option. The *x* axis tick sets the position, label, length, and style. The *y* axis tick sets the position, a null label, and length. The length of the ticks is given in a coordinate system that has {0,0} at the lower-left and {1,1} at the upper-right of the `PlotRange`.

```
In[117]:= Show[
            Graphics[
              Table[Circle[{Random[ ], Random[ ]},0.05],{10}]],
              Axes -> True,
              Ticks -> {{{0.2, a,{0.5, 0.0},{Dashing[{0.02}]}}},
                        {{0.2, "",{0.5, 0.0}}}}]
```

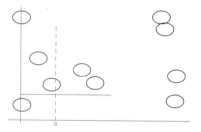

This function can be used for setting the ticks.

```
In[118]:= tfun[x0_, x1_] :=
            Range[x0, x1, (x1-x0)/5]
```

It is more convenient to exploit the different settings of the `Ticks` option by using a *Mathematica* function.

```
In[119]:= Show[
            Graphics[
              Table[Circle[{i,i},0.25],{i,4}]],
              Axes -> True,
              Ticks -> {tfun, tfun}]
```

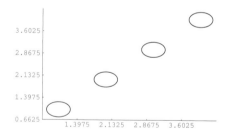

The package `ExtendGraphics`Ticks`` defines a *Mathematica* function that allows detailed control of the positions and labels and styles of tick marks.

20.5 Generating Graphics Objects

There are many ways that `Graphics` objects can be generated in *Mathematica*. These include constructing them directly with *Mathematica* expression-building commands such as `Table` and `Map`, or using graphics commands such as `Plot`. This section will review the most important graphics commands that result in `Graphics` objects.

In *Mathematica* Graphics objects can be created by any of the tools that construct *Mathematica* expressions.

```
In[120]:= Graphics[
              Line[
                 Table[{r Sin[r 2Pi], r Cos[r 2Pi]},
                     {r,1,4,0.01}]]]

Out[120]= -Graphics-
```

A call to Show displays the object.

```
In[121]:= Show[%]
```

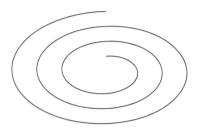

▶ *Plot and ParametricPlot*

Plot is one of the basic *Mathematica* graphics commands. It builds and then displays a Graphics object. Plot[*fun*, {*x*,*x_s*,*x_f*}] will plot a representation of *fun* for *x* from x_s to x_f.

Plot for a single function.

```
In[122]:= Plot[Sin[x]^2/x, {x, -5,5}]
```

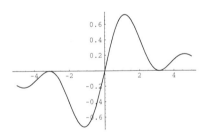

The result of Plot is a Graphics object.

```
In[123]:= Head[%]
Out[123]= Graphics
```

Plot can take more than one function. The use of the option PlotStyle would help to distinguish these plots.

In[124]:= **Plot[{HermiteH[3,x], HermiteH[4,x]}, {x, -2,2}]**

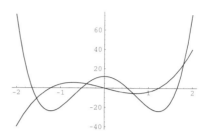

ParametricPlot is another basic *Mathematica* graphics command which also builds and displays a Graphics object. ParametricPlot[{fun_x,fun_y}, {t,t_s,t_f}] will plot the locus of points {fun_x,fun_y} for t from t_s to t_f.

A cycloid plotted by ParametricPlot. The result is also a Graphics object.

In[125]:= **ParametricPlot[{t-Sin[t], 1-Cos[t]}, {t,0,8Pi}]**

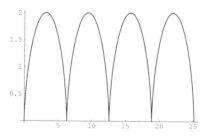

ParametricPlot can also plot several parametric functions. The use of the option PlotStyle would help to distinguish these plots.

In[126]:= **ParametricPlot[**
       {(2+Cos[t]) {Cos[t], Sin[t]},
        (1+2Cos[t]) {Cos[t], Sin[t]}}, {t,0,2Pi}]

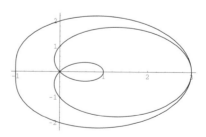

ParametricPlot is particularly suited to drawing plots defined in non-rectangular forms such as those defined in polar forms. This is the basis of the function PolarPlot defined in the standard package Graphics`Graphics`.

Plot and ParametricPlot both have a number of options that are not options of Graphics. These options control styles and how the functions are evaluated. They alter the actual graphics object that results rather than how it should be viewed.

These options are different for Plot than for Graphics. The default setting of Axes is different, but the others are entirely new options. ParametricPlot has the same options as Plot.

In[127]:= **Complement[Options[Plot], Options[Graphics]]**

Out[127]= {Axes -> Automatic, Compiled -> True, MaxBend -> 10.,

      PlotDivision -> 30., PlotPoints -> 25, PlotStyle -> Automatic}

Compiled

The Compiled option of Plot and ParametricPlot controls whether or not *Mathematica* will use the internal compiler to evaluate the function being plotted. Generally, compilation will make the function evaluation faster.

MaxBend, PlotDivision, and PlotPoints

These options are concerned with the adaptive plotting algorithm used by both Plot and ParametricPlot. The aim of adaptive plotting is to make a smooth picture while minimizing the number of points at which the function is evaluated. It does this by first calculating the function at a number of sample points and then looking at each of these to see if more points are needed. This decision is made for each point q by taking the points on the left and right, p and r. The angle between the two line segments, Line[{p,q}] and Line[{q,r}], is then calculated. If the angle θ is more than MaxBend the line segments will be divided. This is demonstrated in the following figure.

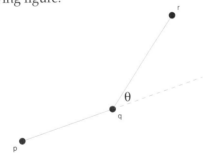

The points actually used to generate the angle compared with MaxBend are scaled so that the *x* and *y* ranges are each one unit. This means that even when the range of points in *x* and *y* are very different, an adequate selection of points is made.

The range of values in *x* and *y* is quite different but the selection of points makes a smooth plot.

In[128]:= `Plot[Im[Cos[Sqrt[n(n-1)] Pi] (-1)^n/n^2], {n, 20, 25}]`

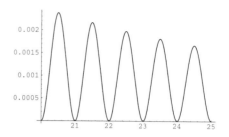

One consequence of this rescaling is that as a line becomes horizontal or vertical more points are evaluated. This is because the algorithm does not know whether the line is nearly horizontal (or vertical) because of the overall scale of the picture or because the line really is horizontal (or vertical). For these lines it will lead to more points being sampled than for diagonal lines.

In[129]:= `ParametricPlot[{Sin[t], Cos[t]}, {t, 0, 2Pi}]`

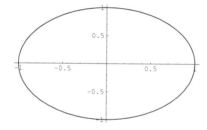

The sample points chosen by the adaptive algorithm can be displayed.

In[130]:= `Show[% /. Line[pts_] :> Map[Point, pts]]`

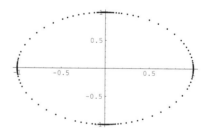

Thus the points chosen around the circle are not uniformly distributed. More points are selected when the line is horizontal or vertical to make sure that scale problems do not affect the result.

When MaxBend is increased the resulting
plot may not be smooth.

In[131]:= **ParametricPlot[**
        x {Cos[x], Sin[x]}, {x,0,2Pi}, MaxBend -> 45]

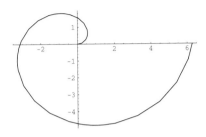

Decreasing MaxBend makes the plot
smoother.

In[132]:= **ParametricPlot[**
        x {Cos[x], Sin[x]}, {x,0,2Pi}, MaxBend -> 1]

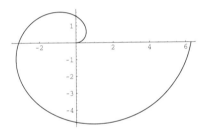

The division of line segments to meet the requirement set by MaxBend does not continue indefinitely.
The function being plotted may have some singularity that causes very rapid oscillation. An alternative
mechanism for the adaptive algorithm to terminate is provided by PlotDivision. When the distance
between adjacent points reduces to less than 1/(PlotPoints PlotDivision) of the range no more sub-
division is carried out.

This function oscillates more and more
rapidly as x approaches 0.
PlotDivision allows the adaptive
algorithm to terminate.

In[133]:= **Plot[Sin[1/x], {x,-1,1}]**

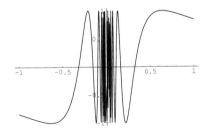

Setting PlotDivision to 1 makes the adaptive algorithm terminate immediately.

In[134]:= `Plot[Sin[1/x], {x,-1,1}, PlotDivision -> 1]`

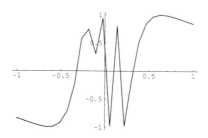

Setting PlotDivision to 500 makes the adaptive algorithm try very hard. Of course for this function the task is impossible since a smooth plot can never be generated.

In[135]:= `Plot[Sin[1/x], {x,-1,1}, PlotDivision -> 500]`

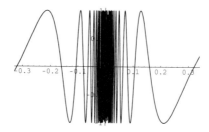

Generally it is not necessary to alter the setting of PlotDivision or MaxBend. The control that is most important is the PlotPoints option. This controls the initial selection of points. If the function oscillates many times between each point in the initial selection then parts of the plot may appear to be smooth when they are not.

This function oscillates rapidly over the range and one of the peaks is missed.

In[136]:= `Plot[Sin[x], {x,0,60Pi}]`

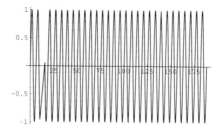

When the PlotPoints option is
increased the picture is improved.

In[137]:= **Plot[Sin[x], {x,0,60Pi}, PlotPoints -> 50]**

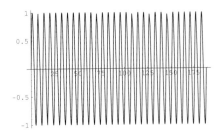

The problem is that the function is not being sampled with sufficient frequency to detect all the oscillations. When this happens it can be detected by visual inspection and corrected by increasing the PlotPoints option. Of course, with some trial and error it is possible to construct a function that will fool the adaptive algorithm. Such a specially chosen function is quite easy to construct.

This will be used to collect the initial
points that Plot chooses.

In[138]:= **pts = {};**

The points are collected as a side effect of
the computation of the plot function.

In[139]:= **Plot[AppendTo[pts, x]; x, {x,0,1}]**

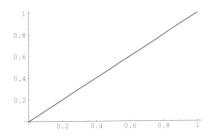

Now a polynomial is generated from
these points. This polynomial is zero at
each of the initial points that Plot
chooses.

In[140]:= **poly = Apply[Times, pts-x]**

Out[140]= $(4.16667 \ 10^{-8} - x) \ (0.0400752 - x) \ (0.0830294 - x)$

$(0.123596 - x) \ (0.163368 - x) \ (0.204426 - x) \ (0.244689 - x)$

$(0.28624 - x) \ (0.326995 - x) \ (0.366954 - x) \ (0.4082 - x)$

$(0.448651 - x) \ (0.488306 - x) \ (0.529249 - x) \ (0.569396 - x)$

$(0.61083 - x) \ (0.651469 - x) \ (0.691312 - x) \ (0.732442 - x)$

$(0.772777 - x) \ (0.8144 - x) \ (0.855226 - x) \ (0.895257 - x)$

$(0.936575 - x) \ (0.977098 - x) \ (1. - x)$

When the plot is made it is flat. 1 is added to the polynomial to lift it off the *x* axis.

In[141]:= `Plot[1 + poly, {x,0,1}]`

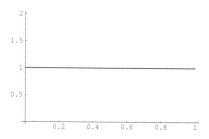

If the PlotPoints option is changed then the true nature of the polynomial is revealed.

In[142]:= `Plot[poly, {x,0,1}, PlotPoints -> 24]`

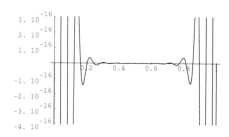

PlotStyle

The PlotStyle option allows individual plots to be identified. This is especially useful when several functions are plotted. PlotStyle -> {*style₁*, ... } sets *style₁* for the first plot and so on. *style₁* should be a list of style directives.

Setting the style for Plot.

In[143]:= `Plot[{HermiteH[3,x], HermiteH[4,x]}, {x, -2,2},`
             `PlotStyle -> {{}, {Dashing[{0.02}]}}]`

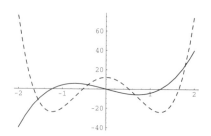

Setting the style for ParametricPlot.

```
In[144]:= ParametricPlot[
              {(2+Cos[t]) {Cos[t], Sin[t]},
               (1+2Cos[t]) {Cos[t], Sin[t]}}, {t,0,2Pi},
              PlotStyle -> {{}, {Dashing[{0.02}]}}]
```

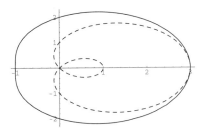

▸ *ListPlot*

ListPlot will plot a list of points. It is very suitable for making a basic data plot.

This is a set of data for ListPlot.

```
In[145]:= d = Table[{i, Sin[i]}, {i,0,2Pi,.1}];
```

ListPlot will plot the data.

```
In[146]:= ListPlot[d]
```

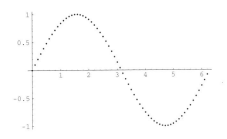

As with Plot and ParametricPlot, ListPlot has options that are not passed directly onto the resulting Graphics object.

These options are different in ListPlot from Graphics. The default setting of Axes is different, but the others are entirely new options.

```
In[147]:= Complement[Options[ListPlot], Options[Graphics]]

Out[147]= {Axes -> Automatic, PlotJoined -> False,
          PlotStyle -> Automatic}
```

PlotJoined

PlotJoined will cause lines to be drawn through the data.

In[148]:= `ListPlot[d, PlotJoined -> True]`

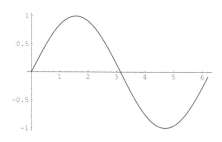

PlotStyle

PlotStyle sets the style for the plot.

In[149]:= `ListPlot[d,`
　　　　　`PlotJoined -> True,`
　　　　　`PlotStyle -> Dashing[{0.02}]]`

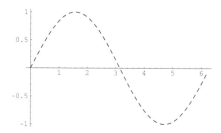

▶ *Packages*

There are many *Mathematica* packages that generate `Graphics` objects to produce a wide variety of pictures. Chapter 4 page 63 and the *Guide to Standard Packages* both have many examples of the functions in these packages.

Chapter 21
Graphics3D Reference

This chapter is intended to be a reference for `Graphics3D` objects. It is intended to give a description of all the functionality together with examples. It is not intended to provide instruction in how `Graphics3D` objects should be used. This is done in Parts I, II, and III of *Mathematica Graphics*.

21.1 Basic Structure

`Graphics3D[`*prims*`, `*opt*$_1$`, `*opt*$_2$`, ... ]`   `Graphics3D` object with primitives and options

The structure of `Graphics3D` objects.

`Graphics3D` objects are provided to represent three-dimensional graphical structures. The basic structure is that the first argument holds three-dimensional graphics primitives. This is followed by zero or more arguments that must be options or lists of options. The following are some examples of `Graphics3D` objects. Any one of these could be displayed with a call to `Show`.

A `Graphics3D` object with one primitive and no options.	`In[1]:= `**`Graphics3D[Line[{{0,0,0}, {1,1,1}}]]`** `Out[1]= `-Graphics3D-

A `Graphics3D` object with a list of two primitives and one option.	`In[2]:= `**`Graphics3D[`**
	     `{Line[{{0,0,0}, {1,1,1}}],Point[{2,2,2}]},`
	     `Axes -> True]`
	
	 `Out[2]= `-Graphics3D-

These `Graphics3D` objects can be displayed with a call to `Show`.	`In[3]:= `**`Show[%]`**

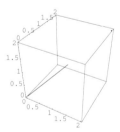

21.2 Primitives

There are many primitives that can be used inside `Graphics3D` objects. This section describes their basic operation along with relevant examples. Chapter 9 also discusses three-dimensional graphics primitives, detailing how they can be generated with the tools that are provided by the rest of *Mathematica*.

▷ *Point, Line, and Polygon*

`Point[p]`	a point drawn at p
`Line[{p₁, p₂, p₃, ... }]`	a line through $p_1, p_2, p_3, \ldots$
`Polygon[{p₁, p₂, p₃, ... }]`	a polygon with vertices $p_1, p_2, p_3, \ldots$
`Polygon[pts, norm]`	a polygon with normal *norm*
`Polygon[pts, norm, edges]`	a polygon with normal *norm* and edges *edges*

`Point`, `Line`, and `Polygon` primitives.

A *Mathematica* expression that represents a point.

```
In[4]:= Point[{5,5,5}]
Out[4]= Point[{5, 5, 5}]
```

The point can be converted to a `Graphics3D` object and then displayed with a call to `Show`.

```
In[5]:= Show[Graphics3D[%]]
```

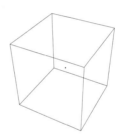

A `Line` primitive representing a random walk can be contructed with `FoldList`.

```
In[6]:= Line[FoldList[Plus, {0,0,0},
                Table[Random[ ]-0.5, {100},{3}]]];
```

Again a call to `Show` will display it.

```
In[7]:= Show[Graphics3D[%]]
```

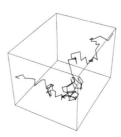

A sequence of points to make into a `Polygon` primitive.

```
In[8]:= pts = Table[{Sin[t], Cos[t],1}, {t,0.,2Pi-Pi/3,Pi/3}];
```

A Polygon primitive is related to a Line primitive. The interior of the path is filled in.

In[9]:= **Polygon[pts]**

Out[9]= Polygon[{{0., 1., 1}, {0.866025, 0.5, 1},

{0.866025, -0.5, 1}, {1.22461 10^{-16}, -1., 1},

{-0.866025, -0.5, 1}, {-0.866025, 0.5, 1}}]

In[10]:= **Show[Graphics3D[%]]**

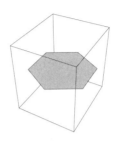

The normal vector can be specified.

Chapter 11 page 214 has more examples of changing the normal vector.

In[11]:= **Polygon[pts, {1,0,0}];**

In[12]:= **Show[Graphics3D[%]]**

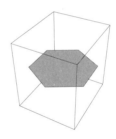

A normal vector of Automatic means that the default normal is to be used.

In[13]:= **Polygon[pts, Automatic];**

In[14]:= **Show[Graphics3D[%]]**

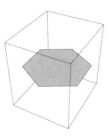

Specifying a style for the edge can leave out the edge at various points. This is useful for making composite polygons.

```
In[15]:= Polygon[pts, Automatic,
                {True, False, True, False, True, False}];
```

```
In[16]:= Show[Graphics3D[%]]
```

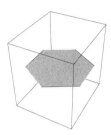

In Version 2.2 (or earlier) *Mathematica* the three-dimensional Polygon primitive was restricted to one argument that specified the outline. It was not possible to specify the normal or different styles for each component of the edge.

▷ *Text*

Text[*expr*, *pt*]	text form of *expr* centered at *pt*
Text[*expr*, *pt*, {x_{off}, y_{off}}]	text form of *expr* with offset {x_{off}, y_{off}}
Text[*expr*, *pt*, {x_{off}, y_{off}}, {x_{vec}, y_{vec}}]	text form of *expr* rotated along vector {x_{vec}, y_{vec}}
Text[FontForm[*expr*, {*font*, *size*}], *pt*]	
	text form of *expr* in font {*font*, *size*}

Arguments of the Text primitive.

In Graphics3D the Text primitive is very similar to a two-dimensional primitive except that it is specified with a three-dimensional coordinate. In a sense it is not really a three-dimensional object. It is a two-dimensional object situated at the projection of a point. The text cannot be considered for hidden surface computations and is rendered after all the other primitives irrespective of whether it is at the front or at the back of the picture. The alignment and rotation options are considered in the plane of the page into which it is rendered. This means that in some abstract sense the Text primitive is lacking in three-dimensional realism. In some abstract sense this is indeed a limitation. However, in a practical sense it is very useful. It allows attractive labels to be placed in a graphic. It is thus an enhancement to a group of primitives. This topic is discussed further in Chapter 9 page 158.

If the Text primitive were a true
three-dimensional object it would be
obscured by the Cuboid.

```
In[17]:= Show[
            Graphics3D[
               {Text["My Label", {0,1,0}],
                Cuboid[{0, 0, 0}]}]], Axes -> True]
```

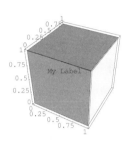

Options of the Text primitive also work for Graphics3D. The Offset coordinate specification is not valid. In Version 2.2 (or earlier) *Mathematica* the Text primitive did not possess options.

This section will not list all the workings of the Text primitive since they are very similar to the way that it works in two dimensions. All of the examples in two dimensions can be used in three dimensions.

A two-dimensional Text primitive.

```
In[18]:= txt2d = Text["This is a string", {2,2}]

Out[18]= Text[This is a string, {2, 2}]
```

The two-dimensional primitive can be
displayed.

```
In[19]:= Show[Graphics[txt2d]]
```

This is a string

The two-dimensional primitive can be
converted to three dimensions.

```
In[20]:= txt3d =
            txt2d /. Text[t_, pt_, s___] :>
                        Text[t, Append[pt, 0], s]

Out[20]= Text[This is a string, {2, 2, 0}]
```

The three-dimensional primitive can be displayed as a Graphics3D object.

In[21]:= **Show[Graphics3D[txt3d]]**

Thus examples of the Text primitive from the Graphics reference chapter can be converted to Graphics3D examples.

In this example the Background and DefaultFont options of Text are set.

In[22]:= **Show[**
    Graphics3D[
        {Line[Table[{t Sin[t], t Cos[t], 0},
                    {t,0,20Pi,.2}]],
        Text["3D Spiral", {0,-40,0},
            Background -> Automatic,
            DefaultFont -> {"Helvetica", 6}]}]]

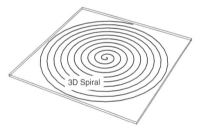

In this example the FormatType and Background options are set.

In[23]:= **Show[**
    Graphics3D[
    {Line[Table[{x, 0, Sin[x]^2/x}, {x, -2,2,.2}]],
    Text[Sin[x]^2/x, {1,0,2/3},
        FormatType -> TraditionalForm,
        Background -> Automatic]}]]

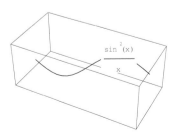

▶ *Cuboid*

Cuboid[*pt*]	Cuboid with left-back-bottom at *pt* and sides of 1 unit
Cuboid[pt_0, pt_1]	Cuboid with left-back-bottom at pt_0 and right-front-top at pt_1

Uses of Cuboid.

Cuboid primitives can be specified by one corner.

```
In[24]:= Show[
            Graphics3D[
              {Cuboid[{-1,-1,-1}], Cuboid[{1,1,1}]}]]
```

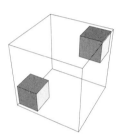

Cuboid primitives can be specified by both corners.

```
In[25]:= Show[
            Graphics3D[
              {Cuboid[{-1,-1,-1}, {0,0,0}],
               Cuboid[{0,0,0}, {1,1,1}]}]]
```

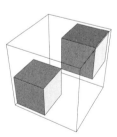

This is a directed random walk.

```
In[26]:= walk =
           Map[Cuboid,
             FoldList[Plus, {0,0,0},
               Table[If[Random[ ] > 0.5, 1,0], {30},{3}]]];
```

The Cuboid primitive is useful when solid objects should be drawn in three dimensions.

In[27]:= **Show[Graphics3D[walk]]**

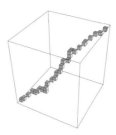

21.3 Style Directives

Style directives cause a change in the style in which primitives are rendered. They change the size of points and lines, make lines dashed, and alter the color. The style directives in three-dimensional graphics work in analogous fashions to the way that they work in two dimensions. The directives that control sizes, such as Thickness, PointSize, or Dashing, are not three-dimensional sizes they are two-dimensional sizes added to help visualize the objects. This makes them similar to the Text primitive.

▶ *Size Directives*

PointSize[*s*]	size for points
AbsolutePointSize[*s*]	absolute size for points
Thickness[*t*]	thickness for lines
AbsoluteThickness[*t*]	absolute thickness for lines
Dashing[{*d*}]	dashing for lines
AbsoluteDashing[{*d*}]	absolute dashing for lines

Size style directives.

A line with a thickness 5% of the width of the picture.

In[28]:= **Show[**
      Graphics3D[
         {Thickness[0.05], Line[{{1,1,1}, {2,2,2}}]}]]

A line with a dashing pattern 5% of the width of the picture.

In[29]:= `Show[`

      `Graphics3D[{Dashing[{0.05}], Line[{{1,1,1},`
      `{2,2,2}}]}]]`

In addition to dashing lines in primitives, `Dashing` and `AbsoluteDashing` can also be used as a style specification for options such as `AxesStyle`, and in `EdgeForm`.

▸ *Color Directives*

Colors can be used on three-dimensional `Point` and `Line` primitives. When they are used on `Polygon` or `Cuboid` primitives it is necessary to switch off the simulated lighting model. This is described in detail in Chapter 11 page 213.

`GrayLevel[g]`	gray
`RGBColor[r, g, b]`	*red, green, blue* color
`Hue[h]`	*hue* color
`Hue[h, s, b]`	*hue, saturation, brightness* color
`CMYKColor[c, m, y, k]`	*cyan, magenta, yellow, black* color
`SurfaceColor[d]`	diffuse color
`SurfaceColor[d, s]`	diffuse and specular color
`SurfaceColor[d, s, n]`	diffuse and specular color with specular exponent

Color directives.

A collection of gray points.

```
In[30]:= Show[
           Graphics3D[
             {GrayLevel[0.5], PointSize[0.02],
              Table[Point[{Random[ ],Random[ ],Random[ ]}],
                {10}]}]]
```

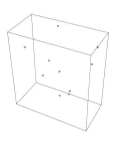

```
In[31]:= Show[
           Graphics3D[
             {RGBColor[1,0,0], Line[{{0,0,0}, {1,1,1}}]}]]
```

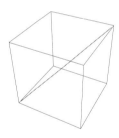

To use a color directive directly with Polygon or Cuboid the lighting must be switched off.

```
In[32]:= Show[
           Graphics3D[
             {GrayLevel[0.5], Cuboid[{0,0,0}]}],
           Lighting -> False]
```

▷ *SurfaceColor*

SurfaceColor works with the lighting model to specify a complex shading model for surfaces. It is fully described in Chapter 11 page 222.

▷ *EdgeForm and FaceForm*

EdgeForm and FaceForm allow individual styles for the edges and faces to be specified.

EdgeForm[*style*]	style for the edges of Polygon primitives
FaceForm[*style*]	style for the faces of Polygon primitives
FaceForm[*style_f*, *style_b*]	styles for the front and back faces of Polygon primitives

The style directives EdgeForm and FaceForm.

```
In[33]:= Show[
            Graphics3D[
              {EdgeForm[Thickness[0.001]],
               FaceForm[GrayLevel[0.5]],
               Cuboid[{0,0,0}]}],
            Lighting -> False]
```

21.4 Graphics3D Options

▷ *AmbientLight*

The AmbientLight option sets the value of ambient light used in the computation used for the lighting model. Chapter 11 page 213 discusses this in detail.

▷ *AspectRatio*

The default setting of the AspectRatio option is Automatic, which ensures that the projection from three dimensions to two dimensions is as set by the various options that control it. There is nothing useful to be gained from changing it.

▷ *Axes*

Setting the Axes option to True causes axes to be drawn.

```
In[34]:= Show[
            Graphics3D[Line[{{0,0,0}, {10,10,10}}]],
            Axes -> True]
```

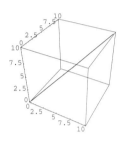

▷ *AxesLabel*

The AxesLabel option adds a label to the axes. Here only one axis is labeled.

```
In[35]:= Show[
            Graphics3D[Line[{{0,0,0}, {10,10,10}}]],
            Axes -> True,
            AxesLabel -> "Z-axis"]
```

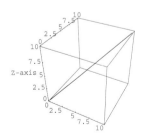

Labels can be added to all the axes.

```
In[36]:= Show[
           Graphics3D[Line[{{0,0,0}, {10,10,10}}]],
           Axes -> True,
           AxesLabel ->
             {"X-axis", "Y-axis", "Z-axis"}]
```

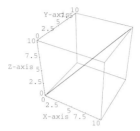

The font of the labels can be controlled with either FontForm or DefaultFont.

▷ *AxesEdge*

The Axes option for three-dimensional graphics draws axes around the box. For any given axis there are four possible edges that can be used. The actual edge chosen is set by the AxesEdge option.

The default setting of Automatic causes axes at the front to be drawn.

```
In[37]:= Show[
           Graphics3D[Line[{{0,0,0}, {1,1,1}}]],
           Axes -> True,
           AxesEdge -> Automatic]
```

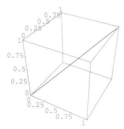

Here three different specifications are used. The *x* axis uses the default method, no *y* axis is drawn, and the *z* axis is drawn on the edge with maximum *x* and *y* values.

```
In[38]:= Show[
            Graphics3D[Line[{{0,0,0}, {1,1,1}}]],
              Axes -> True,
              AxesEdge -> {Automatic, None, {1,1}}]
```

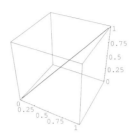

▸ *AxesStyle*

AxesStyle sets the style of the axes. Here they are drawn in gray.

```
In[39]:= Show[
            Graphics3D[Line[{{0,0,0}, {1,1,1}}]],
              Axes -> True, Boxed -> False,
              AxesStyle -> GrayLevel[0.5]]
```

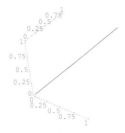

▸ *Background*

Background sets the background color of the picture.

```
In[40]:= Show[
            Graphics3D[Line[{{0,0,0}, {1,1,1}}]],
              Background -> GrayLevel[0.5]]
```

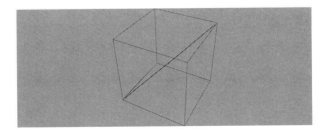

▷ *Boxed*

The Boxed option determines whether or not a box is drawn around the graphic. Here no box is drawn, making it difficult to see this as three-dimensional.

```
In[41]:= Show[
            Graphics3D[Line[{{0,0,0}, {1,1,1}}]],
              Boxed -> False]
```

▷ *BoxRatios*

BoxRatios determine the relative ratios of the box around the image. They are the three-dimensional analog of AspectRatio.

```
In[42]:= Show[
            Graphics3D[Line[{{0,0,0}, {4,1,1}}]],
              BoxRatios -> {2,5,1}]
```

A setting of Automatic gives the same scale in *x*, *y*, and *z*.

```
In[43]:= Show[
            Graphics3D[Line[{{0,0,0}, {4,1,1}}]],
              BoxRatios -> Automatic]
```

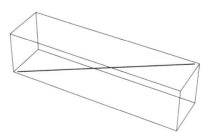

BoxRatios are discussed in detail in Chapter 10 page 180 on coordinate systems.

▸ *BoxStyle*

BoxStyle sets the style in which the box will be rendered.

```
In[44]:= Show[
            Graphics3D[Line[{{0,0,0}, {4,1,1}}]],
              BoxStyle -> GrayLevel[0.5]]
```

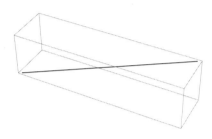

▸ *ColorOutput*

ColorOutput forces the output to come out in gray, it is described in Chapter 11 page 224.

```
In[45]:= Show[
            Graphics3D[{RGBColor[1,0,0],Line[{{0,0,0},
          {1,1,1}}]}],
              ColorOutput -> GrayLevel]
```

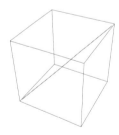

▸ *DefaultColor*

DefaultColor sets the default drawing color.

```
In[46]:= Show[
            Graphics3D[Line[{{0,0,0}, {1,1,1}}]],
              DefaultColor -> GrayLevel[0.5]]
```

▸ *DefaultFont*

The font used for text is controlled by the DefaultFont option.

```
In[47]:= Show[
            Graphics3D[Line[{{0,0,0}, {1,1,1}}]],
              Axes -> True,
              DefaultFont -> {"Helvetica", 6}]
```

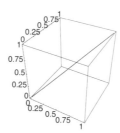

The default value of DefaultFont is $DefaultFont and this works in the same fashion as it does for Graphics.

▸ *DisplayFunction*

The DisplayFunction option determines what is done with graphics objects when they have been assembled. Its operation is equivalent to the DisplayFunction option of Graphics.

▶ *Epilog*

The Epilog option specifies Graphics primitives to be rendered after the main object. This is how two-dimensional primitives not available in Graphics3D can be included.

```
In[48]:= Show[
            Graphics3D[Line[{{0,0,0}, {2,2,2}}]],
            Epilog -> Text["Label", {0.5,0.3}]]
```

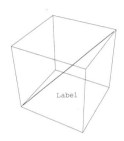

▶ *FaceGrids*

The FaceGrids option specifies that a grid is to be drawn on the faces of the box.

```
In[49]:= Show[
            Graphics3D[Line[{{0,0,0}, {2,2,2}}]],
            FaceGrids -> All]
```

Individual specifications can be given. {-1,0,0} draws a grid on the minimum *x* face and {0,1,0} draws a grid on the maximum *y* face.

```
In[50]:= Show[
            Graphics3D[Line[{{0,0,0}, {2,2,2}}]],
            FaceGrids -> {{-1,0,0},{0,1,0}}]
```

FaceGrids can be drawn when the
graphic is not boxed.

```
In[51]:= Show[
            Graphics3D[Line[{{0,0,0}, {2,2,2}}]],
              Boxed -> False,
              FaceGrids -> {{-1,0,0},{0,1,0}, {0,0,-1}}]
```

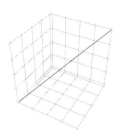

A grid on the minimum *x* face is drawn
for *x* and *y* values of {0,1,2}.

```
In[52]:= Show[
            Graphics3D[Line[{{0,0,0}, {2,2,2}}]],
              FaceGrids -> {{{-1,0,0},{{0,1,2},{0,1,2}}}}]
```

▶ *Lighting*

The Lighting option controls whether
the simulated lighting model is used.
The color directive is ignored since the
lighting is used.

```
In[53]:= Show[
            Graphics3D[
            {GrayLevel[0.5],
              Polygon[{{0,0,0}, {0,1,0},{1,1,0}}]}],
              Lighting -> True]
```

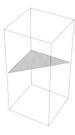

When the simulated lighting model is not used the color directive applies to the Polygon primitive.

```
In[54]:= Show[
            Graphics3D[
            {GrayLevel[0.5],
                Polygon[{{0,0,0}, {0,1,0},{1,1,0}}]}],
            Lighting -> False]
```

Chapter 11 page 213 discusses the use of simulated lighting by *Mathematica* in detail.

▸ *LightSources*

The LightSources option sets the positions and colors of the light sources used in the computation used for the lighting model. Chapter 11 page 213 discusses this in detail.

▸ *PlotLabel*

PlotLabel specifies a label to place at the top of a picture.

```
In[55]:= Show[
            Graphics3D[Line[Table[Random[ ], {10}, {3}]]],
            PlotLabel -> "A Random Line"]
```

The font used for the PlotLabel can be set with either FontForm or DefaultFont.

▷ *PlotRange*

PlotRange of Automatic specifies that a
representative sample of points is to be
shown. The point which lies away from
the line is not shown.

```
In[56]:= Show[
           Graphics3D[{Line[Table[Random[ ], {20}, {3}]],
                       Point[{5,5,5}]}],
           PlotRange -> Automatic]
```

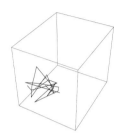

PlotRange of All specifies that all points
should be included in the picture.

```
In[57]:= Show[
           Graphics3D[{Line[Table[Random[ ], {20}, {3}]],
                       Point[{5,5,5}]}],
           PlotRange -> All]
```

Specifications pertaining to each
dimension can be made.

```
In[58]:= Show[
           Graphics3D[{Line[Table[Random[ ], {20}, {3}]],
                       Point[{5,5,5}]}],
           PlotRange -> {{0,5},{0,5},{0,5}}]
```

▷ *PlotRegion*

PlotRegion specifies an internal sub-region where the picture will be displayed.

```
In[59]:= Show[
            Graphics3D[Line[Table[Random[ ], {20}, {3}]]],
            PlotRegion -> {{0,0.5},{0,0.5}},
            Background -> GrayLevel[0.5]]
```

▷ *Plot3Matrix*

The Plot3Matrix is an advanced option that sets the transformation matrix to be used in rendering three-dimensional objects. It is described in Chapter 10 page 194 on coordinate systems.

▷ *PolygonIntersections*

PolygonIntersections -> True instructs *Mathematica* that the resulting Graphics3D object should be composed of non-intersecting primitives.

```
In[60]:= Show[
            Graphics3D[
              {Polygon[{{-1,-1,0},{-1,1,0},{1,-1,0}}],
               Polygon[{{-1,0,-1},{-1,0,1},{1,0,-1}}]}],
            PolygonIntersections -> False]
```

Out[60]= -Graphics3D-

The result consists of different primitives that do not intersect with each other.

```
In[61]:= Short[First[%], 5]
```

Out[61]//Short=

{EdgeForm[], FaceForm[RGBColor[0.543807, 0.324062, 0.531531]],

   Polygon[{{-1., 0., -1.}, {-1., 0., -1.97993 10^{-16}},

   {1., 0., -1.}}], <<14>>, Polygon[{<<3>>}],

   {GrayLevel[0.], Thickness[0.002],

   Line[{{0., -3.75676 10^{-16}, 0.}, {1., -1., -3.17867 10^{-16}}}]}}}

▸ *Prolog*

The Prolog option specifies Graphics2D primitives and style directives to be rendered before the main graphics object.

```
In[62]:= Show[
            Graphics3D[Line[{{0,0,0}, {2,2,2}}]],
            Prolog -> Text["Label", {0.5,0.3}]]
```

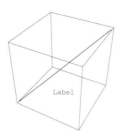

Since they are rendered before the main graphics object the option is not very useful.

▸ *RenderAll*

Setting the RenderAll option to False will use a different three-dimensional renderer. It uses one that attempts to minimize the size of the PostScript that is output.

```
In[63]:= Show[
            Graphics3D[Line[{{0,0,0}, {2,2,2}}]],
            RenderAll -> False]
```

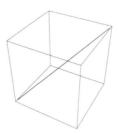

▸ *SphericalRegion*

The SphericalRegion option controls the way that the picture is scaled onto the page. It is described in Chapter 10 page 193.

```
In[64]:= Show[
            Graphics3D[Line[{{0,0,0}, {2,2,2}}]],
            SphericalRegion -> True]
```

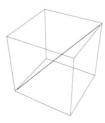

▶ *Ticks*

Ticks -> Automatic states that tick marks should be drawn on axes.

```
In[65]:= Show[
            Graphics3D[Cuboid[{0,0,0}]],
            Axes -> True, Ticks -> Automatic]
```

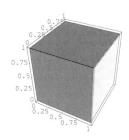

The option works in a very similar fashion to the two-dimensional option except that there are specifications to be given for three axes.

```
In[66]:= Show[
            Graphics3D[Cuboid[{0,0,0}]],
            Axes -> True,
            Ticks -> {Automatic, None, {.2,.4,.6,.8}}]
```

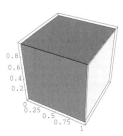

▶ *ViewCenter, ViewPoint, and ViewVertical*

The ViewCenter, ViewPoint, and ViewVertical options are used to determine the projection from three dimensions to two dimensions. They are described in Chapter 10 page 185 which discusses coordinate systems.

21.5 Generating Graphics3D Objects

There are several ways that Graphics3D objects can be generated in *Mathematica*. They can be constructed directly with *Mathematica* expression building commands such as Table and Map or they can be formed as the result of the graphics command ParametricPlot3D.

Graphics3D objects can be created by any of the tools that construct *Mathematica* expressions.

```
In[67]:= Graphics3D[
              Line[Table[{r Sin[r 2Pi], r Cos[r 2Pi],0},
                  {r,1,4,0.01}]]]
```

```
Out[67]= -Graphics3D-
```

A call to Show displays the object.

```
In[68]:= Show[%]
```

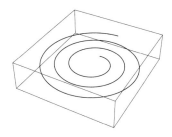

The main built-in function that generates Graphics3D objects is the ParametricPlot3D command.

▶ *ParametricPlot3D*

ParametricPlot3D is the main built-in function that constructs and then displays Graphics3D objects.

ParametricPlot3D[{f_x, f_y, f_z}, {t, t_s, t_f}]
        plot the space curve parametrized by {f_x, f_y, f_z} over {t, t_s, t_f}

ParametricPlot3D[{f_x, f_y, f_z}, {u, u_s, u_f}, {v, v_s, v_f}]
        plot the surface parametrized by {f_x, f_y, f_z} over {u, u_s, u_f} and {v, v_s, v_f}

Arguments of ParametricPlot3D.

A space curve generated by
ParametricPlot3D.

In[69]:= **ParametricPlot3D[{Sin[t], Cos[t], t/8}, {t,0,8Pi}]**

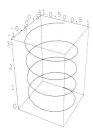

A surface generated by
ParametricPlot3D.

In[70]:= **ParametricPlot3D[**
    {Sin[t] Cos[p], Sin[t] Sin[p], Cos[t]},
    {t,0,Pi}, {p,0,2Pi}]

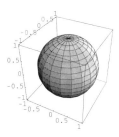

A fourth argument can be given to
control the style of the surface.

In[71]:= **ParametricPlot3D[**
    {Sin[t] Cos[p], Sin[t] Sin[p], Cos[t], Hue[t]},
    {t,0,Pi}, {p,0,2Pi}]

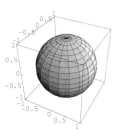

ParametricPlot3D has a number of options that are not options of Graphics3D. These options
control styles and how the functions are evaluated. They alter the actual graphics object that results rather
than how it should be viewed.

These options are different for ParametricPlot3D than for Graphics3D. The default setting of Axes is different and the others are entirely new options.

```
In[72]:= Complement[
               Options[ParametricPlot3D], Options[Graphics3D]]
Out[72]= {AmbientLight -> GrayLevel[0.], Axes -> True,
    Compiled -> True, PlotPoints -> Automatic}
```

Compiled

The Compiled option of ParametricPlot3D controls whether or not *Mathematica* will use the internal compiler to evaluate the function being plotted. Generally, compilation makes the function evaluate faster.

PlotPoints

The PlotPoints option of ParametricPlot3D controls the number of points at which the function is sampled. The default setting of Automatic gives 75 evaluations for a space curve and 20 evaluations in each iterator in a surface. Increasing its value will result in a finer image.

Changing the PlotPoints results in a finer image.

```
In[73]:= ParametricPlot3D[
               {Sin[t] Cos[p], Sin[t] Sin[p], Cos[t]},
               {t,0,Pi}, {p,0,2Pi}, PlotPoints -> 30]
```

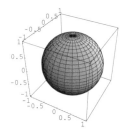

Different values of PlotPoints can be given for each iterator.

```
In[74]:= ParametricPlot3D[
               {Sin[z] Cos[p], Sin[z] Sin[p], z},
               {z,-Pi,Pi}, {p,0,2Pi}, PlotPoints -> {40,30}]
```

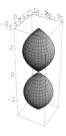

21.6 Converting Graphics3D Objects

Graphics3D objects can be converted to Graphics. This is done automatically by Show if a Graphics object is combined with a Graphics3D object. Chapter 12 discusses the conversion of *Mathematica* graphics objects in detail.

A simple Graphics3D object.

In[75]:= **Graphics3D[Cuboid[{0,0,0}]]**

Out[75]= -Graphics3D-

It is now converted to Graphics.

In[76]:= **Graphics[%]**

Out[76]= -Graphics-

Displaying with a Frame axis confirms that it is indeed a Graphics object.

In[77]:= **Show[%, Frame -> True, AspectRatio -> True]**

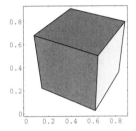

Chapter 22
SurfaceGraphics Reference

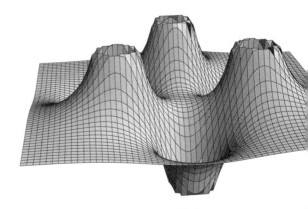

This chapter is intended to be a reference to `SurfaceGraphics` objects. It describes what they are and how they work. It is not intended to instruct how they should be used for visualization, which is done throughout the other parts of *Mathematica Graphics*.

22.1 Basic Structure

`SurfaceGraphics` objects are provided to represent three-dimensional surfaces. They have a special compact representation that can be rendered faster than the more general three-dimensional representation `Graphics3D`. They also possess certain special features (for example coloring with a user-defined function) that are not part of `Graphics3D` objects. In general, `SurfaceGraphics` objects are not designed to be built directly. The reason for this is that the tools `Plot3D` and `ListPlot3D` are perfectly adequate to generate them in most situations. One reason for building them directly would be to extend the way that they work. There have been a number of examples of this in *Mathematica Graphics*, such as in Chapter 13 page 250.

`SurfaceGraphics[{{`z_{11}`,`z_{12}`,... },{`z_{21}`,`z_{22}`,... },... }, ` *options*`]`

surface with heights z_{ij}

`SurfaceGraphics[`z_{array}`, {{`c_{11}`,`c_{12}`,... },{`c_{21}`,`c_{22}`,... },... }, ` *options*`]`

surface with heights and colors

The structure of `SurfaceGraphics` objects.

The basic structure of `SurfaceGraphics` objects is that the first argument is an array of the height of the surface. The points of the surface form a grid of equal-sized rectangles in the xy plane. An optional second argument holds information to color the surface. This is followed by zero or more arguments that must be options or lists of options. The first argument is an array of z values only. The x and y values are determined by the setting of the `MeshRange` option.

A SurfaceGraphics object is generated. Normally ListPlot3D would be a better way to do this.	*In[1]:=* **SurfaceGraphics[{{0,0,0},{0,1,2},{0,2,4}}]** *Out[1]=* -SurfaceGraphics-
The surface can be displayed by Show.	*In[2]:=* **Show[%]**

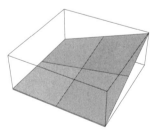

Looking at the surface from directly above demonstrates that it represents a regular rectangular grid.

In[3]:= **Show[%, ViewPoint -> {0,0,200}]**

A surface with color information for each segment.

In[4]:= **SurfaceGraphics[**
{{0,0,0}, {0,1,2}, {0,2,4}},
{{Hue[0], Hue[0.4]}, {Hue[0.7], Hue[0.9]}}]

Out[4]= -SurfaceGraphics-

A surface with color information at each point of the surface[1].

In[5]:= **SurfaceGraphics[**
{{0,0,0}, {0,1,2}, {0,2,4}},
{{Hue[0], Hue[0.4], Hue[0.6]},
{Hue[0.2], Hue[0.6], Hue[0.9]},
{Hue[0.3], Hue[0.9], Hue[0.5]}}]

Out[5]= -SurfaceGraphics-

A surface with color information for each segment of the surface. There are also two options.

In[6]:= **SurfaceGraphics[**
{{0,0,0}, {0,1,2}, {0,2,4}},
{{Hue[0], Hue[0.4]}, {Hue[0.7], Hue[0.9]}},
MeshRange -> {{0,2}, {0,2}},
Axes -> True]

Out[6]= -SurfaceGraphics-

The *x* and *y* values are set by the MeshRange option.

In[7]:= **Show[%]**

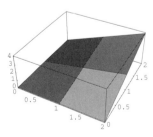

The surface that is represented by a SurfaceGraphics object is quite simple. It cannot intersect with itself and there will be at most one point on the surface over any given point in the *xy* plane. This means that

---

[1]As was noted in Chapter 11 page 210, in Version 2.2 *Mathematica* SurfaceGraphics would not accept a color array of the same dimensionality as the height array.

when it is rendered a fast algorithm for three-dimensional rendering can be used. The parts of the surface furthest from the ViewPoint are rendered first and those closest are rendered last. When Graphics3D objects are rendered they must use a more complex algorithm that detects when primitives intersect and must be broken into the constituent parts.

22.2 SurfaceGraphics Options

SurfaceGraphics objects have a number of options that can be altered by an appropriate call to Show. Many of these options are also options of Graphics3D and work in an analogous fashion. Some options of SurfaceGraphics objects are different from Graphics3D.

These are options of SurfaceGraphics that are different from Graphics3D.

```
In[8]:= Complement[
            Options[SurfaceGraphics], Options[Graphics3D]]

Out[8]= {BoxRatios -> {1, 1, 0.4}, ClipFill -> Automatic,
    ColorFunction -> Automatic, HiddenSurface -> True,
    Mesh -> True, MeshRange -> Automatic, MeshStyle -> Automatic}
```

These are options of Graphics3D that are different from SurfaceGraphics.

```
In[9]:= Complement[Options[Graphics3D], Options[SurfaceGraphics]]

Out[9]= {BoxRatios -> Automatic, PolygonIntersections -> True,
    RenderAll -> True}
```

In this section the options of SurfaceGraphics that are different will be documented. The other options will behave in an analogous fashion to their counterparts for Graphics3D.

▶ *ClipFill*

A SurfaceGraphics object can be built with Plot3D. The PlotRange setting here includes the entire surface.

```
In[10]:= Plot3D[Sin[x] Sin[y], {x,0,2Pi}, {y,0,2Pi}]
```

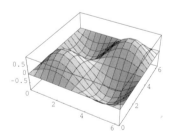

Changing the PlotRange option has left out some of the surface. The behavior at these points is determined by the option ClipFill. The default value is to fill with polygons.

*In[11]:= * **Show[%, PlotRange -> {-.5, .5}]**

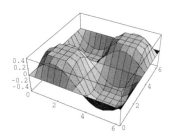

Setting the ClipFill option to None causes no fill to be used.

*In[12]:= * **Show[%, ClipFill -> None]**

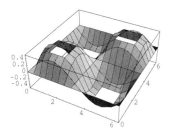

Setting the ClipFill option to a color specification colors the fill with that color.

*In[13]:= * **Show[%, ClipFill -> Hue[0]]**

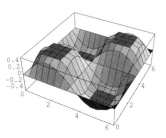

Different colors can be given for the bottom and top fills.

*In[14]:= * **Show[%, ClipFill -> {GrayLevel[0], GrayLevel[1]}]**

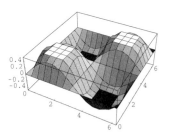

▸ *ColorFunction*

The default setting of ColorFunction is
Automatic and this will use the simulated
lighting model to shade the surface.

In[15]:= **Plot3D[x y (x∧2 - y∧2)/(x∧2 + y∧2),**
　　　　　　　{x,-1,1},{y,-1,1}, PlotPoints -> 40]

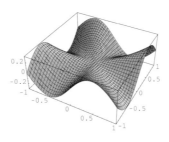

Setting the ColorFunction option allows
the surface to be colored according to its
height.

In[16]:= **Show[%, ColorFunction -> Hue]**

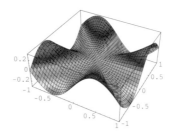

The values passed to the ColorFunction are scaled from the values in the height array for each segment of the surface. First all the vertices of the segment are averaged. This value is then scaled by a linear function generated from the PlotRange. The function scales the minimum value of the z PlotRange to 0 and the maximum to 1. A representation of the scaling function can be given.

The scaling function used to pass
values to the ColorFunction.

In[17]:= **ScaleFun[z_, z0_, z1_] := (z-z0)/(z1-z0)**

▷ *HiddenSurface*

Setting the HiddenSurface option to
False draws a wire frame picture.

In[18]:= **Plot3D[Sin[x y], {x,0,2Pi},{y,0,Pi},
            HiddenSurface -> False]**

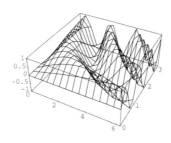

▷ *Mesh*

Setting the Mesh option to False causes
no mesh to be drawn on the surface.

In[19]:= **Plot3D[Sin[x y], {x,0,2Pi},{y,0,Pi},
            Mesh -> False]**

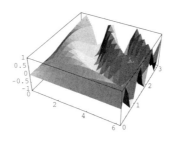

▷ *MeshRange*

The MeshRange option sets the range of
values in *x* and *y*.

In[20]:= **ListPlot3D[Table[Sin[x y], {y,0,Pi,.2},{x,0,2Pi,.4}],
            MeshRange -> {{0,2Pi},{0,Pi}}]**

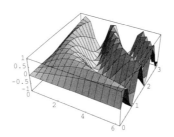

▸ *MeshStyle*

The MeshStyle option sets the style in which the mesh is drawn.

```
In[21]:= Plot3D[Sin[x y], {x,0,2Pi},{y,0,Pi},
             MeshStyle -> Thickness[0.008]]
```

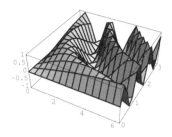

22.3 Generating SurfaceGraphics Objects

There are two main functions that build SurfaceGraphics: Plot3D and ListPlot3D. They are described in this section. Chapter 11 page 207 also describes the color aspects and Chapter 18 page 471 describes the use of ListPlot3D for generating surfaces from three-dimensional numeric data.

Plot3D[f, {x, x_s, x_f},{y, y_s, y_f}]	plot the surface defined by the function f
Plot3D[{f, col}, {x, x_s, x_f},{y, y_s, y_f}]	
	plot the surface and color with col
ListPlot3D[{{z_{11}, z_{12}, ... }, ... }]	plot the surface over a grid of points
ListPlot3D[z_{array},{{c_{11}, c_{12}, ... }, ... }]	
	plot the surface over a grid of points with specified colors

Arguments of Plot3D and ListPlot3D.

▸ *Plot3D*

Plot3D evaluates the function over the specified range. It then constructs and plots the surface over these points.

```
In[22]:= Plot3D[Sin[x] Sin[y], {x,0,2Pi},{y,0,2Pi}]
```

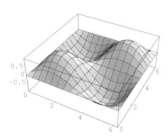

Plot3D will also accept a function as a second argument to shade the surface.

In[23]:= **Plot3D[{Sin[x] Sin[y], RGBColor[x/(2Pi), y/(2Pi), 0]},**
{x,0,2Pi},{y,0,2Pi}]

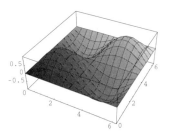

Plot3D has a number of options that are not present in SurfaceGraphics.

In[24]:= **Complement[Options[Plot3D], Options[SurfaceGraphics]]**

Out[24]= {Axes -> True, Compiled -> True, PlotPoints -> 15}

Compiled

The Compiled option of Plot3D controls whether or not *Mathematica* will use the internal compiler to evaluate the function being plotted. Generally, compilation makes the function evaluate faster.

PlotPoints

The PlotPoints option of Plot3D controls the number of points at which the function is sampled. The default setting is 15 and this can be increased to produce a finer picture.

Increasing the PlotPoints allows a finer picture to be generated.

In[25]:= **Plot3D[Sin[x] Sin[y], {x,0,2Pi},{y,0,2Pi},**
PlotPoints -> 30]

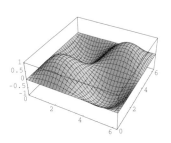

▸ *ListPlot3D*

The form of the data that are accepted by ListPlot3D is described in detail in Chapter 18 page 471.

In[26]:= **data = Table[Sin[x] Sin[y], {y,0,2Pi,.2},{x,0,2Pi,.2}];**

ListPlot3D plots a surface over a rectangular array of data. The MeshRange option can give the axes correct labels.

In[27]:= **ListPlot3D[data, MeshRange -> {{0,2Pi},{0,2Pi}}]**

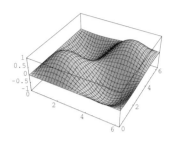

ListPlot3D has the same options as SurfaceGraphics but the default value of the Axes options is different.

In[28]:= **Complement[Options[ListPlot3D],**
      Options[SurfaceGraphics]]

Out[28]= {Axes -> True}

22.4 Converting SurfaceGraphics Objects

SurfaceGraphics objects can be converted to a variety of different forms. The conversion to Contour-Graphics or DensityGraphics works since the representation of these objects is very similar. The conversion of *Mathematica* graphics is discussed in more detail in Chapter 12.

In[29]:= **s = Plot3D[Sin[x] Sin[y], {x,0,2Pi},{y,0,2Pi},**
      PlotPoints -> 30]

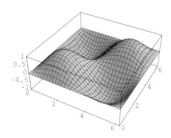

The data in a SurfaceGraphics object can be used to form a ContourGraphics or DensityGraphics object.

In[30]:= **ContourGraphics[s]**

Out[30]= -ContourGraphics-

The ContourGraphics object is
displayed.

In[31]:= **Show[%]**

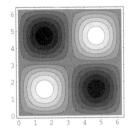

A Graphics3D object can be generated
from a SurfaceGraphics object.

In[32]:= **Show[Graphics3D[s]]**

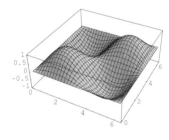

Chapter 23
ContourGraphics Reference

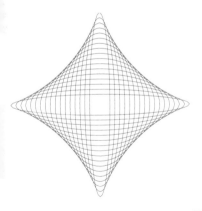

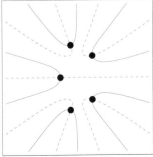

This chapter is intended to be a reference to `ContourGraphics` objects. It describes what they are and how they work. It is not intended to instruct how they should be used for visualization, which is done throughout the other parts of *Mathematica Graphics*.

23.1 Basic Structure

`ContourGraphics` objects are provided to represent plots of contours lines. There is no absolute requirement for a separate object for contour plots; they could be represented by `Graphics` objects. However, having a special structure means that options specific to contour plots can be changed by a call to `Show`. In general, `ContourGraphics` objects are not designed to be built directly. The reason for this is that the tools `ContourPlot` and `ListContourPlot` are perfectly adequate to generate them in most situations. One reason for building them directly would be to extend the way that they work. There have been a number of examples of this in *Mathematica Graphics*, such as in Chapter 13 page 250.

$\texttt{ContourGraphics}[\{\{z_{11}, z_{12}, \dots\}, \{z_{21}, z_{22}, \dots\}, \dots\},\ options]$

heights from which to generate contours

The structure of `ContourGraphics` objects.

The basic structure of `ContourGraphics` objects is that the first argument is an array of the z values of the three-dimensional data. This data forms a grid of equal-sized rectangles in the xy plane. This is followed by zero or more arguments that must be options or lists of options. The x and y values of the data are determined by the setting of the `MeshRange` option.

A `ContourGraphics` is generated. Normally `ListContourPlot` would be a better way to do this.

$In[1]:= \texttt{ContourGraphics}[\{\{0,0,0\},\{0,1,2\},\{0,2,4\}\}]$

$Out[1]= \texttt{-ContourGraphics-}$

The contours can be displayed by `Show`.

$In[2]:= \texttt{Show}[\%]$

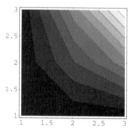

The algorithm that constructs contours from a `ContourGraphics` object is quite simple. As explained above the data are held as a grid of points that form a sequence of rectangles in the xy plane. Each rectangle is tested to see if a contour crosses one of its edges. The point at which the contour crosses the edge is determined by an interpolation technique. Since the contour enters it must exit the rectangle and enter another. The exit point and the successor rectangle are found and the process repeated until the contour leaves the grid or joins itself in a loop. In this way the contour line can be formed.

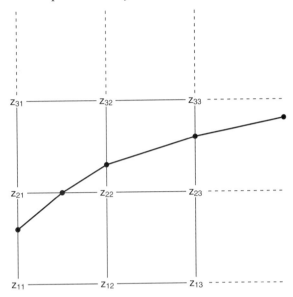

Forming a contour across a sequence of rectangles.

The figure demonstrates that the contour is found to be between z_{11} and z_{21}. This rectangle is searched and an exit is found between z_{21} and z_{22} indicating the rectangle to be searched next. The whole process is then repeated.

When all the contour lines have been generated a further process must be carried for shaded contour plots. This involves forming polygons from the lines and then sorting to make sure that when they are rendered the biggest ones are drawn first. For some earlier versions of *Mathematica* this process could be quite slow and the plot may work better as an unshaded plot. This can be done by setting the ContourShading option to False.

23.2 ContourGraphics Options

ContourGraphics objects have a number of options that can be altered by an appropriate call to Show. The data shown in a contour plot is three-dimensional data while the picture itself is two-dimensional. Many of the options of ContourGraphics come from Graphics and work in an analogous fashion. For example, the AspectRatio option changes the shape of the picture. Some options of ContourGraphics objects are different from Graphics.

These are options of ContourGraphics that are different from Graphics.

```
In[3]:= Complement[
            Options[ContourGraphics], Options[Graphics]]

Out[3]= {AspectRatio -> 1, ColorFunction -> Automatic,
    ContourLines -> True, Contours -> 10, ContourShading -> True,
    ContourSmoothing -> True, ContourStyle -> Automatic,
    Frame -> True, MeshRange -> Automatic}
```

In this section the unique options of ContourGraphics will be documented. A number of options of ContourGraphics have different default values. The AspectRatio is 1, giving a square picture, and Frame axes are drawn, ensuring the axes do not interfere with the picture.

▷ *ColorFunction*

The default setting of ColorFunction is Automatic and this uses a gray shading between contour lines.

```
In[4]:= ContourPlot[x y (x^2 - y^2)/(x^2 + y^2),
            {x,-1,1},{y,-1,1}, PlotPoints -> 30]
```

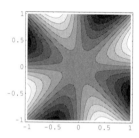

Setting the ColorFunction option uses the function to shade.

```
In[5]:= Show[%, ColorFunction -> Hue]
```

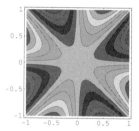

When ContourShading is False no
shading is carried out.

In[6]:= **Show[%, ContourShading -> False]**

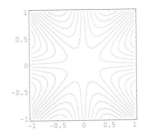

The values passed to the ColorFunction are scaled from the values of the contour lines and the minimum and maximum z values of the PlotRange. The lowest value is the midpoint between the lowest contour and z_{min}; this gets scaled to 0. The highest value is the midpoint between the highest contour and z_{max}; this gets scaled to 1. The intermediate points are the midpoints between the appropriate contour lines. All the values are scaled with a linear function so that the minimum and maximum values are 0 and 1 respectively. This can be represented by the *Mathematica* function where vals are the contour lines and z1 and z2 are respectively the minimum and maximum z values of the PlotRange.

The scaling function used to pass
values to the ColorFunction

```
In[7]:= ColorFunctionValues[vals_List, {z1_, z2_}] :=
            Module[{p1, p2, pf, res},
              p1 = (z1 + First[vals])/2. ;
              p2 = (z2 + Last[vals])/2. ;
              pf = p2 - p1 ;
              res =
                Table[
                  ((Part[vals, i] + Part[vals, i+1])/2. - p1)/pf,
                  {i,Length[vals] - 1}] ;
              Join[{0}, res, {1}]
            ]
```

The way that the values of the contours are determined is described in the material that follows on the Contours option.

▶ *ContourLines*

When the ContourLines option is set to
False no contour lines are drawn.

In[8]:= ContourPlot[x^2 y + x y^2,
                  {x,-2,2},{y,-2,2}, ContourLines -> False]

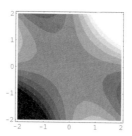

▶ *Contours*

The Contours option determines the
values at which contour lines are drawn.
It can be set to a list of the actual values.

In[9]:= c = ContourPlot[x y,
              {x,-2,2},{y,-2,2},
              Contours -> {-3, -2, -1, 0, 1, 2, 3}]

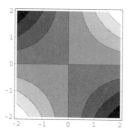

The Contours option can also be set to an
integer that specifies the number of lines
to be drawn.

In[10]:= Show[c, Contours -> 6]

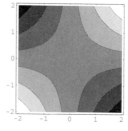

When the setting of the Contours option is an integer the actual lines are determined from the z
values of the PlotRange. This is done so that the lines are equally spaced with half a space between
z_{min} and the lowest line and half a space between the highest line and z_{max}. This is demonstrated in this

Mathematica function where n is the number of contour lines to be calculated and z1 and z2 are respectively the minimum and maximum *z* values of the PlotRange.

The actual contours chosen are determined from the *z* component of the PlotRange.

```
In[11]:= FindContours[n_Integer /; n > 0, {z1_, z2_}] :=
           Module[{zinc},
              zinc = (z2 - z1)/ (n + 1) ;
              Table[i, {i, z1 + zinc, z2 - zinc, zinc}]
              ]
```

With the contour plot c with six contours they will be calculated for these values.

```
In[12]:= FindContours[6, Last[FullOptions[c, PlotRange]]]

Out[12]= {-3., -1.8, -0.6, 0.6, 1.8, 3.}
```

A package that automatically labels contour plots is described in Chapter 15.

▷ *ContourShading*

ContourShading determines whether or not there is shading between the contour lines.

```
In[13]:= ContourPlot[x y,
              {x,-2,2},{y,-2,2},
              ContourShading -> True]
```

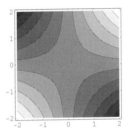

```
In[14]:= Show[%, ContourShading -> False]
```

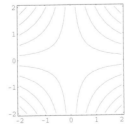

▷ *ContourSmoothing*

ContourSmoothing of False means that a linear interpolation technique is used to determine the contours.

```
In[15]:= ContourPlot[x^2 - x y^2,
              {x,0,3},{y,-3,3},
              ContourShading -> False,
              ContourSmoothing -> False]
```

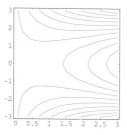

ContourSmoothing of True uses a cubic interpolation technique.

```
In[16]:=
        Show[%, ContourSmoothing -> True]
```

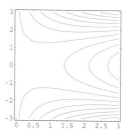

A package that will generate smooth contour plots as well as surface and density plots is described in Chapter 13 page 250.

▶ *ContourStyle*

The ContourStyle option gives a style
for the contour lines. A style can be given
to all the lines.

```
In[17]:= ContourPlot[x y,
              {x,-2,2},{y,-2,2},
              ContourShading -> False,
              ContourStyle -> Dashing[{0.02}]]
```

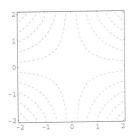

Styles can be given to different contour
lines. Here a style of {} gives the default
(a solid line) to the lowest contour, the
next is dashed, the next is drawn in
default, and so on.

```
In[18]:= ContourPlot[x y,
              {x,-2,2},{y,-2,2},
              ContourShading -> False,
              ContourStyle -> {{}, {Dashing[{0.02}]}}]
```

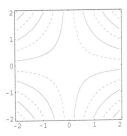

▶ *MeshRange*

The MeshRange option sets the range of
values in *x* and *y*.

```
In[19]:= ListContourPlot[
              Table[Sin[x] Sin[y], {y,0,Pi,.1},{x,0,2Pi,.1}],
              MeshRange -> {{0,2Pi},{0,Pi}}]
```

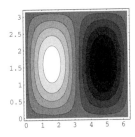

▸ *PlotRange*

The PlotRange option of ContourGraphics is different from the PlotRange option of Graphics since the former can take three components. The first two specify the x and y components of the PlotRange and work the same as for Graphics. The last specifies the z component of the PlotRange. This controls the generation of contour lines and the scaling of points for the ColorFunction. Contour lines that do not lie within the range of the z component of the PlotRange are not shown.

The default PlotRange setting of Automatic is used.

```
In[20]:= ContourPlot[(x^2 y^2) ( 1 + Sin[y] Sin[x]),
                    {x,-2,2},{y,-2,2}, ContourShading -> False]
```

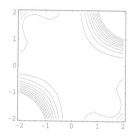

Changing the z component of the PlotRange allows different features to be picked out.

```
In[21]:= Show[%, PlotRange -> {-0.5, 0.5}]
```

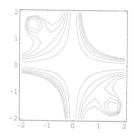

23.3 Generating ContourGraphics Objects

There are two main functions that build ContourGraphics: ContourPlot and ListContourPlot. This section describes them both.

> ContourPlot[f, {x, x_s, x_f},{y, y_s, y_f}]
>
>   generate contours from the function f
>
> ListContourPlot[{{z_{11}, z_{12}, ... }, ... }]
>
>   generate contours over a grid of points

Arguments of ContourPlot and ListContourPlot.

▶ *ContourPlot*

ContourPlot plots contours defined by a function.

In[22]:= ContourPlot[Sin[x] Sin[y], {x,0,2Pi},{y,0,2Pi}]

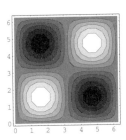

ContourPlot has a number of options that are not present in ContourGraphics.

In[23]:= Complement[
                Options[ContourPlot], Options[ContourGraphics]]

Out[23]= {Compiled -> True, PlotPoints -> 15}

Compiled

The Compiled option of ContourPlot controls whether or not *Mathematica* will use the internal compiler to evaluate the function being plotted. Generally, compilation makes the function evaluate faster.

PlotPoints

The PlotPoints option of ContourPlot controls the number of points at which the function is sampled. The default setting is 15 and this can be increased to produce a finer picture.

Increasing the PlotPoints allows a finer picture to be generated.

In[24]:= ContourPlot[Sin[x] Sin[y], {x,0,2Pi},{y,0,2Pi},
                PlotPoints -> 30]

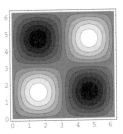

▶ *ListContourPlot*

In[25]:= data = Table[Sin[x] Sin[y], {y,0,2Pi,.2},{x,0,2Pi,.2}];

ListContourPlot will plot contours from a rectangular array of data. The MeshRange option makes sure that the axes are properly arranged.

In[26]:= ListContourPlot[data, MeshRange -> {{0,2Pi},{0,2Pi}}]

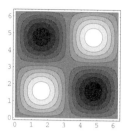

ListContourPlot has the same options as ContourGraphics.

In[27]:= Complement[Options[ListContourPlot],
              Options[ContourGraphics]]

Out[27]= {}

23.4 Converting ContourGraphics Objects

ContourGraphics objects can be converted to a variety of different forms. The conversion to Surface-Graphics or DensityGraphics works since the way that all these objects hold their data is very similar.

In[28]:= c = ContourPlot[Sin[x] Sin[y], {x,0,2Pi},{y,0,2Pi},
              PlotPoints -> 30]

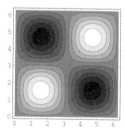

The data in a ContourGraphics object can be used to form a SurfaceGraphics or DensityGraphics object.

In[29]:= Show[SurfaceGraphics[c]]

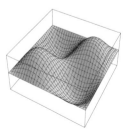

Graphics primitives can be generated from a ContourGraphics object.

In[30]:= **Graphics[c]**

Out[30]= -Graphics-

When these Graphics primitives are displayed the result is identical to the original contour plot.

In[31]:= **Show[%]**

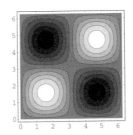

Chapter 12 discusses the conversion of *Mathematica* graphics objects in detail and shows many applications of the feature. In particular, the ability to generate graphics primitives from a contour plot has many uses, which is demonstrated in a wide variety of examples throughout *Mathematica Graphics*.

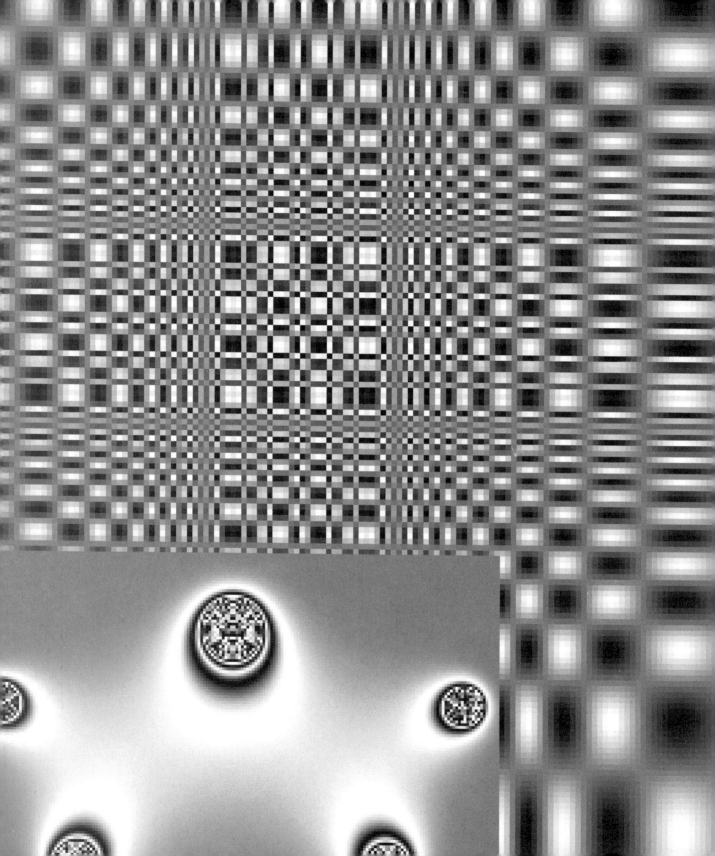

Chapter 24
DensityGraphics Reference

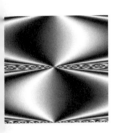

This chapter is intended to be a reference to DensityGraphics objects. It describes what they are and how they work. It is not intended to instruct how they should be used for visualization, which is done throughout the other parts of *Mathematica Graphics*.

24.1 Basic Structure

DensityGraphics objects are provided to represent plots of raster data. It is not required that there be a separate object for density plots; they could be represented by Graphics objects. However, having a special structure means that options specific to density plots can be changed by a call to Show. In general, DensityGraphics objects are not designed to be built directly. The reason for this is that the tools DensityPlot and ListDensityPlot are perfectly adequate to generate them in most situations.

DensityGraphics[{{z_{11},z_{12},... }, {z_{21},z_{22},... },... }, *options*]

                               values to use for a raster image

The structure of DensityGraphics objects.

The basic structure of DensityGraphics objects is that the first argument is an array of the *z* values of the three-dimensional data. This data forms a grid of equal-sized rectangles in the *xy* plane. This is followed by zero or more arguments that must be options or lists of options. The *x* and *y* values of the data are determined by the setting of the MeshRange option.

A DensityGraphics object. The values
of the raster are the first argument.

In[1]:= **DensityGraphics[{{0,0,0},{0,1,2},{0,2,4}}]**

Out[1]= -DensityGraphics-

In[2]:= **Show[%]**

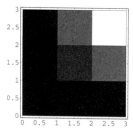

▶ *What Is a Density Plot?*

A density plot shows a rectangular plot that consists of a grid of smaller rectangles each being colored according to the value of a function. These small rectangles can be thought of as generalized pixels (they are different from the pixels of a computer display). A density plot can be compared to a shaded contour plot. One important difference is that, for a density plot, every sample point has its own contour line around it. Often a density plot works well when a contour plot works badly, while a contour plot works well when a density plot works badly. For a function that is rapidly changing, a density plot may well be better than a contour plot. When the function is smooth and flat a contour plot will often be better.

Here the regions where the function changes rapidly do not interfere with the rest of the picture.

```
In[3]:= DensityPlot[Sin[x/ Sin[y]],
            {x,-Pi,Pi}, {y,-Pi,Pi},
            PlotPoints -> 30, Mesh -> False]
```

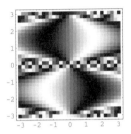

This contour plot of the same function is very congested making it hard to comprehend. The contours pile up in those regions where the function changes rapidly.

```
In[4]:= ContourPlot[Sin[x/ Sin[y]],
            {x,-Pi,Pi}, {y,-Pi,Pi}, PlotPoints -> 30]
```

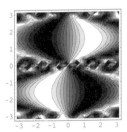

The function is so flat that there are few features in this plot.

```
In[5]:= DensityPlot[Sqrt[x y] ,
            {x,0,1}, {y,0,1},
            PlotPoints -> 30, Mesh -> False]
```

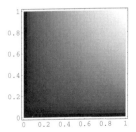

This contour plot of the same function gives a good idea of how the function behaves.

```
In[6]:= ContourPlot[x y,
            {x,0,1}, {y,0,1}, PlotPoints -> 30]
```

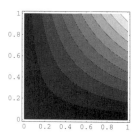

24.2 DensityGraphics Options

DensityGraphics objects have a number of options that can be altered by an appropriate call to Show. The data shown in a density plot are three-dimensional data but the picture is two-dimensional. Many of the options of DensityGraphics come from Graphics working in an analogous fashion. For example, the AspectRatio option changes the shape of the picture. Some options of DensityGraphics objects are different from Graphics.

These are options of DensityGraphics that are different from Graphics.

```
In[7]:= Complement[
            Options[DensityGraphics], Options[Graphics]]

Out[7]= {AspectRatio -> 1, ColorFunction -> Automatic,
         Frame -> True, Mesh -> True, MeshRange -> Automatic,
         MeshStyle -> Automatic}
```

In this section the unique options of DensityGraphics will be documented. A number of options of DensityGraphics have different default values. The AspectRatio is 1, giving a square picture, and Frame axes are drawn, ensuring the axes do not interfere with the picture.

▶ *ColorFunction*

The default setting of ColorFunction is Automatic which uses a gray shading.

```
In[8]:= DensityPlot[(x^2 - y^2)/(x^2 + y^2),
            {x,-1,1},{y,-1,1}]
```

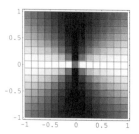

Setting the ColorFunction option uses the function to shade.

In[9]:= **Show[%, ColorFunction -> Hue]**

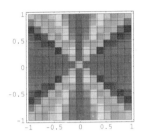

The default setting of ColorFunction is used.

In[10]:= **DensityPlot[Exp[1- x^2 - y^2] (-12 x y + 8 x^3 y^3),**
{x,-3,3},{y,-3,3}]

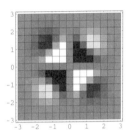

A special ColorFunction can pick out certain parts of an image and change the contrast.

In[11]:= **Show[%,**
ColorFunction ->
(If[# < 0.5, RGBColor[0,1,0],
RGBColor[2 (#-0.5), 0, 0]]&)]

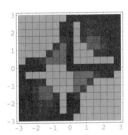

The values passed to the ColorFunction are scaled from the data so that the minimum and maximum values of the z component of the PlotRange scale to 0 and 1 respectively.

▸ *Mesh*

The Mesh option controls whether or not a mesh is drawn over the data. When the number of points is large the mesh is better omitted.

```
In[12]:= DensityPlot[(x^2 - y^2)/(x^2 + y^2),
            {x,-1,1},{y,-1,1}, PlotPoints -> 30,
            Mesh -> False]
```

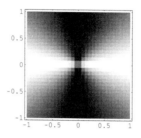

▸ *MeshRange*

The MeshRange option sets the range of values in x and y.

```
In[13]:= ListDensityPlot[
            Table[Sin[x y], {y,0,2Pi,.1},{x,0,Pi,.1}],
            MeshRange -> {{0,Pi},{0,2Pi}}, Mesh -> False]
```

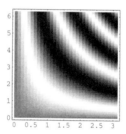

▸ *MeshStyle*

The MeshStyle option sets the style that is used for the mesh.

```
In[14]:= DensityPlot[(x^2 - y^2)/(x^2 + y^2),
            {x,-1,1},{y,-1,1},
            MeshStyle -> {Dashing[{0.02}]}]
```

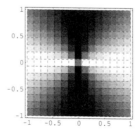

▸ *PlotRange*

The PlotRange option of DensityGraphics is different from the PlotRange option of Graphics since the former can take three components. The first two specify the *x* and *y* components of the PlotRange and work the same as for Graphics. The last specifies the *z* values of the PlotRange. These control the scaling of points for the ColorFunction. Points with a value that is not within the *z* values of the PlotRange are not shown.

The default PlotRange setting of Automatic is used.

In[15]:= **d = DensityPlot[(x^2 y^2) (1 + Sin[y] Sin[x]),**
{x,-2,2},{y,-2,2}, Mesh -> False]

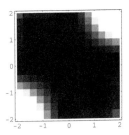

Changing the *z* component of the PlotRange allows different features to be picked out.

In[16]:= **Show[d, PlotRange -> {-0.5, 0.5}]**

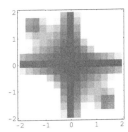

Using a non-linear ColorFunction can also help to change the contrast across an image.

In[17]:= **Show[d, ColorFunction -> (GrayLevel[Sqrt[#]]&)]**

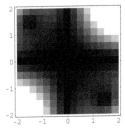

24.3 Generating DensityGraphics Objects

There are two main functions that build `DensityGraphics`: `DensityPlot` and `ListDensityPlot`. This section describes them.

> `DensityPlot[f, {x, x_s, x_f},{y, y_s, y_f}]`
>
> generate a density plot from the function f
>
> `ListDensityPlot[{{z_{11}, z_{12}, ... }, ... }]`
>
> generate a density plot from a grid of points

Arguments of `DensityPlot` and `ListDensityPlot`.

▶ *DensityPlot*

`DensityPlot` plots a density plot from a function.

In[18]:= `DensityPlot[Sin[x/Sin[y]], {x,-Pi,Pi},{y,-Pi,Pi}]`

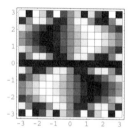

`DensityPlot` has a number of options that are not present in `DensityGraphics`.

In[19]:= `Complement[`
          `Options[DensityPlot], Options[DensityGraphics]]`

Out[19]= `{Compiled -> True, PlotPoints -> 15}`

Compiled

The `Compiled` option of `DensityPlot` controls whether or not *Mathematica* will use the internal compiler to evaluate the function being plotted. Generally, compilation makes the function evaluate faster.

PlotPoints

The `PlotPoints` option of `DensityPlot` controls the number of points at which the function is sampled. The default setting is 15 and this can be increased to produce a finer picture. When the `PlotPoints` are increased it is often good to switch off the mesh.

Increasing the PlotPoints allows a finer picture to be generated.

```
In[20]:= DensityPlot[Sin[x/Sin[y]], {x,-Pi,Pi},{y,-Pi,Pi},
            PlotPoints -> 40, Mesh -> False]
```

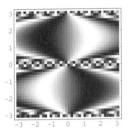

▶ *ListDensityPlot*

```
In[21]:= data = Table[Sin[x/Sin[y]],
            {y,-Pi,Pi,.2},{x,-Pi,Pi,.2}];
```

ListDensityPlot will plot a density plot from a rectangular array of data. The MeshRange option is set to make sure that the axes are properly arranged.

```
In[22]:= ListDensityPlot[data,
            MeshRange -> {{-Pi,Pi},{-Pi,Pi}}]
```

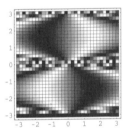

ListDensityPlot has the same options as DensityGraphics.

```
In[23]:= Complement[Options[ListDensityPlot],
            Options[DensityGraphics]]
Out[23]= {}
```

24.4 Converting DensityGraphics Objects

DensityGraphics objects can be converted to a variety of different forms. The conversion to Surface-Graphics or ContourGraphics works since the way that all these objects hold their data is very similar. Chapter 12 discusses the conversion of graphics objects with many examples showing why it is useful.

In[24]:= d = DensityPlot[Sin[x] Sin[y], {x,0,2Pi},{y,0,2Pi},
        PlotPoints -> 30]

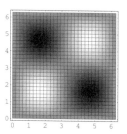

The data in a DensityGraphics object can be used to form a SurfaceGraphics or DensityGraphics object.

In[25]:= **Show[SurfaceGraphics[d]]**

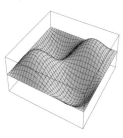

Graphics primitives can be generated from a DensityGraphics object.

In[26]:= **Show[Graphics[d]]**

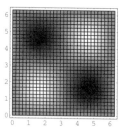

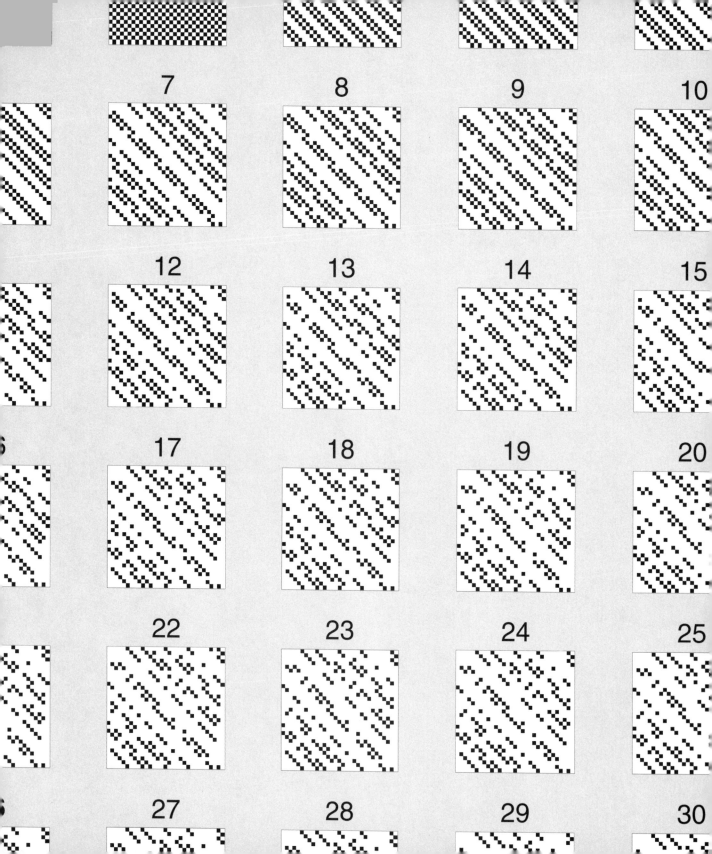

Chapter 25
GraphicsArray Reference

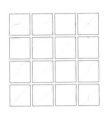

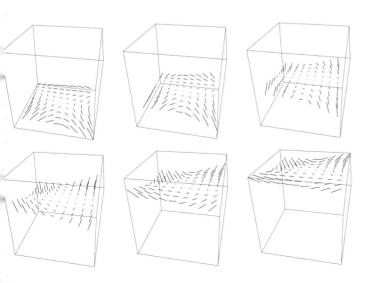

This chapter is a reference for GraphicsArray objects.

25.1 Basic Structure

The aim of the GraphicsArray object is to represent an array of graphics objects. They are generated by building them directly from the constituent graphics objects.

GraphicsArray[{g_1, g_2, ... }]	a horizontal line of graphics objects g_i
GraphicsArray[{{g_1}, {g_2}, ... }]	a vertical line of graphics objects g_i
GraphicsArray[{{g_{11}, g_{12}, ... }, ... }]	an array of graphics objects g_{ij}

The structure of GraphicsArray objects.

Three graphics objects are generated.

```
In[1]:= Table[
           Plot[Sin[x]^n, {x,0,2Pi},
               DisplayFunction -> Identity], {n,3}]

Out[1]= {-Graphics-, -Graphics-, -Graphics-}
```

The three pictures are plotted side by side.

```
In[2]:= Show[GraphicsArray[%]]
```

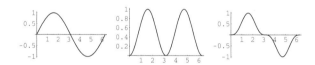

An array of pictures is generated.

```
In[3]:= Table[
           Plot[Sin[x]^m + Cos[x]^n, {x,0,2Pi},
               DisplayFunction -> Identity], {m,3}, {n,4}]

Out[3]= {{-Graphics-, -Graphics-, -Graphics-, -Graphics-},
         {-Graphics-, -Graphics-, -Graphics-, -Graphics-},
         {-Graphics-, -Graphics-, -Graphics-, -Graphics-}}
```

The array of objects is plotted.   *In[4]:=* **Show[GraphicsArray[%]]**

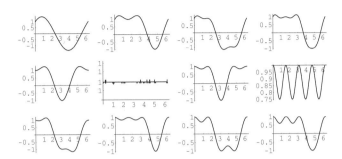

25.2 GraphicsArray Options

GraphicsArray objects have a number of options that can be altered by an appropriate call to Show. The type of picture that is displayed is a Graphics object and the options of GraphicsArray are derived from Graphics.

<table>
<tr><td>These are options of GraphicsArray that are different from Graphics.</td><td>

In[5]:= **Complement[**
                    Options[GraphicsArray], Options[Graphics]]

Out[5]= {AspectRatio -> Automatic, FrameTicks -> None,
       GraphicsSpacing -> 0.1, Ticks -> None}
</td></tr>
</table>

In this section the unique options of GraphicsArray will be documented. A number of options of GraphicsArray have different default values. The setting of the Ticks and FrameTicks options is None, ensuring that when axes are drawn no tick marks are displayed.

In[6]:= **Table[**
                Plot[Sin[x]^n, {x,0,2Pi},
                    DisplayFunction -> Identity], {n,3}]

Out[6]= {-Graphics-, -Graphics-, -Graphics-}

A frame is included around the picture. $In[7]:=$ **Show[GraphicsArray[%], Frame -> True]**

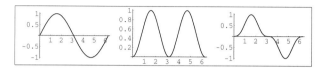

▸ *GraphicsSpacing*

$In[8]:=$ **Table[**
        Plot[Sin[x]^m + Cos[x]^n, {x,0,2Pi},
            DisplayFunction -> Identity], {m,2}, {n,2}]

$Out[8]=$ **{{-Graphics-, -Graphics-}, {-Graphics-, -Graphics-}}**

The GraphicsSpacing option controls the space between the sub-images. Here no space is left.

$In[9]:=$ **Show[GraphicsArray[%], GraphicsSpacing -> 0]**

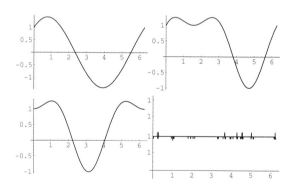

Here the space in the *x* direction is a tenth of the distance across an image. The space in the *y* direction is two tenths.

In[10]:= **Show[%, GraphicsSpacing -> {0.1, 0.2}]**

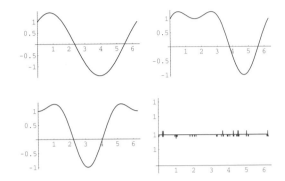

▸ *Changing Sub-Image Options*

When the options of a GraphicsArray are changed with Show this only changes the options of the GraphicsArray object itself. In order to change the options of the images a replacement rule must be applied. Chapter 7 page 107 discussed the use of replacement rules, as well as other details of *Mathematica* programming. Probably it is better to make images with the correct options to start with. This example shows how the options can be changed if the array has already been made.

In[11]:= **Table[**
    Plot[Sin[x]^m + Cos[x]^n, {x,0,2Pi},
     DisplayFunction -> Identity], {m,2}, {n,2}]

Out[11]= **{{-Graphics-, -Graphics-}, {-Graphics-, -Graphics-}}**

The sub-plots each have different PlotRange settings.

In[12]:= **Show[GraphicsArray[%]]**

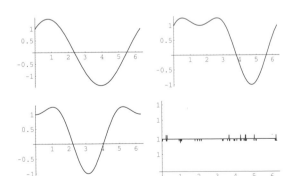

Now the scale is the same for all the
images and the picture is improved.

```
In[13]:= Show[% /.
            GraphicsArray[obj_, opts___] :>
               GraphicsArray[obj /. (PlotRange -> _) :>
                  PlotRange -> {-1.5,1.5}]]
```

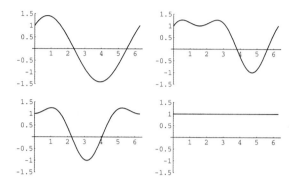

Chapter 26
Rendering and Exporting Graphics

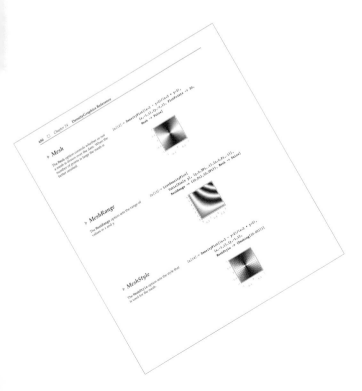

This chapter describes how *Mathematica* graphics objects are rendered. It continues to discuss the techniques that can be used to export *Mathematica* graphics to other applications. The first two parts concern the kernel commands Show and Display, and the latter parts cover tools provided as part of the *Mathematica* front end. A short description of the front end is provided in Chapter 6.

The tools that *Mathematica* provides to export graphics can be divided between those available from the notebook and those from the non-notebook front ends. The notebook front end provides tools that are easier to use in their basic forms. However, when these tools don't provide the correct functionality or don't work properly they are very hard to alter. In contrast, the non-notebook front end provides tools that are harder to use but ultimately more flexible. For example, they can be controlled by a program as opposed to the notebook tools that require manually selecting menu items. Fortunately most versions of *Mathematica* come with both sets of tools and it is possible to take advantage of both approaches.

▸ *Graphics File Formats*

The later sections of this chapter will talk about the various graphics formats that are used by different applications. One way to classify these formats is whether or not they are bitmap formats. A bitmap format contains a grid of pixels that drawn together show a picture. A non-bitmap or object format contains a description of objects that are to be drawn to form a picture. A bitmap format has a fixed resolution and when drawn at a different resolution the appearance of the picture usually degrades. An object format can be drawn at any size or resolution without degrading the appearance. An object format can be turned into an image format by a process called rasterization; when it is viewed on a screen or printed it must be rasterized.

The description of graphics primitives that *Mathematica* uses is an object format. Other object formats are PICT, PostScript, or Windows Metafile. Bitmap formats include TIFF and ppm. Most object formats also include a bitmap representation and sometimes this is inserted in a file to allow an application to display a simple representation of the contents without having to go through all the steps of rendering. A good description of graphics file formats is given in *Graphics File Formats*, D.C. Kay and J.R. Levine. When *Mathematica* graphics are to be exported it is often worthwhile to be aware of whether or not a bitmap format is being used.

26.1 Show

The first section of this chapter will describe the command Show, which is one of the most important commands for working with all types of graphics objects. Show does three things: it invokes the DisplayFunction, it processes options, and it combines graphics objects. The first one of these is the most important.

▸ *Calling the DisplayFunction*

When Show receives a graphics object as an argument it determines the setting of the DisplayFunction option. It then builds an expression using this as the head and the graphics object as the argument. This is returned as the result and it may then evaluate further. The typical default value of the DisplayFunction is set to make a picture appear. The actual setting of the `DisplayFunction` is described in the next section on `Display`.

This uses the default setting for the `DisplayFunction` option; a picture appears.

```
In[1]:= Show[
            Graphics[Line[{{0,0}, {1,1}}]]]
```

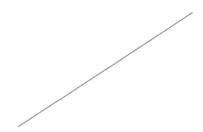

Now the `DisplayFunction` is changed to take the first element of the graphics object.

```
In[2]:= Show[%, DisplayFunction -> First]

Out[2]= Line[{{0, 0}, {1, 1}}]
```

It is important to note that no mention of PostScript has been made to this point. `Show` calls a *Mathematica* function determined by the `DisplayFunction` option. This happens to be set in *Mathematica* to call a function that generates PostScript. However, there is no reason why the `DisplayFunction` could not be set to call some other way of rendering graphics. Of course, work would be necessary to develop this but if it were done, everything in *Mathematica* graphics would work in the new way.

▸ *Processing Options*

In addition to calling the `DisplayFunction`, `Show` also carries out options processing. It is this functionality that allows an option to be set by making a call to `Show`.

A `Graphics` object is built with one option included.

```
In[3]:= Graphics[Line[{{0,0}, {1,1}}],
            DisplayFunction -> Identity]//InputForm

Out[3]//InputForm=
    Graphics[Line[{{0, 0}, {1, 1}}], DisplayFunction -> Identity]
```

Now an option is changed with a call to `Show`. The new option is included in front of the old options. This is how `Show` can change an option setting.

```
In[4]:= Show[%, Axes -> True]//InputForm

Out[4]//InputForm=
    Graphics[Line[{{0, 0}, {1, 1}}],
        {Axes -> True, DisplayFunction -> Identity}]
```

▸ *Combining Graphics Objects*

The last functionality that `Show` provides is to combine graphics objects. The ability of *Mathematica* to convert and combine graphics objects has been used throughout the text and is the topic of Chapter 12.

Two `Graphics` objects are built.

```
In[5]:= (g1 = Graphics[Line[{{0,0}, {1,1}}]];
         g2 = Graphics[Point[{2,2}]]);
```

A call to Show combines the two
Graphics objects.

In[6]:= **Show[g1, g2]**

Looking at the result in InputForm it is
clear that the two Graphics objects
have been combined.

In[7]:= **InputForm[%]**

Out[7]//InputForm=
Graphics[{Line[{{0, 0}, {1, 1}}], Point[{2, 2}]}, {}]

In this example two Graphics objects were combined. This was particularly easy since all that was necessary was a concatenation of the primitives. Sometimes the objects have to be converted into some common form before this can be done. In this case Show will decide what conversion is necessary and carry it out. A number of examples of this are given in Chapter 12.

26.2 Display

When a picture is generated by *Mathematica* it is done in two steps. First the graphics object is converted into PostScript by the kernel command Display. This PostScript is then passed to an external program that actually draws is on the screen. By using PostScript as a common medium *Mathematica* ensures that graphics works in a similar way on all platforms[2].

Display is actually invoked by the setting of the DisplayFunction option. As was described earlier in this chapter one of the functions of the kernel command Show is to find this setting and use it. It is to be noted that the *actual* setting of the DisplayFunction option varies from system to system. What follows is a generic description that will explain the principles underlying specific settings.

Display is the lowest level kernel graphics function that is invoked when graphics are produced. Consequently, rules are sometimes attached to it when some special new meaning is to be given to part of a graphics object. An example of this was presented in Chapter 13 page 267, where a new way to position labels in plots was implemented by a rule on Display.

The option that determines how
graphics output is produced.

In[8]:= **Options[Graphics, DisplayFunction]**

Out[8]= {DisplayFunction :> $DisplayFunction}

---

[2]It is possible to initialize *Mathematica* so that graphics are not generated into PostScript but are rendered in some other way. The description here applies to the default ways that are provided with *Mathematica*. The alternative would require a significant development effort.

This value of $DisplayFunction is a pure function that calls Display. Pure functions are described in Chapter 7 page 110.

```
In[9]:= $DisplayFunction

Out[9]= Display[$Display, #1] &
```

Display is the actual kernel command that produces PostScript. It is used in the DisplayFunction above to send PostScript to $Display.

```
In[10]:= ?Display

Display[channel, graphics] writes graphics or sound to the
    specified output channel.
```

$Display is set so that the binary motifps is launched and then has PostScript written into it. This result is machine dependent.

```
In[11]:= $Display

Out[11]= !motifps -h '400' -w '400' -T 'Mathematica Graphics:\
    Out[11]'
```

A graphics object is generated for an example.

```
In[12]:= g = Graphics[Line[{{0,0},{1,1}}]]

Out[12]= -Graphics-
```

This converts the graphics object to PostScript which is written into the file tmp.ps.

```
In[13]:= Display["tmp.ps", g]

Out[13]= -Graphics-
```

The result of Display is the original graphics object.

```
In[14]:= InputForm[%]

Out[14]//InputForm= Graphics[Line[{{0, 0}, {1, 1}}]]
```

The contents of the file `tmp.ps` can be displayed.

```
In[15]:= !!tmp.ps

%!
%%Creator: Mathematica
%%AspectRatio: .61803
MathPictureStart
/Mabs {
Mgmatrix idtransform
Mtmatrix dtransform
} bind def
/Mabsadd { Mabs
3 -1 roll add
3 1 roll add
exch } bind def
%% Graphics
/Courier findfont 5.5   scalefont   setfont
% Scaling calculations
0.02381 0.952381 0.014715 0.588604 [
[ 0 0 0 ]
[ 1 .61803 0 0 ]
] MathScale
% Start of Graphics
1 setlinecap
1 setlinejoin
newpath
.5 Mabswid
[ ] 0 setdash
0 0 m
1 0 L
1 .61803 L
0 .61803 L
closepath
clip
newpath
0 g
.02381 .01472 m
.97619 .60332 L
s
% End of Graphics
MathPictureEnd
```

The result of these commands is to convert the `Graphics` object into PostScript and to write this into a file. Alternatively the PostScript could have been written with some other communication mechanism such as a pipe, or through *MathLink*.

One important point about the PostScript generated by `Display` is that it is not complete PostScript, it lacks the definition of certain operators. These definitions must be added for the output to be rendered by a generic PostScript device such as a printer. The PostScript interpreters that are supplied with *Mathematica* are initialized with these definitions. In addition, utility programs that add the necessary PostScript operators are also supplied. In most cases there is no need to explicitly use these utilities since everything is set up so that graphics work with no special action being taken. In certain unusual circumstances it is useful to know how to add these definitions. The tools that do this are described later in the chapter.

An important point about `Display` is that it has no inverse that reverses the process of converting a graphics object into PostScript. A file containing PostScript cannot be un-rendered back into the kernel. In the case of *Mathematica* pictures there is no need to do this since the PostScript must originally have been generated from a *Mathematica* object. Thus, keeping the *Mathematica* procedures will allow the graphics object and the PostScript to be regenerated at any time. For some types of graphics, such as three-dimensional graphics, converting back to a `Graphics3D` object would not be possible since PostScript does not contain all the information, such as depth information, that was present in the original object. Just as there is no such thing as an uncompiler that takes a compiled binary and regenerates the original C or Fortran code, there is no un-renderer for *Mathematica* PostScript.

The rest of this chapter will look at the tools that are provided by the notebook and non-notebook front ends to export *Mathematica* graphics.

26.3 Notebook Graphics Formats

In order to see how the notebook front end can export graphics it will be useful to review the different ways that graphics can be stored in a notebook. When the kernel displays a graphics object it creates PostScript and this is sent to the front end. The actual text of the PostScript is stored in a graphics cell in the notebook. When a graphics cell is created the PostScript is rendered to form the picture. When the picture is resized the PostScript can easily be re-rendered into the new size.

There are alternatives to keeping PostScript in a graphics cell. It can be converted to a variety of different formats that are listed in the table below. The formats that are available are those that are native to the system under which the front end is running. The conversion is made by choosing the appropriate item from the **Graph** menu.

Notebook Version	Formats Supported
Macintosh	PICT, Bitmap PICT, Embedded PostScript PICT
Windows	Bitmap
X Windows	Ximage, Pixmap
NeXT	Bitmap

Alternative front end graphics formats.

Apart from PICT and Embedded PostScript PICT these are all bitmap formats. Converting the images to a bitmap format can, in certain circumstances, use less memory to keep than the original PostScript. This is especially true for pictures where many objects are overlaid on top of each other, as with certain three-dimensional pictures. Once conversion to a bitmap image has been made the picture will not rescale smoothly as it did before.

The conversion to these formats can also be used as a prelude to writing into a file. If the graphic has been converted into a PICT or a Bitmap format then these will set the format of the file. The next section describes writing a graphic into a file.

26.4 Exporting Graphics: The Notebook Front End

The simplest way to export a graphic from *Mathematica* is to print it. As described in Chapter 6 page 91 printing works in the typical way for an application of the system on which the front end is running. If the graphic is to be included in another application it must be exported from *Mathematica*, either directly into the application or into a file that is then imported.

▷ *Exporting by Copy and Paste*

A graph can be selected and copied from a graphics cell in the usual way. When this is done a version of the graphic is saved. If the **Paste** command is then given an attempt will be made to paste the graphic at the current insertion point. If the insertion point is in a *Mathematica* notebook at a position where a new cell will be created, then a graphics cell is created containing the picture. When the insertion point has been switched to a new application the behavior is more complex since the application must be capable of accepting graphics. If it can accept graphics then the contents of the cell may need to be modified to be inserted. The way this works is different on different types of computers.

Macintosh

When a *Mathematica* graphic is pasted into an application on the Macintosh it will, by default, be converted to a bitmap PICT format. PICT is a standard Macintosh format for graphics, and is an object-based format of primitives such as lines and polygons. The bitmap PICT represents the picture as a bitmap object. The bitmap is in most circumstances the most compact representation for a graphic. However, it will probably not appear well when the picture is rendered on a higher resolution device such as a printer.

There are two other PICT based formats that can be used, basic PICT or PICT with Embedded PostScript. The basic PICT converts the PostScript into actual PICT objects and these can be manipulated by certain Macintosh applications. PICT with Embedded PostScript is a PICT bitmap that contains the original PostScript. When this is printed the picture will appear the same as the orginal picture in *Mathematica* and will probably have the highest quality of these formats.

The actual format that is used depends upon whether the cell has been converted and how the front end defaults have been set. If the graphics cell has been converted into some other format, as was described in the previous section, then the new format will be pasted. Thus if the cell has been converted to PICT with Embedded PostScript, that will be pasted. If the cell has not been converted then a default will be used. The original setting is bitmap PICT. This can be changed by altering the settings in the **Convert Clipboard** item of the **Edit** menu. The documentation describes how this can be done.

Microsoft Windows

A *Mathematica* graphic can be pasted into an application on Microsoft Windows with the **Paste Special** command of the **Edit** menu. When this is selected a dialog box will request the type of image to be pasted. The choices include metafile and bitmap. The bitmap is more compact but will appear less pleasing when the document is printed.

NeXT

When a graphic is pasted into an application on the NeXT it will either be in a PostScript or a TIFF format. Either of these can be accepted by many NeXT applications. If it is not accepted then nothing will be inserted. Since *Mathematica* graphics are generated as PostScript which is the natural graphics format for the NeXT there are few issues of conversions. These work easily and produce pleasing results.

X Windows

Under X Windows there are extremely few applications that are capable of accepting graphics through copy and paste[3]. Thus, in order to export graphics from the X Windows front end it is necessary to use a file format.

▸ *Encapsulated PostScript File*

An alternative to pasting a picture directly into an application is to save the picture in a file. A common and useful format of file is an Encapsulated PostScript (EPS) file. There are many applications that can import an EPS file. When this is done the imported picture will be placed in the parent document. The application that imported the picture may not contain the ability to render PostScript. So that it can show a representation of what the picture would look like the EPS file usually contains a bitmap that an application can render to give some idea of its appearance. When the document is rendered on a PostScript device such as a printer the actual PostScript of the picture and not the bitmap is used.

On the Macintosh front end an EPS file is created from a *Mathematica* graphic by selecting the graphic and using the **Copy** command to copy it to the clipboard. Then the **Convert Clipboard** item of the **Edit** menu should be invoked. This brings up a dialog box under which an option to save an EPS file can be chosen.

On the NeXT front end a similar procedure is followed. The graphic is selected and copied. Then the **Convert Pasteboard** item of the **Edit** menu should be invoked. This brings up a dialog box under which an EPS file can be written.

Under Microsoft Windows an EPS file is generated by selecting and then copying a graphic and choosing the **Export** command under the **File** menu. When this is selected a dialog box comes up and saving the graphic as an EPS file can be chosen.

The Version 2.2 X Windows front end has no capability to save a *Mathematica* picture in an EPS file. However, this can be done by using the binary **rasterps** to write the file directly from the kernel. A description of this is given later in this chapter in the section on exporting graphics from the kernel page 676.

▸ *Adobe Illustrator File*

An alternative file format for a *Mathematica* graphic is the Adobe Illustrator file format. A file saved in this format can be imported into Adobe Illustrator and certain other applications. When it is imported the graphic is visible as it may be when EPS is imported. However, the actual elements of the graphic such as lines, text, and polygons can be edited and manipulated. This means that extra embellishments for labeling can be added to a picture and that the positions and appearance of existing objects altered. This ability to interactively edit a graphic can be very useful for certain types of work.

An Adobe Illustrator file can be written by following steps similar to those described for writing EPS, the difference being that an Adobe Illustrator file is chosen instead. Only the Macintosh and Microsoft

---

[3]The *Mathematica* notebook front end running under X Windows can paste graphics into another copy of the *Mathematica* front end.

Windows front ends can write Adobe Illustrator files. For the NeXT and X Windows front ends it is necessary to do this directly from the kernel, as is described in the next section.

▸ *Other File Formats*

There are a number of machine-specific formats in which the various notebook front ends can save graphics. Thus, the Macintosh can save a file with a PICT image, the NeXT can save a file with a TIFF image, and the Microsoft Windows version can save a Windows Metafile rendering of a graphic. The documentation that comes with individual front ends describes the different ways that files in these formats can be saved.

26.5 Exporting Graphics: The Kernel

An alternative to using the notebook front end to export graphics is to use the kernel. This will be necessary when a notebook front end is not available or if it lacks some particular feature. Exporting graphics in this way can be considered as a feature of the non-notebook front end even though it may be the kernel that is actually involved in conjunction with certain ancilliary tools of the non-notebook front end.

The main tool provided to work with PostScript is called **rasterps**. This is a compiled binary that exists for all versions of *Mathematica* except the Macintosh[4]. A simpler tool, available on Unix workstations, is called **psfix**. This is not a compiled binary but a shell script. Since **psfix** is simpler it will be discussed first.

▸ *psfix*

psfix is a Unix shell script that works as a filter adding PostScript definitions to *Mathematica* PostScript. These examples will only work on versions of *Mathematica* that have **psfix**. If **psfix** is not present then **rasterps** can be used instead.

This is a graphics object for demonstration.	`In[15]:= g =`
	`        Plot[Sin[x] + x, {x,-10, 10},`
	`            DisplayFunction -> Identity]`
	`Out[15]= -Graphics-`

The graphic is turned into *Mathematica* PostScript which is written into the file tmp.mps.	`In[16]:= Display["tmp.mps", g]` `Out[16]= -Graphics-`
psfix is run on the file tmp.mps and the result directed into tmp.ps. This could also be run from a shell command-line rather than from within *Mathematica*.	`In[17]:= Run["psfix tmp.mps > tmp.ps"];`

---

[4]The Microsoft Windows version of *Mathematica* is not shipped with **rasterps**. However, the DOS version of **rasterps** runs under Windows and is available from *MathSource*.

The first 10 lines of the file are
displayed. The file tmp.ps contains
valid PostScript and could be rendered
by a PostScript device.

```
In[18]:= TableForm[
             ReadList["tmp.ps", Record, 10],
             TableSpacing -> {0,0}]

Out[18]//TableForm= %!PS-Adobe-2.0 EPSF-2.0
                    %%BoundingBox: 72 72 540 720
                    %%Creator: Mathematica
                    %%CreationDate: Sat Aug 13 11:18:00 CDT 1994
                    %%EndComments
                    /Mathdict 150 dict def
                    Mathdict begin
                    /Mlmarg 1.0 72 mul def
                    /Mrmarg 1.0 72 mul def
                    /Mbmarg 1.0 72 mul def
```

The file that results from these steps, tmp.ps, could be sent to a generic PostScript device such as a printer. A more sophisticated use of **psfix** is to define a printing command to work from the kernel that would combine several steps. This is actually how printing to a PostScript printer is implemented on non-notebook workstation versions of *Mathematica*. The command that will print graphics is called PSPrint. It will be demonstrated in these examples.

```
In[19]:= ?PSPrint
PSPrint[-graphics-] sends graphics to a printer.
```

A plot is made to be printed.

```
In[20]:= Plot[Sin[x] + x, {x,-10, 10}]
```

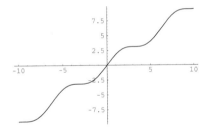

This will send the plot to the default
printer.

```
In[21]:= PSPrint[%]
Out[21]= -Graphics-
```

This shows the implementation of
PSPrint on a Unix workstation version
of *Mathematica*.

```
In[22]:= ??PSPrint
PSPrint[-graphics-] sends graphics to a printer.

PSPrint[x_] := Display["!psfix | lpr", x]
```

PSPrint is defined in terms of the command Display. As described earlier this takes a graphics object and writes a stream of PostScript to the specified channel. Here the channel is defined as a pipe to **psfix** by prepending it with an exclamation point. After **psfix** has added the definitions the result is piped to the printer command, **lpr**. This will send the PostScript to the default printer and if this is a PostScript device the picture will be printed. If the printer does not understand PostScript then **rasterps** should be used instead. This is described later in the section and also in the documentation.

Options of psfix

There are several options for **psfix** that set the size of the picture, the size of margins, and whether or not to print in landscape mode.

-width x	width of image in inches
-height *numbery*	height of image in inches
-lmarg *numberx*	width of left margin in inches
-rmarg *numberx*	width of right margin in inches
-bmarg *numbery*	height of bottom margin in inches
-tmarg *numbery*	height of top margin in inches
-land	print in landscape mode
-epsf	produce an EPS file

Options of **psfix**.

PSPrint does not provide any mechanism for setting these options. Since its definition is so simple, it can easily be rewritten to include some different option setting. An example will be given that changes the command-line options of **psfix** so that no margins are placed around the picture. It also sets an option of **lpr** to send the output to a printer named "newton".

Here PSPrint is redefined so that no margin is drawn around the picture and the output goes to the printer called newton.

```
In[23]:= PSPrint[x_] :=
            Display[
                "!psfix -lmarg 0 -rmarg 0 -tmarg 0 -bmarg 0 |
                lpr -Pnewton", x]
```

▶ *rasterps*

The tool **rasterps** is a compiled binary that is also available to work with *Mathematica* PostScript. There are command-line options to **rasterps** that are similar to those of **psfix**. In addition a format option allows a wide range of different output formats to be generated. Because of this ability to produce different formats **rasterps** is more powerful than **psfix**.

-T *string*	use *string* as the title
-width *number* x	width of image in inches
-height *number* y	height of image in inches
-xdpi *number*	x resolution in dots per inch
-ydpi *number*	y resolution in dots per inch
-file *filename*	output to go to *filename*
-format *dev*	output to be in special format

Some of the options of **rasterps**.

ps	PostScript
eps	Encapsulated PostScript
psimask	PostScript imagemask format
hplj.150	HP LaserJet at 150 dpi
hplj.300	HP LaserJet at 300 dpi
epsonfx	Epson FX printer
xbitmap	X bitmap file
ppm	Portable pixmap

Some settings for the format option of **rasterps**.

These are only some of the values for the format option; a complete list is given in the appropriate user manual. **rasterps** can work in a similar way to the examples of **psfix** that were demonstrated earlier. By setting the format option it can do other things that **psfix** cannot. For example, it can produce output for an HP LaserJet printer.

This is a graphics object to use for demonstration.

```
In[24]:= g =
             Plot[Sin[x] + x, {x,-10, 10},
                 DisplayFunction -> Identity]

Out[24]= -Graphics-
```

The graphic is turned into *Mathematica* PostScript and written into the file tmp.mps.

```
In[25]:= Display["tmp.mps", g]

Out[25]= -Graphics-
```

rasterps is run on the file tmp.mps and the result directed into tmp.hp. This could also be run from the shell command-line rather than from within *Mathematica*.

```
In[26]:= Run["rasterps -format hplj.75 tmp.mps > tmp.hp"];
```

The result of these steps is to produce a file, `tmp.hp`, that could be printed on an HP LaserJet printer. They can be combined into a *Mathematica* function analogous to PSPrint.

A function that prints *Mathematica* graphics on an HP LaserJet printer.

```
In[27]:= HPLaserPrint[g_] :=
            Display["!rasterps -format hplj.75 | lpr", g];
```

Encapsulated PostScript and Adobe Illustrator Files

An EPS file can be produced by **rasterps**. This is done by setting the format option to EPS. In Version 2.2 *Mathematica* an error of **rasterps** made it necessary to set the *x* and *y* resolution to be 72 dots per inch. A *Mathematica* function that generates an EPS file can be written and is quite similar to PSPrint.

EPSExport uses **rasterps** to write a representation of a graphics object into an EPS file.

```
In[28]:= EPSExport[file_, g_] :=
            Display["!rasterps -width 3 -height 3 -xdpi 72
               -ydpi 72 -format eps > " <> file, g]

In[29]:= g = Plot[Sin[x], {x,0,2Pi},
               DisplayFunction -> Identity]

Out[29]= -Graphics-
```

The function EPSExport writes EPS into the file `tmp.eps`.

```
In[30]:= EPSExport["tmp.eps", g]

Out[30]= -Graphics-
```

The first 10 lines of `tmp.eps` are displayed.

```
In[31]:= TableForm[
            ReadList["tmp.eps", Record, 10],
            TableSpacing -> {0,0}]

Out[31]//TableForm=

%!PS-Adobe-2.0 EPSF-2.0
%%BoundingBox: 0 0 216 216
%%Creator: Mathematica
%%CreationDate: Sat Aug 13 11:18:11 1994
%%EndComments
%%BeginPreview: 216 216 1 216
%00000000000000000000000000000000000000000000000000000000000
%00000000000000000000000000000000000000000000000000000000000
%00000000000000000000000000000000000000000000000000000000000
%00000000000000000000000000000000000000000000000000000000000
```

AIExport uses **rasterps** to write a representation of a graphics object into an Adobe Illustrator file.

```
In[32]:= AIExport[file_, g_] :=
            Display["!rasterps -width 3 -height 3 -xdpi 72
               -ydpi 72 -format ai88 > " <> file, g]
```

These two functions, EPSExport and AIExport, demonstrate how the functionality of the notebook front end to export graphics objects into different formats can be reproduced by the kernel. If there is no notebook front end or if the front end lacks this functionality this is how graphics objects can be exported.

▶ Bitmap Files

There are several bitmap formats into which **rasterps** can output graphics. One of these, the portable pixmap (ppm) format, is extremely useful for converting into other formats. There is a large collection of freely available software for converting ppm files into many different formats such as TIFF or PICT. One place to obtain these utilities is from *MathSource*; sending the request "find ppm" will return the relevant information.

An example will be given here of using two of the utilities that can be built from the library on *MathSource*. One is **anytopnm** which converts a pixmap file to a pnm file, and the other is **pnmtotiff** that converts a pnm file to a Tag Image File Format (TIFF) file. TIFF is a bitmap file format that is supported by a wide variety of applications.

A demonstration graphics object.	`In[33]:= g = Plot[Sin[x], {x,0,2Pi},`
	`                        DisplayFunction -> Identity]`
	
	`Out[33]= -Graphics-`

TiffExport produces PostScript, rasterizes this into a ppm file, runs **anytopnm**, and then **pnmtotiff** to result in a TIFF file.	`In[34]:= TiffExport[file_, g_] :=`
	`             (Display["!rasterps -format ppm > tmp.ppm", g] ;`
	`              Run["anytopnm tmp.ppm > tmp.pnm"] ;`
	`              Run[StringJoin["pnmtotiff tmp.pnm > ", file]] ;`
	`              Run["rm tmp.ppm; rm tmp.pnm"];`
	`              g)`

The graphics object g is written out as a TIFF file.	`In[35]:= TiffExport["file.tiff", g]`
	
	`pnmtotiff: computing colormap...`
	`pnmtotiff: 2 colors found`
	
	`Out[35]= -Graphics-`

This example of the function `TiffExport` will not work unless the binaries **anytopnm** and **pnmtotiff** exist and are available. One problem with the function as it is written is that it will delete any existing file that is called `tmp.ppm` or `tmp.pnm`. An improvement would be to write these in some temporary directory.

▸ *Video Output*

There are several ways that a *Mathematica* animation can be converted to produce video output. One way would be to use the Macintosh front end to produce a QuickTime movie. The QuickTime movie can then be converted to video in a number of ways, such as converting it to MPEG.

▸ *Output as DXF*

Drawing Interchange Format, DXF, is a standard file format for CAD programs. It is also used by many raytracing graphics programs as an interchange format. The standard package `Utilities`DXF`` will write three-dimensional *Mathematica* graphics into a DXF file. This functionality allows *Mathematica* graphics to be imported into CAD programs.

The DXF package is loaded.	`In[36]:= Needs["Utilities`DXF`"]`

A `Graphics3D` object is made to be saved in a DXF file.	`In[37]:= g =`
	`             Graphics3D[{Polygon[{{0,0,0},{1,0,0},{0,1,0}}]}]`
	
	`Out[37]= -Graphics3D-`

The DXF file is written.

```
In[38]:= WriteDXF["tmp.dxf", g]

Out[38]= tmp.dxf
```

▸ *Output as ThreeScript*

ThreeScript is a three-dimensional graphics file format developed by Wolfram Research and used by a few applications. A ThreeScript file can be written by loading the package `Graphics‘ThreeScript‘`. Since the development of *MathLink* there has been less need for applications to use a custom file format in which to save three-dimensional graphics.

The ThreeScript package is loaded.

```
In[39]:= Needs["Graphics‘ThreeScript‘"]
```

A `Graphics3D` object is made to be saved in a ThreeScript file.

```
In[40]:= g =
            Graphics3D[{Polygon[{{0,0,0},{1,0,0},{0,1,0}}]}]

Out[40]= -Graphics3D-
```

The ThreeScript file is written.

```
In[41]:= ThreeScript["tmp.ts", g]

Out[41]= tmp.ts
```

▸ *MathLink*

The last method for exporting *Mathematica* graphics from the kernel that will be mentioned in this chapter is *MathLink*. Using *MathLink* it is possible to export actual *Mathematica* graphics objects to an external application. If the external application has some graphics object description then it may be relatively easy to convert *Mathematica* primtives to these objects. Of course, to do this will require the development of some code.

An example of this is the connection between *Mathematica* and the Advanced Visualization System (AVS). This works by exporting three-dimensional graphics objects to the AVS geometry visualizer. This is done by redefining the `DisplayFunction` option of `Graphics3D` and `SurfaceGraphics` to be a function that writes primitives over *MathLink*. As a consequence, when three-dimensional plotting commands such as `Plot3D` or `ParametricPlot3D` are carried out instead of pictures appearing in the PostScript interpreter via `Display` they appear in AVS. The interesting feature of this is that most of the three-dimensional packages and commands work just as before except that the graphics are drawn by a different system. Changing the `DisplayFunction` makes it straightforward to redirect graphics output. The tools to connect between *Mathematica* and AVS are available from *MathSource*.

Appendix A.1
ExtendGraphics Installation

This first section of the appendix describes how the `ExtendGraphics`' packages on the diskette included with *Mathematica Graphics* can be installed on a computer[1]. This involves copying material from the diskette, in some cases unpacking an archive, and adding the location of the packages to the *Mathematica* path variable `$Path`. In the case of Microsoft Windows or DOS a file must be loaded into *Mathematica* to set up a mapping to Microsoft Windows filenames. In the case of Unix or the NeXT the *MathLink* binaries must be built for the *MathLink* packages to work. These binaries are already built for Microsoft Windows and the Macintosh.

▷ *Installing from the Diskette*

The diskette is written in a DOS format, which can be read by computers running Microsoft Windows or DOS, by Macintosh computers, and by Unix and NeXT machines. On the diskette are three archives: one for Microsoft Windows and DOS called `TWJPACKS`, one for the Macintosh called `TWJPACKS.HQX`, and one for Unix and the NeXT called `TWJPACKS.SHR`. There is also a `README.TXT` file containing the same instructions that appear here.

Microsoft Windows and DOS

The files are not actually in a special archive but simply in a directory called `TWJPACKS`. This directory should be copied over to drive `C:`, this can be done by first creating a `TWJPACKS` directory, `MKDIR C:\TWJPACKS`, and then copying files, `XCOPY/S B:\TWJPACKS C:\TWJPACKS`. If some other location is used this description must be altered accordingly. There is no need to build the *MathLink* binaries, which have already been built. However, for these binaries to work the appropriate *MathLink* files must be made available. This can be done by copying the files `MLINK16.DLL`, `MLINK32.DLL`, `MLLCL16.MLL`, `MLLCL32.MLL`, `MLTCP16.MLL`, `MLTCP32.MLL` from the *Mathematica* directory into the `WINDOWS\SYSTEM` directory. An alternative location is in the `EXTENDGR` directory.

Macintosh

The `TWJPACKS.HQX` archive should be copied over to one of the locations that are commonly used for loading software on the computer. To read the diskette it may be necessary to use a program such as the Apple File Exchange (AFE) program. When this is done no special file translation should be selected. One possible place for the archive is directly on drive `Macintosh HD`. Of course, this may not exist on your computer or be convenient. In either of these cases some other location should be used. The archive is encoded in a BinHex4 format and it is necessary to decode it with a utility such as Compact Pro or Stuffit

---

[1]The packages are also available on *MathSource*.

Expander. This is the way *MathSource* sends Macintosh material and it can be consulted for information on how to obtain a suitable decoder if one is not available.

When the archive has been decoded it will form the file `TWJ_Packages.sea`. This self-extracting archive can be unpacked by double clicking on its icon. This produces a dialog box; the **Extract** button in this box should be clicked and then the archive will be unpacked. This will build a collection of folders and files; the actual structure that will be built is listed at the end of this appendix. There is no need to build the *MathLink* binaries, which have already been built. When these binaries are run on the PowerMacintosh the *MathLink* library must be made available. This can be done by copying the file MathLinkLibrary from the folder where *Mathematica* is found to the Extensions folder of the System folder. An alternative location is in the ExtendGraphics folder.

If a decoder for BinHex4 files is not available it is possible to use the DOS files by copying over the `TWJPACKS` directory. When this is done, text translation should be selected to convert CR/LF pairs to CR. After this the filenames will be those suitable for DOS rather than the Macintosh. However a *Mathematica* package, `MACFILES.M` is provided to rename them. Entering `Get["Macintosh HD:TWJPACKS:MACFILES.M"]` to *Mathematica* will load this file. You will be asked where to put the resulting `TWJ_Packages`, the recommended place is also on `Macintosh HD`. The package will then make the necessary copying of files from DOS to Macintosh filenames. One disadvantage of this is that the *MathLink* binaries are not copied over, they are only available in the BinHex4 archive.

Unix and NeXT

The `TWJPACKS.SHR` archive should be copied over to one of the locations that are commonly used for loading software on the computer. It may be necessary to copy the archive to some other computer and copy from this to the target machine. If the latter stage is done by ftp then this should be done in binary mode to prevent any translation of the file. One possible place for the archive is `/usr/local`. Of course, this may not exist on your computer or be inconvenient. In either of these cases some other location should be used. The archive can be unpacked by typing `/bin/sh TWJPACKS.SHR` into a shell. This will build a collection of directories and files, the actual structure that will be built is listed at the end of this appendix.

After the files have been extracted the *MathLink* binaries should be built from the source code. For example the `mandelbrot` binary should be built from the file `mandelbrot.tm`. The source code contains information on how these should be built. Typically this involves using the shell script `mcc` provided with *Mathematica*.

▸ *Using the ExtendGraphics Packages in Mathematica*

When an archive has been installed from the diskette the packages can be used in *Mathematica*. For this to work the *Mathematica* global variable `$Path` *must* be set. It is easy to set `$Path` and it is probably sensible to do this in the `init.m` file that is loaded when *Mathematica* starts up. Since the conventions of naming files are different on Microsoft Windows, Unix and NeXT, or the Macintosh, they will be described differently. There should be no error messages when these operations are carried out.

Microsoft Windows and DOS

The steps described here assume that the archive was copied directly onto drive `C:`. If some other location was used then the following description must be altered to reflect this. `C:\TWJPACKS` contains a file

DOSGRAPH.M and a directory EXTENDGR that contains the ExtendGraphics packages. $Path must be set to include the directory TWJPACKS. After the path is set the file DOSGRAPH.M must be loaded to make sure that the proper files can be loaded. This is necessary since filenames on Microsoft Windows or DOS are restricted in length and are case insensitive. *Mathematica* provides a mechanism to avoid these restrictions and use a uniform package naming convention on all computers. For further information refer to the main *Mathematica* book Chapter 2.10 or the introduction to the *Guide to Standard Packages*.

The directory containing the ExtendGraphics packages is added to the path. The double backslash is necessary to set the path properly.	*In[1]:=* `AppendTo[ $Path, "C:\\TWJPACKS"];`
The file that makes sure the correct files are found is loaded.	*In[2]:=* `Get["DOSGRAPH.M"]`

Now that the system has been set up you can proceed to the section that describes how to confirm that the packages have been properly loaded. When these tests have been carried out with no errors the ExtendGraphics packages have been successfully installed. The steps to set $Path and to load the DOSGRAPH.M file can be placed in `init.m`.

Macintosh

The steps described here assume that the archive was unpacked directly on drive Macintosh HD. If some other location was used then the following description must be altered to reflect this. The archive unpacked to produce a folder Macintosh HD:TWJ_Packages. This contains the folder ExtendGraphics which contains a set of packages. $Path must be set to include the folder TWJ_Packages.

The folder containing the ExtendGraphics packages is added to the path.	*In[1]:=* `AppendTo[ $Path, "Macintosh HD:TWJ_Packages"];`

Now that the system has been set up you can proceed to the section that describes how to confirm that the packages have been properly loaded. When these tests have been carried out with no errors the ExtendGraphics packages have been successfully installed. The step that sets $Path can be placed in `init.m`.

Unix and NeXT

The steps described here assume that the archive was unpacked in the directory /usr/local. If some other location was used then the following description must be altered to reflect this. The archive unpacked to produce a directory /usr/local/TWJ_Packages. This contains the directory ExtendGraphics which contains a set of packages. $Path must be set to include the directory TWJ_Packages.

The directory containing the ExtendGraphics packages is added to the path.	*In[1]:=* `AppendTo[ $Path, "/usr/local/TWJ_Packages"];`

Now that the system has been set up you can proceed to the section that describes how to confirm that the packages have been properly loaded. When these tests have been carried out with no errors the ExtendGraphics packages have been successfully installed. The step that sets $Path can be placed in `init.m`.

▶ *Testing the Installation of the Packages*

The installation of the packages can be tested by evaluating these commands. If any of these examples do not work or if any errors are detected the packages have not been installed properly or the the version of *Mathematica* does not support some of the features that are being used. For example, the *MathLink* examples will not work on certain older versions of *Mathematica*.

The geometry package is loaded.

```
In[2]:= Needs["ExtendGraphics`Geometry`"]

In[3]:= tri = Polygon[{{4,5},{2,1},{9,5}}];
```

If this does not work then the packages have not been installed properly.

```
In[4]:= Show[Graphics[{Boundary[tri], InCircle[tri]}]]
```

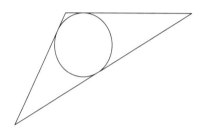

Now the package containing the function MandelbrotImage is loaded. This uses a *MathLink* binary to calculate images of the Mandelbrot set.

```
In[5]:= Needs["ExtendGraphics`Mandelbrot`"]
```

If this does not work then the *MathLink* binary has not been installed or the version of *Mathematica* does not support *MathLink*.

```
In[6]:= Show[MandelbrotImage[{-2,-1.5}, {1,1.5}, 50, 10]]
```

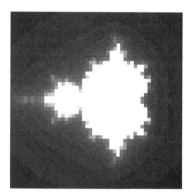

On the Macintosh there are some situations that can cause the *MathLink* binaries to fail to launch. One is if the binary is already running; in this case you should halt this running version, for example with its **Quit** menu item. Another reason is if there is insufficient system memory for the binary to launch; in this case you should quit from some other applications. On the PowerMacintosh the MathLinkLibrary must be copied into the system folder as described earlier in this appendix. Clicking on the icon from the Finder may help you to determine why a binary is failing to launch.

▶ *Summary of Files*

Here is a summary of the files that are part of the electronic component. Since the file naming conventions of Microsoft Windows or DOS are different from those on the Macintosh, Unix, or the NeXT they are described in a different section.

Macintosh, Unix, and NeXT Filenames

`TWJ_Packages`	main directory

`ExtendGraphics`	directory of *Mathematica* packages and *MathLink* files

Contents of `TWJ_Packages`.

`CheckPlot3D.m`	`Master.m`
`ComponentPlot.m`	`NonConvexTriangulate.m`
`ConstrainedContour.m`	`Plot.m`
`Contour.m`	`PointSubstitute3D.m`
`CorrelationPlot.m`	`SimpleHull.m`
`Delaunay.m`	`SmoothGraphics.m`
`FieldLines.m`	`SurfaceGraphics3D.m`
`Geometry.m`	`Ticks.m`
`Geometry3D.m`	`Transform.m`
`Label.m`	`TriangularInterpolate.m`
`LabelContour.m`	`View3D.m`
`Mandelbrot.m`	

Mathematica packages in `ExtendGraphics`.

`EAEdata.m`	`SuperConductor1.m`
`Ionization.m`	`SuperConductor2.m`
`Streakdata.m`	`USVotingData.m`

Data files in `ExtendGraphics`.

Source	binary (not distributed for Unix or NeXT)
`contour.tm`	`contour`
`delaunay.tm`	`delaunay`
`mandelbrot.tm`	`mandelbrot`

MathLink files in `ExtendGraphics`.

Microsoft Windows and DOS

Microsoft Windows and DOS do not support filenames that have more than eight characters with a three character extension. In addition they are not case sensitive. Other computer systems support longer filenames. The file `dosgraph.m` contains translations between long *Mathematica* names and short DOS names. It is essential that this file is loaded before any `ExtendGraphics` packages. There is no need to actually know what the filenames actually are. When the packages are loaded into *Mathematica* the full name should always be used. This is always done when the packages are used in the text.

`TWJPACKS`	main directory

`EXTENDGR`	directory of *Mathematica* packages and *MathLink* files
`DOSGRAPH.M`	file of filename translations

Contents of `TWJPACKS`.

Microsoft Windows filename	*Mathematica* name
`EAEDATA.M`	`ExtendGraphics`EAEdata``
`IONIZE.M`	`ExtendGraphics`Ionization``
`STRKDATA.M`	`ExtendGraphics`Streakdata``
`SUPCOND1.M`	`ExtendGraphics`SuperConductor1``
`SUPCOND2.M`	`ExtendGraphics`SuperConductor2``
`USVOTING.M`	`ExtendGraphics`USVotingData``

Data files in `EXTENDGR`.

Microsoft Windows filename	*Mathematica* name
CHECKP3D.M	ExtendGraphics`CheckPlot3D`
COMPONP.M	ExtendGraphics`ComponentPlot`
CONSCONT.M	ExtendGraphics`ConstrainedContour`
CONTOUR.M	ExtendGraphics`Contour`
CORRPLOT.M	ExtendGraphics`CorrelationPlot`
DELAUNAY.M	ExtendGraphics`Delaunay`
FIELDLNS.M	ExtendGraphics`FieldLines`
GEOMETRY.M	ExtendGraphics`Geometry`
GEOMET3D.M	ExtendGraphics`Geometry3D`
LABEL.M	ExtendGraphics`Label`
LABLCONT.M	ExtendGraphics`LabelContour`
MANDBROT.M	ExtendGraphics`Mandelbrot`
MASTER.M	ExtendGraphics`Master`
NCONTRI.M	ExtendGraphics`NonConvexTriangulate`
PLOT.M	ExtendGraphics`Plot`
PNTSUBS.M	ExtendGraphics`PointSubstitute3D`
SIMPHULL.M	ExtendGraphics`SimpleHull`
SMTGRAPH.M	ExtendGraphics`SmoothGraphics`
SRFGRAPH.M	ExtendGraphics`SurfaceGraphics3D`
TICKS.M	ExtendGraphics`Ticks`
TRANSFORM.M	ExtendGraphics`Transform`
TRIINTE.M	ExtendGraphics`TriangularInterpolate`
VIEW3D.M	ExtendGraphics`View3D`

Mathematica packages in EXTENDGR.

Source	binary
CONTOUR.TM	CONTOUR.EXE
DELAUNAY.TM	DELAUNAY.EXT
MANDBROT.TM	MANDBROT.EXE

MathLink files in EXTENDGR.

Appendix A.2 ExtendGraphics Reference

This section of the appendix is a brief reference to the `ExtendGraphics`` packages that are described in *Mathematica Graphics* and are available on the diskette. Each package is listed with a short description of its functionality. The relevant sections of the book where the package is used and referred to are also given. In addition there is a brief description of each of the functions defined in the package. For the packages `Geometry`, `Geometry3`, `LabelContour`, and `View3D`, which contain several functions defined and used over many pages, references to one or more pages are given for each function. The description of the other packages is more localized in the text and separate references are not required for each function.

▸ *CheckPlot3D*

The package `ExtendGraphics`CheckPlot3D`` provides a function to generate surfaces that are colored with alternating rectangles of black and white. The package is used in Chapter 10 page 184.

`CheckPlot3D`	draws a checkered surface plot

▸ *ComponentPlot*

The package `ExtendGraphics`ComponentPlot`` provides functions to plot ternary component mixtures. The package is described in Chapter 13 page 271, which includes material on the programming techniques that are used.

`ComponentListPlot`	plots a triangular picture of ternary mixtures
`ComponentGraphics`	graphics object returned by `ComponentListPlot`
`Grid`	option of `ComponentGraphics` that draws a triangular grid
`GridStyle`	option of `ComponentGraphics` that sets the style of the grid

▶ *ConstrainedContour*

The package `ExtendGraphics`ConstrainedContour` provides a function to construct contour plots subject to an inequality constraint. The package is described in Chapter 13 page 256, which includes material on the programming techniques that are used.

`ConstrainedContourPlot`	draws contours that meet a constraint

▶ *Contour*

The package `ExtendGraphics`Contour` extends the built-in function `ListContourPlot` to work on irregular data sets. The package is described in the section on three-dimensional data visualization in Chapter 18 page 482. The package uses a *MathLink* binary that must be built and in the proper place for the package to work.

`ListContourPlot`	draws contours over irregular points

▶ *CorrelationPlot*

The package `ExtendGraphics`CorrelationPlot` takes a multidimensional data set and makes an array of plots of each dimension plotted against each other. The package is described in the section on multidimensional data visualization in Chapter 18 page 495, which includes material on the programming techniques that are used.

`CorrelationPlot`	generates an array of correlation plots
`Labels`	option of `CorrelationPlot` that gives labels
`TickFont`	option of `CorrelationPlot` that gives the font for labels

▶ *Delaunay*

The package `ExtendGraphics`Delaunay`` provides functions to generate Delaunay triangulations in the plane. The package is used frequently throughout *Mathematica Graphics*. The basic topics are introduced in the computational geometry section of Chapter 16 page 402. The functions are used for visualization in Chapter 18 page 474. The package is based upon a *MathLink* binary that must be built and in the appropriate place for the functions to work.

`ConvexHull`	returns the convex hull
`ConvexHullPlot`	plots the convex hull
`Delaunay`	generates the Delaunay triangulation
`DelaunayVertices`	returns the indices of the Delaunay triangles
`TrianglePlot`	plots the Delaunay triangles
`TriangulatePoints`	returns the points of the Delaunay triangles

▶ *FieldLines*

The package `ExtendGraphics`FieldLines`` calculates the lines that are generated by a field. The package is described in the section on visualizing vector fields with field lines in Chapter 19 page 516. Earlier sections in Chapter 19, starting on page 516, cover the mathematical basis for calculating field lines and the programming techniques used by the package.

`AddArrow`	adds `Arrow` primitives to two-dimensional lines
`FieldLine`	generates field lines from a two-dimensional vector field
`FieldLine3D`	generates field lines from a three-dimensional vector field

▸ *Geometry*

The package `ExtendGraphics`Geometry` contains many functions for basic results in two-dimensional geometry. The functions in the package are described in the section on geometric results in Chapter 16 page 383. Both the mathematical basis for these results and their implementation in *Mathematica* are covered.

Area	returns the area of a triangle, defined page 391
Bisector	returns the bisector of two lines, defined page 392
Boundary	returns the boundary of a triangle, defined page 375
CenterOfGravity	determines the center of gravity of a triangle, defined page 390
ClosestPointOnLine	returns the point on a line closest to a second point, defined page 385
ImplicitLine	represents an implicit line, defined page 373
InCircle	returns the inscribing circle of a triangle, defined page 392
IntersectionPoint	returns the point of intersection of two lines, defined page 383
LineLength	returns the length of a line segment, defined page 374
Medians	returns the medians of a triangle, defined page 390
NormalVector	generates a normal vector, defined page 372
OutCircle	returns the circumscribing circle of a triangle, defined page 394
Perimeter	returns the perimeter of a triangle, defined page 391
PointInCircleQ	tests if point lies in a circle, defined page 398
PointInTriangle	determines if a point falls in a triangle, defined page 388
PointOnLineQ	tests if a point falls on a line, defined page 384
SideOfLine	determines which side of a line a point falls, defined page 387
ToImplicit	converts an implicit to an explicit line, defined page 374
ToLine	converts an explicit to an implicit line, defined page 373
VectorLength	returns the length of a vector, defined page 371

▶ *Geometry3D*

The package `ExtendGraphics`Geometry3D`` contains many functions for basic results in two-dimensional geometry. The functions in the package are described in the three-dimensional geometry material covered in Chapter 17 page 428. Both the mathematical basis for these results and their implementation in *Mathematica* are covered.

`Clip3D`	clips three-dimensional primitives with a plane, defined page 441
`ClosestPointInPlane`	returns the point in a plane closest to a second point, defined page 431
`ConvexPolygon`	generates a convex polygon, defined page 446
`EmbedIn3D`	embeds two-dimensional points into three-dimensional space, defined page 438
`Extrude`	extrudes a polygon to form a solid, defined page 453
`IntersectionPoint`	returns the point of intersection of two lines and a line and a plane, defined page 429 and page 433
`NonConvexPolygon`	generates a non-convex polygon, defined page 452
`OrthogonalVectors`	generates orthogonal vectors, defined page 415
`ParallelProject`	projects points into a plane, defined page 436
`ParallelProjectTo2D`	projects points into a plane, defined page 437
`Plane`	represents a plane, defined page 417
`PlaneComponents`	generates the components of a plane, defined page 417
`PointInPlaneQ`	tests if a point lies in a plane, defined page 431
`SideOfPlaneQ`	determines which side of a plane a point falls, defined page 432
`ToPlane`	returns the plane of best fit, defined page 434
`ToPolygon`	converts a plane to a polygon, defined page 417

▶ *Label*

The package `ExtendGraphics`Label`` extends the way that labels can be added to *Mathematica* graphics with the option `PlotLabel`. It is described in Chapter 13 page 268, which includes material on the programming techniques that are used. There are no new functions added by this package.

▸ *LabelContour*

The package ExtendGraphics`LabelContour` provides functions to label shaded and unshaded contour plots. The package is the topic of Chapter 15 page 348.

ContourDisplayFunction	a display function that will automatically label contour plots, used page 365
HeightName	option of LabelContourLegend that names the height used in the legend, used page 359
LabelContourLegend	places a legend next to a contour plot, used page 358
LabelContourLines	places labels on contour lines, used page 348
LabelFont	option of LabelContourLines and LabelContourLegend that sets the font used for labels, used page 356
LabelPlacement	option of LabelContourLines that determines how the labels are placed, used page 352
LegendPosition	option of various graphics functions that sets the position of the legend, used page 362
LegendSize	option of various graphics functions that sets the size of the legend, used page 362
PointFactor	option of LabelContourLines that determines how the labels are placed, used page 354
PointSkip	option of LabelContourLines that determines how the labels are placed, used page 355

▸ *Mandelbrot*

The package ExtendGraphics`Mandelbrot` provides functions to generate images of the Mandelbrot set. It uses a *MathLink* binary that must be built and in the proper place for the package to work. ExtendGraphics`Mandelbrot` is described in Chapter 13 page 285, which includes material on the programming techniques that are used.

GetMandelbrot	generates a bitmap representation of the Mandelbrot set
MandelbrotImage	generates a graphics object representation of the Mandelbrot set

▶ *NonConvexTriangulate*

The package `ExtendGraphics`NonConvexTriangulate`` provides a function to triangulate non-convex outlines. It is described in the computational geometry section of Chapter 16 page 406.

`NonConvexTriangulate`	generates a non-convex triangulation

▶ *Plot*

The package `ExtendGraphics`Plot`` extends the built-in function `Plot` to deal with singularities. It is described in Chapter 13 page 246, which includes material on the programming techniques that are used. There are no new functions added by this package.

▶ *PointSubstitute3D*

The package `ExtendGraphics`PointSubstitute3D`` provides functions to replace three-dimensional point primitives with solid objects. It is described in Chapter 13 page 280, which includes material on the programming techniques that are used.

`LineSubstitute`	inserts solid objects at the points of `Line` primitives
`PointSubstitute`	replaces `Point` primitives with solid objects

▶ *SimpleHull*

The package `ExtendGraphics`SimpleHull`` provides functions to generate convex hulls. It is described in the computational geometry section of Chapter 16 page 400. The same functions exist in `ExtendGraphics`Delaunay`, the difference being that `ExtendGraphics`SimpleHull`` does not use *Math-Link*.

`ConvexHull`	returns the convex hull
`ConvexHullPlot`	plots the convex hull

▶ *SmoothGraphics*

The package ExtendGraphics`SmoothGraphics` provides functions to generate smooth surface and contour plots. It is described in Chapter 13 page 250, which includes material on the programming techniques that are used.

SmoothGraphics	generates smooth surface and contour plots

▶ *SurfaceGraphics3D*

The package ExtendGraphics`SurfaceGraphics3D` provides general three-dimensional data plotting functions. The package is described in the three-dimensional visualization section of Chapter 18 page 475. It uses the Delaunay triangulation package.

GridSort	sorts data into an array
ListSurfacePlot3D	plots a surface over the points
SurfaceGraphics3D	graphics object returned by ListSurfacePlot3D
TriangleSort	sorts data into an array

▸ *Ticks*

The package `ExtendGraphics`Ticks` provides functions for generating sophisticated tick marks. It is described in Chapter 13 page 260 and page 264 with material on the programming techniques that are used. Also, it is used in Chapter 14 page 321 and page 343.

`MajorLength`	option of `TickFunction` that sets the length of major tick marks
`MajorStyle`	option of `TickFunction` that sets the style of major tick marks
`MinorLength`	option of `TickFunction` that sets the length of minor tick marks
`MinorStyle`	option of `TickFunction` that sets the style of minor tick marks
`TextFunction`	option of `TickFunction` that processes tick mark labels
`TickFunction`	function to use with the `Ticks` and associated options
`TickLabels`	option of `TickFunction` that sets tick mark labels
`TickNumbers`	option of `TickFunction` that sets the number of major and minor tick marks
`TickPosition`	returns *nice* positions for tick marks
`TrimText`	a function to use with `TrimText` that trims tick mark labels

▸ *Transform*

The package `ExtendGraphics`Transform` provides functions to carry out affine transformations on two- and three-dimensional objects. It is described in the transformation sections of Chapter 16 page 382 and Chapter 17 page 427. These include material on the programming techniques that are used.

`HomogeneousMatrix`	converts a matrix to a homogeneous matrix
`HomogeneousMultiply`	multiplies a vector by a transformation matrix
`HomogeneousRotation`	generates a rotation matrix
`HomogeneousScale`	generates a scale matrix
`HomogeneousShear`	generates a shear matrix
`HomogeneousTransform`	applies a transformation matrix
`HomogeneousTranslation`	generates a translation matrix

▶ *TriangularInterpolate*

The package ExtendGraphics`TriangularInterpolate` provides functions for interpolation of irregular three-dimensional data. The package is described in the computational geometry section of Chapter 16 page 405 and in the three-dimensional visualization section of Chapter 18 page 480. It uses the Delaunay triangulation and the general three-dimensional surface plotting packages.

InterpolateSurface	smooths a SurfaceGraphics3D object
TriangularInterpolate	generates a function for approximating irregular data
TriangularInterpolating	a function that approximates irregular data

▶ *View3D*

The package ExtendGraphics`View3D` provides functions to work with *Mathematica* three-dimensional graphics. It is used in Chapter 10 page 187 and Chapter 11 page 220.

ColorLights	a set of colored LightSources, used page 221
NormalDisplayFunction	a DisplayFunction that inserts normals in Polygon primitives, used page 220
Plot3Matrix	generates the four-dimensional transformation matrix used by *Mathematica*, used page 194
ProjectVector	applies a four-dimensional transformation matrix to a vector, used page 194
SetColorLights	sets the LightSources to use colored lights, used page 220
SetNormalDisplayFunction	sets the DisplayFunction to insert normals in Polygon primitives, used page 220
SetOldDisplayFunction	restores the default DisplayFunction, used page 221
SetOldLights	restores the default LightSources, used page 221
SetWhiteLights	sets the LightSources to use white lights, used page 223
ViewPointFromUser	converts a ViewPoint from user coordinates, implemented and used page 187
ViewPointToUser	converts a ViewPoint to user coordinates, implemented and used page 187
WhiteLights	a set of white LightSources, used page 223

Appendix A.3
Loading Mathematica Packages

The last section of the appendix reviews how packages can be loaded into *Mathematica*. The material here is shown to supplement the earlier sections of the appendix. These show how to install the ExtendGraphics packages and give a brief description of their contents. This section of the appendix will show how packages can be loaded, describe problems that can arise, and demonstrate the Master` package.

▶ *Loading Packages*

The concept of packages was introduced in Chapter 4 page 63, where it was demonstrated how they could be loaded with Needs["cont`"]. It is possible to use an actual filename in place of the context name, "cont`", but since filenames are machine-specific this practice is discouraged[2].

The package Graphics`Shapes` is loaded.

In[1]:= **Needs["Graphics`Shapes`"]**

The function MoebiusStrip was defined in the package and can be used to plot a Moebius strip.

In[2]:= **Show[Graphics3D[MoebiusStrip[ ]]]**

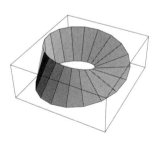

An alternative way to load a package is with Get["cont`"]. This is different from Needs in that the latter only loads a package if it has *not* already been loaded. In contrast Get *alway* loads a package.

The package Graphics`ComplexMap` is loaded.

In[3]:= **Get["Graphics`ComplexMap`"]**

---

[2]For example, if actual filenames were used in this text then every time a package was loaded it would have to be demonstrated for each different type of filename.

The function CartesianMap shows the effect of a function, in this case Tan, on numbers in the complex plane.

In[4]:= **CartesianMap[Tan, {-Pi/3,Pi/3},{-Pi/3,Pi/3}]**

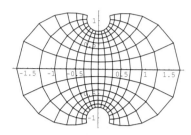

Generally if a fully functioning package is to be loaded Needs is the appropriate function. Get is useful for developing packages.

```
Needs["cont`"]          load package only if it is not loaded
Get["cont`"]            load package always
```

Uses of Needs and Get.

▶ *Shadowing Errors*

If a function is used before the package is loaded then a shadowing message will be generated and the function will not work, (for example, if the LogPlot function is used before the package Graphics`Graphics` is loaded).

Since LogPlot has not been defined this does not produce a plot.

In[5]:= **LogPlot[10^x, {x,1,3}]**

Out[5]= LogPlot[10^x, {x, 1, 3}]

Now the package is loaded. However, a different symbol LogPlot has already been defined and this interferes with the one introduced in the package.

In[6]:= **Needs["Graphics`Graphics`"]**

```
LogPlot::shdw:
   Warning: Symbol LogPlot appears in multiple contexts
     {Graphics`Graphics`, Global`}; definitions in context
     Graphics`Graphics` may shadow or be shadowed by other
     definitions.
```

LogPlot still does not work.

In[7]:= **LogPlot[10^x, {x,1,3}]**

Out[7]= LogPlot[10^x, {x, 1, 3}]

One simple solution is to remove the erroneous symbol.

In[8]:= **Remove[LogPlot]**

Now that the erroneous symbol has been removed the real LogPlot will work.

In[9]:= **LogPlot[10^x, {x,1,3}]**

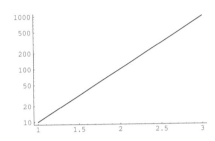

▶ *Using the Master Package*

An alternative method to avoid this problem is to load the relevant `Master`` package. This will load each package automatically as the symbols that it defines are used. Generally the master package should be loaded at the beginning of a *Mathematica* session. This may be done conveniently in an initialization file such as `init.m`.

The master package for ExtendGraphics` is loaded.

In[10]:= **Needs["ExtendGraphics`Master`"]**

Now when a command is executed the appropriate package will be loaded.

In[11]:= **CheckPlot3D[Sin[x] Cos[y], {x,-Pi,Pi},{y,-Pi,Pi}]**

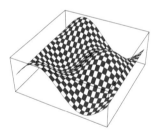

Bibliography

Churchill, R.V., and J.W. Brown. *Complex Variables and Applications*. New York: McGraw-Hill, 1990.

Foley, J., A. van Dam, S. Feiner, and J. Hughes. *Computer Graphics: Principles and Practice*, Second Edition. Reading, MA: Addison-Wesley, 1990.

Glassner, A.S., ed. *Graphics Gems*. Boston: Academic Press, 1990.

Gray, Alfred. *Modern Differential Geometry of Curves and Surfaces*. Boca Raton, FL: CRC Press, 1993.

Greenwood, Addison. *Science at the Frontier: Volume 1*. Washington, DC: National Academy Press, 1992.

Jones, Maldwyn A. *The Limits of Liberty: American History 1607-1980*. Oxford: Oxford University Press, 1983.

Kay, D.C., and J.R. Levine. *Graphics File Formats*. New York: Windcrest/McGraw-Hill, 1992.

PostScript Language Reference Manual, Second Edition. Reading, MA: Addison-Wesley, 1990.

Tufte, E.R. *The Visual Display of Quantitive Information*. Cheshire, CT: Graphics Press, 1983.

Tukey, J. *Exploratory Data Analysis*. Reading, MA: Addison-Wesley, 1977.

Wells, David. *The Penguin Dictionary of Curious and Interesting Geometry*. London: Penguin Books, 1991.

Wolfram, Stephen. *Mathematica: A System for Doing Mathematics by Computer*, Second Edition. Reading, MA: Addison-Wesley, 1990.

Index

Mathematica® Graphics

REGISTRATION CARD

Since this field is fast-moving, we expect updates and changes to occur that might necessitate sending you the most current pertinent information by paper, electronic media, or both, regarding *Mathematica Graphics*. Therefore, in order to not miss out on receiving your important update information, please fill out this card and return it to us promptly. Thank you.

Name: _____

Title: _____

Company: _____

Address: _____

City: _____ State: _____ Zip: _____

Country: _____ Phone: _____

E-mail: _____

Areas of Interest / Technical Expertise: _____

Comments on this Publication: _____

_____

_____

_____

☐ Please check this box to indicate that we may use your comments in our promotion and advertising for this publication.

Purchased from: _____ Date: _____

☐ Please add me to your mailing list to receive updated information on *Mathematica Graphics* and other TELOS publications.

☐ I have a   ☐ 486 computer   ☐ 386 computer   ☐ Macintosh   ☐ NeXT computer

   other _____

TELOS THE ELECTRONIC LIBRARY OF SCIENCE

PLEASE TAPE HERE

FOLD HERE

NO POSTAGE
NECESSARY
IF MAILED
IN THE
UNITED STATES

BUSINESS REPLY MAIL

FIRST CLASS MAIL PERMIT NO. 1314 SANTA CLARA, CA

POSTAGE WILL BE PAID BY ADDRESSEE

THE
ELECTRONIC
LIBRARY
OF
SCIENCE

3600 PRUNERIDGE AVE STE 200
SANTA CLARA CA 95051-9835

Library of Science
Riverside, NJ
Fri 28 July 1995
$24.97 + 5.24 post/hndlg
   also $1.50 tax